My World As A Jew

By the same author:

A Century of Judaism in New York
  (New York, Congregation B'nai Jeshurun, 1930)
Toward a Solution
  (New York, G. P. Putnam's Sons, 1940)
Shanah be-Yisrael, an account of Dr. Israel Goldstein's year of service as treasurer of the Jewish
  Agency
  (Jerusalem, World Confederation of General Zionists, 1950)
Brandeis University— Chapter of Its Founding
  (New York, Bloch Publishing Co., 1951)
American Jewry Comes of Age: Tercentenary Addresses
  (New York, Bloch Publishing Co., 1955)
Transition Years, New York–Jerusalem, 1960–1962
  (Jerusalem, Rubin Mass, 1962; published in Hebrew as *Shenot Ma'avar*, 1963)
Israel at Home and Abroad
  (Jerusalem, Rubin Mass, 1973)
Jewish Justice and Conciliation: History of the Jewish Conciliation Board of America, 1930–1968
  (New York, Ktav Publishing House, Inc., 1981)
Jewish Perspectives: Selected Addresses, Sermons and Articles, 1915–1983
  (in press)

Festschriften:

Two Generations in Perspective: Notable Events and Trends 1896–1956, essays dedicated to Dr. Israel
  Goldstein on the occasion of his sixtieth birthday
  (New York, Monde Publishers, Inc., 1957)
Studies in the History of Zionism (Pirké Meḥkar be-Toledot ha-Tziyyonut), essays presented to
  Dr. Israel Goldstein on the occasion of his eightieth birthday by the Hebrew University's Institute
  of Contemporary Jewry
  (Jerusalem, World Zionist Organization, 1976)

My World As A Jew

The Memoirs of Israel Goldstein

VOLUME 2

Herzl Press
New York • Cornwall Books • London

Cornwall Books
440 Forsgate Drive
Cranbury, NJ 08512

Cornwall Books
25 Sicilian Avenue
London WC1A 2QH, England

Cornwall Books
2133 Royal Windsor Drive
Unit 1
Mississauga, Ontario
Canada L5J 1K5

Library of Congress Cataloging in Publication Data

Goldstein, Israel, 1896–
   My world as a Jew.

   Includes index.
   1. Goldstein, Israel, 1896–   .   2. Rabbis—United
States—Biography.   3. Zionists—United States—
Biography.   I. Title.
BM755.G63A37   1983   956.94'001'0924   [B]   82-42621
ISBN 0-8453-4780-2 (volume 2)

Printed in the United States of America

Contents of Volume 2

Illustrations in this volume appear in two groups,
between pages 128–129, and 256–257.

My World As A Jew

9

A Voyage of Discovery: 1958–59

Traveling at home and abroad seems to have occupied a substantial portion of my life. I must have covered many hundreds of thousands of miles in my time, by land, sea, and air, either alone or accompanied by my wife and sometimes by our children. Airlines, navigation companies, and travel agencies no doubt regarded me as one of their best customers. Almost always, however, whenever I would board a plane or ship, it was in the public interest. For the most part, my journeys were until recent years meant to serve the interests of the Jewish people.

Our globe-trotting in the summer of 1958 fell into that category. The first three weeks of July were spent in various Latin American countries, where I conducted a mission on behalf of the Western Hemisphere Executive of the World Jewish Congress. During the last week of that month I attended a meeting of the WJC in Geneva and then proceeded to London for a meeting of the Conference of Jewish Organizations.

Our next stop was Rio de Janeiro, where Bert and I ran into a fiesta on July 1: Brazil's national soccer team had just returned in triumph after winning the World Cup, and the streets of Rio were crammed with multitudes of exultant soccer fans. Over the next couple of days in that bustling metropolis, we met a number of old friends, including the local director of the WJC, Dr. V. Winterstein, and Israel's ambassador, Arie Aroch, who sought relief and relaxation from his diplomatic work through painting—a field in which he later achieved wide recognition as an eminent Israeli artist.

I noted that the Brazilian *kehillah* now included several thousand recent Jewish immigrants from Egypt and North Africa. Considering that there were numerous Arabs living in Rio de Janeiro, it was remarkable to see the illuminations and bunting along many of the streets in honor of Israel's tenth anniversary.

Brazilian Jewry was on the increase, headed toward some 150,000 within the next decade. About two-thirds of the *kehillah* were to be found in Rio and São Paulo. This latter city was the venue of a Zionist conference I addressed in the course of a subsequent visit to Brazil in March 1960, when I met leaders of the various Zionist groupings.

Buenos Aires, the capital of Argentina, was our next destination. Two important

9

conferences took place there—one called by the World Jewish Congress and, following that, another organized by the World Confederation of General Zionists, one of my major Zionist commitments.

Resolutions on Argentinian Jewry and Israel, adopted by the WJC conference, were brought to President Arturo Frondizi by a special delegation. In the course of our meeting with him, I observed that the WJC had decided to hold its conference in Argentina because it had the fourth largest Jewish community in the world, well over 450,000 Jews at that time. I also took occasion to thank President Frondizi for the friendly attitude he maintained toward Israel. In reply, he assured us that no racial discrimination would be tolerated during his regime and that many Jews occupied high positions in the Government by virtue of their ability. He expressed satisfaction over the holding of our conference in Argentina, and he further assured us that his Administration would always remain well disposed toward Israel, "because every decent man must acknowledge what he owes to his parents."

Despite this favorable official attitude, I detected no little uneasiness among the Jews with whom I spoke, regarding the future of their *kehillah*. Many of them were far from enthusiastic about Jewish functionaries in Government posts, fearing that such prominence might be followed by an anti-Semitic backlash. They also spoke of a mounting campaign of incitement against Argentinian Jewry by local Arab agitators.

At the WJC conference, which was chaired by its head in Argentina, Dr. Moshe Goldman, there were extensive discussions concerning the entire Jewish position in Latin America. Regarding the menace of anti-Semitism, encouraging reports were received from representatives of the 140,000-strong Jewish community of Brazil, the second largest *kehillah* on the South American continent. Jewish and Zionist activities there, however, needed considerable strengthening. It was interesting to hear that the Brazilian Minister of Education, supported by the Roman Catholic archdiocese, had taken the initiative in having the offensive definition of "Jew" (as, *inter alia*, "a usurer") eliminated from the Brazilian Portuguese dictionary. It took twenty more years for modifications of similar anti-Jewish allusions to appear in editions of the *Oxford English Dictionary*.

While revisiting Brazil in 1960, I was especially impressed by a magnificent new synagogue complex in São Paulo, complete with swimming pool and *mikveh* (ritual bath), and by the Jewish day schools I saw there. Since my trip coincided with the Festival of Purim, I joined members of the local Bnei Akiva (Religious Zionist) youth movement at the reading of the *Megillah* they organized, and also attended a Purim ball at the sumptuous Hebraica Club. Included in the local Brazilian Jewish community were about 7,000 Yordim (Israeli emigrants), a number of whom were active in fund-raising campaigns for the Medinah. Most of them claimed that they would ultimately return to Israel.

Our journey home from Buenos Aires in July 1958 included one-day stopovers in Santiago, Chile (where we were told that five hundred *halutzim* were preparing for Aliyah); Lima, Peru; Panama City; and Miami. Back in New York, I had just

enough time to catch my breath before flying on to Geneva the following day, for sessions of the World Jewish Congress Executive, which lasted from July 23 to 28.

It was a significant occasion, as the newly affiliated delegates of Hungarian Jewry were present for the first time as full-fledged members and another Jewish delegation had come from Poland as observers. The Hungarian representatives alluded to the planned publication of a history of their *kehillah*. In my report on South American Jewry I made the recommendation that steps be taken to publish a Spanish translation of the Hebrew Bible and a Spanish-Yiddish dictionary.

The long arm of Communism could be detected in the course of our deliberations. When a tenth anniversary tribute was paid to Medinat Yisrael, the Polish and Hungarian delegates took care to absent themselves from the hall.

Three fortieth anniversaries were noted by Bert and me in the summer of 1958. My graduation from the Jewish Theological Seminary, my election to the pulpit of Congregation B'nai Jeshurun and our marriage in the synagogue of my congregation had all taken place in June and July 1918. Toward the end of the year, the completion of my fourth decade as rabbi of Congregation B'nai Jeshurun was marked by a dinner held at the Plaza Hotel in New York City, on December 11, 1958. Governor Averell Harriman, Senator Herbert H. Lehman, Professor Louis Finkelstein, and Dr. Nahum Goldmann were among the principal speakers, and President Dwight D. Eisenhower sent a message of congratulations. A chair in practical theology was established in my name at the Jewish Theological Seminary.

Bert and I decided to celebrate these important milestones by embarking on a world tour. Our intention was to combine "business"—Jewish business, of course— with pleasure, and to familiarize ourselves with people and places in some of the more remote parts of the world, with especial reference to far-flung Jewish communities.

One of the collateral aims of our planned round-the-world trip was to sound out eminent personalities whom we hoped to meet, as to the feasibility of establishing a World Academy for Peace. This was a cherished idea of mine to which I had devoted considerable thought. A memorandum on the subject, which I had drawn up, had been sent to a number of political, intellectual, and spiritual leaders in the United States, Latin America, Great Britain, Europe, and Israel. Most of them responded favorably, some enthusiastically. Eleanor Roosevelt thought it "inspiring," Lord Boyd Orr wrote that it "could make a worthwhile contribution," and Bishop G. Bromley Oxnam hailed this "thrilling proposal, at once creative and courageous."

Utopian though it may have appeared to some, this World Academy, as I envisaged it, would serve as a useful auxiliary for the promotion of world peace. Existing international bodies left much to be desired. The UN itself was hampered by widely recognized limitations, being composed of sovereign states that were usually motivated by their own short-range interests. The scheme I proposed would, I urged, serve as a useful adjunct. It envisaged the formation of a prestigious body comprising about twenty-five of the world's foremost personalities of intellectual and spiritual stature, wise in their understanding of human affairs and of Nobel Prize caliber, who would be eligible for membership not by virtue of any official position they held, but on the strength of their life records and achievements as men and women dedicated to the welfare and advancement of humanity—and who could be relied upon to exercise independent judgment.

Among those whom I suggested as members of the World Academy were Martin Buber, Edmond Fleg, Gilberto Freire, Nahum Goldmann, Jacques Maritain, François Mauriac, Philip Noel Baker, J. Robert Oppenheimer, Bishop G. Bromley Oxnam, Eleanor Roosevelt, Bertrand Russell, Albert Schweitzer, and Adlai Stevenson. Albert Einstein, alas, was no longer in the land of the living. Two of the outstanding personalities from the Far East were Toyohiko Kagawa of Japan and Dr. S. Radhakrishnan of India, provided they held no public office. I was in quest of suitably qualified personalities from Communist bloc countries, the Muslim world, and Africa.

The members of this Academy would meet once a year, for a period of one month, in a neutral country such as Sweden or Switzerland, where the atmosphere would be free of political pressures. The most ominous threats to world peace could then be discussed, and proposals could be formulated to deal with them. Members would, of course, have no authority to impose any solutions, but, hopefully, the moral authority of their pronouncements would carry weight with peoples and governments, perhaps even with the United Nations Organization itself. The moral and spiritual leaders of mankind could thus take part in an ongoing collective effort to safeguard world peace and to reduce the dangers of war. For all its limitations, such a body and such an effort would, I believed, make a significant contribution toward the attainment of world peace.

My proposal would not depend upon any particular individual or individuals. Every generation produces men and women of surpassing moral stature. Greatness is born ever anew, and sooner or later it gains recognition. There would always be a reservoir from which to draw for the composition of such a World Academy for Peace. Unlike the Nobel Peace Prize scheme, moreover, it would offer no prizes. The members of the World Academy for Peace would be politically independent and untrammeled by obligations to governments, and they would have to be citizens of the world, willing to give their utmost in the service of humanity.

My plan concluded with the suggestion that one day each year be set aside for prayer and meditation on world peace, in which people of every race and creed might join together. An appropriate date for this purpose would be September 2, the anniversary of the end of World War II. On that day, it would be timely to communicate the annual findings of the World Academy for Peace to a world eagerly awaiting the new era when, in the words of Isaiah (2:4), "nation shall not lift up sword against nation, neither shall they learn war any more."

Nothing that has transpired since 1958 has led me to change my opinion or to modify my basic approach. If anything, events have strengthened my conviction that

such an academy for peace, outside the framework of the United Nations and hence unfettered by its built-in limitations, remains a promising instrument in the service of the greatest of all human causes, peace among men and nations.

Other aspects of my journey were more specifically Jewish, related in the main to my lifelong religious and Zionist commitments.

The New York Board of Rabbis entrusted me with the mission of bringing to Jewish religious leaders a special message of greetings, coupled with the announcement of its plan for the building of an international synagogue at New York's Idlewild Airport, since renamed in memory of the late President John F. Kennedy. The Board gave me a set of handsome scrolls which, in the course of our travels, I delivered to Chief Rabbis Isaac Halevi Herzog of Israel, Israel Brodie of Great Britain, Marcus Melchior of Denmark, Israel Porush of Australia, and Louis Rabinowitz of South Africa.

Thus laden with considerable spiritual baggage, we parted from a group of friends who had accompanied us to the airport on January 1, 1959, when we set out on the first leg of our transcontinental journey—the flight to San Francisco. A highlight of the weekend we spent in the Golden Gate city was a family reunion with our son, Avram, and his wife, Dora, their children, Margaret, Dan, Joshua, and Michael, and my brother and sister-in-law, Morris and Adeline. My brother's twenty-fifth anniversary as rabbi of Temple Sherith Israel in San Francisco was to be observed about a month later, in February, and I gladly anticipated it by addressing his congregation at a Sabbath eve service. Morris had published *Thus Religion Grows: The Story of Judaism* in 1936, and had generously dedicated it to me. His other book, *Jesus in the Jewish Tradition*, appeared in 1950.

The 2,100-mile hop across the Pacific to Hawaii offered time for both rest and reflection. Three weeks earlier, on December 13, I had completed what was, by any standard, a long span in the rabbinate and in public and Jewish communal service. During the forty years that had elapsed since 1918, when I had delivered my inaugural sermon at B'nai Jeshurun, I had grappled with three major challenges. One was serving and strengthening Jewish religious and national values through the synagogue, the home, and the Jewish school. The second was active identification with the Zionist movement. The third was the inculcation of civic and human values, the cultivation of the American heritage at its best. How far, I wondered, had my endeavors succeeded? What impact had my own limited "mission" made on the broad mass of Jews among whom I had labored in all those years?

Introspection, they say, is good for the soul. At any rate, the flight from San Francisco and its Golden Gate to the golden sunshine of Hawaii provided an opportunity for some soul-searching.

In planning our world tour, Bert and I had mapped out an itinerary embracing lands and peoples that would broaden our perspectives. Some of these countries we had visited before, and we looked forward to meeting old friends; others would be new to us, and we hoped to make new acquaintances and to learn about new modes of life and thought. We were intent on glimpsing something behind the façade, in

Asia and Africa, where the "new faces in old places"—so much at variance with our experience in the West—might enrich our knowledge of the human species.

Above all, we looked forward to learning more than we had known previously about Jewish life in the more remote outposts of the Diaspora.

So it was that we embarked upon our journey, which lasted for eight months and would bring us back to New York only for Rosh Hashanah, early in the following September.

From Honolulu to Karachi

Our first destination, Hawaii, had still not achieved statehood at the outset of 1959 and was a U.S. territory. Just seven months after our visit, in August 1959, the islanders gained their objective when Hawaii was admitted to the Union.

The foundations of Jewish life there had been laid at the beginning of the twentieth century and, by the end of World War I, about 300 Jewish families resided in Hawaii. Of these, only a third joined the synagogue established in Honolulu. Since it often proved difficult to find enough males for the *minyan*, women were allowed to make up the quorum for prayer. As Temple Emanu-el, this congregation officially became Reform in 1951. I was told that some 1,000 Jews were affiliated with the temple and that the total Jewish population on the islands was probably three or four times that number. Assimilation in this multiracial environment had made severe inroads among the local *kehillah*. We were intrigued to learn that one Chinese family rejoiced in the surname of Goldstein. The head of this Goldstein clan, it transpired, had only discovered the Jewish provenance of his name when he was in his fifties!

One evening, in the course of our stay, I was invited to address what was, by local standards, a "capacity" audience of about 200 Jewish residents and visitors. My chosen topic was the function of the World Jewish Congress and of its primary affiliate, the American Jewish Congress. Before our departure, we made a trip to Pearl Harbor, where a surprise Japanese air attack on the U.S. fleet had precipitated America's entry into World War II, in December 1941.

Japan was the next country on our route. At first sight, the vast urban expanse of the capital, Tokyo, was overwhelming. I had visited many great cities all over the world in my time, but never one so teeming with dense masses of humanity. Broadway, Fifth Avenue, and the other main streets of Manhattan were, by comparison, tranquil thoroughfares.

We were also to see much of ancient Japan in the course of our stay, including Nara, the first capital, cradle of the nation's arts and literature; Kyoto, where I was surprised to discover so much image worship in Buddhism; and Nikko, a famous mountain resort, with its Shrine of the Three Monkeys which "see no evil, hear no evil, speak no evil."

In Tokyo, we met with U.S. Ambassador Douglas MacArthur, nephew of his namesake, the famous American general of World War II days, who had commanded the U.S. armed forces in the Pacific area. The ambassador, an affable man, engaged me in a far-ranging discussion of current affairs, including matters affecting Israel. His late father-in-law, Senator Alben W. Barkley, who had been a friend of mine and a consistent supporter of Israel, had served as Vice-President of the United States after Harry Truman's election as President for a second term in 1949.

The Jewish community in Japan had begun to take shape after refugees had found their way there in the wake of the Bolshevik Revolution. At the time of our visit, there were about 1,000 Jews in Tokyo, but only 100 families belonged to the local congregation. I was told that it was difficult to obtain Japanese citizenship and that only one Jew in the whole of Tokyo held it. Among the Jewish residents were some former refugees from Nazi-occupied Europe who had arrived by way of Harbin and Shanghai, as well as a number of American Jews who represented U.S. business interests in Japan.

The leading Jewish industrialist, Shoul Eisenberg, who had fled from Nazi-occupied Europe, conducted a flourishing business in metals and had an important business outlet in South Korea. His wife, a Japanese woman, was a proselyte to Judaism and they had sent their children to be educated in Orthodox schools in Switzerland. As Mr. Eisenberg was away from Tokyo when we arrived, he arranged for one of his executives to extend courtesies to us.

On Friday evening, we attended services at the Jewish community center. Although the ritual was Orthodox and the rabbi was a graduate of Jews' College in London, men and women were allowed to sit together. The worshipers that night included Israel's minister to Japan, Emile Najar, and his vivacious wife, Aviva. Their helpfulness and hospitality did much to make our visit a memorable and pleasant one. It was an unusual experience to observe a number of young Japanese women in the congregation, who took part in the prayers and responses. I learned that they were converts to Judaism who had married American Jewish servicemen.

I preached a sermon on the theme of communal responsibility for Jewish survival. The following week, I also delivered a sermon at Sabbath services in Yokohama, Japan's major port, to which Chaplain Matthew Simon of the Jewish Welfare Board escorted us as guests of the Zim Shipping Company of Israel. In contrast to Tokyo, organized Jewish life in Yokohama dated back almost a century, to 1861. We learned that Zim had ordered two large tankers from local shipyards, each costing about $9 million, and that Japanese imports of potash and phosphates from Israel pointed to the likely development of commercial ties between the two countries. Religious services in Yokohama were held in the Protestant chapel, and Ambassador Najar sat with Chaplain Simon and myself on the pulpit.

For me, one of the outstanding occasions during our stay in Japan was the meeting Ambassador Najar arranged with Prince Mikasa, the third and youngest brother of Emperor Hirohito. Though a member of the imperial family, Prince Mikasa was a noted liberal. He had little patience for court ceremonial. Like the Catholic Church, the Japanese imperial family comprised a variety of trends, so that whichever might gain the upper hand could always find a suitable candidate for the throne. The Japan Socialist party backed Prince Mikasa. If they ever came to power, he would be their man. Labor unions were strong and well organized in

Japan, but some of their "Socialist" leaders were under marked Communist influence.

Although members of the imperial family had lived modestly since the end of World War II, Prince Mikasa lived even more modestly than the rest. His house was unpretentious, simply furnished, and located in what appeared to be a lower-middle-class neighborhood. The interior was cold and only a small electric heater set in the fireplace provided any warmth. His wife, I was told, devoted herself entirely to their home and to the welfare of their six children.

Like many Japanese, the prince was short and slender, and also ascetic in appearance. He was a bookish man, concerned with spiritual matters. Throughout our conversation, I was impressed by the extent of his knowledge of Judaism. He had become interested in it, he explained, out of a desire to understand Christianity, and this desire had led him to study the origins of the Christian faith and its scriptural basis, the Old Testament. When he mentioned how greatly he had been struck by the connection between the soil, the religion, and the reverence for ancestors in Judaism, I could well appreciate the role of his Japanese background in predisposing him to such an attitude. Prince Mikasa, it appeared, occasionally attended Jewish religious services and communal functions.

I opened the conversation by mentioning the fact that his interest in Jewish studies was known and respected. I then stated that, as a rabbi and former president of the Synagogue Council of America, my main interests were religious and that, as an American, I was anxious that there should be good relations between our two countries. Americans, I said, usually thought of other nations in economic and political terms, but I would like them to think also in spiritual terms and to try to understand other religions. I added that, in my view, the search for world peace needed an extra spiritual and cultural dimension, and in that connection I referred to my proposal for a World Academy for Peace.

On the topic of Israel, I stressed my special concern for the Medinah not only as a politico-national Jewish entity, but also as a fulcrum of spiritual values. That, I said, was also the approach of leaders such as David Ben-Gurion, who saw Israel as part of Asia, as well as of the West. Thus, geographically, historically, and spiritually, Israel could serve as a bridge between East and West.

Emile Najar was present during this interview, which lasted for about one hour. Among other things, we discussed the prospects for peace between Israel and the Arab world. I heard that Professor R. J. Zwi Werblowsky of the Hebrew University's Department of Comparative Religion had recently visited Japan, where he made an excellent impression. One particularly welcome fact I learned at the time, and which, I hope, still holds true, was that Japan provided no foothold for anti-Semitism.

A brief interlude in Hong Kong, the outpost of the free world adjacent to Communist China, provided us with a couple of amusing examples of the quirks often encountered in Jewish nomenclature. Our host for Friday night dinner, whose family had immigrated from Baghdad, was the only Moshe Cohen in the Hong Kong telephone directory. One could scarcely imagine the surname "Cohen" playing such a unique role in most other areas of the English-speaking world, even apart from New York or London. Curiously enough, our table companions included a Mr. Isaac Eastman. Delicate inquiry enabled us to discover that, far from being a Gentile, Mr. Eastman was in fact a Syrian Jew originally named Mizrahi. He helped us get our bearings in Hong Kong and nearby Kowloon.

There were some 200 Jews in Hong Kong. Jewish communal life there was on the decline, offering little hope for the future. They had a *shohet* and *mohel*, but no rabbi. Services took place on Sabbath mornings only; half of the Jewish adults did not attend synagogue on the High Holy Days; and no more than five local families observed *Kashrut*. When I went on Sabbath morning to the Ohel Leah Synagogue, which shared the same premises as the Jewish Club and had been built in 1900 by the Sassoons in honor of their mother, Leah, barely a *minyan* was present and only one woman came to worship. Prayers were held early, to enable the men to leave for business at the usual hour. How different it must have been, I thought, in earlier days, when the Sassoons and the Kadoories—proud, observant Jews—had made outstanding economic and philanthropic contributions to the British crown colony. Judaism was clearly on the wane in Hong Kong.

In Bangkok, the capital of Thailand, we gazed at a panorama of Buddhist temples with colored tile roofs and gilded spires, interspersed with handsome public buildings. Prominent among these were the walled royal palace and Chulalongkorn University on a bend of the River Me Nam. Scores of Buddhist priests with begging bowls perambulated the streets.

During our stay in Bangkok, the wife of the newly accredited Israel ambassador, Mordecai Kidron, was kind enough to escort us on a round of the temples, some of which were truly fantastic in appearance. One Buddha we saw was cast of solid gold and weighed eight tons; another, the renowned Reclining Buddha, is one of the major sights of Thailand.

No organized Jewish community existed in Bangkok. What few Jewish residents there were attended High Holy Day services at the home of Dr. and Mrs. P. B. Jacobson. One of the best-known ophthalmologists in that part of the world, Dr. Jacobson had served as honorary consul of Israel until Ambassador Kidron was accredited two months before our arrival. He had been resident in Bangkok for a long time and now acted as local representative of the World Jewish Congress.

The U.S. ambassador arranged for us to meet Prince Wan, Thailand's delegate at the UN, where he had once served as President of the General Assembly. He turned out to be a courtly and affable host. Our discussion was concerned mainly with the position in Southeast Asia, with particular reference to Thailand itself, which was then receiving American aid, but it also touched upon that country's relations with Israel.

A picturesque feature of the Thai capital was the thriving commerce and shopping aboard floating markets on the Me Nam (Chao Phraya) river, along which we cruised. Situated about twenty miles from the mouth of the river, Bangkok has an extensive harbor along the banks. Being the headquarters of SEATO and the Asian center for many UN agencies, notably UNESCO, it is a rather cosmopolitan city and draws visitors from many parts of the world. To our great surprise and pleasure, we ran into Warren Silver, who was then serving as first secretary at the U.S. embassy in New Delhi and had arrived in Bangkok for a conference. Some months later, we were to meet him again in Delhi, where he and his mother were living. Warren, an outstanding product of our religious school at B'nai Jeshurun, had displayed rare intellectual and literary gifts as a youngster. He entered the State Department and went on to various diplomatic posts overseas. Following his New Delhi assignment, he took up one additional foreign assignment and then, after his retirement, devoted himself to writing historical novels and plays.

Rangoon was next on our itinerary. For sheer exoticism and the stylized beauty of its pagodas and temples, the Burmese capital yielded little to the other Asian cities through which we had come.

There was abundant evidence of the excellent relations that existed between Burma and Israel. A large number of Israeli experts were stationed in the country at the time of our visit, advising on a wide range of economic activities, including construction work, irrigation, pharmaceuticals, shipping, and even poultry-raising. Israel had in fact established a tangible presence in Burma, perhaps second only to that of the United States, which provided considerable grants-in-aid. There was great admiration for Israel among the Burmese. Some fifty or sixty of them were currently in Israel, studying various specialized fields of technology. David Hacohen, Israel's first ambassador in Rangoon, played a notable part in establishing this pattern.

On the Burmese side, U Nu, the country's preeminent statesman, had been the architect of this close cooperation with Israel. He had paid an official visit to Israel in 1955, when he was Prime Minister. President Itzhak Ben-Zvi was to repay the compliment by visiting Burma some time after we were there in 1958. The U.S. embassy arranged an interview for me with U Nu, who had been replaced by General Ne Win as Prime Minister in 1957, and who appeared to be living in self-imposed seclusion. Ne Win put an end to Israel-Burmese cooperation in 1963, when he embarked on a policy of "neutralism," although trade between the two countries remained largely unaffected.

My meeting with the ex-Premier was defined as a discussion between a religious leader from abroad and a Burmese religious leader—presumably in order to spare U Nu any political embarrassment. Though out of power and office, and despite his spiritual credentials, he was suspected of planning a political comeback. Indeed, whereas the Ne Win regime and the military establishment in particular were strongly anti-Communist, U Nu was thought to be playing along with the extreme left in order to regain power. I heard that the new Government that had taken over two months earlier, after ousting U Nu, had succeeded in cleaning up entrenched corruption and the black market, incidentally reducing the high cost of living. I was also told that juvenile delinquency no longer constituted a serious problem in Burma.

On meeting U Nu at his party headquarters, I was impressed by his gracious personality, his cheerful, radiant countenance, and his penetrating eyes, which reflected not only keen intelligence but also a friendly, outgoing spirit. He then appeared to be a man in his early fifties.

At the outset of our conversation, I said that, although I was active in political affairs on the American scene and in relation to Israel, I considered myself primarily a religious leader, and that my approach to him was to a leader of Buddhism. Alluding next to my program for a World Peace Academy, I suggested that men such as himself would be sought out for membership, provided they did not hold public office. U Nu's eyes twinkled, lighting up his round countenance, as he smilingly interjected that he still remained a political figure. He thought my idea worth exploring and asked, "What about India?"

"Pandit Nehru is India's outstanding personality," I replied, "but he is also the political leader of his country today, and must therefore be ruled out."

My next point was that democracy involved the solving of basic economic problems. What more could the United States do, I asked, to win the minds and hearts of people in this part of the world? U Nu asked me to elaborate on what I meant by America's winning "the minds and hearts of people."

"America was founded with a vision for humanity," I answered. "It stood for something in the eyes of the world, but in recent years that image has become blurred. At present, most people associate the United States with gadgets and bad movies."

At this point, U Nu opened up and said, "But America must believe in democracy and must support it elsewhere in the world. It must prove clearly that democracy is better than Communism. It dare not compromise." U.S. support for Chiang Kai-shek's regime had been responsible, he went on, for the Communist victory in China. When Burma, in turn, was under the menace of a Communist takeover in 1948, he and his supporters had told the Burmese people, "We have seen what Communist dictatorship means. We offer you democracy. We have no weapons, no guns." Yet democracy fought and won the ideological battle.

Before we parted, I expressed appreciation to U Nu for having pioneered the system of cooperation with Israel. He smiled when I remarked that two relatively small countries were more capable of free and fruitful cooperation than a great power with a small one. He asked to be remembered to Ben-Gurion.

In some ways, U Nu reminded me of Ben-Gurion. Both men were crafty, yet of spiritual caliber, and each might be called "the father of his country." Ben-Gurion met with U Nu a few years later, in 1961, while on an official visit to Burma.

The local Jewish community, established by immigrants from Persia and India in the early nineteenth century, had once numbered several thousand but had declined to a few hundred souls. The first synagogue, in Rangoon, had been built in 1857. An unfortunate dispute over communal property had split the *kehillah* before we arrived, and I made an unsuccessful attempt to resolve the congregational squabble. Since they had mostly refused to take Burmese citizenship, preferring to retain the British passports they had obtained in pre-independence days (before 1948), the Jews of Burma were not held in especially high regard by the authorities.

Israel had a very capable envoy in Dr. Daniel Lewin. He had left Germany for

Palestine as a youth and, with his wife, had once been a kibbutznik. As consul in Vienna after the establishment of the Medinah, he had been instrumental in launching the scheme for the remains of Theodor Herzl to be transferred to Jerusalem.

Ties with Israel also figured prominently in a talk I had with an old friend, Robert R. Nathan, the U.S. economist, who was then in Rangoon as the head of a group advising the Burmese Government on financial matters. Nathan had helped Israeli officials to establish contacts with the U.S. Administration in the late 1940s and the early 1950s, and had also served as consultant to the Jewish Agency Executive in some of its economic programs.

From Burma, we flew on to Karachi, in what was then the larger, western portion of Pakistan. Following the bloody civil war in 1947, the Indian subcontinent had been divided between a largely Hindu republic of India and the two predominantly Muslim regions of Baluchistan (West Pakistan) and East Bengal. The seaport of Karachi, near the delta of the River Indus, became the chief city—though not the legislative capital—of Pakistan, which remained part of the British Commonwealth and, because of its Western-oriented regime, came under the protective wing of the United States.

A dozen years of independence had failed to instill more than lip service to the ideals of democracy. Corruption was still rife, and the country's military regime faced an uphill task in its admittedly vigorous attempt to eliminate the blight. Standards of efficiency were appalling, while health and education remained woefully backward; disease and sickness were rampant, and the average life span did not exceed thirty-five years. Illiteracy constituted another national problem. Grim poverty was widespread and visible in the shantytowns and hovels occupied by the indigenous population and by hordes of Muslim refugees from India. Pakistan's refugee problem was then certainly the largest in the world, as a result of the 1947 partition, which had taken place amid a welter of indiscriminate butchery.

At the time of our visit, there were about fifty million people in Pakistan's two widely separated provinces. The population of Karachi itself had swelled from about 300,000 twelve years earlier to more than two million after the influx of refugees. In a way, however, the divided state's geopolitical problems were eased when East Pakistan declared its independence, as the Republic of Bangladesh, in the 1970s.

I obtained a good deal of background information from my talks with U.S. embassy officials and from private individuals. It added up to a disheartening picture.

A five-year development plan was making very slow progress. The United States had to channel about $200 million annually to Pakistan, apart from military aid, in order to cope with the most pressing needs and help maintain some semblance of economic stability. Yet in spite of this generosity, there was an undercurrent of bitterness toward America, typical of the beneficiary's attitude vis-à-vis the benefactor, coupled with strong resentment over the larger volume of aid the United States was giving to India. American support for Israel also aroused indignation in this overwhelmingly Muslim country.

We received a warm welcome from the tiny local Jewish community. On the evening after our arrival in Karachi, some 250 of the 400 souls whom it comprised, including young people and schoolchildren, assembled in the Magain Shalome Synagogue, which had been erected in 1893. This meeting was followed by a reception in an adjoining hall, where the president of the congregation extended greetings. We were happy to learn that many of the young people were going to Israel, by way of India, in order to train in *hakhsharot* for agricultural settlement there. A remarkably high spirit was maintained by the community, which had a great asset in the Israeli *shaliaḥ*, who taught Hebrew to adults and children alike. Their cantor led the singing of Israeli songs, and the evening concluded with *Hatikvah*. I was impressed by the fact that *Hatikvah*, the Zionist and Israeli national anthem, was sung with the windows of the hall wide open—despite the unfriendly Muslim environment.

Although there was religious freedom in Pakistan, the leaders of this Bene Israel community had no confidence in the future. They could not forget how, following the proclamation of Israel's establishment in 1948, local agitators had led a riotous mob into the synagogue, where the Holy Ark and the Torah scrolls were desecrated and other acts of vandalism took place. Many Jews promptly left for India, whence they proceeded to Israel. For most Jews in Pakistan, this was the standard Aliyah route. To help and care for the Olim, the Jewish Agency maintained offices in Bombay, India, where such immigrants first arrived from Karachi.

Two Visits to Iran

The beginning of February found us in Teheran, on the first of our two visits to the kingdom of Iran that year. On this occasion, we stayed only a couple of days and laid the groundwork for a longer tour in the spring. Arrangements were made for Bert and myself to be received by the Minister of the Shah's court, Hussein Ala, a former Prime Minister and onetime Iranian ambassador to the United States, who was known for his liberal outlook.

Introducing myself as vice-president of the World Jewish Congress, I expressed the appreciation felt by the Jewish people, and especially by American Jewry, for the Shah's humanitarian policy of allowing Jews fleeing from Iraq, Afghanistan, and other lands to pass through Iran on their way to Israel. Hussein Ala spoke positively about Israel and its spirit of initiative, and made admiring reference to Jewish contributions in many fields. "They are the best," he said, and laughed when I remarked, "They are also the best rabbis."

Iran was then laying plans to observe the twenty-five hundredth anniversary of King Cyrus's accession to the throne of Persia. I pointed out that the WJC was interested in this event, in view of the prominent place Cyrus occupies in Jewish history as a liberal monarch who authorized Jews to hold important posts in his Government and who, at the same time, permitted those who so desired to return to their ancestral homeland, Judea. "We regard the Shah of Iran today as one who follows that tradition," I added.

The next day was the anniversary of Shah Mohammed Riza Pahlavi's escape from an attempt on his life, and services of thanksgiving were held in all houses of worship, including Iran's synagogues. We visited two of these in the *Mahalleh* (Jewish quarter) of Teheran, where a special prayer was recited for the reigning monarch. At every mention of his name, there was much enthusiastic applause from the packed congregations. We also went to a third synagogue, where Chief Rabbi Yedidiah Shofet, head of the Beth Din, addressed the worshipers.

The *Mahalleh*, which then had about 7,000 inhabitants, was in most respects similar to all such Jewish ghettos in the East, with open water troughs lining the alleyways and the obvious lack of any sewerage, although conditions were better than in the *mellahs* of Morocco which we had seen not long before. Teheran's *Mahalleh* had four families living off each courtyard, under which lay enclosed cesspools.

The American Jewish Joint Distribution Committee and its devoted staff were doing a remarkably fine job in caring for the Jewish poor. Prenatal and postnatal care was provided, mothers were looked after in the hospitals, children's crèches were maintained, Arab-style toilets had been installed, and women had been taught to fetch water from the city faucets and to boil it. Hygienic methods had also been introduced in the *kasher* meat markets. As a result, infant mortality among the Jews stood at one per thousand, as compared with seventy per thousand among the general population.

The organizations set up by the JDC included a women's social-service group and a teachers' seminary for local Jewish youth, to which the *kehillah* contributed one-fifth of the operational budget. The JDC also financed the ORT vocational-training school. A well-equipped sports club catered to large numbers of the youth. Apart from the JDC, the Jewish Agency, the World Jewish Congress, ORT, Otzar Hatorah, and the Alliance Israélite Universelle were active in Iran. Otzar Hatorah provided religious education at afternoon classes, teaching modern Hebrew as well as biblical Hebrew and prayers. The Alliance Israélite, long the patron of Jewish education in North Africa and Asia, continued to make an important contribution to the Jewish cultural survival of this *kehillah*.

It was obvious that the 80,000 Jews of Iran held the Shah in high esteem. His authority was widely recognized as a stabilizing factor in a land where Muslim Shi'ite fanaticism and reaction lay just below the surface. The Jews linked their welfare with his, and their prayers at Sabbath services for his health and prosperity were recited with wholehearted devotion.

We were gladdened by the sight of Israel once again, when we arrived at Lod Airport on Friday afternoon, February 6. Our two-week sojourn in Israel was spent relaxing among friends and touring. Everywhere, there was evidence of thriving activity—new settlements, projects, and factories, a new power station and a deep-water harbor at Ashdod.

The first Shabbat morning, President Itzhak Ben-Zvi invited me to attend his synagogue and a Talmud *shi'ur* with him, and then to come for *Kiddush* to his home. He told me of a delightful incident in the course of his official visit to the Netherlands some time back. A dinner was given in honor of the Presidential couple by Queen Juliana and her consort, Prince Bernhard. Upon taking their seats, the Ben-Zvis saw that an unopened bottle of wine had been placed beside each guest's plate. When the President inquired as to the reason for this, Prince Bernhard smilingly replied, "We know that, according to Jewish law, a Gentile is not supposed to pour wine for a Jew." What an example of royal courtesy!

Bert and I called on David Ben-Gurion, to whom we related something of our journeyings and experiences, including the interviews with Prince Mikasa in Tokyo and with U Nu in Rangoon. Israel's Prime Minister, in his turn, gave us an enthusiastic account of a countrywide tour he had made the previous day. On his favorite topic of Aliyah, "the Old Man" made a prophetic statement, saying he was confident that the turn of Soviet Jewry would come next. When I asked him what grounds he had for this belief, he answered, "The Rumanian Jews would not be coming in such large numbers if the USSR didn't want them to."

"But what about Egypt's attitude?" I asked. "Won't Nasser protest?"

"The Russians don't need Nasser," he replied. "Nasser needs them."

"How about the money required to transport and absorb such an influx of Olim?" was my next query. He dismissed it with a wave of his hand. "Money is Eshkol's problem—he's the Minister of Finance. *I'm* interested in Jews."

On the eve of our departure for London in the third week of February, I spoke at a meeting convened by the Israel Executive of the World Jewish Congress. It was, I said, a new experience for us to arrive in the Medinah from the Orient. "Coming to Israel from the U.S., one is aware of how much still needs to be done economically, agriculturally, and industrially, to bring Israel's standards up to America's, although the progress has been remarkable. Coming from the Far East, however, the comparison—except for Japan—is all in Israel's favor. One can understand, therefore, why it is that some of the Asian and African countries are seeking Israel's practical cooperation."

In conclusion, I observed:

> The warmth of the welcome we received from Jews everywhere testified to their desire for contact with the rest of World Jewry. In some instances, I came across practical problems—the need for a rabbi, Hebrew teachers, a *Sefer Torah* or prayer books—and I tried to be of assistance.
>
> It feels good to be here in Israel after visiting those small and dwindling Jewish communities in the Far East. Yet as long as they live there, we must help them in their struggle for survival, especially with the Jewish education of their children. The World Jewish Congress feels this to be one of its responsibilities, and Israel has an important part to play in its fulfillment.

My week-long tour of the United Kingdom, on behalf of the Joint Palestine Appeal, included speaking engagements in London, at the inaugural JPA campaign dinner, and in Manchester, Liverpool, Leeds, and Glasgow. British Jewry had always impressed me as more Zionist in sentiment and practice than American Jewry. Bearing in mind the lower rate of tax exemption for charitable donations allowed in Great Britain, the Jews there, on the whole, showed even greater generosity than their American brethren. They were also a tightly knit community, more ingrown Jewishly than their counterparts in the United States.

On the train journey to the North of England, I found myself sharing a compartment with Colonel (later, Major-General) Avraham Yoffe, commander of the IDF force that had captured Sharm el-Sheikh during the Sinai Campaign a little over two years previously. Credit for the success of that military operation, he said, was due primarily to General Moshe Dayan, who had not only shown himself to be a brilliant chief of staff, but an officer who displayed consideration for all of the men under his command. One night, Yoffe related, he was sleeping near his jeep in the desert not far from Sharm when he was awakened by a buzzing overhead. Looking up, he saw a small reconnaissance plane, from the cockpit of which a voice called, "Is that you, Avraham?"

"Yes," he replied, "who's that?"

"It's the father of Yael and the husband of Ruth," came the answer. "How are you doing? It wouldn't hurt to move a little faster!"

Six hours later, Yoffe's men took the important strategic headland at the mouth of the Red Sea.

Back in Israel, prior to the next stage of our world tour, Bert and I shared the thrill of witnessing the arrival of a shipload of Rumanian immigrants at Haifa. Some disquieting news had been filtering through the Iron Curtain regarding the prospects of further Aliyah from Rumania. Apparently, the authorities in Bucharest were clamping down on the flow of emigration because of their annoyance over a statement made by Ben-Gurion (much the same as what he had told Bert and me a fortnight earlier), to the effect that Jews were able to come from Rumania because the Russians were not opposed to it. Any suggestion that they could not be independent of the Soviet Union in their policies and actions evidently aroused the sensitivity of the Rumanian Government.

Every vessel that berthed at Haifa in the 1950s with new immigrants aboard was an occasion for nationwide rejoicing. My wife and I arrived at the quayside in time to see how the Olim were being processed. Most of the preliminaries had been completed by Jewish Agency officials on board ship even before they docked. After disembarkation, the newcomers were taken to the places of residence for which they had signed up, and they received food packages to tide them over the first few days. Prior to our own arrival, President and Mrs. Ben-Zvi had come to greet a large number of Olim on another incoming ship. Where else in the world, I reflected, would people coming to a new land be welcomed by the head of state?

As we stood on deck, watching the immigrants choked with emotion as they gazed at the Haifa skyline for the first time, Bert turned to one woman laden with hand baggage and asked, in Yiddish, if she was a Zionist. The woman gave a negative shake of her head. "Then why did you come?" Bert asked.

"It's our land, isn't it?" was the reply. "That's why we came."

A few days later, I attended a function at the Habimah Theater in Tel Aviv to mark the centenary of the birth of Sholem Aleichem. I happened to mention this event on the following Shabbat, when lunching at the home of Dr. Abraham Granott, president of the Keren Kayemet Le-Yisrael. My few words prompted a charming reminiscence by Miriam Granott of a childhood meeting with the great Yiddish author. Her father, Rabbi Chaim Tchernowitz, the renowned Talmudic scholar and author (better known as Rav Tza'ir), had taken her along when visiting Sholem Aleichem, who was spending the summer with his family at Montreux, on the shores of Lake Geneva.

While her father was busy talking to the family, Miriam slipped away and wandered into the famous author's workroom, where he was writing at an elevated desk resembling a pulpit. It was a sunny day, and through the windows of the room a delightful view of the lake and mountains could be seen. The little girl was surprised to find an open black umbrella—not a parasol—perched like a canopy over his desk.

"A gut morgen!" Sholem Aleichem said in greeting.

After an appropriate response, Miriam asked, "Why do you have that umbrella there?"

"Well, you see," he explained, "outside it's a beautiful sunny day. How can I write about my sorrowing, suffering people? So the umbrella is there to put me in the proper mood."

Resuming our world tour, Bert and I flew back to Iran in March. That month can be quite chilly in the northern highlands, where Teheran is situated. The Iranian capital stands at an elevation of around 4,000 feet and bitterly cold winds blow in from the Caspian Sea region some seventy miles away. There was more than a nip in the air, therefore, when we returned for a brief stay in Iran en route to India.

At Teheran Airport, we met a group of Iranian, Indian, and Pakistani Jews who were about to leave on the plane to Tel Aviv. The sight of these Olim constituted a timely reminder of the role played by Medinat Yisrael in the life of Jews throughout the world. We went over to bid them Godspeed and a safe flight. They returned our greetings and, with an impulsive gesture, bent to kiss our hands. It was a touching introduction to many other encounters that awaited us in Iran and in the other distant lands for which we were bound.

Isfahan, a religious center filled with mosques in central Iran, has all the ambience of a bygone age. It was the capital of Persia from the sixteenth to the eighteenth centuries, and had more than a quarter of a million inhabitants at the time of our visit. A Jewish community was already established there in the Sassanid period, fifteen centuries ago, and during the Caliphate Isfahan's Jewish quarter was so populous that it was known as "the City of the Jews." Despite recurrent persecutions, a strongly religious and flourishing Jewish communal life was maintained for hundreds of years. In the nineteenth century, however, Isfahan Jewry faced new threats from the Baha'i movement and Christian missionary organizations. The establishment of an Alliance Israélite school helped to strengthen the *kehillah*.

We heard on our arrival that the Jewish population had dwindled from some

12,000 in 1948 to about 3,500, and 2,000 of these still lived in the old ghetto. Some places in that decrepit quarter were even more horrifying than the hovels we had seen in the *mellah* of Casablanca. The vast majority of the Jews in recent times had been poverty-stricken, and it was from this section of the community that the Olim had come to Israel. At a meeting held in our honor in a synagogue hall, we learned that some 400 Iranian Jews were preparing for Aliyah immediately after Passover.

Shiraz, in southwestern Iran, has aptly been called "the city of carpets and flowers." It is hard to say which are more gorgeous—the floral displays in its parks and gardens or the exquisite patterns woven by craftsmen plying their ancient trade. Shiraz was a smaller town than Isfahan, but its Jewish community of some 8,000 souls—most of whom still lived in the *Mahalleh*—amounted to at least five percent of the general population. Judeo-Persian literature flourished there in medieval times, but the more recent history of this *kehillah* was similar to that of Isfahan and there had been substantial Aliyah since the late nineteenth century. A network of Jewish educational institutions maintained the fabric of communal life. We met a number of the Shiraz Jews at a get-together in one of their schools, where we gained a further insight into the impoverished state of a once great and thriving center of Diaspora Jewish life.

On a plain some forty miles to the northeast of Shiraz lay the ruins of Persepolis (Takht-i-Jamshid, as it is called today), which had been the ceremonial capital of Darius I, Persia's "Great King." Susa, the biblical Shushan, was situated 300 miles to the northwest; Ecbatana (the modern Hamadan), Darius's summer capital, where the reputed tombs of Esther and Mordecai are to be found, lay even farther away. At Persepolis, we saw all that remained of this ancient glory of the Achaemenid Empire—the huge surviving pillars of Darius's "hall of a hundred columns," the great double stairway leading to the top of the palace, and marble friezes depicting Persian warriors and a lion in the act of killing a bull. Here, too, lay the vast plazas across which chariots must once have been raced at the behest of the "King of Kings" or his satraps. This great complex of buildings bore mute witness to the architectural grandeur of a remote past. Although the actual site retained some importance as an urban center until the Islamic period, Alexander the Great, marching to India in 330 B.C.E., poured scorn on the once mighty empire and its monarch by conquering the Persian armies and devastating Persepolis. The shattered remains told their own story.

On our return to Teheran, I was informed by the U.S. embassy that Hussein Ala had confirmed the arrangements for Bert and myself to be received in audience by Shah Mohammed Riza on the morning of March 15. We arrived at the appointed hour and were escorted through spacious gardens and several rooms of the palace before being ushered into the royal presence.

The Shah, a handsome, dignified person, was informally dressed in civilian attire. A shock of dark hair, peppered with flecks of gray, although he was only forty, heightened the monarch's youthful appearance. Mohammed Riza Pahlavi had been on the throne of Iran since the age of twenty-two, in 1941, following the abdication of his father. With disarming informality, he showed us to a chair and sofa before sitting beside us, rather than behind a desk.

In cultured English accents, the Shah asked us how long we had been in his country and what we had seen. I told him that we had arrived six days earlier, on our second visit to Iran in a couple of months, and that we had already been to Isfahan, Shiraz, and the ruins of Persepolis, capital of Darius the Great and his son, Xerxes, whom many identify with King Ahasuerus of the Bible. I went on to say how glad we were that our visit to Iran coincided with World Brotherhood Week, as I was active in the movement and had met with several of its leaders in the course of our recent travels. The Shah was interested to hear this, since he held the office of honorary president of the World Brotherhood Movement's Iranian branch, while Hussein Ala, the royal chamberlain, was vice-president.

"I have been in touch with the Jewish communities here," I remarked, "and it is moving to observe the reverence and affection in which Your Majesty is held by the Jews of Iran, who sincerely believe that their future depends on you."

"We have always shown respect and tolerance toward other faiths," the Shah replied, "believing that people should be able to follow their own way of life."

I then turned to the forthcoming twenty-five hundredth anniversary of the founding of the Persian Empire by Cyrus the Great. "In Jewish history he is remembered as a liberal ruler," I said, "liberal in the treatment of his Jewish subjects and liberal in permitting those who so desired to return to Judea in order to help rebuild the Jewish commonwealth there. We feel that Your Majesty's Government honors that tradition." I also took occasion to point out that my mission was primarily on behalf of the World Jewish Congress, which represented Jewish communities in more than sixty countries and had a recognized status in the United Nations.

At this point, the Shah interjected that the anniversary was still some way off. He thought that the appropriate date, according to the Jewish calendar, might be a year ahead of the Persian reckoning. Conceivably, therefore, the celebrations in Iran might begin around March 25, 1961, but nothing had been fixed so far. "One year more or less matters little in the perspective of two and a half millennia," I remarked, citing the recent three thousandth anniversary of the founding of Jerusalem by King David, on which occasion one scholar had opined that it was being celebrated a year short of the proper date. The Shah found this amusing and laughed heartily. I may have reminded him of a similar discussion in palace circles.

I went on to say that the World Jewish Congress, anticipating the Jewish people's interest in this historic event, might give thought to the formation of an international committee to mark the occasion, because of Cyrus's decree permitting the Jewish return from exile in the sixth century B.C.E. Jewish communities everywhere would be encouraged to join in the celebration. I ventured to suggest that, if the stimulation of tourism were to form part of Iran's plan, Israel's experience might prove helpful, as it had just experienced a boom in tourism during its tenth anniversary year, at a time when tourism had suffered a marked decline elsewhere. My suggestion interested the Shah, who stated that one reason for delaying matters was the fact that Iran still had insufficient hotels and motels to handle a large influx of visitors from abroad.

As far as any advice or help from the World Jewish Congress was concerned, he believed that the head of the Iranian Information Bureau in New York might serve as a liaison. Once or twice during our conversation, the Shah alluded to "possible developments in the next few years," which might have some influence on the planning of Cyrus's anniversary. Although we both steered clear of any discussion concerning relations between Israel and Iran, I took note of his remark that "there have been tensions between Iran and the Arab states, but we are Muslims nonetheless."

In general, Iran's monarch impressed me as a shrewd, liberal man, inclined to be friendly toward Israel and the Jewish people, but guarded in his statements.

At the termination of our audience, I went to thank Hussein Ala for arranging it. I also sought permission for the issue of a press report incorporating my suggestions vis-à-vis the World Jewish Congress and stressing the need for an appropriate reference to Jerusalem. I urged Hussein Ala to read the biblical mention of Cyrus in the first chapter of the Book of Ezra. Were Iran to arrange an international conference of historians during the festive period, I said, it would surely be appropriate to invite Israeli scholars as well. To this he agreed. The tourism idea also impressed him.

As finally approved by Hussein Ala, however, the press statement omitted any mention of possible cooperation by the WJC. Nor was there any reference to Israel and Jerusalem. It merely reported my audience with the Shah, to whom I had brought greetings from the World Jewish Congress on the forthcoming celebrations, and mentioned the fact that Cyrus the Great had an honored place in Jewish history. The World Jewish Congress, my abbreviated statement added, was appreciative that the Shah's regime continued that noble tradition.

A sad postscript must be written. These events took place some two decades before the overthrow of the Shah. When the revolution in Iran took on a fanatical religious guise, under the Ayatollah Khomeini, Jews were among the first to suffer. A prominent victim was the president of the Iranian Jewish community, Habib Elghanian, whom the new rulers executed for "corruption and treason." One of his alleged crimes was his link with Israel. How tragic it is, in retrospect, that many of the well-to-do Jews of Iran failed to heed the call of Zion, and left it for their poorer brethren to make Aliyah.

From Bombay to Singapore

Our next destination was India. Nothing we had read beforehand prepared us for the staggering immensity of what we encountered. There is an incredible gap between the splendor of India's past, which bedazzles the eye, and the appalling spectacle of impoverishment and misery among its present-day teeming multitudes. Our route lay across a breathtaking geographical canvas: Madras and Hyderabad, with their fine university campuses; Agra and its fantastic "jewel palace," the Taj

Mahal; the holy city of Benares, with its shrines and temples and the broad River Ganges, to which millions of pilgrims flock in search of healing and spiritual purification; Jaipur, known as the "Pink City" because all of its buildings are painted that color; and the spacious boulevards and handsome edifices of the capital, New Delhi, which bears the architectural imprint of the British Raj. Such were the ornamental trappings of Mother India.

Yet, behind this sumptuous façade, the tangible evidence of squalor and misery shocked us. Skinny hands held out begging bowls and starvation lurked in the shadow of elaborate marble palaces. While visiting Calcutta, in West Bengal, we saw homeless folk sleeping in doorways and entire families camping out in the open, emaciated caricatures of the human species. Around them lay the tokens of an extravagantly wealthy past, like so many monumental exclamation points dotting the annals of countless epochs.

Our introduction to the essential character of India, with its array of disparate castes and religious sects, came when we arrived in Bombay, the country's urban gateway to the Arabian Sea. It had a multifarious population of nearly four million, constituting one enormous human mosaic of Hindus, Jains, Parsees, and Buddhists, with a scattering of Muslims and Jews. An unimaginable mass of people crowded every inch of the sidewalks, spilling over into the roadway. Although twelve years had elapsed since partition, many of these pitiable dregs of mankind were still, to all intents and purposes, refugees from West Pakistan. Most of them were dressed in little better than rags, and cripples afflicted with various deformities abounded. Who could fail to be horrified by the spectacle of vast multitudes living in conditions of near-famine? Begging attained epidemic proportions, and one could not walk anywhere for more than a few seconds without glimpsing a scrawny hand stretched out for alms.

This living chronicle of bleak hardship, penury, and distress bore witness to a virtually unparalleled failure of social justice on the most massive scale. We were, however, also motivated by a deep concern for those segments of our own people which had, in some miraculous fashion, survived all the chronic ills and economic pressures of the Indian environment.

The evening after we landed at Bombay Airport on the plane from Teheran, a reception was held for us at the Jewish Club under the auspices of the Central Jewish Board of Bombay. Mr. Meyer Nissim, president of the community and a former Mayor of Bombay, chaired the proceedings. The local *kehillah* then numbered some 15,000, of whom around four-fifths belonged to the Bene Israel community. Jewish communal life revolved around the ten synagogues, two schools, Maccabi sports association, YMHA and YWHA, B'nai B'rith and Bene Israel Women's Organization. A *shali'aḥ* of the Jewish Agency's Torah Education Department conducted a teacher-training program for boys and girls. Vigorous activity was maintained by the Bombay Zionist Association. Philip Cohen, the Jewish Agency's devoted Aliyah director, told us that about one thousand persons left each year for Israel.

We heard from another source that the Baghdadi Jews, who had immigrated in recent times from Syria and Iraq, were inclined to look down on the indigenous Bene Israel, whose status as Jews had been recognized by the Israel Chief Rabbinate. The Bene Israel claimed descent from Galilean Jews of the second century B.C.E. They lived in miserable conditions, one family to a room, as we discovered on visiting their slum quarters.

At one time, however, Bene Israel Jews had enjoyed a greater degree of prosperity. Sha'ar ha-Rahamim ("Gate of Mercy"), the oldest synagogue in Bombay, had been built in 1796 by the brothers Samuel and Isaac Divekar. The origin of this synagogue constituted a fascinating piece of Jewish history. The Divekar brothers had served in the Anglo-Indian army as officers, Samuel attaining the rank of *subadar* (captain), and they fell into enemy hands during the British campaign against Mysore, a principality in southern India. As they were about to be condemned to death, the notorious Sultan of Mysore, Tippoo Sahib, asked to what caste they belonged.

"We are Bene Israel," the brothers replied.

The Muslim ruler had never heard of such a caste, but his wife, who was better informed, told him that it was mentioned in the Koran. Samuel and Isaac Divekar were spared and were subsequently released in an exchange of prisoners. On returning to Bombay, they built the Sha'ar ha-Rahamim Synagogue in thanksgiving for their deliverance, and they became active in communal affairs. Two thoroughfares were named for them: Samuel Street, where the synagogue was located, and Isaac Street.

Sha'ar ha-Rahamim could accommodate 300 worshipers, but although a large congregation attended High Holy Day services there, the turnout on Sabbaths was rarely more than fifty. A *mikveh* stood nearby. The aristocratic Baghdadi Jews, now reduced in number, had built more splendid houses of worship, Magen David and Keneseth Eliahoo, in the second half of the nineteenth century. These, together with a number of hospitals, schools, and other institutions in Bombay, bore witness to the philanthropic endeavors of David Sassoon and his family.

The Bene Israel of Konkan had lived for centuries in complete isolation from the rest of Jewry. Many aspects of Judaism, even the festivals of Hanukkah and Purim, were unknown to them until the eighteenth century. Their prayer books followed the traditional rite, however, and included a Marathi translation. The local Hindu population dubbed them *Shanwar Telis*, "Sabbath-observing oilmen," because they pressed and dealt in oil and abstained from work on Saturday. Bene Israel children, at the Bombay Jewish day school we visited, were taught Marathi, Hindi, English, and Hebrew.

The Jews of Bombay mostly earned their livelihood in trade and commerce. The immigrant German and East European element had established a Reform congregation, but lacked a house of worship. Their minister was Rabbi Hugo Gryn, who in later years accepted a call to the West London Synagogue in Upper Berkeley Street. We met Rabbi Gryn and his wife when we were invited to dinner at the home of the

Israeli consul, Avshalom Caspi, where the other guests included Mr. and Mrs. Rajah Singh, brother-in-law and youngest sister of Mrs. Nehru, the Prime Minister's wife.

Even usually well-informed people in India displayed a woeful ignorance of matters concerning Judaism and Israel. This was evident from the naïve questions put to me by a *Bombay Times* reporter who came for a press interview. "What is a rabbi?" he asked.

An ancient Jewish community we visited was that of Cochin, a seaport on the Malabar coast at the southwestern tip of the Indian subcontinent. The state of Kerala, in which Cochin lies, had a population of nearly fourteen million, with Trivandrum (formerly, Travancore) as its capital. At the previous election, the Communists had been returned to power by a narrow majority. Christians made up nearly one-third of Kerala's population, whereas they constituted only 2.5 percent in the rest of the country.

Bert and I were wreathed in garlands by the group that welcomed us at the airport. It was led by Shabdai Samuel Koder, the recognized head of all Jewish communities in southern India and son of a distinguished father who, in his time, had received many honors for his services to Cochin.

The "Jews' Synagogue" is one of the famous historical sites in that part of the world. Jewish settlement on the Malabar coast dates from antiquity, and a copper plate deposited in the Paradesi Synagogue of the "White" Jews records that they once received special privileges. The early *kehillah* resided about twenty miles from Cochin, but moved there following the arrival of the Portuguese, who systematically persecuted the Jews until Dutch forces took control in 1663. Under the protection of the Rajah of Cochin, Jew Town was established in 1567 and a synagogue was built there a year later. This house of worship, the Paradesi Synagogue, was destroyed by the Portuguese before they left. It was rebuilt in 1664, and a clock tower with Hebrew numerals on the dial was added to the structure in 1761. On display inside the synagogue is a golden crown, which the Maharajah presented to the Cochin Jews in 1763, and the Chinese porcelain tiles paving the floor were laid the same year. At the time of our visit, the *kehillah* numbered about 1,000 persons.

Other synagogues to which we went on Purim were that of the "Black" Jews in Ernakulam, situated on Jews' Street, where many of them lived, and one belonging to the more aristocratic "White" Jews in Cochin. According to local tradition, the "Black" Jews were descendants of converted slaves or concubines. The synagogue of the "White" Jews, a veritable gem dating from 1565, contained a beautifully carved Ark with one Torah scroll enclosed in a golden *tik* (case), a centrally placed *bimah* and another at an upper level used for sounding the shofar, a glorious chandelier and Chinese blue tiles of eighteenth-century manufacture.

Alongside this building stood the palace of the Maharajah who had protected the Jews against Portuguese attacks. We were shown copper plates, taken from the vaults, which were said to go back to 370 C.E. They recorded in Tamil the edict of protection granting autonomy to the Jews within a certain area. On the occasion of his state visit in November 1956, Emperor Haile Selassie of Ethiopia presented a carpet to the Jews of Cochin, and told the community leaders that his own people traced their descent from the ancient Judeans.

One of the purposes of my visit to the Cochin region was to see what further possibilities for Aliyah existed there. Those Jews from Ernakulam who had so far emigrated to Israel had enjoyed a successful Klitah. The elders of the community implored me to expedite the Aliyah of the remaining Ernakulam Jews, and their pleas accompanied us to the airport. I brought back their message to the Jewish Agency in Jerusalem.

We were told that good relations prevailed among all sections of the population, and that Hindus often came to Jewish homes at Purim and exchanged gifts with their hosts. Almost the entire Cochin Jewish community later emigrated to Israel. Devoted Jews, earnest and hardworking, they have established flourishing settlements in the eastern Shefelah.

The local Rotary Club, at which I spoke one evening, had a mixed membership of Christians, Muslims, Hindus, and Jews. During question time, I was asked to explain the nature of the cooperative movement in Israel. The fact that to be a kibbutz member was optional, and that there was no state compulsion to join, impressed the non-Jews in my audience.

India's foremost spiritual and intellectual leader was, by general consent, the Vice-President, Dr. Sarvepalli Radhakrishnan. I was glad to hear, therefore, on our arrival in Madras, capital of the state of that name, that the Vice-President had his residence there. We were briefed by Arthur and Shirley Isenberg, who were connected with a Ford Foundation project to publish and distribute good books in translation. They were in Madras for a short stay. We discovered to our delight that Arthur Isenberg had been a classmate of our son and son-in-law at Harvard.

At dinner one evening, the conversation turned to my plan for a World Peace Academy, which I said I would like to discuss with Dr. Radhakrishnan. One of the guests kindly arranged an appointment for us. The Vice-President's home turned out to be a modest, simply furnished apartment. He gave us a friendly welcome and then sat on the couch with his legs folded under him, in accordance with local custom. Then we talked.

That same morning, we had heard the speech delivered by the Vice-President at the centenary celebration of the International Red Cross, and I had been impressed by its lofty moral and spiritual tone. Alluding to his address, I said that many of the points he had made I could identify in terms of my own Jewish tradition. I took occasion to quote the text, "I have set before thee life and death, the blessing and the curse; therefore choose life, that thou mayest live, thou and thy seed." To my surprise and delight, he interrupted me and said, "Deuteronomy!"—which was, indeed, the source (Deut. 30:19).

Dr. Radhakrishnan went on to express regret over the fact that his official duties prevented him from visiting universities in other countries, as he would have wished. To bring Israel into the picture, I observed that President Itzhak Ben-Zvi felt similarly restrained. In many ways, Israel and India were alike in their ideas and ideals, I said, and one could not help wondering why there were no diplomatic relations between them. "There ought to be," he replied, and added that he was discussing the matter with the Prime Minister.

When I told him of my planned World Academy for Peace, he welcomed the idea and the plan. With evident regret, he said that people such as he would not be eligible to serve on it because they were holding public offices.

Turning next to India's program of agricultural reform, which was opposed by vested interests, the Vice-President disclosed that Government officials had been sent to the villages in order to explain its purpose. There were currently, he noted, seven million "explainers" on similar errands in Communist China.

It was refreshing to meet someone of Dr. Radhakrishnan's high intellectual and moral caliber who displayed a broad liberal outlook and was so obviously unaffected by the power and authority he enjoyed.

I had no way of knowing what kind of future lay in store for the dark-haired lady clad in an elegant sari who received me in her New Delhi office one afternoon in early April. Indira Gandhi, a handsome woman who had just turned forty, was then nearing the end of her term as president of India's Congress Party. With her olive complexion, clean-cut features, and the mark of her high caste painted on her forehead, she exuded that dignity and charisma which, seven years later, would raise her to the premiership of her country.

Speaking in cultured English, she gave me to understand that politics held no great attraction for her and that she would prefer to go back to her former work in the country villages and education. Mrs. Gandhi remarked that there were now forty women in Congress and other spheres of public life, but she also made this interesting observation: "In the United States, women find fulfillment in many areas, in addition to the home. In India, however, women find outside fulfillment only in politics."

The Government did not adopt a doctrinaire position on agricultural reform, she stated. "If someone has a better idea, let him come forward with it." There was no question of resorting to compulsory measures, as the Government prided itself on maintaining the democratic process. When I asked whether India could learn anything from other countries, Mrs. Gandhi affirmed that Israel had done an excellent job in cooperative farming, but that conditions there were different. She claimed that India's masses were better off than they had been ten years previously. Then they only had loincloths; now they had clothing. Mahatma Gandhi, the great nationalist leader and advocate of passive resistance, had adopted the loincloth, she said, not only as a protest against British-made goods, but also because it was less subject to tax. These days, however, people in India were demanding more.

I mentioned that on the previous day I had seen the U.S. ambassador, Ellsworth Bunker, and Mrs. Gandhi immediately praised him as a man who showed a great understanding for the Indian people. Americans sometimes came with money, and also with ideas and projects unsuited to the circumstances in her country, she told me. It was her belief that people from the United States who came on aid missions to India should be trained on the spot to learn and appreciate local requirements.

The next morning, we had an appointment with India's Prime Minister, Jawaharlal Pandit Nehru, Indira Gandhi's father. He had been in office for twelve years. Tall, lean, and ascetic in appearance, Pandit Nehru was dressed entirely in white and his distinctive white cap remained on his head throughout our half-hour interview in the Ministry for External Affairs. He was in his seventieth year, but looked younger. I handed him a letter of introduction from U.S. Supreme Court Justice William O. Douglas, which he read through carefully. "Mr. Douglas is a very good friend of ours," he remarked.

In answer to my opening question as to whether progress in India could be achieved voluntarily, he went into a lengthy disquisition. His five-year plan was a unified system, he said, encompassing agriculture, irrigation, industry, and mechanization. It could not be implemented piecemeal, in sections, and everything had to be integrated as a working unit. "Birth control is also part of our program," he added, "but that will take another generation to become effective."

Nehru agreed that a huge capital outlay would be required, and that the United States should be made more fully aware of how much needed to be done. He smiled in approval of my remark that both countries were fortunate to have men such as Ellsworth Bunker and Chester Bowles representing the U.S. in India.

At that time, a Buddhist visionary named Vinoba Bhave, hailed as "the Walking Saint of India," had been going on foot from place to place in an effort to persuade landowners to give part of their estate to poor farmers, and a veritable grassroots movement around him had sprung up. Mrs. Gandhi had spoken of this development when we met, but felt that getting people to part with some of their land was not enough. Money had to come from somewhere in order to make proper use of the soil.

Pandit Nehru also referred to the Bhave movement, which he termed a uniquely Indian phenomenon. The very act of walking from village to village appealed to the masses and produced a response. It thus created an atmosphere conducive to the Government's programs, regardless of the area or quality of the land donated. "Other peoples commit lunatics to asylums," the Prime Minister quipped. "We worship them."

I then ventured to remark, "Some of your problems remind me of those which Israel has faced. Among the Indians whom I have met, there is a feeling of goodwill and respect for Israel. I wonder, therefore, why there are no proper diplomatic relations between these two countries."

Although I feared that he might flare up, the Prime Minister retained his composure and replied calmly, even apologetically, "There *is* a feeling of goodwill toward Israel," he said, "and there is no logical reason for the absence of diplomatic relations. Israelis sometimes come here to cooperate, of course, and some of our people go to Israel. We will shortly be sending an official delegation to study the cooperative movement there."

One day, he declared, there would be a peace agreement between Israel and the

Arab states. The Arabs had to realize that Israel could not be wiped off the map. "If diplomatic relations had been established when India recognized Israel, it would have been one thing," Nehru added. "At this time, however, it might be interpreted as an unfriendly, aggressive move against the Arab world." Even in the internal conflicts that beset the Arabs, he pointed out, one group often accused its opponents of being secretly pro-Israel.

I thanked the Prime Minister for his friendly remarks and then sought his reaction to my peace plan. He thought that it had much to commend it, but feared that it would prove difficult to bring such a group of personalities together. Moreover, he said, they might lack familiarity with the political background to some of the issues they would be called upon to discuss.

"What gives us the courage to propose a scheme that appears to be unrealistic," I answered, "is that the practical men, the statesmen, have not devised a solution to the problem."

It was now 11:30 A.M., and the cabinet was awaiting Pandit Nehru for its daily session to begin. He parted from us with a cordial handshake.

From subsequent conversations in India I learned that Nehru's aim was for every village to have three basic institutions—a *panchayat* (religious council), a cooperative, and a school. Only then, in his view, could the new India's foundations be established securely.

Vedanta is the central philosophy of Hinduism. Visits we paid to two *ashrams* (religious retreats) made it clear to us that Hinduism makes no protest against social injustice, as Judaism emphatically does. Rather, it enables the masses to become reconciled to their misery, impoverishment, and disease by instilling faith in *Karma*—the power generated by each individual's actions, which, according to both Hindus and Buddhists, perpetuates reincarnation and predetermines his fate and punishment in this life (and in future existence), in retribution for past offenses. This was, to my mind, a form of "opium for the masses," inducing them to accept centuries of degradation and suffering without a murmur of complaint. Such Eastern fatalism naturally gave rise to no prophets of justice and righteousness on the biblical pattern.

I had an hour's conversation with the *swami* ("master" in Hindi) at one *ashram*, a man of about sixty who spoke good English and was quite familiar with Western as well as Indian culture. "How can I find salvation?" someone asked, and his answer was, "By getting rid of the 'I.'" To discard ambition, desire, family ties, and possessions seemed to be the core of Vedanta. "Everything must be merged with God, like a bottle of water emptying into the sea, or the extinction of a flame." *Nirvana* (heaven), the *swami* explained, was the state in which the "I" became totally one with God. All religions could be found in Hinduism, he asserted. There was much in Judaism, Christianity, and Islam he found acceptable.

We spent a pleasant week in Kashmir, despite the turmoil in that much-troubled state over the Muslim majority's demand for union with Pakistan, to which there was stern resistance by India. At that time of the year, early April, the route was normally impassable, but we were fortunate to arrive safely in Srinagar, Kashmir's summer capital.

Our hotel there was a houseboat on the River Jhelum, comprising five nicely furnished rooms and a spacious deck. Attached to it, on a smaller boat, were the kitchen and the servants' quarters. For the modest rental of five dollars per day, we thus had all the comforts of a hotel, as well as personal service and the added advantage of free movement and mooring up and down the river. There was even a "taxi" service, provided by skiffs, which conveyed us to the shore and the main road.

Carefully preserved in a mosque along the river was a hair which, according to the faithful, came from the beard of Mohammed. It was encased in glass and could be viewed by the public, though only on religious festivals. It did not require much imagination to picture vast crowds of pilgrims standing up in boats along the Jhelum river to behold from a distance that treasured relic—a hair from the beard of the Prophet!

On April 10, one day after our return to New Delhi, I called on Acharaya Jiwatram Kripalani, leader of the Indian Socialist Party. His group was the third largest in the national assembly, ranking next to the dominant Congress Party and to the Communists. Unlike the Communists, India's Socialist Party constituted a loyal opposition.

An adroit politician by repute, Kripalani was then close to seventy-one. He had served as a professor at Bihar and Benares universities, and during his long political career he had held leading posts in the Congress Party before crossing the floor to join the Socialists. Kripalani had written some important books about Mahatma Gandhi, whom he revered, and had once served as president of the Indian National Congress.

Oddly enough, his wife, who was present during the conversation at their home but took no part in it, held office as secretary of the Congress Party. Their daughter, who had spent three months at Deganyah and Nahalal while visiting Israel two years earlier, was more outgoing and gave me an enthusiastic account of her stay. All three impressed me as advanced intellectuals.

"What exactly is the difference between your faction and the Congress Party?" I asked my host.

"Only the emphasis," he replied. "We are pragmatic, not doctrinaire Socialists."

"Something like Mapai?" I ventured.

"Yes," he agreed. Kripalani was aware of the ideological parallel, as he had also visited Israel, where he had met President Ben-Zvi, David Ben-Gurion, Moshe Sharett, and leaders of the Histadrut.

In the course of our talk, he told me that his countrymen appreciated U.S. economic assistance, but resented the military aid the Americans gave to Pakistan, because it compelled India to spend so much on armaments. "We Indians like the American people," he said, "but not American policy." The two outstanding personalities in India were, he stated, Vice-President Radhakrishnan and Vinoba Bhave, the land reformer. Kripalani believed that the latter's approach deserved to be followed in other underdeveloped countries.

The next point on our itinerary was Katmandu, capital of the Himalayan kingdom of Nepal. Like Benares in India, Katmandu has a holy river flowing through its confines. In the case of Benares, it is the mighty Ganges, with smoke-plumed funeral pyres lining its banks and vast numbers of people in search of healing in its remarkably pure waters; whereas Katmandu lies at the confluence of the Bashanmati and Baghmati tributaries of that sacred stream.

There is a marked difference between the populations of these two cities. The people of Benares are of Aryan (Indo-European) stock, while those of Nepal are of mixed Indian and Mongol descent. We found the Nepalese to be friendlier, more easygoing folk, while impoverishment was visibly worse even than in India.

Buddha himself was born in India, near the Nepal border, which may be why Katmandu had more Buddhist shrines than private homes. An outstanding example was the splendidly adorned Golden Temple. Countless prayer wheels could be seen along the sidewalks of the capital. These cylindrical devices contained myriads of written prayers which, on being revolved on their axis, served to invoke the deity's name millions of times over. Also characteristic were the Monkey Temples, where these creatures—held to be sacred—were allowed to roam about as they pleased. Other shrines were decorated with human fertility symbols.

Nepal's pastoral economy could be gauged from the large quantities of produce brought to the markets of Katmandu. Barefoot peasants laden with bundles of wood or bags of rice arrived in droves, having made their way on foot over distances of up to fifty miles. A grain market was located in the plaza-like area fronting the Temple of the Goddess of Agriculture, on what was evidently the capital's main thoroughfare. Land taxes to the Government, we were told, took the form of bags of rice.

Buddhist monks were present in vast numbers. In one of the temples we visited, they carried enormous animal horns, which, it appeared, were blown on special occasions.

During our stay in Katmandu, Nepal's postal authorities issued the first stamps of that kingdom, indicating a gradual change in its status vis-à-vis India, since Indian stamps had been in use hitherto.

Calcutta, the chief city and capital of West Bengal, was our last port of call in India. For almost a century and a half, until 1912, it had served as India's capital under the British Raj, and nearly one-third of its teeming population had originally taken refuge there from Pakistan. The 1,200 members of the local Jewish community amounted to no more than a tiny drop in that vast ocean of humanity. At one time, there had been three times as many Jews in Calcutta, but most of them had either made Aliyah or sought better economic opportunities in Europe, America, and Australia.

Rabbi Ezekiel N. Musleah, a native of Calcutta, who came to welcome us, was a graduate of the Jewish Theological Seminary, where he had been a classmate of William Berkowitz, my associate rabbi at Congregation B'nai Jeshurun in New

York. His ability as an educator and youth leader was not fully appreciated by the local Jews. The Magen David Synagogue, where he officiated, had been generously endowed by David Joseph Ezra, a relative of the wealthy and influential Sassoon family. Built in 1884, it was said to be one of the largest synagogues in the Far East. A room behind the Ark overflowed with Torah scrolls in beautiful cases, some of which were adorned with semiprecious stones. A veritable treasure house of Jewish ceremonial objects lay before us there.

Baghdadi Jews had founded the city's *kehillah* in the early nineteenth century. They made it a flourishing center of Jewish cultural life, and a Jewish press operated in Calcutta for several decades. One other feature distinguished the community— the large number of Jews who had made their mark in the professions, as well as in commerce. Two schools were maintained by Calcutta Jewry at the time of our visit, one for boys, who received free tuition, and another for girls, who could apply for the many scholarships available. The total number of pupils at these schools was 250.

Our sightseeing tour included an inspection of the Jain temple. Jainism may be described as a kind of Reform wing of the Buddhist religion. Inside this temple was a hall lined with straight and convex mirrors, which reflected ten images of the beholder. Bert and I took turns multiplying ourselves, and I felt bound to tell our hosts, Mr. and Mrs. Bernard Jacob of Calcutta, "This would make an excellent addition to any small Jewish congregation. It could immediately turn one Jew into a *minyan!*"

Passover was now a week away and we prepared to leave India for points farther to the east. Before our departure from New York, we had planned our itinerary in such a way as to spend *Pesaḥ* in a Jewish community large enough to provide the opportunity of attending *Sedarim* and synagogue services during the week commencing April 22, 1959. According to our original plan, we were to have celebrated the festival on the Indonesian island of Bali, but a Mr. Ezekiel of Djakarta wrote to inform us that there were no Jews to be found in Bali and that Passover provisions could not be obtained even in the city of Djakarta. We found a suitable alternative, therefore, in Singapore, which had a community of nearly 700 Jews. Like so many other places in the Far East, this *kehillah* had once been more populous, but there had been considerable emigration to other parts of the world since the end of World War II.

Among those who met us on our arrival were Mr. and Mrs. Douglas Blaufarb of New York, whose parents were especially close friends of ours. Douglas was on the U.S. embassy staff and he, his wife and their four children lived in a delightful home at the far tip of the Malay Peninsula.

No sooner had we settled in at the famous Raffles Hotel, named for the British founder of this onetime Straits Settlement, Sir Stamford Raffles, than Maurice Gareh, secretary of the Jewish Welfare Board, called to see us. He explained that we would be receiving an invitation to participate in the *Seder* arranged by Mrs. Nissim, daughter of the late Sir Manasseh Meyer, a leader and benefactor of

Singapore Jewry half a century earlier, who had risen to fame and fortune in it. The Meyer and Nissim families were Sephardim of Baghdadi origin.

Before paying our respects to Mrs. Nissim, Bert and I took a stroll over to the impressive office building her father had erected in the commercial center and which bore his name. It was adorned with a huge Shield of David, carved in stone, bearing witness to his Jewish pride. We learned that Manasseh Meyer had arrived in Singapore almost without a penny, and had later bought up land at three pence an acre. In addition to his religious and philanthropic work, he had established the first Zionist society in the Far East.

Mrs. Nissim was a grand, matriarchal figure and her home was large and imposing. Among the guests at our first luncheon there, and later on at the *Seder*, were a number of young Jewish seamen from a British merchant ship in the harbor. Mrs. Nissim had been raised in the Orthodox tradition and she played a leading role at the *Seder*, reciting portions of the *Haggadah*, in which all of us had the opportunity to participate. She read the familiar passages with dignity and fluency in a delightful Sephardic accent.

Early the next morning, from our hotel window, we noticed a chauffeur-driven automobile drawing up outside and a butler stepping out, carrying on his head what looked like a variety of pots. A few minutes later, there was a knock on our door and the butler entered, bringing us the day's supply of Passover victuals. This courtesy was repeated daily throughout the festival, constituting a new "high" in our experience of hospitality from fellow Jews.

While worshiping in the Maghain Aboth Synagogue, which had been built in 1878, we heard that Singapore had another, privately endowed house of worship, Chased-El, which Sir Manasseh Meyer had erected in 1904. He had provided for its maintenance in his will, leaving instructions that a *minyan* be hired on a permanent basis and be called for every morning—Sabbaths and festivals included. Local Sephardi practice, incidentally, allowed for conveyance by rickshaw on Shabbat. There were few worshipers in the Chased-El Synagogue, apart from members of the family and their hired *minyan*, and we attended the services there only once.

An amusing story told to us involved the synagogue's Hindu janitor. On one occasion, when he fell ill, he prayed to his god but no help was forthcoming. He then entered the synagogue, approached the Holy Ark and pleaded, "O Jewish God, I have faithfully taken care of your house of worship. Now that I am sick, please help me." The janitor recovered. Since then, apparently, the God of Israel has rated very high with that particular Hindu.

Another local personality whose hospitality we enjoyed was David Saul Marshall, a prominent Labor politician and attorney, who had served as Chief Minister of Singapore but now devoted himself to his law practice. He had also been president of the Jewish Welfare Board for seven years. A tall, impressive man, then about fifty years of age, Marshall owned a splendid estate overlooking the sea and, though a bachelor, ran an excellent household. The day we lunched with him there, we found ourselves in the company of Mr. and Mrs. Rajah Singh of Bombay, whom we had already met in India. They expressed criticism of Pandit Nehru's extreme anti-

British policies. Mrs. Singh spoke admiringly of Israel and mentioned that she was writing a book about the country. She was friendly with Avshalom Caspi, the Israeli consul in Bombay.

The island of Singapore, which achieved independence in the 1960s as a state within the Federation of Malaysia, and then as a separate republic, was one of the world's largest ports, almost comparable to New York and Liverpool in its importance. Polynesians, Chinese, and Dravidians (of Indian stock) formed the bulk of Singapore's multiracial population. It was clear from our talks with various people that Communist infiltration was a major concern, posing a threat to regional stability.

The next stage of our journey took us by air to an entirely different society, largely of Western origin, when we headed for Australia.

10

Year of Parting: 1959–60

When we left the continent of Asia, the spectacle of ossified traditions and plodding ways of life, visible in the Indian bullock cart, beast-driven waterwheels, and seagoing junks with their huge sails, gave way to vastly different panoramas. The decadence and lethargy of a timeless civilization were now replaced by the pace and energy of a modern, forward-thrusting society.

Australia and New Zealand, two dominions within the British Commonwealth, were far younger and less populated countries than the United States, but their urban developments bore a specious resemblance to those of North America. The first settlers in Australasia had also started from scratch, as it were, taking possession of a virgin territory filled with promise, where they only needed to work hard at the beginning in order to assure themselves of the kind of life that could never have been theirs back home in far-off England.

A Visit to the Antipodes

The convicts brought ashore at Botany Bay following the establishment of the first British penal settlement there in 1788 scarcely imagined that they would be the forerunners of a bustling and prosperous commonwealth "down under." In less than two centuries, however, Botany Bay was to become a mere annex to the rapidly growing suburban hinterland of Sydney, in the state of New South Wales.

Inevitably, a sprinkling of half a dozen Jews—not even a *minyan*—formed part of the incoming group of unwilling immigrants who disembarked from the British transport vessels. One of these Jewish pioneers, a Londoner named John Harris, eventually secured his freedom and, as the colony's first policeman, became the founder of Australia's constabulary. It took thirty more years of sparse Jewish immigration before the fledgling *kehillah* managed to establish a burial society. There was a larger influx during the 1830s, mainly from England, which led to the founding or consolidation of new Jewish communities in the Antipodes. Subsequent waves of Jewish immigration during the gold rush period of the 1850s and in the wake of the Russian pogroms helped to strengthen congregational life.

Our own landing on Australian soil was at Melbourne, capital of the state of Victoria, several hundred miles distant from the country's largest metropolis, Syd-

41

ney. We found Melbourne to be a pleasant, modern city of 1,500,000 inhabitants, situated in the area where Captain James Cook had made his first explorations and had claimed the newly discovered continent for the British crown in 1770. Our visit to the Antipodes was in fact a detour made at the request of the Keren Hayesod–United Israel Appeal in Jerusalem, which wished me to conduct its annual campaign there while touring that part of the world. A reception party of some fifty, representing all the local Jewish organizations, awaited us at the airport when we arrived in the afternoon of May 18, 1959.

We soon learned Australian Jewry's vital statistics. The community numbered about 65,000 souls, of whom some 30,000 lived in Melbourne and 25,000 in Sydney. The remainder were to be found in Perth, Brisbane, Adelaide, Canberra, and a score of minor *kehillot*. Until the early twentieth century, almost twenty-five percent of the Jews had been scattered throughout the country in small towns and rural areas. This phenomenon had inevitably led to considerable intermarriage, a problem that the lack of rabbis, Hebrew teachers, and Jewish women served to aggravate. It was only when fairly large numbers of Jews from Central and Eastern Europe began arriving in the 1930s that this ominous trend was arrested. Thereafter, religious life, Jewish education, and Zionist activity had undergone a revival, and Boards of Deputies (established in all states of the dominion apart from Tasmania) joined in setting up the Executive Council of Australian Jewry in 1944. Between 1933 and 1954, the *kehillah* had doubled in size, and about forty percent of the Jews in Melbourne, for example, had come as refugees from Nazi Germany and occupied Europe.

Since its early beginnings, Australian Jewry had acknowledged the authority of the British Chief Rabbinate and had tended to follow the ritual and tradition of London's United Synagogue. Judaism was a "respectable" religious denomination in this dominion, congregations enjoyed prestige in the general community, and freedom of opportunity enabled Jews to take an active part in public affairs, including the state governments and legislatures. Sir John Monash had commanded the Australian armed forces in Western Europe and the Middle East during World War I, and Sir Isaac Isaacs had been the first Australian-born Governor-General in 1931–36. I was told that a university in Melbourne had been named in honor of Monash and that almost every Jewish home in Australia had a Jewish National Fund blue and white box. Most Jews were affiliated with synagogues, eighty percent belonging to Orthodox and twenty percent to Liberal (Reform) congregations.

Our first weekend "down under" found us across the sea in New Zealand, a remarkably scenic country where North Island is tropical, with lush vegetation and hot springs, and South Island is Alpine in character, with snow-covered mountains, lakes, and glaciers. The history of Jewish settlement in this dominion was akin to that of Australia, New Zealand's first organized *kehillah* having been established in Auckland in 1840, upon the country's annexation by Great Britain. A short-lived gold rush during the 1860s had led to the founding of Jewish communities in Christchurch and Dunedin, and in smaller towns where there were no longer any traces of Jewish life. At the time of our visit, there were fewer than 4,500 Jews in the country, mainly because of a restrictive immigration policy that limited admission to persons of British origin. Even during the Nazi period, only a very small number of Jewish refugees had been allowed into New Zealand, and assimilation and intermarriage were predictably rife. Organizationally, the *kehillah* resembled that of Australia, albeit on a much smaller scale. All but one of the congregations were Orthodox. Jews played a prominent role in public life, the professions, business, and farming. Sir Julius Vogel had twice served as Prime Minister in the 1870s, and Sir Michael Myers had been Chief Justice of New Zealand from 1929 until 1946.

Christchurch, on South Island, was our first stop. There were about 250 Jews living in the city, although only a score of them attended Friday evening services in the synagogue. During dinner at the rabbi's home, we were told that a former spiritual leader of the community had devised a formula in the writing of a *ketubbah* (marriage contract) to avoid mentioning the city's proper name, which Orthodox Jews found distasteful. He styled it "Canterbury," the name of the provincial district in which Christchurch lies. Another Orthodox rabbi had called the city "Ch-Ch-" in a *ketubbah*.

The Maori origins of New Zealand were much in evidence during our tour. A friend whom we met in Auckland took us on a four-hour drive to see one of the natural wonders of North Island—the bubbling thermal springs of Rotorua. It was amusing to hear that one of the early Jewish settlers had married a Maori princess and that one night, at a society ball, she had appeared clad in his discarded *tallit*.

While on North Island, we traveled by rail to Wellington, the dominion's capital. It had a Jewish population of about 1,500. I heard that Jewish education was mostly of the Sunday school type and that the more Jewishly conscious members of the community would like to move to larger *kehillot* in Australia and elsewhere. At the Keren Hayesod *magbit* gathering in Wellington, which resulted in a substantial increase over the previous year's total, I stressed the importance of a more intensive Jewish education for the children.

An interview with Prime Minister Walter Nash had been arranged for me, and one of the facts brought to my attention in advance was that Anzac (Australian and New Zealand) servicemen had established friendly contacts with the Yishuv in Palestine during both World Wars. I took occasion, therefore, to emphasize my own appreciation of the warm regard that both the Prime Minister and the people of New Zealand continued to display toward Israel, and to say that the Jews of the United States were gratefully aware of New Zealand's vote in favor of the UN partition resolution in November 1947. Our conversation then veered to other matters. I detected some negative religious undertones in the remarks made by Mr. Nash, especially from his veiled references to Jesus and the Jews of his day. At the same time, however, he voiced the opinion that the prophet Isaiah was the greatest man who ever lived. The explanation was forthcoming when I learned subsequently that Nash had been a lay preacher before entering politics.

During our stay in Wellington, I also called on the U.S. ambassador. He told me that New Zealand was dependent on America for its security, as Great Britain had withdrawn its forces from the South Pacific.

After leaving Wellington, we visited Auckland, the country's largest city, which had a population of over 400,000, including almost 2,000 Jews. David Nathan, a Sephardi Jew from London, had founded the *kehillah* there and his descendants remained prominent in Auckland's commercial life and Jewish communal affairs. We called on Lawrence Nathan, president of the (Orthodox) United Synagogue of New Zealand, an affiliate of the World Jewish Congress. A Magen David adorned the façade of the Nathan family's place of business. Exhibited inside was the *ketubbah* drawn up for Mr. Nathan's grandparents in 1841, a year after Auckland had been established.

The Jewish community was a prosperous one, and it had a fine house of worship, the Princes Street Synagogue, built in 1885. Rabbi Alexander Astor had been serving as this Orthodox congregation's minister for nearly three decades. There was also a small, newly established Liberal congregation, with a rabbi.

One impressive character whom we met in Auckland was Sir Ernest Davis, a stalwart and well-spoken man of eighty-six, who had twice been elected Mayor of the city. He was one of the leaders of the *kehillah* and owned several hotels. Sir Ernest had unfortunately lost both his wife and his son. At a Keren Hayesod fundraising affair I addressed, he announced his son's bequest of £100,000 for hospitals in Israel. The principal was to remain invested in New Zealand and the yearly income of about £5,000 would be remitted to the hospitals.

Our first destination in Australia on returning from New Zealand was Brisbane, a port in the state of Victoria famous for its "Gold Coast," the country's finest beach. Our host there was a Mr. Newhouse. As a young man, he had served in the Jewish Legion in Palestine and he was now the Zionist "powerhouse" in Brisbane. We observed that a number of Jewish homes there bore names such as "Hatikvah." The Keren Hayesod—United Israel Appeal meeting at which I spoke produced a fortypercent increase over the previous year's income.

From Brisbane we proceeded to Melbourne, arriving in time for the celebration of Yom Ha-Atzma'ut. The festivities were preceded by a service of thanksgiving at the Toorak Road Synagogue of the Melbourne Hebrew Congregation. Rabbi Israel Porush, senior minister of the Great Synagogue in Sydney, presided. I delivered to him the scroll and greetings entrusted to me by the New York Board of Rabbis. A special message was brought by Moshe Yuval, Israel's ambassador in Australia, who was also accredited to New Zealand.

Apart from myself, those who participated in the Yom Ha-Atzma'ut service were three local Zionist leaders, Max Freilich, J. Solvey, and Samuel Wynn, president of the Zionist Federation of Australia and New Zealand. Accompanied by Mr. Wynn, Bert and I visited Bet Weizmann, an impressive center of Jewish activity in Melbourne. It was interesting to hear that the Zionist Federation had been established as recently as 1927, in the teeth of strenuous opposition by Sir Isaac Isaacs and other "Anglo-Jewish" anti-Zionist grandees, whose stronghold was for many years the St. Kilda Synagogue in Melbourne. Rabbi Israel Brodie, then senior minister of the Melbourne Hebrew Congregation and later Chief Rabbi of the British Commonwealth, had served as the Federation's first president and Sir John Monash had been honorary president. I already knew, of course, that Herbert Evatt, Australia's delegate to the UN, had done much to secure the partition resolution in 1947, when he was chairman of the UN Ad Hoc Committee on Palestine.

The next day, we visited the Mount Scopus War Memorial College, established in 1948, which then had an enrollment of more than 1,000 pupils. Our host there was Maurice Ashkanasy, a prominent lawyer and the acknowledged lay leader of Australian Jewry, who represented his community at the Claims Conference and had secured a considerable measure of support from that body for the school. Mount Scopus, which grew rapidly and would become reputedly the world's largest Jewish day school, offered a program of broad secular and compulsory Jewish studies. The tuition fees covered only part of the actual maintenance cost per pupil, the remainder being borne by the community fund. This fine school was located on a thirty-acre site, which included a sports field. Impressed by what I saw during our visit, I urged Melbourne's Jewish leadership to encourage the establishment of similar day schools in other Australian *kehillot*, and to expand the existing program so as to provide a department for the training of Jewish teachers who would serve other communities in Australasia.

Alongside the growth of synagogue life, in fact, Melbourne was the scene of much Jewish educational pioneering. Apart from Mount Scopus College, there were several hundred pupils attending Moriah College, the strictly Orthodox Hungarian Adass Israel Congregation's day school, and the Lubavitch movement's yeshivah. Further educational work was conducted by the Mizrahi organization, which had its own synagogue.

At the Keren Hayesod appeal dinner, which I addressed that same evening, contributions once more showed a substantial increase over those of the previous year.

In Sydney, our hosts were Max Freilich and Sidney Einfeld, M.P. Inspired by the visit to Mount Scopus College in Melbourne, I urged them to start work on a comparable Jewish day school of their own. I also addressed the Jewish Board of Deputies of New South Wales. We had the pleasure of meeting Professor Julius Stone, a world-renowned authority on international law and jurisprudence, who had been raised in Leeds, England. He was active in the Sydney Jewish community and in Zionist affairs.

As in Melbourne, there was a large number of thriving Jewish congregations in this "cradle of Australian Jewry," the majority of them Orthodox. Joseph Barrow Montefiore, a cousin of Sir Moses Montefiore, had served as first president of the original Jewish congregation in Sydney, which gave rise to the city's Great Synagogue, an impressive structure built in 1878.

Mr. Einfeld took us to see Premier Joseph J. Cahill of New South Wales, who told us of his ambitious plans for the opera house and concert hall. The Lord Mayor of

Sydney tendered us a reception and expressed a warm regard for Israel, which he had visited. A brief visit to Canberra, the federal capital, enabled us to meet Australia's Acting Prime Minister, Mr. John McEwen, who was deputizing for Premier Robert Menzies while the latter was away in the United States. I expressed appreciation of the Government's immigration policy, which had made it possible for thousands of Jews to come from less friendly or promising shores, and thanked Mr. McEwin for his friendly attitude toward Israel. We also visited the U.S. ambassador.

Back in Sydney, we participated in the Keren Hayesod dinner, which was attended also by Moshe Yuval, Israel's minister plenipotentiary. Contributions again topped those raised in the previous year. Australian Jewry, we heard, was also engaged in raising funds to build suitable premises for a new Israel embassy in Canberra.

Adelaide, the capital of South Australia, was our next stop. The small Jewish community there included a fair proportion of former refugees from Hitlerism and a substantial group of Egyptian immigrants. We took part in the *kehillah*'s Israel Independence Day celebration.

On our arrival in Perth, the capital of Western Australia, we were met at the airport by a group of boys and girls from the local branch of Habonim, who danced the Hora and sang *Hevenu Shalom Alékhem*. Although Perth's Jewish community was the third largest in the country, about 3,000 in number, it was one of the most isolated *kehillot* in the world, situated 1,400 miles from its closest neighbor, Adelaide. The Jews who established Perth's Hebrew congregation in 1892 mostly came from Eastern Europe or Palestine. There was also a small Liberal congregation. We had "competition" during Sabbath eve services on Friday night, when the Reverend Billy Graham launched one of his high-powered evangelical crusades. In this Jewish community the Brachler family played a leading role. The rate of intermarriage was disturbingly high. We saw a Jewish war memorial in Perth, apparently the only one of its kind in Australia. Bert and I addressed fund-raising meetings in the course of our stay.

Throughout the fortnight we spent in the Antipodes, many Jews referred to their sense of isolation from the mainstream of Jewish life, yet it was evident that they enjoyed living in a large, easygoing country with few tensions. Anti-Semitism there was minimal. In most places, however, a low-key type of Jewish existence predominated, and the communities had to face mounting assimilation and an ominous rate of marriage out of the faith. I was told that the number of such dropouts now exceeded twenty-five percent of the entire community. The one factor of Jewish significance that dominated life in Australasia and united Jews there was Medinat Yisrael, and their pride in its achievements.

The flight to South Africa, our next destination, took thirty hours, with an overnight stop on the small British island colony of Mauritius in the Indian Ocean. To at least two passengers on the aircraft, my wife and myself, Mauritius recalled a sorry chapter in the history of British Mandatory rule over Palestine, when the 1939

White Paper restrictions on Jewish immigration were being rigidly and brutally enforced.

A group of over 1,500 refugees from the Nazi terror, comprising Czechoslovak, German, and Austrian Jews, had been deported from Haifa after their arrival there aboard an "illegal immigrant" ship, the S.S. *Atlantic*. They reached Mauritius on December 26, 1940, fifteen months after the outbreak of World War II. The men were confined to a prison in the town of Beau Bassin, while the women were kept separately in adjacent huts. Nearly 130 of these unfortunate people had died of tropical diseases in the course of their imprisonment. A notable part was played by South African Jewry and by the Jewish Agency in the effort to alleviate their misery. It was not until after VE-Day, in 1945, that they were released and eventually permitted to go to Palestine, this time as free Olim.

The surface area of Mauritius was a mere 720 square miles. Its population consisted of Indians, Malays, and some Chinese and Europeans. Although English was the official language of this mountainous, volcanic island, a French (Creole) dialect was mainly spoken. As in other out-of-the-way places, we scanned the local telephone directory that evening in our hotel, but found no subscribers with Jewish-sounding names whom we thought it worthwhile trying to contact.

Jewish Life in Southern Africa

We flew into Jan Smuts Airport, near Johannesburg, on the morning of Monday, June 1, and were met by Gabriel Doron, the Israel consul-general, and a delegation of Jewish community leaders. Our halt in Mauritius had prevented us from attending the biennial conference of the South African Zionist Federation, which had opened on the previous night, but Bert and I at least had the consolation of having been in a place bound up with recent Zionist history.

South Africa, then still part of the British Commonwealth, had a Jewish population of about 112,000.* From the earliest days of White settlement at the Cape of Good Hope, there had been some form of Jewish association with the country. Portuguese Jewish cartographers had been of assistance to Vasco da Gama in his voyage of discovery in 1497, and Jewish merchants in Amsterdam had been involved in the Dutch East India Company's colonization of the Cape in 1652. The handful of Jews who actually settled there in the early days abandoned Judaism, however, since only Protestants were admitted by the Dutch. Professing Jews began arriving in some numbers only after the British took control of the area in 1806, and they came mainly from England and Central Europe. One such pioneer, Nathaniel Isaacs, who explored what was to become the province of Natal and met the Zulu king, Chaka, published an account of his adventures there in 1836. The "mother congregation" of Cape Town, established in 1841, built its first synagogue eight years later and called it "Tikvath Israel," a name alluding to the Cape of Good Hope.

*I am grateful to my friend, Dr. Gabriel Sivan, for some historical details in this chapter.

A fresh impetus for settlement was created, first by the Kimberley diamond fields in 1869 and later by the discovery of gold on the Witwatersrand in the 1880s. Those who arrived in search of the fabled riches included Jews from the United States and Australia, as well as from Europe. Until then, Jews had lived mainly in the Western Cape or in Grahamstown and Port Elizabeth to the east. The great tide of Jewish immigration came after 1881, however, when stories of the new *Goldene Medine* reached dozens of small communities in Russia, which had been swept by the czarist pogroms. Within twenty-five years, from 1880 until 1905, South African Jewry increased tenfold. The newly arrived "greeners" often settled in small towns and rural areas, where they earned their livelihood as peddlers and shopkeepers. Most of them came from Lithuania and they soon outnumbered the older Anglo-German Jewish families, imbuing the South African Jewish community with its present-day "Litvak" aspect and tradition. This had its impact on religious life, cultural activity, and Zionism, but most of all on the organizational structure of the *kehillah*.

I was particularly interested in the almost unique Zionist record of South African Jewry. Even before Herzl had convened the First Zionist Congress at Basle, there were Hovevei Zion societies in Southern Africa. The S.A. Zionist Federation, established in 1898, was renowned for its efficiency, fund-raising record, diversified program, and devoted staff. It grouped together all the Zionist parties and three vigorous halutzic movements (Habonim, Bnei Akiva, and Betar), as well as a powerful Women's Zionist Council with branches throughout the country and the Maccabi sports organization. Although the Government allowed no tax concessions, South African Jewry made the world's highest per-capita contributions to Zionist funds in the Israel United Appeal (IUA). SAZF projects in Israel included investment and housing schemes, generous endowments (especially at the Hebrew University) and a large office in Tel Aviv that assisted the proportionately numerous South African Olim. Local Zionist initiative had also promoted the development of several fine Jewish day schools.

From the outset of our visit, however, I was struck by the fact that the Jewish leaders with whom we spoke shied away from the vexed issue of apartheid. Israel and everything to do with the Medinah seemed to be the focus of their attention, perhaps because they thought these matters were of primary interest to us. Only later, when our hosts found that we would like to know more about the general social and political climate in South Africa, did they and we begin to discuss it.

That first evening in Johannesburg, we were the dinner guests of some dozen Jewish community leaders and their wives. Among them was Chief Rabbi Louis Isaac Rabinowitz, a splendid, liberal-minded Orthodox personality, with whom we forged a lasting friendship that has continued since we and our wives made Aliyah over twenty years ago. Mrs. Rabinowitz was a daughter of the late Chief Rabbi Moshe Avigdor Amiel of Tel Aviv, the eminent Mizrahi leader. Her husband, though forthright in expressing his views, appeared to enjoy much popularity and esteem in his *kehillah*.

As a result of our conversations with various people on controversial political matters, we were able to gain a better understanding of the local scene. Although the staunchly pro-Zionist Jan Christiaan Smuts had been defeated at the elections in 1948, the Nationalist Government headed by Dr. Daniel Malan, which replaced his Administration, had maintained cordial relations with Israel—because the Afrikaners were Bible-loving people, we were told, and had a great belief in biblical prophecy. During the Nazi period, there had been some anti-Jewish agitation by extremists, but such hate propaganda was now of little significance, according to my informants. There was no "collective" Jewish stand on apartheid, although many sympathized with the courageous Helen Suzman, a United Party M.P. who later represented the Progressive Party in South Africa's Parliament. Although only one Jew had ever achieved cabinet rank, there had been many Jewish mayors, especially in Johannesburg, and Jews were prominent in literature and the arts, music and the theater, economic life, journalism, medicine, and the judiciary.

A short while earlier, a Christian group had urged voters in the forthcoming elections to support only those candidates who were "good Christians," but in face of Jewish protests the group's leaders had apologized, stating that they actually meant "religious men." We also heard that, as a direct result of the racial barriers between Black, White, and "Colored" South Africans—and because even Afrikaans- and English-speaking people had limited social contact—assimilation and intermarriage were not major problems for the Jews of South Africa.

To my mind, however, this Jewish community was balanced on a tightrope, and I had the impression that some of its leaders, aware of my liberal views, were none too eager for me to meet with Prime Minister Hendrik Verwoerd. "If I were advising South African Jewry," I took occasion once to say, "I would not urge them to pack right now, but to start buying valises."

The Zionist Centre, an imposing multistory building on De Villiers Street, near the downtown business section of Johannesburg, had been opened about a year before our visit. From there, the S.A. Zionist Federation and its many constituent bodies conducted their operations. Edel Horwitz of the dominant General Zionist group, the United Zionist Association (UZA), was about to succeed Israel Dunsky as chairman of the Federation. Dunsky, a scholarly Zionist and member of a prominent family in nearby Germiston, had decided to retire in order to make Aliyah.

I gathered that many of those contemplating emigration at the time were thinking about Australia and the United States, as well as about Israel. Yet South African Jewry, by and large, considered itself to be the world's premier Zionist community.

Our first working assignment was in Durban, situated on the shores of the Indian Ocean in the province of Natal. South Africa's third largest city, with a population of well over half a million, Durban had a large and busy harbor and was of metropolitan proportions. Thanks to its semitropical climate and excellent beaches, it was one of the country's favorite holiday resorts. We commented to our guide on the wide streets and avenues, and were told that they had been laid before the invention of horseless carriages, when carts drawn by oxen needed plenty of room in which to turn around. Some time later, while in Rhodesia, we heard that Cecil Rhodes had planned the city of Bulawayo on the same basis.

As elsewhere in the Union, Durban's population was divided into separate ethnic groups, each with its own residential areas, and apartheid was strictly observed. Having previously assumed that this form of segregation was insisted upon by the Afrikaners, we were rather intrigued to find it in Durban, where most of the White South Africans were of British stock. Apart from the Whites and the Black Africans (mainly of the Zulu tribe in Natal), there were also large numbers of Indians and "Coloreds." The "Coloreds," people of mixed race, were looked down upon by all of the other groups.

We were taken to meet a canon of the Anglican Church who was a Zulu. While speaking with him, I mentioned my friendship with Dr. Martin Luther King and organizational ties with the National Association for the Advancement of Colored People in the U.S. One question I put to him concerned the attitude adopted by the Anglican Church toward apartheid. "We consider it a sin," he replied. I then asked if his people had a leader of stature such as Gandhi. He told me that Chief Albert Luthuli, a future Nobel Peace Prize laureate, was such a leader. The authorities had recently banned his political activities in the African National Congress, and there was no one of comparable status to replace him.

Although a few Jews, notably the famous Nathaniel Isaacs, had lived thereabouts in the first half of the nineteenth century, it was not until 1883 that a *kehillah* had been established in Durban. An unusually high proportion of the local Jewish families were of English immigrant descent. At the time of our visit, there were about 5,000 Jews there, and they had two Orthodox congregations, one Progressive (Reform) temple, and a Jewish day school. The Durban Jewish Club, located near the seafront, was a large and impressive center of activity. Bert and I addressed several Jewish groups there before returning to Johannesburg.

Within a decade of its foundation in 1886, there were already over 6,000 Jews living in South Africa's future metropolis. Johannesburg then lay in the independent Boer Republic of the Transvaal and, following the establishment of the first Jewish congregation in 1887, a second house of worship was opened by President Paul Kruger, with whom Transvaal Jewry maintained friendly relations. Two eminent rabbis who had served the community were Joseph H. Hertz, who went on to become Chief Rabbi of the British Empire, and Judah Loeb Landau, a noted Hebrew writer. By 1959, when we were visiting the country, well over 57,000 Jews—half of the Union's Jewish population and about ten percent of the White group in Johannesburg—lived in the city. They were prominent in its civic, cultural, and business life, as M.Ps. representing local constituencies, and in the professions. An extraordinarily high proportion of both the faculty and student body at the English-speaking University of the Witwatersrand, where Chief Rabbi Louis Rabinowitz served as professor of Hebrew, were Jews.

Johannesburg was the headquarters of an impressive array of Jewish religious, cultural, educational, social, and philanthropic organizations. The Federation of

Synagogues had under its umbrella nearly all of the Orthodox congregations in the Transvaal, Orange Free State, Natal, and Eastern Cape. It maintained the Chief Rabbinate and Beth Din, conducted a training program for rabbis, (non-ordained) ministers, and *shoḥatim,* and published a weekly newspaper, one of four Jewish weeklies in the city. I learned that eighty percent of synagogue-affiliated Jews in the community attended Greater Johannesburg's score of Orthodox congregations. The remaining twenty percent had joined three congregations affiliated with the South African Union for Progressive Judaism, which Rabbi Moses Cyrus Weiler had mainly been responsible for creating. In practice and ritual, the Progressive movement was closer to American Conservative Judaism than to Reform, and unlike Reform in general it had always been staunchly Zionist.

On the domestic scene, the South African Jewish Board of Deputies represented and defended the interests of the *kehillah.* It conducted its own program of adult education, organized youth and student activities, maintained Johannesburg's Jewish Museum, and published a cultural monthly, *Jewish Affairs.* Namie Philips, chairman of the Executive Council, invited me to address a meeting of the Board and I spoke primarily about the World Jewish Congress, with which they were affiliated. The Board's officers, though proud of South African Jewry's outstanding financial contribution to Medinat Yisrael, told me that their campaign for local needs, organized through the United Communal Fund, received inadequate support because of the major emphasis on Zionist causes. I asked them whether Jews felt secure in the country. Their answer was that Jews *qua* Jews had no real problem, but that they might have to face difficulties in the future as Whites and Europeans.

Towering sandy mine-dumps line the horizon in Johannesburg, which is the world's largest producer of gold. At one time, Jewish "Randlords" such as Barney Barnato, a rival and then an associate of Cecil Rhodes, had played a major role in the goldmining industry of the "Reef." Our visit presented us with the opportunity to visit a gold mine and so, one morning, Bert and I went down 2,700 feet on one of the regular tours. Apart from the supervisors, all of the labor force was Black. The miners received about fourteen dollars a week, in addition to their food and lodging. They came in from their distant homesteads and even from across the border, for periods of several months at a time, leaving their families behind them. In this way, money could be saved to improve conditions of life back home. The miners were accommodated in special compounds, ten or more to a room. Tribal dances organized at regular intervals on Sunday mornings provided both the laborers and the spectators with some welcome recreation.

After addressing a number of Zionist groups in Johannesburg, we left for a visit to Cape Town, South Africa's legislative capital. Like Johannesburg, Cape Town had fine public buildings and lovely suburbs, but the Union's second largest city offered more splendid vistas, with the Atlantic Ocean surrounding the Cape Peninsula and Table Mountain—often covered by its cloudy "tablecloth"—dominating the background.

We visited the Parliament, where we learned that one Jewish member of the House, Hymie Miller of the United Party, which constituted the main opposition at the time, had served as Mayor of Johannesburg. The Cape Colored population still returned members to the House, but it was subsequently disfranchised. Sir Ernest Oppenheimer, the German-born founder of the country's largest diamond industry, had also sat in Parliament. After marrying his second wife, he became a Catholic, but Harry F. Oppenheimer, the son of his first marriage, was a Jew by birth and now headed the family business. Like his late father, he was the United Party M.P. for Kimberley. We were told that Harry Oppenheimer had helped to promote the diamond industry in Israel.

With a Jewish population of close to 25,000, Cape Town had the second largest *kehillah* in South Africa. The United Council of Orthodox Hebrew Congregations in the Western Cape and South-West Africa was the counterpart of Johannesburg's Federation of Synagogues and maintained its own Chief Rabbinate and Beth Din. There were about a dozen congregations in and around Cape Town, all but one or two of them Orthodox. National Zionist and communal organizations had local branches, but there were also a few autonomous bodies. The new Jewish day school, Herzlia, was making good progress and had an enrollment of 750 pupils.

In the course of our stay, we called on Israel's ambassador, Yitzhak Bavly, who spent six months of the year in Cape Town and the other six months in Pretoria, the Union's administrative capital.

On Friday evening, we had dinner with the Sagorskys. Dr. Deborah Sagorsky, originally from Johannesburg, had served as president of the Women's Zionist Council of South Africa. In answer to our question as to what future awaited the Jews there, they said that they were not afraid of anti-Semitism, since Jews formed part of the "European" community. For Shabbat morning services, we went to the beautiful Gardens Synagogue, built in 1905, which stood close to the Parliament and the city library. Next door to it was the original synagogue, dating from 1849, which served as a museum of Cape Town Jewry. Chief Rabbi Israel Abrahams, the Orthodox community's spiritual leader, was professor of Hebrew at the University of Cape Town.

We were also entertained by Judge Joseph Herbstein and his wife. He was Judge President of the Cape Supreme Court, a veteran Zionist, and a onetime friend of Ze'ev Jabotinsky. The Herbsteins had a married daughter in Israel and later, upon his retirement from the bench, they made Aliyah. Almost every Jewish family in South Africa appeared to have relatives in Israel. The vice-chancellor of Cape Town University was another guest at their home. He told us that White and Black students attended lectures together at the university, but that social contact between the two groups was not permitted there. I addressed a public meeting that night before we returned once more to Johannesburg.

Our tour of the city and its various institutions included a visit to the King David School in the suburb of Linksfield, which had primary and secondary divisions. It stood on a sixty-acre site—even larger than that of Mount Scopus College in Melbourne—and, like its Australian counterpart, it had magnificent sports facilities. There were over 1,000 children enrolled, with a long waiting list. Although no financial aid was provided by the South African Government, increasing numbers of Jewish parents wished to send their children to Jewish day schools because of their high academic standards and prestige. A branch of King David had therefore been opened across town in the suburb of Victory Park. All the instruction was Israel-oriented, and a number of the Hebrew teachers had been trained in the Rabbi J. L. Zlotnik Teachers' Seminary. Yeshiva College, with an enrollment of several hundred pupils, had developed from a Bnei Akiva yeshivah founded by the South African Mizraḥi Organization in 1951. Altogether, we heard that there were about 5,000 children receiving an intensive Jewish education in Johannesburg.

At West Park Cemetery we saw an impressive memorial to the six million victims of the European Holocaust. It had just been unveiled there and its design, by a leading sculptor, Herman Wald, incorporated three giant pairs of hands clutching six-foot-high shofarot that formed a triple arch. Prominent in the center were the Hebrew words, *Lo Tishkaḥ* ("Do not Forget!")

Nettie Davidoff, a friend from our Jewish National Fund days in New York, arranged a two-day visit for us to the Kruger National Park, South Africa's famous game reserve. Vast numbers and varieties of wild beasts abounded there, and we learned that this wildlife sanctuary—the largest of its kind in the world— encompassed an area equivalent to that of Israel. We were glad to be accompanied by Nettie and her husband, Hyman Davidoff, a former Labor Party M.P.

Our next destination was Pretoria. On the way there from "Jo'burg," we saw the massive Voortrekker Monument, completed in 1949, which honors the Boer pioneers who had made the Great Trek from the Cape to escape British domination and founded the short-lived South African Republic. Pretoria was the capital of the Transvaal as well as the country's administrative capital, and the Union Buildings housing sessions of Parliament were most impressive. Our guides on this tour were Israel Dunsky, outgoing chairman of the S.A. Zionist Federation, and Zvi Infeld, its executive secretary. They told us that Pretoria was known as the "Jacaranda City" because of the 50,000 jacaranda trees planted there which scatter glorious mauve blooms from late spring.

Pretoria's 3,000 Jews maintained three congregations, two Orthodox and one Progressive. The Carmel Jewish School was scheduled to open there very soon. As far as South Africa's other medium-sized *kehillot* were concerned, Port Elizabeth alone had a Jewish day school. We learned that there were communities of 500 or more Jews in Bloemfontein, capital of the Orange Free State; East London, Grahamstown, and Kimberley in Cape Province; and in Benoni, Germiston, Krugersdorp, and Springs in the Transvaal. A special department of the Board of Deputies provided religious guidance and services for the small country communities.

We returned from Pretoria in time to attend services at the Great Synagogue on Wolmarans Street, near Johannesburg's city center, ushering in the Festival of Shavu'ot on June 11. Chief Rabbi Louis Rabinowitz, basing his sermon on the first of the Ten Commandments, spoke out against the Government's denial of basic human rights to the Black population and against the prevalent treatment of agricultural workers. He mentioned some instances where he had interceded successfully with Jewish farmers. The Chief Rabbi's uncompromising liberal stand was not welcomed by all members of the Jewish community, but his position and authority were unchallenged.

I took occasion during a visit to his home to present Rabbi Rabinowitz with the scroll I had brought on behalf of the New York Board of Rabbis.

One day while we were in Johannesburg, we visited Bishop Ambrose Reeves, who was a thorn in the flesh of the Nationalist Government because of the opposition of the Anglican Church to its racial policies. We gathered that the Catholic bishop was also highly critical, though less aggressive in his pronouncements, while the Methodists were timid. A leading activist in the African National Congress was a young man from a prominent Zionist family, Ronald Segal, who later fled the country to avoid arrest in March 1960.

We spent one pleasant evening at the home of Leslie Frankel, a friend of Hyman Ross, vice-president of my congregation in New York. Mr. Frankel and I talked a good deal about the Hebrew University, in which he was becoming increasingly interested. He later headed the local branch of the Friends of the Hebrew University.

Toward the end of our stay, we were the guests of Israel and Muriel Maisels, both of whom were actively involved in Jewish communal affairs. Mr. Maisels had served as president of the Jewish Board of Deputies and was to be elected chairman and, later, president of the S.A. Zionist Federation, while his wife was a future president of the Women's Zionist Council. Still only in his midfifties, he was acknowledged to be South Africa's foremost lawyer and, two years after our visit, became a justice of the High Court of Southern Rhodesia.

From South Africa we went on to our next destination, the Rhodesias, Northern and Southern. I was interested to learn that Jews had served in the columns dispatched by the great "empire builder," Cecil Rhodes, to occupy Matabeleland and Mashonaland in the 1890s. A number of his close friends and associates had been Jews, and they had played a leading part in the development of the territory. Mining, agriculture, and the tobacco trade, and the clothing, hotel, and furniture industries all owed much to Jewish enterprise and investment.

In the granite hills of the Matopos, about thirty miles from Bulawayo, we visited the tomb of Rhodesia's founder. Local Ndebele (Matabele) tribesmen regarded this spot as a haunt of benevolent spirits and from it, in his lifetime, Rhodes obtained his "view of the world." The burial site was overwhelming in its sheer simplicity. A plaque bearing his name lay flat on the ground over the tomb, which was surrounded by huge boulders standing like guardians.

Although there was much to see in the country, we had allowed only a short time for our visit and confined our stay to Bulawayo. The first Jewish community there had mainly comprised Lithuanian and Russian immigrants, but the country's growing prosperity had later attracted English, South African, and German Jews as well. A *kehillah* had been established in Bulawayo in 1894 and three years later the present synagogue of the Bulawayo Hebrew Congregation was built. Rhodesian

Jewry had been strongly Zionist from the outset, and Bulawayo's Chovevei Zion Society was one of the oldest in the world, having been founded in 1898, shortly after the First Zionist Congress. Samuel Rabinovitz was the veteran Zionist personality at the time of our visit. Both the Rhodesian Zionist Council and the Rhodesian Jewish Board of Deputies had their headquarters in the city, and we met with their leading representatives. Communities in Northern Rhodesia also participated in the work of these two bodies.

Southern Rhodesia then had a Jewish population of about 6,500, which was beginning to decline because of the uncertain political situation. There were 3,000 Jews living in Bulawayo, 2,500 in the capital, Salisbury, and the remainder were divided among three small *kehillot*, Gatooma, Gwelo, and Que Que. The Jewish community in Salisbury would soon outstrip that of Bulawayo in numbers, despite the overall process of erosion. Its Hebrew Congregation had been founded in 1895, mainly on the initiative of Joseph van Praagh, an early mayor, who had first arrived on foot, crossing the jungle, from Beira on the coast of Mozambique. While Bulawayo had a small Progressive congregation, Salisbury boasted a considerable Sephardi one comprising about one-third of the city's *kehillah*. They mostly came from the island of Rhodes in the Aegean and had separated from the Ashkenazim to form their own community in 1931.

There was a new Jewish day school in Bulawayo and another was about to open in Salisbury. Both cities had elected a number of Jewish mayors.

The Prime Minister of the Federation of Rhodesia and Nyasaland was Sir Roy Welensky, a former union leader and Rhodesian heavyweight boxing champion, whose father had been a "Litvak" immigrant. Though Jewish on his father's side only, he counted himself part of the Rhodesian *kehillah*. A form of apartheid existed in both parts of the territory, but it was not rigidly enforced and there was no racial discrimination at the universities. All population groups could vote in elections, but only in theory, since the education test and a minimum-income requirement barred most Black Africans from the polling booths. No more than two Africans sat in Parliament.

Sir Roy Welensky favored a system of partnership between the Federation's Black and White citizens, but his hopes were doomed to failure. It became apparent from my conversations that the White population felt uneasy about the political outlook and believed that a takeover by the Black majority could not be too far distant. In fact, however, with the collapse of the Federation in 1963, Nyasaland and Northern Rhodesia became the independent Black republics of Malawi and Zambia, within the British Commonwealth, whereas Southern Rhodesia continued to be governed by a White minority, which broke with Great Britain under a "Unilateral Declaration of Independence" (UDI) and retained power for another fifteen years. New elections held after a protracted guerrilla war then resulted in a Black majority government in the remaining portion of Rhodesia, now styled Zimbabwe.

In common with the 250,000 other White Rhodesians, the Jews whom I met there in 1959 showed no great inclination to move. The Zionist youth movements, however, were strong and a number of their graduates were leaving for Israel. Although Jewish adults were not communicative about future plans, I did sense among them more than a passing interest in Aliyah.

The multiplicity of our impressions while visiting Southern and East Africa was such that no easy value judgments could be made. From the visual aspect— magnificent scenery, great rivers and lakes, vast wildlife reserves and national parks, the majestic Zambezi and the Victoria Falls—nothing could have been more exciting. Yet because we were imbued with a sensitivity to issues of social justice and the inalienable rights of the individual, our tour of the region was, in measure, a depressing experience.

There were about 1,200 Jews in Northern Rhodesia when we arrived there, but our contacts with them were minimal. The first *kehillah* had been established in Livingstone, near the Victoria Falls, in 1905. Thereafter, other Jewish congregations had sprung up in Lusaka, where Jews pioneered in cattle-raising and farming, and in smaller towns such as Kitwe and Ndola, where they made an important contribution to the development of the territory's Copper Belt. No permanent rabbis served these scattered communities, which nevertheless maintained links with the larger *kehillah* in Southern Rhodesia.

It was while Bert and I were in Livingstone that we finally resolved upon a fateful course of action we had been pondering ever since that first year of Medinat Yisrael, when we were living there. Our Aliyah would not be delayed any longer. We agreed that a letter should be sent to the board of Congregation B'nai Jeshurun, notifying them of my intention to retire from the rabbinate of the congregation on the last day of December 1960, so that the two of us might make our home in Israel. The date in question was still eighteen months away, but we felt that a goodly measure of advance notice should be given. The lengthy period of travel, during which I was relieved of my normal burden of pressing daily obligations, had crystalized our decision.

As I once had occasion to tell my congregants in New York, I was not contemplating retirement for the reason given by Groucho Marx, the motion-picture comedian, who, when asked why he and his brothers were quitting stage and screen, replied, "As always in our career, we are anticipating the public demand." My reason for doing so was perhaps best explained in a statement I subsequently made to our congregation and friends:

> I am retiring so that my wife and I may fulfill a long-cherished desire to spend the Sabbath of our lives mostly in Israel, a hope born in us eleven years ago when, after my year of service as Treasurer of the Jewish Agency, we purchased a plot of land on which to build our future home.
>
> Our enchantment with Israel is in no wise a disenchantment with America, the land of our birth. . . . But the Jew in me is older than the American, and Israel is the cradle of my faith and people. It is the Holy Land, and Jerusalem is the Holy City. It is the Bible Land. And, having seen the prayer of nineteen centuries fulfilled in our time, we want to be part of that fulfillment. . . . Obviously, Israel is the place where Judaism can be lived more fully than anywhere else on earth. This is *hagshamah*, the highest form of Jewish self-fulfillment.

I felt that my colleague, Rabbi William Berkowitz, who had been associated with me at B'nai Jeshurun for the past ten years, was qualified to be my successor and to assume the full burden of the rabbinate in our congregation. During the period of our collaboration, he had grown in stature and had won respect, friendship, and devotion as one of the outstanding younger rabbis in New York City.

From Kenya to the Congo

Meanwhile, our trek through the wilds and the more developed parts of Africa continued. On June 18, my sixty-third birthday, we stopped over in Nairobi, the capital of Kenya and East Africa's most flourishing commercial center. With a population of a quarter of a million, it was one of the largest cities between Johannesburg and Cairo. We found it hard to believe that Nairobi, with its pleasant, equable climate, lay only one hundred miles away from the equator. It sprawled out on a plateau 5,000 feet above sea level.

At the airport we were met by three prominent members of the Nairobi Jewish community—Israel Somen, the honorary consul for Israel, and Mr. and Mrs. Jacob Hirschfeld, representatives of one of the pioneer Jewish families thereabouts. Somen, a successful industrialist, was a former president of the Board of Kenya Jewry and of the Nairobi Hebrew Congregation. This *kehillah*, which was served by a rabbi who doubled as Hebrew teacher, comprised about 150 families.

Hirschfeld was descended from Jews who had helped found Rishon Le-Zion in 1882. He himself had settled in Nairobi following his marriage to Rita Block, who was born in the town. Her father, Abraham Lazarus Block, had come with his Jaffa-born wife to Kenya in 1903, when he was a young man of nineteen. After many years in farming, he had founded a department store and begun to expand his business interests. The Stanley Hotel, where we stayed in Nairobi, was one of two he owned there. He gave generously to local, Jewish, and Israeli causes.

That first evening, we went with Mr. and Mrs. Block to services at the Nairobi synagogue, a handsome new structure with seating for 300 worshipers and a Magen David emblem displayed both outside the building and within. An earlier synagogue had been built there in 1913. Mrs. Hirschfeld later gave a dinner in our honor at the Jewish communal hall.

As the pioneer of this *kehillah*, Abraham Block was well informed about local affairs and he maintained that the Blacks would take control of the country within a decade. Only four years were to elapse, in fact, before Jomo Kenyatta headed an independent Black regime there in 1963. Block also told us that there was no apartheid system in Kenya or other forms of segregation. Africans could enter any hotel or restaurant they pleased, and only refrained from doing so for cultural or economic reasons.

He provided us with some fascinating personal footnotes on the historical background to the proposed Uganda Scheme, which had rocked the Zionist movement well over half a century earlier. Although the land offered for Jewish settlement by Great Britain's Colonial Secretary, Joseph Chamberlain, was styled "Uganda," that territory became part of British East Africa only after World War I. The actual settlement area envisaged was in the region now known as the "White Highlands" of Kenya, and comprised about 2,000 square miles of land. When Chamberlain had come forward with the idea of what Herzl was to call a *Nachtasyl* (temporary refuge), the White settlers and officials met and the British Governor of the protectorate raised strenuous objections. Abraham Block, youthful though he was at the time, answered the Governor so convincingly that the latter was persuaded to change his mind. Because of unrelenting opposition to the Uganda Scheme, on the part of Russian Zionists especially, it had, of course, never become more than a paper proposal for a solution to Jewish homelessness.

When I urged Mr. Block to publish his memoirs, he told me that he had already dictated nine chapters, covering the period from 1903 to 1912, and also disclosed that there were documents of Jewish interest in the official archives at Nairobi. Unfortunately, however, his manuscript was lost. Since then, other works have appeared on the history of the Jews in Kenya.

A cordial greeting in Hebrew, "*Shalom, sh'mi Somen, ani Yehudi kattan!*"— "Welcome, I am a little Jew named Somen!," came from an unexpected quarter when we entered the Somens' home. It was uttered by their parrot, obviously a bird well trained in Jewish ways. Israel Somen had been in the country for about thirty years, had twice served as Mayor of Nairobi, and was a city alderman at the time of our visit. He was a good friend of Tom M'boya, the Black nationalist leader, who later assumed a ministerial post in the Government set up by Jomo Kenyatta after independence.

Just as there had been many more Whites in Southern than in Northern Rhodesia, so too, in Kenya, there were more European settlers than in neighboring Uganda and Tanganyika, where the Whites were mostly Government personnel whose move, when the time came, would mean only a transfer to other colonial posts. Mr. Somen, a man of liberal outlook, believed that the Africans should be helped to proceed toward eventual self-government. He also thought that the White settlers in Kenya would be needed for a long time, in order to provide the necessary skills. Unlike the Indian segment of the population, which had its roots in an older culture, the Black Africans were amenable to Western civilization. Somen was a trustee of the multiracial Royal Technical College, where there were few White students, and saw every advantage ensuing from an integrated Kenyan society. It was a somewhat unpopular opinion for any European to express at a time when the Mau Mau insurrection had brought death and injury to many Whites.

He took us on a tour of Nairobi's industrial areas, which were fairly well developed. He himself manufactured and sold furniture, and in front of his store on one of the main streets we saw a blue and white shield adorned with the Menorah emblem and a sign reading, "Consulate of Israel." Following Kenya's independence, diplomatic relations with the Jewish State were firmly established.

At the end of our three-day sojourn in Nairobi, Mr. George Farkas, secretary of the local *kehillah*, drove us to the airport, where we were to emplane for Kampala. Mr. Farkas, a chemist by profession, had arrived in Kenya over twenty years earlier as an immigrant from Europe. He told us that the area proposed to Herzl by the British Government in 1903 lay close to the railroad leading to Uganda, and was scarcely large enough to support a substantial population. We were also informed of a philological curiosity in the local African dialects. Some of the tribes, he said, used words of clearly Hebraic origin to denote certain numbers, such as ten, twenty, thirty, and forty. It was his belief that they bore witness to the influence of Jewish traders or travelers on the East African coast, some twelve or thirteen centuries earlier.

Our next stop was Uganda. A small delegation of Jews from Kampala, the capital, was awaiting us at Entebbe Airport. Their first words of greeting were an announcement of the sum they had just managed to raise for the Keren Hayesod in their latest campaign. It was wryly amusing to hear them talk longingly about the advantages of living in a large Jewish community. "In Israel?" I asked. No, they meant Nairobi.

Uganda, in 1959, was a British protectorate, although it had its own parliament. The European population consisted mainly of British colonial officials and their families, together with a large number of missionaries—Catholic, Protestant, and Seventh-Day Adventist. As in Kenya, Europeans were not allowed to own land.

Kampala was built on seven hills, each of which was occupied by one or more imposing structures. Among these were Makerere University, the best in East Africa, which included a medical school and had 1,500 students; the royal palace; the House of Parliament, which faced a broad avenue; a mosque; and the Catholic and Protestant cathedrals. There were also some Hindu temples.

The local Jewish congregation, a tiny one, had difficulty in assembling a *minyan*. There was no rabbi or minister and so, when a boy was born, a surgeon whose father had been a *shammash* (synagogue beadle) in London performed the circumcision and recited the appropriate blessings. Altogether, there were precisely thirteen Jewish families in Kampala, yet they contrived to maintain some level of Jewish activity.

We spent about a week in Uganda and visited all of its four principalities, each of which was under the nominal rule of a "king." According to our hosts, the country would attain independence in five years. In fact, however, it took only three years, as in 1962 the Governor was replaced by a President, Sir Edward Mutesa II, the former Kabaka (king) of Buganda, and Dr. Milton Obote became Prime Minister. Buganda remained an autonomous unit within the territory for some time, but the situation changed radically in the ensuing decade and the onetime kingdom was absorbed into Uganda. Sir Edward Mutesa II was eventually deposed and Dr. Obote then succeeded him as President, only to be ousted in his turn by the monstrous Idi Amin.

The history of this part of the world had long been a turbulent one. We were interested to learn that, in the five-year period from 1952 until 1957, a Jew had been responsible for altering its course. He was the Governor, Sir Andrew Cohen, a high-ranking British civil servant who, as Undersecretary of State at the Colonial Office, had wisely foreseen the need to prepare Great Britain's African colonies for their approaching independence. Upon his installation as Governor in Kampala, Sir Andrew had chosen to take the Jewish form of the oath of allegiance. Though never officially a Zionist, he had played an active part in the upbuilding of the Yishuv, as chairman of the London Economic Board for Palestine.

Sir Andrew Cohen's decisive role in Ugandan affairs was evident when, in 1953, he deposed Edward Mutesa II from the throne, owing to what was described as a clash of wills between the Kabaka and the Governor over a nationalist political issue. At the end of that year, Mutesa was stripped of his authority and dispatched forthwith to London without being allowed to say goodbye to his family or to tell them what had happened. Although Sir Andrew Cohen had followed the instructions issued by Whitehall, his abrupt action precipitated a crisis that took years to simmer down. Toward the end of 1955, when constitutional reforms in Uganda were introduced, the Kabaka was permitted to return. At the time of our visit, Sir Andrew was Great Britain's representative on the UN Trusteeship Council.

Our itinerary took in such areas as Murchison Park, a splendid big game reserve, and Murchison Falls. The lodge we occupied in the former was located on the very bank of the River Nile and had been built especially for the visit of Queen Elizabeth, the British Queen Mother, two years previously. Sitting outside in the cool of the evening, we were able to catch sight of an assortment of wild animals on the other bank. There were ten hippos on land and others in the water, swimming around with their calves. Herds of elephant and impala, warthogs and other animals could also be seen.

From Murchison Park we drove about 150 miles through lush hilly country, lined by plantations and truck farms, to Fort Portal, capital of Toro. The town lay south of Lake Albert, on Uganda's frontier with Belgian Congo. We learned that most of the original territory of Toro had been handed over by the British to Belgium in 1910 without consulting its inhabitants, who were now demanding that it be returned.

Our driver-guide, a genial and informative African named Sahide, told us of an amusing incident during World War I. Neighboring Tanganyika was then part of the protectorate of German East Africa, and the boundaries were far from well defined. British headquarters sent instructions to local district officers ordering them to arrest all enemy subjects. Radio contact being nonexistent in those days, news of the outbreak of war in Europe and of its progress often took some time to reach the more remote localities. One party of British officials went through the game reserve, detaining any aliens whom they found there. The game warden in charge of the operation finally telegraphed back to headquarters: "Have arrested nine Germans, four Frenchmen and three Belgians. Please inform us with whom we are at war."

Shortly after driving into Fort Portal, we noticed a group of men in colorful African robes standing outside a building that turned out to be the Legislative Chamber. As they all spoke English, I struck up a conversation with them and inquired about a relatively impressive structure not far away from us. They told me that it was the palace of King George Kamurasi Rukidi III, Omukama of Toro. "Could we have an audience with His Majesty?" I ventured to ask. Within fifteen minutes, everything had been arranged by one of the Prime Minister's aides, and the king's brother escorted us up the hill to the residence, an imposing bungalow in the middle of a compound surrounded by a reed fence.

We were received at the entrance by the king's son, who ushered us into the royal presence. I was advised to greet His Majesty with the word, *Kali,* meaning "It's all yours," and when I did so, he laughed with delight. King George was a big man, six feet tall and weighing probably more than 200 pounds. He wore a business suit, and I was thankful that I had had the foresight to change my brown sport shirt for a jacket, tie, and white shirt before appearing before him.

He received us cordially and without ceremony. Evidently under the impression that the title prefixed to my name meant that I was a physician, he immediately sought my medical advice about his gout. It took a little time to explain to him the nature of my doctoral degree, but even then he insisted on giving me one of a number of carbon copies he had on file of a report drawn up by the doctors who had examined him in London.

His Majesty then proceeded to enlist my help in another area. His son, our escort, had been awarded a scholarship at Wagner College, Staten Island, New York, providing for room and board as well as tuition, but some way had to be found to pay for the cost of the trip, which amounted to around $600. I promised to do my best to assist, and could not help feeling that this interview had assumed all the elements of a stage comedy.

That impression was reinforced when Bert asked the king what his religion was.

"Protestant," he answered, and then asked us, "What is yours?"

Now at the outset of our talk, while disclaiming the qualifications of a medical doctor, I had told him that I was a rabbi, but apparently he had not grasped the religious significance of this term.

"We are Jewish," Bert replied, to which he rejoined, "It's all the same!"

So ended Act One of this African comedy.

The curtain rose on Act Two several months later, in New York, following our return home. One morning early in November 1959, I was pleasantly surprised to receive a telephone call from the king of Toro, asking me to drop in and see him at the Chatham Hotel, where he was staying. When I called there some days later, as arranged, a most friendly welcome awaited me—as well as a renewed request for the amount to defray his son's travel expenses. The college scholarship, it appeared, was being kept open for the royal student.

From His Majesty's suite, I telephoned a number of contacts and succeeded in arranging for the fare to be paid by a Jewish foundation, and in interesting other educational bodies in the young prince's welfare.

During the hour I spent with King George Rukidi III, I surmised that the most pressing reason for his trip was a course of treatment he was receiving for the ailment about which I had been mistakenly consulted in Toro. Ostensibly, however, he was in New York for weightier matters. While we were talking, he called up his financial representative, who turned out to be a Jewish lawyer. This man served as an adviser not only to the king of Toro, but also to the rulers of Buganda and Ankole in regard to economic concessions in their domains. He maintained similar contact with the Government of Sudan and with Dr. Nnamdi Azikiwe ("Zik"), the Nigerian nationalist leader who became that country's Prime Minister after it achieved independence in 1960.

The lawyer subsequently told me that the king of Toro, though a pensioner of the British administration, held title to extensive tea and coffee plantations that would eventually come into his possession. Whether they ever did, I have no way of knowing.

Our next stopover was in the province of Ankole, situated in northern Uganda. There was a considerable hubbub there when we arrived, as a teachers' conference was scheduled to begin. The king and queen of Ankole had honored it with their patronage. This provided us with the opportunity for our second royal reception, but it proved less dramatic than the first.

From Uganda we crossed into Belgian Congo, traveling along a route that wound through a dense bamboo forest once inhabited by gorillas, which, we were told, could often be seen until hunting expeditions had driven them far from human gaze.

A memorable experience at this stage of our African tour was the visit we paid to a pygmy encampment in the Beni Ituri forest, an immense region 37,500 square miles in area. The pygmies averaged no more than four feet in height and lived in tiny huts like so many oversize dog kennels. They wore only loincloths. One pygmy woman nursing a doll-sized baby at her breast added an amusing touch to the scene when she took part in a tribal dance. Every now and then, she would hand over the infant to a man (presumably the father), so as to perform the complicated steps without hindrance.

These pygmies were an utterly unself-conscious, carefree group of people, but apparently untamable. An attempt by the Belgian authorities to settle them in agriculture had proved a failure, as they had all returned to the bush in the end. A life of hard, steady work was not for them.

On the evening of the same day, we attended another pygmy dance program inside a nearby cave. The cave was huge and the accoustics were perfect—resoundingly so. A stage had been set up and electric lights were strung across the whole length of the cave. No less fantastic than the dances themselves was the long line of bats hanging by their claws from the electric wires, a spectacle that added a weird visual effect to the proceedings.

Our interest in the exotic aspects of Africa did not, of course, make us forgetful of our quest for remote points of Jewish settlement. "Communities" would be too grandiose a term for the mini-kehillot, sometimes numbering a handful or two of Jews, scattered around most parts of Black Africa.

Upon our arrival in Stanleyville, a town in eastern Belgian Congo, we proceeded to search the local telephone directory for Jewish names but failed to locate any until the hotel clerk mentioned that a Mme. Sarfatti was a Jewess. She came to see us and introduced herself as a physician who served as president of the local WIZO society. Two other ladies accompanied her.

The first Jewish settlers in the country arrived in 1907 from South Africa, and were mostly recent immigrants from Europe and Palestine. These Ashkenazi pioneers were soon joined by Sephardim from the island of Rhodes and the Greek mainland. After World War II, there had been a fresh influx of Jews from Europe and Rhodesia. At the time of our visit, there were about 2,500 Jews in Belgian Congo and of these one-half were to be found in Elisabethville, far to the south, which boasted a synagogue, a rabbi, a Jewish community center, and various Zionist organizations. The 200 Jewish children attending government schools in Elisabethville were able to receive tuition there in Hebrew and in Jewish studies from Jewish teachers paid by the state. Léopoldville, the capital, had about six dozen Jewish families.

In Stanleyville, however, there were only fifteen Jewish families, about fifty souls in all. No organized congregation existed there, still less a rabbi, and Jewish children received their religious education in the government schools—from a Protestant teacher! Nevertheless, this tiny *kehillah* held services on the High Holy Days and raised about $6,000 in an annual fund-raising drive for Israel.

That same evening, the three ladies who had come to our hotel returned with their husbands to spend more time with us. We learned that they and the other local Jewish families looked for guidance and moral support to the comparatively large *kehillah* in Elisabethville, which made up a substantial percentage of that city's White population. Bert and I tried to impress upon them that their future in Belgian Congo seemed far from promising, and that they ought to be planning Aliyah to Israel.

"It would be hard to uproot ourselves once again," one of the men told us. "After all, we have important business interests here and the country is rich in natural resources—gold, diamonds, copper, wolfram, and cotton. The present unrest will die down."

I countered by pointing out that it is the political extremists who usually seize control of newly independent countries. While admitting the truth of that statement, our visitors could only foresee difficulty in settling elsewhere, including Israel. The same opinion was expressed by a few other Jews in the import-export business, onetime immigrants from Rhodes, whom we met later. "How can we expect to make a living in Israel?" one of them asked somewhat rhetorically.

Ever since Belgian Congo became independent in 1960, first under the name of Congo-Kinshasa and then as the Republic of Zaïre, I have often wondered about the fate that lay in store for those Jewish merchants in the African interior. From Léopoldville, Elisabethville, and Stanleyville (subsequently renamed Kinshasa, Lubumbashi, and Kisangani), most of the Jews "with so much to lose" had to depart amid scenes of violence and disorder, compelled to rebuild their lives and businesses in South Africa and, in a few cases, even in Israel. As far as I know, few of them were able to return.

Our final stop in the country was at Léopoldville, some 250 miles east of the Atlantic Ocean, where we met the leading Jewish resident, Henri Maurice Alhadeff. A portly gentleman who had immigrated from Rhodes before World War I, he headed a prosperous import-export firm, also maintained a home in Central Park

South in New York, and had previously been honorary consul for Israel in Elisabethville.

Mr. Alhadeff was now devoting a good deal of his time to his hobby, native arts, encouraging local Africans to develop their talents in drawing, painting, and sculpture. He supported a group of about a dozen artists, each of whom received from him the equivalent of twenty dollars a week, a handsome stipend at that time.

One Sunday morning while we were his guests, Bert and I met these craftsmen when they came to see him with their weekly output. He had begun the project five years earlier with a gallery in a store, where the objets d'art fashioned by his protégés were exhibited and sold to tourists. In this way, Alhadeff was able to promote indigenous art forms and to provide the struggling artists' families with a livelihood. His own town house (he had another home out in the country) was cluttered with paintings and sculpture executed by the African "pensioners."

A West African Finale

On the last stage of our journey through the "Dark Continent," we flew to West Africa, beginning our tour in Ghana. Under British rule, the territory had been known as the Gold Coast, probably because Africans had once brought gold down to the ships with them to pay European traders for goods. The name *Ghana* recalled a West African empire that had flourished from the fourth to the thirteenth centuries, and from it (or a kindred term) derived *Guinea*, a name applied by Europeans to the entire littoral stretching from Gambia to Angola, whence the British gold coin ("guinea") first minted in the seventeenth century.

Ghana had achieved independence as a republic within the British Commonwealth about two years prior to our visit. In 1959, when Dr. Kwame Nkrumah was its Prime Minister, a strong personality cult was obviously developing around the nation's leader. Monuments in public squares, the names of thoroughfares, coins stamped with his image, sycophantic headlines in the Ghanaian press, streamers and inscriptions—all bore the hallmark of a one-man regime.

The people were good-looking and friendly and, on the surface, Ghana's economy seemed to be thriving. Accra, the capital and main seaport, was still the commercial center of West Africa and its traditional gateway to the Atlantic trade routes. Rumor had it that the adored leader ("Nkrumah, live for ever!" chanted his followers), who was soon to become Ghana's first President, wished to create a federation of West African states—including Nigeria—with himself, presumably, as head of state.

In the end, however, fate decreed otherwise. Not only did Nkrumah fail in that objective, but even in his own country he fell from power in 1966. New political circumstances, and the effects of corruption in any dictatorship, combined to bring about his overthrow. When we were visiting Ghana, of course, Nkrumah was the preeminent symbol of national unity, the hand that had fashioned a state out of quarreling tribes. When last heard of, he was an exile in Sékou Touré's leftist Republic of Guinea, which had been part of French West Africa until 1958.

Accra had a sizable Israeli colony of experts in various fields, and it grew for more than a decade subsequently, until Arab economic and political pressure led to a break in relations between Israel and most of Black Africa in 1973. Israeli enterprise, talent, and industry were impressively evident there in 1959, ranging from agricultural projects to the infant Black Star navigation company.

Shortly after our arrival in mid-July, we were invited to dinner by Israel's ambassador to Ghana, Ehud Avriel, an outstanding diplomat who, until 1948, had served as an effective European representative of the Jewish Agency. Gifted with high intelligence and considerable charm, Avriel had a clear perception of the issues in West Africa and the nature of his tasks arising from them. He was one of the architects of Israel's diplomatic thrust in that part of the world and, following various promotions, left the Foreign Ministry to become chairman of the Zionist General Council in 1968.

The Israel embassy arranged for us to be received by the king of Ashanti, whose seat was in Kumasi, the provincial capital. We heard that this was an especially prosperous region because of the cocoa plantations which furnished Ghana with seventy percent of its gross national revenue.

The Asantahene, Chief of Chiefs of the Ashantis, was Sir Osei Agyeman Prempeh II. He had occupied the "Golden Stool" for twenty-eight years and wore the traditional African robe. Although Nana ("Grandfather") Prempeh usually spoke with visitors through an interpreter, he addressed us directly in English without proving very communicative. Nonetheless, we were left in no doubt about his warm feelings for Israel, especially when I conveyed personal regards from Ambassador Avriel, whom the king remembered with much pleasure.

Israel's popularity in Ghana at that time was pinpointed amusingly enough for us by the report that a Ghanaian official who had been in Israel on a study tour, and whose wife had given birth to a son there, had named him "Sabra."

Such esteem for the Medinah was no less evident in Liberia when we arrived in the capital, Monrovia, a couple of days later. To judge by the large construction projects there, in which both Israeli and Liberian finance was involved, Israel had been playing an important role in the West African state's development. We heard admiring comments on the high standards maintained by the resident Israeli experts and on the excellent quality of goods imported from Israel.

Liberia, an independent republic for well over a century, had been founded in 1822 by the American Colonization Society to help freed slaves wishing to reestablish themselves in Africa. Monrovia was named for James Monroe, fifth President of the United States, who had once headed the society. American influence remained noticeable, extending even to the local coinage. The Israelis whom we met there all showed the highest regard for Liberia's President, William V. S. Tubman.

We learned that the envoys of a number of countries often met at the home of Israel's ambassador, Ḥanan Yavor. They knew that he was remarkably well informed about Liberian affairs and so looked to him for information that might otherwise have proved difficult to gather. One notable personality whom we met at dinner as guests of Ambassador Yavor and his wife was Ms. Angy Brooks, who served for many years as Liberia's UN delegate and as president of the World

Organization of Women Lawyers. Ms. Brooks proved to be a woman of dynamic character, highly intelligent and eloquent. She was then around forty years of age. In the course of our table talk, she paid tribute to President Tubman for having furthered "Women's Lib" in the country and for having given many opportunities to others of her sex for advancement in their careers.

Some piquant items of information also came our way. The captain of Prime Minister Kwame Nkrumah's newly acquired yacht was an Israeli, Commander Dvir, and Nkrumah had just ordered a larger and more luxurious craft. Dvir had in fact taken us on a tour of inspection of the present yacht while we were in Ghana. We next learned that the captain and crew of President Tubman's yacht were also Israelis. To hear these seaman conversing in Hebrew was a pleasant and surprising experience.

Ambassador Yavor told us the story of Simon Simonovitch, an East European Jew who had arrived in Monrovia as a refugee in 1940. Having established a flourishing business, he had married a Danish non-Jewess and died at the age of sixty-four, a year before our visit. Simonovitch, a close friend of President Tubman, had been honorary consul for Israel prior to the accreditation of Hanan Yavor. He had left the sum of $20,000 to the Medinah in his will. Both the President of Liberia and the ambassador of Israel sat up all night at his deathbed. While the funeral was in progress, President Tubman had ordered that all flags in Liberia be flown at half-mast.

Our brief stay in Monrovia marked the end of our African adventure. At the airport, before catching our plane to Lisbon, we met President Tubman, who had come with his daughter to welcome his two student sons on their return from a summer vacation in England.

In completing this tour of several weeks' duration through the "Dark Continent," we felt that our journeying there had been especially worthwhile at a time when so many African states were either in the process of emerging from colonial rule or were on the verge of achieving their independence by nationalist activities and uprisings.

After the conclusion of our world tour in November 1959, I went to Washington in order to acquaint the U.S. State Department with my impressions of the Asian and African countries we had visited. One point I stressed was the extent of constructive aid being extended at the time by Israel to countries such as Burma, Ghana, and Liberia, particularly in developing local agriculture and industry, as well as in helping to develop a new managerial class. Many Afro-Asian states, mindful of European colonial policies in the recent past, greatly appreciated this form of assistance. More than one American embassy had expressed satisfaction with this relationship, and I surmised that the State Department might have hinted to U.S. diplomatic representatives abroad that they should encourage such cooperation with the Israelis.

As on previous occasions, I also wrote a confidential report to Israel's Foreign Minister, Golda Meir, outlining some of my general impressions and conversations with various national leaders. Like the State Department, Israel's Foreign Ministry had alerted its embassies and legations to our impending arrival, and this courtesy had helped to make our visits more interesting and worthwhile.

In a talk I gave on Kol Zion La-Golah, the overseas service of Israel Radio, in January 1960, I stressed the fact that Medinat Yisrael not only served as a cohesive force holding Diaspora Jewish communities together, but also enhanced non-Jewish esteem for these *kehillot* in many parts of the world. Anti-Semitism was of negligible significance in the countries my wife and I had visited recently, but the Zionist sentiment and religious traditionalism characteristic of many such far-flung Jewish communities required the fortification of teachers' institutes to stem the tide of assimilation and intermarriage. I also pointed out that Judaism was a *terra incognita* even for most intellectuals in Asia and Africa, who tended to regard Jews as "a sort of Christian sect." A serious effort should be made to correct such misconceptions and to promote a better understanding of Judaism among peoples outside Europe and the Americas.

Israel's relations with the countries of Black Africa were then being cemented. They were promoted in the following year by the International Conference on Science in the Advancement of New States, convened at Rehovot and presided over by Israel's Minister of Education and Culture, Abba Eban, who at that time was also president of the Weizmann Institute of Science. It seemed that a period of hope and promise had opened for the newly independent African nations, with dynamic Israel aiding and advising them out of its own successful experience.

How sad it was for both sides that members of the Organization of African Unity (OAU), which had received Israel's ungrudging moral and material support, broke off diplomatic relations with Medinat Yisrael in 1972–73, at the behest of Arab governments motivated by considerations other than Black Africa's best interests. There are now signs, however, that a number of OAU countries have begun to seek a rapprochement with Israel.

More "Jewish Business" in Europe

Our journey around the globe, which had brought us into contact with so many and such varied Jewish communities, eventually terminated in Stockholm, where a week-long assembly of the World Jewish Congress took place in August 1959. Before arriving in Sweden, however, Bert and I had spent ten days in Portugal, to which we flew on the return trip from Dakar in Senegal, West Africa. One memorable feature of our stay in Estoril and Lisbon was the friendship we struck up with Professor Moses Bensabat Amzalak and his wife. One afternoon, by an odd coincidence, the guest of honor at a bullfight in Lisbon to which they took us was Emperor Haile Selassie of Ethiopia.

Professor Amzalak, then a man in his late sixties, was a versatile scholar who had headed the Portuguese Jewish community for many years. He was rector of the Technical University in Lisbon, which had faculties of agronomy, architecture, economics, engineering, and veterinary medicine. His own specialized field was economics, but he wrote authoritatively on Jewish cultural and historical subjects as well and had published, among other works, a study of *Hebrew Typography in 15th-Century Portugal*. At the time of our visit, he was working on another study, "The Economics of the Old Testament." In the course of his career, Professor Amzalak served as president of the Portuguese Academy of Sciences and represented Portugal's intellectual community in the Senate. He had received honorary degrees from many universities and colleges abroad.

From 1933, when Hitler assumed power in Germany, Professor Amzalak had been involved in the efforts to rescue Jews suffering persecution and in danger of their lives. As a friend of President Antonio de Oliveira Salazar, Portugal's head of state, and as the outstanding Jew in that country's public life, he had influenced the official policy of granting visas to Jews in Nazi-dominated Europe, which enabled them to enter Portugal as refugees after the French collapse in 1940 and, during the latter part of World War II, as temporary residents in transit to other countries of the free world. Thousands of Jewish refugees and wayfarers had passed through Lisbon throughout the Hitler era, when Portugal's neutral status made it a useful staging post to the Western Hemisphere, and the Lisbon *kehillah* had organized a relief committee, with Amzalak at its head, which worked with the help and guidance of the American Jewish Joint Distribution Committee and the Hebrew Immigrant Aid Society.

Our host, Professor Amzalak, also told us that he had managed to persuade Salazar to instruct consuls in lands under Nazi occupation to validate all Portuguese passports held by Jews (even though many of these documents were known to be far from "kosher"), and to see to it that the holders be allowed to leave for Portugal. Such consular protection, as I was already aware, had helped to save large numbers of Jews—especially in Nazi-occupied Hungary—from the gas chambers.

While staying in Lisbon, we were intrigued to discover that the only Cohen listed in the telephone directory who professed Judaism was a *ḥazzan* of that name. All the remaining Cohens, amounting to over a column of subscribers, were Roman Catholics! Thus, when the cantor left Portugal shortly thereafter, only non-Jews continued to bear that ancient Hebrew title. It was a bizarre sidelight on the pervasive Marrano presence in Spain and Portugal.

Professor Amzalak gave us an up-to-date account of the Marrano revival in northern Portugal and the eventual collapse of that high-minded, but unsuccessful effort.

Although people in the outside world had believed that crypto-Judaism no longer existed in Portugal by the beginning of the twentieth century, a Polish mining engineer named Samuel Schwarz had come across a secret Marrano group near Belmonte in 1917. While Schwarz was telling of his discovery, Captain Arturo de Barros Basto, a hero of the 1910 revolution, came from Oporto to the newly established synagogue in Lisbon and announced that he was searching for the religious faith of his ancestors. As a child, he had been initiated in certain Marrano beliefs and practices by his grandfather. Barros Basto, now a thirty-year-old army officer, underwent circumcision and launched a campaign for the revitalization of Portuguese Judaism. He received encouragement and support from Jews in Great Britain and, with funds donated by Sir Elly Kadoorie and by the Sephardi congregations in London and Amsterdam, he established a new *kehillah* of his own in Oporto, where a fine synagogue and an associated religious college were built in 1929. Through "missionary" work in the towns and villages of northern Portugal, where Marrano roots lay deep, and through a series of works on Judaism that he published in Oporto, the center of his movement, Captain de Barros Basto seemed likely to win back many thousands to the religion of their forefathers, particularly since Portugal's anticlerical regime looked kindly on his endeavors.

In an excess of zeal, he overreached himself, however, and began to act as a rabbi, rendering decisions on ritual matters and performing circumcisions with the aid of surgeons. Some Jews denounced him, and Orthodox rabbinical authorities abroad withheld their recognition of his Jewish religious leadership. When the Catholic Church regained power and influence under a right-wing government, the protests against him mounted still further. Barros Basto was advised to withdraw from the Marrano revival campaign and most reluctantly he did so, whereupon the movement he had founded started to disintegrate.

It was a heartrending, melancholy episode in recent Jewish history. The noble captain, whom Cecil Roth once hailed as "The Apostle of the Marranos" in a book of that title, died two years after our visit to Portugal, in 1961, a lonely and embittered man.

Modern Jewish communal life in Portugal, we learned, dated from the end of the eighteenth century. A small *kehillah* had been established in Lisbon around 1813, but did not obtain full recognition from the authorities there until 1892. Ten years later, Congregation Sha'arei Tikvah was erected in the capital, although no outward signs of identification as a house of Jewish worship were permitted until the revolution of 1910 abolished the disabilities of non-Catholic denominations. After World War I, the original community (mainly Sephardic) was swelled by a large influx of Ashkenazim from Eastern Europe and, during World War II, about 45,000 Jewish refugees from Nazi-occupied lands made periodic, brief appearances in Lisbon. Most of the 1,000 Jews in Portugal were living in the capital when we were there, although there were tiny *kehillot* in Oporto and Faro, as well as perhaps 2,000 or 3,000 surviving adherents of the Marrano revival movement.

We were the guests of the Lisbon Jewish community one evening, after *Ma'ariv* in the Sha'arei Tikvah Synagogue. The audience was a mixed one—Jewish families long resident in Portugal, others of Eastern European origin, and a few Israelis, including the consul and his wife. In the course of my remarks, I eulogized Israel's Ashkenazi Chief Rabbi, Dr. Isaac Halevi Herzog, who had died a few days earlier, on July 25. Some of the Ashkenazi Jews present asked me to say a few words in Yiddish and I was glad to oblige.

After the meeting, Professor Amzalak told me of a curious incident involving a Portuguese Jew's marriage ceremony in Lisbon. He had come to it wearing *tefillin*, as was customary in his crypto-Jewish tradition, but also with several crucifixes attached to his person. The bridegroom fortunately raised no objection when Professor Amzalak urged him to remove the Christian emblems and swathe himself in a *tallit!*

Our next stop was Stockholm, where the World Jewish Congress assembly was scheduled to begin its deliberations in August. The attendance exceeded all previous records, with representatives of *kehillot* from more than forty-five different countries participating. Matters of interest and substance occupied the agenda, notably Soviet Jewry, and the venue was particularly appropriate, since Sweden was the closest one could get to the USSR on neutral territory. At the gala opening in Stockholm's impressive city hall, greetings were extended by the Prime Minister, the Mayor, and spokesmen for various UN agencies. Our working sessions took place in the Swedish Parliament building.

This assembly had been organized with the help of Hillel Storch, the indefatigable WJC representative in Sweden. His activities, together with those of other communal leaders who had established contacts with Reichsführer Heinrich Himler and various prominent Nazis, had saved thousands of Jews from the death camps. Sweden, in common with its Scandinavian neighbors, had played a notable part in rescuing Jews and other victims of Hitlerism.

International Jewish gatherings of this type provide an opportunity for other meetings and discussions on Jewish problems not directly related to the agenda of the convened assembly. One reason for these extramural activities is the fact that a high proportion of world Jewish leaders often appear on two or more platforms "wearing different hats." Thus, in Stockholm, our World Confederation of General Zionists held an informal conference of its own, with Rose Halprin of the United States, Michel Topiol of France, Kalman Sultanik of Israel, and other WJC delegates participating.

At the assembly proper, Dr. Nahum Goldmann, in his presidential address, dwelt upon the growing dangers of assimilation in the USSR, where many Jews were losing their ethnic identity, some by choice and others by the pressure of circumstances.

That evening, I chaired a session on "Cultural Pluralism in the Modern World." Among those participating in the discussion were Pierre Lebar of UNESCO, Professor Morris Ginsberg of London University, Father Jean Daniélou of the Institut Catholique in Paris, and Thomas Diop of Senegal, representing the African Society for Culture.

On the following morning, Dr. Binyamin Eliav, head of the Eastern European desk in Israel's Foreign Ministry, spoke about the Soviet campaign against religion in general and against Judaism in particular. A full-scale debate ensued. It was common knowledge at the time that *Siddur ha-Shalom*, the "Peace Prayer Book" issued by Rabbi Solomon Schliefer of Moscow, amounted only to a propaganda gesture, as the limited number of printed copies did not circulate among Russian Jews.

A symposium on "The Jewish State and the Jewish People," chaired by Israel Sieff, was held on the Tuesday evening. The two participants were Moshe Sharett and Professor Salo Baron. Sharett made the point that Israel's policy must be to avoid interfering with Jewish communities abroad, although dangers menacing Diaspora *kehillot* could not be ignored. Baron declared that anti-Semitism had lost much of its impact on the Jewish people because of the existence of Israel, which would promote *Kibbutz Galuyyot*, the ingathering of the exiles, not only physically but culturally as well. He thought it likely that Israel would open up a new era of Jewish cultural development.

Another symposium, in which Professor Akiba Ernst Simon, Dr. Aaron Steinberg, and Judah Pilch took part, was devoted to Jewish education. It pointed up a substantial growth in the number of Jewish children receiving a Jewish education and the need for its content to be improved and increased. Professor Simon expressed the opinion that Israeli youth had an inadequate feeling of solidarity with the rest of the Jewish people.

At this session, the centenary of Sholem Aleichem was marked.

In view of our planned Aliyah at the end of December 1960, I announced my decision to relinquish the chairmanship of the WJC Western Hemisphere Executive, which I had held for the past ten years. I was then elected honorary vice-president of the World Jewish Congress, a post I continued to hold for many years thereafter. Samuel Bronfman, president of the Canadian Jewish Congress, was chosen to succeed me as chairman of the Western Hemisphere Executive.

Before leaving Stockholm for Central Europe, I held a press conference at which I elaborated on my proposal regarding a World Academy for Peace. It seemed appropriate to do so in the city where the Nobel Peace Prize is awarded each year.

Our visit to Czechoslovakia in mid-August was both enlightening and depressing. Fourteen years after the end of World War II, that country's surviving Jewish community presented a tragic spectacle, physical destruction by the Nazis having been followed by spiritual paralysis under the Communist regime that had seized power in 1948. Out of a prewar Jewish population of some 360,000, fewer than 20,000 remained in Czechoslovakia. Prague, the capital, where there had been 56,000 Jews in 1939, now had only about 5,000. The remainder had either been deported and murdered or else had fled the country. Contact with other Jewish communities abroad, even in the Communist bloc, was almost nonexistent; no Aliyah or emigration was permitted; and, even several years after the Slánský Trial, Jews were still the target of much hostile propaganda.

Our hosts, from whom we obtained basic information and guidance around the city and its Jewish communal institutions, were Rabbi E. Davidovič and Rudolf Iltis, secretary-general of the Council of Jewish Communities in Bohemia and Moravia. In the prevailing Stalinist atmosphere, of course, they were obliged to speak guardedly to us, but the evidence of our own eyes was sufficient to complete any gaps. Chief Rabbi Gustav Sicher, who had spent the war years in Palestine, was not accessible because of his advanced age and ill health.

The Czechoslovakian Government, having done away with Jewish communal autonomy, now financed the religious institutions to a diminishing extent and paid for the upkeep of the synagogues, although state policy was naturally atheistic. A handful of rabbis, cantors, and *shoḥatim* received salaries from this budget. Jewish "religious" education was imparted to no more than fifty Jewish children in state schools by a teacher assigned for the purpose. Officially, at least, no Bar Mitzvah instruction was given and no religious marriages took place.

We visited the historic Jewish quarter of Prague, where not only the old synagogues were located but also the offices of the *kehillah*, a home for the aged, and a *kasher* restaurant. We were told that the Jewish community center's large hall was used for weddings, Purim celebrations, and Passover *Sedarim*. Miraculously, the architectural treasures of this 1,000-year-old community had survived the Holocaust only because the Nazis had been intent on using them as part of a "Central Museum of the Defunct Jewish Race," a project that seems to have originated in the mind of Reichsprotektor Reinhard Heydrich, the SS chief and leading planner of the "Final Solution." All nine synagogues in the ghetto had therefore been made to serve as warehouses for looted ritual objects and, by the end of World War II, one of the world's richest and most extensive collections of Judaica had been housed there.

Prague's Jewish quarter formed an important and integral part of the city's cultural history, as the Communist authorities were well aware. The Jewish Town Hall, or Rathaus, which had been rebuilt in 1765, was remarkable for its two clocks. One of these, above, was a regular timepiece with Roman numerals, but the lower one bore Hebrew numerals and the hands moved counterclockwise.

Close by stood the various historic places of worship, some of them dating back many centuries. Bert and I were most eager to see the Altneuschul ("Old-New Synagogue"), Europe's oldest surviving house of Jewish prayer, which is still in use. Designed in Gothic style, it was built around 1270. The inside wall bore the traces of bloodstains, grim evidence of a massacre that took place in the fourteenth century, when the local Jews were accused of poisoning the wells. Thereafter, the stains were left on the wall and not painted over, as a perpetual reminder of the ghastly event. A more heartening relic on view there was the banner emblazoned with a Magen David, which Emperor Ferdinand III presented to Prague's *kehillah* in 1648, as a token of appreciation for the heroism displayed by Jews in the defense of their city against the invading Swedes.

A persistent legend associates the Altneuschul with the *Maharal* of Prague, Rabbi Judah Löw ben Bezalel, and the *golem* (robot in human shape) he allegedly created there at the end of the sixteenth century. According to this legend, Rabbi Löw fashioned the *golem* to act as his servant and defend the Jewish population, but he was obliged to restore it to its original clay when it ran amok, endangering the innocent as well as the guilty. There is no historical basis for the *golem*'s link with the *Maharal* of Prague, but this curious tale has given rise to a number of modern works in art and literature.

The Pinkas Synagogue, built in 1535, stood near this ancient monument. It was being renovated by the Czech Government as a memorial to Bohemian and Moravian Jews who had fallen victim to the Nazis. Inscribed on the walls of this synagogue, the second oldest in Prague, were more than 77,000 names.

Within the ghetto area, we were shown the old Jewish cemetery, now disused, on three-quarters of which Prague's city council had erected buildings. Bodies had been exhumed and reburied in the remaining space, twelve deep, and the tombstones—many of historical interest and importance—were all crowded together. There was a new Jewish cemetery on the outskirts of the capital.

While in Prague, we attended Shabbat eve services at the Altneuschul, where there was a hired *minyan*.

On the following Sunday, Mr. Sattat, the Israeli chargé d'affaires, drove us to the town of Terezín, about forty miles north of Prague. Under its German name, Theresienstadt, it had been one of the largest Nazi concentration camps during the years 1941–45, but its function had been distinct from that of all the other camps. Jews transported to Theresienstadt—from Czechoslovakia, Germany, Austria, and one or two other Western lands—had included many elderly and "privileged" people, such as Jews eminent in public life or who had been decorated for gallantry during World War I. When rumors of Hitler's genocide program began to circulate at the height of World War II, the Nazis converted Theresienstadt into a showplace ghetto, complete with the false paraphernalia of normal life, and even made movies there for screening at home and abroad. Unsuspecting officials of the International Red Cross who toured the camp later reported on how "well" the inmates were being treated.

In fact, however, Theresienstadt merely assured those incarcerated there of a slower death. Well over half of the 150,000 Jews who passed through its walls were subsequently deported to extermination centers in Poland, and a further 33,000 died of starvation, torture, or disease in this "showplace." The assimilated majority were the first to succumb, whereas the minority of Orthodox and Zionist prisoners maintained a higher level of morale. By the time of the liberation, only about ten percent of those sent to Theresienstadt still remained alive.

Signs in the cemetery preserved next to the wartime ghetto indicated that 110,000 persons were buried in mass graves. We also saw a monument erected by the Council of Jewish Communities in Bohemia and Moravia, enumerating all the countries from which the victims had been transported to Theresienstadt.

On another day in the course of our visit, we went to the village of Lidice, not far from Prague, which has acquired a place in history as a symbol of Nazi vindictiveness and ferocity. Reichsprotektor Reinhard Heydrich, who was Adolf Eichmann's boss, had already won infamy as organizer of the *Kristallnacht* outrages and of the murderous Nazi Einsatzkommandos when he was appointed Governor of Bohemia and Moravia in 1941. As a result of his peculiarly brutal reign of terror there, Heydrich was nicknamed "the Hangman." Following his assassination by Czech patriots in May 1942, thousands of Jews were immediately transported to death camps and an Einsatzkommando unit drove to Lidice, where one of Heydrich's suspected assailants was thought to be living. The men were lined up and shot, the women were deported, and the entire village was razed to the ground. Like Oradour-sur-Glane in France, where the 1,000 inhabitants were also murdered in a Nazi reprisal measure over two years later, Lidice has become a byword for the kind of atrocity perpetrated against civilian populations by forces of the Third Reich.

Before leaving Prague, we visited the U.S. ambassador, John Moore Ellison, who told us that relations with Czechoslovakia were at a low ebb. A statue of the late

Soviet dictator, Josef Stalin, erected by the Czech Government two years after Khrushchev's revelations at the Twentieth Party Congress in 1956, bore witness to the regime's unrepentant Stalinism. Ambassador Ellison informed us that the standard of living in Czechoslovakia was higher than in any other Communist bloc country.

Our next stop was Vienna. We spent our first evening in the home of the Israel ambassador, Yeḥezkel Sahar. Many Israelis were there, including David Hacohen, who talked about his experiences as Israel's envoy in Burma.

The local *kehillah*, numbering about 12,000, was almost equally divided between Austrian Jews who had returned to Vienna after World War II and former refugees and DPs who had escaped from Poland, Hungary, and other parts of Eastern Europe. As yet, of course, there was no large-scale Jewish immigration from the Soviet Union. Austria's Chief Rabbi, Dr. Akiba Eisenberg, headed the Israelitische Kultusgemeinde, together with its lay president, Emil Maurer, who represented the non-Zionist Social Democratic majority in the Jewish communal body.

We attended Sabbath morning services at the old Stadttempel on the Seitenstettengasse, located near Vienna's historic Jewish quarter. It was the only major synagogue in the Austrian capital that had escaped destruction on *Kristallnacht* in 1938. We learned that Emperor Francis I (not to be confused with the "good Kaiser," Franz Josef, who reigned from 1848 until 1916 and was well disposed to the Jews) had only permitted the construction of Vienna's Stadttempel on condition that it would bear no outward resemblance to a synagogue. Thanks to the sermons of its first rabbi, Isaac Noah Mannheimer, and the musical service pioneered by its *ḥazzan*, Salomon Sulzer, this congregation had steered a moderate, traditional course between strict Orthodoxy and Reform, and had set the tone for other leading synagogues in the Austro-Hungarian Empire.

The attendance, about one hundred men and the same number of women, was unusually large, since a Bar Mitzvah was being celebrated that Shabbat and a bridegroom was "called up" to the Torah.

Chief Rabbi Eisenberg informed us that almost every Jew in Vienna belonged to the Kultusgemeinde and paid a communal tax for the maintenance of local Jewish institutions. The *kehillah* also received a measure of support from the Claims Conference. Talmud Torah schools were conducted by the Austrian branch of Agudat Yisrael, but there was also a strong Mizraḥi element in the Orthodox section of the community. Vienna's Zionist offices and Jewish charitable organizations were housed in the synagogue building on the Seitenstettengasse.

That evening, Ted Feder told us about the work of the Joint Distribution Committee, which provided support for Jewish schools and refugees. He said that there was close cooperation between the JDC and the Jewish Agency in Vienna, and that HIAS assisted those who wished to settle in countries other than Israel. The Kultusgemeinde, having recently sold the Rothschild Hospital, had sent part of the proceeds to Israel and had devoted the remainder to local needs. We heard from the Jewish Agency's Aliyah *shali'aḥ* that if Jews arriving from the Soviet Union with a visa for Israel decided to go elsewhere, they were free to do so. A colleague of his told us about organized groups of Olim from Rumania, who were allowed to spend no more than twelve hours in Vienna before being sent on to Naples, where they were to board ships bound for Haifa.

During our stay in Austria, we made a point of visiting the site of the former Nazi death camp at Mauthausen, some twelve miles southeast of Linz. Originally intended for Austrian anti-Nazis, Mauthausen soon became the place where anti-Nazis from all occupied countries received the harshest form of treatment prescribed. Inmates had built the high walls surrounding the camp and were compelled to drag heavy stones up the 186 steps of the notorious "stairway of death," at the top of which they looked down on the *Wienergraben,* a huge quarry. On their way up or down, Nazi guards often beat the weaker prisoners to death. Captured Russian soldiers and Czechs deported to Mauthausen after the assassination of Heydrich were subjected to particular brutality.

In May 1941, the first group of 400 Jews from Amsterdam arrived by way of Buchenwald: within three days, all of them had died at the quarry. Many were herded to the edge and then were forced to jump off; other prisoners took their own lives there rather than undergo further torture. The SS guards employed various methods for disposing of their victims—hurling them into the abyss, shooting them in the nape of the neck, injecting them with poison, and gassing them. No cemetery existed for the disposal of their remains. Until mass evacuations from camps in Eastern Europe began in 1944, no Jew survived longer than three days in Mauthausen. Altogether, more than 330,000 prisoners were deported to this dreadful place from Poland, Russia, Yugoslavia, Italy, Holland, and Belgium. No one ever escaped over the electrified walls and only a small minority survived.

We saw monuments erected there by various European governments, but there was no memorial to the Jewish dead—not even a plaque, such as there was in Theresienstadt. On the walls and doors of what had been the Jewish barracks, Jewish visitors had written tributes of their own in Hebrew, Yiddish, Polish, German, and Hungarian. Apparently, the Russians, who had liberated Mauthausen in 1945, were not disposed to identify any of the victims as Jews, although a very high percentage of these martyrs had been Jewish.

I could not help wondering how many Jews traveling in Austria since the war had taken the trouble to visit this death camp, so close to Salzburg, where the music festivals continue to receive Jewish patronage.

It is surely a grave lapse on the part of our world Jewish organizations that they fail to urge American and other Jewish tourists in Europe to include in their itineraries visits to the former Nazi concentration and death camps. That doleful aspect of recent Jewish history tends, unfortunately, to be almost completely overlooked. How many of us have ever taken time out to see the blood-soaked ground on which, a mere generation ago, millions of our people were butchered or burned to ashes? My own visits to Auschwitz, Dachau, Mauthausen, Theresienstadt, and other sites have convinced me that such experiences must be shared by all Jews. If veterans' and ex-servicemen's organizations can organize tours of the military cemeteries in France and elsewhere, honoring the dead of both World Wars, so can and so should Jewish bodies throughout the world sponsor pilgrimages to those places where our own kith and kin died, simply because they were Jews.

By September 1, 1959, we were homeward bound at last, on our way through Paris to New York. The day after our arrival in Paris, President Eisenhower came on an official visit. He and President Charles de Gaulle were applauded by vast crowds as they drove together down the Champs Elysées.

On the following morning, we visited the Memorial to the Unknown Jewish Martyr, which had been dedicated in 1956. Isaac Schneersohn was the initiator of this project and I served as a member of the international committee of sponsors, managing to secure an allocation for it from the Claims Conference. The Memorial contains the Tomb of the Unknown Jewish Martyr and, next to Yad Vashem, the world's largest collection of archives and documents relating to the *Sho'ah*. It is located near the historic Jewish quarter of Paris, known locally as the *Pletzel*. Municipal plans called for the removal of a building which then obscured the view of the River Seine, and for the laying of a garden in front of the monument.

Schneersohn guided us through the Memorial, which forms part of the Centre de Documentation Juive Contemporaine. It was an impressive structure. The names of all the Nazi camps were recorded on a bronze cylinder set against a huge marble wall and, on the lower floor, each of the six crypts contained ashes from one of those camps. On the upper floor, we saw photographic exhibitions of the Nazi atrocities, as well as the original copy of Hitler's last will and testament, in which he reiterated that the Jews "are an international source of poison." There was also a catalogue room and a library containing over 1,000 books on the Nazi period.

The Memorial building and the activities that take place there receive financial support from the Claims Conference and from local sources. I did not get the impression that many people visited this monument, and I made various suggestions as to how it might be brought to the attention of Jews traveling abroad.

Return to Familiar Ground

As the Pan-American airliner bringing us home from Paris circled over New York harbor prior to landing at Idlewild, I was assailed by a medley of feelings generated by the realization that this particular return to our native soil, after so many scores of homecomings from places overseas, heralded the approaching end of an epoch in our lives. On the one hand, I longed to see the old familiar faces of our immediate family and of friends and congregants after so long an absence abroad, nostalgia for the past increasing as awareness of the imminent break became more acute. On the other hand, I was filled with anticipation—and not a little apprehension—because of the manifold preparations that lay immediately before us in starting a new chapter in our lives, Aliyah to Israel, at an age when most people would be inclined to take things easy and rest on their laurels.

So much had to be completed before the time for our departure would arrive. We had to wind up our affairs, professional, personal, and social, before bidding farewell to our accustomed mode of life in the United States—though not to the U.S. as such, since we planned to make frequent return visits to America after our Aliyah. Sixteen months remained to us in New York, and we sensed that the curtain was beginning to fall on the crowded, busy scenes of our lifetime on American soil.

Upon our return, the board and members of Congregation B'nai Jeshurun, as well as many colleagues in a variety of organizations, began urging that we reconsider our decision to leave for Israel. As I made it clear to them, however, our determination to proceed with the arrangements for our Aliyah was unalterable.

At a "Welcome Home" Sabbath morning service on September 19, I devoted my sermon to the topic, "Asia and Africa in Transition." Addressing our congregants on behalf of Bert and myself, I emphasized our "feeling of intensified appreciation of America and its way of life" and our new awareness of the struggle for Jewish survival in remote corners of the earth where Israel was playing a major role "in endowing Jewish lives with spirit and content."

Subsequently, in December, *The New York Post* published my reflections on our recent world tour, with special reference to the U.S. position in the newly emergent Afro-Asian states. I pointed out that Soviet influence in those areas of the world was frequently offset by heavy-handed Communist methods, and that *The Ugly American*, a current best-seller, had exaggerated U.S. diplomatic shortcomings. I urged that efforts be made to promote greater cultural ties and to train American diplomatic representatives who would be conversant with the language and customs of the countries in which they served. The critical danger zone, to my mind, was India, where vastly increased economic aid was essential. In Africa, there would be a future for the White inhabitants only if the former European colonial powers joined forces with the United States in devising some new type of Marshall Plan. At this stage, I believed, the Western form of democracy was unsuited to most Afro-Asian states, which were not yet ready for such a system of government. My conclusion was that our principal goals must be a fuller understanding of their particular problems, coupled with a readiness to offer practical assistance.

For the moment, however, the daily concerns of the present submerged our thoughts about the future. Within a day or two of our return to New York, I plunged into my customary schedule of synagogue activities, pastoral visits, and public affairs, both Jewish and general. My primary concern, of course, was the congregation, which had been entrusted to the devoted care of my associate, Rabbi William Berkowitz, during our prolonged absence abroad. Charles H. Silver, who had succeeded Jacob Sincoff as president in 1957, was achieving wide recognition as president of the Beth Israel Hospital and he was also destined to make his mark as president of the New York Board of Education. Another prominent figure in our congregation, Louis Lefkowitz, had been elected Attorney General of the State of New York in 1957.

A meaningful experience that winter was the centennial observance of the delivery by Dr. Morris J. Raphall, a nineteenth-century predecessor of mine as rabbi of Congregation B'nai Jeshurun, of the first prayer to be recited by a Jewish spiritual leader before the U.S. House of Representatives, on February 1, 1860. Dr. Abraham G. Duker, president of the College of Jewish Studies in Chicago, had first suggested the idea of such an observance to Congressman Sidney R. Yates of Chicago, who then came forward with the proposal that I be invited to Washington. Although acceptance meant my having to forego an important meeting in Europe, I felt that this historic occasion was too significant to be missed.

My prayer, on Monday, February 1, 1960, opened the session of the House of Representatives at noon. The Speaker of the House, Congressman Sam Rayburn, presented the officiant. I had donned full ceremonial attire, rabbinical robe, cap, and *tallit*, as Dr. Raphall had done a century earlier. My prayer was as follows:

Lord, Creator, Father,

"This is the day which the Lord hath made that we should rejoice and be glad thereon."

We pray Thee, make Thy light to shine upon this day which we joyfully mark as the one hundredth anniversary of a prayer intoned within this legislative hall for the first time by a teacher of the Jewish faith, Rabbi Morris Jacob Raphall. It was a day as meaningful for America as for the household of Jacob, tokening not only religious freedom and equality but interreligious fellowship.

How better can we remember that day than by calling to mind some of the prayerful words then uttered?

"Lord! Great and manifold have been Thy bounties to this highly favored land. Heartfelt and sincere are our thanks. . . . It has been Thy gracious will that in this Western hemisphere there should be established a Commonwealth after the model of that which Thou, Thyself, didst bestow on the tribes of Israel, in their best and purest days. The Constitution and the institutions of this Republic prove to the world that men created in Thine image and obedient to Thy behests are not only capable—fully capable—of self-government, but that they know best how to combine civil liberty with ready obedience to the laws, religious liberty . . . with sincere respect for individual rights."

While those words had and have a timeless ring, other words of that prayer reflected the ominous tensions of the time when our nation, riven by strife, was on the threshold of a tragic civil war.

O Lord Whose Name is One, we thank Thee that today our nation stands before the world one and indivisible. May it stand not only in the panoply of might but in the splendor of spirit, not too proud to acknowledge its own blemishes and seek to correct them, and not too meek to aspire to the role of world leadership by example, in helping to lift burdens of oppression, poverty, ignorance and disease, wherever the uplifting hand is needed and welcomed. May we begin at home by cleansing our own habitations from the germs of hatred and prejudice. And may we join forces with the vigilant safeguarding of goodwill everywhere, aware that the toleration of evil paves the way for evil's domination.

We thank Thee that the restoration of Zion, a prayer and a dream a hundred years ago, has come to fulfillment in our time with the noble help of these United States. Grant that out of Zion shall go forth again the Law and the word of God out of Jerusalem.

In a hundred years, thanks to the progress of science, the ends of the earth have come together across the barriers of time and space. Grant Thy children the moral wisdom to match proximity with neighborliness.

In a hundred years the inventions of destruction have left us no alternative to peace. Grant us the will to pursue peace relentlessly and the inventiveness to surmount the obstacles in the way.

Sustain with Thy blessing the President of these United States and all who conduct the affairs of government. May Thy face be turned unto our beautiful America and unto Thy children everywhere.

May it be Thy will that one hundred years hence America shall yet stand unsurpassed as a citadel of human fellowship and a fortress of peace and freedom in a free and peaceful world.

Adonai oz le-ammo yitten, Adonai yevarekh et ammo va-shalom. The Lord endow us all with strength, the Lord bless us all with peace. Amen.

Following my invocation, a number of senators, congressmen, and special guests attended a luncheon given by Representative Emanuel Celler in the Speaker's dining room. While responding to the greetings extended by Congressman Celler, who presided, and by Senator Everett Dirksen, I reconstructed the background to Rabbi Raphall's prayer a century earlier, and I noted the progress made since then in civil rights and intergroup relations in the United States.

A curious set of circumstances had prevailed at the time when Rabbi Raphall delivered his prayer. The division of forces within the House of Representatives, between those who favored the abolition of slavery and those who opposed it, was so even that it had proved impossible to elect a Speaker and thus conduct the business of the House. Day after day, the roll call produced the same evenly balanced division and no presiding officer could be elected.

It so happened that on the very day of Rabbi Raphall's appearance before Congress, when his prayer was greeted with awed silence, the deadlock was broken and a Speaker was finally elected on the forty-fourth ballot. Newspaper reporters who wired the outcome to their papers added: "The rabbi's prayer did it!"

On the morning after my invocation in the House of Representatives, accompanied by Senator Jacob Javits, who introduced me, I was received at the White House by President Dwight D. Eisenhower. He recalled his presence in 1954 at the dinner held in New York to commemorate the three hundredth anniversary of Jewish settlement in the United States. I presented to him a copy of my book, *A Century of Judaism in New York*, in which Rabbi Raphall's prayer is cited.

Before leaving Washington that afternoon, I called at the embassy of Israel for a chat with the minister plenipotentiary, Ya'acov (Jacob) Herzog. He was delighted to hear about our impending Aliyah and offered to help us in any way possible.

One day toward the end of February, while he was visiting New York, Zalman Shazar, acting chairman of the Jewish Agency in Jerusalem, came in to see me. He urged me to take over the American branch of the Jewish Agency's Department for Education and Culture in the Diaspora, of which he held the portfolio on the Jerusalem Executive. I regretfully declined the offer, on the ground that I wished to divest myself of as many responsibilities as possible, so as to arrive in Israel without prior commitments.

This was by no means my first meeting with Shazar, whom I had known and admired for many years, since the time when he had been prominent on the Jewish and Zionist world scenes as Zalman Rubashov.*

Zalman Shazar was one of the galaxy of eminent personalities who saw merit in my proposed establishment of a World Academy for Peace. Since first broaching the idea in 1958, I had received various forms of encouragement. Thus, early in March 1960, Dr. Ralph Bunche, a great American and a dedicated international public servant, telephoned me in response to a letter I had written to him on the subject. He was strongly in favor of the idea, but urged that the members of such an Academy should stay together for longer than the month each year I had envisaged.

On June 30, while attending a Jewish education conference in Paris, I took occasion to discuss my plan with François Mauriac, the celebrated French Catholic writer and intellectual. Mauriac, then a man of seventy-five, exercised considerable moral authority and differed from many of his friends on the left by stressing his pro-Jewish attitude. During the five-year legal battle known as the Finaly Case, he had opposed the official Catholic line and had demanded that the kidnapped war orphans be returned (as they eventually were) to the fold of Judaism and to their Jewish relatives in Israel.

Mauriac approved my peace proposal, but wanted to know how it could be implemented. He particularly urged that the World Academy for Peace should deal with the Arab-Israel conflict and the war then raging in Algeria. Anticipating the difficulty in finding suitable Muslim participants, he suggested that membership of the Academy be offered to a Professor Massignon of the Collège de France, who enjoyed a high reputation in the Muslim world.

A few days later, on July 5, I had an appointment in London with Professor Arnold Toynbee, the British historian. He, too, welcomed my proposal, although he doubted whether intellectuals would exert much influence on world public opinion. Toynbee felt that at least one eminent Muslim should be invited to join the Academy.

I also had a meeting in London with Philip Noel Baker, the British Socialist thinker and politician, who agreed that there could be no hope for mankind if the value of moral authority were to be downgraded. He approved the list of names I had already drawn up, but also recommended a Professor Hussein of Cairo. In his opinion, J. Robert Oppenheimer was in some ways equal in stature to Albert Einstein. Noel Baker proved to be far more enthusiastic about the scheme than Toynbee, declaring that the World Academy for Peace might serve as an important auxiliary to the UN and help mold public opinion throughout the world.

An opportunity to renew my proposal and to bring it before the wider public came later that summer, on August 6, the fifteenth anniversary of the atomic bomb attack

*On Zalman Shazar, see chapter 17.

on Hiroshima. I was among those who addressed an outdoor gathering of about 3,000 people, predominantly of the younger generation, at a Hiroshima Day rally on the UN Plaza in New York, sponsored by the Sane Nuclear Policy group.

The speakers included a Cornell University professor of physics, Theodore Bikel, the Jewish actor and folk singer, and representatives of the Protestant Council of New York and of the Sane Nuclear Committee. Prior to the actual meeting, an Episcopal minister from the Cathedral of St. John the Divine and a clergyman from the Protestant Council joined me for a prayer period in the Meditation Room of the United Nations building.

In the course of my address, I spoke of man's failure so far to heed the tragic lessons of Hiroshima and Nagasaki, and of the challenge to religion this represented. Transposed into modern terminology, the message of Isaiah and Micah to our own nuclear generation was: "Transform the missiles of destruction into missions of salvation to the underdeveloped areas of the earth, to help develop their economic resources, cure poverty, and heal disease." It was not enough, I said, merely to abolish the weapons of mass destruction. Men needed to build up concepts and instrumentalities of peace for the solution of international disputes. "This is the road of morality," I declared. "This is the road of sanity." Then, after a detailed outline of my plan for the World Academy, I concluded as follows:

> Collective effort in the field of medical research has brought tremendous good to mankind in the healing and prevention of disease. Is it too much to hope that collective effort in the struggle against war may also be productive of good results?
>
> Of fundamental importance is the universal rejection of the premise that war is inevitable. The first step toward abolishing war is the faith that war can be abolished. Faith, therefore, becomes the first essential in the achievement of a warless world.

At about this time, I went to see Lawrence Finkelstein, vice-president and executive director of the Carnegie Endowment for International Peace. It turned out that he had celebrated his Bar Mitzvah in my congregation well over twenty years earlier, in 1938. I told him about my talks with various eminent men and women, and of the interest Ralph Bunche had expressed. Finkelstein was able to identify Noel Baker's "Professor Hussein" as the blind Egyptian scholar and religious educator, Taha Hussein, and he warmly commended the choice of such a candidate. He also stressed the importance of adding a few personalities from the Communist states to our panel. In his view, the Academy should not address itself to immediate problems, where it might prove ineffective, but rather to longer-range issues that would be likely to crop up over the next ten or fifteen years.

A month and a half later, I called on Paul Hoffman at his office in the UN Secretariat building to discuss my proposal. He appeared to favor a scheme that would be initiated by the World Brotherhood Movement. I told him of a previous conversation with Dr. Everett R. Clinchy, head of the National Conference of Christians and Jews, who had indicated that the World Brotherhood Movement would like to sponsor the projected Academy for Peace. Hoffman cautioned me about the difficulty of bringing together a group of people, each of whom would probably offer a plan of his own.

One further step toward my goal came in November, not long before Bert and I left to settle in Israel. A luncheon was then arranged at the Harmonie Club in New York by a mutual friend, Raymond Rubinow, who was executive director of the J. M. Kaplan Fund, the other guests being Dr. Joseph E. Johnson, president of the Carnegie Endowment for International Peace, and the vice-president, Lawrence Finkelstein. They expressed some doubts about the workableness of my proposal and wanted to study it further before undertaking any commitment. In reply, I said that if the idea had moral value, it must be given a try in the hope that it might lead somewhere, since no plan, not even the most richly endowed, had as yet attracted international attention and support.

There, unfortunately, the matter rested.

I have gone to some length in describing this proposal of mine and my efforts, hitherto fruitless, in its behalf, because I felt then—and continue to feel—that an enterprise of this kind, so basic, albeit so complicated, merits the widest possible support, regardless of the prospects for its success. The ideal itself—the vision of universal peace—is one of Judaism's fundamental contributions to the fellowship of mankind. It deserves to be nurtured continuously and unremittingly, in the hope that eventually a solution will be found to the world's most challenging and most vital problem.

An unusual personality whom I met in New York in the late spring of 1960 was Dr. Setsuzo Kotsuji, the eminent Japanese Hebraist, who had embraced Judaism a year previously at a ceremony in Jerusalem, where he took the name Avraham. It came as a surprise to learn that the Kyoto-born, American-educated man of youthful, dapper appearance, on whom I called at the Park Plaza Hotel, was actually sixty-one years of age. According to some reports, he had been tutor in Jewish studies to the Emperor's youngest brother, Prince Mikasa.

As a teenager, Kotsuji had abandoned his ancestral religion for Christianity while attending the American Presbyterian College in Tokyo. Earlier still, however, at thirteen, he had become interested in Judaism after reading a Japanese translation of the Bible. The Book of Leviticus made a deep impression on his young mind, it appeared, because of its detailed ritual ordinances for the *Kohanim*, which appealed to this descendant of Shinto priests.

Shintoism, he told me, had no holy book: it was handed down from generation to generation through ritual observance. I mentioned my talk with Prince Mikasa in Tokyo and the latter's remark that Judaism had aroused his interest on two accounts—the strong character of the Patriarchs, and the connection between religion and the soil. Kotsuji agreed with my surmise that there might be a parallel in Shintoist ancestor worship and its national aspect.

He described how, after taking his Bachelor of Divinity degree in Semitics at the Pacific School of Religion in Berkeley almost thirty years earlier, he had begun to study Hebrew in Japan, where he became a lecturer in both Hebrew and Old Testament. On the eve of World War II, he had been of assistance to Eastern European Jewish refugees seeking a temporary haven in his country and, in 1943, had published a book to acquaint the Japanese public with Judaism and the Jewish people. Eventually, after the war, he had perfected his Hebrew in Israel and then felt impelled to fulfill his religious yearnings by becoming a proselyte in the Holy City.

Dr. Kotsuji, who now made regular lecture tours of the United States but who divided his time mainly between Israel and Japan, regarded Medinat Yisrael as the home of an exceptionally "cheerful" form of nationalism. It displayed none of the gloomy aspects of ghetto life, such as he had come across in his reading of modern Jewish literature.

"Was there any feeling of resentment among the Japanese because of your conversion to Judaism?" I asked.

"Not at all," he replied, "the exact opposite occurred. Much to my surprise, while I was in Israel last year, members of my family were greatly honored in Japan, probably because people felt that I had taken a courageous step, and was the first of my nation to do so."

Dr. Avraham Kotsuji continued his religious and educational activities for some years after our meeting and published his autobiography in 1964. He died in October 1973, and his body was flown to Israel for interment in Jerusalem.

The future of American Jewry was uppermost in my thoughts as the time for our Aliyah approached. Within the space of a fortnight, in May 1960, I delivered three addresses on this theme before the conventions of the Rabbinical Assembly of America, the National Federation of Men's Clubs of the United Synagogue, and the Synagogue Council of America.

Speaking at Grossinger's, the famous Jewish resort hotel in New York State, on May 9, I urged fellow members of the Rabbinical Assembly to make communal organization one of their urgent priorities:

> The time is overdue for placing again on the agenda of the American Jewish community the urgency of establishing a representative body which would play the same role in the United States as is played by the Board of Deputies in Great Britain, the Canadian Jewish Congress in Canada, the DAIA in the Argentine, and similar bodies in France, Australia, South Africa and other countries. The experience we have had with the American Jewish Congress forty years ago and with the American Jewish Conference fifteen years ago can stand us in good stead in preparing a new attempt, since the former is within our memory and the latter is within the personal experience of many of us. . . .
>
> It would be a sign of the maturity of the American Jewish community if it could recognize that the Jewish people, and American Jewry, which is one of its primary components, are confronted by a long-range crisis which can be as devastating as an acute crisis. "Jewish Survival" has a prosaic sound, but in essence it is a dramatic confrontation with forces both malevolent and benevo-

lent, which threaten not only Jewish continuity, but the character and content of Jewish survival. Indeed, it is one of the critical shortcomings of Jewish leadership that it waits for acute crises to spur it into cohesiveness.

I went on to observe that American Jewry, now more united than ever before, was ready for this step. A central representative body on the American Jewish scene would have to concern itself with a variety of issues—the mobilization of support for Israel, the plight of Jews in areas such as Eastern Europe and North Africa, the fight against resurgent anti-Semitism, the protection of civil rights and liberties, and the deepening and strengthening of Jewish education. To tackle these and a host of other problems, American Jewry needed "a high command" that would lay plans and implement measures for its future, thereby doing away with the unseemly spectacle of several Jewish bodies all claiming to speak on behalf of the world's largest *kehillah*.

The role of the synagogue in contemporary Jewish life, upon which I touched in this address, was dealt with more fully in my two other addresses. Speaking at the third General Assembly of the Synagogue Council at Columbia University on May 22, I listed the major commitments of American Jewry in the following order of priorities: synagogue affiliation and Jewish education; philanthropy; Israel; anti-defamation activities; concern with other Jewish communities throughout the world; contacts with non-Jewish bodies in the U.S.; and the protection of racial and religious minority groups. It was my view that the current trend toward greater religious identification and observance of the *mitzvot*—even outside of the Orthodox camp—would continue for at least another decade, and this Jewish religious revival, superficial though it might seem, should not be discounted. Nevertheless, in view of the fact that spiritual values and the sanctity of the Jewish home were undergoing a decline, American rabbis should cease congratulating their congregants on mere outward demonstrations of "Jewishness," and should become more self-searching, critical, and demanding. From larger numbers of committed American Jews might come the "saving remnant" that would preserve the essential fabric of the Jewish community.

In the course of my address before the annual convention of the National Federation of Men's Clubs at Kiamesha Lake, New York, on May 10, I emphasized the importance of religious leadership and spokesmanship on the American Jewish scene. Having posed the question, "Are Jews a religious denomination, an ethnic group or something else?," I pointed out that none of the attempted definitions truly defined a "peculiar people" that did not fit into the conventional rubrics of categorization. At the same time, however, religion had been the Jew's historic contribution to civilization, and his most significant credential in non-Jewish eyes, especially in the United States. If, as Jewish secularists tried to claim, the Jew's status depended on ethnic or other characteristics, it would become insignificant in American life. Alongside religion, the synagogue—with all its ancillary rabbinical, lay, educational, social, and philanthropic arms—conferred status upon the American Jew. "The synagogues of the United States represent nearly one million Jewish homes," I said. "This is a vast constituency. Hence, his religion is not only the most valuable credential of the American Jew. It is also his most substantial and most conspicuous commitment."

The State of Israel presented a contrasting picture, for despite the political influence of one or two religious parties and certain hallmarks of Judaism in its daily life and national institutions, Israel was not a theocracy and religion was not the unifying force that it had become in America and other Diaspora communities. Yet, on second thought, one had to realize that the Medinah itself was a primary and powerful factor making for Jewish survival. "As long as the Jewish State will continue, the Jewish identity of its citizens will be guaranteed," I declared.

Reverting to America, I challenged the right of secular Jewish bodies to usurp functions and activities that should be the prerogative of religious leaders and spokesmen. Thus, matters concerning Jewish relations with Christian religious bodies must be handled by the Synagogue Council of America and not by a secular Jewish organization motivated by ambition for prestige. It would require strong religious leadership to put the intruders in their place. Nor could the religious voice be excluded from a whole gamut of social and political concerns, for otherwise Judaism would be reduced to "a weekend exercise in worship instead of being a daily guide to practical conduct." It was, therefore, my conviction that religious leaders should play a role in every Jewish "summit" activity, in every organized endeavor to deal with matters of top priority in Jewish life, on both the national and the international level. Like the wise men of ancient Israel who had failed to erect the Tabernacle without the guiding hand of Moses, "the secular technicians of Jewish life, no matter how gifted, cannot build an enduring structure without the master touch of religious inspiration."

Meanwhile, the campaign of Senator John F. Kennedy for the Presidency of the United States in the summer of 1960 gained my wholehearted support. His youth and liberalism appealed to me, as to vast numbers of other Americans. The New York Liberal Party, in which I continued to play an active role, endorsed his candidacy and tendered him a luncheon in New York on June 23. I was accorded the privilege of sitting beside him, so as to have an opportunity to speak with him about Israel.

At the outset of our conversation, I mentioned the fact that my son, Avram, and son-in-law, Paul Olum, had been among his classmates at Harvard. Senator Kennedy was frank enough to say that he did not recall them, but charming enough to add, "I'm sure they were top students in our class, far above me." Actually, while he was right about them, he was (according to my "sources") unduly modest about himself.

The youthful Presidential candidate, only forty-three at the time, displayed charm and eloquence, handled himself with aplomb, and proved affable, frank, and outgoing. His good looks were an additional asset. The audience was greatly impressed, especially during the question-and-answer period that followed his speech. More than one of us reflected at the time that, if elected to office, John Fitzgerald

Kennedy would not only be the youngest President ever, but also the first Catholic to hold that post.

In the course of the luncheon, Alex Rose suggested to me, *sotto voce*, that I write a letter to Kennedy, seeking his views on issues related to the Middle East. He would then, no doubt, reply with a personal statement. The same procedure had already been followed by the Republican candidate, Senator Richard M. Nixon, in his answer to an inquiry by Label Katz, the president of B'nai B'rith.

This idea appealed to me and I took it up with Senator Kennedy, who was agreeable. Several weeks elapsed while various drafts were being considered. In the interim, the Democratic Party convention nominated him as its candidate for the Presidency. While preparing the letter, I consulted Arthur J. Goldberg, the distinguished labor lawyer, who later was named an Associate Justice of the U.S. Supreme Court and, thereafter, chief U.S. delegate to the United Nations. I also sought the advice of I. L. ("Si") Kenen, executive director of the American Israel Public Affairs Committee. Finally, an acceptable text was approved and, on August 1, 1960, I wrote to the senator.

Kennedy replied nine days later, in a letter from which I would like to quote a few relevant paragraphs:

I am glad that your letter gives me the immediate opportunity to state in somewhat greater detail my views on American policy with regard to Israel and the Middle East.

The section on the Middle East of the platform just adopted at the national convention of the Democratic Party sets out a just and reasonable course for American—and, indeed, world—policy in this important area. The platform is one I am proud to advocate and will do all within my power to implement.

The senator then went on to cite that section, which read as follows:

In the Middle East we will work for guarantees of independence for all states. We will encourage direct Arab-Israel peace negotiations, the resettlement of Arab refugees in lands where there is room and opportunity for them, an end to boycotts and blockades, and unrestricted use of the Suez Canal by all nations.

We urge continued economic assistance to Israel and the Arab peoples to help them raise their living standards. We pledge our best efforts for peace in the Middle East by seeking to prevent an arms race, while guarding against the dangers of a military imbalance resulting from Soviet arms shipments.

Protection of the rights of American citizens to travel, to pursue lawful trade and to engage in other lawful activities abroad, without distinction as to race or religion, is a cardinal function of the national sovereignty.

We will oppose any international agreement or treaty which, by its terms or practices, differentiates among citizens on grounds of race or religion.

Thereafter, the Democratic candidate set forth his own specific approach to these policy matters:

While all phases of the platform on Middle East problems are important, it seems to me that the central, overriding problem in the Middle East is the problem of achieving peace in the area. The persistence of the Arab states in maintaining a "state of war" against Israel is clearly the root cause of the discriminations you cite. The starting point, therefore, for an effective, realistic American policy designed to preserve peace and extend the free way of life in the Middle East is to come to grips with this threshold obstacle. American diplomacy must be directed toward ending the "state of war" in the Middle East, and this undertaking should have a very high priority in a Democratic Administration.

The necessary first step, as I see it, is to bring about a conference of the contending states in which they undertake by mutual negotiation to resolve the outstanding problems that are crucial to each side. Such a meeting could be meaningful—and even decisive—if it stemmed from a desire to provide the conditions for a just and mutually beneficial *modus vivendi*, and to see the Arab states renounce the "state of war" and begin peace negotiations with Israel based upon the principle of recognition of the integrity and independence of all the states concerned.

While this will be our firm objective, it is also important that a Democratic Administration take immediate steps to eliminate discrimination on grounds of race, religion or color practiced against Americans abroad.

In the course of the campaign, I will be discussing with the American people my views of international problems and programs, and I expect that my speeches will contain amplification of the matters I have discussed above. I hope my views will enjoy your support and I shall look forward to hearing from you again.

With every good wish, I am

Sincerely
[signed] John F. Kennedy

It was a forthright approach to the problems with which Israel and the Zionist movement were then grappling, and the Presidential nominee's statement was greatly appreciated by those of us involved.

The extent to which the Democratic election promises were kept is, of course, another matter, and one that must be judged on its own merits.

A Series of Farewells

As the autumn of 1960 approached and the time for our departure drew near, various suggestions and proposals were made to me with regard to my future sphere of activity, but I postponed any final decision until after we had taken up residence in Israel. My hope was, however, that whatever might lie in store for me there, I would find some way to play a useful role at the Israel end of the bridge between Diaspora Jewry and the Medinah, having served heretofore at the American end. I especially looked forward to maintaining the connection with my beloved congregation, B'nai Jeshurun, by returning once a year for the High Holy Days, and to keeping my bonds with the American Jewish community ever fresh and strong.

There were, however, still local responsibilities that had to be discharged, threads to be tied together, and personal affairs to be wound up. One event of importance in that category, toward the end of the year, was the one hundred thirty-fifth anniversary observance of my congregation. Rabbi William Berkowitz was chiefly responsible for working out and directing the festive program. It was marked by a special Sabbath service on November 19, at which I preached the anniversary sermon, and by the Thanksgiving Day service five days later, when New York's Mayor, Robert F. Wagner, delivered the principal address.

Another notable event of this period was the American Zionist Assembly, convened by the American Zionist Council. It marked the first public appearance in the U.S. of Moshe Sharett as the newly elected chairman of the Zionist and Jewish Agency Executives. He staunchly defended the existence, purpose, and value of the World Zionist Organization, which was then being subjected to some carping criticism by prominent Israelis—notably, of course, David Ben-Gurion. Sharett maintained that the WZO was a unique organization fulfilling a unique role, and that Aliyah and adult Jewish education must be in the forefront of its programs.

I also had a series of consultations with leaders of Conservative Judaism in the United States, aimed at securing their participation as observers in the forthcoming World Zionist Congress in Jerusalem. Those involved were Rabbis Louis Finkelstein, Simon Greenberg, Edward Sandrow, Wolfe Kelman, and Bernard Segal, who held the leading positions in the Jewish Theological Seminary, the Rabbinical Assembly, and the United Synagogue of America, respectively. My talks with them, unfortunately, proved inconclusive.

The New York Board of Rabbis, by contrast, decided unanimously to accept an invitation to send a fraternal delegation to the Zionist Congress, and I was glad so to inform Dr. Nahum Goldmann, president of the World Zionist Organization.

The time had now come for a round of public farewells. My last meeting with the board of trustees of Congregation B'nai Jeshurun took place on November 3, when I offered some parting suggestions. One of these concerned a new prayer book. The *siddur* in current use, prepared eighty years earlier by Rabbi Henry S. Jacobs, contained a rather inadequate English translation. I had hesitated to prepare a new edition, as this would have necessitated my drastically revising not only the English translation, but part of the Hebrew text as well. I felt that I had no right to undertake such a task on my own, nor was I sure that I had the moral right to precipitate a controversy over what might become a vexed issue within our congregation. It was one thing to draw up a liturgical guide for special occasions, as I had done in the past, for the late Friday evenings or Sunday morning lectures and for Thanksgiving Day and Brotherhood Day services. These did not impinge on the sanctity of Jewish tradition. A revised prayer book for the regular Sabbath, Festival, and High Holy Day services, however, was an entirely different matter, and so I refrained.

Rabbi Berkowitz, my associate rabbi and designated successor, agreed to my suggestion that the prayer book sponsored by the United Synagogue of America be adopted. Our recommendation met with the approval of the congregation's board.

A graduate of the Jewish Theological Seminary, William Berkowitz had served

Congregation B'nai Jeshurun with great devotion and effectiveness over the preceding ten years, first as assistant rabbi and later, from 1954, as my associate. He revealed special talents in the parallel fields of children's and adult education. His emphasis on weekday instruction, aiming for the establishment of a Jewish day school that would combine religious and secular studies, eventually resulted in the successful implementation of this project. Similarly, the stress he laid on adult Jewish education, notably in the programs of the men's club and the sisterhood, found expression in cultural forums that attracted wide attention and large audiences. These forums, with the participation of distinguished American Jewish and Israeli personalities, crystalized in B'nai Jeshurun's Institute of Adult Jewish Studies. Under the direction of Rabbi Berkowitz, Dr. Herbert Greenberg served ably and devotedly as principal of our religious school. At the same time, my associate's wife, Florence, another onetime Philadelphian, played an active role in the sisterhood, under the effective presidency of Mrs. Jacob Schwartz.

Throughout this period, Cantor Robert H. Segal continued his splendid work as *ḥazzan*. He established the B'nai Jeshurun Choral Society, which enhanced the musical aspects of our services on Sabbaths and Holy Days. The Choral Society, under his skilled direction, gave an annual concert of Jewish music.

In 1949, when my wife and I had given serious thought to remaining in Israel after my year of service there, the congregation had found it impossible to release me until they could be sure of a satisfactory replacement. Now, eleven years later, they were satisfied that Rabbi Berkowitz could be entrusted with the full weight of responsibilities in the congregational rabbinate, and so they consented to my retirement. I was named rabbi emeritus and was asked to return annually to New York for the High Holy Day season.

Looking ahead to the congregation's future, I foresaw problems immediately before it, since the neighborhood in which our synagogue was located had begun to decline, and many families had either already moved or would soon move to the East Side. It would be prudent, therefore, I believed, to look around for a suitable plot on that side of Manhattan: our new synagogue could be built there, while the existing premises on the West Side could be utilized as long as they still filled a need.

Even before the decline of the neighborhood became so manifest, I had several times proposed that such steps be taken, but the board had not been able to mobilize itself for such an undertaking. I then turned to Chancellor Louis Finkelstein of the Jewish Theological Seminary, with the suggestion that the JTS help finance our East Side project, which would surely prove of benefit to the Seminary and to Conservative Judaism, but no response was forthcoming. The congregation was left with no choice, therefore, and had to make the best of the situation, in the hope that the neighborhood might ultimately improve.

One advantage did accrue from B'nai Jeshurun's existing location. Many parents, dissatisfied with the public schools, began to think positively about sending their children to an all-day Jewish school on the lines envisaged by Rabbi Berkowitz, and his efforts toward that goal met with success.

It was my sad duty, shortly before the end of November, to attend a memorial assembly for one of my oldest and closest friends, Gershon Agron, who had died "in harness" as Mayor of Jerusalem. *The Palestine Post*, which he had established as an English-language daily on December 1, 1932, had won renown under his editorship and, from 1950, had continued (as *The Jerusalem Post*) to mirror the Israeli, Jewish, and world scenes. One year after Gershon's death, a number of his friends met in the suite occupied by Moshe Sharett at the Savoy Hilton, New York, to launch an appropriate memorial project—a press center in his name, for which the Jerusalem municipality had donated a splendid plot overlooking a park in the heart of the city. Sharett was the honorary chairman of this project, while Meyer Weisgal and I served as co-chairmen.

Heading the roster of farewell gatherings arranged prior to our departure for Israel was a dinner given by the congregation on December 6, 1960, at the Hotel Pierre, in honor of my designation as rabbi emeritus. Over 700 people attended. The guests, among whom was the Mayor of New York, Robert F. Wagner, represented all shades of opinion and every sphere of national, civic, and public life, both Jewish and non-Jewish, in which I had at one time or another taken an active part. Charles H. Silver, president of Congregation B'nai Jeshurun, and Samuel Blumberg, chairman of the board of trustees, served as co-chairmen of the evening and were among the speakers. Rabbi Max D. Davidson, president of the Synagogue Council of America, gave the invocation, Rabbi William Berkowitz acted as toastmaster, and Cantor Robert Segal recited the grace.

Among the distinguished guests who paid tribute to my wife and myself were former Senator Herbert H. Lehman; Professor Paul R. Hayes, chairman of the New York Liberal Party; Roy Wilkins, executive secretary of the National Association for the Advancement of Colored People; Dr. Everett R. Clinchy, president of the National Conference of Christians and Jews; Professor Louis Finkelstein, chancellor of the Jewish Theological Seminary; Rose Halprin, my cherished Zionist colleague, who was then acting chairman of the Jewish Agency Executive's American Section; Dr. Joachim Prinz, president of the American Jewish Congress; and Avraham Harman, Israel's ambassador to the United States.

In her response, Bert dwelt on some of the personal, family aspects of my ministry and on the part played by the women of B'nai Jeshurun in its congregational life and in broader spheres. She offered our hospitality in Jerusalem to congregants who would visit us.

My own "Farewell to the Community" expressed our thankfulness for the outpouring of congregational and community-wide devotion. I took occasion to pay my tribute to the congregation itself, around which our lives had been woven for the past forty-two years, to the lay leaders who had "made it possible for their rabbi to serve the world as his synagogue and humanity as his pulpit," and to my younger colleague and successor, Rabbi William Berkowitz, whose ability and devotion had enabled me to demonstrate that I was not "the indispensable man."

In concluding my brief address, with a touch of humor, I remarked:

My adoring congregants have nominated me for almost every office in Israel, beginning with the Presidency. I haven't heard the nominations seconded by the Israeli electorate. For us, it is enough to fulfill the *mitzvah* of *Yishuv Eretz Yisrael*, to live there and let time take its course.

Among the hundreds of messages received, the most meaningful to me were those from President-elect John F. Kennedy and from Israel's Prime Minister, David Ben-Gurion.

Kennedy wired the following:

Keenly regret I cannot attend the dinner honoring Dr. Goldstein. His unselfish devotion to community affairs and his long service in causes dedicated to human welfare make the dinner a fitting tribute to him. I would have liked to join you in that tribute. I know that the farewell dinner is just the beginning for Dr. Goldstein and I wish him continued success in his efforts for international peace and for greater and greater civil rights for all humanity.

Ben-Gurion cabled:

It gives me great pleasure to send my greetings to you and your wife on the occasion of your forthcoming Aliyah to Israel. For many years you have been in the forefront of Zionist and Jewish activities and it is difficult to find one sphere of American Jewish life in which you have not been either initiator, organizer or educator. Your activities in these varied fields and your great contribution without bounds to the State of Israel have made their impact on American Jewish life. I feel sure that your decision to settle in Israel will serve as an example to many American Jewish leaders and that many years of fruitful work lie ahead of you in the State of Israel.

Equally gratifying was a letter I received a few days later from Professor Horace M. Kallen of the New School for Social Research, who was regarded as the outstanding Jewish philosopher on the American scene and as the intellectual leader of the American Jewish Congress. "I am hoping," he wrote, "that your role in Israel will be, like your role here, to join to your devotion to that heroic and hazardous utopian endeavor your commitment to the principles of religious and intellectual liberty, and the orchestration of diversities, which made you the outstanding American as well as the most understanding rabbi among the Jewish people of our country."

My last Sabbath morning service, on December 10, at which I preached the sermon, was attended by a congregation that filled the main synagogue and the auditorium of B'nai Jeshurun's Community Center, overflowing into the street outside. Many people, including Meyer and Shirley Weisgal, were unable to gain admittance. The *Kiddush* reception that followed in the ballroom very nearly became a stampede. Many young couples were accompanied by their children. One lady brought her youngsters, down to the age of three, to have a look at the rabbi who had officiated at the weddings of their parents and grandparents. Some of those present recalled having heard me preach my first sermon in 1918. It was an overwhelming personal tribute to my forty-two and a half years of service to the congregation and to the community at home and abroad—a tenure twice as long as that of any of my predecessors.

In the course of my farewell address, I outlined the credo that had governed my approach to Judaism and Jewish peoplehood. Although the board members of B'nai Jeshurun had never been "yes-men," I said, they had always displayed tolerance and respect in according me the freedom of the pulpit, even in those early years when some of my preachments had not met with universal approval. As a result, the congregation and its officials had not only "permitted themselves to be educated," but had also "been at my side in all my endeavors to make the world a little better."

I then went on to say:

We go to Israel with considerable baggage, the baggage of our American idealism interwoven with Jewish traditions. We feel that there is an affinity between that small great democracy and this large great democracy. The Old Testament which emanated from that land was at the founding of this land. Israel and America together represent a way of life which must find wider and wider currency in our time. We shall try to help to build the bridge between these two democracies, between these two important Jewries. . . .

I have a vision of world peace. Some of you know about that vision—not only a vision, a plan. I shall probably fail in it, but there is nothing more worth failing in. And living in Zion, I feel it would be appropriate to dedicate oneself from Zion to world peace and world brotherhood. This is what Zion is supposed to be. This is the Zion, the *Yerushalayim shel ma'lah*, in which are invested the highest hopes of humanity.

Jerusalem beckons with its glamor—a glamor which we have tasted more than once—with its exhilarating air, its inexhaustibly varying contour, the mystic glow of its twilights and, hovering over all, the fourth dimension, history, in which Jerusalem is unrivalled. When I bade farewell to Jerusalem eleven years ago, after a year's stay, I said, "Again and again we shall return to thee, but finally we shall settle in the midst of thee, O Jerusalem." And now we are going to fulfill that pledge.

Yevarekhekha mi-Tziyyon—The Lord bless you out of Zion.

The flurry of events during the next eight or nine days included a television interview with Dr. Ormond Drake, highlighting the congregation's one hundred thirty-fifth anniversary and my retirement, as well as a series of farewell receptions by the Jewish Agency (at 515 Park Avenue), Israel Bonds, the New York Board of Rabbis, the Hadassah Women's Zionist Organization, and the Claims Conference. The Labor Zionist Pioneer Women's organization held a luncheon for Bert, their retiring president.

Symbolically, our last public appearance was at the annual Israel Bonds Ḥanukkah festival, of which I had been chairman since its inception, held at Madison Square Garden on the evening of December 18. "The Menorah kindled in Israel by the Maccabees of old, whom we commemorate this week," I affirmed, "has been a

Menorah of religious freedom whose rays have been shed upon the foundations of our American Republic. This Menorah, kindled in our time by Medinat Yisrael, is spreading its rays of freedom, courage and idealism to peoples everywhere who are at liberty to receive its light."

At the conclusion of my brief address, I said not "good-bye" but *au revoir—Shalom* and *Le-hitra'ot*—to a capacity audience of almost 20,000. We then drove through a snowstorm with a police motorcycle escort, which enabled us to reach Idlewild Airport in time to board our plane for Europe and Israel. One long, eventful chapter in my life and career had just closed. Another was about to open.

11

A Foothold in Jerusalem: 1961–67

Bert and I were by no means strangers in Jerusalem. Over a period of more than thirty years, during which we had made more than thirty visits to the country, many memorable experiences had been shared in Eretz Yisrael. At the time of our first visit, in 1928, I had come as president of Young Judea and as the still youthful rabbi of New York's second-oldest Jewish congregation. Two decades later, when I served as treasurer of the Jewish Agency immediately after the establishment of the State of Israel and when Jerusalem became our temporary home, I had reached early middle age and what then seemed the height of my career. Now, as 1960 drew to a close, I came as the former rabbi of B'nai Jeshurun and an *Oleh Ḥadash*, a new immigrant in Israel, looking forward not to leisurely retirement but to a life of strenuous Jewish service, of personal and Jewish fulfillment, in our old-new homeland.

On bidding farewell to the congregation, I had expressed our feelings in this way:

> My wife and I are moving from beauty to beauty, from beautiful America and beautiful B'nai Jeshurun to beautiful Israel and beautiful Jerusalem. We are going to Israel because, being of the generation which has seen a dream of nineteen centuries come true, we could not be at peace with ourselves unless we had a part in the fulfillment of that dream.

So it was that when I came to Jerusalem's City Hall a few days after our arrival and, in the presence of Mayor Mordecai Ish-Shalom, signed the official register (a ceremonial act I had performed several times in the past), I was conscious of the fact that this time I was writing: "Yisrael Goldstein, *Yerushalmi*."

Our arrival in Israel had been timed to coincide with the opening of the 25th Zionist Congress, which also marked the centenary of the birth of Theodor Herzl. The Congress began impressively in Binyanei ha-Umah, Jerusalem's new convention center, with Dr. Nahum Goldmann's presidential address, Ben-Gurion's stirring appeal to the idealism of Jewish youth in the Diaspora, and other highlights. There were, however, some less agreeable features, such as poor organization and the obvious disparity in age between the veteran leaders of the World Zionist Organization and the majority of the rank-and-file delegates. The Lavon Affair, an Israel security mishap that projected Ben-Gurion into the role of unrelenting prosecutor, also had a negative impact on Congress debates.

My old colleague, Dr. Joachim Prinz, then president of the American Jewish Congress, had issued a call for the dissolution of the WZO and its replacement by another body. I could see no effective substitute for the Zionist Organization and thought it unworthy of Dr. Prinz, a ranking Jewish leader and a self-proclaimed Zionist, to make such damaging statements at a time when the WZO was far from moribund and was confronted by great and historic challenges.

Whereas certain aspects of this Congress might justly be criticized, there were nevertheless many positive achievements. These included a new and fruitful relationship between the WZO and the Israel Government, the emphasis placed on Aliyah, and the importance given to youth and educational work in the *Golah*. Clearly, the strengthening of Jewish education in Diaspora communities would reinforce the barriers against assimilation, promote identification with Israel, and serve as an incentive to Aliyah. The 25th Congress might prove to be a major turning point, if only the new Actions Committee would implement its major decisions. Such a program would require a massive budget, as well as steadfast adherence to Zionist principles and faith in Israel's destiny, but the presence of leading Diaspora Jewish organizations was another significant and positive factor I regarded as an encouraging development.

There was a good deal of political maneuvering behind the scenes with regard to the filling of certain key Zionist posts. Moshe Sharett, who succeeded Berl Locker as chairman of the Jerusalem Executive, managed to close the deliberations on a high note of positive achievement. Nahum Goldmann was reelected as president of the World Zionist Organization.

My own address to Congress, delivered in Hebrew, was entitled "The Zionist Movement in America—Realities and Potentials." In it I stressed the need for American Jews to place the concerns of World Jewry above purely local considerations. I also expressed unease over the fact that American Jewry's financial support for Israel, channeled through the United Jewish Appeal and Israel Bonds, was now mainly in the hands of non-Zionists. This had weakened the position of Zionism in the United States. With my own Aliyah fresh in my mind, I urged overseas delegates not to be oversensitive to the Zionist concept of *Golah:*

> It is merely a reflection of the sober truth that only in Israel, because it is the historic Jewish Homeland and because it is the only land where Jews are the majority civilization, can a Jew find his highest self-fulfillment as a Jew. I am willing to state categorically that, as I see it, there is nothing in Zionism which cannot be proclaimed from the housetops and which is not consistent with the highest human values and concepts. It was so in the days of the Hebrew Prophets, who pioneered the integration of nationalism and internationalism. And it is so in the era of Medinat Yisrael today.

The speech was well received, particularly by Moshe Sharett and Zalman Shazar, who told me later: "This shows that you will overcome every difficulty."

The Shabbat following the opening of Congress happened to coincide with the last day of the secular year, December 31, 1960. That morning I attended services at the Yeshurun Synagogue, where it transpired that a rather unusual Bar Mitzvah celebration was scheduled to take place. The parents of the Bar Mitzvah boy were members of Temple Israel, a prominent Reform congregation in Hollywood, and their rabbi, Dr. Max Nussbaum, had come with them to witness the boy's "calling up" to the Torah in this Orthodox Israeli synagogue. I could not help noticing that, while Professor Yosef Yoel Rivlin's instructive words to the Bar Mitzvah were appreciated by the congregation, they were lost on the American youngster, who knew little or no Hebrew.

Later, after attending a *Kiddush* in the boy's honor, I went on to the home of Alexander Eliash, president of the Yeshurun Synagogue. Here, I became involved in a vigorous discussion of the Synagogue and State issue, which would preoccupy me increasingly as time went by. It was my contention that there was room in Israel for the Conservative and Reform streams of Judaism—not the imported brands, but in some *totzeret ha-Aretz* form, "Made in Israel." What particularly irked me in the Orthodox house of worship was the separate seating for men and women, as well as the liturgical references to animal sacrifices and the hope for their restoration in a rebuilt Temple.

My remarks drew a sharp response from Zalman Shragai, a colleague on the Jewish Agency Executive and a former Mayor of Jerusalem, who was a veteran leader of Ha-Po'el Ha-Mizraḥi. He cited in his counter-argument the example of Zvi Luz, son of Knesset Speaker Kadish Luz (a Mapai stalwart), who had become *dati* while studying at Bar-Ilan University and who had married a religious girl. When young Israelis turn to religion, Shragai claimed, they go "all the way" and become Orthodox.

Within the next few months, as part of my voluntary course of Israel orientation and social integration, I made a special effort to see as much as possible of the many varieties of synagogue life and worship available in the country. My usual guide in Jerusalem was Professor Moshe Davis. A weekend in Tiberias gave me the opportunity of praying with Oriental Jews, with Slonimer Ḥasidim, and with youngsters of the Karlin-Stolin Ḥasidic dynasty whose *davvening* was vociferous. On another occasion, at Kiryat Zanz, a suburb of Netanyah, I was able to familiarize myself with the institutions of the Klausenburger Rebbe.

Back home in Jerusalem, it was a refreshing experience to visit the Italian Synagogue, with its elegant 250-year-old furnishings from the historic community of Conegliano Veneto, and to attend modern Orthodox services at Bet Hillel, where the lively (and mainly young) congregation filling the hall included a large number of girls in the *ezrat nashim*.

One Friday evening, Bert and I went to Bet ha-Ḥalutzot for services organized by a predominantly Reform group under the leadership of Shalom Ben-Chorin, the author and journalist. Men wore *kippot*, an American prayer book (with Hebrew text and English translation) was used, and there was instrumental (piano) accompaniment. The Har-El (Progressive) Congregation later developed from this group, whose services did not impress me. Nor, despite my friendship with Rabbi Jack J. Cohen, did I join the Reconstructionist congregation, Mevakshé Derekh, when it was subsequently organized in Jerusalem. For all my personal attachment to Professor Mordecai M. Kaplan and my adherence to most of his views, I never shared the

Reconstructionist movement's negative approach to the Chosen People concept. Moreover, whereas the Synagogue had been my foremost priority in the United States, because of its indispensable importance for Jewish survival, I felt that in Israel there were also other important factors making for Jewish continuity.

So it was that Bert and I generally attended Orthodox services near our place of residence in Jerusalem during the dozen years following our Aliyah. At first, I went mostly to the Yeshurun Synagogue, but sometimes also to Hechal Shlomo, the Chief Rabbinate center built with funds provided by our old friend, Isaac Wolfson. When we moved to our permanent home in Talbieh, I began frequenting the Sephardi Congregation Yissa Berakhah on Jabotinsky Street. Later, when Rubin Mass, the publisher, initiated the establishment of a new Ashkenazi synagogue in our neighborhood, I joined him. Despite my non-Orthodoxy, I felt a *Klal Yisrael* obligation to support this type of neighborhood congregation, which met the needs of the local residents. It was only years later, in 1972, when a synagogue was opened in the Center for Conservative Judaism at the corner of Agron and Keren Hayesod Streets, that we finally joined a congregation embodying our own religious preferences.

Our first few weeks in Israel were replete with new feelings and new perspectives. Some of my diary notes summarizing the day's activities indicate an elevation of spirit:

> I arose early to a misty morning. From our hotel room I looked out over the hills of Moab in the distance. It seemed like the beginning of the world. Every minute the composition changed, like an organ whose keys were shades of light. When the sun appeared, it looked like the moon shrouded by mist, its cold light bringing into view the mountains and the Dead Sea barely visible on the horizon. Then the sun became higher and brighter, and more of the landscape came into view. It was a scene which left me angry at my sense of frustration over not being able to find words to describe what I felt. No wonder this has been the city of visions. . . .

There was much to be done. Like all new immigrants, our first concern was finding a home. On an earlier visit to Israel, we had chosen a plot of land on which to build, only to discover at a later stage that the entire area had been set aside for the Hebrew University's new campus at Givat Ram. And so, after moving into a hotel and then into an apartment rented from Professor Yigael Yadin (who was on sabbatical leave at the time), we resumed our search. In time, we found a site close to Gan ha-Shoshannim, the municipal Rose Garden, which commanded a view of the road from Jerusalem to Bethlehem. With Bert supervising every detail of planning and construction, our new house began to take shape from the plans of our architects and friends, Dan and Raphael Ben-Dor, while our good friend Ḥaim Krongold took care of all the legal problems involved. Rassco, the construction company owned partly by the Jewish Agency, was entrusted with the building operations. By Tu bi-Shevat of 5722, celebrated on January 21, 1962, we were ready to lay the cornerstone of our future home at 12 Pinsker Street in Talbieh. Following Rabbinic custom, we planted saplings in the garden for each of our seven grandchildren—four pines for the boys and three cypresses for the girls. It was a memorable day in our lives.

By the time we were able to take up residence in the middle of the next year, our small grove of trees was beginning to provide shade for the Jerusalem stone walls of our new home. On June 5, 1963, Bert and I arranged a formal *Ḥanukkat ha-Bayit* housewarming and held a reception that lasted from afternoon until late evening. Our daughter, Vivian, and her husband, Professor Paul Olum, together with their three children, Judith, Joyce, and Kenneth Akiba, came specially from Ithaca, New York, to be with us on this occasion. Hundreds of friends attended the dedication. The guests included President Zalman and Raḥel Shazar, Knesset Speaker Kadish Luz, Finance Minister Levi Eshkol (who would shortly succeed David Ben-Gurion as Prime Minister), Chief Rabbi Itzḥak Nissim, and justices of the Israel Supreme Court. We were also happy to welcome children and staff members of the Israel Goldstein Youth Village in Katamon, headed by Ze'ev and Hadassah Schickler, the director and his wife.

This housewarming was, of course, a great family event, setting a seal on our Aliyah and providing an earnest of our new life in Israel.

Thereafter, we kept open house in Jerusalem and, over the years, we have welcomed a stream of relatives, friends, and congregants from the United States and other lands of the Diaspora, as well as the many friends whom we have made in Israel.

I had not come as an Oleh with any clear idea of what part I would play as a citizen of the Jewish State. One thing, however, was certain. As I had told the New York Board of Rabbis before we left the United States, it was not my intention to function as a rabbi:

> I do not feel the same compulsion in Israel as I do in America to practice this calling. In America, the Synagogue and the Rabbinate are indispensable instruments of creative Jewish survival. In Israel, the existence of the State itself is the primary guarantee of Jewish survival.

I knew that there would be no shortage of worthwhile tasks from which to choose.

At the same time, I retained a number of my organizational responsibilities, such as the presidency of the World Confederation of General Zionists, my positions in the World Jewish Congress, the Conference of Jewish Organizations, and the Conference on Jewish Material Claims against Germany, and my presidency of the Jewish Conciliation Board of America. Apart from the maintenance of such organizational contacts and of personal friendships, the arrangement I had made with Congregation B'nai Jeshurun to return annually for the High Holy Days, and the fact that our children and grandchildren were still "over there" in the United States, made the prospect of our periodical return visits to America as definite as any prospect could be. Far from cutting ourselves off from the American scene, we had simply moved from one end of the bridge to the other. Yet Israel was now our permanent commitment. Bert and I became citizens of Israel while retaining our U.S. citizenship.

The question as to what my major responsibility in Israel would be was not long in presenting itself. Indeed, the first proposal had come from Dr. Nahum Goldmann, president of the WZO, almost as soon as we arrived in the country. He had then asked me to take the chairmanship of the Jewish Agency Executive in Jerusalem. During and after the Zionist Congress, however, I observed that the "party key" system which governed the composition and workings of the Zionist Executive often reduced its efficiency. Though urged by all the Zionist factions to accept the chairmanship, and despite a headline in *The Jerusalem Post* assuring its readers that I would do so, I declined the offer, but agreed to serve as a member of the Jerusalem Executive of the Jewish Agency.

Another overture was then made by Moshe Kol, leader of the Independent Liberal Party, who offered me that faction's No. 2 seat in the Knesset if I would join its ranks. Kol thought this a natural choice for me to make, since I had been active politically in the New York State Liberal Party, of which I had been a founder and continued to be honorary vice-president.

Again, I felt obliged to decline, this time on the grounds that, as president of the World Confederation of General Zionists, I owed it to my constituency to retain that position and thus, by definition, could not also be active in Israeli politics.

Somewhat later, however, when the chairmanship of the Keren Hayesod-United Israel Appeal was offered to me, I agreed to accept it, since this post, in my judgment, presented an important and manageable challenge. It was my firm belief that the Keren Hayesod had not yet reached the stage of full development and that it was producing an income far below its true potential. Given freedom of action, I felt capable of expanding this organization and its operations. I was confident that my experience of fund raising in the United States would prove helpful and that my recent travels had given me some valuable knowledge of the Keren Hayesod communities throughout the world.

Thus, within a few months, I was plunged into new and challenging responsibilities.

Very soon, I found myself becoming involved in a number of collateral activities. Some of these stemmed from my Keren Hayesod duties and from membership in the Jewish Agency Executive. I joined the board of Yad Vashem, the national memorial to victims of the European Holocaust; took my place in Hakhsharat ha-Yishuv, the Israel Land Development Company, and in Otzar Hityashvut ha-Yehudim, the mother company of Bank Leumi Le-Yisrael; and became a governor of the Hebrew University and of the Weizmann Institute of Science.

Other involvements, both public and private, followed in the course of time. They included work for the rescue of Ethiopia's vanishing Black Jews, a cause to which I had given wholehearted support thirty years previously as chairman of the American Pro-Falasha Committee, and for the Israel Interfaith Committee, of which I would eventually become an honorary president.

Another "portfolio," which I finally accepted at the urgent request of Mayor Mordecai Ish-Shalom, was the chairmanship of the Jerusalem Artists' House. A hut near the King David Hotel had served as headquarters of the Association of

Jerusalem Artists, but more suitable premises became available when the Bezalel Museum was transferred to a new building in the Israel Museum complex. Though ready to help, I made it a condition of my acceptance that the artists' club suspend the Friday night activities, which I found religiously objectionable. My first task was to refurbish the old Bezalel building and make it a congenial place for the display of pictures and exhibits. Then, with the assistance of other committee members, I developed a Friends of the Artists' House group to raise funds and provide continuing support. The Jerusalem Artists' House became a much-frequented center for exhibitions and social gatherings. Interestingly enough, Raḥel Rabinowitz, who served as executive director, later became Moshe Dayan's second wife. I remained chairman of the Artists' House project for a period of five years and was succeeded by Mr. Ish-Shalom.

My frequent visits to towns, villages, kibbutzim, and moshavim up and down the country brought me face to face with problems of the young. I was impressed by the Youth Aliyah institutions that the several segments of the Zionist movement maintained, each in accordance with its ideology.

There were also children living in the slums of Jerusalem and other places who sometimes wandered unsuspectingly into Christian missions, where a Hebrew greeting and a tasty snack were offered in the hope of converting at least a few of these boys and girls into "Messianic Jews." Keren Yaldenu, a nonpolitical voluntary organization headed by Malkah Frankel, had set up a handful of Jewishly motivated clubs to combat this menace, but their resources were such that only a fraction of the youngsters on the streets could be reached. Visiting Keren Yaldenu institutions in Jerusalem, I was made aware of their needs and endeavored to be helpful.

It was a great pleasure to follow the progress made at the Jerusalem Youth Village bearing my name. Founded in 1949, during my term of office as treasurer of the Jewish Agency, Ḥavvat ha-No'ar ha-Tzioni (the Zionist Youth Farm, as it was known to Israelis) had developed magnificently under the direction of Ze'ev Schickler, who together with Moshe Kol—then head of Youth Aliyah—was its co-founder. The Youth Village occupied seventy *dunams* of land in the Katamon area of Jerusalem and accommodated 600 boys and girls aged twelve to eighteen. It was not only their home but also their school, providing vocational as well as academic training, and from it the senior pupils graduated into the Israel Defense Forces.

Each visit to the Village gave me new insights into the merit of its particular approach to Aliyah. A few weeks after settling in Jerusalem, Bert and I lunched there with a group of children from Hungary, Poland, Rumania, the Soviet Union, Morocco, Tunisia, and Iraq. Nine boys of varying ethnic backgrounds had recently celebrated their Bar Mitzvah in a neighboring synagogue. One of them was in tears because his mother, fearful of losing a day's pay or even her job if she took off work, had not been present at the Bar Mitzvah ceremony. They had all prepared short essays describing life in their countries of origin. One boy had written:

I was born in Poland. When I was seven, I went to school. The older boys beat me up. When I broke the hand of one of them, the whole gang pounced on me and almost ate me alive. When I was nine, I came here—*le-moladeti*—to my Homeland. Here life is good.

That little composition spoke volumes.

To be the "Daddy" of this Youth Village has been one of my most rewarding experiences, and I have gladly devoted to it no little amount of my time and attention. It gave us enormous pleasure to attend a reunion of *Ḥavvah* graduates in June 1964 and to see in that happy gathering wives, husbands, and children of our former wards.

More than a decade had passed since I had last lived in Israel and so, before taking up my new duties with the Keren Hayesod, I made it my business to travel around the country and reacclimatize myself to the national and local scenes. As already indicated, much of my time was spent visiting kibbutzim, moshavim, and development towns, worshiping in the synagogues of many different Jewish communities, and meeting and talking both with *vatikim*, veteran Israelis, and with recent immigrants.

The Association of Americans and Canadians in Israel held its annual convention in Tel Aviv that year and the first Sunday evening in March found Bert and myself seated next to Prime Minister David Ben-Gurion at the opening banquet. I had often commended the AACI's vital work in the field of immigrant absorption. In my maiden speech as a new immigrant, I congratulated the AACI on its fine record of achievement but deplored the low priority given to Aliyah by Zionists in the United States. I also expressed my belief that the inculcation of spiritual and religious values was an essential part of Zionist idealism. Our dinner-table talk with Ben-Gurion yielded some characteristic "B-G" aphorisms, notably his suggestion that the Zionist Organization of America change the first word in its title to "Jewish."

In the course of his address at the AACI convention, Ben-Gurion made reference to President John F. Kennedy's Peace Corps and observed that Israel had set the pattern for aid to the underdeveloped Afro-Asian states. In regard to Aliyah, he asserted that Israel needed Jewish intellectuals trained in the West and quoted a remark by Albert Einstein to the effect that American Jewish scientists would come to Israel because they had not been made to feel at home in the United States.

"When I met Dr. Robert Oppenheimer," Ben-Gurion went on, "I asked him the same question. He was not as optimistic as Einstein had been, although he thought that quite a few might come. Oppenheimer said that he himself had not felt welcome in the U.S. during the McCarthy era, and added that, had he been younger, he would have settled in Israel."

Ben-Gurion quoted Oppenheimer as having told him: "Life has no meaning in the United States. It has meaning in Israel."

Social engagements and talks with leaders of intellectual and religious life kept me fully occupied. We were invited to lunch one day at the home of Maurice Jaffe, the director of Hechal Shlomo. Since his guests included the Japanese ambassador and his wife, I spoke of our visit to Japan, where we had seen an Israeli tanker being built in one of the shipyards, and also made warm reference to Prince Mikasa and to Professor Setsuzo Kotsuji. The conversation then turned to the Herzog-Toynbee debate, which had been transmitted by Kol Yisrael (Israel radio) the previous night. We all agreed that Dr. Ya'acov Herzog had more than held his own in this contest, demolishing Professor Toynbee's notorious arguments concerning the Deir Yassin "massacre," responsibility for the Arab refugee problem, and the "fossilized" Jewish people. Toynbee had, in fact, been compelled to admit that the term *fossil* was misleading. He now claimed that the Jews must be more adaptable to new circumstances, more self-critical, and more responsive to the demands of Hebrew prophecy.

One of my most interesting encounters at this time was with an erudite young Sephardi rabbi, Ovadyah Yosef. As a child in the early 1920s, he had come to Jerusalem from Baghdad. He had later gained distinction both as a scholar and as a courageous champion of Jewish rights in Egypt, where he served as Deputy Chief Rabbi for a brief spell. Now a member of the Jerusalem Beth Din, he was often mentioned as a potential Chief Rabbi of Israel. Rabbi Yosef was not too well informed about American Jewry, as I soon gathered from our talk. When I identified myself as a Liberal rabbi from "Schechter's Seminary," he scarcely knew who Schechter was and had never heard of Louis Finkelstein.

He invited me to accompany him to the *shi'ur* he was due to deliver. On our arrival at the appointed place, about two dozen men were awaiting him. Rabbi Yosef discussed the laws of Passover, seasoning his remarks with a number of instructive stories about the saintly Rabbi Yisrael Salanter.

In retrospect, one aspect of our meeting was somewhat ironical. A volume of Rabbi Yosef's Responsa that he showed me contained a glowing *haskamah* (approbation) from the Rishon le-Tziyyon, Sephardi Chief Rabbi Itzhak Nissim. Having glanced at it, I said: "Rabbi Nissim considers you a *mekil*, one lenient in judgment. Apparently, he himself is a *mahmir*, a rigorist!" My host laughed, but offered no comment. More than a decade later, when Ovadyah Yosef became the Sephardi Chief Rabbi of Israel, some of his pronouncements were anything but lenient.

I had two meetings with Professor Martin Buber during our first twelve months in Israel. Buber's short physical stature belied his towering moral status. An impressive white beard framed his sensitive face and piercing blue eyes. He seemed to radiate greatness.

Nearly ten years earlier, in November 1951, Buber had come to New York as a guest of the Jewish Theological Seminary, where he delivered that year's Israel Goldstein lectures on "The Appeal to Religion," "Judaism and Civilization," and "The Dialogue between Heaven and Earth." Now I was a guest in his home in Abu Tor, overlooking the precipitous descent of the Valley of Hinnom, with the walls of the then Jordanian-ruled Old City beyond. Speaking slowly in English, he seemed to weigh every word.

"Are you a religious man?" Buber asked me, "—and I don't mean Orthodox."

When I told him that my criteria for the judgment of values were certainly religious criteria, my answer prompted a disquisition by my host on the failure of the spirit, on the contrasting qualities of David Ben-Gurion ("a man of power politics") and of Itzḥak Ben-Zvi ("a man suited to his position"). Pursuing his theme, Buber also contrasted the quality of life in the United States with that in Israel.

"In the United States," he affirmed, "life is easy and meaningless. Here it is difficult and meaningful. For geopolitical and political reasons, Israel has developed in a way that is not conducive to spiritual values. Some of the manifestations which have developed here are even dangerous. It may take two generations before the complexion will change. The spirit most often has not been successful, has failed; but, like a plant which decays and which in decaying enriches the earth to bring forth blossoms, so often is the spirit."

He believed that the era of *tzena*, austerity, had promoted certain spiritual values in the young Jewish State that were lacking in this era of an artificially prosperous Israel.

Passover, the "Season of our Freedom," was the first of the three annual Pilgrim Festivals Bert and I looked forward to celebrating in Jerusalem. It was ushered in that year on a Sabbath eve, Friday, March 31, and we were invited to attend our first *Seder* in Israel as new Olim at the home of Chief Rabbi Nissim. It was a large gathering—about three dozen people apart from the host's family. Among the other guests present were two old friends from New York, Rabbi David de Sola Pool of Congregation Shearith Israel and his wife, Tamar, a former national president of Hadassah; Professor Daniel Moynihan, a Christian friend of Israel who, years later, would gain renown as America's champion of sanity at the United Nations; and the Cuban ambassador and his wife, who were Jews. Apparently, Fidel Castro thought it only natural to appoint a Jew as his country's envoy to Israel.

I was impressed by the unfamiliar Sephardic customs observed at the *Seder*, especially designed to involve and attract the attention of the younger members of the household. One of the subjects brought up for discussion was the question of the Falashas, a "lost tribe" of Israel living in virtual bondage. Although Rabbi Nissim did not consider as difficult the halakhic problems involving their acceptance as Jews, he believed that their social integration would present many difficulties and therefore he did not favor bringing them to Israel at the time. Another topic discussed was the propriety of inserting in the *Haggadah* narrative a reference to the six million Jews martyred in Nazi-occupied Europe. The Chief Rabbi felt that any such insertion would be out of place, not only because Passover commemorated a miraculous deliverance of our people (as well as their earlier sufferings under Pharaoh) but also because a special date, 27 Nisan, had been set aside for Yom Ha-Sho'ah, Holocaust Memorial Day, in Israel.

A radio news bulletin on the morning of April 12, 1961, brought the announcement of the first man in space, Soviet astronaut Yuri Gagarin, whom Russian scientists had put into orbit around the globe and then brought safely back to earth again. That same day, the trial of Adolf Eichmann opened at Jerusalem's Bet Ha-Am. What a lesson, I thought, demonstrating how low man can sink on the moral plane and how high he can rise scientifically!

Eichmann had been living under an assumed name in Buenos Aires since 1950. Once tracked down there, he had been captured by agents of the Mosad and secretly flown to Israel in May 1960. There was a temporary strain in relations with Argentina, but international opinion favored the archcriminal's abduction and trial. Indeed, in a display of rare unanimity, both the United States and the Soviet Union had joined forces in supporting Israel's dramatic coup. Eichmann was brought before the Jerusalem District Court and charged with crimes against the Jewish people and against humanity. Supreme Court Justice Moshe Landau was the presiding judge, and Dr. Robert Servatius, a West German lawyer, defended the accused.

Jerusalem seemed to become the focus of world attention overnight, with journalists and radio and television teams milling around the scene of the trial. For Israelis, it was an especially poignant moment. According to one report, a crippled survivor of the Holocaust raised himself up from his wheelchair in a Jerusalem hospital and, pointing to the heavens, declaimed the opening verse of Psalm 94: *El-nekamot Adonai, El nekamot hofi'a!* ("Lord God of retribution . . . shine forth!"). Prior to its opening broadcast of the trial from Bet Ha-Am, the BBC played a recording of *Shema Yisrael*, the age-old proclamation of Jewish faith and martyrdom, which so many of Eichmann's victims had recited on their way to the gas chambers.

I attended the judicial proceedings on the first day and watched Eichmann—the chief executive of Hitler's "Final Solution"—standing in the prisoner's dock, with the Menorah, emblem of the reborn Jewish State, confronting him on the opposite wall. This dramatic image sprang to mind ten days later in Herzlia, where I delivered an address in Yiddish at the annual reunion of former displaced persons from the Bergen-Belsen concentration camp. In considering the manifold implications of this event, I said:

> The significant aspect of the Eichmann Trial is that, for the first time in Jewish history, the Jews of the world as a people are not without a defender and an accuser and that Medinat Yisrael is here to appear on behalf of the Jewish people.

The opening of the trial coincided with the eve of Yom Ha-Sho'ah, Holocaust Memorial Day. That night I went up to Mount Zion, close to the Old City walls, where *Lel Shimmurim*—a kind of watch night—was being observed. About fifty men, including many elderly Yemenites who had never had to face the Nazi horrors, were studying, reciting Psalms, and saying *Kaddish*. Young people came to look around, or simply to be on Mount Zion. On such an evening, with Jerusalem still divided, the Old City (to quote Tennyson's phrase) seemed "so near and yet so far."

Yom Ha-Sho'ah provided the army of "media men" covering the Eichmann Trial with additional material for their viewers, listeners, and readers. Among the ceremonies at Yad Vashem that attracted special attention was the reinterment, in the morning, of the ashes of martyrs from various death camps. These were solemnly buried in the floor of a memorial wing, the Ohel Yizkor, during the official dedication at which I was present the same evening. Several thousand people—including the President, members of the Government, the Knesset and the Jewish Agency, and the diplomatic corps—watched as six large candles were lighted in memory of the six million.

Holocaust Memorial Day observances began at twilight, when huge torches were kindled. Dr. Aryeh Kubovy, the head of Yad Vashem, presided and Abba Eban was the main speaker. Psalms were read, *Kaddish* was recited and, as the Ohel Yizkor was lit up, four searchlights pierced the sky. Two groups of soldiers came forward with torches and a guard of honor marched into the hall where the ashes had been buried. As the *Azkarah* memorial prayer was intoned by a cantor, weeping could be heard amid the vast audience. It was a fantastic sight, possible nowhere else on the face of the earth. The entire proceedings were conducted with a dignity and a solemnity befitting the occasion.

Throughout 1961, as the Eichmann Trial ground on to its final stages, Israel's Attorney General and chief prosecutor, Gideon Hausner, pursued the accused with shattering documentary evidence, the testimony of survivors, and questions designed to force this embodiment of Nazi satanism into the admission that he had been no petty bureaucrat who "merely obeyed orders." Successive eyewitness accounts of the unparalleled atrocities for which Adolf Eichmann was directly responsible made what had seemed beyond belief all too believable. One day in court was enough to make anybody realize what it was to be a Jew, outlawed, degraded, hunted down, and finally slaughtered, in territories conquered by the Third Reich.

In the end, it was established beyond all shadow of doubt that Eichmann had outdone even his superiors in the planning and fiendish implementation of that genocidal program known in Nazi jargon as the "Final Solution of the Jewish Problem." On December 14, Adolf Eichmann was convicted and sentenced to death. After his appeals, first against the verdict and then for clemency, had been rejected, he was hanged at Ramleh Prison on June 1, 1962, and his cremated remains were scattered over the Mediterranean, lest they contaminate the soil of the Holy Land.

At one point during the trial, I happened to dine with Gideon Hausner, who spoke about the letters he had been receiving from Sabras telling him that they now understood how it was that those six million Jews had died. The Eichmann Trial fulfilled an immensely important educational purpose by creating a sense of kinship with Jews all over the world, and by answering questions that had troubled Israeli youth accustomed to Jewish statehood and to the capabilities of a tough fighting army. "What the Ministry of Education could not do," Hausner concluded, " we did." Years later, he succeeded in recapturing much of the trial's drama and anguish in a volume entitled *Justice in Jerusalem*.

There were, however, certain questions that remained unanswered. Why was nothing done by the Allies to halt the mass slaughter? How could they have ignored heartrending appeals for the bombing of Auschwitz and of the railroads leading to the gas chambers and crematoria? Would such inhuman callousness have been displayed by Western statesmen and generals if Hitler's principal victims had not been Jews? These and similar questions, made even more burning by the release and publication of wartime state documents, continue to haunt us.

In May 1961, I was officially installed as chairman of the Keren Hayesod. Meeting with the entire head-office staff before actually taking charge, I recalled that my first extra-congregational involvement as a young rabbi in New York forty years previously had been as a worker in the ranks during America's inaugural Keren Hayesod campaign. In those early years, I had come to know of Arthur Hantke, Leib Jaffe, Leo Hermann, and other leaders of the Keren Hayesod.

Over the next few weeks, my new responsibilities kept me fully occupied. I then set out on my first trip abroad since our move to Israel.

One of my first appointments after arriving in the United States was at New York University, where I received an honorary Doctor of Laws degree on June 7. Thoughts of Israel, the Land of the Bible, were uppermost in my mind when I spoke of the bonds between New York and Jerusalem at the NYU dinner held on the eve of the commencement exercises:

> It was interesting to read the other day that a college valedictory was spoken in Latin. In the Hebrew prayer book there is a prayer: "Renew our days as of old." This renewal of an old custom, of delivering addresses in Latin at graduation exercises, should have a sequel.
>
> Perhaps some day NYU would consider permitting or encouraging a graduation address also in Hebrew, as was done in the early American colleges where Hebrew held a place alongside Greek and Latin in the curriculum and in the graduation exercises. Indeed, the curriculum of New York University in its first years included Hebrew and Rabbinic literature among the compulsory studies. It is to the credit of the President and officers of NYU in our time that, under the guidance of Professor [Abraham I.] Katsh, it has been the first university to teach modern Hebrew.

In the citation that accompanied my honorary degree I was particularly moved by the following passage:

> But for him, there would be no Brandeis University. But for him, not only American Jewry but the interfaith movement would be infinitely poorer. An ardent, lifelong Zionist, he has lived to see the age-old prayer of Israel for a national homeland come to indefeasible fruition, and he can well rejoice in his own assiduous part in that consummation.

A few days later, at the Chicago College of Jewish Studies, I again donned academic dress to receive an honorary Doctor of Hebrew Letters degree. It was bestowed by President Abraham G. Duker. My acceptance speech emphasized the need for more Jewish content and motivation in the life of the American Jew, which could only be met by a thoroughgoing change of values and approach leading to "A Higher Priority for Jewish Education as a Community Responsibility."

The underlying theme, namely, the danger that Jews and Judaism would be swallowed up by an alien environment and culture, was one that I found particularly appropriate to the situation facing me during my travels through the *kehillot* of North and South America, primarily on behalf of the Keren Hayesod. In my address to a Zionist conference in Santiago, Chile, delivered on August 23, I drew a distinction between the eternal influences that had enriched Jewish civilization and the sociocultural infiltrations that were now undermining wide sections of Diaspora Jewry:

I am afraid we are beginning to see this kind of assimilation even in Latin America, where we thought Jewish life was safe from such dangers.

No Zionist *kinnus* [assembly] can shut its eyes to this internal danger to Jewish *kiyyum* [survival], since the primary aim of Zionism is the survival of the Jewish people. Even the Jewish State is secondary to the Jewish people, and the chief purpose of the Jewish State is to help ensure the survival of the Jewish people. If I had to give a comprehensive definition of Zionism, I would say that Zionism is the active commitment to the creative survival of the Jewish people and to the Jewish State as an indispensable instrument toward that end.

There were occasional welcome intervals between my official engagements for visits with our children and grandchildren in Ithaca, New York, and in Stanford, California.

On August 16, I went to see U.S. Secretary of Labor Arthur Goldberg in Washington. I had a briefing session with Israel Ambassador Avraham Harman prior to this meeting. Israel was ready to enter into direct negotiations with the Arab states over the refugee problem, but the Kennedy Administration—anxious not to appear too pro-Israel—was currently endeavoring to be "impartial," despite clear evidence of the Arabs' real intentions.

Arthur Goldberg received me cordially. I told him of my warm feelings toward President Kennedy, but said that his handling of the Arab refugee issue was rather disconcerting. The refugees would never be allowed to determine their own future, but would be terrorized by the Arab governments into returning to what was once Palestine in order to create trouble for Israel. In his search for a peaceful solution, Kennedy had sent letters to the various Arab rulers, but King Hussein of Jordan, the only one who bothered to reply, had insisted that the reason there was no peace in the Middle East was the existence of the State of Israel. It was my belief that however many concessions Israel might make, the Arabs would keep demanding more, until the Jewish State was entirely at their mercy.

Goldberg stated that he had not discussed these matters directly with the President, but had gathered that he was trying to fulfill his election promise to achieve some progress in the Arab-Israel dispute. He disclosed that, after his recent talks with Kennedy, Ben-Gurion had appeared to be satisfied. Goldberg hinted that Vice-President Adlai Stevenson's well-known coolness toward Israel might have something to do with the current U.S. line, although Stevenson would have to abide by any policy changes determined by the President.

Before I left, Arthur Goldberg asked my advice about what specific points he should make in the address he was due to deliver at the Hadassah convention. I suggested that a restatement of President Kennedy's pre-election stand on questions affecting Israel would be especially welcome at the time.

It had been a frank and informative discussion, and I felt that the Secretary of Labor could be counted as a genuine friend in the U.S. Administration.

With the arrival of the High Holy Days in September, I honored the pledge I had made to spend Rosh Hashanah and Yom Kippur with my former congregants at B'nai Jeshurun. As rabbi emeritus, I shared the pulpit with Rabbi William Berkowitz, both in the main synagogue and at the overflow services in the Community Center. A different prayer book that Rabbi Berkowitz had introduced was now used for the first time. Despite its undeniable qualities, I thought it too Orthodox for this particular congregation.

My sermon for the New Year had a topical theme, "Space Man and Inner Man." In it, I reviewed some of the past twelve months' events from my new standpoint as a Jerusalem resident:

> You see, therefore, how one living in Israel has a point of vantage from which to observe the entire human panorama, and to observe it not as a matter of curiosity but as a matter of vital concern. For in one way or another, everything which happens in the world affects Israel. Israel is a sensitive seismograph.

Then, reverting to my central motif, I dwelt on the technological race between the two Great Powers, the dangers confronting humanity in the nuclear age, and their challenge to man's faith in Providence. "If religion," I said, "does not bridge the gap between man's scientific attainments and his moral power to use them for good and not for evil, for life's enrichment and not for destruction, then it will have forfeited its credentials."

On September 16, it was my pleasant duty to install Rabbi Berkowitz as spiritual leader of Congregation B'nai Jeshurun. The installation ceremony took place on *Shabbat Shuvah*. Congratulatory messages were received from President John F. Kennedy and Israel's ambassador, Avraham Harman. Charles H. Silver, the congregation's president, Chancellor Louis Finkelstein of the Jewish Theological Seminary, and Rabbi Martin Berkowitz (my successor's brother) were the principal speakers. The new incumbent's address followed my charge to him, as rabbi emeritus. I expressed the hope that he would enjoy the same degree of loyalty and affection from his congregants that I had been fortunate to enjoy for more than forty years.

Two days later, I made a brief visit to Philadelphia in order to attend the fiftieth anniversary of my high-school graduation class. A larger and more modern building now housed the school, which was run on coeducational lines. Most of the surviving members of my old class arrived to participate in a full day's program. I spoke to the pupils and, at a dinner in the evening, delivered an address to my fellow alumni, who appreciated the fact that I had come all the way from Jerusalem.

We were soon homeward bound aboard the S. S. *Israel*. Our fellow passengers included a group of Habonim and Young Judea youngsters who would be spending a year in Israel, partly on kibbutz. During Sukkot, I talked with them about the meaning of the festival. A lively debate on Zionism and Aliyah then ensued. At the service held on Simḥat Torah, I was privileged for the first time in my life, as a layman, to serve as the *Ḥatan Torah* ("Bridegroom of the Law").

On Friday, October 6, after two weeks on the high seas and more than four months abroad, we docked at Haifa. The city looked beautiful as we approached it. Arriving in Jerusalem, we entered our new apartment rented from Professor Yigael Yadin. On the following Sunday, I began work in my newly reconstructed office as world chairman of Keren Hayesod.

Platforms and Policies

I had little idea of what lay ahead for me. Instead of a leisurely retirement, there would be a full decade of activity in the service of Zionism—involving the establishment of new friendships, the forging of new links with Israel, the promotion of Jewish life and values, and much periodic travel throughout the world. In that coming decade, and during the twelve years following my relinquishment of office, there would also be the challenges, tragedies, and exhilarations resulting from Israel's three military confrontations with its enemies: the Six-Day War, the War of Attrition, and the Yom Kippur War.

We would see Israel respond to those challenges, overcome the dangers, extend its borders, make vast economic strides, and, in its fourth decade, undergo a momentous change of government and begin peace negotiations with its major adversary.

Looking back now, as I complete these memoirs twenty-two years later, such manifold changes strike me with particular force. There have been, and there continue to be, numerous "ups and down"—in Aliyah from the free world and from the Soviet Union, in Israel's status within the world community, in various phenomena affecting the quality of our nation's life—yet the progress achieved is virtually without parallel. True, the Zionist vision has dimmed in certain respects, but in others Zionist aspirations have been fulfilled.

The story of my decade of Keren Hayesod activity from 1961 to 1971 constitutes a separate portion of this record (see chapter 13). There were, however, other involvements, both public and private, which had a significance of their own and which, therefore, properly belong to this narrative.

On the Monday afternoon following our return from New York, the cornerstone of Bet Agron, the Jerusalem Press Center, was laid. Moshe Sharett presided at the ceremony and Justice Minister Dov Joseph, who had been military governor of Jerusalem during the 1948 siege, was among those present. In a brief tribute to Gershon Agron, I spoke of our childhood friendship in Philadelphia. I said that journalists were better qualified than I to assess his contribution to Israel as editor of

The Palestine Post, and that others could better describe his services to Jerusalem as the city's Mayor. However, I did recall his important services in later years as an emissary to the Diaspora:

> Wherever he came, he not only reflected the light of Zion but radiated it to Jews and non-Jews. His warm, sparkling personality captured many hearts and his brilliant, untrammeled approach captivated many minds. Gershon disarmed antagonists, converted neutrals into partisans, and partisans into enthusiasts. . . . If the purpose of journalism, in its highest sense, is not only to inform and entertain but to enlighten, interpret and guide, then Gershon was the journalist *par excellence*.

There could be no more appropriate living monument to the integrity, dedication, and human qualities of such a man than a meeting place such as Bet Agron. The next day, some of us joined his widow and children in visiting his grave at the Har ha-Menuḥot cemetery, near the western approach to the capital.

By an odd coincidence, at the end of the same week I was called upon to address the Journalists' Club and chose as my subject the Keren Hayesod mission I had recently undertaken in the Western Hemisphere. My assessment of the strengths and weaknesses of the U.S., Canadian, and Latin American Jewish communities pointed to one great common denominator among them: "the feeling, sometimes conscious but more often subconscious, that we are one people with one destiny and that the Jewish State is the heart which pumps vitality into Jewish life everywhere."

My orientation tours, which kept me *au fait* with the country's development, led me to different areas of Israel. On one occasion at about this time, I was able to see the place where a new town was to be built in the Judean Desert. Our party, headed by JNF Chairman Ya'akov Tsur, included the British ambassador, Patrick Hancock, and his wife. The site designated for the new town of Arad occupied half a million *dunams* and was crossed by pipelines carrying water and gas. It lay a few miles east of the biblical city of Arad, an archaeologist's paradise.

Our guide, Arie (Lova) Eliav, director of the Arad Region Development Project and a onetime member of the Israel embassy staff in Moscow, had previously headed the project that brought Lachish into being. Using a map spread out on a rock, he explained how everything had been planned and where the future town's housing areas, shopping center, and schools would be located. The plan called for an eventual population of 10,000 and for road links with other parts of the country, to be built by the Keren Kayemet, which would make it possible to drive to or from Jerusalem in an hour and a half. Some 200 Olim were scheduled to settle in Arad in the following spring.

At the time of our visit in October 1961, the black tents of Negev Bedouin provided the only sign of human presence thereabouts. "It sounds incredible," said Mrs. Hancock, the British ambassador's wife, "but I'm sure it will be exactly as planned. That's the way Israelis do things."

She was right, of course. Arad is now a thriving urban center, mainly populated by Sabras and much favored as a vacation and health resort because of its bracing climate.

This experience stood me in good stead when Ya'akov Tsur and I were guest speakers at a meeting of Brit Rishonim, the association of veteran Zionists, in Tel Aviv the following week. It was held to commemorate the twentieth anniversary of the death of Menaḥem Mendel Ussishkin, Tsur's illustrious predecessor as head of the Jewish National Fund. I recalled my first encounter with Ussishkin in 1931 and the impact of his personality, which had moved me to accept the presidency of the American JNF and thus launched me on my career of Zionist leadership. Then, after surveying Ussishkin's permanent legacy to the Zionist movement and Israel, I paid tribute to his enduring principle that land be owned by the nation and prepared for settlement:

> If the Keren Kayemet's program of land reclamation and border settlement was one of the factors which determined the boundaries of present-day Israel, much of the credit belongs to Ussishkin's vision. . . . He did not live to see Medinat Yisrael, but as long as it survives, his guidance, his dedication, his stubborn will and his work will live.

The presiding officer at this meeting was Rabbi Mordekhai Nurock, a venerated Zionist and Mizraḥi leader. As a member of the Knesset and of the Israel Government, Rabbi Nurock was one of the very few who had previously sat in a foreign parliament. His unique distinction was to have been called upon to form a new Latvian cabinet in 1926, as head of the Minorities' Bloc in that Baltic republic.

A few days after the Ussishkin *Yahrzeit* meeting, I was invited to a third JNF engagement. This time, however, it was a tribute to the living—Senator Hubert H. Humphrey—in whose honor a forest was being dedicated near Jerusalem. The future Vice-President of the United States and I were old friends and political allies. On the way to the ceremony, we discussed his recent visit to Lebanon and Jordan and a forthcoming Middle East debate at the UN.

In my remarks at the dedication of the Hubert H. Humphrey Forest, I said that the senator's espousal of Israel's cause was of a piece with his liberalism in domestic policies and his humanitarianism in the sphere of aid to emerging, underdeveloped states. It was peculiarly fitting that his name should be implanted in the Freedom Forest, dedicated by Americans in honor of their foremost sons:

> The trees which here will strike root, spread their branches and clothe the bare hills, will be an evergreen song of tribute to a man who loves Israel because he loves mankind and who understands that Israel, in reclaiming the soil of our people, has kindled a light whose rays enlighten and inspire other peoples seeking redemption.

A message of greeting from the Keren Hayesod to "her older sister," the Keren Kayemet Le-Yisrael, rounded off this series of speaking engagements within the Zionist "family" that I undertook during my first year in office. It was the sixtieth anniversary celebration of the KKL-JNF, held in the Hebrew University's Wise Auditorium on January 2, 1962. Ben-Gurion, Yosef Weitz, and I delivered the principal addresses. The most refreshing aspect of this jubilee was the participation of settlers from two kibbutzim and one moshav established on KKL land.

From the very outset, I was conscious of the need to create a favorable image for the Keren Hayesod within Israel, as well as abroad. One welcome step in this direction was taken by the Jerusalem City Council toward the end of 1961. The lower stretch of King George Avenue, running from the junction below Hechal Shlomo down to the King David Street intersection, was renamed Rehov Keren Hayesod, thus balancing old-established Keren Kayemet Street, which flanks the Jewish Agency building higher up the road. Moshe Ussoskin, director-general of the Keren Hayesod at the time, had a great part in bringing this about.

One of my concerns was with the Israeli press—and particularly with the mass-circulation afternoon dailies, *Maariv* and *Yediot Aharonot*. I took the matter up with Arie Dissentchik, the chief editor of *Maariv*, in Tel Aviv. He promised us more news space and introduced me to one of his star reporters, Shalom Rosenfeld, who served as his deputy and subsequently became the paper's editor in chief. I then spoke with *Yediot*'s editor, Dr. Herzl Rosenblum. In the course of our talk, I aired my opinions about Israeli youth and religious tradition and, to my surprise, Rosenblum blithely remarked that he never stepped into a synagogue. I continue to be astounded by such alienation from Judaism on the part of many leading Israeli opinion makers.

David Ben-Gurion had his own unique approach to these matters. His love for the Hebrew Bible was paramount. Every Saturday evening, upon the termination of Shabbat, a Bible study circle met in the Prime Minister's home. When I attended this *Hug Tanakh* from time to time, it was impressive to see both observant and nonobservant participants studying Torah and imbibing knowledge from some eminent Bible scholar. Some years later, I decided to take an interest in Ben-Gurion's favorite project, the World Jewish Bible Society, and to support the Jerusalem Bible Center proposal, which was one of his cherished dreams. The moving spirit in these activities was Dr. Haim Gevaryahu.

Another farsighted scheme, which would remain unfulfilled, was outlined to me in mid-November of 1961 by Rabbi Louis I. Rabinowitz, whom I had last met two years earlier in South Africa. Having retired from his position as Chief Rabbi of the Transvaal and Orange Free State, and having made Aliyah, Louis (as we all knew him) had become closely associated with the Yeshurun Synagogue and was now conducting a vigorous campaign overseas for the building of a central "cathedral" synagogue that would be worthy of Israel's capital. His plan called not only for a beautiful edifice but also for the kind of religious community center with which Olim from the West were familiar. Unfortunately, in spite of his enthusiasm and strenuous efforts, the scheme was never realized. It remains to be seen whether the new Jerusalem Great Synagogue, adjoining Hechal Shlomo, will prove to be more than a spacious and resplendent house of worship.

Rabbi Rabinowitz eventually found his niche as deputy chief editor of the *Encyclopaedia Judaica* and as the Deputy Mayor of Jerusalem.

The "Living Newspaper" was a popular form of discussion providing enlightenment (and also a measure of entertainment) on Friday evenings. I had the novel experience of taking part in one of these periodical postprandial symposia toward the end of our first year in Jerusalem. The topic scheduled was British Jewry. The meeting took place under the auspices of the World Jewish Congress, and my fellow panelists were Moshe Pearlman, Dr. Aryeh Tartakower, and Dr. Geoffrey Wigoder. A large Jewish delegation, headed by Lady Reading and Maurice Orbach, M.P., had just arrived from the United Kingdom and formed a considerable portion of the audience.

My own contribution to the proceedings dealt with the Anglo-Jewish community's influence on the development of American Jewry. I referred to the early history of my former congregation, B'nai Jeshurun, and to the shaping of Jewish communal life in nineteenth-century America. I also made mention of the exemplary role of British Jewry in its response to the Damascus Affair of 1840, the Mortara kidnapping case of 1860, and the czarist pogroms, as well as the wartime events preceding the Balfour Declaration of 1917. "It was," I said, "English Jewry which created the precedents for American Jewry's sense of responsibility in providing not only relief but also political intervention for the benefit of Jews in other parts of the world."

Despite its numerical preponderance, the American Jewish community still had something to learn from British Jewry, I concluded. There was in the United States no representative body comparable to the Board of Deputies of British Jews, which, since 1760, had retained its uniqueness and distinction throughout the world. "The absence of such a body," I said, "is responsible for much of the confusion and duplication on the American Jewish scene in both domestic and foreign affairs." Those who resisted the establishment of such a body resorted to the shibboleth of "democracy," yet true democracy—which would shake their own entrenched positions in American Jewish life—was what they really feared. One could only hope that the organizational pattern of British Jewry would some day be emulated across the Atlantic.

A contrasting discussion that took place about seven months later, in June 1962, found me seated in the audience for once and not (happily!) on the platform. This time, American Jewry was the main focus of interest, an American Jewish Congress delegation had organized the debate or "dialogue," and Dr. Joachim Prinz was the principal contender. Sparring first with Abba Eban and then with Ben-Gurion, Prinz made three basic assertions: that American Jewry had no reason to doubt that a long future lay ahead of it, that there would never be a substantial Aliyah from the United States, and that Hebrew would never become the second language of Jews in the Diaspora.

These claims were, of course, designed as a counterblast to Ben-Gurion's much-publicized and equally trenchant views about the Israel-Diaspora relationship. At the AACI convention earlier in the year, Ben-Gurion had revealed his unfamiliarity with the American Jewish scene when he maintained that American Jews were not at all religious and that they attended synagogue "for social reasons." As one of those who had promptly refuted this view, I felt bound to agree with the stand made by Dr. Prinz on that particular issue. Indeed, when addressing the Association of Retired Americans in Israel on December 24, 1961, I had emphasized the all-embracing significance of the American synagogue and called for a broader interpretation of its function in Israel's daily life. I believed that a whole new field of religious pioneering awaited young rabbis trained in the West.

Between my public engagements, I was working on a new volume of selected addresses delivered in New York, Jerusalem, and other cities over the past two or three years. Eventually, my book was published in Jerusalem by Rubin Mass under the title of *Transition Years* and a Hebrew edition appeared as *Shenot Ma'avar*. President Itzhak Ben-Zvi and his wife, Rahel Yannait, whom we often visited, gave a small reception at their home to mark the book's publication.

Toward the end of the month, I flew to Paris on Keren Hayesod business that would take me to Brussels, Stockholm, Geneva, and Zurich, also enabling me to visit our Aliyah installations in Marseilles, Naples, and Vienna.

At the National Conference of Aide à Israël in Paris, Chief Rabbi Jacob Kaplan recalled the help I had managed to provide for Jewish children in Paris in 1945, and I alluded to those times in my address. The burden of my message was that to be proud of Israel and to be "a good Jew at heart" was not good enough. The traditional bond of Jewish mutual responsibility obligated one to render practical assistance. Despite its growing prosperity, the Jewish community in France had not yet risen to the challenge. Echoing Weizmann's historic cry, "Jewish people, where art thou?," I asked my audience, "Where are the Jews of France?" The point got home. From Baron Guy de Rothschild down, contributors to the *magbit* pledged much greater support.

About ten days later, I surveyed the arrangements for Olim in Vienna. Compared with the transit facilities made available to North African Jews in Marseilles, those provided for immigrants arriving from the Soviet Union were more ample, though less geared to the family unit. The Austrian authorities were very helpful, presumably anxious that these Russian Jews should not remain in the country longer than necessary. That was also our concern, chiefly because the representatives of HIAS (the American Hebrew Immigrant Aid Society) appeared to encourage these new arrivals to settle in the United States or other Western countries. Our people in Vienna were constantly on the alert, preparing food, beds, and train tickets to Naples at all hours of the day and night.

Some of the Russian Olim had harrowing stories to tell. One man, having completed the registration formalities, had waited twelve years for his exit visa. When he and his wife received it at long last, they discovered that their seven-year-old daughter was not included. "I'm sorry, there's nothing you can do about it," a Soviet official told them. The man pleaded that they had sold most of their belongings and given up their apartment in a provincial city, that only three days remained before the date fixed for their departure, and that something should be done about their daughter's emigration permit.

"Let her stay here," the official replied. "We can give her a better education than she will receive in Israel."

"That's out of the question," said the father. "She's our only child and we won't go without her."

"Then make another application," suggested the official.

"But it's taken us twelve years to have *this* one approved!" the desperate father rejoined.

"So wait another twelve years," was the callous answer.

The poor Jew fainted on the spot. Luckily, however, everything was fixed up in the end. Other families were not so fortunate.

Watching these Olim from the other side of the Iron Curtain, as they carried their precious few *pekkelakh* on to the train in Vienna, I had a sudden vision of those other trains that had once left for Auschwitz, bearing a human cargo destined for slaughter. Here were the happy faces of Jews who would soon be seeing the last of Europe, a continent drenched with the blood of their kinfolk. They could travel in relative comfort and dignity to rebuild their lives in a free Jewish State. It would not be easy, and problems of adjustment awaited them, but their children would have a secure future in Israel.

At the end of the following week, after my return to Israel, I visited the site of Carmiel, a new development town in Galilee which, like Arad, was expected to have a population of about 10,000. Here, not a few of those Soviet Olim would eventually make their homes.

Bert and I had an enjoyable and uniquely varied celebration of Purim that year. To begin with, we were the guests of Rabbi Simḥah Melammed, secretary of Jerusalem's Persian Jewish community, who took us to hear the reading of the *Megillah* in the main synagogue of Jews hailing from Iran. We then visited two other Persian congregations and a Bukharan synagogue in the same quarter. From there we proceeded to Me'ah She'arim for a Ḥasidic rendering of the Esther Scroll. Customs varied considerably: whereas the Ḥasidim banged seats and benches every time the wicked Haman's name was mentioned, the Persian and Bukharan Jews mostly fired toy pistols. We rounded off our evening with a celebration at the Youth Village.

The last week of March found me in Scandinavia, where I attended the opening of the Claims Conference in the Danish capital. The choice of Copenhagen as the center for this meeting was a tribute to the Danish people's heroic resistance to the Nazi invaders and their protection and rescue of the imperiled Jewish community. As Dr. Leni Yaḥil, an Israeli scholar, emphasized in a paper she delivered at the conference, such identification with the Jews by the Danish population, frustrating Nazi aims, showed what might have been achieved in other occupied countries during World War II.

Dr. Nahum Goldmann's conference address was devoted to the practical aspect of Jewish material claims against Germany over the previous decade. Although

900,000 cases were still pending, the restitution payments made so far—to Israel, Jewish communities, and individual Jewish victims of the Nazis throughout the world—more than justified the original decision to begin negotiations with the Federal German Republic. Goldmann warned, however, that the settlement of claims had already cost the West Germans three times the amount originally estimated—about 22 billion deutsche marks. They were now "sick and tired of the whole matter," and even Chancellor Konrad Adenauer was less receptive than he had once been.

Subsequent reports at this Claims Conference indicated that virtually no Jews had been allowed to leave the Soviet Union in 1961, that the Joint Distribution Committee was endeavoring to supply Russian Jews with *matzot* and other religious items, and that it might be possible to erect a Jewish monument at Treblinka if the Polish Government would agree to accept the necessary amount from the Claims Conference and the JDC.

Copenhagen's Jewish community numbered about 5,000 souls. Unlike the Swedish and Norwegian *kehillot*, Danish Jewry was not particularly affluent and Zionistically it was lukewarm. On one occasion, when Golda Meir was planning a visit, the Jewish communal leaders expressed opposition to members of the local Bnei Akiva (religious Zionist) youth movement's greeting her in their blue and white uniforms, and it was only after she threatened to cancel her trip that they changed their tune.

Over lunch, I told Chief Rabbi Marcus Melchior that the Jews of Denmark needed "shock treatment" because of their appalling record of support for the Keren Hayesod. He thought that an outstanding *shalia'aḥ* might help, but also felt that a closer study of the position was advisable. I met his son, Bent Melchior, then head of the Scandinavian Jewish Youth Federation, who had volunteered to fight in Israel's War of Liberation. A graduate of Jews' College, London, he became Chief Rabbi of Denmark after the death of his father in 1969.

Since anti-Semitism was a negligible factor in Scandinavian life generally, the one real danger Jews faced there was assimilation. Intermarriage had almost reached epidemic proportions, and many Christians prided themselves on having a Jew in their family. Israel's ambassador, Harry Levin, was convinced that Danish Jewry would die out within another generation or two. In Helsinki, my next port of call, I found an even more disastrous situation. Only ten percent of Jews there married within the Jewish community, and most "Jewish" children had unconverted Finnish mothers. The local congregation had no rabbi, yet somehow managed to run a small Jewish day school, where I was delighted to hear older pupils conducting a discussion about the kibbutz—in Hebrew.

Despite its delicate position, with persistent Soviet interference in its political affairs, Finland maintained warm relations with Israel, which encompassed trade and a favorable voting record at the UN. My press and radio interviews in Helsinki drew a parallel between Finland's desire for peace and freedom and Israel's similar aspirations. In general, I was left with a very uneasy feeling about what lay in store for the Jews of Scandinavia. A fair number had made Aliyah, it appeared, and some Finnish Olim were specialists in agriculture.

Several days later, at a meeting of the Jewish Agency Executive in Jerusalem, Dr. Nahum Goldmann presented his report on the Claims Conference. Most of what he had to say concerned the position of Soviet Jewry, based partly on information received "from the inside." Nikita Khrushchev and his predecessors, convinced that Judaism and the Jews would vanish from the face of Russia, had sought ways of hastening that process. In fact, however, their tactics had boomeranged: many young Soviet Jews, hitherto ignorant of their ancestral culture and traditions, now felt the urge to identify themselves as Jews, and tens of thousands had milled around the main synagogues in Moscow and Leningrad on the Simḥat Torah festival. Goldmann painted an even rosier picture of Jewish life in places such as Tashkent and the Caucasus region, notably Georgia. There, religious observance remained strong and even young people could be found in the synagogues. Paradoxically, the one place of unrelieved gloom was Birobidzhan in far eastern USSR, where Stalin had established his abortive "Autonomous Jewish Republic." Of that grandiose scheme practically nothing remained.

I had a number of private talks with Dr. Goldmann at this time. On the issue of Soviet Jewry, he told me at the beginning of the year that he could have seen—and, presumably, influenced—Khrushchev several times, had it not been for his presidency of the World Zionist Organization. This, he said, hampered any approach he wished to make to the Kremlin. He also predicted that the French would gain influence in the Arab world and turn their backs on Israel.

Goldmann disclosed that he intended to withdraw from the American scene and would divide his time between Israel and Switzerland. As long as Ben-Gurion remained in office, however, he would neither become an Israeli citizen nor enter Israel's political life. On the Russian Jewish issue again, he was opposed to attacks on the Soviet Union. He detected a more liberal approach by the Kremlin, as evidenced in Yiddish theatrical performances, some Russian translations of works by Sholem Aleichem and Mendele Mokher Seforim, and the publication of *Sovetish Heymland*. A Yiddish literary journal, newly established to fend off outside pressure, *Sovetish Heymland* was actually a faithful mouthpiece of the Communist Party. Its editor, Aaron Vergelis, was the kind of stooge whom I would subsequently meet in Russia in August 1963.

Nahum Goldmann's greatest fear seemed to be that the Soviets would write off all Jews as anti-Russian and would one day sever diplomatic relations with Israel. That blow fell not many years later, yet more Jews have left the USSR since then than during the nearly twenty years that preceded the break.

As Passover drew near, Bert and I went to see some of the preparations being made for the festival in two or three of Jerusalem's religious neighborhoods. We were impressed by the efficiency and cleanliness visible in the bakeries where *matzot* were made and baked by hand. One bakery had been taken over for the day by students from a yeshivah, who prepared their own *matzot* and sang traditional songs as they worked.

We spent the week of Passover in Eilat and for part of the time enjoyed the hospitality of *Tzahal*, the Israel Defense Forces. Brigadier General Avraham Yoffe came to greet us at our hotel and took us to his army base for the *Seder*. There being no regular chaplain to lead the services, another army officer took charge. About 200 soldiers were present. Everyone received a copy of the *Haggadah*, an amalgamation of the Ashkenazi and Sephardic-Oriental traditions, especially prepared by Rabbi Shlomo Goren, the IDF's Chief Chaplain. It allowed for a good deal of responsive reading.

General Yoffe conducted the *Seder* splendidly and led the singing throughout. He was destined to become one of the heroes of the Six-Day War on the Egyptian front and later entered politics in the Land of Israel Movement and as a member of Knesset, representing the Likud. We finished the *Seder* by 11:00 p.m. and informal dancing ensued, but Bert and I returned to our hotel. I felt nostalgic for the *Sedarim* we had celebrated in our former home in New York and looked forward to holding our own *Seder* "next year in Jerusalem."

During the intermediate days of the festival, I attended services in a variety of local synagogues—Ashkenazi, North African, and Yemenite. Eilat's mayor came to tell us about the town and we paid a visit to the harbor. On Shabbat, General Yoffe, his wife, and daughter were our guests for lunch. The next day, he took us on a trip into the mountains and showed us some military fortifications and one of the battlegrounds on which he had fought during the 1956 Sinai Campaign. The scenery was fantastic, reminiscent of the Painted Desert in the U.S.

The thirteenth anniversary of the liberation of Eilat was celebrated with a military parade and the signing of a treaty of friendship with the mayors of three East African ports, one in Kenya and two in Tanzania. Later that night, the entire shore was illuminated for a performance of the Solomon and Sheba story. As the Queen of Sheba arrived by boat, she was greeted by a fireworks display on the shore. It was a spectacular and memorable highlight of our Passover holiday in Israel's southernmost city.

After our return to Jerusalem, I had a number of meetings with British Zionist leaders then vacationing in Israel. J. Edward ("Teddy") Sieff discussed Keren Hayesod affairs with me and said that he wanted to move the JPA offices to a new building away from 77 Great Russell Street. Eventually, the whole British Zionist operation left historic No. 77 and found a spacious new home in Rex House. Sieff also offered to lend us one of his efficiency experts from Marks and Spencer. My talks with Isaac Wolfson were also helpful. Chief Rabbi Israel Brodie said that his colleagues in the British rabbinate were mostly committed to the JNF and would need to be coaxed into working in support of Keren Hayesod.

On May 9, we went to Tel Aviv for the Israel Independence Day parade, which turned out to be a display of military strength and not quite what I had anticipated. We attended a luncheon there in honor of Angela Ulanova, one of the last surviving leaders of the October (Bolshevik) Revolution. At the age of ninety-two, she was still remarkably alert and her reminiscences were fascinating. Listening to her recite poetry in Russian, French, and German, I could visualize the type of rich and privileged Jewish home in which she had been raised. A phrase here and there revealed her knowledge of Yiddish.

After the Bolsheviks had seized power, Madame Ulanova became Lenin's secretary and worked closely with his immediate associates, including the archrivals, Trotsky and Stalin. "Unlike Trotsky, who could not master his personal ambitions, Lenin was a selfless idealist," she claimed. "Lenin never seemed to be aware of his own greatness. The cause meant everything to him, and he was ruthless in its pursuit, but he suffered pangs of remorse when instances of cruelty came to his notice."

Eventually Angela Ulanova could no longer go along with Lenin's principle that "the end justifies the means." She decided to leave Soviet Russia. "I asked him for the necessary documents," she told us, "but he said, 'You don't need any: you're better known here than I am.' It was only when he walked out to the gate with me that I understood what he meant. I was the one whom the guard on duty saluted. He didn't recognize Lenin, who always came in through the gate with a worker's cap over his face."

Since leaving Russia, she had lived in Italy and at one time befriended Mussolini, thinking that he was a Socialist like herself. She had never married. One gathered from our table talk that Madame Ulanova was a good friend of Norman Thomas and had a high regard for Walter Reuther, the American labor leader, whom she considered to be a Socialist. Her impressions of American Jewry were quite mistaken, and I told her so. Her attitude toward Israel and its dominant Labor Party she did not disclose.

The fashioning of links between Israel and visitors from overseas, particularly Americans, is a vitally important task and one I have eagerly pursued whenever possible. In July 1962, I addressed the New York University Professors' Workshop in Israel, a predominantly non-Jewish group led by Professor A. I. Katsh. After reviewing the Law of Return and its implications, Israel's cultural life and its political system, the relationship of State and Religion, and the nation's sense of purpose, I stressed the need for patient understanding of the country's special problems:

> If you find a good deal of inefficiency in the country, a good deal of bureaucracy and possibly a lack of courtesy, compared with American standards, then try to understand that life here is much harder than in the United States, that Israel has not had a long tradition of skills, that most of the people are recent immigrants who have not had the time to adjust themselves, that leisure, which is the soil of good manners, is practically non-existent, and that a large part of the population is engaged in a tough daily struggle for existence.
>
> Israel is a nation geared to showing its best qualities under the stress of emergency. To reverse the popular adage ascribed to Israelis, I hear them saying, "The impossible things we do right away; the difficult things take a little longer."

A three-day visit to Amsterdam in May, when I presided over a conference of the

World Confederation of General Zionists, afforded a welcome opportunity to see the main places of Jewish interest in that city. I attended Sabbath services in the historic Portuguese Synagogue, which established the religious pattern for all other Western Sephardic congregations. A youngster happened to be celebrating his Bar Mitzvah that morning. I was told that even boys under the age of thirteen could be "called up" to read the *haftarah*.

Like millions of others, I had read and been moved by *The Diary of Anne Frank*, a unique chronicle of the Holocaust recorded by one of its child victims. Since the building in which Anne and her family had remained hidden for over two years now served as a museum and youth center, I was anxious to visit it before leaving Amsterdam. Over dinner on Friday night, however, I heard that many people in Holland were far from enthusiastic about the to-do over the Anne Frank House and thought that Anne's father, Otto Frank, had exploited her memory for commercial purposes. Mrs. DeVries, the wife of my host, spoke of the daughter whom she had lost in one of the Nazi concentration camps and clearly resented Mr. Frank's negative attitude toward Israel. The Israel ambassador, Ḥanan Cidor, advanced the view that the martyred diarist's symbolic importance outweighed other considerations.

Making up my mind to see things for myself, I went to the building on the Prinsengracht which had served as Otto Frank's business premises. A bell rang as I passed through the door and, for a moment, I felt a cold tremor, recalling Anne's description of how she felt each time that bell rang: it might announce the arrival of the Gestapo. Masking the entrance to the upper part of the house, where the Franks and their fellow escapees lived in hiding, was a false door covered with a large map of Java (from where Otto's firm imported spices). Beyond this door were steps leading up to the two floors and attic that meant safety until the fugitives were betrayed. Whenever they wanted to talk, they went up to the attic. I saw a little map in the *Achterhuis*, on which were pinned tags showing the position of the Allied and German armies as the war progressed and information came through on their secret radio.

So Anne, Mr. and Mrs. Frank, Margot, Peter, and the rest managed to survive until August 1944, when the Gestapo finally did come to arrest them. The fact that Anne Frank's diary had illuminated one tiny part of the colossal tragedy was impressive.

Downstairs, on the exhibition floor, there was a bust of Anne Frank with a quotation from her diary: "I still believe that people are good."

A few days after my return to Israel, a meeting of the Zionist General Council (Actions Committee) opened at Binyanei ha-Umah. President Ben-Zvi made a point of attending, but Prime Minister Ben-Gurion and Foreign Minister Golda Meir were noticeably absent. It was perhaps fortunate that Abba Eban, representing the Government as Minister of Education and Culture, laid particular stress on the duty of our youth to acknowledge the historic role of the Zionist movement. Not content with his boycott of the Actions Committee meeting, however, Ben-Gurion sent a letter recommending that the WZO amend its title to leave out the word *Zionist*. This had a depressing effect on the closing session.

My next mission for Keren Hayesod, to Brazil, Argentina, and Uruguay, was scheduled for the latter part of June. Before leaving, I made an appointment with Golda Meir at the Foreign Ministry, with a view to securing for the Keren Hayesod a greater measure of cooperation and assistance from Israel's diplomatic representatives abroad. She was receptive to my plea.

An important Keren Hayesod appointment which I finally settled on the eve of my departure was that of Shimshon Y. Kreutner as our new European director, replacing Sam Segall. "Shai" Kreutner had an excellent record as a senior executive in the WZO, and he was to display unflagging devotion, enthusiasm, and loyalty in his post throughout the years ahead.

"Argentine Jewry facing the Test" was the theme of my address before the DAIA (Delegación de Asociaciones Israelitas Argentinas) in Buenos Aires on June 26. The weeks preceding my visit to Latin America had witnessed a recrudescence of anti-Semitic and neo-Nazi violence in Argentina—presumably a response to Israel's capture and trial of Adolf Eichmann, who had been executed at the beginning of the month. Most frightening of all was the inaction of the Argentine police, which seemed bent on discrediting the Jewish victims rather than apprehending their assailants. The fact that this *kehillah* of nearly half a million was then observing the hundredth anniversary of Jewish settlement in the country lent a grim irony to the latest events.

While congratulating Argentine Jewry and its representative body, the DAIA, on standing their ground with dignity and courage, I warned that the Jewish position in Latin America generally could be expected to deteriorate still further. Revolutionary elements, inspired by the Castroist example, might well exploit the yawning gap between the "haves" and the "have-nots"—and the Jews, a "distinguishable, stubborn and successful minority," were in a particularly exposed situation. Their troubles would be compounded by religious prejudice and racist forces in the region. This diagnosis was not meant to "frighten Jews into Aliyah," but to promote a new Jewish communal strategy: practical assistance for those wishing to settle in Israel, together with the planning of a more meaningful Jewish life for those who chose to remain.

I felt bound to express some constructive criticism of Argentine Jewry, based on firsthand observation. Even more serious than anti-Semitism was the menace of assimilation. Less than half the children of school age attended Jewish day schools, and young Jews studying at the universities were "exposed to the prevailing radical winds." No organized attempts had been made to cope with these problems. Furthermore, I pointed out, "yours is a secular community." The synagogue must become more than a house of worship, where the youth did not feel at home because the rabbi had no idea how to communicate with them, and where there was no provision for broader communal, cultural, or social activities.

After welcoming the recent establishment of a rabbinical seminary in Buenos

Aires, under the direction of Rabbi Marshall Meyer, as one step in the right direction, I concluded:

> If anti-Semitism continues to be a phenomenon in this part of the world, modern rabbis will be needed to give Jews the spiritual and intellectual strength to resist its corrosion, to resist with the mind as well as the heart. *"Barukh she-lo asani goy,"* blessed is the Jew who can say that he did not have to wait for the non-Jew to make him Jewish. . . . The promise of a future of Jewish self-fulfillment for you and your children lies in the Promised Land, now the Land of Fulfillment.

Looking back some two decades later, I have reason to believe that the situation has improved in a few respects. Anti-Jewish manifestations in Argentina have not disappeared, but there have been improvements in Jewish communal life and many more Olim have come to Israel.

In March 1962, the Jewish Agency Executive had accepted a proposal to mark the tenth *Yahrzeit* of Dr. Chaim Weizmann by naming in his memory the hall in the Jewish Agency building where the Zionist Actions Committee met and where Weizmann had been chosen as first President of Israel. It was my privilege to deliver a memorial address at the dedication of the Weizmann Room on November 13 of that year. Speaking in Hebrew, I offered a few personal impressions of our beloved leader, particularly in regard to his influence on American Jewry during the years preceding the establishment of Medinat Yisrael.

"To Jews and non-Jews alike," I said, Chaim Weizmann had been "a name, a presence and a purpose." In the course of a manifold career, rich in idealism and practical wisdom, in statesmanship and scientific achievement, he had played a decisive role in three historic developments—the securing of the Balfour Declaration in 1917, the establishment of the Keren Hayesod in 1920, and the first move to broaden the Jewish Agency in 1929. I had a vivid recollection of the impact each of these events had exerted on the Jews of the United States.

It was my belief that a fortuitous combination of time and circumstance sometimes determines the moment in history when the providential event takes place. "Weizmann was luckier than Herzl, in that the conjuncture of circumstances favoring the establishment of the Jewish National Home happened in his lifetime." Yet he, more than any of his contemporaries, had deserved to be sworn in here as Israel's first President. Those of us who had worked at his side, who had argued and debated with him, and who had alternately criticized and admired him, had been privileged to have a share in Israel's chapter of Genesis, walking with him through the storm and darkness until we emerged into the light and could say, "It was night and it was morning—the first day."

From time to time, it has been my sad duty to pronounce a *hesped* (memorial address) in tribute to Zionist leaders or friends of Israel and the Jewish people. Three such personalities whom I had occasion to memorialize during the 1960s—all cherished friends and colleagues in the American Zionist movement—were Ḥayim Greenberg, Louis Lipsky, and Stephen S. Wise (see chapter 17).

On December 12, 1962, at a meeting of the Israel-America Society in Tel Aviv, I had the privilege of recalling Eleanor Roosevelt's service to humanity in general, and to Israel and World Jewry in particular. As one who had been honored by her friendship and who had been associated with some of her civic endeavors, I called her "a true citizen of the world." What gave special poignancy to the occasion was the fact that my wife and I had last met her only in February, when we had attended a private function in her honor at the home of Abba and Suzy Eban. Mrs. Roosevelt had then expressed the wish that Americans of today could somehow recapture the feeling their ancestors must have had after 1776 and which the Israelis now experienced—that they were making history.

Eleanor Roosevelt had rightly been described as "the great wife of a great man," America's thirty-second President. As Roosevelt's eyes, ears, and legs, she had helped him to overcome his physical disabilities and to become a crusader for social justice. In so doing, she herself had become involved in the human problems affecting America and, ultimately, the entire world. There were occasions when she took the liberty of expressing her views publicly on controversial issues, even when they did not coincide with those of her husband. During the Nazi period, her castigating voice had infuriated Hitler's propaganda chief, Josef Goebbels. Years later, her criticism of anti-Jewish discrimination in the Soviet Union had not endeared her to the Stalinists. She had actually grown in stature after Roosevelt's death. State Department officials cringed before her furious attacks on their surrender to Arab pressure, and she had a share in influencing President Truman's decision to grant immediate recognition to Israel in May 1948. She had paid three visits to Israel and had served as the world patroness of Youth Aliyah.

Believing profoundly in the American Dream and in the dignity of man, Eleanor Roosevelt had made her greatest single contribution through her work for and in the United Nations, where she steered the Universal Declaration of Human Rights through the General Assembly. "Perhaps the most telling of the worldwide tributes paid to her memory," I concluded, "comes from her friend and comrade-at-arms in the battle for a more decent world, Adlai E. Stevenson, who said, 'She would rather light candles than curse the darkness.'"

There were other significant occasions for remembrance. The Lincoln Day observance at Bar-Ilan University on February 12, 1963, enabled me to take stock of the progress made by this center of higher learning since the dedication ceremony I had attended there in 1955. It was encouraging to find that Bar-Ilan, while religiously motivated, was maintaining a broad syllabus and high academic standards. The Lincoln Day exercises, held annually on the Ramat Gan campus, forged an additional Israeli link with the spiritual heritage of America.

I referred in my address to Abraham Lincoln's deep roots in the Hebrew Bible and drew some lessons for contemporary Israel from his intertwining of moral and political concerns. In the economic, religious, and cultural spheres, I said, even the smallest instances of discrimination must be eliminated. "To paraphrase the words of Lincoln, a nation cannot remain half-privileged and half-underprivileged." The world also could not remain half-slave and half-free. By extending a helping hand to yesterday's submerged African peoples, Israel was strengthening its credentials in the international sphere.

A month later, while visiting the United States, I was able to see the realization of a project that the New York Board of Rabbis had initiated in 1958 and of which I had been one of the earliest sponsors. This was the new International Synagogue at New York's Idlewild Airport. The International Synagogue was formally inaugurated at a dinner celebrating the occasion on March 10. As one of its honorary presidents, I was delighted to bring special greetings "from Zion, Jerusalem and Israel." In the course of my remarks, I said:

> The Synagogue in America gives the Jewish community a status in the general Christian community, a status far out of proportion to its numbers. In this age, and in a country which is so public-relations conscious, the Synagogue has a public relations value of which even the non-Synagogue Jew is a collateral beneficiary. . . . The International Synagogue will be a token of worldwide Jewish brotherhood united around its greatest and noblest common denominator, Judaism.

Standing alongside Protestant and Catholic chapels at what has since been re-named Kennedy Airport, one of the world's aerial crossroads, the International Synagogue tokens the religious equality underlying American democracy. A rabbi is constantly on duty there and daily religious services are held for the benefit of Jewish passengers and airport staff. The synagogue houses a museum of Jewish ceremonial objects and provides facilities for Jewish celebrations. "According to Jewish law," I observed, "the Ten Commandments were given in flying letters. It should be made possible, therefore, for the *mitzvot* to be observed by 'flying Jews.'" The existence of such a house of worship provides that opportunity, and it reinforces the international credentials of the Jewish people.

Six weeks later, on April 23, 1963, Israel mourned the death of its second President, Itzhak Ben-Zvi. His passing robbed the State of a great father figure, whose pioneering Zionism, upright character, scholarly achievements, and true humility won universal respect and affection. Symbolic of the nation's love and sense of bereavement was the presence at the burial services of delegates from Israel's agricultural settlements, who deposited bags of earth in Ben-Zvi's open grave.

Zalman Shazar, who was sworn in as third President of the State, brought a luster of his own to that high office. I often felt that it exacted a heavy price in terms of the limitations placed on his self-expression as a writer and orator. It would be untrue to say that Shazar disliked his new role; indeed, he seemed unhappy about parting from it when his second five-year term drew to a close. The years of his Presidency brought him cherished opportunities to renew his many bonds with the far-flung Diaspora, and on such missions his phenomenal memory stood him in good stead.

In consequence of his many new responsibilities, Shazar pressed me to relieve him of the presidency of Brit Ivrit Olamit, the World Hebrew Union. I protested that one such as myself, still struggling to master the Hebrew language, was scarcely the right man for the job. Undismayed, Shazar jokingly answered, "That's fine. It should encourage others to struggle, too!" Finally, in deference to his express wish, I accepted this post for the duration of his Presidency.

When Shazar retired in the spring of 1973, it was my privilege to help raise a $200,000 fund for the publication of a "Shazar Library." The plan was initiated by Professor Moshe Davis, head of the Institute of Contemporary Jewry at the Hebrew University, and our colleague in this project was Dr. Eliahu Elath, former president of the Hebrew University and onetime Israel ambassador in Washington, D.C., and London. Our object was to collect and edit for publication the various discussions concerning world Jewish affairs that had taken place in Bet ha-Nasi, the President's House, during his incumbency. Shazar was moved literally beyond words by this gesture.

I think it fair to say that although I felt inadequate, I took my presidential responsibilities toward the Brit Ivrit Olamit seriously enough. At Zionist Congresses and Actions Committee meetings, my unswerving position had been that the WZO would not live up to its Zionist title unless it were to budget more realistic sums for the cultivation of Hebrew, as well as for general Jewish education in the Diaspora. Accordingly, I now drew up a series of recommendations covering everything from the strengthening of the Jerusalem office to audiovisual aids and an annual *Yom Ivri* ("Hebrew Day") on Eliezer Ben-Yehudah's birthday. I mentioned some of these points at the Los Angeles convention of Hadassah in August 1964, with particular reference to the woman's role in Hebrew education and culture.

On September 3, in New York, I spoke before the Histadrut Ivrit of America, the World Hebrew Union's "largest and most important constituency." I said that the 500,000 Zionist-affiliated homes throughout the United States constituted a tremendous field for implanting the Hebrew word, and that it was up to the Zionist leadership in America to set the tone. If opinions differed as to whether one could be a Zionist without making Aliyah, surely involvement in Hebrew culture was an important criterion for the right to such a title. After enumerating my priorities and suggestions, I called for a new "aristocracy of achievement" in American Jewish life:

> The first President of Columbia University wrote in his diary that he taught his grandson Hebrew every day so he would "grow up to be a gentleman." Jewish children today and Jewish parents can become, by the acquisition of the Hebrew language and culture, the truest cultural heirs of their great Jewish past, the truest cultural kin of their brothers and sisters of Israel, and, what is most important of all, the vanguard in the battle for Jewish cultural-spiritual survival in the Diaspora.

Behind the Iron Curtain: From Bucharest to Warsaw

In the past few years, during my travels through Europe, Latin America, South and Central Africa, Australasia, and the Far East, I had been able to gain firsthand impressions of the battle for Jewish existence and survival, outside the two thriving major centers of Jewish population in Israel and the United States. What was needed to complete the picture, however, could only be supplied by a study tour behind the Iron Curtain.

On Thursday, July 18, 1963, Bert and I set out on a month-long trip to the Soviet Union and three of its Eastern European satellite countries. The first stage of our journey took us to Rumania, Hungary, and Poland, and the second to the USSR. We visited Bucharest, Budapest, Warsaw, Cracow, Moscow, Leningrad, Kiev, and Odessa, as well as the former Nazi death camps at Auschwitz (Oświęcim) and Treblinka in Poland. To the best of my knowledge, I was the only member of the World Zionist Executive who entered those Communist states at the time and who conducted some meaningful talks with representatives of the Soviet Government. The conclusions I drew from these various fact-finding tours were submitted after our return to the Executives of the Jewish Agency and the World Jewish Congress. I shall have more to say later about these reports.

The main purpose of my journey was to obtain firsthand information about the Jewish communities and their problems in the Soviet bloc. It was also intended, however, as a mission of fraternal goodwill to as many Jews as I could reach in that area of the world, where they felt cut off from the majority of their Jewish brethren.

In general, I was impressed by the fact that these Communist states did not constitute the sort of monolithic bloc we in the free world tended to visualize. Living standards had improved and, compared with most Western countries, vast strides had been made in terms of free higher education and the provision of inexpensive cultural facilities. On the economic, political, and social planes, conditions varied from one state to the next and, inevitably, these variations were reflected in the spheres of Jewish communal life.

Bucharest, the Rumanian capital, had once been renowned as the "little Paris" of Eastern Europe. With its well-dressed citizens and attractive stores, it still retained something of that character, but one felt the pressure of a vigilant regime. An atmosphere of fear and suspicion prevailed among the Jews whom we met, their experience having apparently been that anyone with whom one spoke might prove to be an informer in the pay of the authorities.

It was an impressive experience to visit the Israel embassy in Bucharest at that period of increased Aliyah and to witness the handling of those Jews who had received an official permit to leave the country and who needed all kinds of help— moral, material, and sometimes also medical. I spent hours there, observing the method of processing these would-be Olim. Many complained of anti-Semitism, not government-inspired but spontaneous, which was one of the compelling motivations for their emigration. Jews were not allowed to absent themselves from work on the High Holy Days, they suffered various forms of discriminatory treatment once they applied for Aliyah, and some had to wait as long as twelve years before their applications were granted. Valuables would be taken from them at the airport. Considerable sums of money were charged for renovating the apartments vacated by emigrants, so that the new tenants might receive them in good condition.

I asked one young man, a construction worker from a small Rumanian town, why he had decided to leave for Israel. "I'm the only Jew in the whole plant," he told me. "Whenever anything goes wrong, they always say I am to blame."

There were then about 170,000 Jews in the country, nearly half of that number in Bucharest. Dr. Moshe Rosen, the Chief Rabbi, was overseas when we visited Rumania, but his wise and effective leadership was visible in the smooth functioning of Jewish communal life and institutions. The Federation of Communities of the Mosaic Religion, as Rumania's central *kehillah* was designated, managed to operate hundreds of synagogues and several dozen slaughterhouses for *kasher* meat, as well as *mikva'ot* (ritual baths), a *matzah* factory, a communal restaurant in Bucharest, religious schools, and other facilities. The Chief Rabbi had secured concessions from the Government to provide Jewish children with some essentials of a religious education, and we saw boys at a talmud torah being prepared for their Bar Mitzvah. Dr. Rosen was then, and he still is today, the oustanding and most influential personality in Rumanian Jewry, its spiritual guide and spokesman in the National Assembly, and—uniquely in the Communist bloc states—the *kehillah*'s advocate before the Government and its official link with Jews and Jewish organizations abroad.

I had an amusing experience a day after our arrival, when I went to the main "Choir Synagogue" in Bucharest, without giving anyone there advance notification. The *shammash* (sexton), noticing an unfamiliar face, greeted me and asked who I was. When I introduced myself as chairman of the Keren Hayesod and a member of the Jewish Agency Executive, he escorted me to a seat in one of the front rows near that of the *gabbai,* the warden of the congregation, who then arranged for me to receive the *aliyah* of *hamishi,* the honor of being called fifth to the reading of the Torah.

Opening the prayer book in front of me for the Sabbath morning service, I found that this *siddur* was the postwar (1946) edition published by the World Jewish Congress and bearing the editorial stamp of Dr. Marcus Ehrenpreis, the late Chief Rabbi of Sweden, who had been one of the leaders of the WJC. I happened to mention to my neighbor, the *gabbai,* that I was actively involved in the World Jewish Congress as its vice-president, whereupon he summoned the *shammash* and told him to change my *aliyah* from *hamishi* to *shelishi* (third), a more prestigious honor. This "promotion" indicated the respective local ratings of the two leading world Jewish organizations.

When reciting the blessings over the Torah scroll, I emphasized my Sephardic pronunciation of the Hebrew in order to let everyone present know that I was a visitor from Israel.

In Hungary, where, on July 23, we began the next stage of our trip, the political atmosphere seemed much more relaxed. Here, the regime headed by János Kádár was apparently popular. Having learned his lesson from the 1956 uprising, Kádár, we were told, had extended a considerable measure of freedom to the country's population.

Around 60,000 Jews were living in the capital, Budapest, and an additional

10,000 were scattered throughout the rest of the country. From what I heard, thousands more constituted an unofficial fringe element, not having registered as Jews with the Central Board of Hungarian Jewry. As in Rumania, there was an extensive network of Jewish communal institutions, but here they were administered by two parallel religious trends—the *Neolog* or "Reform" (which was, in practice, Conservative) and the strictly Orthodox. As a result of the Holocaust and the subsequent Aliyah of most surviving Orthodox Jews, the *Neolog* trend now constituted the overwhelming majority.

In spite of Hungary's liberalized regime, the Jewish communal leadership was sensitive politically, especially where overseas visitors were concerned. Shortly after our arrival, Endre Sos, the president of the *kehillah*, and another official who accompanied him, came to see me at our hotel. I had already been told that Sos made a point of issuing anti-Israel statements in order to curry favor with the Hungarian Government, and that Dr. Imre Benoschofsky, the Acting Chief Rabbi of the *Neolog* trend and a onetime Zionist, followed a similar line, not wishing to prejudice his chances of being appointed Chief Rabbi. Subsequently, we learned that Sos dutifully submitted reports to the authorities about Jewish visitors and that their rooms were often searched.

My conversation with Sos touched on the matter of German restitution payments and also served to brief me about the situation of Hungarian Jewry, which was—predictably—depicted in a rosy light. Sos affirmed that the prospects for Jewish survival in this country were much better than in Rumania, where the community was in the process of emigrating, or in Poland, where only 30,000 Jews remained. He said that some 1,500 boys celebrated their Bar Mitzvah each year in Hungary and that an equal number of girls were confirmed on the Festival of Shavu'ot. Both churches and synagogues received financial support from the Hungarian Government.

Sos, I gathered, was a writer of some repute on Jewish and general history, had a private library of 6,000 books, and enjoyed high favor in Government circles. He took us to visit some of the principal Jewish institutions in Budapest. We saw the *(Neolog)* Jewish Theological Seminary, the principal synagogue on Dohány Street, and the Jewish Museum. In its palmy days, the seminary had trained upwards of 150 students every year; now there were fewer than a dozen. Under its present director, Dr. Sándor (Alexander) Scheiber, who was away when we called, the seminary was valiantly maintaining itself as the only rabbinical school and Jewish scientific institute in the Communist world.

I was intrigued to discover that the building which houses the Jewish Museum, adjacent to the Dohány Street Temple, occupies the site of Dr. Theodor Herzl's birthplace. There was a bust of Herzl in the entrance hall. Each year, I was told, the Israeli minister, together with the leaders of the Hungarian Jewish community, took part in a private memorial ceremony on Herzl's *Yahrzeit*, laying wreaths in homage to the founder of political Zionism in the city of his birth.

The Jewish Museum contained two ancient Jewish tombstones dating from the Roman period and documents illustrating Hungarian Jewry's involvement in the

1. **International Synagogue at Idlewild (now Kennedy) Airport, New York. General view of Synagogue.**

2. **International Synagogue. The author, presenting scroll from the New York Board of Rabbis to Israel's Ashkenazi Chief Rabbi, Dr. Isaac Halevi Herzog, during his world tour in 1959.**

3. **Presenting scroll to Dr. Israel Brodie, Chief Rabbi of the British Commonwealth, 1959.**
   Krongold photo, London.

4. Presenting scroll to Professor Louis I. Rabinowitz, Chief Rabbi of the South African Federation of Synagogues. Eli Weinberg photo, Johannesburg, South Africa.

5. Centenary Prayer before the House of Representatives in Washington, D.C., February 1, 1960. Pictured before the ceremony *(right to left):* Congressman Emanuel Celler, Congressman Abraham Moulter, Congress Chaplain Bernard Broskamp, the author, Bert Goldstein, and *(3rd from left)* Professor Abraham G. Duker. Harris & Ewing photo, Washington, D.C.

6. **Centenary Prayer before House of Representatives. President Dwight D. Eisenhower inspects a copy of Dr. Goldstein's book,** *A Century of Judaism in New York*, **presented to him by the author, February 1, 1960. Also pictured** *(in center):* **Senator Jacob K. Javits. Associated Press photo.**

7. **New York University President Carl Newson conferring an honorary degree on the author, June 7, 1961. William R. Simmons photo, New York.**

8. At Congregation B'nai Jeshurun, New York, on the eve of the author's retirement, December 1960. *New York Herald Tribune* photo.

9. Dedication of the Jewish National Fund Forest in Israel honoring Senator Hubert H. Humphrey, October 29, 1961. The senator and his wife are seated to the left.

10. Youth Aliyah reception for Eleanor Roosevelt at the International Cultural Center for Youth in Jerusalem, February 26, 1962.

11. Dedication of the Weizmann Room in the Jewish Agency building, Jerusalem, December 13, 1962. On the dais *(left to right)*: Ya'akov Tsur, the author, Zalman Shazar, Moshe Sharett, and Kadish Luz. Jewish Agency Archives photo, Jerusalem.

12. **Keren Hayesod** *magbit* **campaign addresses in Europe. Paris, 1962** *(left to right):* **Dr. Vidal Modiano, Chief Rabbi Jacob Kaplan, Raymond Vallier** *(partly obscured),* **and Israel Ambassador Walter Eytan. Jacques Zelter photo, Paris.**

13. **Keren Hayesod campaign addresses. Intercontinental Hotel, Geneva, 1964, with** *(left to right)* **Jean S. Brunschvig, Baroness Nadine and Baron Edmond de Rothschild. Photo Centre photo, Geneva.**

14. At a reception for Levi Eshkol in Jerusalem, April 1964.

15. Brit Ivrit Olamit (World Hebrew Union) convention in Jerusalem, December 1964. Pictured *(right to left)*: Mayor Mordecai Ish-Shalom, Yitzhak Harkavy, the author, President Zalman Shazar, Professor Aryeh Tartakower *(standing)*, and Kadish Luz.

16. Keren Hayesod dedication ceremonies in Israel. With Frances and Harry Browner at the Louis and Jeannette Altschul *ulpan* hostel in Beersheba, April 17, 1963. Jewish Agency Archives photo, Jerusalem.

17. Keren Hayesod dedication ceremonies. Kiryat Wolfson housing project in Akko, April 20, 1966. Preceded by Lady Edith Wolfson *(left)* and Mrs. Miriam Eshkol, the author walks in procession with Sir Isaac Wolfson.

18. Keren Hayesod dedication ceremonies. Kiryat Wolfson housing project in Jerusalem, June 20, 1971. Leonard Wolfson addresses the gathering, with *(seated, left to right)* Mayor Teddy Kollek, Prime Minister Golda Meir, the author, Pinḥas Sapir, Louis A. Pincus, Mrs. Leonard Wolfson, and David Young of the Wolfson Foundation.

19. United Jewish Appeal World Leadership Conference at the Waldorf-Astoria Hotel, New York, 1965. Pictured *(left to right):* the author, Astorre Mayer (Italy), Gregorio Faigon (Argentina), Baron Guy de Rothschild (France), Max Fisher (U.S.A.), Djamshiel Kashfi (Iran), and Samuel Bronfman (Canada).

20. With President Zalman Shazar at a Lubavitch (Ḥabad) Ḥasidic celebration, Kfar Ḥabad, November 29, 1966. N. Abramovitz photo, Tel Aviv.

21. President Lyndon B. Johnson receives the author at the White House, following Dr. Goldstein's prayer before the U.S. Senate in Washington, D.C., February 21, 1967.

22. Members of the Jewish Agency Executive at the Western Wall in July 1967, after the
Six-Day War and Jerusalem's reunification. Pictured *(left to right)*: Raya Jaglom,
Avraham Ciegel, Arye L. Dulzin, M. Ben-Zion Meiri, Eliyahu Dobkin, André Narboni,
the author, and Zivia Lubetkin. Jewish Agency Archives photo, Jerusalem.

23. Keren Hayesod delegation presenting a gift to General Yitzhak Rabin, Israel's Chief of
Staff, December 1967. Pictured *(left to right)*: Nora Aviad, Rabbi Morton M. Berman,
General Rabin, Michael Barzilay, the author, Yitzhak Rogow, Moshe Ussoskin, and the
general's aide. Keren Hayesod photo, United Israel Appeal Photo Archives, Jerusalem.

24. Arriving in Brussels, "on Keren Hayesod business," December 1967. Pictured *(left to right)*: S. J. Kreutner, the author, Israel Ambassador Emile Najar, Pinḥas Sapir, and Belgian campaign chairman Léon Maiersdorf.

25. Dedication of the Israel Goldstein Chair in the History of Zionism and the New Yishuv, at the Hebrew University, December 25, 1967. On dais *(left to right)*: Professor Moshe Davis, Dr. Nahum Goldmann, Professor Nathan Rotenstreich, President Zalman Shazar, Hebrew University President Eliahu Elath, Chief Justice Simon Agranat, Professor Sir Isaiah Berlin, and Dr. Yisrael Kollat. David Harris photo, Jerusalem.

26. Memorial assembly, March 1, 1968, to mark the 20th anniversary of the Arab terrorist bomb outrage at the Keren Hayesod building in Jerusalem. Dr. Goldstein recalls the
tragedy; seated next to him *(left to right)* are Dr. Dov Joseph, Governor of Jerusalem
during the Arab siege, President Zalman Shazar, General David Shaltiel, former
Haganah intelligence chief and IDF commander in Jerusalem during the War of Liberation, and S. J. Kreutner.

27. Distinguished guests of the Keren Hayesod in Jerusalem. Prince Emanuel of Liechten-
stein, bringing a gift from his people to Israel, March 10, 1968.

28. **Distinguished guests of the Keren Hayesod in Jerusalem. Rumania's Chief Rabbi, Dr. Moshe Rosen, in conversation with the author, March 9, 1969. Photo-Emka Ltd., Jerusalem.**

29. **Inspecting *matzot* prepared for the Samaritan Passover celebration on Mount Gerizim, April 1968. Amram ben Yitzḥak, the Samaritan High Priest, stands next to the author.**

nineteenth-century struggle for Hungary's independence, as well as a fine collection of Jewish ritual objects. One section was devoted to the Holocaust, in the course of which about 600,000 Hungarian Jews had been deported to the Nazi death camps. A photograph of Adolf Eichmann confronted by Gideon Hausner at the trial in Jerusalem set an appropriate seal on this display. The museum maintained contact with Yad Vashem and its curator was the sister of Acting Chief Rabbi Benoschofsky.

Of the 400 synagogues, large and small, which once functioned in Budapest, only about one-tenth remained, and many of these were really small prayer houses or *shtiblakh*. Most of the larger synagogues belonged to the *Neolog* religious trend. I was greatly impressed by the Dohány Street Temple, a vast cathedral-like structure, built in nineteenth-century Moorish style with twin turrets. It had four balconies and seated nearly 3,500 congregants. Even more spacious than Temple Emanu-El in New York, it is easily the largest synagogue in Europe and may well be the world's largest Jewish house of worship. A plaque inside this edifice acknowledged the assistance of the Claims Conference in renovating the synagogue after World War II. I was told that several hundred people attended services there every Sabbath eve, and that the smaller congregation on Shabbat morning worshiped in an adjacent chapel.

Not far away were the offices of the Central Board of Hungarian Jewry. Outside, in the courtyard, we saw the mass graves of 2,400 Jews who died during the Nazi occupation at the end of the war and who could not be buried in the cemetery across the Danube because, by then, the bridges had been destroyed. A memorial plaque in the courtyard also commemorated Hannah Szenes, the Zionist poet and martyr, who was born and raised in the Hungarian capital. As a Haganah volunteer, she had parachuted into Yugoslavia in March 1944 and then joined Tito's partisans. Three months later, in an attempt to organize Jewish resistance and rescue operations, she crossed the border into Hungary, but was arrested and tortured by the Fascists. Eventually, on November 7, 1944, Hannah Szenes was executed by a firing squad. Her remains had been reinterred on Mount Herzl in 1950.

Among the other institutions maintained by the Jewish community in Budapest were a yeshivah for Orthodox rabbinical students, a Jewish secondary school, a hospital for 240 patients, and a splendid home for the aged. Both the hospital, which was administered by the *Neolog* majority, and the home for the aged, which was under Orthodox management, scrupulously observed the laws of *Kashrut*. We talked to some of the Jewish women who volunteered to work for the *kehillah* in various spheres—philanthropic and youth activities, festival programs and so forth. It was hard to believe their claim that intermarriage was virtually nonexistent, but I did not entirely discount the stories they told me about religious consciousness among sections of the Jewish youth.

On the eve of our departure for Poland, we were tendered a dinner on the grounds of the Jewish hospital, which had a *kasher* kitchen. The official leaders of the Budapest Jewish community were present, and Endre Sos presided. I was particularly impressed by the remarks made by the Orthodox Chief Rabbi, Jenö Schück, whom I had already met at the Jewish communal offices. Behind the learned texts which he cited, I thought I discerned a message. The impression I gathered was that he may have been helpful in making available *matzot* and Jewish religious articles to *kehillot* in Soviet Russia.

Rabbi Benoschofsky, the *Neolog* community's spiritual leader, was not available for contacts or conversations. Perhaps he was being wary.

I came away from this visit to Hungary with the impression that its regime was perhaps the most liberal among the Communist bloc states, and that there were substantial differences between countries within the Soviet orbit.

It was surprising to find that very few restrictions governed emigration from Hungary, and that Jews applying for exit visas were not penalized as they were in Rumania and the Soviet Union. Physicians, engineers, and other professionals whose services the country needed did find it hard to obtain visas, but the Jews were not singled out for discriminatory treatment in this respect. Aliyah had slowed to a mere trickle, however, since nearly half of Hungary's Jewish population had passed the age of retirement and, as pensioners, were loath to exchange their modest degree of economic security for an uncertain future in Israel.

The same was true of the tiny Jewish community in Poland, which had been reduced to 30,000, a mere one percent of its prewar population, since almost everyone who wished to leave for Israel had done so. Israel Ambassador Avigdor Dagan gave me a thorough briefing soon after our arrival in Warsaw, on July 25, and told me that all the signs pointed to a rapid strengthening of the "radical" (i.e., reactionary) group within the Polish United Workers' Party. In regard to Jewish religious and cultural matters, Premier Wladyslaw Gomulka had been pursuing a fairly liberal policy in recent years, but the upsurge of "radicalism" might well bring an anti-Semitic campaign in its train. That had certainly been the case in the past.

Jewish Communists played a leading role in Government ministries and cultural affairs. They also dominated what remained of organized Jewish life, as we would soon discover. Some prominent Jewish Communists were the worst enemies of their own people, in the Russian Yevsektsiya tradition. One such was Dr. Juliusz Katz-Suchy, twice Poland's delegate to the UN, who now served as professor of international law at Warsaw University. It sometimes happens that members of the same family adopt conflicting political ideologies. Katz-Suchy's elder brother, Dr. Benzion Katz (Benshalom), was a colleague of mine in Jerusalem, where he served as director of the Jewish Agency's and Youth Heḥalutz Department. A year later, in 1964, he was appointed rector of Tel Aviv University. Katz-Suchy himself became one of the chief victims of the anti-Jewish purge, at the time of the Six-Day War, and spent his last years as an exile in Denmark.

Religious life was at a low ebb in Polish Jewry, although a "Union of Jewish Congregations" (Va'ad ha-Kehillot) enjoyed official recognition. The contrast with what I had seen in Rumania and Hungary, and even with what I would later find in the Soviet Union, was horrifying. Practically no rabbis or learned laymen remained, genuinely pious individuals were debarred from holding office in the few synagogues still functioning, and those in charge were persons of no account who made a living from their "religious" tasks. On Sabbaths, it was difficult to muster the necessary *minyan*, and even on the High Holy Days the only worshipers were old people who no longer had to work. I was told that a few teenagers and children came to synagogue on festivals when food or gifts were distributed. More such evidence of the ebbing away of Judaism would come to light during our week in Poland. Today, in retrospect, that visit was more a pilgrimage into the past than a tour of the bleak, depressing present.

Ambassador Dagan stated that about 500 Polish Jews left for Israel each year and that the only restriction placed in their way by the authorities was the minimal amount of personal possessions they could take out of the country. Intermarried couples were denied exit visas, since experience had proved that they could not adjust to life in Israel and usually returned to Poland. One Jewish official, who proved to be unusually frank, told me that the Jewish Communists discouraged Aliyah for fear of losing their "constituency." This accounted for the negative reporting of matters concerning Israel in the local Yiddish press. He referred to his own generation as "The Last of the Mohicans."

I learned subsequently that the Kultur-Gezelshaftlikher Farband, the Communist-oriented Cultural and Social Union of the Jews in Poland, maintained seven state-aided Yiddish schools, a soup kitchen, and one or two Jewish restaurants where *Kashrut* was not observed, and conducted summer camps for members' children. The Farband also published books, the *Folks-shtimme* newspaper (which appeared about four times a week), and *Yidishe Shriften*, a monthly that received Government support. There was also the remarkable Warsaw Jewish Theater, which attracted a large number of younger Jews and even non-Jews, who were supplied with earphones in order to follow the Yiddish performance in Polish translation. The Government had its own reasons for providing this theater with an exceptionally generous subsidy.

We took the opportunity to visit the ORT school and toured its workshops. Many of the graduates joined cooperatives, we were told, which were sponsored by the Kultur-Gezelshaftlikher Farband and employed 1,700 Jewish workers. ORT played an important part in vocational training, and the JDC gave it some financial support. Once the Polish Government was satisfied that the JDC was nonpolitical, and brought coveted dollars into the country, it offered all kinds of financial incentives and concessions in spite of its uneasiness about local Jewish sentiment toward Israel.

One of my first calls was at the Jewish Historical Institute, which faces an empty plaza on which the Warsaw Great Synagogue—the Tlomacka Street *(Deutscher) Shul*—had stood before the Nazis destroyed it. That synagogue was the city's most impressive Jewish structure and, in its heyday, Cantor Gershon Sirota and preachers such as Samuel Poznanski and Moses Schorr had ministered there to vast and enthusiastic congregations.

The Institute's director, Professor Berl Mark, was away at the time, although I managed to see him on a later occasion. Financial support was mainly provided by the Polish Government, but a small grant was also made by the Joint Distribution Committee. Inside, there was a permanent exhibition of Jewish ceremonial objects, together with *pinkasim* (record books) of various Polish communities, books and manuscripts relating to the last two and a half centuries of Jewish history in the country, and a pictorial exhibit of the Nazi occupation and Holocaust era. We were shown the huge milk cans in which Emanuel Ringelblum hid his wartime diaries, as well as other manuscript works and records. The Ringelblum archives were kept in a specially protected room, copies having been sent to Yad Vashem. After the collapse of the Warsaw Ghetto revolt, the Ringelblums were sheltered by a Christian family on the "Aryan" side of the notorious wall, but they and their protectors were finally arrested and murdered by the Germans in March 1944. I was informed that the Institute corresponded with YIVO in New York and with the Memorial to the Unknown Jewish Martyr in Paris, as well as with Yad Vashem, and supplied all of them with photostat material.

That same afternoon, we visited the site of the Warsaw Ghetto, where new apartment blocks for workers were beginning to intrude. We saw streets, or the wreckage of streets, which the revolt had made famous—Gęsia, Nowolipki, Zamenhofa—and the small stone monument over No. 18 Mila Street, where the last Ghetto fighters perished in their underground bunker. No trace of the wall remained, but the building in which the *Judenrat* was housed and the Pawiak Prison, which served as Gestapo headquarters, still stood in ruins. Just outside the northern perimeter of the Ghetto was the *Umschlagplatz*, where tens of thousands of Jews were assembled for deportation to the death camps. On Ghetto Heroes' Square stands the central memorial to the Jewish underground fighters whose uprising dramatized the plight of Jewry in occupied Europe. This granite monument was executed by Nathan Rapaport and unveiled on April 19, 1948, the fifth anniversary of the Warsaw Ghetto revolt. It carries inscriptions in Hebrew, Yiddish, and Polish and bears massive black sculptures and reliefs portraying victims of the Nazis and members of the Jewish Fighters' Organization, including a young man with his fist upraised. Not far away, we also visited the historic Jewish cemetery of Warsaw, which in some miraculous fashion survived the Nazi depradations and destruction.

It was a traumatic experience, which present-day realities did nothing to relieve. Towering over the city, and visible from all parts, was the twenty-five-story Palace of Culture erected by the Soviet Union, Warsaw's most hated building, for which the Poles themselves may have had to foot the bill. Public housing was much inferior to Israel's and there was little evidence of economic progress in the streets and stores. Returning to our hotel, I was surprised to find *Haaretz* on display at the newsstand. Someone told me that Jaffa ("Assis") orange juice was the most popular and widely recommended brand imported by Poland.

The next morning, we attended Shabbat services at the Twarda Street Synagogue, Warsaw's only remaining Jewish house of worship. The building had survived because a German officer used it during the war years to store a mass of items he had looted. About fifteen men were present in the synagogue. I was called up to the Torah, and they made *Kiddush* over vodka after the services. An average of one Bar

Mitzvah a year took place, I heard. The JDC provided some small measure of support. Unlike its Hungarian counterpart, the Polish Government was not interested in maintaining Jewish religious life.

That Saturday evening, the JDC's Warsaw representative, a Mr. Kahanne, took Bert and myself to dinner. He told us that the Catholic Church retained its power and influence in Poland. Were it not for the Jewish Communists, religious education and even a few yeshivot could be organized by the *kehillah*. Yiddish language and some Jewish history formed part of the syllabus in the seven Jewish schools, but Hebrew and Bible were not taught. Kahanne said that whereas everything was closed for Christmas, Jewish institutions in Poland were kept open on Yom Kippur.

The next day, July 28, we left Warsaw for Cracow, the ancient capital of Poland, which in former times had been one of the leading centers of Jewish life in Europe. Cracow prides itself on having the oldest university in the land and more ancient churches than any other Polish city. In the historic old part of the town, we saw the graves of the Jagiellon kings and the tomb of Tadeusz Kosciuszko, the Polish patriot who fought with George Washington during the American Revolution.

A Mr. Fischgrund, head of the local Kultur-Farband, escorted us on our sightseeing tour. His brother, whose acquaintance we had already made, held a similar position in Warsaw. To our pleasant surprise, there were not a few places of Jewish historical interest to be visited in Cracow. Preeminent among these was the Rema Synagogue, dating from 1553, which preserved the memory of Rabbi Moses Isserles (Rema), the great codifier, whose halakhic additions made Caro's *Shulḥan Arukh* the standard legal guide for Ashkenazi Jewry. Three other synagogues had also survived the Nazi occupation. The oldest of all, the *Hoykher Shul*, had been turned into a museum of Jewish life and the Holocaust. Another, where Chief Rabbi Osias Thon, the Polish Zionist leader, had preached in pre-Hitler days, had—like the Twarda Street Synagogue in Warsaw—been used to store Nazi loot, and thus escaped destruction.

Cracow's old Jewish cemetery had been renovated with the help of the JDC. Apart from a number of mass graves, mute testimony of the Nazi occupation, we saw the tombstones of Rabbi Isserles, the "Tosafot Yom Tov," and Dr. Thon. The inscription on the last was in Polish and I was asked to supply an appropriate Hebrew text, since there was only one rabbi in the entire country and none of the local Jews had a command of the holy tongue.

Later that day, Fischgrund, his wife, and his fifteen-year-old stepdaughter joined us at our hotel. He gave me a Hebrew book published by his late father, who had been a rabbi and scholar, and he wrote a dedication on the flyleaf. It was a commentary on *Pirké Avot*, the Mishnaic "Ethics of the Fathers," including the famous *Tosafot* of Rabbi Yom Tov Lipmann Heller, head of Cracow's Beth Din in the seventeenth century, whose burial place we had seen a few hours previously. The gift symbolized Fischgrund's own tragic predicament: this man, son of a rabbi, had lost a teenage daughter in the Holocaust and could find no consolation in a stepdaughter who clearly did not wish to be reminded of her Jewish heritage.

I gathered that relations between the Yiddish Kultur-Farband and the small

Jewish religious community in Cracow were far from cordial. A furniture manufac-
turer named Jakubowicz, the only learned and pious layman, was leading the fight
to keep Judaism alive thereabouts. Apparently, he and his friends still scoured the
nearby forest for Jewish remains so as to ensure that these would receive Jewish
burial among the mass graves of their cemetery. Such last honors to the dead were a
striking example of *ḥesed shel emet*, the "act of true kindness" not performed for the
sake of a reward. Jakubowicz, who devoted much of his time to Cracow's Jewish
monuments, was planning to leave for Israel within the year. After his departure, I
reflected, little more than the dying embers of a glorious Jewish past would remain.

At Oświęcim, an hour and a half's journey from Cracow, lay the most elaborate
and notorious of all the Nazi extermination camps—Auschwitz. In the course of my
talks in Warsaw with Israel Ambassador Dagan, U.S. Ambassador John Cabot, and
others, I had already raised the issue of a Jewish pavilion to commemorate the
specific Jewish dimension of Hitler's murder program and portray it to visitors from
all parts of the world. Permission had been received for the erection of a memorial at
Treblinka, where 800,000 Jews had been done to death, but at Auschwitz, where
many more Jews had perished, their conspicuous martyrdom was not acknowledged.
Such an omission could no longer be tolerated.

There was abundant evidence of muddled thinking on the part of the Polish
Government. The Poles would not allow Israel to erect a memorial at Auschwitz, on
the pretext that Israel—as a foreign country—represented neither Polish Jewry nor
the Jewish people as a whole. Yet Czechoslovakia, Hungary, and even East Germany had been allocated space at Auschwitz for national pavilions depicting the
fate of their citizens in this place of mass slaughter. Nor would the Poles enter into
negotiations with the World Jewish Congress or accept "tainted" (West German)
reparations money from the Claims Conference. Premier Gomulka had nevertheless
hinted that Dr. Nahum Goldmann would be given an official welcome, as chairman
of the Claims Conference, if he attended the dedication of a Jewish monument at
Treblinka—on which occasion the Poles would mention the contributions made by
the Claims Conference and the WJC.

The American ambassador, to whom I subsequently reported my visits to Auschwitz and Treblinka, promised to do whatever he could to help.

Approximately four million human beings, about half of them Jews, had perished
in Hitler's chief death camp. We entered Auschwitz by way of the gate bearing the
sardonic legend, *Arbeit Macht Frei*—"Work Liberates." What we saw there has
become so familiar to Jews of today that only a few remarks need be made. Auschwitz has been preserved as a vast, overwhelming museum of satanic cruelty and
annihilation. Tens of thousands of lives were snuffed out there in a single day. We
saw the exhibits: seventeen tons of hair shorn from women and children, and the
materials woven from it; mountains of shoes; luggage from a score of countries;
incredible masses of spectacles; piles of *tallitot;* other personal effects too numerous
to mention; and, most horrifying of all, the torture chambers and the walls where
multitudes were lined up and shot.

Two miles away, at Birkenau, where the crematoria had reduced tortured bodies to cinders, we toured the furnaces, saw the ditches where human remains were burned when the ovens could not cope with the daily load, and found ourselves stepping on the ashes that still remained. We were told that, at times, the blood ran two inches deep in the execution yard.

Our guide, a former inmate of the camp, related the story of one Jewish girl whose mother had refused to undress for her "shower" in the gas chamber. When the SS officer in charge began tearing off the woman's clothes, the girl kicked him, grabbed his pistol, shot him dead, and then wounded two other Nazis before she was overpowered. The official version of this incident was that the SS man was accidentally shot when the Germans fired at rioting prisoners. It would have been unthinkable to admit that a representative of the *Herrenvolk* had been shot down by a mere Jewess. That nameless girl deserved, I felt, to be remembered with our many other unknown heroes and martyrs on Yom Ha-Sho'ah.

There was a monument at Auschwitz, paid for by the JDC, depicting two hands raised toward the sky but displaying no Jewish symbol. At Birkenau, we did find an unimpressive, weatherbeaten little memorial bearing, in Polish, Yiddish, and Hebrew, the inscription: "To the Millions of Jews who were exterminated by Hitler." That kind of tribute spoke for itself. We were informed, however, that an international monument was planned and that Israel would be represented on the organizing committee.

From Auschwitz to Treblinka in northeastern Poland, new road and rail links had been built in time for the twentieth anniversary of the Warsaw Ghetto Uprising, which had been marked by various commemorative events three months before our arrival. A large monument engraved with a Menorah and a mausoleum had been set up in Treblinka. Jewish tombstones bore the names of the victims' places of origin, but no Magen David could be seen, although the graves in the adjoining Christian cemetery displayed crosses. The previous April, members of the visiting Israeli delegation had reverently gathered some of the Jewish ashes for reinterment at a moving ceremony held later at Tel Aviv's Naḥalat Yitzḥak burial ground.

After our return to Warsaw, Ambassador Avigdor Dagan told me that it would cost only about $10,000 for the World Jewish Congress to establish a permanent Jewish exhibit at Auschwitz. We agreed that pressure should be exerted for the construction of such a pavilion, where the Jewish aspect of Hitler's genocide program could be explained and where Israel's role in providing a haven for the surviving remnant could be properly acknowledged.*

Some criticism was leveled at the JDC for leaving too much control of subsidized Jewish activities in the hands of Jewish Communists. There were many small Polish

---

*A Jewish pavilion was officially dedicated at Auschwitz on April 17, 1978. Dr. Nahum Goldmann headed a large delegation of Jewish representatives from all parts of the world, including the Soviet Union, at the opening ceremony. My friend and colleague, Kalman Sultanik, was among those present and he noted the pavilion's failure to depict Jewish heroism (the ghetto revolts), to record Jewish cultural achievements prior to the *Sho'ah*, or to reflect the role of Holocaust survivors in defending and building the State of Israel. After the opening ceremony, however, Polish President Henryk Jablonski did acknowledge Jewish contributions to the enrichment of Poland's culture.

towns where Jewish tombstones were still used for paving and where Jewish cemeteries had been neglected. It was especially galling to find that the one Polish newspaper that regularly disseminated anti-Israel propaganda was the Yiddish *Folks-shtimme*—which American Jewry kept alive through disbursements from the Joint Distribution Committee. I thought it best to use my influence in the Claims Conference by way of the World Jewish Congress, rather than the JDC.

Two of my most illuminating meetings in the Polish capital, on the eve of our departure, were with Hersh Smolar, editor of the *Folks-shtimme*, and with Professor Berl Mark. Smolar, an ardent Communist, strongly opposed the idea of a special Jewish exhibit at Auschwitz, asserting that the Jewish tragedy could be represented adequately in each of the scheduled European pavilions. He "did not know" about the absence of Jewish symbols at Treblinka and "had nothing against" the Magen David. Professing to see "an awakening of Jewish consciousness" among the youth, he was sanguine about the future. With regard to his paper's uniquely anti-Israel line, Smolar declared that the *Folks-shtimme* was appreciative of "constructive developments" in the Jewish State and only criticized those matters which conflicted with Poland's "world outlook." I was flabbergasted to hear him say, "We *do* welcome strikes in Israel and other Socialist manifestations." Like many of his Jewish comrades, Smolar was destined to suffer disgrace and expulsion from the party in the late 1960s. Ironically, this notorious anti-Zionist found refuge in Israel in 1971.

Professor Mark proved to be a very different type of Jew. His Institute possessed many fine Jewish art works that the authorities might allow him to have exhibited in Israel, and some of these might even be permitted to remain there. His daughter was visiting Israel as a tourist at the time, and it was his cherished hope that she would marry and settle there. That was the one reason accepted by the Polish Government for one of their nationals failing to return from an overseas trip. It was most unlikely that his wife, who was in charge of the archives at party headquarters, would ever be granted an exit visa. The Communist Kultur-Farband was not highly regarded by the Polish Government, he said, but they did manage to create difficulties, for example, in regard to Aliyah and the Auschwitz Jewish memorial. Mark was convinced that the Soviet bloc exhibits would deliberately gloss over Jewish losses in the Holocaust, and he urged that pressure be maintained on the Polish authorities through their ambassador in Washington, who would be sensitive to American public opinion. Moscow allowed the satellite countries a good deal of autonomy in the running of their internal affairs. He had a poor opinion of *Sovetish Heymland*, but thought that the very fact of its existence was important. In contrast to the situation in Poland, many young Russian Jews were now learning Hebrew, albeit privately, he said.

This interview with Professor Mark, a vital man in his middle fifties who wished to be remembered to President Shazar, was the best and most informative talk I had during my stay in the country. He died, an unwilling captive there, in 1966.

Poland, it seemed to us, was one vast Jewish graveyard. Our visit, as I have suggested, became a melancholy pilgrimage into the distant and recent Jewish past, filled with many grim reminders of how nations had stood by indifferently while millions of our brethren were being slaughtered. I could only hope that some, at least, of those who still survived on Poland's bloody soil would make a new Jewish life for themselves in Israel, and not in some distant corner of the *Galut*.

Jewish Survival in the USSR

Over thirty years had elapsed since my previous visit to the Soviet Union. Hence, it was with no little anticipation of seeing the changes which had meanwhile occurred that we emplaned for Moscow on August 1. What mainly engaged our attention was the extent to which there had been an upsurge in Jewish national feeling in Russia. I was anxious to discover how the ordinary Jew in the street would react when I spoke to him, always assuming that it would be possible to draw him out in an atmosphere dominated by official watchfulness, and this at a time when the long-suppressed feeling of affinity with fellow Jews—especially with Israelis—was beginning to emerge once more, like the early flowers of spring after a hard winter.

Our contacts with Soviet Jewry were made in the streets and in public parks, in the synagogues and in Jewish cemeteries where people came to visit the graves of departed relatives. Congregations in the USSR were invariably under the supervision of lay chairmen, the *gabba'im*, who evidently had to be persona grata with the authorities and who spared no effort to ensure that "foreign" Jews would have no contact with local worshipers. In accordance with this rule, I was always escorted to the section reserved for overseas visitors whenever I attended Sabbath services in one of the synagogues. To overcome this form of segregation, I managed to be present at the early-morning service on weekdays, when elderly folk were generally the sole worshipers, before the *gabbai* would arrive. This practice afforded an opportunity for some informal conversation—conducted, of course, in Yiddish. Even so, these brief discussions took place in a furtive atmosphere.

I received some useful advice from Yosef Tekoa, Israel's ambassador to the Soviet Union at that time, who suggested that we carry an El Al airline travel bag with us whenever possible. This would—and did—encourage Jews to strike up a conversation. We also followed his advice in regard to speaking Yiddish, rather than English.

While sightseeing in Moscow during the first half of August, Intourist guides took us to the places of general interest. With its broad avenues, imposing structures, and historic monuments, the Soviet capital was a beautiful metropolis. We toured Red Square, the Kremlin, and Lenin's mausoleum, where overseas visitors such as ourselves enjoyed the privilege of entering ahead of the endless lines of local people. Stalin's grave, located next to those of other Soviet leaders at the edge of the Kremlin walls, was something of a comedown. Moscow University was housed in a towering, thirty-three-story building, and we heard that about one-third of its 30,000 students were accommodated in dormitories at very modest cost. One department store was larger even than Macy's in New York, and the Metro (subway) stations were astonishingly ornate—resplendent with paintings and sculptures, which were no doubt meant to impress tourists as well as Muscovites and other Russian citizens.

We spent enjoyable evenings at a puppet theater, at the Moscow Opera House and at the circus. Here, we had enlightening private conversations with a Jewish woman who listened to Yiddish broadcasts from Israel and with a former member of Solomon Mikhoels' State Jewish Theater, who had been spared by Stalin's anti-Jewish terror campaign. Whether by coincidence or otherwise, a number of our taxi drivers also proved to be Jewish.

The permissiveness that governed relations between the sexes during the early period of the Soviet regime seemed to have vanished. A woman convicted of soliciting as a prostitute could be sentenced to imprisonment in Siberia. A cheerful atmosphere prevailed at the Palace of Marriage, where we saw brides and grooms awaiting their turn in separate rooms. The facilities included shops for the purchase of wedding rings and jewelry, and a reception hall for use after the ceremony. The registrar in charge was a good-looking woman who addressed each couple after the marriage contract had been signed in the presence of witnesses, but no one "gave the bride away" and no wedding march was played. Two rings were brought in an elegant receptacle for the bride and bridegroom to bestow upon each other, after which those present showered congratulations on the newly married couple.

This wedding palace was a concrete expression of the atheism fostered by the Soviet state, which lost no opportunity to deride religious belief. Decades of Communism had not weaned all Russians away from Christianity, however, and the churches of various denominations that we visited on our first Sunday were crowded with worshipers. We would find that Judaism and the synagogue had fared far worse in the USSR.

According to official estimates, of the two and a half million Jews in the USSR, about 240,000 lived in Moscow. From what I heard, upwards of 400,000 was a more likely total of Jews living in the Soviet capital. Having come furnished with a basic list of problems concerning Jewish national and religious rights in the USSR, I was anxious to see Yekaterina Furtseva, the Soviet Minister of Culture, but the U.S. ambassador told me that the whole complex of Jewish issues fell under the jurisdiction of several ministries, and that Madame Furtseva would most probably not receive anyone arriving from the West "on Jewish business." Officially, a Jewish problem did not exist in the Soviet Union. Whenever anyone raised the matter, Negro rights in the United States were brought up as a counter-issue. "But there's all the difference in the world," I pointed out. "The American Government is fighting for Black and minority rights in the U.S. What positive interest do the Soviet authorities take in the welfare of their Jewish minority?"

As in Warsaw, I outlined my scheme for a World Peace Academy to the American ambassador, who told me that U.S. Vice-President Adlai Stevenson was arriving in Moscow the next day to discuss the Atomic Test-Ban Treaty. He made warm reference to Yosef Tekoa, his Israeli diplomatic colleague, and advised me to see Henry Shapiro, the local United Press correspondent, who might be able to arrange a meeting with a high-ranking Soviet official. Shapiro, who came over to our hotel a couple of nights later, remembered our previous meeting in Kiev more than three decades earlier, in 1932. It was his impression that Premier Nikita Khrushchev had no understanding whatsoever of Jewish rights and wrongs, and that the relaxation of international tensions would not be conducive to improved Soviet relations with Israel. Nevertheless, Shapiro was willing to try to make some approaches on my behalf, and one of these proved successful.

On our first Shabbat morning in Moscow, we attended services at the Great Synagogue on Arkhipova Street, where the mandatory segregated seating awaited us. Some 400 worshipers were present—more than usual, since it was *Shabbat Naḥamu*, just after the fast of Tish'ah be-Av. I received *aḥaron*, the final *aliyah* to the Torah, and a former colleague of mine in the American rabbinate was honored with *maftir*. Upstairs, in the women's gallery, a tourist handed a prayer book she had brought to one of the women, but a synagogue official appeared from nowhere and appropriated it. Chief Rabbi Yehudah Leib Lewin, a tall, impressive man, officiated. He was then close to seventy, but I took him to be a good ten years younger. After the services, I managed to arrange an appointment with him at nine o'clock on the following morning. Many of the Russian Jews exchanged *Shalom* greetings with us as we left.

Later, over lunch at the Israel embassy, we were told that members of the diplomatic staff had been compelled to refrain from distributing *tallitot* and *siddurim* outside the Great Synagogue, as this aroused attention and adverse comment. The recipients allegedly sold these religious items. To avoid unpleasantness, Israeli diplomatic personnel now left such articles inside the synagogue. At the time of the original furore, Israel's Chief Rabbi Itzḥak Nissim had sent an official protest to the Soviet authorities, and the embassy staff had greatly appreciated his firm stand. We also heard that a check was made of all comings and goings at the Israel embassy, and that anything of importance was therefore discussed in the open air and not in a car, which might be "bugged" by some device.

Instead of returning to the Great Synagogue later that Sabbath, we went to a Ḥasidic *shtibl*, where about thirty men were present, mostly pensioners. The presiding rabbi, a member of the famous Twersky family, which had a branch in America, had applied with his wife for an exit visa to Israel. His son-in-law, whom I also met there, had similar hopes of making Aliyah and asked me to help. Rabbi Mordecai Ḥanzin, it transpired, already had a brother in Israel who served as Chief Rabbi of Petaḥ Tikvah. I imagined that such a family connection might prove useful in submitting an application to leave the country. Rabbi Ḥanzin, who worked in Moscow University's Hebrew Department, was kept busy as secretary of the *kehillah* and as Chief Rabbi Lewin's amanuensis. "Lewin is a nobody, afraid of his own shadow," Ḥanzin told me, "but Rabbi Twersky is a genuine spiritual leader." Several other people had already hinted that the present Chief Rabbi of Moscow lacked both the learning and the personality of his predecessor, Rabbi Solomon Schliefer.

As we participated in the third Sabbath meal, *Shalosh Se'udot*, with its bread, herring, and beer, and sang *Zemirot*, Rabbi Hanzin asserted that Jewish religious life in the Soviet Union was becoming weaker year by year. He also contradicted the statement made by Professor Mark in Warsaw about the numbers of Russian Jews studying Hebrew and Yiddish in private. After the *Havdalah* ceremony at the Sabbath's termination, we were about to return to our hotel by car when several of the elderly Jews rushed to intercept us. *"Nemt unz mit aykh nakh Yisroel!"* they pleaded in Yiddish. I was deeply affected by such appeals to rescue the aged Prisoners of Zion, especially since I knew that little could be done at the time. It was a cry that would haunt me throughout my visit to the Soviet Union, and for months and years thereafter.

The next morning, as arranged, I had the first of my two private conversations with Chief Rabbi Lewin. These afforded an insight into Jewish conditions in Moscow, which, for the most part, typified the situation of Russian Jewry as a whole. One did not need to look hard in order to see how heavily the burden of responsibility as a religious leader in Soviet Jewry weighed upon this man. He did not impress me as the kind of spiritual champion who would fight valiantly for Judaism and Jewish rights under a Communist regime. Fear was reflected in his constantly shifting eyes, and the dilemma facing him must have contributed to the deterioration of his health.

Rabbi Lewin was at pains to assure me that he had good reason to hope that the Jewish religious position would improve. This outward optimism governed his answers to my queries regarding the need for an additional burial ground, facilities for *shehitah*, the provision of *kasher* meat and of *matzot* before Passover, and similar problems. The Moscow yeshivah that Chief Rabbi Schliefer had been allowed to open in 1957 had now trained about three dozen religious functionaries—all but one or two of them as *shohatim*, ritual slaughterers. When I asked why only six students were presently enrolled in the yeshivah, Rabbi Lewin claimed that these trainees (mainly from Georgia, I later discovered) had difficulty in finding accommodations. "Our Government is an atheistic one," he added, "and the Christian seminaries have much the same story to tell." A new edition of *Siddur ha-Shalom*, the "Prayer Book of Peace" issued by Rabbi Schliefer, had been held up because offset printing was "difficult." The Soviet authorities maintained that there were "not enough" Jews to warrant the establishment of a synagogue federation in the USSR.

One of the other matters I raised was the right of Jewish religious leaders to attend religious conferences outside the Soviet Union. Rabbi Lewin affirmed that he had been granted permission to attend an Agudat Yisrael convention in Zurich one month previously, but that ill health had prevented him from doing so. "A diplomatic illness," I said to myself at the time, but I subsequently learned that he had in fact suffered a heart attack prior to his intended departure for Switzerland. My earnest advice to Rabbi Lewin was that whenever an opportunity next presented itself to attend such a conference, especially were it to take place in some neutral country, he should make every effort to attend—not only for the sake of his own prestige, but also because such participation would prove a source of encouragement to Jews inside and outside Russia, and because it would reflect well on the Soviet regime.

In retrospect, it is interesting to recall that Chief Rabbi Lewin visited the United States five years after our conversation, in 1968, albeit as the honored guest of the anti-Zionist American Council for Judaism! In February 1969, moreover, official permission was granted to the committee of the Moscow Great Synagogue to invite rabbis from Israel and other Western countries to attend the celebration of the Chief Rabbi's seventy-fifth birthday.

Our tête-à-tête was interrupted by the arrival of the Government-appointed Jewish communal functionary known as the *gabbai*, who burst into Rabbi Lewin's office without knocking. He calmly sat down and listened to what was being said. Naturally, the *gabbai's* presence had a dampening effect on our discussion and I soon left.

However much allowance had to be made for the difficulty of his position, I was still convinced that the Chief Rabbi could obtain far more from the Soviet authorities if he were to display more courage and tenacity in making legitimate demands. A firmer stand would not involve such serious risks in the Khrushchev era as would have been the case in Stalin's time, and a number of legal provisions and precedents concerning other religious denominations might be cited. Someone had told me about the religious fortitude displayed by "Gruzinian" (Georgian) Jews when they were threatened with the conversion of their synagogue into a cinema. As a direct result of their outcry, not only was the synagogue left undisturbed but the authorities even added an extra floor to the building. My parting words to Rabbi Lewin drew no reply, nor did I expect one in the circumstances.

Israel's ambassador had just returned from a trip to Minsk and Kiev, where Jewish feelings were stronger than in Moscow. When we dined with Mr. and Mrs. Tekoa that Sunday evening, we were told that young as well as older people came to visit the mass graves near those cities on Tish'ah be-Av and to recite memorial prayers. A number of them had come over to his car and spoken frankly about Russian anti-Semitism. One woman, who had belonged to a Zionist youth movement and who had been sentenced to imprisonment, said to Tekoa: "The news we hear on the radio about Israel is the breath of life to us."

The ambassador stated that the present regime's aim was to assimilate Russian Jewry rather than eliminate anti-Jewish prejudice. "When the Churches sell candles, the authorities turn a blind eye," he declared, "but when the Jews sell *matzot*, they call it speculation." Precisely because the Soviet Government wanted to keep the Jewish issue quiet, it must constantly be aired. Jewish and non-Jewish protests outside the USSR fortified the morale of Soviet Jewry, but such protest campaigns had to be on a high level. I asked if it would be possible for President Shazar to intervene with the Russian authorities in order to secure exit visas to Israel for Rabbis Twersky and Ḥanzin and their families. Tekoa thought that something could be done.

Bert and I left next morning for Odessa, making an overnight stop in Yalta en route. We met some Brazilian Jewish tourists in this Crimean coastal resort. They and their Soviet relatives were generally satisfied with Khrushchev's liberalization program, but attributed the rise of Jewish national sentiment among the youth to endemic Russian anti-Semitism.

It was interesting to hear the wife of an Associated Press correspondent speak of the antireligious prejudice she encountered because she wore a cross. The youngsters who jeered at her had learned their atheism courses very thoroughly. One young man told me that he was specializing in Arabic at the university because the Government was fostering Near Eastern relations and studies. Clearly, Hebrew and Israel did not form part of this cultural scenario for the Russians. Another youth, who coveted one of my sport shirts, found the wrong customer: he offered me a Russian ikon in exchange.

We arrived in Odessa on Tuesday, and explored its cultural monuments. The art museum had a fine collection of Western and Oriental paintings and other objets d'art and I found that the municipal library's stock of two and a half million volumes included some post-Revolutionary Yiddish "proletarian" works. Most of the old and rarer Hebrew books had been sent to Moscow.

There were reputedly 150,000 Jews living in Odessa, about one-quarter of the total population. Until the early 1920s, this had been the second largest Jewish community in the Russian Empire, an outstanding center of Jewish cultural life and Zionist activity. We paid two midweek visits to the synagogue, where we met the spiritual leader of Odessa Jewry, Rabbi Izrail Shvartzblatt. Much younger in appearance than the average Russian *rav*, perhaps about fifty, he claimed to have studied at the famous yeshivah of Slobodka and to have headed another yeshivah in Warsaw. He was, in point of fact, the one rabbi known to have been ordained by the late Chief Rabbi Solomon Schliefer of Moscow. I also met the Government-appointed president of the congregation and gathered that *balebos* was the local Yiddish nickname for a *gabbai*.

My second visit to the synagogue coincided with the first *minyan*'s conclusion of the morning service. Glasses of *branfen* (brandy or other strong drink) were being handed out, although the *balebos* normally in charge was said to disapprove of the practice. One of the worshipers, who had studied at the famous seminary of Chaim Tchernowitz (Rav Tza'ir) in Odessa, warned me that the *balebos* would paint a glowing picture of Jewish religious life, misrepresenting the true situation. I was also told that only a few Russians had tried to save Jews from the Nazis in Odessa, that the graves of Mendele Mokher Seforim and other eminent personalities could be seen in the Jewish cemetery, and that many people baked their own *matzot* at home before Passover. Very few boys celebrated their Bar Mitzvah and Jews rarely attended synagogue before retirement from their jobs, for fear of losing them.

I had another word with Rabbi Shvartzblatt, who had lost all his family in the Holocaust and now had twin daughters by a second marriage. Despite this typically tragic background, he kept a smiling face and seemed to be a devoted communal leader. Each day between the afternoon and evening services, he conducted a *shi'ur* for those attending synagogue. When the principal *balebos*, a vigorous man in his midfifties, came in, I jokingly remarked: "It's good to see your young and energetic rabbi—I caught him learning!" Only later, when I returned to Moscow, did someone inform me that Rabbi Shvartzblatt was a Government stooge who aimed to become Chief Rabbi of Moscow after Yehudah Leib Lewin. The consensus was that such a promotion would make things even worse for Soviet Jewry.

As I was about to leave, the *balebos* urged: "Come again! It's warm here in *shul*." His emphasis of the heating spoke for itself.

My most unusual experience in Odessa took place at the Jewish cemetery, when I went to visit the grave of Mendele Mokher Seforim (Shalom Ya'akov Abramovich), one of the fathers of modern Hebrew and Yiddish literature. A one-legged man offered to be my escort and to recite the traditional *El Malé Raḥamim* (memorial) prayer at the graveside. I promptly accepted his offer. The man obviously mistook me for a Jewish author, when he followed the custom of invoking the intercession of the departed on behalf of the living. I say this because he added a special plea in Yiddish to the standard prayer: "Reb Mendele, be a *melitz yosher* [true advocate] for the writer standing here before you, so that he may be protected against sickness and imprisonment!" That well-intentioned and pathetic plea shed startling light on the everyday apprehensions of ordinary Soviet Jews.

Kiev, the historic capital of the Ukraine, was an hour's journey from Odessa by air, and we arrived just before the weekend. As usual, Bert and I did some sightseeing and were introduced to the subway, which was not as elaborate as Moscow's, but no less elegant. An impressive Memorial to the Unknown Soldier stood near the city center. We saw Jewish names such as "Friedman" and "Markovich" among those listed as having served as officers and who fell in Kiev's defense during the "Great Patriotic War" against Nazi Germany.

One of my first calls was at the Intourist office, where I asked about visits to Babi Yar. "There's nothing to see there," we were told, "and no tours are available." When we insisted on going to that place of Jewish martyrdom, the Intourist official said that we would have to make our own arrangements. Earlier, in Moscow, Ambassador Tekoa had pointed out that the site of the Babi Yar massacre had been cemented over, and that no trace of what took place there now remained. It was another of those Russian Jewish "unmentionables," but deeply rooted Ukrainian anti-Semitism may well have played a part in this affair. Significantly, *Judaism without Embellishment*, one of a series of hate-mongering works by Trofim Kichko, was published with the imprimatur of the Ukrainian Academy of Sciences in the year of our visit to Russia, 1963. At any rate, we did manage to visit Babi Yar just before our scheduled return to Moscow.

While Kiev's main synagogue, the *Shnaydersher Shul*, was under repair, services were taking place at the smaller *Sukhovitzki Shul*. I first went there on Friday morning, when I found about a hundred elderly men worshiping downstairs. Two *gabba'im* and a *shammash* formed a wall around me and kept me under constant surveillance. Eventually, after obtaining the address of the Jewish cemetery, I decided to make my escape. According to reliable sources, the president of this congregation proved to be one of the most compliant agents of the Soviet authorities.

On Sunday, however, I managed to circumvent the local *balebos* and his confederates by arriving very early for morning prayers. There were three *minyanim*, and as one quorum finished *davvening*, another began. My conversations with the "regulars" ranged over a variety of topics—from local conditions to the possibility of being reunited with close relatives overseas. It was enlightening to compare their answers to certain questions with those which one of the *gabba'im* later supplied. When I asked if Bar Mitzvah ceremonies took place, they said, "No," whereas the *gabbai* said, "Very few." When I then asked whether there had been enough *matzot* available on Passover, they said, "Yes, but we have to bake them privately," whereas he told me that Jews were also allowed to bake *matzot* for fellow Jews if the flour was supplied, but could charge only for the baking. Like Russian Christians who baked sacramental wafers, Jews were not permitted to earn money on the side by baking *matzot*. "Two years ago," the *gabbai* added, "*matzot* were produced by a Government bakery, but our people insisted that they were not *kasher* for Passover because the same machinery had been used to produce bagels only a short time before, so most of the purchasers were non-Jews."

Information received by specialists on Soviet Jewish affairs indicates, however, that the baking of *matzot* was totally banned in Kiev from 1960 until 1966, and that any infringement of this rule resulted in a jail sentence.

The *gabbai* or *fervalter* (synagogue "manager") with whom I spoke that morning told me that some local markets received supplies of *kasher* meat and that observant Jews had advance notice of where it could be bought. When the old Jewish cemetery was scheduled for redevelopment, he had helped Rabbi Twersky of Brooklyn to arrange the transfer of the remains of some of his relatives, their coffins and tombstones, to a new burial ground. If such action was possible in Kiev, I reflected, the Chief Rabbi of Moscow could surely endeavor to achieve the same results. Paradoxically enough, the Jews of Kiev had not been able to appoint any successor to their former rabbi, Abraham Panitch, and had to make do with *fervalter* whom the Soviet authorities found suitable.

Babi Yar, which we visited later that day, is a ten-acre site on the outskirts of Kiev. Over 33,000 Jews had been mowed down in its ravine by Nazi machine-gunners on the last two days of September 1941. It was to claim many more victims, not all of them Jews, before the SS tried to obliterate all traces of the mass slaughter that had taken place there. A new housing development had been undertaken in the vicinity and there was nothing to indicate that the whole area was surrounded by a multitude of nameless graves. Yevgeni Yevtushenko's recent protest poem had focused attention on the Government's failure to establish a permanent memorial on the site, but both state and municipal authorities remained adamantly opposed to such a monument. The whole ghastly story, updated to 1970, was eventually told by A. Anatoli (Kuznetsov) in his "documentary novel," *Babi Yar*, the complete, uncensored version of which appeared after the author's escape to Great Britain. For some strange reason, the Central Committee of the Ukrainian Communist Party—led first by Nikita Khrushchev and then by Nikolai Podgorny—considered that the 70,000 Jews and perhaps half that number of Ukrainians murdered in the ravine did not deserve any kind of memorial. Anti-Semitism was undoubtedly a factor, though conceivably not the only one. In any case, official Soviet policy has been to suppress evidence of a specifically Jewish martyrdom under the Nazis; and this policy was maintained during Stalin's "anti-cosmopolitan" campaign and even during the post-Stalin "thaw," when Khrushchev became Prime Minister and Podgorny, the Soviet President.

As far as I was able to judge from my own personal contacts, anti-Semitism was endemic in the Russian population. For example, the floor housekeeper at one of the hotels where we stayed was a Jewish widow who lived alone in a one-room apartment. It was pitiful to hear her describe the kind of misery inflicted on her by malicious anti-Jewish neighbors. By contrast, two of our guides seemed proud of the fact that they were married to Jews and had Jewish family connections. One was bound, of course, to make allowance for statements made by Intourist personnel, with overseas visitors in mind.

A considerable amount of popular anti-Semitism undoubtedly sprang from envy and might also have been a residue of Church indoctrination—practically the sole element of Russian Orthodox doctrine which still retained its hold on the masses. Another factor, already mentioned, was the intense, widespread Russian national-ism, which made young Jews feel that they were outsiders. This would account for their pursuit of Jewish identification and solidarity, demonstrated in those vast crowds outside the main synagogues on religious festivals and the throngs surround-ing the Israel embassy limousine with its Menorah pennant. Despite the often abusive newspaper references to Israel, these young Jews now cherished an im-mense admiration for the Medinah. Its establishment had contributed greatly to the Jewish national resurgence in the Soviet Union.

No popular hostility toward a minority group can flourish unchecked in the USSR unless it is encouraged—or receives tacit approval—at the highest level. It is safe to assume that all questions affecting Soviet Jewry are still decided at the highest level—within the Praesidium of the Communist Party.

While sightseeing in Kiev, we had an amusing and not uncharacteristic discus-sion with our Intourist guide. A diligent sort of girl, not content with revealing the glories of her own city, she also prepared us for some of the outstanding treats awaiting us elsewhere. These included a peace monument in Moscow, which, she said, bore a beautiful inscription: "And they shall beat their swords into plow-shares."

I asked if she knew where that phrase originated. She thought for a moment and then answered, "It's from an ancient Greek poem."

"Are you quite sure?" I persisted.

"No, not absolutely," she replied, somewhat embarrassed.

I then suggested that she check the matter with her Intourist supervisor and let me have some precise information that afternoon, when we were to resume our tour.

At the appointed time, our conscientious guide returned with the details requested. The quotation, she declared, was from the New Testament. "No," I rejoined, "as a matter of fact, it's from the Hebrew Bible—chapter 2, verse 4, of the Book of Isaiah. You told us you were a college student. Don't you also study the Bible?"

"We're not religious, so we don't," she said.

"Well," I replied, "in America we're not Communists, but in our colleges we are taught to know something about the *Communist Manifesto*. It is part of the intellectual equipment of an educated person, even one opposed to Communism. Please convey this message to your superior at Intourist."

I very much doubt if she did.

On returning to Moscow, I gave my impressions of the places we had visited to the U.S. ambassador and his aide, who both said that the analysis confirmed what they already knew about the problems confronting Soviet Jewry. I was more than ever anxious to speak with Culture Minister Furtseva, and the ambassador suggested that I make a direct approach through Intourist. Finally, I told him that while in the United States on my return journey to Israel I would speak in favor of continued protests against the Soviet Government's Jewish policy. He said to me, "Why not? Plenty of Americans are concerned about these matters."

Meanwhile, Henry Shapiro had fulfilled his promise to help me and so, before making a second appointment with the Chief Rabbi, I called at the office of the Committee for Soviet-American Relations, where I introduced myself as a former vice-chairman of Russian War Relief in the United States during World War II. They advised me to discuss the issues I outlined with a senior official at the Council for Religious Minorities. I met the deputy director, Mr. Bukharin, a day or two later.

After stating my credentials and emphasizing American Jewry's influence on U.S. public opinion, I produced my list of questions and went over them with Bukharin point by point. They dealt with the need for a Chief Rabbinate of the Soviet Union and the granting of permission for Jewish religious leaders to attend rabbinical conferences outside the USSR; provisions for the marketing of *kasher* meat; more adequate arrangements for the baking of *matzot* and distributing them in time for Passover; the urgent need for new Jewish cemeteries, especially in Moscow; more generous facilities for the Moscow yeshivah and its students; and the reprinting of *Siddur ha-Shalom*, Rabbi Schliefer's prayer book.

It soon became apparent that Bukharin was either remarkably ignorant about the matters I raised in our discussion or deliberately lying when he answered. I subsequently wrote to him from New York, reminding him of the various points made in our conversation and asking for his written confirmation. Needless to say, I never received a reply.

Having already encountered leading Jewish Communists in Poland, I was interested to compare their attitudes with those adopted by their counterparts in the

Soviet Union. At the offices of *Sovetish Heymland*, the Yiddish-language periodical, I was disappointed to find that Aaron Vergelis, the chief editor, was not in Moscow. His deputy, Abraham Gonter, spent some time with me, however, and I also met other members of the editorial board, all of whom proved to be energetic apologists for the Soviet regime.

They told me that *Sovetish Heymland* had uncovered new talents in various parts of the USSR and that 25,000 copies of each issue were printed. About a thousand people, young and old, had recently attended a function under the paper's auspices. When I asked whether a Yiddish theater could be reestablished in Moscow, they said that would depend on sufficient popular support for such a move.

Gonter and his colleagues wanted to hear my impressions of the USSR and were somewhat truculent about the World Jewish Congress and its role. What right, they asked, had the WJC to speak in the name of Jews in Russia or anywhere else? "The same right that Jewish organizations had to speak out on behalf of German Jewry in the Hitler period," I replied. A mordant note was struck when I asked about the treatment of matters concerning Israel in the *Heymland*. Their laconic answer reminded me of what Hersh Smolar had asserted in Warsaw. "Of course we are interested in Israel," they assured me. "We always devote space to labor strikes over there!"

In regard to freedom of religious expression in the Soviet Union, they cited the example of Russian Muslims who received permission to make the *Hajj* to Mecca. I could not resist asking whether Jews were similarly enabled to make pilgrimage visits to Jerusalem on Passover, Shavu'ot, and Sukkot. "We think such arrangements are possible," they ventured, but they knew as well as I did that they were lying.

My most fascinating conversation in Moscow was with Ilya Ehrenburg, the eminent Jewish author and journalist, a much-courted favorite of the Soviet hierarchy and a frequent guest at Kremlin receptions. Though an active revolutionary in his youth, he had spent twenty years of his life in Western Europe after the first stage of the Bolshevik Revolution, returning to the USSR only in 1941. Ehrenburg had thereafter remained steadfastly loyal to the regime—and unscathed—even during the worst Stalinist purges and terror campaigns, and he now stood out as one of its principal literary apologists.

His Moscow apartment, comprising several well-furnished rooms, was hung with paintings. I noticed a few by Picasso and a Chagall self-portrait. At the time of our meeting, Ehrenburg was in his early seventies and seemed to be in reasonably good health. I thought Yiddish would be our *lingua franca*, but he barely understood it and, since my French was inadequate, we spoke through an interpreter.

Ehrenburg believed the appearance of *Sovetish Heymland* to be a step in the right direction, which might promote fresh literary creativity. He was doubtful whether the nucleus for a permanent Yiddish theater existed in Moscow. "Mikhoels and Zuskin were first-rate actors," he observed, "but there are no longer the talents here to build up a regular clientele. A Yiddish theater might conceivably attract audiences for the first few months, because of the novelty, but it would probably lose its appeal. Any closure would then do irreparable damage to Jewish prestige and to Yiddish culture."

Our conversation turned to the poet Yevgeni Yevtushenko, a non-Jew who had depicted the Jewish agony in his moving poem, "Babi Yar." Ehrenburg was critical of the fact that this young writer, still only thirty years of age, had subsequently compromised his genius by revising the last few lines of his elegy in order to retain official favor. "Had he refused to do so," said Ehrenburg, "the worst that could have happened would have been his having to wait a few extra months for the publication of his next book." Pointing to himself as an example, my host indicated that "the storm eventually blows over."

Ehrenburg confessed that he had no knowledge of modern Hebrew or Yiddish literature, but would be interested to read Israeli authors such as Agnon or Hazaz in translation. Among other contemporary Jewish writers in the West, he was acquainted with Edmond Fleg and I mentioned that this French Jew was a friend of mine. In parting, I suggested the motto: "Jewish writers of the world, unite!"

Before leaving Moscow, I had another chat with Henry Shapiro, the United Press correspondent, who told me that he and his wife planned to visit Israel in two months' time. He believed that Ilya Ehrenburg had been unjustly condemned by Jews outside the Soviet Union and told me that Ehrenburg had joined Mikhoels in attempting to win reprieves from Stalin for Jews condemned in "show trials." Apparently, despite his manic suspicion of Jews, Stalin had displayed a curious fondness for the eminent Jewish writer.

Khrushchev's program of liberalization had downgraded party ideologists and brought technocrats to the fore, thus making it unlikely that there would be a reversion to Stalinist terror. Shapiro was nevertheless convinced that the new upsurge of Russian nationalism had led to a sense of alienation among younger Soviet Jews, who now felt strongly about their own national status and their links with Israel. In one respect, he proved to be mistaken. "There is no likelihood of the USSR permitting full-scale Aliyah," he opined, "because of the foreseeable Arab reaction to such a policy."

On Thursday, August 15, we flew to Leningrad on the final lap of our journey through Eastern Europe. We spent the next two days touring the many places of cultural importance in this beautiful city, which Peter the Great founded in 1703. From then until the outbreak of World War I, it was known as St. Petersburg (Peterburg); for a brief period (1914–24) it was styled Petrograd, but meanwhile yielded its status as the Russian capital to Moscow in 1917; and, after the death of the first Soviet dictator, it was finally renamed Leningrad.

The influence of eighteenth-century French and Italian architects, artists, and sculptors was unmistakable, especially in Rastrelli's magnificent Winter Palace. We visited the museums of the Hermitage, a splendid miniature Louvre overlooking the River Neva, where the gorgeous rooms and chandeliers, lovely Gobelin tapestries, and rich collection of paintings—by Italian Renaissance masters, nineteenth-century French artists, and others—were a delight to see. The equestrian statue of Peter the Great and the palaces and cathedrals also left a powerful impression. A half-hour's drive from the city brought us to Peterhof, a palace facing the Gulf of Finland, which, with its beautiful park and fountains, reminded us of Versailles. This area had been Nazi-occupied territory during the thirty-month siege of Leningrad, which was lifted only in February 1944.

Much less to our taste was the Museum of Religion and Atheism, housed in what had once been a cathedral. Most of the displays were meant to inculcate atheistic ideas and we saw a few antireligious caricatures. One small exhibit devoted to Judaism included a picture of the Leningrad Great Synagogue and a Simḥat Torah scene of rejoicing. Our guide, who proved to be a Jewess, assured us that synagogues and churches had closed down in Russia because they no longer served any purpose in an atheistic society. At first she said that Jews were less inclined to attend their places of worship than Christians were, but then contradicted herself by stating that, if Jews took off work in order to go to synagogue on Shabbat, "it would be held against them."

Shortly after our arrival in Leningrad, I paid my first visit to the Great Synagogue in the hope of meeting Rabbi Ḥayyim Klebanov, the eighty-four-year-old spiritual leader of the city's Jewish congregation, but was told that he happened to be away on vacation. A greatly beloved figure, Rabbi Klebanov had been exiled to a forced-labor camp during the Stalinist period. Under the present, somewhat more liberal regime, he had been freed and restored to his former office.

Returning to the synagogue on Friday evening, I was able to meet its president, Meyer Freiman, who proved to be the most genial of all the *gabba'im* we encountered in the Soviet Union. He had succeeded Gedaliah Pechersky, a very popular and dynamic lay leader, whom the Jews of Leningrad remembered as a man sincerely devoted to the synagogue and its affairs. Pechersky had received a seven-year jail sentence in 1961 for "maintaining contact with a foreign embassy"— Israel's legation, of course. Bearing in mind that Freiman, his replacement, was almost certainly hand-picked by the Soviet authorities, I treated his statements with a degree of caution. He claimed to have been active in congregational affairs for close on fifty years.

The 200,000 Jews of Leningrad, though numbering far fewer than the community in Moscow, were economically in a stronger position. Freiman informed me that his *kehillah* provided a generous share of the 40,000 roubles needed for the upkeep of the Moscow yeshivah each year.

With obvious pride, he showed me around the synagogue, one of the largest in Europe and certainly the most impressive Jewish house of worship we had seen in Russia. I gathered that, apart from the services in the main building, two smaller congregations also prayed in adjoining premises each Sabbath morning. There was a library of 60,000 Jewish books and, attached to the congregation, a *mikveh*, a slaughterhouse, and a *matzah* bakery, although use of the last had been banned the previous year. Those parents who could arrange leaves of absence from work held occasional Bar Mitzvah celebrations at the synagogue. Freiman maintained that no problems had been encountered with regard to Jewish burial; only two years previously, they had been able to acquire a new and separate portion of a larger cemetery. As president of the Jewish Conciliation Board in America, I was interested to learn that the Leningrad Synagogue ran its own Bet Mishpat ha-Shalom, and that many domestic disputes were brought before this Jewish court.

Our conversation gave me the opportunity to ask Freiman the same questions I had raised with Chief Rabbi Lewin and with Bukharin, the Soviet official in Moscow. As far as the issue of an "All-Union" Chief Rabbinate and Jewish religious organization was concerned, the *gabbai* disclosed that this had been one of the points discussed by representatives of various Russian *kehillot* when they were in Moscow six years earlier to attend the funeral of Chief Rabbi Schliefer. He and his colleagues had urged that a central Jewish authority be established in Leningrad, but the other delegates expressed opposition and the talks proved abortive. When I ventured to suggest that Moscow, being the capital, was therefore the proper location for such a body (just as it was for other religious denominations), Freiman agreed and said that he and his friends would change their stand whenever the matter could be dealt with again.

The Jews of Leningrad were, it appeared, dissatisfied with Chief Rabbi Lewin's administration of the yeshivah in Moscow. The current decline in student enrollment there was attributable to a lack of suitable accommodations, and Freiman was ready to conduct a fund-raising campaign to build the dormitories needed, but the Chief Rabbi seemed fearful of assuming such a responsibility. No less aggravating, said Freiman, was the fact that the yeshivah trained cantors, slaughterers, and the like, but hardly any rabbis. Properly qualified *rabbanim*, he felt, should be the first priority.

In answer to my question about *aliyah le-regel* pilgrimages to Jerusalem, Freiman pointed out that the main obstacle was the high cost involved. "Who can afford to pay $2,000 or more?" he enquired, "and who will admit that he can afford such a sum?" A few elderly people had done so in the past, making all the obligatory payments and arrangements in the USSR and stating that they were going to see (the late) Rabbi Tzvi Pesaḥ Frank of Jerusalem, but this was not a practical proposition for the vast majority of Soviet Jews. There was no question of young people applying, since they would immediately be suspected of not wishing to return.

My last query related to the much-needed new edition of Rabbi Schliefer's *Siddur ha-Shalom*. Here, Freiman had a rather curious tale to tell. In 1960, it seemed, the Government had provisionally agreed to authorize a reprint but wanted to have a Russian translation for someone to check. The text submitted was a translation of the *nusaḥ Sefard* ritual and the official who subsequently read it soon found discrepancies between this and the original *(nusaḥ Ashkenaz)* edition. Because of these differences, permission to reprint the *siddur* had been withheld. An appeal was to be made against this decision, with the assurance that all sections of the community would be amenable to use of the first text and translation, if the authorities so insisted.

As for what the future might bring, Freiman expressed a weird kind of optimism.

"If Jews managed to survive as Marranos in Spain," he declared, "they can survive here in Russia as well." "*Az okh un vey,*" I thought. "The very comparison makes one shudder!"

In general, however, my impression of this *gabbai* was a positive one. Much of what he had to say tallied with the information I had previously gleaned elsewhere. Since Jewish religious leaders could obviously obtain more for their communities if they demanded what they were entitled to have under Soviet law, I urged Freiman to convey this important message to Rabbi Klebanov and to Chief Rabbi Lewin, who had evidently paid only one visit to Leningrad.

In the course of our tour of the major Russian cities, I availed myself of the opportunity to inspect the Judaica and Hebraica sections of the municipal libraries. The most important of these proved to be the Leningrad Public Library, which, with its thirteen million volumes, is the third largest in the world. More than 75,000 items of Jewish interest, in Hebrew, Yiddish, and other languages, were listed in the catalog, and the library's collection of rare Jewish manuscripts was universally renowned.

I learned that Professor K. B. Starkova, a non-Jewess, who taught in the Institute for African and Asian Studies, was an acknowledged expert on medieval Jewish poetry. She and five assistants were then working on manuscripts from Granada and other Jewish material relating to the Golden Age in Spain. I saw a fourteenth-century text by Ralbag (Rabbi Levi ben Gershom), the Bible commentator, philosopher, and mathematician, which my friend, Professor Abraham Katsh, had been eager to consult.

Not surprisingly, most of those employed in the Judaica and Hebraica sections of the public libraries were Jews. When talking to them, I always made a point of urging them to enter into correspondence with other major Jewish libraries abroad— in the United States, Great Britain, and Israel, for example—so as to exchange information and microfilms, and also to make available duplicate books and periodicals. Later, on my return from the USSR, I contacted libraries in the United States and Israel, suggesting that they take the initiative in establishing such vital contacts.

Our last day in the Soviet Union, August 17, was a Shabbat and there were some 300 worshipers in the Great Synagogue of Leningrad that morning. Freiman had told me that something like 40,000 Jews packed the adjoining streets on Kol Nidré night and on Simḥat Torah. I was honored with an *aliyah* to the Torah and was handed a copy of the Jewish calendar published by the congregation; 20,000 copies were printed annually for distribution, not only in Leningrad but in other major centers as well.

It was *Shabbat Mevarekhim,* the Sabbath preceding the month of Elul, and the customary *Yehi Ratzon* prayer for God's blessing of this New Moon was recited. The *ḥazzan* laid particular emphasis on the words, "May He who wrought miracles for our fathers . . . speedily redeem us, and gather our exiles from the four corners of the earth, even all Israel united in fellowship." That invocation set an apt seal on our month behind the Iron Curtain and on our series of moving encounters with the "Jews of Silence."

From Leningrad we flew home via Helsinki and Copenhagen, then over the North Pole to Alaska, San Francisco, New York, and Tel Aviv.

In the course of the next twelve months, I gave press conferences and was invited to address a succession of meetings on our Eastern European tour before many audiences in Israel and other parts of the world. For President Shazar, Moshe Sharett, and the Jewish Agency Executive I also prepared special reports. Using a combination of firsthand evidence and official statistics, I repeatedly stressed that what was being demanded for the Jews of the Soviet Union, who constituted one-fifth of World Jewry, was identical with what was accorded to Jews in other Communist bloc states. Criticism of the "liberal" post-Stalin regime would mount unless its policy of cultural genocide vis-à-vis Russian Jewry would be abandoned. Why, I asked, should Jews not enjoy the same rights granted to the various Christian denominations and to Muslims? Within the past six years, Christian Bibles and editions of the Koran had been published and republished in the USSR, whereas not a single copy of the *Tanakh*, the Hebrew Bible, had been printed in Russia since 1917. There was one place of worship for every 2,000 Orthodox Christians, one for every 500 Baptists, but only one for every 25,000 Jews—yet more synagogues were being closed down.

Speaking at the Engineers' Club in Tel Aviv on February 28, 1964, I stressed the guarantees written into the Soviet Constitution and the United Nations Charter on Human Rights. The unjust and unequal treatment meted out to Jews as a group in the Soviet Union called for unrelenting protest and exposure. And there was one final demand, made in the name of enlightened international standards, the right to go elsewhere. "There are," I argued, "scores of thousands of Jews in the USSR who have relatives abroad, many of them in Israel. Their right to emigrate is a fundamental human right." All things considered, the one sure road to Jewish survival for those spiritually oppressed Jews behind the Iron Curtain was Aliyah.

A Sense of History

After having spent the High Holy Days with our congregants and friends at B'nai Jeshurun in New York, it was relaxing to be back home in Israel shortly before the Sukkot holidays. We found on our arrival that Ze'ev Schickler and some other people from the Youth Village had very thoughtfully put the finishing touches to the *sukkah* erected on the balcony of our new house. A number of children from the neighborhood came to look at it, and we were glad to extend hospitality to them. In the course of the festival, our guests included Viscount Edwin and Lady Hadassah Samuel, Moshe Sharett, Max Nurock, Sir Jack and Lady Cohen of London, and Max Kopstein of Chicago.

As a non-Orthodox rabbi, I had made a point of attending the dedication exercises of the new American Reform center in Jerusalem on July 7, 1963, about ten days before we left for our visit to Eastern Europe. Headed by Dr. Nelson Glueck, the moving force behind its construction, Hebrew Union College's Biblical and Archaeological School was inaugurated in the presence of David Ben-Gurion, Israel's Prime Minister, and U.S. Ambassador Walworth Barbour. In later years, we became friendly with two leading figures at the Jerusalem campus of HUC, Professor Ezra Spicehandler and Rabbi Asher (Richard) Hirsch. A return to more traditional norms has been visible in some sections of the Reform movement, and it is intriguing nowadays to see a few of the HUC students wearing crocheted *kippot*.

On the eve of Hoshana Rabba, a markedly different religious experience awaited me when I visited the celebrated *Nazir*, Rabbi David Cohen, in his *sukkah*. My escort was his son, Rabbi She'ar Yashuv Cohen, who subsequently headed Jerusalem's Harry Fischel Institute for Talmudic Research and who now serves as Chief Rabbi of Haifa. With his traditional white garb and snowy beard, the *Nazir*, a disciple of Rav Kook, was an imposing figure. He gave a two-hour *shi'ur* that ended at midnight, dealing with a portion from the Zohar, the "Bible of the Kabbalists." His extensive knowledge of modern science and philosophy was impressive. After the *shi'ur*, a few *pizmonim* (hymnlike compositions) were sung, one of which had been written by the *Nazir* himself about forty years earlier. A violinist played Hasidic melodies in the course of the evening. All in all, this proved to be a most unusual Sukkot experience.

The next evening was Simḥat Torah, and we went to see the *Hakkafot*—Torah scroll processions—in Me'ah She'arim. Our first encounter there was with Rabbi Amram Blau and his fanatically anti-Zionist Neturei Karta sect. I later danced with pious Jews of a different stamp, Hasidim of the Karlin-Stolin dynasty.

With the conclusion of the festive season, each new week brought the usual round of public business and official engagements. At a meeting of the Jewish Agency Executive in October, part of the agenda was devoted to Israel's relations with South Africa. These had worsened because of Israel's firm stand against apartheid in UN debates. Reports from South Africa indicated that the outcome might be of serious consequence to our Keren Hayesod campaigns in the Republic. The South African Zionist Federation's representatives at this meeting were apprehensive, and critical of some Israeli leaders for making "unhelpful" policy statements.

In reply, Moshe Sharett pointed out that Israel's stand on this issue not only accorded with that of Western opinion, but also represented the deep feelings that Jews throughout the world had toward racial discrimination.

While in agreement with Sharett, I was also aware that Israel had been strengthening commercial and diplomatic ties with Third World countries, especially in Black Africa. This found expression in the state dinner that the President tendered to the Congolese leader, President Kassabuvu, in December. Only a year previously, the late President Ben-Zvi had been warmly received in Congo-Kinshasa (subsequently renamed Zaïre), and now Israel had apparently agreed to train Congolese troops as parachutists. Kassabuvu made a felicitous speech at the dinner. We could scarcely foresee the collapse of Israel's African policy ten years later, as a result of combined Arab and Soviet pressure. Whereas Zaïre, for example, severed diplomatic relations with Israel on the very eve of the Yom Kippur War, South

Africa drew closer to the Jewish State and their economic collaboration developed significantly. Israeli experts, however, continued to assist a number of Black African countries that were later said to be on the point of restoring their diplomatic ties with Israel.

At the end of November, I toured various new development areas as the guest of the Jewish Agency's Settlement Department. Two villages close to the Lebanese border, Dovev and Avivim, were located on sites previously abandoned by Jewish settlers and now housed Olim from Morocco. When we stopped at Avivim, which had been provided with a synagogue and a regional school, I was thrilled to discover among these pioneering families some of the Jewish village folk I had met in the Atlas Mountains while visiting Morocco in December 1953. A few of them also recognized me. Unhappily, both these frontier outposts were destined to suffer murderous attacks by Arab terrorists operating from across the border, but the hardy mountain Jews refused to budge. They were, and are, true *halutzim*.

On a strategic height in the heavily Arab-populated "Little Triangle," overlooking the Irron Valley, the first Jewish settlement had been established by a Nahal group, and here we were joined by Ya'akov Tsur, chairman of the KKL-JNF, Yosef Weitz, and General Avraham Yoffe. Four years later, in 1967, this *hityashvut* would become a civilian kibbutz affiliated with our (General Zionist) Ha-No'ar Ha-Tzioni movement. At that point, its development was largely financed (through the JNF) by the Jewish community of Miami, Florida, hence the like-sounding Hebrew name given to it—Mei Ammi, "Water of My People."

While we were there, a JNF official related the gist of a conversation he had had with an Arab teacher who was instructing his fellow Bedouin in agricultural methods. They had originally lived in Beersheba, but were now settled near Mount Tabor. The JNF man asked why they had come such a long distance and the Bedouin teacher's answer was in the best Zionist tradition: "One must do one's stint of *halutziut*."

The most tragic and melancholy event of 1963 was the assassination of President John F. Kennedy in Dallas. The news came over the radio at 10:00 A.M. (Israel time) on Friday, November 22. I immediately sent cables to Vice-President Lyndon Johnson and to my congregation, B'nai Jeshurun. I was so agitated that I could not sleep that night. For the first time since our Aliyah, I yearned to be with my former congregants and with fellow Americans. And so, the next morning, I walked over to attend Shabbat services at Hebrew Union College in King David Street. The services were conducted by Rabbi Jakob Petuchowsky, professor of rabbinics at the parent college in Cincinnati, who was on a visit to Israel at the time. He made reference to Kennedy's assassination.

On Sunday morning, I signed the condolence book at the U.S. consulate in West Jerusalem and, in the afternoon, I did the same at the American embassy in Tel Aviv. There were already 10,000 signatories. That evening, at ZOA House, I eulogized the late President at a meeting of the Tel Aviv branch of the Association of Americans and Canadians in Israel. Although Soviet Jewry had been my scheduled topic for the following Thursday at the Haifa Rotary Club, I changed it to a memorial address on President Kennedy. The Tel Aviv branch of the AACI arranged a solemn memorial assembly on Sunday, December 8, when the first secretary of the U.S. embassy and the national president of the AACI paid tribute to Kennedy. I delivered the main address and also eulogized Senator Herbert Lehman and Rabbi Abba Hillel Silver, both of whom had passed away during the preceding ten days.*

At the Haifa meeting, where I spoke as one who had known John F. Kennedy, worked for his election to the Presidency, and enthused over many of his policies, I stressed the courage and integrity of the man whose entry into the White House had been a landmark in American politics. The first Catholic to be elected to the highest office in the land, President Kennedy was one of America's most cultured heads of state. I went on to say:

> His Inaugural Address, one of the briefest and most meaningful ever to have been delivered, contained a pungent exhortation valid for the citizens of all nations: "Ask not what your country can do for you—ask what you can do for your country." His few years in office exceeded the expectations even of his admirers, and his stature grew with his facing and overcoming of problems. To President Roosevelt's New Deal, and President Truman's Fair Deal, President Kennedy added the slogan of the New Frontier, making it a ringing challenge to himself and others to open up new frontiers of social, economic and racial justice and of world peace. His admiration and friendship for Israel stemmed from his recognition that Israel was one of the new frontiers of human progress which could serve as an example to many other nations.

In Israel, President Zalman Shazar was impressing himself more and more upon the minds and hearts of his people. Shazar transformed Bet ha-Nasi, the modest Presidential residence, into a center of intellectual and artistic life. He also managed to persuade Ben-Gurion to move the weekly Bible study group to Bet ha-Nasi, and I participated in its Saturday evening meetings from time to time. One Shabbat morning in November, I attended services in his honor at the Metivta Synagogue near our home, where addresses of welcome were delivered by Rabbi Eliyahu Pardes and Eliyahu Eliachar, the religious and lay leaders respectively of Jerusalem's Sephardi community. Echoing the Songs of Songs (3:11), a choir of boys added a touch of regal dignity with their singing of *Tze'enah u-re'enah ba-Melekh Shelomoh*—"Come forth and gaze upon King Solomon."

Menashe Eliachar, Eliyahu's younger brother, achieved distinction as president of the Jerusalem Chamber of Commerce (from 1950), and in many other civic enterprises.

At the beginning of Ḥanukkah, in the second week of December, President Shazar officially welcomed a group of more than 100 Catholic archbishops, bishops, and other clergymen who were on a pilgrimage to their holy places in Israel. The

*On Abba Hillel Silver, see chapter 17.

historic nature of this event, I reflected, was that a people constituting a religious and ethnic minority everywhere else on earth extended, in its own homeland, full minority rights to a religion with hundreds of millions of adherents throughout the world.

This sense of history in the making in Israel was enhanced when Pope Paul VI made a three-day pilgrimage to the Holy Land in the first week of January 1964. It was the first papal visit to Eretz Yisrael since ancient times. After arriving in Jordan on January 4, the Pope then entered Israel by way of the Mandelbaum Gate, where President Shazar accorded him an official and ceremonious reception. I was among the thousands lining the roadside at the western entrance to the capital when Pope Paul and his entourage were met by Mayor Ish-Shalom and members of the City Council. In accordance with Jewish tradition, they offered bread and salt to their distinguished visitor. Chief Rabbi Itzḥak Nissim had sent a message of greeting, but he was not present at the ceremonies. The streets were crowded, but the applause was muted. Most people seemed merely curious.

The second Vatican Council was then in the middle of its deliberations, and the attitude adopted by the Church toward non-Christian faiths was high on the list of topics for discussion. The thought that passed through my mind was the answer to a topical question. Why had the Jewish State a great contribution to make to the normalization of Jewish-Christian relations? Because exile had supposedly been our punishment for the crucifixion of Jesus, and now the very existence of the State of Israel had done away with the tag of "punishment for Jewish villainy."

At the Mandelbaum Gate, Pope Paul defended Pius XII against the charges made by Rolf Hochhuth in his play, *The Deputy,* which had aroused much resentment in Catholic circles. Throughout his brief twelve-hour visit, Pope Paul never referred to the Jewish State as "Israel." After 1967, however, when Jerusalem was reunified and all of the Holy Land west of the Jordan passed under Israeli control, a less coldly correct attitude became apparent in the Vatican. At any rate, President Shazar struck a note of Jewish dignity when, in his greetings to the Pope, he quoted Micah 4:5—"Though all the peoples walk each one in the name of its god, we will walk in the name of the Lord our God for ever and ever."

In fairness to Paul VI, it should be added that the *Nostra Aetate* declaration, with its statement on Christianity's Jewish roots and on the continued importance of the Jewish people, was issued during his pontificate. Pope Paul was not of the same cast as his remarkable predecessor, John XXIII, who had saved Jews from the Nazis, had shown an uniquely warm regard for Jews and Judaism, and had initiated the more enlightened Jewish policy of the Catholic Church. Yet it was Paul VI who, supporting Cardinal Bea, overcame the opposition of ultra-conservative prelates to the "winds of change" blowing down Vatican corridors.

Early in the new year, Keren Hayesod business necessitated my departure for Great Britain and Western Europe. Israel Sieff, senior member of the Marks and Spencer "family," sat alongside me on the plane and we discussed subjects ranging from World Jewish Congress affairs to problems of Jewish education. On our arrival at London Airport on January 12, Lavy Bakstansky, the tireless general secretary of the British Zionist Federation, was there to greet and brief me.

A tight schedule had been prepared for my visit. Over the next few days, I addressed the Federation's honorary officers, describing my recent visit to the Iron Curtain countries, and also spoke at a number of Joint Palestine Appeal meetings in the London area. My first port of call in the provinces was Birmingham, where Alec Coleman made the JPA appeal. The vote of thanks extended to me was witty and apposite. It was proposed by the Reverend Sidney Gold, senior minister of Birmingham's old-established Singers Hill Congregation, who recalled an episode in Victor Hugo's novel, *Les Misérables*, where Jean Valjean, the hero, steals a pair of silver candlesticks from the home of his benefactor, the bishop. "Now," said Gold, "a Jewish bishop has come, he has taken our silver, and the community offers him a vote of thanks!" The next morning, before proceeding to my next rendezvous, I was received by Birmingham's Jewish Lord Mayor.

In Liverpool, I recalled the wartime meeting I had addressed there during the blackout. Gerald Strong, the local JPA chairman, took good care of me. Now, as then, Liverpool was an excellent Zionist city, contributing much to Israel in terms of finance and Aliyah. Merseyside Jewry had also "exported" religious leaders to many parts of the English-speaking world. Rabbi Isser Yehudah Unterman, Liverpool's onetime communal *Rav*, was to be installed shortly as the Ashkenazi Chief Rabbi of Israel. It was gratifying that people remembered my visits to Liverpool in 1949 and in 1959.

Returning to London on Friday, I addressed a luncheon meeting of the World Jewish Congress (British Section) Executive. The next morning, I attended Sabbath services at the Central Synagogue on Great Portland Street, where Sir Isaac Wolfson was president. Later, while dining with the Wolfsons at their apartment nearby, I learned that my host had almost clinched an important oil deal in the Soviet Union when he was told that no supplies must reach Israel, whereupon he promptly broke off his negotiations.

Since Aliyah and Hebrew are two basic points in my Zionist *Shulḥan Arukh*, I was glad to accompany Levi Gertner, the Jewish Agency's education director, to a Saturday night function where I addressed a Hebrew-speaking circle. Two days later, I was invited to record two talks in Hebrew, on my impressions of Eastern Europe, for the BBC's Overseas Service. Before leaving for Paris on January 22, I gave briefings to Zionist keyworkers in London and Manchester.

My few days in the French capital were mainly devoted to organizational matters. Fund raising became part of my business again in Belgium. The campaign dinner held in Brussels, and attended by Israel Ambassador Emile Najar and his wife, was also graced by the presence of Gaston Eyskens, a former Belgian Prime Minister, who had once played host to Ben-Gurion. He delivered a warm address, in the course of which he called for Israel's admission to the European Common Market.

From the Jewish angle, Antwerp is very different from Brussels. Nearly all of the Jews are of Eastern European origin and many, including large groups of Ḥasidim, arrived there after World War II. The community was split between the modern Orthodox *Shomré Hadass* congregation and the ultra-Orthodox *Machsiké Hadass*, each with its own network of synagogues, *Kashrut* authorities, and educational institutions. Zionist families, including Antwerp's strong Mizraḥi following, were affiliated with the *Shomré Hadass*, which prided itself on a fine central synagogue on Van den Nestlei. The rival congregation's membership largely comprised Agudat Yisrael supporters. The exclusively Orthodox complexion of Antwerp Jewry remains unique in Western Europe.

It was fascinating to visit the Diamond Exchange, an overwhelmingly Jewish environment, where the members' restaurant served *kasher* meals. I was told that every deal, whether for an average sum or for hundreds of thousands of dollars, was closed with the Yiddish phrase, *"Mazzel un Brokhe!"*—"Good luck and Blessing!" Even non-Jews closed deals with this formula.

My stay in Belgium prompted a certain Mr. Chanania to write me a letter describing his wartime experience as a Jew hiding from the Nazis in occupied Holland, and the effect produced on him by a broadcast talk on Purim which I had recorded for the BBC (see chapter 4).

One of my rewarding experiences while touring various countries on behalf of Keren Hayesod was meeting hundreds of Jewish communal leaders and forging bonds of friendship with many of them. Among the personalities who greatly impressed me was the Italian industrialist, Astorre Mayer. An enthusiastic Hebraist, he served as honorary consul for Israel in his native city, Milan, and he also helped to establish the Haderah Paper Mills in Israel.

Another Jewish communal figure, whose acquaintance I first made when visiting Geneva during my campaign tour, was Nessim Gaon. A man of wealth, spirit, and leadership, he played an increasingly important role in Jewish affairs. Nessim Gaon now serves with distinction as president of the World Sephardi Federation. To Sephardim in Israel and throughout the world, he has been a great patron and champion.

Preeminent among the world's Jewish nobility is the house of Rothschild, with its branches in London and Paris. My travels had brought me into contact with Baron Guy de Rothschild, the senior member of the Paris family, whose cousin, Alain, had succeeded him as president of the Consistoire, the religious "establishment" of French Jewry. Baroness Bethsabée de Rothschild, a patroness of the arts, was soon to found Batsheva, a dance company bearing her Hebrew name, in Tel Aviv. As yet, however, I had not had the opportunity to meet their younger cousin, Baron Edmond, a namesake of his illustrious grandfather—the philanthropist whom Israelis style "the Father of the Yishuv."

This opportunity presented itself when I came to Geneva for the *magbit* and attended a campaign dinner at the new Intercontinental Hotel. Baron Edmond de Rothschild, then in his late thirties, was the host and his wife and mother accompanied him. Though committed primarily to Israel Bonds, he responded to my appeal. His wife was interested in learning Hebrew and I offered some suggestions. They had a six-month-old son, Benjamin. When I ventured to suggest that the Baron establish something in the child's name, he told me about his idea to set up a school for diplomatic service and administration in Israel. Our conversation then switched to Zionism. "I'm not a Zionist," said the Baron, "but I believe that there is no future for the Jewish people without Israel." His definition of non-Zionism amused me. "In that case," I replied, "I am a member of your 'non-Zionist' club."

Jean Brunschvig, the splendid chairman of our *magbit* in Geneva, had no reason to complain of that evening's appeal, a 250-percent increase over the previous year's total. Baron Edmond was leaving the next day for Israel, where he was to open a new hotel in Caesarea. My wife and I accepted his invitation to attend the opening ceremony. It is worth mentioning that the Baron headed the Comité de Solidarité avec Israël from 1967.

Meetings of the Claims Conference generally coincided with those of COJO and the World Jewish Congress, enabling the participants to attend a number of different organizational sessions within a period of a few days. Thus, after concluding my Keren Hayesod business, I often had the opportunity to participate in other meetings and to discuss with colleagues the whole gamut of issues facing Israel, the Zionist movement, and World Jewry. The several bodies meeting in the same city had an interlocking leadership, and it was usually Dr. Nahum Goldmann who presided over their deliberations.

On March 4, 1964, a week-long meeting of the Claims Conference opened in Brussels. Nahum Goldmann had already told me of his plan to use most of the last German payment to establish a cultural fund and to help finance Bet ha-Tefutzot, the Museum of the Jewish Diaspora, which he planned to build and develop in Israel. The cultural fund soon acquired impressive dimensions as the Memorial Foundation for Jewish Culture.

While in Brussels, I also attended sessions of the World Jewish Congress at which we heard reports on the rising tide of anti-Semitic agitation in Latin America. Unstable economic and political conditions posed the main threat to Jews in Argentina. The activities of the Arab League, neo-Nazi propaganda, and the attitude of the Catholic Church were additional disturbing factors throughout the Central and South American region.

A separate report on South Africa indicated the concern felt by Jews there over the withdrawal of Israel's diplomatic representative from Pretoria. Even before Sharpeville and the Soweto riots, most Jews believed that a clash between repressed Blacks and dominant Whites could not be avoided, yet no increase in Aliyah had been discerned.

Subsequently, at a meeting of COJO, Moshe Sharett spoke about the Russian scene and Dr. Gerhart Riegner surveyed the latest round of contacts with the Vatican. Label Katz, reporting on developments in the United States, disclosed that both the American Jewish Committee and the Synagogue Council had agreed to join the Presidents' Conference. This was a significant turning point in the quest for American Jewish unity.

Together with Moshe Sharett, I left Brussels in mid-March to visit the Monumenta Judaica exhibition in Cologne. Near the Rhine, crowned by the world's highest spire, stood Cologne Cathedral, the famous *Kölner Dom*, which took more than five centuries to complete. In another part of the city where Chancellor Konrad

Adenauer had served as Bürgermeister (Mayor) until the Hitler era, we saw and visited the Cologne Synagogue, newly restored after its destruction by the Nazis. For me, this synagogue had a special importance, because it was here that Dr. Adolf Kober had ministered between the two World Wars. He and his family had found refuge in New York after receiving affidavits from my congregation, B'nai Jeshurun, and he remained associated with us until his death in 1958. I also helped him to secure a research fellowship from the German Claims Conference. After the end of World War II, Dr. Kober was made an honorary citizen of Cologne and a street was named there in his honor.

Two thousand years of Jewish history and culture in the Rhineland were reflected in the Monumenta Judaica exhibits. These portrayed ancient Jewish settlements of the Roman period, Christianity's debt to Judaism, evidence concerning "ritual murder" charges and persecution by the Church, economic and social life, Jewish craftsmanship and some old Passover *Haggadot*. Among the modern exhibits I saw a photostat of the letter in which Theodor Herzl wrote that, had he known of the proto-Zionist essays by Moses Hess and Leon Pinsker, he would not have published his own book, *The Jewish State*.

Cologne had staged this exhibition with typical German thoroughness, and a comprehensive, illustrated guidebook was available. Ironically enough, Dr. Kober had organized the Jewish section of an earlier and general exhibition on Rhenish history in 1925, some years before the eclipse of German Jewry.

Shortly after my return to Israel, intensive discussions took place between WZO leaders and Government ministers with regard to the Zionist movement's effectiveness in the Diaspora. It was alleged that the Israel Government itself had contributed to the Zionist Organization's declining prestige. Among those who made practical suggestions were Labor Minister Yigal Allon, who believed that Zionist values must be reemphasized in order to discourage Yeridah, and Education Minister Zalman Aranne, who called for the establishment of training schools to prepare Israelis for teaching posts in the *Golah*. Levi Eshkol, who had succeeded Ben-Gurion as Prime Minister the preceding June, advocated the formation of a Jewish Peace Corps when he addressed the Zionist General Council that same week.

The urgent need for a coordinated worldwide program of Jewish education, which I reiterated during my travels abroad, also loomed large in my address when I took part in a World Jewish Congress symposium on July 14, entitled "Israel and the Diaspora." My fellow panelists were President Eliahu Elath and Professor Moshe Davis of the Hebrew University and Professor Baruch Kurzweil of Bar-Ilan University. I urged that the overseas *kehillot*, the World Zionist Organization, and Medinat Yisrael all had a vital role to play. "The Jewish people," I concluded, "needs a well-planned program of Jewish survival. But in addition to a strategy of Jewish survival, it needs a High Command representing its two segments, Israel and Diaspora Jewry."

A year earlier, in 1963, Bert and I had celebrated Passover in Jerusalem with a *Seder* in our new home in Talbieh. Our guests on that occasion had included the governor of the Bank of Israel, David Horowitz, the British ambassador, the U.S. consul general, and their wives. Also present was the ambassador of the Ivory Coast, for whom we had managed to obtain a *Haggadah* with French translation.

This year, however, we were invited to join Meyer and Shirley Weisgal at the Weizmann Institute in Reḥovot, and I conducted part of the *Seder* in their home. Apart from U.S. Ambassador Walworth Barbour, most of those who came were executives and benefactors of the Weizmann Institute, notably Dewey Stone, chairman of the board of governors, and his wife, Sir Isaac and Lady Wolfson, the Clores, the Feinbergs, the Goldenbergs, and the Wixes. Abe Feinberg had brought the Coca-Cola industry to Israel. The following morning, I accompanied Sir Isaac Wolfson to Passover services in Reḥovot. After the termination of Shabbat and *Yom Tov*, Bert and I drove to Tel Aviv, where we saw and enjoyed the Hebrew stage version of *My Fair Lady*.

The next morning we left for Eilat. There we met Robert Sherwood of Geneva and his wife. Mr. Sherwood was providing financial backing for a new desalination process. There was one desalination plant in Eilat, designed by Alexander Zarchin, an Israeli engineer and inventor.

Later in the year, we saw Israel's main water carrier at Tabgha, near Tiberias, on Lake Kinneret, where enormous pumps raised the water to a level sufficient to propel it through Israel along pollution-free canals.

It was a pleasant change to be unhampered by overseas commitments during the spring and summer of 1964. A number of interesting events took place at about this time. Two which I attended in an official capacity were Holocaust Memorial Day, on April 9, and (three days later) the installation of Tel Aviv's Chief Rabbi, Isser Yehudah Unterman, as Ashkenazi Chief Rabbi of Israel. A special Holocaust Day program was arranged by the Jewish National Fund in the Martyrs' Forest, where I spoke on behalf of Yad Vashem.

The post of Ashkenazi Chief Rabbi had been vacant since the death of Dr. Isaac Halevi Herzog in 1959. As world chairman of Keren Hayesod, I had been invited to act as one of the new Chief Rabbi's escorts at the induction ceremony, held in the presence of President Zalman Shazar and a distinguished gathering, at Hechal Shlomo. The sounding of shofarot in counterpoint, the fine singing of a cantor and choir, and the attendance of Christian and Muslim religious dignitaries all contributed to an impressive ceremonial event. Rabbi Unterman was enthroned on a canopied rostrum, with the Rishon Le-Tziyyon, Sephardi Chief Rabbi Itzḥak Nissim, seated next to him. Prime Minister Levi Eshkol, the Religious Affairs Minister, Dr. Zeraḥ Warhaftig, and Rabbi Nissim delivered the most important addresses, next to that of the new Chief Rabbi.

I was also present at the opening of Yad ha-Rav Maimon, about two months later. This new institute in Jerusalem perpetuated the memory of Rabbi Yehudah-Leib Maimon, a founder of World Mizraḥi and friend of Rav Kook, who had served as Israel's first Minister of Religious Affairs. His able son-in-law, Yitzḥak Raphael, presided at the opening ceremony. David Ben-Gurion, Rabbi Zvi Yehudah Kook (son of the late Rav Kook and a future spiritual mentor of Gush Emunim), Interior

Minister and National Religious Party leader Ḥayyim Moshe Shapira, and Moshe Sharett were the principal speakers. Ben-Gurion's address was full of affectionate reminiscences. He spoke of Rabbi Maimon's two great loves—*ahavat Yisrael* and *ahavat Torah*—and stressed the need for Jewish unity across religious differences.

Israel Independence Day that year had its focus in Beersheba. We arrived there on Wednesday, April 15, the eve of Yom Ha-Atzma'ut. After dinner, Bert and I left our hotel to see the dancing and a fireworks display. The Beersheba we had known in 1948–49—a small town with some 2,000 inhabitants, nearly all of them Arabs— was now a city of 62,000 people, nearly all Jews, and the capital of the Negev. On the following day, we saw an impressive, superbly organized military parade, the highlight of which was a display by the Israel Air Force.

One week later, we had a dinner party at our home for two visiting Jewish writers from the United States, Chaim Grade and Charles Angoff. Our other guests included Ethel Agron, Rina Nikova, and Gideon Rafael of the Israel Foreign Ministry. Grade, an eminent Yiddish poet and novelist, had grown up in Vilna, Lithuania, and as a *yeshivah-bokher* had studied under Rabbi Avraham Karelitz, the celebrated Ḥazon Ish. Lithuanian Jewish life and the Holocaust were recurrent motifs in his writings. I had heard him lecture on these just two days before, when Professor Dov Sadan introduced him to the audience. He was on his second visit to Israel, as the guest of President Shazar, and he spoke rhapsodically about Safed and the kibbutzim he had seen.

Quite by chance, I happened to meet Chaim Grade a fortnight afterwards, when we were both visiting Kfar Ḥabad. This village, near Ramleh, was established by Lubavitcher (Ḥabad) Ḥasidim in 1949, and it has since become the educational and industrial center of their movement in Israel. There were about eighty families living there at the time. We saw printing and carpentry shops and a large yeshivah, as well as a girls' vocational school. Unlike the Neturei Karta fanatics whom they derided, the Ḥabadniks proved friendly and tolerant, although there was no disguising their eagerness to convert other Jews to their particular religious outlook.

Knowing that Rabbi Menaḥem Mendel Schneersohn, the current Lubavitcher Rebbe, lived and remained in New York's Williamsburg area, I asked some of the villagers why he had never visited Israel. "When there is something to be done here which only he can do, then he will come," they replied. I asked if he had any children and they said, "No, but all the Ḥasidim are his sons and daughters."

For all my differences with the Ḥasidim and their mystical philosophy, I do share their fondness for music. My taste, however, embraces everything from *Ḥazzanut*, the art of the synagogue cantor, to opera, ballet, and the symphony concert. I retain affectionate memories of that great cantor, "Reb Yossele" (Josef) Rosenblatt. It was also my privilege to address the Cantors' Assembly held in the Hebrew University's Wise Auditorium one evening in July 1964.

A musical event in a class of its own was the concert given by the Israel Philharmonic Orchestra in 1961, when Pablo Casals appeared as guest conductor in Jerusalem. The great cellist was then in his mideighties, but still vigorous, although he had to conduct the orchestra from a specially constructed high chair. Ben-Gurion presented him with a medal. It was a rare experience to see so much courage and humanity combined with the musical genius of a master.

In January 1964, Leonard Bernstein came to Israel for a performance of his *Kaddish* Symphony. We gave a luncheon for him at our home, when Jennie Tourel (the mezzo-soprano) and Hannah Rovina (Israel's leading actress) were our other guests. In May, we attended a reception for Arthur Rubinstein at the home of Golda Meir, following a concert by the virtuoso pianist. Rubinstein, who proclaimed his love for Israel, said that his father had been a friend of Nahum Sokolow and had written for *Hatzefirah*. "I am a chauvinistic Jew," he declared. "All the great musicians are Jews!" On the following day, a chair in musicology was established in his name at the Hebrew University in appreciation of the fact that Rubinstein had never taken payment for his concerts in Israel. Less than a fortnight later, we were among those invited to honor Isaac Stern at a reception given by Dr. Dov Joseph and at a luncheon given by the governing board of the Israel Philharmonic Orchestra.

Another musical occasion, in mid-June, led to an interesting encounter. We had decided to spend a long Shavu'ot weekend at the kibbutz guest house at Kiryat Anavim, a few miles west of Jerusalem, and also to attend the annual Bach festival in nearby Abu Ghosh. The Arab village of Abu Ghosh takes its name from a predatory sheikh who once extracted money from passing travelers thereabouts. Its inhabitants had cooperated with the Haganah and Lehi fighters during the British Mandate period, remained loyal to Israel in the War of Liberation, and had prospered. An old Crusader church in the village contains archaeological evidence of the fact that the Roman Tenth Legion, which besieged Jerusalem on the eve of the Temple's destruction, once encamped in the area.

We met Haj Musa Abu Ghosh, the *mukhtar* (headman), who ran a café in the village and who introduced us to his brother. The latter, a graduate of Brandeis University, had taken a doctorate in political science at Princeton. His thesis dealt with self-government in Arab villages, and he was then seeking a post at one of Israel's universities. When Dr. Subhi Abu Ghosh spoke about the need for better educational facilities there, I promised to raise the matter with the appropriate authorities. This promise I kept, and satisfactory results were obtained.

This was the time of year when I customarily visited installations supported by the Altschul Foundation in various parts of the country, together with other institutions in which I took a close interest. One of these was Moshav Udim, near Netanyah. Another was Kibbutz Ha-Solelim, about half of whose settlers had immigrated from the United States and other English-speaking lands. I was shown around by David Ben-Nahum, a fellow Philadelphian. We talked, among other things, about religion. My host thought that there would be a future in Israel for a modernized interpretation of Judaism and he asked why the Jewish Theological Seminary did not send emissaries to kibbutzim such as his own. I shared his view and continued to press the matter when speaking with colleagues in the Conservative rabbinate who were visiting Israel.

Professor Louis Finkelstein, chancellor of the Seminary, was one of those with whom I discussed such ideas. His major concern, however, appeared to be the

Israel Chief Rabbinate's refusal to recognize marriages and divorces performed under Conservative auspices in America. At one stage, Chief Rabbi Nissim had seemed agreeable to some sort of accommodation, but later he had retreated from that position. Finkelstein was unwilling to force the issue. He did not respond to my proposal of rabbinical *halutziut,* and I told him that, in my view, Reform was taking command of the "protestant" movement in Israel.

On one occasion, three years after our Aliyah, when Louis Finkelstein came to have tea with us one Shabbat afternoon in June 1964, I had the satisfaction of hearing him say, "I was wrong to think you would not stay in Israel, but would return to New York."

Earlier that month, the tenth *Yahrzeit* of Professor Louis Ginzberg was observed at the Seminary's Jerusalem Student Center in Neveh Schechter. The great scholar's distinguished son, Dr. Eli Ginzberg, offered an evaluation of his late father. I was intrigued to hear some little-known facts concerning this great-grandnephew of Rabbi Eliyahu ben Shlomo Zalman, the famous Gaon of Vilna. When he came from America to spend a year (1928–29) as visiting professor of Halakhah at the Hebrew University, Louis Ginzberg had been unhappy about Zionist handling of the Arabs. Presumably, his attitude had been similar to that of Magnes, Buber, and other intellectuals of the Brit Shalom group. Eli Ginzberg also disclosed that when his father, a graduate of several Lithuanian yeshivot, first came to teach at Hebrew Union College, the contract was canceled by Rabbi Isaac M. Wise, the "Father of American Reform," because Louis Ginzberg's approach to the Bible was "too radical"! HUC's loss had clearly been the Seminary's gain.

There were two other occasions for special remembrance in 1964. One was the first *Yahrzeit* of the late President Itzhak Ben-Zvi. Bert visited his grave on Mount Herzl, while I attended a meeting of Yad Ben-Zvi at the residence of President Shazar and a memorial assembly at Bet Ha-Am, where Knesset Speaker Kadish Luz delivered a eulogy.

The reinterment of the remains of Ze'ev Jabotinsky proved to be a momentous event. In his will, written some time before his death in 1940, Jabotinsky had stipulated: "My remains will be transferred to Eretz Yisrael only on the instructions of a Jewish Government." Since the founding of Israel, Ben-Gurion had remained implacably opposed to any such transfer, but Prime Minister Levi Eshkol had now decided to fulfill the Revisionist leader's last request. As Moshe Sharett reported at a meeting of the Jewish Agency Executive in April, Dr. Eri Jabotinsky, only son of the deceased, wished his father to be buried next to Theodor Herzl. It was, however, impossible to arrange this. In every other respect, the Israel Government strove to honor Jabotinsky's memory and it accorded him a state funeral.

On July 9, the coffin, which had been flown to Israel from New York and had then received public homage in Jerusalem's Independence Park, was taken to Mount Herzl, with stops en route at Hechal Shlomo and the Knesset. Members of the Betar youth movement, as well as Israeli soldiers, lined the approaches to the cemetery. Rose Halprin and I went as representatives of the World Conferation of General Zionists. It was fitting that Menahem Begin, the Herut Party leader, delivered the principal memorial address. Those present included President Shazar, Prime Minister Eshkol, the Chief Rabbis, Government ministers and Knesset members, and the heads of the WZO and the Jewish Agency. Ben-Gurion was conspicuously absent.

At the end of July, I left for Geneva to attend another meeting of the Claims Conference executive committee. Our main business was concerned with the new Memorial Foundation for Jewish Culture, established on the initiative of Dr. Nahum Goldmann. It was to serve as a living memorial to the six million Jews who had perished in the Nazi Holocaust. An endowment of $22 million had been obtained, consisting of residual funds donated by the Conference on Jewish Material Claims against Germany. The principal objects of the Foundation are to foster Jewish scholarship, to train young Jews for communal service, to support university programs of Jewish studies, and, in general, to work for the preservation and transmission of Jewish culture throughout the world. Allocations are made to cover only a small proportion of the total cost of any project. The Foundation has since its inception placed special emphasis on grants to encourage documentation and research on the Holocaust. Its board of trustees comprises representatives of major Jewish organizations thoughout the world, reflecting all the significant trends in Jewish life.

At a subsequent session of the Memorial Foundation held in the summer of 1966, Nahum Goldmann emphasized some of its main priorities. He stated that there were thirty vacancies for professors of Jewish studies at American and European universities. To fill these posts, more young Jews must be encouraged to qualify as scholars in the field. Time and money should not be frittered away on insignificant matters. I was gratified to note one practical outcome—a substantial allocation of funds to the Jewish Agency for the enlargement of the Hayim Greenberg and Rabbi Gold institutes, which train teachers and youth leaders for service in Diaspora communities.

Soon after my return from Western Europe in the early part of 1964, the Reverend Peter Schneider called to tell me about a new interdenominational "club" he was planning to establish. The Rainbow Group would consist of seven Jews, seven Protestants, and seven Catholics, and he was eager for me to join. Once I had satisfied myself that he and his Christian associates had no ulterior, conversionist motives, I agreed to become involved in this fellowship. My own experience as one of the founders of the National Conference of Christians and Jews in America and of the International Conference of Christians and Jews had predisposed me to genuine interreligious dialogue.

There were also other reasons that motivated my decision to join the Rainbow Group. I believed that in Israel, where Jews are the majority, they owe a special debt of honor to religious minorities. Here, the Jewish majority did not have to worry about safeguarding its own position, as was the case with Jewish communities abroad. Whatever usefulness it might possess, this interfaith "club" could become a meaningful model of interfaith relations and its repercussions might be felt abroad.

In Israel, moreover, I felt more at ease with Christian friends and colleagues than in the United States. There, I had often heard talk of the "five-o'clock barrier," which divided Jews from Christians at the end of the working day. Although this had not been my own experience, I nevertheless recognized it to be true in a general sense.

As an Israeli Jew, I felt the need of the Rainbow Group's spiritual comradeship, extending across denominational lines.

The Rainbow Group commenced its activities in 1965, with a limited membership of ten Jews and ten Christians. Its first chairman was Dr. R. J. Zwi Werblowsky, professor of comparative religion at the Hebrew University. He did much to provide it with the desired imprimatur. Two of its leading Christian spokesmen were the Most Reverend George Appleton, the Anglican Archbishop in Jerusalem, and Father Marcel Dubois.

Monthly meetings take place, at which the reading of a paper is followed by open discussion. An atmosphere of mutual confidence governs the proceedings. There are Catholic and Protestant members of the Rainbow Group with whom I would not hesitate to discuss any matter affecting Jewish-Christian relations.

As an independent source of opinion and information, the Rainbow Group performed valuable services for Israel during the Middle East crisis of 1967 and after the Six-Day War. In cooperation with the Department of Christian Communities of the Israel Ministry of Religious Affairs and the Israel Foreign Ministry's Ecclesiastical Affairs Department, this group also does much to enlighten Christian pilgrims and visitors from overseas. Its widely read "Christian Comment" feature, published monthly in *The Jerusalem Post*, reappears in a large range of periodicals outside Israel.

Several years later, in 1971, the Rainbow Group provided the impetus for a revitalization of the Israel Interfaith Committee. Unlike the Rainbow Group, this committee has a few Muslims and Druzes among its sponsors. The Israel Interfaith Committee has undertaken enlightenment and social action programs, has arranged visits to Arab population centers, and has been active in organizing and promoting a variety of lectures, conferences, and symposia. Part of its ongoing work has involved explaining Judaism and the Jewish experience to Arabs, Afro-Asian visitors, and Western Christians, as well as familiarizing Jews with the tenets of Christianity and Islam. These wide-ranging activities take place within the framework of meetings and seminars, including an annual symposium on a subject of major relevance to the Interfaith Committee. Its representatives are often sent abroad to participate in international conclaves.

Jewish members of the Committee's executive have included Professor Zwi Werblowsky, Dr. André Chouraqui, and Professor Shmaryahu Talmon. Among its most active non-Jews have been Archbishop Appleton, Father Marcel Dubois, Father Joseph Stiassny, and the Reverend Dr. Douglas Young. Dr. Young, a Baptist clergyman and staunch Israeli patriot who headed the Holy Land Bible Institute on Mount Zion, was awarded the title of *Yakir Yerushalayim*, Honored Citizen of Jerusalem. The devoted secretary of the Interfaith Committee throughout the years has been Joseph Emanuel.

I have considered it a privilege to serve for many years as one of the honorary presidents of the Israel Interfaith Committee.

As was our custom, my wife and I spent the summer vacation period of 1964 in the United States, visiting with our children, grandchildren, and other kin, and renewing old acquaintances. Nevertheless, I found myself attending meetings of the Jewish Agency Executive in New York, involved in the problems of the Histadrut Ivrit, and addressing an occasional gathering of the American Jewish League for Israel (a constituent of the World Confederation of General Zionists). I also maintained my contact with the Jewish Conciliation Board of America. That summer, I flew to Los Angeles for Hadassah's "Salute to Freedom" convention, where I delivered an address. At this convention, Charlotte Jacobson was elected president of Hadassah.

As usual while vacationing in the United States, I appeared with Dr. Ormond Drake in the Columbia Broadcasting System's television program, *The Way to Go*, which presented interviews with religious leaders of all denominations. For some years prior to our Aliyah, Dr. Drake's *Church of the Air* program on Sunday mornings had given me the opportunity of discussing Jewish and Zionist topics, and I welcomed his renewed invitations to do so on our annual visits to the U.S. During the High Holy Days, I shared the pulpit of my congregation with Rabbi William Berkowitz.

On September 14, 1964, Bert and I presented our portraits of Michael Gratz and Rebecca Gratz to the Jewish Theological Seminary Art Center. The presentation took place in the JTS synagogue, with Professor Louis Finkelstein presiding. Rabbi Simon Greenberg accepted the gifts on behalf of the Seminary.

A week later we were back in Haifa, embarking on a sea voyage to the islands of Greece with the Israel Exploration Society, which was celebrating its fiftieth anniversary. The Zim shipping line had been involved in a great deal of controversy that year because of the second, non-*kasher* kitchen installed in one of its new liners, the S.S. *Shalom*, which aimed to attract an international, partly non-Jewish clientele. Fortunately, our ship, the S.S. *Theodor Herzl*, was unaffected by the political and religious storm, and we had a most interesting cruise. On board, Bert and I were in the midst of a bevy of archaeologists, including Professors Yohanan Aharoni, Michael Avi-Yonah, Benjamin Mazar, and Yigael Yadin. We met Professor Mazar again toward the end of the year, at En Gedi, where he was excavating a site of the late biblical period.

My Keren Hayesod duties during the latter part of 1964 and early 1965 took me to several Western European communities, including Sweden. I found Swedish Jewry to be highly assimilated, with a frightening rate of intermarriage. The 300 Jewish families in Göteborg had built themselves a palatial new community center, but the only person qualified to direct its activities whom they had been able to find was a non-Jew. He showed me the library. Most of the Jewish books on the shelves had never been opened; I could almost hear them weep.

In one respect, Swedish Jewry is unique: its Chief Rabbinate and main synagogues are non-Orthodox. Their ritual and approach may be likened to those of Liberal Judaism in prewar Germany or of the *Neolog* community in postwar Hungary, avoiding the extremes of Reform. In Stockholm, the Great Synagogue adhered to this pattern, but there were also two smaller Orthodox congregations and a Jewish day school supported by the Orthodox and the Zionists. Chief Rabbi Kurt Wilhelm, whom I met there, was a graduate of the Jewish Theological Seminaries in both Breslau and New York. He had left for Eretz Yisrael in 1933, and had been one of the founders of Emet Ve-Emunah, a congregation of mainly German Olim in Jerusalem. This synagogue, which I had visited from time to time, was Conservative in affiliation but close to Orthodoxy in its practice. One of its leading spirits has been Professor Akiba Ernst Simon. Rabbi Wilhelm left Israel in 1948, when he was appointed Chief Rabbi of Sweden. Both he and his successor, Rabbi Aharon Philipp, received an authorization to perform marriages from Israel's late Chief Rabbi, Dr. Isaac Halevi Herzog.

The Jewish historical exhibition I had visited in Cologne less than a year previously was fresh in mind when I came to Frankfurt am Main early in 1965. One of the oldest of all German *kehillot*, the Jewish community of Frankfurt had an illustrious history of rabbinic learning and leadership, philanthropic and social endeavor, Jewish cultural life and publishing. Among the eminent Jewish families which originated in this city were the Rothschilds and the Schiffs. Frankfurt had also been the scene of a momentous struggle between religious traditionalists and the extreme Reformers headed by Abraham Geiger in the mid-nineteenth century. It was as a result of that conflict that Rabbi Samson Raphael Hirsch established his separatist Orthodox *Austrittsgemeinde*, which became an influential trend not only in Germany but even further afield. Here, too, in 1920, Franz Rosenzweig founded his popular institute of Jewish studies, the Jüdisches Lehrhaus, where Martin Buber and other scholars first made their reputation. Zionism had had no stauncher champion than Rabbi Nehemiah Anton Nobel, a Mizrahi leader and intellectual, nor Agudism two more dogged exponents than Dr. Isaac Breuer and Jakob Rosenheim. Yet all of this lay in an almost forgotten past. Twenty years after the downfall of Hitlerism, Frankfurt Jewry—though next in size to that of West Berlin—was but a shadow of its former self.

My visit happened to coincide with the twentieth anniversary of the liberation of Auschwitz, and "Do not forget!" was the central theme of the sermon I was invited to deliver in the Great Synagogue of Frankfurt on January 23. Speaking in Yiddish, I recalled my errand of mercy to Holocaust survivors in occupied Germany soon after the end of World War II. Referring to those brave non-Jews who had risked their own lives to save Jews from the Gestapo, and whose actions now brought recognition at Yad Vashem, I said that there had been hundreds of such Righteous Gentiles, yet their numbers only accentuated the extent of collaboration with the Nazis in a dozen or more occupied countries. What had happened at Auschwitz, Bergen-Belsen, Dachau, and all the other death camps must become part of our national memory, like the Temple's destruction and Masada, and must be taught to our children.

There was a profound truth in a saying of the Kotzker Rebbe, *"A gantzer Yid iz a Yid mit a tzerbrokhener Hartz"*—"Only a Jew with a broken heart is a whole Jew."

This "Remember—do not forget" theme was applicable to postwar Germany, I declared. Conscience demanded that there be no statute of limitations on the arrest and prosecution of Nazi war criminals still at large. "What is the hurry?" I asked. "Is West Germany tired of being reminded of those criminals who did not tire of killing Jews?"

The term *Wiedergutmachung,* signifying "restitution," should be taken as a challenge by Jews themselves, I said, to "make good" at least part of the intellectual, spiritual, and psychological damage done to the Jewish people. Two remedies were available—Jewish education and Aliyah:

> My urgent plea to the Jews of Germany is not only to do their part in financial support of the program of *Kibbutz Galuyyot.* . . . That is not enough. You and your children should be in Israel in the nearest possible time. You and your children need Israel in order to fulfill your lives as Jews.

Congregation B'nai Jeshurun celebrated its one hundred fortieth anniversary in May 1966 and I was gratified to receive both a heartwarming personal message from President Zalman Shazar and a letter from Prime Minister Levi Eshkol, extending greetings and mentioning a visit he had once paid to "this historic synagogue steeped in its almost century and half of tradition." Another commemoration of importance to me personally was the forty-fifth anniversary of the Jewish Conciliation Board of America, with which my thirty-five years as president were linked. In response to the pleas of my colleagues, I had agreed to retain my presidency of the Board even after leaving New York for Israel, but the time had come for other hands to take control and I was confident that a suitable successor would be found. The burden of responsibility was not lifted from my shoulders, however, until the annual meeting of the Jewish Conciliation Board in 1968, when Rabbi Julius Mark, of Temple Emanu-El in New York, agreed to take over the presidency.

From time to time during our first few years in Israel, the attempts made by non-Orthodox groups to establish congregations of their own were fiercely resisted by the religious establishment. An alliance of Orthodox and secular forces occasionally prevented such groups from using or hiring premises for worship on Sabbaths and festivals. In an address delivered before the Commercial Club in Tel Aviv at the beginning of February 1966, subsequently reported in *Hayom,* I affirmed that "when a Reform or Conservative congregation, because of the pressure by Orthodox bodies, is denied the possibility of housing in a public building, it blemishes Israel's image not only in the eyes of the world but particularly in the eyes of World Jewry." I also pointed to the instructive example of a proper working relationship between Orthodox, Conservative, and Reform congregations in the United States, as these were represented in the Synagogue Council of America. Another lesson Israel could afford to learn from American Jewry, I stated, was how synagogues might also serve as community centers to attract broader sections of Israeli youth.

Sensitive to the conflicting pressures, the Government of Israel issued a formal statement affirming the basic right of every citizen to freedom of religion. According to this statement, "every person in Israel is entitled to pray wherever he wishes and in the form he wishes." However, despite such reassurances, the fact remains that "religious pluralism" among Jews continues to be a vexed issue in Medinat Yisrael.

During the mid-1960s, new political and economic factors were eroding the security of many Jews in Latin America. While Argentina's neo-Nazis, the *Tacuara*, constituted the most obvious menace, left-wing urban guerillas were attacking people and property, and even old-fashioned graft had begun to assume new and more subtle forms. At a meeting of the Keren Hayesod Directorion in November 1963, someone told us of a man in a certain Latin American country who could only clinch a business deal by bribing a government minister. He sent him a volume of poetry with a dollar bill attached to each page. The minister replied, thanking the man for his gift and stating that he was under the impression that a second volume of the poetry had appeared.

Soon after Passover in the spring of 1966, I was on my way to Brazil. My last visit to that vast republic had taken place four years earlier, but my contacts with the Brazilian Jewish community had kept me in touch with the situation there, which was relatively encouraging. The one untoward development in Brazil had been the enactment of a law banning propaganda that might lead to emigration, and its effect was to hamper our efforts for Aliyah. In April 1964, when news of this law reached the Jewish Agency Executive, I had briefed Deputy Defense Minister Shim'on Peres, who was then about to conduct a *magbit* for us in Brazil. Peres, one of Ben-Gurion's younger confidants, had since left Mapai to become secretary-general of the new Rafi faction in the Knesset. In June of the same year, I had given a luncheon at Bet Shalom, the Keren Hayesod hospitality center in Jerusalem, for Israel Klabin, a young representative of the prominent and wealthy Klabin family, which controlled an empire of paper manufacturing and allied industries in São Paulo. He told me then that his children would only have a future as Jews in Israel. Sixteen years later, in 1980, Senhor Klabin had risen to become Mayor of Rio de Janeiro.

My main speech in Brazil took the form of an Israel Independence Day address delivered in Rio, on April 24, and repeated in São Paulo the next day. I offered some firsthand impressions of Israel's establishment in 1948 and a *tour d'horizon* of the eighteen-year-old State—its political and military achievements, cultural and spiritual dimension, economic development and technical aid to other countries. The Egyptian dictator's latest warlike threats, the Middle East balance of power, and the fate of Soviet Jewry also figured in this speech.

I made a point of emphasizing Brazil's now traditional friendship with Israel and the forthcoming state visit by President Zalman Shazar, in whose honor Brazil later issued a special postage stamp. Aliyah, I said, not only strengthened Israel but also fortified spiritually those communities from which the Olim came. In conclusion, I stressed the need for an enduring partnership between the Jewish State and the communities of the Diaspora—"For we are one people, and our battlecry has been *eḥad:* one people, one God, one homeland, one past, one future."

Back in Israel, I was approaching my seventieth birthday. On June 18, 1966, a large contingent from the Youth Village, headed by Ze'ev Schickler, assembled in the Rose Garden near our home in order to greet me. A few days later, Dr. Nahum Goldmann, Rose Halprin, and Louis Aryeh Pincus, the treasurer of the Jewish Agency, spoke at a luncheon at the Youth Village, which U.S. Ambassador Walworth Barbour also attended. I had called on President Shazar in October 1964 to congratulate him on reaching the age of seventy-five, and he now did more than reciprocate by inviting a small group to Bet ha-Nasi on December 31 to mark my own anniversary.

"At Threescore and Ten" was a logical title for the sermon I delivered at Congregation B'nai Jeshurun on September 17, *Shabbat Shuvah*, during our annual visit to the United States. In essence, this *derashah*, inspired by the injunction of Moses in the portion of the week to "remember the days of yore and pay attention to the years of every generation," was my *ḥeshbon ha-nefesh*, appropriate to the season of spiritual stock-taking and self-criticism, and a recounting of those values I cherished most dearly. Rabbi Berkowitz welcomed me to the pulpit and Professor Mordecai Kaplan and Father George B. Ford, a wartime U.S. chaplaincy colleague, were present in the synagogue.

In the second half of July, after attending a meeting of the Conference of Jewish Organizations in Geneva, I had paid an official visit to Spain as world chairman of the Keren Hayesod. Bert accompanied me. Señor Max Mazin, president of the Madrid Jewish community, was leaving for his summer vacation when I called, but we received a warm welcome from several other members of the *kehillah*, which mainly comprised Ashkenazi and North African Jews.

A modest community center housing a synagogue and located inconspicuously off a broad avenue had been serving the Madrid *kehillah* for some years past. I spoke there on Friday night. After an initial greeting in Hebrew, I switched to English and commended their support of the *magbit* and their youth and educational program. A small Jewish school with about sixty pupils and a popular summer camp were maintained by the community. It opened a new and larger community center and place of worship in 1968, when a rabbi was appointed. He must have been the first religious leader of Spanish Jewry since the Expulsion of 1492. On the following Sunday, we visited Camp Masada, about half an hour's drive from Madrid. Two groups of sixty children each, ages seven to sixteen, spent consecutive periods of three weeks there. They hoisted the Spanish flag and they sang *Hatikvah* when the Israeli flag was raised. The boys all wore *kippot*. *Shaḥarit* services were held each day and grace after meals was recited. Through such activities, we were told, even the parents became more involved in Jewish communal life.

Our visit to Toledo, the ancient capital of Spain, was a voyage into history. The cathedral and the paintings of El Greco were most impressive. What interested us more particularly, however, was the rich evidence of Jewish life prior to the Expulsion. Next to what had once been the royal palace stood the restored El Tránsito Synagogue, built in 1357 by Don Samuel ben Meir Halevi Abulafia, treasurer of Pedro the Cruel. From 1497 it was used as a church, but the building has been declared a national monument and now serves as the Museum for the History of the Jews in Spain. Designed in Moorish style, with beautiful arabesques, the synagogue contains a decorative frieze of quotations from the Psalms in Hebrew lettering. A large model of part of the interior can now be seen in Bet ha-Tefutzot, the Museum of the Jewish Diaspora in Tel Aviv.

Street signs in and around the old Jewish quarter of Toledo recall a glorious past. In medieval times, this city was a foremost center of Jewish life and scholarship. Rabbi Moses Ibn Ezra, Rabbi Asher ben Yehiel (the Rosh), and his son, Rabbi Jacob ben Asher, were only three of the many great sages who flourished there. A century before the Expulsion, however, the persecutions of 1391 had virtually destroyed this *kehillah*.

We also visited the house of Don Samuel Halevi, where El Greco is said to have lived at a later stage. There were concealed passages underground, leading to the river, presumably to afford the inhabitants an escape from anti-Jewish mobs. Another and older synagogue, built in 1203, was converted into a church known as Santa Maria La Blanca in 1411. Now also a national monument, it has the characteristic Moorish arches but no inscriptions.

On July 18, the thirtieth anniversary of the outbreak of the Spanish Civil War, we went to the Valley of the Fallen outside Madrid, where we saw a huge monument to those—both Nationalists and Republicans—who died in the fighting.

Later that day, we left Madrid for the city of Palma, on the island of Majorca. In Palma Cathedral, the largest in Spain, we were inspecting various precious objects displayed in the treasury when I noticed among them a beautifully wrought staff surmounted by a silver crown and bells. Something about this particular item intrigued me and I therefore asked the sacristan if he could tell me what it was. "We call it a *Rimonium,*" he answered, "and it is carried by the Archbishop in special processions to the altar." I then explained that this object had clearly been one of the *rimmonim,* finials decorated with silver bells or ornaments shaped like pomegranates, which customarily adorn the upper rollers of a *Sefer Torah*. I was left wondering whether the sacristan would convey this information to the Archbishop.

While sightseeing in the town, we also visited the street of the goldsmiths and silversmiths and entered some of the shops. Such crafts had been a Jewish speciality in Palma during the Middle Ages and had been maintained by their converted (Marrano) descendants, who are known locally as *Chuetas*. About 300 *Chueta* families survive, despite centuries of ostracism and prejudice lingering even today. We discovered a few *Chueta* jewelers, who told us that General Franco had encouraged a tolerant policy toward them. It was extraordinary to think that the racist Spanish doctrine of *limpieza de sangre,* "purity of blood," still dogged these unfortunates. In 1966, the year of our visit, a number of *Chueta* families left for Israel in an attempt to recover their Jewish identity, but they found life in Israel too difficult and eventually returned to Majorca.

We flew back to the mainland for the completion of our tour of Spain. In Barcelona, there was a well-organized Jewish community of Ashkenazim and Sephardim, the latter having immigrated from Salonika and North Africa. We attended Sabbath services in the Barcelona Synagogue, where I addressed the members of the *kehillah*. Their leaders, together with the heads of the Madrid Jewish community, had been received by General Franco the previous year—the first such meeting to be convened by a Spanish head of state since the Expulsion of 1492.

On the final leg of our journey, Bert and I visited Córdoba and Seville. Like Toledo, Córdoba had once been a major center of Jewish intellectual activity and, as in the case of El Tránsito, its fourteenth-century synagogue (also a national monument) displayed friezes adorned with Hebrew passages from Psalms. Rabbi Moshe ben Maimon, Rambam or Maimonides, had lived in Córdoba as a small child and the eight hundredth anniversary of his birth was commemorated by the city in 1935. Two years before our visit, in 1964, a Maimonides Week had been held, in the course of which the municipality erected a statue in his honor. We saw this likeness of the brilliant Jewish philosopher, commentator, and physician in the Plazuela de Maimonides, a square in the old Jewish quarter which bears his name.

Our next destination was Brussels, where I attended meetings of the Claims Conference and the World Jewish Congress, both of them chaired by Dr. Nahum Goldmann. It was my assignment to introduce a symposium on "World Peace and Disarmament," held under the auspices of the WJC Assembly on August 1. The speakers on this occasion were Lord Ritchie Calder, president of the British National Peace Council, William Epstein, general secretary of the UN Disarmament Commission, and Professor Henri Laugier, who represented France on the Executive Board of UNESCO.

In my introductory remarks, I stressed the traditional Jewish pursuit of peace and the concern shown for these problems by world Jewish organizations at the present time. I also took occasion to mention my proposal for the establishment of a World Academy for Peace. East-West tensions and Nasser's warlike measures against Israel were very much in my mind when I said:

> The beating of swords into plowshares and of spears into pruning hooks, transposed into modern language, means the conversion of nuclear energy to peaceful purposes. It is not by chance that Isaiah's text was selected to be inscribed on the wall facing the United Nations headquarters in New York.

An important event in Israel was the dedication of the new Parliament building on August 30, 1966. For years, the Knesset had met in what had formerly been the offices of a bank in downtown Jerusalem. Now, a bequest from the estate of the late James de Rothschild had made possible the transfer to a magnificent structure near the Hebrew University's Givat Ram campus. Heading the procession of overseas dignitaries was the Speaker of the Icelandic Parliament, oldest of all parliamentary bodies, who conveyed greetings on their behalf. He was followed by President Zalman Shazar, Knesset Speaker Kadish Luz, Prime Minister Levi Eshkol, and WZO President Nahum Goldmann. Unfortunately, David Ben-Gurion could not attend because of illness, and his absence was keenly felt.

It was fitting that the widow of James de Rothschild, son of the "Father of the Yishuv," should have been asked to give the concluding address. Her words, which ended with a Hebrew quotation, brought the dedication ceremony to a moving climax. In the light of the full moon, we could see the flags of Israel and many nations fluttering in the breeze. Lighted torches glowed on the surrounding hilltops. Altogether, it was an unforgettable experience. On the following morning, I attended the first session of the Knesset to be held in the new Parliament building.

Later that year, old memories were stirred by the dedication of the Judah L. Magnes Museum on the Berkeley campus of the University of California. It took place on October 2. I had known Dr. Magnes as an ardent Zionist whose gravitation toward religious traditionalism had led him to quit his Reform pulpit at Temple Emanu-El and to serve, very briefly, as rabbi of my congregation, B'nai Jeshurun, in 1911–12. He then became involved in the project to establish a *Kehillah* organization for New York Jewry. It did not succeed. Subsequently, he turned his idealism to the Hebrew University of Jerusalem, serving as chancellor and later as first president of the university from 1925 until his death in 1948. During those years in Eretz Yisrael, Dr. Magnes had been one of the advocates of an unpopular scheme for a binational Palestinian state, with parity between Jews and Arabs.

In anticipation of the museum's dedication, I visited his widow, Mrs. Beatrice Magnes, at her home in Jerusalem. One amusing detail that she supplied added to my overall impression of the man's human qualities: he had been a baseball enthusiast and, on arriving at the Hebrew University, he had made a vain attempt to organize a faculty baseball team.

In my address at Berkeley, I described Judah Magnes as "a shining light to his younger colleagues in the rabbinate, in Zionism, in Jewish community service, in the Hebrew University, and in the dedication to world peace." I also expressed pride in the fact that this new museum would also house the Rabbi Morris Goldstein Library, named in honor of my younger brother, who had just celebrated his thirty-fifth anniversary as rabbi of Congregation Sherith Israel in San Francisco. Exhibits in the Magnes Museum would illuminate aspects of Judaism and of local Jewish history. I expressed the hope that they would thereby help Christians better to understand Jews, and Jews better to understand themselves.

Bert and I had naturally felt the separation from our family in the United States, whom we endeavored to visit each summer. We were all the more delighted, therefore, when Margaret, our son Avram's daughter, came to Israel for an extended visit around this time. She also stayed at Kibbutz En ha-Horesh for a while and there came under the influence of Abba Kovner, the Hebrew poet, who had been one of the Jewish resistance leaders in Nazi-occupied Lithuania. Margaret was the first of our grandchildren to spend time with us in Israel.

We shared the nation's jubilation that October, when it was announced that

Shmuel Yosef Agnon would be awarded the Nobel Prize for literature. "Shai" Agnon was the world's foremost Hebrew writer and the first ever to receive this prestigious award. I had been very moved when he remembered my seventieth birthday, sending me a reprint of one of his Hebrew stories—appropriately entitled *Ha-Shanim ha-Tovot*, "The Good Years"—with a friendly inscription. On the Shabbat morning following the announcement, I walked to Agnon's synagogue in Talpiot, an hour's distance from my home, in order to join him in worship. A special *Kiddush* was arranged there after the services. As we sat around the table, Agnon greeted each of his Talpiot neighbors in turn—there were about twenty of them present—by recounting his family *yiḥus* (lineage), going back several generations. It was an astonishing feat of memory for the seventy-eight-year-old writer.

Agnon's style, combining rabbinic idioms and Jewish mystical elements with the art of a master novelist, has always been a source of wonder to me. I shall long cherish the privilege of having moved within the "four ells" of his presence in Jerusalem.

That autumn, we paid a visit to Nes Ammim ("Banner of the Nations"), a unique Christian moshav situated between Akko and Nahariyah, in northern Israel. There were about a dozen Protestant families from Holland, Germany, Switzerland, and the United States in this interdenominational settlement, established in 1962. Part of their religious commitment is to demonstrate their feeling of solidarity with the Jewish people by doing their best to help build up Israel. The settlers based their moshav's economy on the cultivation of roses and fruit trees. What impressed us in particular was their choice of a site adjacent to Kibbutz Loḥamé ha-Getta'ot, the home of many former World War II ghetto and resistance fighters, and the fact that these Christian friends of Israel had built their own homes so as to face the Holocaust Museum, which stands on the kibbutz.

Early in 1967, before embarking on a Keren Hayesod mission to Mexico, it was my privilege to deliver the prayer opening a new session of the U. S. Senate. The invitation had been sponsored by Senator Jacob Javits of New York. On February 21, I was escorted to the podium by the oldest member of the Senate, Carl Haydn of Arizona, who had served there for fifty-five years.

At six o'clock that evening, I was received by President Lyndon B. Johnson, to whom I presented a copy of my book, *A Century of Judaism in New York*. Our conversation began on a good-humored note when I said, "Mr. President, I trust that the country's economic situation has not worsened since the delivery of my prayer this morning!" "Well," he replied, "some of my advisers have since told me that there are signs of an approaching depression." I said I hoped it was only a coincidence. President Johnson took obvious pride in showing me a chart recording the extent of U.S. aid to Israel over the years, and indicating that this aid had reached its highest level during his Administration.

Five days later, I arrived in Mexico City, where I toured the magnificent Jewish community center. Every Sunday, large numbers of people, both young and old, flocked there to participate in a wide range of social and recreational activities. I was told that as many as 4,000 adults, young people and children spent the entire day in that welcoming environment. This center also served as a venue for a number of Jewish organizations, including the Keren Hayesod, on behalf of which I had come to Mexico.

Not long after my return to Israel, the municipality of Eilat, which was about to celebrate its eighteenth birthday, honored me with the award of honorary citizenship. The citation made mention of the fact that I had influenced leading overseas contributors to our campaign funds, particularly in Great Britain, to establish a variety of community projects in Israel's most southerly urban center. In my response, following the bestowal of this award on March 22, I recalled my first visit, as treasurer of the Jewish Agency in 1949, to the barren site on which Eilat was destined to rise. I said that I had taken a close interest in the city's development and that I would continue to do so, predicting a bright future for Israel's Red Sea port.

As the hostile Arab chorus intensified that spring, I made a point of visiting our kibbutzim in the far north. There, looking upwards, we could glimpse the Syrian gun emplacements above us on the Golan Heights, from which vantage point shells had been raining down on inoffensive Israeli settlements in the valley below. This, although we had no way of knowing it at the time, was but the prelude to the storm.

12

Solidarity and Restoration: 1967–71

There were few outward signs of tension on Israel's nineteenth Independence Day, which fell on May 15, 1967, although the celebrations in Jerusalem were more restrained than heretofore. General Marie-Pierre Koenig, one of the outstanding heroes of the Free French during World War II and a former Defense Minister in the French Government, came to our home on Yom Ha-Atzma'ut. He was president of the Alliance France-Israël and an enthusiastic supporter of our *magbit*. We knew of his devotion to the Keren Hayesod in France; he himself stressed the need to change French Jewry's lukewarm response to our appeal. A truly Righteous Gentile, this valiant Frenchman championed Israel's cause and unceasingly denounced his own country's Middle East policy up to the moment of his death in 1970.

Hitherto, President Charles de Gaulle had termed Israel the "loyal ally" of France, but his obsession with French *gloire* and his resentful attitude toward the "Anglo-Saxon" powers (Great Britain and the United States), coupled with his new diplomatic offensive in North Africa and the Arab world, now resulted in an astonishing *volte-face*. The embargo he placed on arms supplies to the Jewish State would soon be followed by that ominous remark of his concerning *"un peuple d'élite, sûr de soi et dominateur"*—"an elitist, self-confident, and domineering people." Politicians, including a few (such as Michel Debré and Maurice Schumann) of Jewish descent, hastened to follow De Gaulle's pro-Arab line.

It was a pleasant relief at this time to welcome Richard Tucker, the Metropolitan Opera star and eminent cantor, who came to Jerusalem to conduct a Shabbat service in Hechal Shlomo. We arranged a reception for him in our home. The following day, I took him to visit our Youth Village. To hear Richard Tucker sing—and to see him leading them in their songs—was a wonderful experience for our youngsters.

The Six-Day War and Its Legacy

On May 19, acceding to a peremptory demand by the Egyptian dictator, UN Emergency Force units were evacuated from the Sinai border area, the Gaza Strip, and Sharm el-Sheikh. The powerlessness and irresponsibility displayed by UN Secretary-General U Thant were a portent of things to come. As Nasser closed the Straits of Tiran to Israeli shipping, there was a great deal of talk by world leaders but no decisive action to end the blockade. Instead, the Russians spread false reports of Israeli troops massing on the border with Syria, and De Gaulle called for "restraint." Israel was left to its own devices.

The Keren Hayesod–United Israel Appeal launched an emergency campaign throughout the Jewish world, following urgent meetings at the Jewish Agency. My particular task was to begin with the conducting of this special *magbit* in Canada and thereafter, possibly, in Latin America. By the time I reached Montevideo in the second week of June, war had already broken out (see chapter 13).

Under the menace of attack by the Egyptian and Syrian armies, Israel's new Coalition Government—including, for the first time, members of the Herut Party— had vainly appealed to King Hussein not to begin hostilities. When Jordanian artillery opened fire indiscriminately on the morning of June 5, however, West Jerusalem became part of Israel's front line.

I was naturally concerned for Bert's safety. Finding it impossible to contact her by phone, I sent her a telex message from one of our Keren Hayesod offices across the Atlantic. It was only later, after my return to Israel, that I learned how she had been spending her time—either in our air-raid shelter or else as a volunteer driver, conveying soldiers to various points in the Jerusalem area.

On the final leg of my overseas mission, I heard in New York that there was good news from the war front and that the Old City of Jerusalem was now in Israeli hands. I felt a sense of helplessness and frustration at not being in Israel at such a time, but consoled myself with the thought that I was helping to mobilize the financial support of the Jewish people for the embattled Jewish State.

It was exhilarating to see lines of young people, at various stops on my route, anxious to volunteer their services in Israel's defense. Not a few high-minded non-Jews were among them. From New York to Johannesburg and from London to Buenos Aires, Zionist offices were literally besieged by thousands of such volunteers. Some had to wait days in order to find room on a plane. Although there were many who came from Zionist backgrounds and through Zionist organizations, great numbers of idealistic young *mitnadvim* (volunteers) had had no significant contact with organized Jewish life. Their motivation was an elemental one: "We feel we must go to fight for Israel." Altogether, several thousand young Jews arrived in Israel as *mitnadvim* and others were on their way when the war ended. To one anxious parent's cabled request, "Come home!," the son had replied, "I *am* home!"

Hymie Morrison, chairman of the emergency campaign in Great Britain, accompanied me on the flight to Israel. Our plane landed at Lod Airport during the blackout. Back home in Jerusalem, I was relieved to find Bert well and busy making her own contribution to the war effort. The rear of our house was scarred by fragments of a shell fired from the monastery of Mar Elias, on what had been the Israel-Jordan border. One room in the Keren Hayesod building had been completely destroyed.

In spite of the gratifying scenes of Jewish response and solidarity abroad, the dramatic reunification of Jerusalem at the height of the war was something I greatly regretted having missed. I was thrilled to learn of the astounding success achieved by General Yitzhak Rabin, Israel's Chief of Staff, on the southern front, where IDF pilots had caught most of Nasser's powerful airforce on the ground. At bases in Sinai and throughout Egypt, hundreds of enemy planes had been destroyed before they could take to the air, thereby hastening Israel's victory.

Both the Israel Defense Forces and the civilian population had given an excellent account of themselves. We were saddened, however, by the bereavement of good friends whose sons had been killed in the fighting or by news of the injuries inflicted on others.

The last and most difficult stage of the war was then in progress—the battle for the Golan Heights, the Syrian hilltops from which our northern settlements were still under ferocious attack. We all knew that this would be the toughest battle of all, and it proved to be the most savage. Evidence of horrifying Syrian brutality piled up as the IDF pushed forward. When the last battle was won, the entire country breathed a sigh of relief and exaltation. Israel's victory on all fronts in what was destined to be known as the Six-Day War had been swift and decisive.

Together with other members of the Jewish Agency Executive, I toured the newly liberated areas on the Sunday following my return to Jerusalem. We first went to the *Kotel Ma'aravi,* that surviving Western Wall of the Second Temple over which so many Jewish generations had shed tears in the past and which, for that reason, unsympathetic non-Jews had derisively called the "Wailing Wall." Now, hundreds of Jews were streaming to the *Kotel*—young and old, bearded Ḥasidim in their caftans and soldiers in their battledress, religious and secular, all commingled. The spectacle of all those praying, crying, and dancing people, of unity across diversity, was unforgettable. Bulldozers were already tearing down the Arab slums that had disfigured the site for so long, and they would soon lay the foundations of a spacious plaza providing access to many thousands of visitors. We were losing no time in making Jerusalem one united city.

From there we drove to what remained of Gush Etzion, a cluster of four kibbutzim (three of them religious) which, in 1948, had saved Jewish Jerusalem by holding up the Arab Legion's advance. Most of Kfar Etzion's heroic pioneers had been massacred by Arab villagers when forced to surrender, and now only a few ruins told of that grim event. Happily, work on the Etzion Bloc's restoration began soon after the war, when the children of those *ḥalutzim* obtained Government permission to "return to their border." The settlements occupying that site today are more populous and more prosperous than their forerunners.

We passed streams of Arabs making their way back to the homes from which they had fled, mostly women, children, and old men laden with bundles. One group stopped our bus and asked for water. We gave them something to drink and food as well. Everywhere white flags were in evidence. As we approached Hebron, scene of a gruesome massacre of inoffensive Jews in 1929, many Arabs waved to us from their balconies. I did not wave back. I would have respected them more had they not waved at all. Twelve years later, PLO gunmen were to fire at Jews from some of those balconies, and yeshivah students would be their victims once more. In Hebron, we were shown the surrender document, which began with the words, "Welcome to our Israeli conquerors." I confess I did not relish the sycophantic tone.

At Rachel's Tomb, near Bethlehem, I had been asked to read a chapter of Psalms, and at *Me'arat ha-Makhpelah*, the Cave of the Patriarchs in Hebron, I again took out my Bible and recited the relevant portions of the Book of Genesis and the Book of Joshua. For the first time in many centuries, access to the Tombs of the Patriarchs was complete and we were able to walk up all the steps that Jews had been forbidden to tread while Muslims had exercised their intolerant control. Fifty generations had prayed for this moment, I reflected, but was our generation worthy of such a privilege? Perhaps this *zekhut* had been granted to the generation capable of producing an army of Israel that, like the ancient Maccabees, fought with spirit as well as with the weapons of war.

Returning to Jerusalem, we visited Mount Scopus, where the original Hebrew University buildings and Hadassah Hospital had been cut off from Israel for a period of nineteen years.

On the following Shabbat morning, I attended services in the Yeshurun Synagogue. When the reader came to *Shirat ha-Yam*, the liturgical section in *Shaharit* that includes the Song of Moses and the Children of Israel after their crossing of the Red Sea (Exodus 15:1–18), most of the worshipers yelled themselves hoarse and danced in the aisles of the synagogue. I was one of them.

General Uzi Narkiss had commanded the forces that took the Old City and thus ended the prolonged division of Jerusalem. The principal hero of the Six-Day War, General Yitzhak Rabin, the *Ramatkal* (Chief of Staff), had seen all the military operations through to their successful conclusion. As world chairman of Keren Hayesod, I was privileged to head a delegation he received after the hostilities had ended. Rabin subsequently made his name as Israel's ambassador to the United States, as leader of the Ma'arakh (Labor Alignment), and as Prime Minister. His address on Mount Scopus, when he was awarded an honorary degree by the Hebrew University, made a deep impression. It was unusual for a fighting man, in its emphasis of Israel's unceasing quest for peace.

My correspondence files contain letters written at the time by people overseas who could not restrain their admiration for Israel's achievement. One non-Jewish woman wrote: "The Israelis are the heroes of our modern world." An American Gentile said: "The Israelis have given us a 'new testament' to live by." Other spoke of undertaking a course of self-examination and self-criticism, while many ordinary folk confessed that "without Israel there would be no sense or meaning to our lives." Thanks to Israel, we had witnessed a rebirth of Jewish identity and commitment, a sense of at-oneness with the Medinah that would not fade from the Jewish people's consciousness.

On the fast of Tish'ah be-Av we were among the vast crowds thronging the Western Wall. These were stirring times for Israel and for the myriads of Jews who had flocked to the expanded homeland on pilgrimage visits.

In the course of that summer, Bert and I made trips to some of the newly liberated areas, including the Golan Heights, where we reached Mount Hermon. These private excursions began shortly after the Six-Day War, when my brother, Morris, rabbi of Congregation Sherith Israel in San Francisco, paid us a visit. He and his wife, Adeline, were on their first pilgrimage to the Holy Land. I took him with me on a tour of the "West Bank," in the course of which we visited the Samaritans near Nablus, close to biblical Samaria and Shechem. There, we met with the Samaritan high priest, Amram ben Yitzhak, spiritual leader of an ethnic group that claims descent from survivors of the Northern Kingdom of Israel whom the conquering Assyrians permitted to remain in the land. In Roman times, the Samaritans had been powerful and numerous, but over the centuries they had been reduced to a few hundred souls as a result of constant persecution by the Byzantines, Turks, and Arabs. Between 1948 and 1967, one group of Samaritans had held fast to its holiest site on Mount Gerizim, overlooking Nablus, then under Jordanian rule, while other scattered clans had reestablished themselves in Holon, near Tel Aviv. If anything, the protection extended to the Nablus Samaritans by the Hashemite kingdom of Jordan had intensified local Arab hatred for these wretched "infidels."

The high priest told us that he and his people had danced with one of their Torah scrolls in celebration of Israel's victory. He begged me to intercede in their behalf with President Ben-Zvi, who had taken an interest in their welfare even before the establishment of the State, and whom the Samaritans regarded as their special patron. They were obviously unaware of Ben-Zvi's death four years earlier, in April 1963. We were shown the place on Mount Gerizim where they continue to sacrifice the *korban Pesah*, and heard a description of that ancient Passover ritual, which Rabbinic Judaism abandoned after the destruction of the Second Temple.

I recalled my first visit to the Samaritans in 1932, when I had been delighted to receive a gift from the high priest of that period: the opening chapter of *Bereshit*, the Book of Genesis, handwritten in their ancient script.

Just under a year later, in the spring of 1968, Bert and I paid another visit to the Samaritans on the eve of Passover, when we witnessed their paschal sacrifice of sheep on Mount Gerizim. According to their tradition, this is the place God chose for His sanctuary. Amram ben Yitzhak officiated at the ceremony, which drew many curious Jewish visitors. We also saw an ancient Torah scroll they prize and which, they claim, is several thousand years old. Since June 1967, the two branches of the Samaritan community have established close contact, facilitating the increase of marriages and a revival of their communal and religious life.

"World Jewry's Solidarity with Israel in the Six-Day War and After" was the title of an address I delivered before the Commerce and Industry Club in Tel Aviv on July 7, 1967. My speech amplified what I had said at a *Kiddush* given in the capital by President Shazar in honor of Dr. Dov Joseph, David Shaltiel, and others who had been active in the defense of Jerusalem during the 1948 War of Liberation. World Jewry's financial response had been unprecedented, I declared, vastly exceeding all previous records. In Great Britain, virtually every Jewish family had contributed to the emergency appeal. Our victory had enhanced the standing of Jews everywhere. Young and old had flocked to the synagogues. We were now faced with two challenges, I said, the one being enlightened treatment of the defeated Arabs and of places holy to other religions, and the other being a campaign to draw far greater numbers of idealistic Jews to Israel.

I recalled hearing an IDF officer remark that he had felt a personal duty to honor the memory of our European martyrs by showing what Jews could do when they had weapons in their hands. My concluding observation was as follows:

> I believe we are witnessing, thanks to Israel, a renascence of Jewish identity which may be the opening page of a new chapter in Jewish history. I cannot believe that these are fleeting, superficial expressions. I believe they reveal that deep roots of Jewish identity have been exposed by Israel's emergency, which attest to the innermost sense of the Jewish people's identity with Israel, the umbilical cord which will never be severed.

One man who should have been with us in the hour of triumphant vindication, but whom death had snatched from our midst, was Moshe Sharett (see chapter 17). On the occasion of his second *Yahrzeit*, a memorial assembly was held at Bet Ha-Am in Jerusalem, five weeks after the war, on July 16. I reviewed his outstanding services to the Zionist movement and to Israel, emphasizing his many accomplishments, his wisdom, his compassion, and his moral stature. "Moshe Sharett was tested both in victory and in defeat," I said. "In victory he was humble, and in defeat he was uncomplaining. His lifelong Jewish commitments occupied him up to the last hour of his consciousness."

After attending a special session of the Knesset to mark the seventieth anniversary of the First Zionist Congress, I left for New York to spend the High Holy Days with my congregation. On the way, I devoted some time in Western Europe to coordinating plans for the postwar campaigns of the Keren Hayesod. An important event in my life, which took place shortly before Hanukkah, was the dedication at the Hebrew University of the Israel Goldstein Chair in the History of Zionism and the New Yishuv. Funds were provided for this purpose by congregants and friends in New York, to mark my seventieth birthday, which was behind me, and my fiftieth anniversary in the rabbinate, which was immediately ahead. The chair was to be part of the Institute of Contemporary Jewry, headed by my friend, Professor Moshe Davis. Dr. Yisrael Kollat was the designated incumbent of this chair. There were also annual guest lecturers, including Professors Abraham S. Halkin, Krister Stendhal, Milton R. Konvitz, Franklin H. Littell, and Simon N. Herman.

The dedication exercises were held on December 25, 1967. Among those who honored us with their presence were President Zalman Shazar, Dr. Nahum Goldmann, Chief Justice Simon Agranat, and Professor Nathan Rotenstreich, rector of the Hebrew University. Addresses were delivered by Eliahu Elath, the university's president, Professor Moshe Davis, and Dr. Kollat. The principal address was delivered by Professor Sir Isaiah Berlin, who came from the University of Oxford to lecture on "Weizmann as Exilarch." A reception was held afterwards at the home of President Shazar.

Although prophecy has been described as a risky vocation since the destruction of the Temple, I did venture to express a warning and a hope in my response to those who had made possible the establishment of this chair in Zionism:

It would not surprise me if the fundamental Zionist thesis, the unity of the Jewish people around Israel, were to be challenged again, and if the recent animadversions of the head of the French State were to be echoed by anti-Zionists in other countries. In my view, it is not unlikely that Zionism, resting upon a concept of nationalism which is broad and not restrictive, civilized and not dogmatic, will once again be called upon to become a fighting movement in a meaningful sense. Thus will it regain its soul, its vitality and its excitement.

Eight years later, when a resolution equating Zionism with racism was passed by the UN's "permanent majority," that forecast was validated.

On June 9, 1968, just one year after the Six-Day War, the 27th Zionist Congress opened in Jerusalem. Merely by looking at the delegates, and checking the composition of the Executive that was elected toward the end of Congress, one could find encouraging evidence of many new and younger faces in the Zionist movement. For the first time, Aliyah was upgraded to the major concern of the WZO. There was a general feeling that the absorption and integration of new Olim should be streamlined and improved, in the hope that this would promote more substantial immigration from the West. Before long, Aliyah from the United States, the British Commonwealth, Latin America, and other areas increased markedly. Even the trickle of immigration from the Soviet Union was destined to attain considerable proportions.

In many ways, this 27th Congress embarked on a more clearly defined and meaningful course of Zionist activity. Its new Jerusalem Program declared the aims of Zionism to be the unity of the Jewish people and the centrality of Israel in Jewish life; the ingathering of the Jewish people in its historic homeland, Eretz Yisrael, through Aliyah from all parts of the Dispersion; the strengthening of Israel, founded on the prophetic ideals of justice and peace; the preservation of Jewish identity through the fostering of Jewish and Hebrew education and of Jewish spiritual and cultural values; and the protection of Jewish rights everywhere.

As a move toward greater efficiency, I particularly welcomed the reduction in size of the WZO Executive and its infusion with new blood. Credit for this was largely due to the persistent efforts of Louis A. Pincus, who was reelected chairman of the Executive, a post he had assumed after the death of Moshe Sharett. One unresolved matter was the election of a successor to Dr. Nahum Goldmann, who resigned from the presidency of the World Zionist Organization.

The primary *mitzvah* of Aliyah received particular emphasis in my address to a delegation of the New York Board of Rabbis in Jerusalem on August 5. My former colleagues had assembled that day in the Ramban Synagogue, one of the Old City's historic monuments, which the Jordanians had left in ruins. Established in the thirteenth century, this synagogue testified to the fact that its founder, Rabbi Moshe ben Naḥman (Naḥmanides or Ramban), had set a personal example by leaving the *Golah* and settling in Eretz Yisrael. That *mitzvah* of Jewish self-fulfillment should not be lost on the modern rabbi, I urged. Young men training for the rabbinate should spend at least one year in Israel, rabbis already serving congregations should spend at least their sabbatical years here with their families, and those retiring from the rabbinate should come to Israel to enjoy the Shabbat of their lives. A living bridge with their communities of origin would be created by their living in Eretz Yisrael.

An important milestone for Bert and myself was the observance of our golden wedding anniversary on August 15. To mark the occasion, a large contingent of our family flew over from the United States in order to be with us at our *simḥah*. We were delighted to welcome our son and daughter-in-law, Avram and Dora Goldstein, our daughter and son-in-law, Vivian and Paul Olum, my brother and sister-in-law, Isaac and Fannie Goldstein, my sister and brother-in-law, Sarah and Herman Lazarus, and Bert's sister, Grace Volpert. They were joined by Carl and Eleanor Leff, cherished congregants and friends, whom we regarded as part of the family. Representatives of our Jerusalem Youth Village, headed by Ze'ev and Hadassah Schickler, also participated.

Our golden wedding celebration began with a short thanksgiving service at the Hebrew University Synagogue bearing my name. There, Bert and I recited a prayer we had composed especially for the occasion:

WE GIVE THANKS

that our young lives were joined in the twilight of the First World War,
whose end was expected to usher in an era of enduring world peace;

that we were privileged to nurture the Jewish way of life and the dream of Zion
    restored,
in which both of us had been cradled,
and that opportunities came our way to serve and to lead in these endeavors,
subtained by kinship of mind and spirit;

that when the tocsin of the Second World War was sounded
before even the echoes of the First had died down,
and Satan was on the verge of being enthroned,
having ravaged a continent and exterminated the Jews of Europe,
we lived to see his overthrow and destruction;

that when the conscience of the civilized world
put its stamp of approval on the fulfillment of the Zionist dream,
and the youth of Eretz Yisrael sealed that stamp with its blood,
and Medinat Yisrael was established,
we were alive to rejoice and to invest our modest labors
in helping the new, struggling infant born of Jewish dreams and prayers;

that the last seven years of our lives have been their crowning fulfillment,
the Shabbat in which we have been privileged to live in Israel and in
   Jerusalem,
to love them and serve them
with all our hearts, with all our souls and with all our might,
and to share Israel's mortal peril and triumphant victory,
and be part of Jerusalem the Golden reunited.

May it be granted us to walk a little longer, hand in hand,
toward whatever may lie in store,
prayerful that the harbinger of a better dispensation for our people and for the
   human family
may come in our lifetime.

To the Dispenser of the years,
our thanks for the past are intertwined
with our supplications for the future.
Amen. *Selah.*

After this *Tefillat Hodayah* service, we were all invited to luncheon at the Youth
Village. There was a reception that same evening in the garden of our home for 600
of our relatives and friends. President Zalman and Raḥel Shazar headed the array of
guests.

In gratitude for our many blessings, Bert and I endowed a Jerusalem Prize for
Good Citizenship to be awarded annually to Jerusalemites excelling in good deeds
and public-spirited activities. Together with Deputy Mayor Yosef Gadish, Dr. Jack
Karpas, Jacob Maimon, and A. P. Michaelis, Bert served on the committee that
selected recipients of the prize. It has proved helpful in revealing little people who
are doing great things.

To mark our golden wedding anniversary and my fiftieth year of rabbinic leader-
ship in the congregation, a special service was also held at B'nai Jeshurun in New
York on *Shabbat Shuvah*, September 14, 1968. Cantor Robert Segal, who has since
made Aliyah with his family, conducted the services. Apart from my able successor,
Rabbi William Berkowitz, and the congregation's president, Charles H. Silver, the
speakers included Professor Louis Finkelstein, chancellor of the Jewish Theological
Seminary, Dr. Joachim Prinz, honorary president of the American Jewish Congress,
Father George B. Ford, pastor emeritus of Corpus Christi Roman Catholic Church,
and Mrs. Harry L. (Jennie Rothman) Jones, a B'nai Jeshurun alumna, who was then
serving as national chairman of the Women's Division of the United Jewish Appeal.
Our one regret was that Professor Mordecai M. Kaplan had been kept away by
illness.

"A Jubilee Lookaround" would best describe the sermon I delivered. It touched
on some of the highlights of my public career of half a century. After outlining my
credo, my *Ani Ma'amin*, I concluded with a prayer—"for the human family, that it
may dwell in peace; for America, that it may match its wealth with its spirit; for the

Jewish people, that it may long endure; and for Israel, that it may 'flourish as the rose and strike its roots as the Lebanon.' "

These hopes were reiterated in the prayer I was invited to offer at the opening session of the U.S. House of Representatives in Washington on October 3. Congressman William Fitts Ryan, who represented the New York City district in which Congregation B'nai Jeshurun is located, arranged for the invitation.

I felt greatly honored when the Speaker of the House, Representative John McCormack of Massachusetts, stepped down from his rostrum in order to welcome me. He reminisced about the days when American Zionist leaders had been engaged in the struggle for a Jewish commonwealth in Palestine, and he spoke of the pro-Zionist plank which, as chairman of the Platform Committee at the Democratic Party convention in 1944, he had succeeded in having adopted.

Among the congressmen who came up to greet me were Herbert Tenzer, an old friend, and Ogden Reid, whom I had known well in Israel during his term as U. S. ambassador. When I greeted him in Hebrew, he promptly responded in kind.

Altogether, it was a moving finale to the celebration of our anniversaries.

Early in 1969, I made one of my periodic visits to Europe on behalf of Keren Hayesod. My first stop was in Rome, where I met with Chief Rabbi Elio Toaff and the leaders of our *magbit*, and I then proceeded to Milan. There, I was welcomed by the chairman of the Keren Hayesod, Jacob Ghitis, and his wife, Esther, a generous friend of our Youth Village in Jerusalem.

While I was in Brussels on February 26, a radio news bulletin brought the announcement of Prime Minister Levi Eshkol's sudden death. My first impulse was to take the next plane home in order to attend the state funeral, but at the telephone urging of Louis Pincus, chairman of the Jewish Agency Executive, I concluded my tour of the Low Countries.

Levi Eshkol had served Israel with great ability—first in the Jewish Agency, as head of its Agricultural Settlement Department and later as its treasurer, then in the Government, as Minister of Finance, and finally as head of the Coalition Government that guided the nation through the Six-Day War and for some time thereafter.*

By the time I came back to Israel at the beginning of March, Golda Meir had succeeded Eshkol as Prime Minister. In the absence of Louis Pincus, who was abroad at the time, I was privileged to offer her the Jewish Agency's greetings and felicitations at a reception tendered by President Shazar.

Soon afterwards, I conducted a party of journalists on a Keren Hayesod tour of the Golan Heights. Bert and I had been there before, when many Israelis were rushing to visit the "liberated territories." Now there were Israeli settlements dotting the somewhat bleak landscape of Ramat ha-Golan. We inspected some of these new installations. Our tour brought us as far as Kuneitra, virtually a ghost town on the Syrian-Israeli cease-fire line. General David Elazar, commander of the Israeli

---

*On Levi Eshkol, see chapter 17.

forces that had captured the Golan Heights in 1967 (and a future Chief of Staff), addressed our group at a luncheon in Kuneitra.

Mission to the Falashas

On March 24, 1969, I left Israel with Bert for a visit to Ethiopia. In so doing, we fulfilled a long-cherished desire to spend at least part of Passover with the Falashas—the most beleaguered and pathetic of Israel's "lost tribes"—and, if possible, to intercede with Emperor Haile Selassie on their behalf. My interest in their fate had originally been enlisted by Professor Jacques Faitlovitch in 1930, when I became the chairman of the American Pro-Falasha Committee (see chapter 3). Funds were then raised to build and maintain a school for Falasha children on land donated by Haile Selassie, shortly after his accession to the throne and assumption of the title, "Lion of Judah." Subsequent efforts by the various Pro-Falasha committees were only sporadic, especially after the death of Professor Faitlovitch in 1955.

Following Mussolini's conquest of Ethiopia, Haile Selassie had found temporary refuge in Jerusalem, together with other members of the imperial family and various Ethiopian notables. A number of Palestinian Jews had fought under General Orde Wingate, that great friend of the Yishuv, during the British campaign to liberate Ethiopia from Italian Fascist occupation in 1941. They had marched with Wingate in the victory parade that the Negus led through the Ethiopian capital. Haile Selassie warmly appreciated the contribution of Palestinian Jewish soldiers to the liberation of his country, and he had invited some of them to act as Government advisers at that time. Such was the background to Ethiopia's subsequent friendly ties with Israel.

As a new Oleh, at the end of 1960, I found that interest in the Falashas was being maintained by a small group in Israel headed by Professor Aryeh Tartakower. Their most important friend in London was Professor Norman Bentwich, who often came to the Israeli group's meetings. He enjoyed the confidence of the Negus, having at one time served as his legal consultant in drawing up a constitution for Ethiopia. Much encouragement was received from President Itzhak Ben-Zvi and, after him, from President Zalman Shazar.

The Falashas had declined in number over the years. In 1930, Professor Faitlovitch had estimated their population to be somewhere between 50,000 and 70,000, but only about 30,000 Falashas remained by the late 1960s. Christian missionary activity, enlistment in the army, and flight to the cities had been responsible for this decline. A dozen Falasha boys were, however, brought to Israel by Youth Aliyah after the establishment of the State and educated in Kfar Batyah, a children's village supported by American Mizrahi Women. Two of them stayed, but the others returned to Ethiopia, where they became Hebrew teachers. The Jewish Agency's Torah Education Department also sent a few *shlihim* to the religious schools there, for which it provided a modest subsidy.

The meetings Professor Tartakower chaired in Israel were usually attended by a representative of the Ministry of Foreign Affairs. The subject of Aliyah for the Falashas, we were advised, needed to be handled delicately. Dr. Ra'anan Weitz, head of the Jewish Agency's Settlement Department, once proposed that hilly land in the Galilee be set aside for fifty or sixty families. Sporadically, doctors, nurses, and assorted "experts" were dispatched to alleviate the plight of the Falashas in Ethiopia, but there was no coordinated relief or emigration program.

On our departure for Addis Ababa, the Ethiopian capital, Bert and I were accompanied by a good friend, Rosa Krongold, who had relatives living in Asmara.

Ethiopia proved to be a fascinating country for the tourist. We visited Axum, the ancient holy city where monarchs were once crowned, and the seaport of Asmara, where we saw fishing boats on their way to Eilat. There were a few Jewish families in Asmara, including Mrs. Krongold's relatives, Boris Gewirtzman and his brother-in-law, Harry Cahana, who exported canned meat to Israel. *Kashrut* supervision was provided by the Israel Chief Rabbinate.

Addis Ababa impressed us with its fine public buildings, more especially the emperor's palace and the university. Both in the palace and in the parks we saw many reproductions of Haile Selassie's emblem, the Lion of Judah, together with the Magen David motif, often joined to a cross. Several dozen Jewish families were living in Addis Ababa in 1969.

I had several discussions with Israel Ambassador Uri Lubrani, who had given me a preliminary briefing in Jerusalem. He and other members of the embassy staff told me about a new plan for agricultural resettlement which, with Government approval, could take care of more than a thousand Falasha families. Having lost their own land centuries earlier, the Falashas were now eking out a miserable existence as lessees or serfs at the mercy of Christian landowners in the Gondar region, north of Lake Tana. The proposed resettlement scheme would move them to an area near the Sudanese border, and there they would no longer be serfs. It was estimated that an initial investment of $500,000 would be needed to provide all the necessary economic and technical assistance. The Governor of Gondar, whom I met later, expressed support for the resettlement project.

The leader of the Falashas, who guided us on our visits, was Yonah Bogala, a former pupil of Professor Faitlovitch. He directed their Hebrew schools and was his community's main bridge to Israel and the Jewish world. We were surprised to learn that Tedasseh Yaacov, Ethiopia's Minister of Pensions and president of the National Bank, was also a Falasha (related to Yonah Bogala) and that his uncle was the late Taamrat Emanuel, whom I had brought to the United States and who later served the Negus as Undersecretary of State for Education. Although all three of these men claimed descent from the imperial house on their paternal side, they had chosen to be identified with their maternal Falasha ancestry.

Ambassador Lubrani went with me to see Tedasseh Yaacov. We had a lengthy discussion, speaking both Hebrew and English, in the course of which the latter told me that his son was a graduate of Bar-Ilan University, and that he had visited Israel several times. He lost no time in complaining that, as one who had never disguised his origins and sympathies, he should have been consulted about the proposed resettlement scheme for the Falashas. When I mentioned that part of the scheme relating to settlements on the Sudanese border, he was unenthusiastic. His judgment proved sound. Tedasseh Yaacov also criticized the niggardly aid provided by the Jewish Agency. "Israel has abandoned the Falashas," he complained. It was at once an enlightening and a disheartening interview.

The Ethiopians generally believe that they are descended from King Solomon and the Queen of Sheba. The Falashas themselves maintain, however, that their ancestors reached Ethiopia by way of Egypt after the destruction of the First Temple. In appearance, they resemble the people around them, being black in color, with finely chiseled features and kinky black hair. The very term *Falasha*—meaning "wanderer," "exile" or (possibly) "stranger"—points to a different origin. According to many scholars, they are of mixed descent; some of their forefathers were Jews from southern Arabia who arrived in the fourth century of the Common Era, and these newcomers then intermarried with native tribes which had already adopted Jewish customs. The important fact is that the Falashas, who prefer to be known as *Beta Esrael* ("House of Israel"), have valiantly maintained their allegiance to Judaism, albeit in an ancient pre-Talmudic form.

Their sacred literature comprises the whole of the Torah and some Apocryphal and other postbiblical works, which they read in Ghe'ez, a language sacred to the Ethiopians generally. Since the Talmud and Rabbinic Judaism passed them by, they have long observed only the biblically ordained practices. Religious leadership is vested in the *Cahenat* (*Kohanim* or priests), who choose a high priest, and in an order of Nazirites, who serve as teachers and readers of the sacred texts. The Falashas observe Shabbat strictly, practice *shehitah* and circumcision, and lay particular emphasis on the laws of family purity. Their menfolk, too, are scrupulous about ritual immersion. Falasha villages are therefore located near a river or stream. Usually, they are to be found on a hilltop and can be distinguished by the presence of the *mesgid* (synagogue), which is a larger kind of the standard Ethiopian *tukul* or round hut with a conical straw roof.

The Falasha villages are situated mainly in the Gondar region, and the most important of these is Ambober. Here, the most interesting part of our Ethiopian tour awaited us. It took an hour and a half by Landrover to reach Ambober, which lies thirty kilometers from Gondar, since the roads were fit only for travel by mules. We arrived a few hours before the eve of Passover, in time to see the young men coming back from their ablutions in the river. Falasha women were cleaning out their huts and some of them were baking the last of their *matzot* in primitive outdoor ovens. Yonah Bogala, who had come with us as our guide, took us to the Hebrew school, one of those partly supported by the Jewish Agency, where the children greeted us with the songs of Zion. Just before sunset, we saw lines of Falashas coming from neighboring villages to participate in the services that would usher in the Passover festival.

It was now time to take our places in the Ambober synagogue, a comparatively substantial building surmounted by a Magen David. Inside, we were shown their copy of the Torah, a book written in the Ghe'ez tongue on goatskin and wrapped in a cloth. There was also a small Hebrew *Sefer Torah*, draped in a mantle, which Yonah Bogala had brought from Jerusalem and had taught some of the priests to read. The synagogue accommodated several hundred people—the men in one section, the women in another, and the children in a third. It was touching to see some of the older women flinging themselves to the ground and kissing it, their faces turned toward Jerusalem. The service, conducted by the *Cahenat* and led by the high priest, lasted for a little over half an hour. It consisted of a chant in Ghe'ez, accompanied by the gentle beating of a drum and cymbals. The Falashas had, until recent times, offered a *korban Pesaḥ* or paschal sacrifice, but this practice was discontinued when the late Professor Faitlovitch explained that it was no longer customary among Jews in the outside world.

After the service, everyone gathered outside the *mesgid* and I then conveyed our greetings to the assembly in Hebrew. The high priest responded in Amharic, the daily language of Ethiopia. Yonah Bogala, who served as our translator, had brought supplies of *matzot* and wine from the Holy Land, made available by the Israel embassy in Addis Ababa. Children recited the Four Questions and other passages in Hebrew, using copies of an Israeli *Haggadah*. The high priest explained the significance of the Passover festival.

From behind a hill overlooking the village, the full moon had risen, imparting a touch of the exotic to this scene. I felt that this Passover eve also shed light on the characteristic Jewish stubbornness of a strange outpost of our people, where the struggle to maintain some expression of Israel's identity and tradition had persisted throughout the centuries. As we were leaving, one of the priests whispered into my ear in Hebrew: *"Al tishkaḥ otanu!"*—"Don't forget us!" This moving plea is one I have since felt compelled to bring before Jews everywhere.

On April 8, toward the end of Passover, I had an audience with Emperor Haile Selassie at his palace in Addis Ababa. The U.S. ambassador, Mr. Hall, had seen to the arrangements and he introduced me to the Negus.

A short, slightly built man, Haile Selassie wore his military attire with all his decorations. An interpreter was present to translate what I said, but the Negus appeared to understand my English. I told him about my long-standing interest in the Falashas and their welfare, and made appreciative reference to the proposed scheme for their resettlement. In reply, he affirmed his support for this new program and his readiness to protect the Falasha settlers against possible Sudanese attack. He believed, however, that whatever help was extended to the Falashas by Jewish organizations should be extended also to the neighboring Ethiopian population, so as not to arouse invidious distinctions. I assured him that this had always been a principle of Jewish philanthropy. One final remark by the Negus reminded me of what Tedasseh Yaacov had said. I mentioned the fact that the World Jewish Congress was now concerning itself with the plight of the Falashas, whereupon Haile Selassie turned to me and observed, "All of those world Jewish organizations have so far done very little for them."

Soon after our return to Israel, I submitted reports of my visit to President Shazar, the Jewish Agency Executive, and the committee headed by Professor Tartakower. While visiting London on a mission for the Keren Hayesod, I also spoke with Professor Norman Bentwich, who told me that OSE, the world organization for Jewish health and child care, had provided mobile medical units to assist the Falashas with an efficient health program. Several other Jewish organizations, such as ICA (the Jewish Colonization Association), the Alliance Israélite Universelle, and ORT, had rendered some help over the years, and now the Joint Distribution Committee in New York had substantially increased its budget for relief work among the Falashas. I again raised this issue at a meeting of the Conference of Jewish Organizations held in Geneva, on July 19, 1969, urging that properly coordinated action be taken. Unfortunately, this appeal went unanswered.

Four years later, on March 21, 1973, I was visited in Jerusalem by Yonah Bogala, who had been such a helpful guide to us in Ethiopia. A son of his was living in Israel by then. He brought me the latest news concerning the Falashas, indicating that the resettlement scheme had run into difficulties because of harrassment from the Sudanese side of the border. This security hazard eventually resulted in the abandonment of the new Falasha settlements. Meanwhile, the erosion of his people was all too visible throughout the country. Yonah Bogala stated emphatically that only Aliyah could save them. I conveyed this information to Professor Tartakower and to the Jewish Agency. Independent efforts to help the Falashas were being made by David Kessler, chairman of the board of *The Jewish Chronicle* in London, and by Graenum Berger, an executive of the Federation of Jewish Philanthropic Societies in New York.

The religious status of the Falashas was no longer an issue. From Rabbi Azriel Hildesheimer, in 1864, to Rav Kook and Chief Rabbi Herzog, the "saving of a Jewish tribe from the hands of the missionaries" and its restoration in the Holy Land had been the uppermost consideration. Chief Rabbi Nissim had ruled that the Falashas were eligible for Aliyah and that males require only token circumcision. On February 9, 1973, Israel's new Sephardi Chief Rabbi, Ovadyah Yosef, ruled "that the Falashas are Jews, whom it is our duty to redeem from assimilation, so as to hasten their immigration to Israel, educate them in the spirit of our holy Torah, and make them partners in the building of our Holy Land." Ashkenazi Chief Rabbi Shlomo Goren concurred.

At a meeting of Professor Tartakower's committee that I attended in 1975, we were informed that the Falashas could not only come to Israel as Olim, under the Law of Return, but would also receive assistance from the Jewish Agency. A few score individuals who had arrived from Ethiopia appeared to have adjusted well to the climate and had found employment in agriculture and industry. The Negus, however, opposed any organized program of Aliyah.

Since then, conditions in Ethiopia have deteriorated still further. The Lion of Judah, toppled from his imperial throne, is dead and the revolutionary, Moscow-oriented regime that succeeded him has severed all ties with Israel. Driven off the land they worked, enticed by Christian missionaries, demoralized by pillage, rape, and murder, the Black Jews of Ethiopia face possible extinction.

Today, at last, there are welcome signs of a more positive approach to the issue throughout the Jewish world. On November 15, 1979, Prime Minister Menaḥem Begin's Government announced that it would spare no effort to rescue the Falashas and bring them back to Israel. A public campaign has since been launched on their behalf.

Perhaps it is still not too late to fulfill the *mitzvah* of *Pidyon Shevuyim*, the ransoming of captives, by a worldwide and coordinated effort to save the last remnant of the Falashas.

Approaching Retirement

On May 3, 1969, about a month after my return from Ethiopia, I participated in the dedication of Bet Agron, named in memory of my boyhood friend, Gershon Agronsky (as he was then known), founder-editor of *The Palestine Post*, who had died in office as Mayor of Jerusalem. I had spoken at the laying of Bet Agron's foundation stone nearly eight years previously and, at the side of Meyer Weisgal, had helped to raise some of the funds needed for the project. As the home of the Jerusalem Journalists' Association, the Government Press Office, and the Haganah Museum, Bet Agron has become an important center of cultural and social activity in Israel's capital. It is today an imposing five-story building in which local and overseas newsmen can meet, relax, and exchange ideas.

At about this time, we had the pleasure of entertaining President James Hester of New York University, who was on a visit to Israel. Among those who welcomed him at our home were Chief Justice Simon Agranat, Professor Nelson Glueck, head of the Hebrew Union College–Jewish Institute of Religion, Professor Kalman Mann, the medical director of Hadassah Hospital, and Teddy Kollek, Jerusalem's new Mayor.

Something of a *Folksmensh*, a no-nonsense man of the people, Kollek had won his Zionist spurs in the Jewish Agency's Political Department and the Haganah, and had later served for a number of years as director of the Prime Minister's Office and in other important capacities. We had come to know him also as an enthusiastic campaigner for the Israel Museum, to the chairmanship of which he was elected in 1964. A year later, Teddy Kollek had fought a successful municipal election as head of the Rafi list, replacing the incumbent Labor Mayor, Mordecai Ish-Shalom, through a coalition alliance with Gaḥal (the Ḥerut-Liberal bloc) and the Religious Front parties. Skillful both as politician and as administrator, Kollek subsequently realigned himself with the Labor Party and, after the Six-Day War, he became the first Mayor of *Yerushalayim ha-Shelemah*, United Jerusalem. His phenomenal working day, his determination to weld both East and West Jerusalem into one harmonious city, and his ability to "sell" Israel's undivided capital to the world have since made Teddy Kollek an international personality.

We left Israel in August for our usual High Holy Day visit to Congregation B'nai Jeshurun. On the way, I made stops in Montreal and Toronto, to conduct our Keren Hayesod campaigns in those important centers of Canadian Jewry. After my arrival in New York, the board of the International Synagogue at Kennedy Airport honored me with a luncheon. As one of the founders, I had participated in the synagogue's inauguration six years previously, in March 1963.

I also took occasion to meet with the editors of several American Protestant journals whose attitude to Israel during the Six-Day War had left much to be desired. In order to help these Christian opinion makers understand the depth of Jewish religious feeling about Eretz Yisrael, I quoted a selection of passages from the traditional *siddur* referring to Zion and Jerusalem.

Two months later, on November 11, it was my privilege to greet President Shazar on the occasion of his eightieth birthday. Speaking on behalf of the Brit Ivrit Olamit and Keren Hayesod, I extended salutations to Israel's beloved and gifted head of state, the unifier and tribune of his people. The Aramaic term *Safra ve-Sayafa*, "Scholar and Warrior," seemed peculiarly applicable to Zalman Shazar. "Medinat Yisrael has had to live both by the sword *(sayif)* and by the Book *(Sefer)*," I noted. "That has happened before in our history. The Book has been your sword in helping to bring inner security and spiritual glory to our people and to our Medinah. May there be many years of *gevurot*, mighty achievements, ahead of you for the sake of our people and its culture."

A goodly proportion of my time and energy was devoted, in the course of the next eighteen months, to the golden jubilee of the Keren Hayesod and to matters concerning the reconstituted Jewish Agency. Early in 1969, Louis Pincus had told me of his plan for the Agency's reorganization and broadening, to include Jewish leaders who, though active supporters of Israel, regarded themselves as non-Zionists. I then indicated my approval of such a move. The details of what transpired within the Zionist movement at this time, however, properly belong elsewhere (see chapter 13).

On March 6, 1970, a convention of the Central Conference of American Rabbis was held for the first time in Jerusalem. This marked a dramatic turning point in the history of the American Reform movement.

Later that year, when the new University of the Negev was inaugurated in Beersheba, I presided over the exercises marking the laying of the cornerstone for the university's School of Engineering. Participants who spoke on that occasion included Finance Minister Pinḥas Sapir, Mayor Eliahu Nawi of Beersheba, the British ambassador, and the university's rector. Subsequently, this important institution was renamed the "Ben-Gurion University of the Negev."

My overseas missions in connection with the fiftieth anniversary of Keren Hayesod, observed throughout the world in 1970, took me to Great Britain, several European countries, the Western Hemisphere, and Southern Africa. While in Brazil, I made a detour to the new capital, Brasilia, which lies many hundreds of miles inland from Rio de Janeiro and São Paulo. Laid out in the form of an airplane, Brasilia proved to be an ultramodern city with some beautiful public buildings and religious structures. It had been designed by Oscar Niemeyer, Brazil's internationally renowned Jewish architect, who was also responsible for the new Haifa University campus on the summit of Mount Carmel.

For the High Holy Days, I was again with my congregation in New York. On October 4, immediately after Rosh Hashanah and *Shabbat Shuvah*, I left New York to attend the seventy-fifth anniversary celebration of Gratz College in Philadelphia. As on previous occasions elsewhere, I emphasized in my address the need to give Jewish education a much higher communal priority. Hebrew language and literature, the centrality of Eretz Yisrael in Jewish life, and Aliyah as a goal of Jewish self-fulfillment still needed to be interwoven more integrally into the textbooks of Jewish schools, beginning with the lowest grades. Far more trained teachers were still required. Together with Israel, I said, American Jewry must play a greater part in developing the resources for promoting a vital Jewish future.

In June 1971, I received an honorary doctorate from Dropsie University in Philadelphia. The degree was bestowed by Dropsie's president, Professor Abraham I. Katsh, and the hood was placed upon me by the university's senior professor, Solomon Zeitlin, and by Bernard A. Segal, chairman of the board of trustees. At a dinner that same evening, I conveyed greetings from President Zalman Shazar, who had received a similar honor from Dropsie University in the previous year.

My address at this dinner was on "Mordecai Manuel Noah—Pioneer American Zionist: His Relevancy to Our Time." Surveying the life and career of this remarkable Philadelphian, who served as consul to the Barbary States and later as High Sheriff of New York, I touched on his colorful and often stormy activities in the spheres of literature, journalism, and politics. I also alluded to his lifelong membership of Congregation Shearith Israel in New York and to his many friendly contacts with my own congregation, B'nai Jeshurun, during its early decades. Above all, however, I drew attention to the significance of his proto-Zionism, notably the utopian Ararat project on Grand Island in the Niagara river, which was launched with much pomp and publicity in 1825 and ended in a fiasco. I said that for all our reservations about his "City of Refuge" and his curious religious apologetics, Mordecai M. Noah deserved to be remembered as one who urged the restoration of the Jews to their ancient homeland, not as an eschatological hope but as a contemporary realistic possibility; who stressed the importance of agriculture and industry in consolidating Jewish nationhood; and who proclaimed the Christian world's moral duty to support and facilitate the modern Jewish return to Zion. Anticipating by more than a century the Balfour Declaration of 1917 and the UN resolution of 1947, Mordecai Manuel Noah was, I believed, "probably the most interesting, the most versatile, the most baffling, yet withal, the most consistently committed Zionist in American public life of the pre-Herzlian period."

Within the next few months, I received a series of tributes on the occasion of my seventy-fifth birthday. Congregation B'nai Jeshurun arranged a special service at which Rabbi William Berkowitz and Charles H. Silver extended pulpit greetings. As president of the congregation, the latter announced a decision of the board that B'nai Jeshurun's Community Center should henceforth bear my name. As previously while in New York, I availed myself of the opportunity to gain new benefactions for the synagogue and managed to raise $75,000 for its religious school scholarship fund.

On October 1, shortly after the celebration at B'nai Jeshurun, Bert and I were invited to City Hall, where Mayor John Lindsay presented me with the New York City Medallion for Distinguished Civic Service. Apart from Rabbi Berkowitz, President Charles H. Silver, and Board Chairman Leon Singer, who represented my congregation at this ceremony, many leading figures in the civic, political, philanthropic, and religious life of New York were also present. They included leading representatives of the New York Board of Rabbis, the Liberal Party, the National Conference of Christians and Jews, and the National Association for the Advancement of Colored People.

Earlier, in Israel, I had attended the plenary session of the Jewish Agency Executive, which commenced on June 17. My seventy-fifth birthday was marked by a Keren Hayesod reception in the garden of Bet Shalom and a dinner tendered by the World Confederation of General Zionists at the King David Hotel, on Saturday evening, June 19, at which Rose Halprin presided and Ezra Z. Shapiro, Faye Schenk, and Kalman Sultanik were the speakers.

It was my privilege the next day to preside at the dedication of Kiryat Wolfson, a high-rise housing project for Western Olim in Jerusalem. Sir Isaac Wolfson, his son, Leonard, and their families attended. Addresses were delivered by Finance Minister Pinḥas Sapir, Jewish Agency Chairman Louis Pincus, and Mayor Teddy Kollek.

The reconstituted Jewish Agency began its sessions that evening. Three days later, on June 24, I received a moving seventy-fifth birthday tribute at the enlarged body's founding assembly. It was on this occasion that I bade farewell to the Zionist General Council (Actions Committee), where I had played an active role for so many years. Ezra Z. Shapiro was elected to succeed me as world chairman of Keren Hayesod and he assumed his new responsibilities on September 1. My half-century of public service in the Zionist movement was now at an end.

One of the honors I cherish most is the honorary doctorate conferred upon me by the Hebrew University of Jerusalem at a ceremony that took place on Mount Scopus on July 5, 1971. It was especially meaningful to me that the degree scroll was placed in my hands by Avraham Harman, the president of the university. We had become well acquainted in 1948, when we were fellow members of the Jewish Agency Executive and he was in charge of the Department of Information. In later years, between 1959 and 1968, I had known and frequently met Avraham Harman while he served as Israel's very able ambassador in Washington. My esteem for him acquired added dimensions by virtue of my deputy chairmanship of the Hebrew University's board of governors. I observed at close range his dedication, perspicacity, and power of articulating ideas and ideals.

I was one of those invited to speak at the convocation. "Torah from Zion" was the theme of my address. As a lighthouse for human culture, for teaching and research in the sciences and humanities, the university was fulfilling its purpose nobly, I observed. Yet, as its biblical context made clear, the slogan, *Ki mi-Tziyyon tetzé Torah*—"For out of Zion shall come forth Torah," correctly understood, means the inculcation of moral standards governing relationships between men and between nations. That was the realm in which Judaism had made its unique contribution and to which Israel today must be likewise committed. Within Israel, however, one finds behavior patterns and imported Western materialism, which give considerable grounds for concern. It was, therefore, appropriate that a call go forth from Mount Scopus, urging that more serious attention be paid to the moral dimensions of our national life:

> We cannot afford to be *ke-khol ha-goyyim*, like all the nations. Medinat Yisrael must be more than a political end in itself. Zion must have its principal *raison d'être* in the Jewish moral and ethical way of life. *Tziyyon be-mishpat tippadeh*—"Zion must be redeemed through equity, and its returnees through justice."
>
> Who is to teach us, who is to exhort Torah in its essential meaning of giving direction to human life? Even a scientific study of the Bible does not necessarily make one religious. Is it too much to expect that on Mount Scopus and on Givat Ram choice intellects and spirits may come together for the purpose of keeping alive the searchlight of national self-criticism touching our daily lives in Israel? If a group of dedicated men of light and learning were to join in a common concern for our domestic moral climate, theirs would not be voices crying in the wilderness. And their radiating influence would also be felt in Jewish communities abroad.
>
> What I plead for today is for a torch to be kindled on the mountain top.

Nearly a fortnight later, on July 17, we were delighted to attend the Bar Mitzvah of Netanel Warszawski at Ha-Tzvi Yisrael Synagogue, close to our home in Talbieh. The portion that Shabbat morning was *Pinḥas*. Izak and Judith Warszawski, the parents of the Bar Mitzvah, were good friends of mine. They lived in Paris, where Izak was one of the leaders of our World Confederation of General Zionists and an editor of our French affiliate's Yiddish-language newspaper, *Di Tzionistishe Shtimme*.

Two more functions were held that summer to bid me farewell. One was a luncheon arranged by the Jerusalem Journalists' Association, at which Danny Bloch, the chairman, presided and addresses were delivered by old colleagues of mine on the Jewish Agency Executive representing the various Zionist parties— Rabbi Mordecai Kirshblum (Mizraḥi-Ha-Po'el Ha-Mizraḥi), Yosef Klarman (Ḥerut), and Avraham Schenker (Mapam)—and by Jerusalem's former Mayor, Mordecai Ish-Shalom (Mapai).

The other was a ceremony held in Western Galilee on July 29, when the new development town of Carmiel awarded me honorary citizenship. Having already received a similar honor at Eilat on the occasion of my seventieth birthday, I now took pride in this seventy-fifth birthday present. "Henceforth," I observed, "I have a broad stake in Eretz Yisrael—from Carmiel in the north to Eilat in the south!"

A few days later, when I accompanied my friend, colleague, and successor, Ezra Shapiro, to the Keren Hayesod office in Jerusalem and introduced him to the staff as their new boss, I was deeply conscious of the privilege and good fortune that had been mine in strengthening that great powerhouse of Jewish and Zionist endeavor. Thus concluded my five-decade-long active service to the Zionist movement. I would, of course, continue to maintain interest and to be helpful, as far as possible, but I would no longer be subject to constant daily pressures and taxing journeys. An immense weight had been lifted from my shoulders, but I was grateful for the privilege of having borne it.

13

Keren Hayesod:
Instrument for Jewish Creative Survival

These memoirs, in my view, would lack perspective and completeness were I to omit some special account of my long-standing involvement in two causes that have dominated my Zionist career. These causes are the Keren Hayesod, which it was my privilege to head for ten years, and the World Confederation of General Zionists, which I led for a quarter of a century. In serving the Confederation, I was discharging my moral obligation to the furthering of mainstream, Herzlian Zionism; in serving the Keren Hayesod, I was campaigning for the realization of an un-hyphenated Zionism in the interests of Medinat Yisrael and *Klal Yisrael*.

To the extent that the following pages may shed light on these aspects of my Zionist commitment, particularly during the years following World War II, I feel justified in interrupting my narrative.

I did not come to my responsibilities in the Keren Hayesod as a novice. A major portion of my career had been occupied with fund raising for the Jewish National Home before 1948, and for the State of Israel thereafter. My experience had spanned a decade as president of the Jewish National Fund in America and a number of crucial years as co-chairman and then chairman of the United Palestine Appeal, later also as co-chairman of the United Jewish Appeal. Subsequently, my year in Israel (1948–49) as treasurer of the Jewish Agency, and the world tour my wife and I undertook in 1959–60, afforded valuable insight into the local operations of the Keren Hayesod. They also gave me firsthand experience of fund-raising campaigns in the United States and British Commonwealth countries.

Obtaining substantial amounts for an important cause requires professional planning, organization, propaganda, and solicitation. It is a complex business, calling for initiative and imagination, the ability to overcome disappointments and to learn from experience, the challenge of converting apathy into interest, interest into enthusiasm, and enthusiasm into financial support. Fund raising, of necessity, has become a science. The methods employed vary in accordance with the nature of the objective and the clientele. There is, however, one common denominator essential to any successful fund-raising enterprise: the kind of leadership that will inspire confidence and ensure wide support.

My credentials and my accumulated experience over the years no doubt moved influential Zionist circles to endorse and urge my candidacy for the post of chairman of the Keren Hayesod. More important was the fact that I myself felt qualified to tackle such a responsibility. No matter how insistent the urgings of my colleagues, I would never have consented had I not felt that I could make a useful contribution.

There was, however, also a degree of sentiment involved for me in this choice. My first extra-congregational activity as a rabbinical neophyte on New York's West Side in 1921 was as a volunteer "infantryman" in America's first campaign for Keren Hayesod. I had fond recollections of Dr. Chaim Weizmann's visit at that time, of accompanying Naḥum Sokolow to a campaign meeting in New Haven (and helping, partly by carrying his valise and partly by briefing him in advance about the Jewish community he was about to address), and of prevailing upon Ze'ev Jabotinsky to speak at a weekday gathering of my congregants. Indeed, it might be said that I had cut my fund-raising wisdom teeth at the expense, or at any rate in the service, of the Keren Hayesod.

When, after the passage of forty years, I assumed the world chairmanship in 1961, I familiarized myself once again with the Keren Hayesod's historical background.

The concern of Jews in the Diaspora for their brethren in Eretz Yisrael was as old as the Diaspora itself. Once the cherished dream of *Shivat Tziyyon*, the Return to Zion, began to approach realization with the issuance of the Balfour Declaration in November 1917, Dr. Weizmann and his colleagues in the Zionist Organization laid plans for financing a program of immigration and settlement in the Jewish National Home.

There were several varied precedents. In 1899, Dr. Theodor Herzl had set up the Jewish Colonial Trust, which later became a holding company. Early in 1918, two months after the Balfour Declaration was issued, Chaim Weizmann, Naḥum Sokolow, and Jehiel Tschlenow proclaimed the Keren Hakhanah (Preparation Fund), with a quota of one million dollars, of which more than half was raised. Subsequently, in July 1919, a second fund was proclaimed—Keren ha-Ge'ulah (the Redemption Fund)—and this appeal raised close to $4 million.

At the Zionist Conference in London in 1920, three separate proposals were made for the creation of a financial instrument to implement Zionist aims. The first, calling for a national loan, was rejected out of hand by the assembled delegates, since "an appreciable part of the funds collected for the purpose of immigration and colonization would have to be spent on objectives from which no return could be expected." The second proposal, energetically promoted by U.S. Supreme Court Justice Louis D. Brandeis, the leader and spokesman of American Zionism, stipulated that Jews throughout the world would be asked to invest in a financial institution that would operate on a sound businesslike basis, supplying loans to immigrants for the development of private enterprise.

The third proposal, put forward by Dr. Weizmann and his colleagues, called for a campaign for contributions that would bring no financial return to the donor. Weizmann contended that no Jew would invest money in Palestine until economic conditions there provided a reasonable basis for such investments. According to this view, Zionism was a national pioneering enterprise and the Zionist Organization would accordingly seek funds from the entire Jewish people, and not only from the rich.

The resolution that brought Keren Hayesod, the Foundation Fund, into being made an appeal to all Jews, Zionists and non-Zionists alike, for money to finance immigration and settlement in Palestine on a nonprofit basis. The objective of the Fund was to lay the foundations of the Jewish National Home, as well as to encourage business enterprises, in close cooperation with private capital. Contributions to the Keren Hayesod were to be inspired by the ancient biblical tradition of *ma'aser*, giving a tithe (tenth) of one's income.

In October 1920, the new head office of the Keren Hayesod was formally opened at the Zionist headquarters in London, 75–77 Great Russell Street, W.C.1. It remained at that address until 1926, when the office was transferred to Jerusalem. Committees were organized in every country where the size of the Jewish population warranted a campaign. As a result of the Bolshevik Revolution of 1917, however, no committee was established in Russia.

In December 1920, the Keren Hayesod issued its first manifesto, declaring in ringing words the challenge facing every responsible Jew:

> No casual charity will suffice. The exceptional effort which is called for today must take the form of self-taxation—steady, persistent, systematic, inspired by the noble tradition of the tithe. There is no State. The appeal that is about to be made is to the Jewish conscience, and is justified by no power or compulsion; but no Jew worthy of the name will, at this solemn moment, take the responsibility of sheltering himself behind the powerlessness of his people.

When Dr. Weizmann arrived in America in April 1921, the executive of the Zionist Organization of America was firmly opposed to the principle of the tithe. The only group initially to adopt the Keren Hayesod was the Order of the Sons of Zion (now B'nai Zion), whose first public meeting in support of the Fund took place on April 17. Menaḥem Ussishkin and Shmaryahu Levin were the principal speakers. A month later, the Order of the Sons of Zion turned over the sum of $15,000 in cash and another $500,000 in pledges. Lengthy negotiations, however, between the ZOA's president, Judge Julian Mack, and Dr. Weizmann could effect no compromise. Weizmann then took the bold step of unilaterally declaring the establishment of an American bureau of the Keren Hayesod on April 18, 1921. He pinned his hopes on a special convention of the ZOA in two months' time, believing that it would ultimately confirm his decision.

At that convention, Weizmann's action was indeed upheld and the Mack-Brandeis group was defeated. Justice Brandeis accordingly resigned from the presidency of the ZOA. His letter of resignation made it clear that he and his colleagues were not withdrawing from the Zionist movement, but were taking their places in the ranks as "humble soldiers." Not long afterwards, three members of his group—Rabbi Stephen S. Wise, Rabbi Abba Hillel Silver, and Robert Szold—returned to the official Zionist fold. All three eventually became presidents of the ZOA and held other important Zionist positions, including leadership in fund raising. A program of private investment initiated by the Brandeis group was expanded into the Palestine Economic Corporation in 1926, with Bernard Flexner and Robert Szold in the leading positions.

The first president of the American Keren Hayesod was Samuel Untermeyer, an eminent New York attorney, who became prominent in the anti-Nazi boycott campaign during the 1930s. Emanuel Neumann, another future president of the ZOA, served as director-general.

Immediately after the Cleveland convention of 1921, Weizmann embarked on a seven-week campaign across the United States. When it ended, more than $3 million had been collected. Under the agreement laid down by the Zionist Congress, twenty percent of the net proceeds went to the Jewish National Fund.

During the twenty-eight years between the establishment of Keren Hayesod in 1920 and the establishment of Medinat Yisrael in 1948, a total of $143 million was raised and 257 settlements were built with Keren Hayesod resources. World War II imposed particularly heavy demands upon the Jewish Agency and its financial arm, the Keren Hayesod. Yet despite drastically reduced contributions from the European continent, commensurately larger sums raised in Great Britain and other English-speaking countries mitigated such losses.

In the course of Israel's War of Liberation, ten settlements established by the Jewish Agency were destroyed and seventy-six were severely damaged. All of these were later rebuilt with funds provided by the Keren Hayesod. The war of 1948–49 also imposed crushing burdens on Israel's farming community, which was similarly revived by means of allocations from an emergency Keren Hayesod budget.

With the establishment of the State, the Zionist General Council found itself confronted by a vital question when it met in Jerusalem in August 1948: What role should the Jewish Agency play now that Israel was a reality? There could be only one answer: The Agency must proceed with its historic mission of "ingathering," *Kibbutz Galuyyot*. This was to be carried out in two ways. First, the responsibility had to be undertaken for providing the infrastructure whereby Olim would be brought from overseas and helped to settle on the land, and whereby young people and children could be cared for through the Youth Aliyah program. Second, responsibility had also to be undertaken for fostering cultural and spiritual ties between Israel and the Diaspora and for instilling an awareness and appreciation of Jewish and Zionist values.

The Keren Hayesod was the principal financial instrument of the World Zionist Organization for carrying out these important operations. This major financial arm of the Jewish Agency for Israel was the body I was called upon to administer and develop, and to which I chose to dedicate my energies after Bert and I had begun to build a new life for ourselves in Medinat Yisrael.

To mark my appointment as world chairman of Keren Hayesod, a reception was tendered by the Jewish Agency's chairman, Moshe Sharett, on May 15, 1961, both to welcome me and to bid farewell to my immediate predecessor, Eliyahu Dobkin. I expressed my eagerness to undertake the tasks that lay ahead:

> The greater part of my Zionist life has been given to fund raising, to the Keren Hayesod under its various appellations, and to the Keren Kayemet. I am grateful that upon coming to Israel I have not been diverted from this pattern. The reward is a daily reward, the satisfaction of knowing that, at the end of the day, new resources have come from Jews contributing towards the strengthening and consolidation of Israel as a whole and enabling brother and sister Jews to find here their home, their dignity, their freedom and their salvation.

My work began immediately. Initially, for a brief period, I was fortunate to have Sarah Roth as my secretary. Her successor, Ḥasidah Aviad, served throughout the decade of my chairmanship with unusual efficiency and devotion.

In order to familiarize myself with the workings of the organization, its weaknesses and its potentials, and so as to prepare the necessary round of fund-raising campaigns, I planned a tour of countries in Europe and North and South America where the Keren Hayesod was active. Before leaving, however, some of the problems the Keren Hayesod would be facing were clearly delineated. I had already begun tracing them in broad outline after attending sessions of the Jewish Agency Executive and the Zionist General Council in April.

At a meeting of the Va'adat Te'um, the coordinating committee of the Israel Government and the Jewish Agency, chaired by Ben-Gurion, Moshe Sharett reported on the mounting rate of Aliyah. The year 1960 had brought a total of 25,000 Olim. This year, 1961, 32,000 new immigrants were expected and a total of 40,000 was forecast for 1962. (In fact, there were nearly 48,000 Olim in 1961 and more than 60,000 arrived during the following year.) Housing and Development Minister Giora Josephthal then reported that the Government's building program would be able to provide only 6,000 housing units, which would take care of less than half the anticipated need.

The next morning, at a meeting of the Keren Hayesod's Directorion (our new designation for the board of directors), the problem of locating effective *shliḥim* to cope with the growing needs of the Keren Hayesod was raised. We resolved that new people would have to be found, capable of matching the infectious enthusiasm of Shmaryahu Levin, Leib Jaffe, and other such pioneer emissaries of former years.

Clearly, the Keren Hayesod had to aim for a twofold objective: fund raising would have to be increased, and Keren Hayesod organizations around the world would have to be strengthened in order to meet this challenge.

One program I was eager to develop, even before beginning my overseas tour, was a *magbit me'uḥedet*—a united Keren Hayesod–Jewish National Fund appeal in Israel itself. The importance of such a venture lay, I felt, not only in its financial value but also in its psychological impact on the Diaspora. It would stimulate greater efforts on the part of Jewish communities throughout the *Golah* by demonstrating that Israelis were ready to make financial sacrifices over and above the heavy burden of taxation required by the State's defense budget.

With an eye to the American leg of my forthcoming trip, I had in mind a report made by the Council of Jewish Federations and Welfare Funds in the United States after its study mission had returned from Israel. One part of this report read:

> The development of fund raising in Israel on a systematic, voluntary and generous basis would underline for American Jewry even more forcefully the seriousness with which Israel itself views its present needs.

Ya'akov Tsur, chairman of the Directorion of the KKL-JNF, was in complete agreement with this policy. We accordingly put in motion the search for a strong local committee to direct this Israeli *magbit*. The committee was headed by Dr. Ernst Lehmann of Bank Leumi Le-Yisrael, with whom I had worked years earlier during my period as treasurer of the Jewish Agency.

Subsequent developments proved disappointing. On March 22, 1962, there took place in Tel Aviv a conference of the National Committee (Va'ad Artzi) of the United Israel Appeal, representing both the Keren Hayesod and the Keren Kayemet. Although such a Va'ad Artzi had actually been set up in Israel several years previously, it was now hoped to make a stronger effort, to inaugurate a campaign of larger dimensions, and to recruit a new and more dynamic leadership. All of this was intended to signify that greater support would be asked of the Yishuv, which had grown not only in population but in economic capacity as well. However, this united appeal has not fulfilled the hopes set upon it.

When I took office that spring, Keren Hayesod was entering its forty-first year. It had celebrated its fortieth anniversary in December 1960, at a world conference in Jerusalem organized by my predecessor, Eliyahu Dobkin. At that time, it was announced that $750 million had been raised by the Keren Hayesod and United Jewish Appeal since the establishment of the State in 1948 and that, in its forty years of existence, the Keren Hayesod had collected a grand total of $893 million.

In 1960, the entire income of the Keren Hayesod stood at $16 million, representing the total sum received from campaigns in fifty-four countries, excluding the United States. This figure remained stable for a time, until I had effected certain organizational changes. Then the income began to climb steadily. In 1967, mainly in response to the Six-Day War, its income rose to $150 million, a tenfold increase in comparison with 1961. By the time I relinquished my chairmanship in August 1971, it had been stabilized at $70 million per annum. The number of countries in which campaigns were organized had also risen, to sixty-nine.

It should be pointed out that while the Keren Hayesod raised $16 million in 1960, the United Jewish Appeal in the U.S. raised about $40 million. This brought the Jewish Agency's annual income to some $55 million that year. At the same time, however, the Agency's budget was approximately $100 million and it thus found itself unable to finance all the immigration and absorption (Aliyah and Klitah) needs, which had been mounting over the years. A great deal of deficit financing was resorted to, and the Israel Government had to shoulder a large part of the burden by assuming the ultimate financial responsibility for the Klitah program.

The tour of major European Jewish communities that I made soon after taking up my new responsibilities was the one practical way to familiarize myself with the workings of the international Keren Hayesod organization. I immediately had to face a serious problem in France involving the Keren Hayesod representative there. With the help of Ambassador Walter Eytan and of the Jewish Agency's chairman, Moshe Sharett, a reorganization of our work in Europe was put into effect. The European bureau, headed by Sam Segall, a wartime French resistance leader, was transferred to Jerusalem and the Keren Hayesod's Finance Department was moved to Geneva. Subsequently, the French *magbit* (L'Appel Unifié Juif), under the chairmanship of Raymond Wallier, began an upward swing, while the Fonds Social Juif Unifié—which took care of local Jewish needs—continued to show substantial increases from year to year.

Our fund-raising activities in Great Britain, conducted through the Joint Palestine Appeal (JPA), were in the capable hands of Lavy Bakstansky, general secretary of the British Zionist Federation, and his energetic assistant, Harry Shine. Bakstansky, whom I had first met during my wartime visit to London in 1944, also played a leading role in our General Zionist Confederation until his death in 1971.

In New York, I had a meeting with my Zionist Executive colleague, Zalman Shazar, who had just returned from South America. He had opened the Keren Hayesod campaign in Brazil and had also been promoting the cause of Jewish education in Argentina and Uruguay. A former Minister of Education and Culture and Israel's future President, Shazar, half in jest, offered to strike a bargain with me. "I'll support the Keren Hayesod in the Jewish Agency Executive," he said, "if you'll support my work for Jewish education." My reply was that no such deal was necessary. "I'll support Jewish education anyhow, while you will do the same for Keren Hayesod!"

During my absences abroad, the Jerusalem office was supervised by my deputy chairman, Woolf Perry, a Londoner, who retained his post from 1961 until 1968, serving also as a member of the Executive of the Jewish Agency and the World Zionist Organization. Perry had been a vice-president of the Zionist Federation of Great Britain and Ireland, and a vice-chairman of the World Confederation of General Zionists. He eventually returned to London.

The director-general and treasurer of World Keren Hayesod–United Israel Appeal during the initial period of my chairmanship was Moshe Ussoskin. Before coming to Israel, Ussoskin had rendered valuable service in Eastern Europe, particularly in Rumania, as the representative of the American Jewish Joint Distribution Committee there. He had also fostered Aliyah and organized Jewish cooperatives in the Balkans. In Jerusalem, he had commanded Haganah operations and served as honorary secretary of the Jewish Agency Committee for Claims Conference Allocations. Ussoskin's career with the Keren Hayesod, which ended with his retirement in 1968, spanned nearly three decades of able and devoted service.

Within the Keren Hayesod office there were special departments responsible for homogeneous geographical areas, notably Latin America, the European continent, and the English-speaking countries. It was naturally the English-speaking desk that first attracted my attention, not only because of my background but also because it produced by far the largest annual income. Another reason for my interest was the fact that the director of the Department for English-Speaking Countries was a cherished friend and colleague, Rabbi Morton Mayer Berman, who had arrived in Israel from the United States in 1957.

Both in the Jewish Institute of Religion and in the Free Synagogue, Rabbi Berman had worked closely with Dr. Stephen Wise. Later, as rabbi of Temple Isaiah Israel in Chicago, he had achieved positions of leadership in the American JNF, the American Jewish Congress, Labor Zionism, the United Jewish Appeal, and the ZOA. Throughout the period of my chairmanship, Rabbi Berman was frequently asked to lead Keren Hayesod campaigns in Great Britain, where he performed effective services for the Joint Palestine Appeal. Upon the occasion of the Keren Hayesod's fiftieth anniversary in 1970, he wrote *The Bridge to Life*, an authoritative illustrated history of the Keren Hayesod.

In October 1961, I outlined to the board of directors of Keren Hayesod–United Israel Appeal some of the problems confronting our future campaigning, as I had observed them, together with a number of recommendations that I hoped would lead to substantial increases in the funds Israel's development would require in the coming years.

Rejuvenation constituted the most immediate problem. After forty years of fund-raising campaigns and thirteen years of propagandist slogans drumming up support for the new State, the excitement and glamour surrounding the Keren Hayesod appeals had worn thin. Moreover, there was a need for new and younger leadership at the side of the veteran workers and, often, to replace the veterans.

A second issue was that of our budget. Much enthusiasm had been engendered by the mass Aliyah that had flooded Israel during the early years of statehood, and this had produced larger contributions from Diaspora Jewry, but far less than the needs. Absorption facilities were far below standard and an Aliyah of 60,000, with higher standards of Klitah, taxed the fund-raising operations.

There was also the element of competition. Many of our former key workers, together with such new elements as had meanwhile joined the Zionist movement, had become attracted to Israel Bonds—long-term loans to the Government of Israel, at modest rates of interest, which had been launched in the United States by David Ben-Gurion when he first arrived as Israel's Prime Minister in 1951. The Israel Bonds campaign enjoyed an intrinsic advantage in that, while asking not for gifts but for loans, it gave Jews the feeling that their bond purchases were also helping Israel and increasing its absorptive capacity for new immigrants. Morever, in some countries where Jews felt financially insecure, Israel Bonds were regarded as a form of protection not only against local currency devaluation, but also against economic and political uncertainties. To some extent, these investments represented a psychological bulwark for Jews contemplating the possibility of Aliyah.

Another form of competition that had to be faced were the combined campaigns, which took cognizance also of local communal needs. My position was that such local needs were important enough to warrant a special additional effort, and that lumping them together with our own Israel Appeal would inevitably prove costly to the Keren Hayesod.

I urged that Diaspora Zionist leaders accord due priority to the Keren Hayesod, that separate Keren Hayesod campaigns be conducted wherever possible, and that every effort be exerted to enforce Zionist discipline so as to ensure that no deductions would be made from campaign proceeds without the prior consent of the Jewish Agency in Jerusalem. These proposals were to form the basis of our fund-raising policy over the next decade.

During my first years in office, an intensified and concentrated effort was made to secure a more informed involvement of campaign leaders, key workers, and contributors. For Zionist key workers we used the Hebrew term *Askanim*, "volunteer activists." I urged the necessity of preparing new leadership cadres for the future, of setting up committees with younger people, and I stressed the importance of deepening and broadening the awareness of key personnel in regard to Israel's problems and requirements, through study of these at firsthand. To this end, we encouraged the dispatch of study missions to Israel, which met with Government, Jewish Agency, and Keren Hayesod leaders, in order to become personally familiar with the needs related to the responsibilities of the Jewish Agency. Members of these study missions visited installations maintained by the Jewish Agency's Immigration and Absorption Department, as well as agricultural and settlement projects, and they were also afforded the opportunity to visit Israel army installations and to see something of the nation's defense establishment. By 1970, some forty of these missions had been welcomed and hosted by Keren Hayesod.

For the Keren Hayesod communities throughout the world, I inaugurated Yom ha-Askan, an annual Key Workers' Day, in 1963. The particular date chosen was November 29, the anniversary of the UN resolution of 1947 sanctioning the establishment of a Jewish State. The occasion was to be devoted to honoring outstanding Keren Hayesod activists of the preceding year, mobilizing workers for the year ahead, and conveying the latest information about Israel's achievements and future requirements.

Special programs were developed to intensify the involvement of major contributors. One had to do with special projects, through which a donor who gave sums additional to his regular yearly contribution could have his name attached to a specific project for the absorption of immigrants. The 175 special projects that contributors established during the decade of my chairmanship included kindergartens, secondary schools, youth clubs, libraries, community centers, and other facilities for the benefit of new Olim. Some of the outstanding gifts in this category made possible the expansion of existing settlements, the establishment of residential facilities for elderly immigrant couples, the creation of playgrounds for children, and the building of entire housing areas.

Kiryat Wolfson, a new housing project in Akko (Acre), was a splendid example. Named in honor of the British philanthropist and Jewish communal leader, Isaac Wolfson, it was one of the first such undertakings of my Keren Hayesod administration and was financed by the Isaac and Edith Wolfson Trust. Apart from housing,

Kiryat Wolfson provided facilities for educational, religious, and social activities within one massive complex. To encourage good-neighbor relations between Jews and Arabs in Akko, a number of apartments were also set aside for Arab families. Together with Sir Isaac and Lady Wolfson, those present at the opening ceremony included their son, Leonard, and his family, Mrs. Vera Weizmann, J. Edward ("Teddy") Sieff, who was then chairman of Great Britain's Joint Palestine Appeal, David Ben-Gurion, and Labor Minister Yosef Almogi. A second Kiryat Wolfson was later built in Jerusalem.

Another project initiated during my tenure was the introduction of women's divisions. In order to set this in motion, I asked Paulette Fink, who had headed the Women's Division of the United Jewish Appeal in the United States, to visit a number of Jewish communities in Great Britain and Europe. My wife later took the initiative of establishing a women's division in Australia. Gradually, this idea spread. In many other parts of the Keren Hayesod world the innovation became an additional factor in our fund-raising picture.

With the cooperation of the New York United Jewish Appeal, directed by Henry Bernstein, a Hall of Remembrance was established in the Keren Hayesod building in Jerusalem. Its purpose was to honor contributors abroad who had performed exceptional services for Israel in their lifetime and who had made bequests of $5,000 or more to Keren Hayesod or the UJA. Their names are inscribed on wall plaques in the Memorial Hall and are recorded in special Books of Remembrance. The first such plaque, dedicated to Senator Herbert H. Lehman, was affixed at the ceremony inaugurating the Hall of Remembrance in 1964.

An annual cultural event closely associated with our activities was the award of the annual Leib Jaffe Prize for the best Hebrew book in the field of Jewish literature. This prize, inaugurated in 1957, honored the memory of a distinguished Zionist leader and spokesman of the Keren Hayesod who had lost his life in the bomb outrage that destroyed part of the Jewish Agency headquarters in March 1948. During my decade of chairmanship, the Leib Jaffe Prize was awarded to Jewish poets, biographers, and historians.

A constant problem was the need to budget for the increasing burden of immigrant absorption. Aliyah from a particular country might fluctuate from month to month, depending on circumstances beyond our control and even beyond our ability to anticipate. In 1963, for example, a sudden outbreak of anti-Semitism in Argentina brought about the rapid exit of nearly 5,000 Jews from that country. Neither the Jewish Agency nor the Government of Israel was in a position to forecast the rate of immigration, yet both had always to be prepared. Ships and planes needed to be on the alert and housing could not await the arrival of new Olim, but had to be put into construction at least six months ahead.

These were the concerns I emphasized at a European conference of Keren Hayesod held in Zurich at the end of January 1963. After citing the immigration costs and projections for the coming year, I said:

Every immigrant who is properly absorbed paves the way for another immigrant. Everyone who is not adequately absorbed discourages the next one from coming.

Jews must rid themselves of the illusion that somehow there is a *deus ex machina* who will solve these problems and will make good the failures of the Jewish people. Obviously, the Government of Israel is expected to play this role. I wish I knew how to shock Jews out of such an irresponsible approach. The Government, which means the taxpayers of Israel, can hardly meet its own requirements, especially the defense needs. I have heard people complain that we always talk of emergencies. We shall have to continue to talk of emergencies as long as there is no other word in the dictionary to describe the realities of the conditions with which we have to cope.

To those who were always demanding new campaign slogans I offered a list of suggestions—*Hatzalah* (Rescue), *Pidyon Shevuyim* (Redemption of Captives), *Kibbutz Galuyyot* (Ingathering of the Exiles), *Binyan ha-Aretz* (Building of the Land), *Ge'ulat ha-Am* (Redemption of the People). "If these slogans are not enough to stir a worthy Jewish response," I declared, "then, indeed, we are lost!"

In December 1964, on the eve of the 26th World Zionist Congress, a world conference of the Keren Hayesod was held in Jerusalem. It was attended by some 200 of our leaders from more than fifty countries. At that time there were 128,000 contributors to the Keren Hayesod. I was able to report that the preceding four years had witnessed an increase of more than twenty percent in our income, to a total of $167 million. Delegates at the conference's closing dinner heard a written message from Moshe Sharett, chairman of the Jewish Agency, whose illness prevented his attending. Sharett's words embodied a moving tribute to the delegates themselves, whom he saluted as "the Order of Knighthood of the Keren Hayesod and the United Jewish Appeal."

Aliyah figures plummeted during the years 1965–67, falling to less than one-third of what they had been annually during the previous three years. Only 54,700 persons entered Israel directly in that span of time, and the number of Olim declined to a record low of 12,275 in 1967. On the one hand, there was clearly a drying up of the reservoir of Jews in what were called the "lands of distress" (the Soviet bloc countries and the Muslim states), intensified by the refusal of the authorities there to let their Jews go. On the other hand, out of the millions of Jews living in the free world, only 3,300 came from the communities of Western Europe and 4,200 (about half of them Argentinians) from North and South America. The South African Aliyah, numbering 1,425, was proportionately the largest. To compound the problem, unemployment became widespread throughout Israel as a result of an economic recession.

Fund raising had still to be carried on, even more urgently, against this grim background. As an additional method of conveying our needs, our problems and our potentials to the Keren Hayesod *Askanim* around the world, I arranged the publication of a monthly bulletin entitled *Between Us*. In this newsletter, we endeavored to explain the reasons for the current stressful situation: the ending of reparations payments from West Germany, the decline in foreign aid, the sudden increased tension on Israel's northern border, which necessitated additional defense expenditure, and the residual problems that inevitably arose from the immigration of one and a half million Jews in a relatively short period of time.

In the course of my tours overseas at this critical juncture, I was repeatedly confronted by one question: "How does one justify asking for increased donations at a time when Aliyah is on the downgrade?" As I explained in an issue of *Between Us*, it would have been foolish to base a long-term judgment on what might turn out to be a passing phenomenon. Aliyah had to be assessed in terms of years, not months. Bringing Olim to Israel was only the first step: unless this was followed by successful absorption, various dangers would present themselves. Many immigrants would return disillusioned to their countries of origin, or they would write letters home that would discourage their relatives and friends from coming. Moreover, inadequate attention to Klitah would burden Israel's population with malcontents and potentially explosive troublemakers. I felt, therefore, that it would be wise to take advantage of this temporary lull in immigration so as to speed up the absorption of those who had come, but who had yet to be integrated, economically, socially, or otherwise. The respite also afforded an opportunity to tackle various persisting social maladies, such as the overcrowded dwellings and slum areas in Israel's major cities, the prevailing shortage of youth centers and recreational facilities in urban districts, and other, similar shortcomings.

Such, then, was the bleak position as the year 1966 drew to a close and the war clouds began to mass along Israel's borders with the hostile Arab states to the north, south and east. Who, in the last months of 1966 and the early part of 1967, could have foreseen that the entire picture would soon be changed and that one of the most remarkable demonstrations of World Jewry's solidarity with the embattled State of Israel would soon be evinced?

As those first alarming months of 1967 wore on, we were left in no doubt that the very existence of Israel was now in mortal danger. The governments of the surrounding Arab states, led vociferously by Egypt's President Gamal Abdul Nasser, made no attempt to disguise their intentions. By mid-May, these voices had become louder and more menacing, impressing upon us the urgent necessity to mobilize unprecedentedly vast sums for the emergency fund, to relieve the Government of having to pay for the immigrant-absorption program. Keren Hayesod and the United Jewish Appeal faced a challenge of the first magnitude.

In response to Nasser's preparations for all-out war, the Israel Defense Forces began calling up the reserves on May 18. Simultaneously, an emergency campaign fund delegation, Keren Hayesod's special task force, left Israel to alert Jewish communities in the Diaspora to the grave dangers of this new Middle East crisis. Leading this delegation were Israel's Finance Minister, Pinhas Sapir, the Jewish Agency's chairman, Louis Pincus, and its treasurer, Arye L. Dultzin, and I, together with other Government and Jewish Agency personalities and a number of senior IDF officers headed by General Hayyim Laskov. Meetings were arranged at short notice in a series of major cities throughout Western Europe and North and

South America, in order to fix targets for the emergency campaign. The quotas that Sapir allocated to the European communities were usually ten times the amounts raised in 1966, and in most cases these quotas were attained.

It was agreed that I should proceed to Canada forthwith and then go on to Latin America. Sapir and Pincus went to Great Britain, the United States being their next destination; Ya'akov Tsur, the head of the Keren Kayemet, flew to Europe; and Labor Minister Yosef Almogi followed soon afterwards. Moshe Ussoskin, the Keren Hayesod's director-general, remained in Jerusalem to coordinate our activities.

On reaching Canada, I had immediate consultations with Sam Bronfman and the Zionist leadership in Montreal and Toronto, including Sol Granek, director of the Canadian UJA. At this initial stage, new pace-setting contributions were announced. I then flew on to the western provinces of Canada, where I found younger men taking the helm. My objective was to begin campaigning without delay, in the hope that, if significant increases could be achieved there, it would serve as a challenge and incentive to the larger Jewish communities in Ontario and Quebec.

The responses were most encouraging. In Winnipeg, for example, Joe Secter and his campaign committee met with me three times in the course of the day to upgrade their quota in the light of results being obtained by telephone calls and personal visits. We conducted a walking campaign, calling on people at their places of business without giving prior notice. The excitement was contagious. All previous fund-raising records were not only surpassed but multiplied. This experience, in fact, was typical of the response we obtained from Jewish communities, both large and small, throughout the world.

From Winnipeg we telephoned Vancouver and other centers in western Canada so as to prepare them for my visits. When I arrived, I found the ground well prepared for a repetition of the Winnipeg experience. We lost no time in communicating these results to the leaders in the eastern provinces, where the "big money" was to be raised. It was a powerful and challenging stimulus.

I could easily picture similar scenes being enacted all over the world. Diaspora Jewry was responding magnificently to Israel's emergency.

While on the point of flying back to the east, I received a long-distance telephone call informing me that it was thought advisable in Jerusalem that I proceed instead to Montevideo, where Pinhas Sapir was scheduled to meet with the leaders of our Keren Hayesod communities in South America. Revising my plans within minutes, I was soon on board a plane for Uruguay. En route, we had a one-hour stop in Mexico City, where I received the report that our campaign there was going well. A stopover in Buenos Aires provided me with enough time to meet local Keren Hayesod leaders at the airport and check on their initial results. Later, I learned that Sapir and Pincus had been conducting successful airport campaigns with Jewish leaders in many parts of Western Europe, stressing the urgency for immediate preliminary responses to Israel's need.

In Montevideo, I found that Sapir was already conferring with a number of Jewish community leaders from South America. Israel's ambassador to Brazil, Yitzhak

Harkavy, was with them. Sapir's message was characteristically brief and forceful. The response was exhilarating, as one Jewish leader after another assumed responsibility for the quota assigned to his community. Since this was Keren Hayesod territory, I knew that it would be my job to help them fulfill their promises.

By that time, the second week of June, war had already broken out, although there was no clear news yet from Israel. Pinḥas Sapir had a son in the armed forces. My own thoughts were on my wife, Bert, in Jerusalem. A long-distance call came. It was Israel's Defense Minister, General Moshe Dayan, ringing Sapir. The message was brief, but reassuring: *"Ha-kol be-seder"*—"Everything is OK."

With the conclusion of our urgent business, the assembled leaders returned to Argentina, Brazil, Chile, and the other South American republics. I left for Israel, making hurried visits of a few hours' duration, on the way, to our children in the United States.

My one other stopover was in London. There, Michael Barzilay, Keren Hayesod's representative in Great Britain, awaited me and took me to the home of the British campaign's chairman, Hyam ("Hymie") J. Morrison (who years later would become my next-door, oft-time neighbor in Jerusalem). On the following day, I visited Rex House, the new and more spacious headquarters of the British Zionist Federation and Joint Israel Appeal. These offices in Regent Street had replaced the historic but inadequate building in Great Russell Street. At Rex House, Morrison and his colleagues were working feverishly. His wife, Doris, was organizing the women campaigners. In Teddy Sieff, Michael Sacher, Jack Lyons, and Harold Poster, Hymie Morrison had a strong and inspiring team of Keren Hayesod activists.

While I was there, Shimshon Y. Kreutner, our European director, telephoned from Geneva to tell me that the emergency campaign was also doing well across the English Channel. In France, a joint *magbit* had been arranged with the Fonds Social Juif Unifié. Baron Guy de Rothschild subsequently announced that an unprecedented 72 percent of French Jewry had contributed to the appeal.

The Jewish people throughout the world had responded admirably to the crisis. In the United States, the United Jewish Appeal had risen to unprecedented heights. So had the Keren Hayesod communities elsewhere. Indeed, in proportion to their numbers and means, the response of the Keren Hayesod communities was even more impressive.

The reasons for this extraordinary manifestation of worldwide Jewish solidarity with Israel were obvious. Newsreels, television and radio reports, all the paraphernalia of the mass media, had driven home the horrifying significance of the bloodthirsty Arab mobs incited by their glory-seeking leaders; the callous cynicism of the Soviet propaganda machine; the helplessness of the United Nations; and the terrifying possibility of a wholesale massacre of Jews in the Jewish homeland.

Jews everywhere were shocked into action. Over four years previously, in Zurich, I had spoken of Keren Hayesod's *Askanim* as representing "a kind of *Tzahal*, not *Tzeva Haganah Le-Yisrael* (the Israel Defense Forces) but *Tzeva Hatramah le-Yisrael*, the Army of Fund Raisers for Israel." This army had also gone into action, rallying volunteers from the Diaspora, obtaining supplies of urgently needed equipment, and providing additional funds that would enable the Jewish State to fulfill its tasks during the emergency.

Accompanied by Woolf Perry, Moshe Ussoskin, Rabbi Morton Berman, and Michael Barzilay, I visited Israel's Chief of Staff, General Yitzhak Rabin, at his office in Tel Aviv in order to convey the Keren Hayesod's gratitude to the fighting army. We presented him with an original painting of an Israeli paratrooper kissing the stones of the Western Wall. Reproductions of that picture were subsequently awarded to our outstanding workers.

Those of us who were privileged to have had some part in the great drama of June 1967 will never forget it. Outside Keren Hayesod and Zionist offices, Israel embassies and legations in many countries, long lines of contributors stood waiting. Every mail delivery brought thousands of remittances, sometimes from people who had never previously given money to Israel, among them large numbers of non-Jews. In Holland, for example, two-fifths of the contributors were Christian sympathizers. There were recipients of German restitution funds who gave the greater part of their income; elderly folk who brought their life savings; communities and congregations that sold off some of their assets in order to donate their share. Jewish housewives and schoolchildren handed over their savings or found employment so as to earn money for the emergency campaigns. In dozens of cities, women stripped off their jewelry; in Hong Kong, ex-refugees from Communist China brought cash contributions to demonstrate their own solidarity with Israel. Everywhere, there were profoundly moving demonstrations of popular support for Israel's cause.

The emergency campaign fund netted $151,477,500 for the Keren Hayesod, more than twelve times the amount raised in 1966. The total number of contributors rose to 400,000, twice as many as had come forward in any one year previously. These sums had been made available within a matter of days. The scope of this Israel Appeal and of its counterpart in the United States had no precedent in the history of fund raising.

In the wake of this response, the Keren Hayesod organized a series of concerts in a number of Diaspora communities by the Youth Orchestra of Gadna (Gedudé No'ar), the cadet corps of the Israel Defense Forces. Yitzhak Rogow, the director of Keren Hayesod's Information Department, served as the impresario of this project. He had the cooperation of Woolf Perry, my deputy chairman. Mendy Rodan conducted the Gadna Orchestra during its tour, but on a number of occasions the baton was taken by the famous star of stage and screen, Danny Kaye, an untiring and warmhearted friend of Israel. The orchestra gave twenty-four concerts in twenty-two countries throughout Europe and the Americas. It was a project that created a great deal of interest and goodwill overseas.

All in all, World Jewry's response to the 1967 emergency was much broader and deeper than it had been during the Suez crisis of 1956. Nineteen years of Jewish statehood had proved that Medinat Yisrael, despite its shortcomings, had measured up to the great expectations reposed in it and had enhanced the good name of the Jew in the eyes of the world.

One stimulating effect of the Six-Day War, which proved to be of permanent value to the Keren Hayesod, was the emergence of a dynamic young leadership in many communities, men in their thirties who set an example by their own giving and working, and who spurred their elders to greater efforts and more generous responses. As I had occasion to say more than once, this new factor was important not only for Israel, but also for the Jewish future of the overseas communities themselves. From every angle, philanthropic, religious, or Zionist, many of these young men had proved that they constituted a great new potential, and it was clear that persons of their caliber were needed—and should be recruited—by the leaders of their *kehillot*. As a postscript to that evaluation, I should add that they have indeed been so enlisted.

Paradoxically enough, after the experience of June 1967, I learned on October 1 that Pinḥas Sapir, Israel's Minister of Finance, was now contemplating the desirability of merging the Keren Hayesod with other bodies to form one vast fund-raising instrument of the Government and the Jewish Agency, to be known as "Keren Yisrael." Only in Great Britain and Canada, where special circumstances prevailed, would the Keren Hayesod continue to operate under its own name. Sapir's plan was motivated by the continuing need for massive funds and the the emergency campaign's success in uncovering new forces and hitherto untapped resources throughout the world. Prime Minister Levi Eshkol, Dr. Nahum Goldmann, president of the World Zionist Organization, and Louis Pincus, chairman of the Jewish Agency Executive, seemed amenable to this idea.

I expressed firm opposition to such a move, for a variety of reasons. The very name of Keren Hayesod stood for an important tradition; it was the best possible instrument for what had to be achieved and had proved its worth in June; its replacement by some other body, in which Israel's overseas diplomats would be the key figures, would surely be a blow to the morale of all Keren Hayesod *Askanim;* and serious legal problems would arise in respect to tax-exemption benefits in various countries. Far from abandoning the Keren Hayesod, both the Israel Government and the Jewish Agency ought to strengthen it instead. I also insisted that any far-reaching change would need to be ratified by the World Zionist Organization at its next Congress. Moshe Ussoskin and our Keren Hayesod administrative committee gave full backing to this stand.

Fortunately, Prime Minister Levi Eshkol supported my position and it was in large measure because of his attitude that our view prevailed and the Sapir-Pincus merger scheme was dropped. It was a clear-cut victory for the Keren Hayesod, which entered upon a new era, mobilizing new forces and greatly increased funds to relieve the Government of some burdens it had been compelled to shoulder hitherto.

At the same time, however, I did feel the need for some reorganization in the Keren Hayesod's head office. New and younger men were drawn into our work, some of them former army officers with administrative and organizational experience. Others had been active in public service. One major step was the appointment of Shimshon Y. (Shai) Kreutner to the key post of director-general, immediately upon the retirement of Moshe Ussoskin in 1968. Kreutner had joined the Keren

Hayesod after having served effectively in the World Zionist Organization for a number of years as director of the Organization Department. Latterly, he had directed our operations in Europe. Combining European and Jewish culture, he had excelled in his Zionist missions to many parts of the world and had also displayed much ability as secretary of the 24th and 25th Zionist Congresses.

The year following the Six-Day War brought a perhaps inevitable reaction in terms of Keren Hayesod income. The amount raised was $44 million, but our subsequent campaigns netted substantially larger sums—$60 million in 1969–70 and $75 million in 1970–71. From 1920 to 1970, in its first fifty years, the Keren Hayesod had produced a total of $1,600 million through its various campaigns. What we had to show for those years were well over one million immigrants, 490 agricultural settlements, twenty-seven new development towns, the expansion of Israel's cities, and the promotion of industrial development, all of which contributed to a new image of the Jew throughout the world.

In April 1968, Prime Minister Levi Eshkol convened the International Economic Conference in Jerusalem, with the object of devising a new and expanded development program for Israel. Just over a year later, in June 1969, the Jewish Agency sponsored the Conference on Human Needs in Israel (COHN), attended by some 200 leading fund raisers from North America and the Keren Hayesod communities. Meeting in Jerusalem, they hammered out a program designed to meet Israel's urgent requirements in various essential areas, ranging from Aliyah and absorption to social welfare and education. In my message to the Keren Hayesod delegates I said:

> No longer can we meet the vital needs of each immediate year as they arise, nor should we have to face the challenge of each crisis as it occurs. The time has come to plan our work on a thorough study of the total long-range humanitarian needs of Israel, and the constant absorption of immigrants, which are fundamental to the upbuilding of the nation.
>
> We require your counsel, your special knowledge and experience in your many fields of endeavor and, above all, your continual, unwavering dedication to our tasks.

The cooperation eagerly extended by non-Zionist fund raisers abroad inspired Louis Pincus's plan for a broadened composition of the Jewish Agency Executive, which eventually came to fruition.

An important and gratifying event during my chairmanship of the Keren Hayesod–United Israel Appeal was the year-long (1969–70) program of festivities to mark its golden jubilee.* I announced the forthcoming celebration at a special session of the Zionist General Council held in Jerusalem on July 1, 1969. Addresses were then delivered by the Council's chairman, Ehud Avriel, the chairman of the Jewish

---

*Two publications surveying Keren Hayesod's fifty years of achievement were Rabbi Morton Berman's *The Bridge To Life* and Dr. Shlomo Kodesh's *Shekhem Ehad* ("Shoulder to Shoulder"), written especially for Israel's youth. Both appeared in 1970.

Agency, Louis Pincus, and by Sir Barnett Janner, Yitzḥak Ben-Aharon, and Moshe Krone. Three weeks later, at a reception held at the President's house, Bet ha-Nasi, I presented a scroll to President Zalman Shazar formally proclaiming Keren Hayesod's jubilee year.

My address before the Zionist General Council recalled some interesting past history. I pointed out that when the Foundation Fund was established in 1920, the object had been to raise the sum of £25 million sterling over a period of five years. The leaders of the Zionist movement in those far-off days evidently believed that such an amount would suffice to lay the foundations of the Jewish National Home. By 1923, it had become obvious that this target would not be reached and it was then that Dr. Chaim Weizmann issued his challenging and reproachful call: "O Jewish people, where art thou?"

More than once, as I reminded my audience, the Keren Hayesod had been compelled to echo that urgent plea by its principal founder. Yet, when the Jewish State faced its grave peril in June 1967, the entire Jewish people had at last responded: "*Hineni!* Here I am!" A time would come, I ventured to hope, when the three million Jews locked behind the Iron Curtain would be free to leave and join their brethren in Israel. At that point, "the Keren Hayesod will be challenged again and again to arouse the Jewish people to its responsibility." Meanwhile, Jewish communities everywhere were urged to mark the jubilee by intensifying their efforts for Israel.

The celebrations in Israel, under the patronage of President Shazar, included the dedication of a Keren Hayesod Pavilion at the International Fair held in Tel Aviv's showgrounds; a reception in Jerusalem for the mayors of fifty-five towns that had named one of their streets or squares "Keren Hayesod"; and a festive concert by the Israel Philharmonic Orchestra, which had been one of the early beneficiaries of the Foundation Fund. At this IPO concert, held in Binyanei ha-Umah on July 21, Zubin Mehta took the baton and the soloists were Daniel Barenboim (piano) and his wife, Jacqueline Dupré (cello), and Richard Tucker (tenor). A special session of the Knesset was held, in the course of which the Speaker and the Finance Minister conveyed the Israel Government's appreciation to the Keren Hayesod for its fifty years of service to the Yishuv and to the State. The Ministry of Posts issued a commemorative stamp to mark the jubilee incorporating in its design the words *Aliyah, Klitah, Hityashvut*—"Immigration, Absorption, Settlement"; and a Keren Hayesod medallion was distributed to leaders of the State and of the Zionist movement and to *Askanim* and contributors who had rendered meritorious service to the Foundation Fund.

It was my great personal privilege to present a set of the commemorative medallions to a founder of the Keren Hayesod, David Ben-Gurion, at his Tel Aviv home. Another set was presented to the Weizmann House in Reḥovot, to be deposited among the mementos of Israel's first President, whose vision and foresight helped to create the Keren Hayesod and whose unflagging labors in its behalf, the world over, played a large part in its fund-raising achievements. One of these medallions was also presented to the Jabotinsky Museum in Metzudat Ze'ev, Tel Aviv, where it was accepted by Menaḥem Begin, leader of the Ḥerut Party. Jabotinsky had been a member of the first board of the Keren Hayesod, in 1920, and had directed its Information Department.

Celebrations were held outside Israel as well, in major centers of Keren Hayesod activity on five continents. I addressed jubilee functions in Great Britain, Latin America, South Africa, and the United States. In Paris, Geneva, Buenos Aires, Rio de Janeiro, São Paulo and Montevideo, festivities were combined with fund-raising dinners. In New York, Edward Ginsberg, chairman of the United Jewish Appeal, presided over the dinner at which I spoke together with Israel's ambassador, Yitzhak Rabin, and a film depicting Keren Hayesod's fifty years of achievement was screened. My host in London was again Hyam Morrison, and I addressed the opening session of the British Zionist Federation conference. Donald Silk, the chairman of the Federation, Lord Janner, and Eva, Marchioness of Reading, were among those who shared the platform.

An important part was played by Israel's diplomatic representatives abroad in the Keren Hayesod campaigns throughout the decade of my chairmanship and during my many fund-raising tours overseas. The Israel embassy often serves as a focal point from which Jews in the Diaspora receive a spiritual impetus for the conduct of our campaigns, and through it their own status in the eyes of non-Jews is frequently enhanced. Moshe Yuval, whom I had first met ten years earlier in Australia, thus proved very helpful to me, by virtue of his position as ambassador in Peru, when I came to launch the *magbit* there in 1970.

The highlight of that golden jubilee tour was probably my visit to South Africa. Bert accompanied me. Our previous visit, more in the nature of a private tour of the country, had taken place over a decade before and we were aware of many changes. South African Jewry could boast of the highest percentage of children in any Diaspora community who received a good Jewish education. From the outset of the Zionist struggle, South Africa's Jewish community had placed itself on the highway of the great itinerant spokesmen and organizers of the Keren Hayesod—Weizmann, Sokolow, Ussishkin, Shmaryahu Levin, Leib Jaffe, and others of caliber. More than once, their visits had resulted in the securing of important pro-Zionist declarations from General Smuts and his colleagues.

The opening session of the biennial South African Zionist conference took place in Johannesburg on March 26, 1970. Some 400 delegates were present. The principal speakers included Chief Rabbi Bernard M. Casper, Israel's consul general, Itzhak Unna, who subsequently returned with the rank of ambassador, and Judge Israel Maisels, president of the Israel United Appeal. On the platform, I was glad to see former Chief Rabbi Louis Rabinowitz, a good friend of ours in Jerusalem and a valuable emissary for our *magbit*. At the special IUA session over which Julius Weinstein presided, I awarded jubilee medallions to Harry Trobe and Meyer Goldsmith, who had played leading roles in our campaigns over the past fifty years.

It proved to be a lively convention, presaging one or two significant changes within South African Zionism. Under pressure from younger delegates, a resolution was adopted making it incumbent upon the Federation's chairman to leave for Israel "within a reasonable time"—specifically, two years. This was no paper resolution to be honored in the breach. After retiring from his chairmanship of the SAZF in 1972, Solly Liebgott, then also head of the United Mizrahi Organization, did in fact make Aliyah. Another subsequent development, following local Zionist elections in November 1971, was the emergence of Julius Weinstein's Revisionist group as the dominant Zionist faction. Until then, the United Zionist Association, a General Zionist alliance, had been the strongest party in South Africa. In 1978, Harry Hurwitz, senior vice-chairman of the SAZF and another leading Revisionist, left South Africa to become Prime Minister Menahem Begin's chief adviser on overseas information.

In my conference address, I made appreciative reference to South African Jewry's unique contribution to Israel, both financial and in terms of eminent Olim. The $25 million raised in the 1967 IUA campaign was the highest per-capita record in the world. South Africa had raised future leaders and spokesmen of Israel—men such as Abba Eban, Jack Geri, Arthur Lourie, Michael Comay, and Louis Aryeh Pincus. As chairman of the Jewish Agency, Pincus had sent fond greetings to the community of his birth. My own message touched on the potentially even greater contributions this exemplary *kehillah* might make in both spheres. "The Jewish people has been referred to as Israel's inalienable ally," I concluded. That relationship was far more than any alliance or partnership; it was a sense of belonging together, of being bound by a common faith and fate. I believed that "Jews everywhere will cherish the privilege of helping Israel carry its responsibilities, for the sake of our own people and for the sake of a more decent and a more enlightened world."

Several months later, in early November, Prime Minister Golda Meir helped to boost our fund-raising efforts while she was in London. At a reception there tendered by Ambassador Michael Comay and his wife, she received a number of Keren Hayesod leaders from Europe, including Baron Elie de Rothschild of Paris, Nessim Gaon of Geneva, Léon Maiersdorf of Brussels, and Jozef Komkommer of Antwerp. It was my privilege to open and conclude the evening, in which Shai Kreutner was a participant. The responses following Golda Meir's address substantially exceeded the previous year's contributions, in some cases by as much as fifty percent.

Among the leading Keren Hayesod activists in Europe during the period of my chairmanship, Jean Brunschvig of Geneva and Michel (Melech) Topiol of Paris deserve special mention. A past president of the *kehillah* in Geneva and secretary of the Federation of Swiss Jewish Communities, Jean Brunschvig was the mainstay of our *magbit* in western (French-speaking) Switzerland for many years and went on to become honorary president of the Swiss Keren Hayesod. He also played an active role in our General Zionist Confederation and was a generous patron of my Jerusalem Youth Village. Michel Topiol, who served as chairman of the Appel Unifié Juif in France, was a member of the Zionist General Council and later sat on the Jewish Agency Executive. In more recent years, he has achieved prominence as co-president of the World Confederation of United Zionists.

By the end of 1970, I had decided that, upon reaching the age of seventy-five in June 1971, I would resign from the chairmanship of Keren Hayesod and from membership of the Jewish Agency Executive. Having devoted ten good years of my life to the Foundation Fund, having raised its income many times over and its prestige very considerably throughout the Jewish world, it was time for me to retire. Finding a proper successor was no easy task. With the agreement of Louis Pincus and Pinḥas Sapir, and after sounding out Rose Halprin, Kalman Sultanik, Michel Topiol, and other leaders of our Confederation, I finally decided on Ezra Zelig Shapiro of Cleveland, Ohio. He had served with distinction as president of the American Jewish League for Palestine, was an outstanding Hebraist and Zionist leader, and had a splendid like-minded partner in his wife, Sylvia. Both of them were ready to make Aliyah. A distinguished "Anglo-Saxon" gathering, headed by Viscount Edwin and Lady Samuel, welcomed the Shapiros at a dinner in our home almost as soon as they arrived in Jerusalem.

Our choice of Ezra Shapiro proved to be a wise decision.

With the appointment of my successor now settled, I was able to embark on my last Keren Hayesod tours in an easier frame of mind. On one trip, to Caracas, Venezuela, and Rio de Janeiro, I was accompanied by Pinḥas Sapir and Sam Rothberg. The results of our *magbit* were even better than those achieved during the 1967 emergency appeal. I jokingly dubbed Rothberg "SAM Missile No. III," since he was campaigning for Israel Bonds, Keren Hayesod, and the Hebrew University. In Rio we met a number of Jews who had fled Chile when President Allende's leftist regime took control of that country. "How many times must you keep on running?" asked Sapir. "Come to Israel. We shall do everything possible to help you find your place in the Jewish homeland."

My final campaign took me to Australia, where I combined *magbit* appearances with Israel Independence Day speeches in Sydney, Melbourne, and Brisbane. The Yom Ha-Atzma'ut celebrations in Perth had been organized by the local Women Zionists, and it was thus appropriate that Bert, who accompanied me, should deliver the main address there.

Our previous visit to Australia had taken place twelve years earlier, in 1959. We were happy to note significant improvements in the spheres of Jewish education, communal organization, relations with world Jewish bodies, and Zionist activity. Isador A. Magit, who had been born in Harbin, was chairman of the Federal Keren Hayesod–United Israel Appeal of Australia. He had distinguished himself in the emergency campaign of 1967 and was later to become a governor of the Jewish Agency and a prominent friend of the Hebrew University of Jerusalem.

An effective younger leadership had also come to the fore. In absolute figures, the 5,000 Jews who attended Yom Ha-Atzma'ut celebrations in Melbourne were only surpassed in Israel and New York. Proportionately, however, both Melbourne and Sydney could claim the best attendance anywhere in the world: practically every family had representatives at these Israel Independence Day rallies.

My Yom Ha-Atzma'ut address in Melbourne on April 25, 1971, repeated two days later in Sydney, began with a tribute to this remarkable Zionist commitment and to the friendly ties that had linked Australia with Israel ever since the late Herbert Evatt's memorable role at the United Nations General Assembly debates resulting in the partition resolution of November 1947. I devoted the remainder of my speech to a *tour d'horizon* of the world Jewish, Zionist, and Israeli scenes. "The commitment of the Jewish people to Israel is unconditional," I said. "*Altneuland* must never become '*Al-tnay-land*,' a commitment hedged about with conditions. Let the 'gold,' the 'bronze' and the 'light' in the song, *Yerushalayim Shel Zahav*, token the need for the light of understanding, the bronze of resolution and the gold of generous material support."

Following discussions between the World Zionist Organization, Keren Hayesod, and the United Israel Appeal, an "Agreement for the Reconstitution of the Jewish Agency" was approved by the Zionist General Council in February 1970. Dewey D. Stone, then honorary chairman of the United Israel Appeal, played an important part in this development. He was ably assisted by Gottlieb Hammer, executive vice-chairman of the United Israel Appeal. Dewey Stone had helped to launch the successful $100 million UJA campaign in 1945 as well as the first campaign for Israel Bonds. As national chairman of the UJA from 1955 until 1963, and as chairman of the board of governors of the Weizmann Institute from 1944, he had been associated with fund raising for major Israeli causes. It was during these years that Max M. Fisher and other prominent non-Zionists had their first contact with fund raising for Israel through the United Israel Appeal.

Such collaboration on the American scene may be said to have paved the way for even broader and more significant later developments. Thus, under the leadership of Louis Aryeh Pincus, chairman of the Jewish Agency Executive, and Max M. Fisher, chairman of the United Israel Appeal in the United States, the broadened Jewish Agency, comprising both Zionists and non-Zionists, was brought into being.

At this Actions Committee meeting in February 1970, I drew a comparison with the previous, similar attempt in 1929, when Chaim Weizmann and Louis Marshall were the motivating forces and when it had been my privilege to be among those present. Forty years later, however, this move was taking place in vastly different circumstances. Marshall, Warburg, Sir Alfred Mond, and the other non-Zionists who joined the Agency in 1929 had come as individual personalities distinguished in their own right, whereas those who were joining today derived their strength from the great organizations that they led. These organizations would be permanently committed and the enlarged Jewish Agency, therefore, would rest on solid foundations. Furthermore, the very existence of Israel and its centrality in Jewish life sharpened the contrast between the Zurich meeting of 1929 and the Jerusalem meeting of 1970.

On August 24, the Planning Committee for the Reconstitution of the Jewish Agency met to implement the new agreement. Louis Pincus and Max Fisher were the chief participants. Three days later, on August 27, the agreement was initialed by leaders of the WZO, Keren Hayesod, and United Israel Appeal at a ceremony held at Bet ha-Nasi in the presence of Israel's President, Zalman Shazar, and Prime Minister Golda Meir. According to the terms of the agreement, the World Zionist Organization would nominate fifty percent of the members of the reconstituted Jewish Agency; the United Israel Appeal, thirty percent; and the Keren Hayesod communities would designate the remaining twenty percent. The task of preparing the ground for the founding assembly of the enlarged Jewish Agency in the following year was entrusted to the Implementation and Planning Committee, headed by Judge Israel Maisels, honorary president of South Africa's Israel United Appeal (Keren Hayesod), Avraham Schenker of the WZO and Jewish Agency Executives, Melvin Dubinsky, vice-chairman of the United Israel Appeal, and myself, as co-chairman of the Finance Committee. Moshe Rivlin, the Jewish Agency's director-general, served as coordinator.

Some influential Zionists were apprehensive lest this new arrangement lead to a weakening or dilution of the Zionist movement. I did not share their fears. It was my belief that, with the non-Zionists sharing in the massive responsibilities of financing and administering Aliyah, Klitah, housing, land settlement, and similar tasks, the World Zionist Organization would be able to concentrate more effectively on information, youth and pioneering, Jewish National Fund, and similar activities, and especially on Zionist and Hebrew education in the Diaspora and on stimulating Aliyah. A major challenge facing the WZO was the "conversion" of young Jews to the Zionist cause, particularly those students and others in the *Golah* who had been influenced by leftist movements and anti-Israel attitudes. Above all, I believed, we should make every effort to promote their Aliyah. On the broader issue of fund raising, there was little to choose between those who defined themselves as Zionists and those who did not. As a result of the Six-Day War, intensified and expanded support for Israel had swept across all such divisions. We had everything to gain, therefore, by enlisting the active participation of "non-Zionists" in the Jewish Agency's vital program.

The founding assembly of the reconstituted Jewish Agency was held in Jerusalem and opened on June 21, 1971. It was attended by Jewish leaders from all parts of the world. Max Fisher presided. The principal addresses were delivered by Louis Pincus, on behalf of the World Zionist Executive; Edward Ginsberg, for the United Israel Appeal; and by myself, on behalf of the Keren Hayesod.

In conveying greetings to this assembly, I said that my "constituency" comprised sixty-nine different *kehillot* throughout the world, exclusive of the United States. I also thought it worth mentioning that the idea of an expanded Jewish Agency had germinated among leaders of the United Israel Appeal in the U.S., where Zionists and non-Zionists had developed a fruitful cooperation and mutual confidence over the years. "What we have here," I declared, "is an attestation of Jewish unity around Israel." Alluding to the earlier attempt, in 1929, to expand the Agency, I said:

Professor Einstein, on that occasion, remarked in terms of his own scientific vocabulary that the Jewish people was split into atoms. If he were alive today, he would not make such an observation. Partly as a result of the tragic Holocaust, which has become a unifying Jewish memory, but mainly because of the glorious reality of Medinat Yisrael, we are today a more united people than ever before.

Theodor Herzl had affirmed, "We are a people, one people." The Keren Hayesod and the UJA together expressed that unity.

During this time, a reception and a breakfast meeting were arranged by the Keren Hayesod to mark my seventy-fifth birthday. Felicitations were extended by Baroness Alix de Rothschild, a patroness of the Jerusalem Youth Village bearing my name, and by other Keren Hayesod leaders who were in Israel for the assembly.

With this first session of the reconstituted Jewish Agency, the moment for my retirement was now at hand. My beloved friend and colleague, Ezra Z. Shapiro, was ready to take over. At an assembly session over which Sam Rothberg presided, Jewish Agency Chairman Louis Pincus presented me with a Scroll of Honor on the occasion of my retirement from the Agency Executive and the chairmanship of the Keren Hayesod. His accompanying remarks, the address by Rose Halprin and the spontaneous expressions of friendship and gratitude that followed at the gathering, made this farewell a most moving and rewarding experience.

The scroll contained, in part, these words of tribute:

For upwards of fifty years
you have shouldered faithfully the burden of public affairs,
leaving the impress of your personality
on all spheres of life in Israel
and in Jewish communal life in the United States,
as well as in other countries of the world.

In the past decade,
as World Chairman of the Keren Hayesod-United Israel Appeal,
you have contributed greatly to the strengthening of the historical partnership
between Diaspora Jewry and Israel.

As Rabbi and as writer,
as founder of Brandeis University
and as governor of institutions of higher learning in Israel,
you have given top priority to the interests of Jewish education
and have merited universal appreciation.

May you be granted many more happy and fruitful years
and may the Tabernacle of Peace be spread over Israel for ever and ever.

In the course of my response, I spoke of my sixty-three years of continuous Zionist involvement, from the age of twelve. "To have had a share in all of this has been its own reward," I said. "To receive a meed of tribute for something which is its own reward is more than one bargains for. This scroll I shall cherish. I shall consider it a daily reminder not only of finished business but also of the unfinished business to which I am retiring, namely, a little more contemplation, a little more study, and a little more writing, which I have insufficiently exercised while married to the relentless demands of incessant Jewish and human imperatives."

I concluded with a prayer of thanksgiving, inspired by the words of Chaim Naḥman Bialik, the national poet of Eretz Yisrael, that it had been my good fortune to be a part of "the last generation to witness Jewish degradation and the first to experience Jewish salvation."

There were farewell receptions in Tel Aviv, where JNF Chairman Ya'akov Tsur was one of the speakers, and in Jerusalem, where Eliyahu Dobkin presided over a Keren Hayesod Directorion function. I felt and expressed my debt of gratitude to my co-workers, great and small, in the head office of the Keren Hayesod in Jerusalem, and to that great army of volunteers serving throughout the Keren Hayesod world.

My withdrawal from active duty was not, however, the end of my association with the Keren Hayesod. I responded to every call by my successors in the leadership. Assemblies of the reconstituted Jewish Agency undertook tasks of ever-increasing importance. A new and heartening phenomenon was the substantial Aliyah from the Soviet Union. It continued to mount, attaining a monthly figure of 4,000 Russian Olim in the second half of 1973. Despite extortionate "exit fees," harassment, the trial and imprisonment of leading "Prisoners of Zion," and every available form of pressure, Jews could not be deterred from applying to leave for Israel.

The Yom Kippur War of 1973, which caught both Israel and the Jewish people completely by surprise, again shocked World Jewry into action. By the end of that year, under the traumatic impact of a near-disaster transformed into an astonishing victory, the Jews of the Diaspora had contributed a total of $300 million to the Jewish Agency—twice the sum raised during the emergency campaign of 1967, at the time of the Six-Day War.

From 1971 onward, the Keren Hayesod was able to avail itself of my services, whenever they were required. An annual Prize for the Outstanding Volunteer Campaigner was established in my name by the Keren Hayesod, to mark my eightieth birthday in June 1976. On that occasion, Ezra Shapiro announced the decision to award such a prize in the course of a ceremony at Bet ha-Nasi in the presence of Israel's President, Professor Ephraim Katzir, the chairman of the World Zionist Organization, Yosef Almogi, members of the Government, and other distinguished guests.

A particularly hard blow for the Keren Hayesod was the loss of my successor, Ezra Zelig Shapiro, who died on May 14, 1977, a Sabbath morning. The son of a rabbi, Ezra was born in Volozhin and from early childhood lived in the United States. As a lawyer, civic leader, Jewish communal figure, Hebraist, and Zionist, he achieved distinction and renown in the city of Cleveland, Ohio, and nationally. He was one of my close friends and colleagues.

The funeral service took place on the following Monday, May 16, allowing time for Ezra's son and daughter to arrive from the United States. Before the cortege left the Jewish Agency compound, eulogies were delivered by Yosef Almogi, chairman of the Jewish Agency, Itzḥak Navon, chairman of the Zionist General Council, and Rabbi Mordecai Kirshblum, a member of the Jewish Agency Executive. I spoke on behalf of the Keren Hayesod. Shai Kreutner, director-general of the Keren Hayesod, delivered a tribute at the graveside. Among those who paid their last respects at the funeral service were President Katzir and Jerusalem's Mayor, Teddy Kollek.

In the course of my eulogy of Ezra Shapiro I said:

> He rose to national leadership in the Zionist movement, the United Jewish Appeal and Israel Bonds, and he became the founding President of the American League for Israel and, later, the President of the World Confederation of United Zionists. He was for years a leading member of the Council of the World Zionist Organization and he had the historic privilege of chairing the committee which prepared the Jerusalem Program at the Zionist Congress of 1951.
>
> When he and his beloved wife, Sylvia, herself an active, dedicated Zionist of distinguished Zionist lineage and a leader in Hadassah, made their Aliyah in 1971, it was indeed the crowning fulfillment of their lives.
>
> When Ezra became the Chairman of the Keren Hayesod and a member of the Jewish Agency Executive, he entered upon the climax of his Zionist career. His dedication, his ability to work with colleagues and his natural friendliness made him a popular leader throughout the Keren Hayesod world.
>
> During and immediately after the Yom Kippur War, he labored tirelessly at the side of Pinhas Sapir, of blessed memory, in mobilizing the support of the Jewish people. He raised the income of the Keren Hayesod to unprecedented heights.
>
> Alas, for the ship whose captain is no more!

This sad event necessitated the finding of an interim replacement to oversee the Keren Hayesod's ongoing operations. My colleagues in the Confederation urged me to step into the breach. I felt, however, that a younger hand was needed. Faye Schenk, president of the American Zionist Federation, and Philip Granovsky, head of the United Israel Appeal in Canada, thereupon jointly undertook the responsibility until such time as a suitable permanent appointment could be made. This arrangement was subsequently confirmed by the Zionist General Council. Their task was greatly eased during the transition period by the effective continuing service of Shai Kreutner as director-general. Under pressure from my colleagues, I did finally agree to take Ezra Shapiro's place on the World Zionist Executive, pending new elections at the next Zionist Congress.

In March 1978, at the conclusion of the 29th Zionist Congress, Arye L. Dulzin was unanimously elected chairman of the World Zionist Organization. Faye Schenk received one of the portfolios assigned to our Confederation, as head of the WZO's Organization Department. The world chairmanship of Keren Hayesod was assigned to our Confederation's nominee, Dr. Avraham Avi-hai, who had begun his Zionist career as Sid Applebaum, in Toronto, Canada. He had studied at the Jewish Theological Seminary in New York, the Hebrew University in Jerusalem, and Columbia University, where he was awarded his doctorate. In Israel, Dr. Avi-hai had served in the Prime Minister's Office under Levi Eshkol and as a consultant to Jerusalem's Mayor, Teddy Kollek. He had been assistant director for Israel Bonds and vice-provost of the Hebrew University's School for Overseas Students, and had taught both there and at Bar-Ilan University. He was also the author of *Ben-Gurion:*

State-Builder. Dr. Avi-hai's command of English, French, Hebrew, and Yiddish would prove an important asset in dealing with the Keren Hayesod's variegated worldwide constituency.

A new milestone in the history of the Keren Hayesod, its sixtieth anniversary, was proclaimed ceremonially at the President's House in Jerusalem on October 25, 1979. Those present included Chief Rabbi Shlomo Goren and members of the Jewish Agency Executive. As world chairman of Keren Hayesod–United Israel Appeal, Dr. Avraham Avi-hai handed a symbolic key bearing an inscription taken from the Foundation Fund's original manifesto to President Itzhak Navon, who observed that "there are communities around the world where Keren Hayesod is the central, and sometimes the only, Jewish activity." In tribute to its role in the establishment and progress of development towns throughout Israel, Keren Hayesod Days were held in the Upper Galilee center of Kiryat Shemonah and in the Negev town of Dimona. Special missions from France, Holland, and Sweden participated in these events, and additional celebrations were held in Israel and overseas.

It was my privilege to serve as honorary chairman of Keren Hayesod's sixtieth anniversary festivities. Speaking at the inaugural ceremony at Bet ha-Nasi, I felt justified in stating that "as much as Jews have done for the Keren Hayesod, it has done incomparably more for them. The Keren Hayesod has provided them with a channel and a challenge to share in writing the greatest chapter in nineteen centuries of Jewish history, the building of Medinat Yisrael." Having enlarged and strengthened Israel's foundations, Keren Hayesod must now enhance the State's historic role "by helping to make the Jewish National Home a Menorah of light and salvation."

The culminating sixtieth anniversary event in which I participated was held in March 1980, amidst a post-Purim festive atmosphere, in Antwerp, Belgium. There, in Antwerp's Town Hall, and in the presence of Lord Janner, Dr. Avi-hai, Shai Kreutner, and a distinguished Jewish and civic gathering, I presented golden jubilee medallions for distinguished service to Max Fisher of the United States, J. Edward Sieff of Great Britain, Phil Granovsky of Canada, and Fred Hall of Australia.

More in the nature of a "family gathering" was the reception tendered by the Keren Hayesod in honor of its long-serving director-general, S. J. Kreutner, which took place at Bet Shalom in Jerusalem, on December 17, 1979. Dr. Avi-hai presided and I paid tribute to Mr. Kreutner's extraordinary services both to the Keren Hayesod and to Medinat Yisrael over the past two decades.

In retrospect, viewing my sixty years of work for the Keren Hayesod, I am impelled to state my belief that fund raising has an importance far transcending the intrinsic value of the sums raised. This fact is not sufficiently appreciated. A financial contribution, often made casually, under pressure, or out of a sense of obligation to the solicitor, can lead to a permanent ideological and spiritual identification with the cause involved. There have been instances in my experience when contributions solicited by me for a religious institution or for a Zionist cause, given out of personal regard, marked the beginning of a lifelong, active commitment to causes such as the Jewish Theological Seminary, the Jewish National Fund, the Keren Hayesod, or the United Jewish Appeal. It has also happened, in my experience, that the entire course of a man's life has been changed, in a highly positive way, as a result of his casual initiation by way of a response to a fund-raising appeal.

My tribute, therefore, goes out to the fund raisers and the *Askanim*. They themselves are often unaware of the far-reaching consequences, for others and for themselves, which may stem from their initial fund-raising involvements.

Since the Six-Day War of 1967 and the Yom Kippur War of 1973, many younger Israelis have had occasion to revise their attitude toward Diaspora Jewry, in the context of Zionist fund raising. Such Israelis had once dismissed the Keren Hayesod and United Israel Appeal campaigns as "the big *schnorr*." That contemptuous term has practically disappeared from the Israeli's vocabulary. Army officers of all ranks, Sabras, have called to thank us for sending them on missions to Jewish communities abroad, since, as a result of their personal contacts with Jews there, they have come to appreciate World Jewry's identification with Israel in its struggle for survival.

14

General Zionism

As president of the World Confederation of General Zionists for ten years, after it had been formally constituted under that name in 1946, and then as co-chairman with Rose Halprin for the ensuing fifteen years until 1971, I have devoted a sizable portion of my Zionist life to the furtherance and enhancement of this central worldwide Zionist body.

From the beginning, General Zionism has considered itself to be classical Zionism—the Zionism of Herzl and Weizmann, representing the broad, central approach within the world Zionist movement and based on the principles of the Basle Program, enunciated at the First Zionist Congress in 1897. According to this program:

> The aim of Zionism is to create for the Jewish people a home in Palestine served by public law.
>
> The Congress contemplates the following means to the attainment of this end:
>
> 1. The promotion, on suitable lines, of the colonization of Palestine by Jewish agricultural and industrial workers.
>
> 2. The organization and binding together of the whole of Jewry by means of appropriate institutions, local and international, in accordance with the laws of each country.
>
> 3. The strengthening and fostering of Jewish national sentiment and consciousness.
>
> 4. Preparatory steps towards obtaining government consent, where necessary, to the attainment of the aim of Zionism.

Within a decade of the appearance of Herzlian Zionism on the world stage, two distinct trends had separated themselves from the mainstream of the world movement: the religiously motivated Mizraḥi Party (1902) and the Socialist-oriented Po'alei Zion (1906). Unlike these ideologically opposed factions, the General Zionists did not formulate a specific program of their own for the economic and social development of the Jewish homeland, nor did they set about establishing their own institutions in Palestine and initiating their own programs there.

In time, the absence of a General Zionist political machine resulted in a dissipation of its strength in the World Zionist Organization. Thus, in 1921, 73 percent of all delegates to the Twelfth Zionist Congress in Carlsbad were General Zionists, 19 percent were Mizrahists, while the Labor Zionists constituted only 8 percent. Ten years later, at the Seventeenth Congress in Basle in 1931, the General Zionists were split into three groups, together comprising 53 percent of the delegates, while Labor had increased from 8 to 29 percent. This trend, although it slowed somewhat, continued for over two decades, until American Zionists, represented essentially by Hadassah and the Zionist Organization of America, became more consciously General Zionist after World War II.

Adding to the difficulties of the General Zionist movement was its own division into two major streams after World War I: Group "A," faithful to the leadership of Dr. Weizmann, which represented both the middle classes and the General Zionist pioneering settlements; and Group "B," which sought to strengthen private initiative and to establish an organized force to match the growing power of Socialist (Labor) Zionism.

As early as 1929, attempts had been made to set up a world organization of General Zionists, but the vagueness of the proposed platform served only to widen the breach between Groups "A" and "B." On the eve of the Seventeenth Zionist Congress, in June 1931, General Zionist delegates met for another attempt to achieve international unity. Isaac Schwarzbart was elected president of the World Union of General Zionists and a central office was established in Cracow, Poland. This attempt, too, was short-lived and, in 1935, Groups "A" and "B" once more asserted their differing views.

In time, the separate streams began to converge until, in 1939, they were given added impetus by the outbreak of World War II and the imposition of severe restrictions on Jewish immigration by the British Mandatory authorities. According to the White Paper of 1939, the number of Jews allowed into Palestine was to be strictly limited and immigration certificates were to be issued on the basis of financial ability to create a foothold there.

In such a situation, the Mizrahi and Labor Zionist movements, with their well-established international political apparatuses, were able to muster the financial and organizational aid necessary to secure the much-sought-after certificates, enabling numbers of their own supporters to escape from Europe to Palestine. All too often, the unaffiliated General Zionists were left unaided. In Palestine itself, complaints were voiced that the Right* and Left factions, whether in urban or rural areas, were receiving moral and financial support from their ideological kindred organizations overseas, thus enabling them to create power positions in the Yishuv, while the Center was being neglected and left to fend for itself.

---

*Strictly speaking, the Zionist "Right" comprised Ze'ev Jabotinsky's Revisionist movement, for which there was growing support in Europe and in the Yishuv during the 1930s. Between 1935 and 1946, however, the Revisionists distanced themselves from "official" Zionism and maintained their own secessionist New Zionist Organization, which boycotted the Zionist Congresses.

All in all, the conditions during and immediately after World War II were such that the formation of a General Zionist confederation presented itself increasingly as an imperative. The two basic tools needed to make this possible were a large, well-organized membership and the finances to help Jews still requiring assistance in getting to Eretz Yisrael and establishing themselves there.

My own relationship with General Zionism began after the earlier attempts to form a center party in the World Zionist Organization in 1921, and it continued through my activities within the Zionist Organization of America. In 1934, I became a vice-president of the ZOA and, from 1943 to 1945, I served as its president. When I began my term of office, the ZOA had a membership of 68,000. I attempted to build up its membership and its program of activities and to lead the organization toward a more active role within the international Zionist community. By 1945, the strength of the ZOA had more than doubled, and my efforts to bring it into the world General Zionist framework were beginning to bear fruit.

In August 1945, during the World Zionist Conference in London, the first post-war General Zionist assembly was also convened. Only a month before, as mentioned earlier, I had been the first civilian representative of American Jewry to visit the Displaced Persons' camps in Germany. I arrived at the conference fully convinced that there would be no chance of rebuilding the Zionist movement in Europe and channeling it into constructive efforts in Eretz Yisrael without the practical support of the two principal elements in American Zionism—the Zionist Organization of America, of which I was currently the president, and Hadassah, the Women's Zionist Organization of America. This would mean a definite change in orientation, and it did not come spontaneously or easily to our organizations, which had not been closely involved in the past with the organized activities of world General Zionism as such.

The conference included representatives from Australia, Belgium, Canada, Egypt, Eretz Yisrael, France, Great Britain, Greece, Italy, the Netherlands, Poland, South Africa, Sweden, Switzerland, and the United States. The delegates arrived at the unanimous conclusion that the World Union of General Zionists had to be revived and reactivated in the fields of organization and propaganda; that the activities of our comrades in all countries must be guided; that emissaries had to be sent to Europe in order to bolster the movement there; and that the organization must establish a fund enabling it to extend financial help to the halutzic movement in Europe, the new children's homes, and our colonization efforts in Eretz Yisrael.

We sensed that we were entering a new phase in our struggle for independence in Eretz Yisrael and that our movement had to establish itself among the remnants of European Jewry, in organizing them for Aliyah, strengthening Zionism, and expanding our activities in Eretz Yisrael so as to enable us to absorb those who were preparing to come.

It was decided to establish regional offices of the revived confederation in London, headed by Lavy Bakstansky, and in Paris, to be headed by Sam Segall, in collaboration with other Western European colleagues. I was to head the New York office, together with a Hadassah representative. Moshe Kol and Dr. Moshe Sneh were to head our branch in Eretz Yisrael, where our activities were to be coordinated with the Jewish Agency on behalf of our kibbutzim and our middle-class settlements.

At the end of the conference, the executive issued a manifesto to the General Zionists of the world, which read in part:

> General Zionism, which has placed itself in the front-line of the struggle to establish Palestine as a free and democratic Jewish State, calls upon the Jewish people, wherever they may be, to rally to the Zionist flag, to increase their effort and to spare no sacrifice until we shall achieve our aim of bringing to Palestine the remnants of our people and of securing for them a life of freedom in Eretz Yisrael, established as the independent state of the Jewish people. General Zionism considers itself the main factor for national unity, offering a nationwide Jewish policy for the Diaspora and for the Yishuv. General Zionism stresses the foundation of our existence as one people, united by a great historic mission and by a common, cruel fate. It strives to achieve the political, cultural, educational and social unity of those who return to take part in our renewed life in Palestine; it aims at bridging the social differences between the various parts of the Yishuv and its classes through common responsibility and mutual understanding.

A decision was also adopted to convene a world conference of General Zionists in Basle on the eve of the 22nd Zionist Congress, which was scheduled to be held in December 1946.

My term as president of the ZOA ended barely two months after returning from the London conference. In delivering my farewell remarks at the ZOA's national convention, in November 1945, I took the opportunity to speak of the need for a strong world movement of General Zionism:

> From a well-planned, well-organized and well-financed World Confederation of General Zionists, great good can come to the Zionist movement as a whole. In Palestine, the General Zionists, backed by a strong World Confederation, can play a more important part than they are now playing—as a balancing factor amidst the extremes of partisanship. They can wield a wholesome influence by emphasizing and fortifying the general and broader interests of the Yishuv as a whole, while supporting the social gains which distinguish the economy of Jewish Palestine. They can increase the sum total of colonization and industrial opportunities by encouraging and subsidizing their comrades, as the adherents of other parties are being encouraged and subsidized.
>
> Outside of Palestine, the General Zionist groupings can be helped by a World Confederation to function more actively, thus adding to the sum total of Zionist activity in those lands. It is not for the purpose of subtracting strength from other parties but in order to strengthen its own power to serve Zionism, thus adding to the total area of Zionist strength, that there is a need for a strong World Confederation of General Zionists. It means adding to the total effectiveness of the Zionist movement, by building up one segment of it which until now has been tended with insufficient care and vigilance.

This was the first time that such a note had been sounded from a ZOA platform, calling for an ideological and organizational departure from the status quo of American Zionists.

When the 22nd Zionist Congress convened at Basle in December 1946, seven years had passed since the preceding Congress and almost fifty years since the First Zionist Congress had met in that same city. During that period, one-third of the Jewish population of the world had been annihilated and the Zionist movement had disappeared from its former centers of strength. Still, this was the largest Zionist Congress ever held up to that time, and the overall tone was optimistic. There was a feeling that Herzl's prophecy of the Jewish State was nearing fulfillment.

Of the 385 delegates representing over two million shekel payers, the largest delegation was the American, numbering 120 and composed mostly of delegates from the ZOA and Hadassah, both groups now firmly committed to the General Zionist movement.

Just prior to the Congress, General Zionists from all parts of the globe met to establish the World Confederation formally. I was honored to be elected its first president. The executive included Lavy Bakstansky, Professor Selig Brodetsky, Judith Epstein, Rose Halprin, Moshe Kol, Dr. Emanuel Neumann, Rabbi Abba Hillel Silver, and Dr. Moshe Sneh (who subsequently realigned himself with the political Left). Later, we were joined by Dr. Nahum Goldmann, Pinhas Rosen, and Yosef Serlin.

One of the first items of business was a political question which was to be decided at the Zionist Congress, and the General Zionist group had to formulate its own position. The British Government had invited the Zionist movement to send representatives to yet another round-table conference on Palestine. Should the Congress accept? And should it agree to a partition of Palestine, or insist on all of Palestine west of the River Jordan as the territory of the future Jewish State?

Dr. Chaim Weizmann, president of the World Zionist Organization, believed in a policy of moderation and was considered by many to have shown insufficient firmness vis-à-vis the British Government. He favored acceptance of the invitation to attend the conference and was also ready to acquiesce in the partitioning of Palestine.

Our group comprised forty percent of the delegates at the 1946 Congress. At our own General Zionist conference, opinions were divided. Selig Brodetsky, Nahum Goldmann, Yitzhak Gruenbaum, Aliyah Hadashah (the association of immigrants from Germany and Central Europe), Hadassah delegates led by Rose Halprin, Barnett Janner, Judge Louis E. Levinthal, Louis Lipsky, Stephen Wise, and, especially, the British Zionist Federation, all supported Weizmann on both questions. I myself was in the opposite camp—the more militant, anti-British element—which, with the majority of the Americans, headed by Abba Hillel Silver and Emanuel Neumann, carried the day.

At that Congress, Weizmann was not reelected president of the World Zionist Organization. In retrospect, I never felt any regret at having been on the side of those who were responsible for that outcome. On the contrary, I felt that Weizmann's failure to be reelected president of the WZO in 1946 made it possible for him to become the first President of Medinat Yisrael in 1948, since the accession of a stronger leadership—headed by Ben-Gurion and Silver—had resulted in the achievement of a Jewish State.

At the inaugural meeting of our Confederation, it was decided to establish offices in Tel Aviv, New York, and Paris. A World Executive and a World Central Committee were constituted. Those nominated as my vice-presidents were Professor Selig Brodetsky of Great Britain, Bernard Gering of South Africa, Rose Halprin of the United States, Dr. Cornel Janco of Rumania, A. Rabinowitz of Argentina, I. Sachs of Canada, and Yosef Serlin of Palestine. Abraham Krumbein of New York was elected treasurer and Yitzhak Carmin Karpman was appointed general secretary.

A decision of far-reaching importance taken at this first conference of the World Confederation of General Zionists was to establish the movement's Constructive Enterprises Fund, known as the KMK (Keren le-Mifalim Konstruktivi'im), which would serve as the financial instrument of the Confederation. Official endorsement of this move was sought at the Congress, but this proved to be no easy matter and the KMK became involved in bitter disputes regarding the political issues and the new Zionist leadership.

Throughout the Congress, the General Zionists negotiated with the Mapai and Mizrahi groups over the establishment of the fund. We argued that if our movement were denied allocations from central funds, it would be obliged to organize its own independent fund-raising activities—as was the case with the Gewerkschaften Fund of Mapai and its allies and with the Mizrahi Palestine Fund. This would be to the detriment of overall fund raising for Eretz Yisrael, in which the General Zionists of the United States were the major factor. Final approval came only at the eleventh hour, as the Congress was about to terminate. The KMK was thereupon assigned allocations from the United Palestine Appeal in the United States, to compensate for its giving up the conduct of a separate campaign.

The World Confederation of General Zionists had made a good showing of its strength and importance in this first united appearance at a Zionist Congress. As its president, I was proud to be able to return to the United States and report on the vital role that had been played at the Congress by our American delegation. We had emerged with a distinct party consciousness and an organizational framework. In Eretz Yisrael, our aim was to concentrate on the broad national interests of the Jewish people; to foster the development of a unified educational system unfettered by political ideologies; and to ensure equal opportunity, in both immigration and settlement, for all who wished to build their lives in and through the Jewish National Home. Outside of Palestine, the Confederation would seek to build a constituency for which the general interests of the Zionist movement would be the paramount consideration. As the largest group represented at Congress, the Confederation felt a special responsibility to hold the Zionist movement together in the face of inter-party strains and tensions.

At the ZOA's annual convention in New York some months later, I explained the need for our General Zionist Confederation and the role it anticipated playing:

General Zionists, with all their desire for social progress, take issue with Mapai's program of a Socialist state and, with all respect for Jewish tradition, take issue with Mizrahi's program of a state based on Orthodox Judaism. Some General Zionists believe in the center position as a matter of ideology, some as a matter of economic self-interest, others as a matter of temperament. There are still others who are in the center because they are unmoved by any party motivations.

All these are the potential constituency of the World Confederation of General Zionists. Party consciousness has become the pattern of the social order [in Palestine]. Children of tender ages are indoctrinated with party allegiance, be it Mapai, Ha-Shomer Ha-Tza'ir, Mizrahi or Revisionism. Partisanship begets partisanship. The wonder is that there is so much unity in the face of crises such as have confronted the Yishuv. The normal atmosphere, however, is one of abnormal tension.

A good, strong, liberal center group could be a wholesome influence on the life of the Yishuv, since, as the center, it would serve as a balance and a corrective against the extremism at either end.

In Palestine, I said, the General Zionist group was the weakest, while outside of Palestine it was the strongest. Must one assume that the climate of Eretz Yisrael was not congenial, or that its soil was not fertile for General Zionism? In my estimate, most of the General Zionist leaders in positions of authority had not done enough to assure us of the practical equality which came from group strength:

If they innocently believe that the party system should be abolished altogether, let them ask themselves searchingly how the weaknesses of the center group will encourage the other groups to go out of business.

The Confederation's first concentration of effort is on the situation in Palestine. It is axiomatic that every party structure must be based in Eretz. Our Confederation's base is there, but it needs to be strengthened and its segments consolidated. In the administration of funds, the needs of our middle class and of our halutzic group, Ha-Oved Ha-Tzioni, must receive equal consideration, for these must develop side by side as the twin pillars of General Zionism.

The Confederation's next concentration of effort should be upon the European scene, where Jews are straining for Palestine. . . .

The Confederation's third objective is to help strengthen and enlarge the ranks of General Zionism in the Latin American and in the English-speaking countries. . . .

We are proud that the ZOA view has become the majority view of the World Confederation.

Our permanent common ground is (a) our political thesis that the establishment of a Jewish State in the nearest possible future is our first and foremost consideration; (b) our social thesis that the national interest must supersede every party interest in the Yishuv; and (c) our economic thesis that the development of Palestine's maximum absorptive capacity demands that private initiative as well as collective enterprise be encouraged by national funds and institutions.

The first ten years of the Confederation brought about an important change in the status of General Zionism within the World Zionist Organization.

This period marked the revival of the General Zionist idea and influence all over the world. The General Zionist organizations in all countries of the Diaspora were strengthened and fortified by the recognition that they were an inseparable and a leading part of a great world movement that had played, and was continuing to play, a major role in achieving and buttressing Israel's independence.

The first two years of our Confederation's existence were mainly devoted to the struggle of the Yishuv and the world Zionist movement for political independence, a sovereign State. In the United States, the reins of Zionist leadership were held by the General Zionists. They were in a position to play the leading role in the representations made in Washington, and at the United Nations in Lake Success, during the decisive period that reached its climax on November 29, 1947, when more than two-thirds of the UN member states, including the two foremost world powers, voted for the establishment of a Jewish State in Palestine.

Throughout 1947 and 1948, constant appeals for supplementary relief streamed in to the Confederation from General Zionist groups in Europe. The American office received some 4,000 names and addresses of members in Europe, on whose behalf the General Zionist bureau in Paris applied for immediate aid. In response, the ZOA and Hadassah made available a special fund to underwrite the shipment of relief packages to all European countries. Clothing was also supplied to General Zionist groups in Europe and to the Displaced Persons' camps in Cyprus.

It was mainly through the efforts of the General Zionists in the United States that the foundation for the Constructive Fund (KMK) was laid in Eretz Yisrael. Its initial capital came from an allocation of $600,000 from Zionist funds in the United States, to which the Keren Hayesod contributed $100,000 in 1946 and the United Palestine Appeal gave $500,000 in 1947. In 1948, Keren Hayesod and the Jewish National Fund (Keren Kayemet) in the United States approved the request of the American Section of the Jewish Agency for an increased annual allocation of $750,000. These appropriations were made in lieu of separate campaigns which, otherwise, we—like other Zionist parties—would have been obliged to conduct.

The European bureau of the Confederation was opened in Paris on January 1, 1947. From this office, relief work, education, information, and social programs were organized in the liberated lands. In all parts of Europe, the General Zionist *halutz* movement proved to be among the most vital and creative elements in the Jewish communities. Thousands of General Zionists organized in Ha-No'ar Ha-Tzioni prepared themselves in 130 training centers for their eventual life in Israel. A notable part in this effort was played by the children's homes, where many orphaned survivors of the Holocaust found a warm and loving haven. These homes were reservoirs drawn upon by the educational institutions and kibbutzim of Eretz Yisrael, by way of the Youth Aliyah program. Among them was the Israel Goldstein Children's Home in a thirty-eight-room former château near Lyons, in France.

In May 1948, within earshot of a violent exchange of gunfire between Arab attackers and Haganah defenders, the cornerstone was laid for a large housing project in Ramat Gan. This was intended to accommodate 400 families and to include a school, a kindergarten, and other facilities for refugees from Poland. The project was undertaken jointly by the World Federation of Polish Jews and Shikun Ezraḥi, a building company affiliated with our Confederation. It was my privilege to lay the cornerstone together with Emanuel Neumann, president of the ZOA, who was with me to attend a meeting of the Zionist General Council. Avraham Krinitzi, the Mayor of Ramat Gan, and a number of other prominent Zionist leaders spoke at this ceremony. It demonstrated our conviction that intensified Jewish settlement was a most effective response to Arab aggression.

The growing strength of General Zionism in Europe during the closing years of British rule in Palestine and during the initial years of Medinat Yisrael was evident at a conference of our movement attended by delegates from eighteen countries in Europe and North Africa, which was held in Paris in September 1950. This conference established guidelines for future activity. Then, as later, our dominant principle in Europe was not to attempt to wean away the adherents of other Zionist parties, but rather to reach out for new members from the remainder of Europe's Jewish communities, to whom the General Zionist program would make a special appeal.

In order to make contact with these European Jews, we had to print material in three languages—French, German, and Yiddish. One of our primary vehicles was *Di Tzionistishe Shtimme*, a Yiddish weekly published by the European bureau as the official organ of our Confederation. Its editor, Moshe Kalchheim, was the secretary general of our European branch. A French-language monthly, *La Voix Sioniste*, was also inaugurated to cater to the Jewish communities in France, Belgium, Luxembourg, and Switzerland, as well as North Africa. Both periodicals became important sources of Jewish information.

At the same time, we were also able to lay the foundations of a General Zionist organization in Latin America. Our Confederation was one of the foremost Zionist groupings, instilling a consciousness of Zionism in Jews inhabiting that part of the world. Latin American Zionism has since become a significant factor in the Zionist movement as a whole, with Ha-No'ar Ha-Tzioni as one of the largest and most active youth movements on the South American continent.

During my decade as president of the Confederation and, later, as co-chairman with Rose Halprin for a decade and a half, I paid several visits to South America and addressed numerous Jewish gatherings. The youth always presented a special challenge since many, particularly those on the university campuses, could not be reached because of their leftist leanings. There were, however, always enough young Jews prepared for Aliyah to make the effort a rewarding one.

Within the Yishuv, both before and after 1948, General Zionism had its affiliated organizations. Even before the establishment of the State, however, there were two General Zionist camps there, which at times drew apart in a fierce clash of opinions and attitudes, yet at other times moved close to one another and even united in a single framework.

When Jewish statehood came, these differences of opinion were formalized in rival political platforms on the eve of the elections to the first Knesset in February 1949. Two separate parties emerged. One was the group known previously as General Zionists "A," which, together with some of the pro-Labor elements, Ha-Oved Ha-Tzioni and Aliyah Ḥadashah, formed the new Progressive Party, led by Pinḥas Rosen, Dr. Abraham Granott, Moshe Kol, and Zvi Herman and affiliated with the World Confederation of General Zionists. The other group, which had been the "B" wing of General Zionism, merged with Iḥud Ezraḥi to form the General Zionist Party. Its leaders included Peretz Bernstein, Dr. Elimelekh Rimalt, Yosef Saphir, and Yosef Serlin.

Throughout the first Knesset, the Progressive Party was represented almost constantly in the Government coalition. The General Zionist Party, however, stood in opposition. This division frequently gave rise to acrimonious polemics and exacerbated relations between the respective adherents, which unfortunately was also reflected in the World Confederation of General Zionists in Israel and the Diaspora.

The conference of the World Executive of the Confederation, held during the Zionist General Council session in May 1949, decided to appoint a committee to explore the possibilities of reuniting the General Zionist groups in Israel into one party. A negotiating committee of seven members was named: Peretz Bernstein, Yosef Serlin, and Elimelekh Rimalt for the General Zionist Party; Abraham Granott, Pinḥas Rosen, and Moshe Kol for the Progressive Party; and I as chairman. These and succeeding efforts, regrettably, came to naught.

The split in Israel was reflected throughout the General Zionist movement abroad. In the United States, two factions arose—one under Dr. Emanuel Neumann's leadership, the other headed by Rose Halprin and myself and, later, by Ezra Shapiro. A crucial divisive point in the Diaspora was the issue as to whether we should identify with political groups in Israel. The position of our faction in the U.S. was that General Zionists outside of Israel should be clearly dissociated from any political party within the State. Each of the General Zionist parties there had its own policies and politics to pursue. As a result, there were not a few stormy debates at Confederation conferences. The period until 1956 witnessed a deepening of the rift within the Confederation between the Progressives and the General Zionists in Israel. The repercussions were felt in the Diaspora and led to the final split following the 24th Zionist Congress, held in Jerusalem in 1956.

It fell to my lot to make appeals for unity. Whereas I believed that it would be unrealistic to overlook the existence of the two General Zionist groups in Israel, I also held that we could do much more to reduce the area of conflicting partisanship to a minimum and expand the area of common aims to a maximum. I felt that far more emphasis needed to be placed upon the constructive achievements of General Zionism and the tangible accomplishments of our Constructive Fund, the KMK. I urged that if all General Zionist forces in Israel were combined, they would have a good chance of becoming the leading party in the country. I appealed to our constituencies abroad to do their utmost to maintain an attitude of neutrality with regard to the internal disputes in Israel.

Despite our efforts, the strained relations between the two wings culminated in a breakup at the conference of the Confederation held after the 24th Zionist Congress in May 1956. At this conference, the two camps were unable to reach agreement on basic issues. The General Zionist Party and the Progressive Party of Israel—and the majority of the ZOA—were in favor of a policy of "identification," whereby General Zionist groups in the Diaspora would declare their solidarity with a kindred political group in Israel. The other camp, to which I belonged, held that their identification with any political party in Israel was not consonant with the tradition of General Zionism and was bound to divert attention in the Diaspora from the main general tasks of Zionism.

The groups opposed to identification decided to continue the existence of the Confederation without the participating membership of the General Zionist and Progressive parties of Israel. It was decided to reorganize the Confederation along completely new lines as a nonpartisan, Diaspora-based body. The dissenting groups that had opted for identification with the General Zionist Party in Israel eventually adopted the designation, "World Union of General Zionists," and elected Emanuel Neumann as their president.

At a conference held in London on March 9–10, 1958, delegates from many countries officially launched the new and reorganized World Confederation of General Zionists as a separate body. Our Confederation now mainly comprised the Hadassah Women's Zionist Organization of America, the General Zionists of Great Britain, and kindred groups from the European continent, Latin America, South Africa, and Australia. Rose Halprin and I were elected co-chairmen, and I served in that capacity until 1971, when I retired from all official Zionist posts. The executive secretary, later named executive vice-president, was Kalman Sultanik.

A statement setting out our position was issued on that occasion:

> General Zionism—a Zionism unattached to any political party in Israel—has always appealed to vast numbers of the Jewish people in the Diaspora. General Zionism is the current embodiment of classical Zionism.
>
> Today, this non-party concept of independent Zionism is more vital than ever before to the millions of Jews outside of Israel for whom partisan conflicts are remote, and for whom the well-being of Israel as a whole and of the Jewish people as a whole is a primary concern. . . .
>
> Our goal has always been the promotion of liberal, democratic Zionism, which is not linked in any way with Israel's internal political affairs. This is the only kind of Zionism that can have meaning for new generations of Jews in the Diaspora. It is the only Zionism that can encourage creative initiative in the Diaspora and benefit both Israel, the nation, and the Jewish people living outside of Israel. It can best promote knowledge, understanding and support of Israel's culture and national institutions as a whole.
>
> General Zionism has always played an important, indeed a major, role in the world Zionist movement, and today it is more essential than ever before to have such a strong, independent General Zionist bulwark, able to maintain a balance of power and give leadership and direction within the orbit of world Zionism.

General Zionists have invariably deferred to the imperatives of the movement as a whole, frequently to the detriment of immediate party interests. It was, therefore, logical and proper that they should have been the first group to break away from the grip of outmoded formulae and to introduce the philosophy of non-identification with the political parties in Israel. This policy is gaining support and influence in Zionist thinking as the most creative way in which World Jewry can serve Israel as well as Zionism in the Diaspora.

In the United States, there was a notable development when, in addition to Hadassah, which has always remained aloof from the political parties in Israel, the American Jewish League for Israel was formed in 1958, as the principal male constituency of the World Confederation in the United States. Among the founders were my old friends and colleagues, Judge Louis E. Levinthal and Ezra Z. Shapiro, who were the first presidents, and Louis Lipsky, the nestor of American Zionism. The initiative in organizing the League was taken in protest against the ZOA's policy of identification with the General Zionist Party in Israel.

Throughout the organizational maneuverings, both in Israel and the Diaspora, General Zionism's Keren le-Mifalim Konstruktivi'im has continued as the principal instrument of the movement's practical achievements. The first board of directors of the KMK consisted of Peretz Bernstein, Dr. Abraham Granott, Yitzhak Gruenbaum, Zvi Herman, Moshe Kol, Yitzhak Kubowitzki, Sheftel Mirenberg, and myself. Kubowitzki was its executive director. Kalman Sultanik, who before coming to Israel had been active in Europe with Ha-No'ar Ha-Tzioni and the Ihud movement, became his deputy.

The primary objective of the KMK, according to the first article of its statutes, was "to help, support and encourage agricultural settlement in all forms in villages and smallholders' settlements; to establish and/or to cooperate with other factors in the establishment of agricultural settlements in Palestine; in particular, to direct new immigrants to agricultural settlements, and to assist and support agricultural settlers in every possible way."

In all the varied activities of the KMK, emphasis was always laid on the absorption of new immigrants into farming, cooperative enterprises, industry, workshops, and the building trade. Olim were urgently in need of this kind of assistance—more especially the General Zionists among them, who had no special framework to which to turn for supplements to the basic aid that was provided by the major funds. The KMK did not scrutinize the party affiliations of those whom it helped; indeed, a great many of the recipients had no formal political associations whatsoever, and it was precisely the people within that category who were most in need of a helping hand.

General Zionism, which had always done its utmost to further the upbuilding of the country on the broadest possible basis, above and beyond party considerations, was no longer willing to accept a situation that left the General Zionist Oleh without the added care and guidance that other Olim received from their respective party organizations. The KMK extended support to the "little man," whether in trade, industry, or any other field of economic endeavor. While the major funds, Keren Hayesod and Keren Kayemet, helped every new settler with his basic, minimal requirements, it was the additional help provided by the party funds that often spelled the difference between successful and unsuccessful absorption into the life of the country.

In October 1949, as a result of negotiations conducted by Moshe Kol, Yosef Serlin, and Yitzḥak Kubowitzki, an agreement was reached in New York with the Jewish Agency and the ZOA, whereby the annual amount of funds that the KMK would receive and administer was increased to $1,100,000. Of this sum, the ZOA would be allocated $350,000 for its own autonomous constructive projects. A further sum of $150,000 made available by the KMK was to be used by the ZOA, in cooperation with the KMK, for the building of the ZOA House in Tel Aviv, a project successfully initiated and promoted by Daniel Frisch, who was then president of the Zionist Organization of America.

Overall, during the decade between 1946 and 1955, the KMK disbursed some $15 million to various agricultural and industrial enterprises, educational institutions, and housing schemes, in both the private and collective sectors. In the private domain, Ha-Mifdeh Ha-Ezraḥi operated through its affiliated company, Shikun Ezraḥi (Civic Housing), to become one of the major building corporations in the country, and it sponsored a range of diversified cooperative plants that produced everything from tractors to furniture, shoes, and fruit juices.

Through its loan fund, the KMK also attended to the special needs of the middle-class farmers in Israel. The average middle-class farm had an area of about twenty-five *dunams* (six acres). The KMK helped the settlers to raise half the initial cost of the farmsteads, thereby relieving the settlement budget of the Jewish Agency of large amounts it would otherwise have had to disburse. Moreover, it accommodated farmers who had special requirements for developing their holdings.

Organized General Zionism thus became a significant factor in the entire field of practical work in Israel. Through the KMK, members of the world movement were brought into direct contact with the realities of life in Israel by having their attention focused on the practical possibilities of land settlement.

Together with the Jewish Agency, Ha-Mifdeh Ha-Ezraḥi established a loans center, Merkaz Kuppat Gemaḥ (*Gemaḥ* is the Hebrew acronym for *Gemilut Ḥesed*, interest-free loans), which, by 1954, had 267 branches in Israel. Twelve years later, their number had increased to over 300. In 1955 alone, more than 20,000 interest-free loans were granted. Recipients included artisans, small tradesmen, owners of small farmsteads, and the temporarily unemployed. A special feature of this loans center was the aid extended to new immigrants employed in afforestation and other public works, whose pay was at times held up for protracted periods.

Another form of utilitarian help was that afforded by the Idud (Incentive) Loan Society, which had been founded jointly with the Jewish Agency Executive. Idud granted loans directly to Olim and residents of the middle and professional classes for such useful purposes as financial help in the purchase of housing, vocational training, equipment for workshops and light industries, the acquiring of office space, and the provision of modest working capital. Special joint funds were also operated together with various immigrant associations.

Idud conducted its business on a strictly nonparty basis and no political bias was displayed in considering loan applications. Most of the borrowers came from the newly established farm settlements or from immigrant absorption centers. Kibbutzim that absorbed newcomers also received credit to pay for the initial costs of their integration.

When the Progressive Party was established in Israel in 1943 as an affiliate of the World Confederation of General Zionists, Mifalé Ha-Miflagah Ha-Progressivit (MHP) became the third beneficiary of KMK funds. As with Ha-Mifdeh Ha-Ezrahi, this concern was active mainly in the private sector. Its aims were to establish new private agricultural settlements and to further the development of existing ones, to set up immigrant hostels, form cooperatives and collective workshops, and to sponsor loan societies assisting new settlers.

Three agricultural training centers for immigrants from Europe were set up and here such Olim, while receiving basic instruction for their future life on the land, could also work on nearby homesteads to gain practical experience and, at the same time, build their own holdings.

Many constructive achievements can be recorded by Mifalé Ha-Oved Ha-Tzioni (MHH), which became part of the Progressive Party's operation. KMK allocations amounted to some eighty percent of the capital deployed by the MHH. During the War of Liberation in 1948–49, when some of the General Zionist settlements were cut off from the rest of Israel, MHH spent a considerable amount on security, organizing transport, and supplying fuel and vehicles. With the allocation of additional land to the kibbutzim at the end of the war, the purchase of essential machinery was made possible through loans granted by the MHH. It also guaranteed urgently required loans for Ha-Oved Ha-Tzioni settlements.

A new company named Yesodot (Foundations) was set up by Mifalé Ha-Oved Ha-Tzioni in 1950 to plan, develop, and coordinate General Zionist educational institutions. Sponsored by the KMK, which allocated some fifteen percent of its funds to the project, these youth-education institutions have become a source of pride to the movement. Its five youth villages are Magdiel, Aloné Yitzhak (near Kfar Glickson), Nitzanim, Neveh Hadassah (at Kibbutz Tel Yitzhak), and the Israel Goldstein Youth Village in Katamon, Jerusalem. Some 2,000 youngsters receive their education and vocational training in these institutes.

To further the successful absorption of new immigrants for whom the Jewish Agency did not provide permanent dwellings and who were the objects of our particular concern, the KMK set up an immigrants' hostel on Basle Street, Tel Aviv, shortly after the State came into being in 1948. Designed to provide temporary lodging for newcomers until they could find work and permanent housing, the hostel accommodated 120 persons. Named in my honor, it contained an assembly hall, a library, and a restaurant. Hebrew courses, lectures, and tours of the country were organized. General Zionists arriving from many countries were provided with a temporary home, at very modest cost, through its facilities. Eventually, however, as the standard of absorption-center accommodation improved, this center became outdated and the property was sold.

During its early years, Ha-No'ar Ha-Tzioni, the Confederation's youth movement, hewed out a creative path for itself in Zionist activity as well as in the daily life of Israel. Born in Eastern Europe, Ha-No'ar Ha-Tzioni furnished a continuous source of Zionist strength and ḥalutzic Aliyah throughout the stormy years of the Mandate and the dramatic epoch of Aliyah Bet. The movement's ideology sought to shape a better way of life and pattern of service to the Jewish State. It succeeded in establishing eleven settlements.

In the United States, the Plugat Aliyah (General Zionist pioneering) organization was founded and joined the world movement. It conducted a training farm in Poughkeepsie, New York, and a summer camp under canvas on the lines of an Israeli kibbutz. It flourished for a number of years, with the help and guidance of our Ḥalutzic Commission.

In February 1951, an educational institute for Zionist youth leaders was opened at the Israel Goldstein Youth Village in Jerusalem. The participants spent five months in study and travel around the country, using the Village as their base, and four more months at various settlements, where they took part in a work-study program and acquainted themselves with life and work in Israel. The curriculum was so designed as to equip these students with a thorough grounding in Jewish history and culture, Hebrew language, Zionist ideals, Israel's structure and social background, and the principles and practices of youth leadership. In time, this program was superseded by the highly successful Shnat Sherut scheme, which brings hundreds of youngsters each year from Diaspora communities for a year's service in Israel's kibbutzim.

A development of major significance has been the establishment of an independent world Zionist youth movement at a Jerusalem conference sponsored by our Confederation in the summer of 1973. Young Judea, Hashaḥar, and three Latin American organizations joined together in this venture.

Thus, the worldwide General Zionist movement, functioning through its youth affiliates and its numerous practical enterprises, and with the financial help of the KMK, has added a significant dimension to the epic of Zionist pioneering and upbuilding in our ancestral homeland.

My tenure as president of the Confederation ended in April 1956. I continued thereafter as co-chairman, with Rose Halprin, until 1971, when I retired from the chairmanship of the Keren Hayesod and from the Jewish Agency Executive. Ezra Z. Shapiro, who succeeded me as world chairman of Keren Hayesod, was then elected president of our Confederation. Rose Halprin and I were named honorary presidents for life.

Though no longer fully involved since 1971, I have maintained my interest in the progress and achievements of our General Zionist movement and have been heartened by continuing evidence of its growing strength in Jewish communities around the world.

At a special session of the Confederation's World Executive, held in Jerusalem in July 1974, it was unanimously resolved that it be given a new designation—"The World Confederation of United Zionists." This change of name met a long-felt need to avoid confusion with the party-affiliated World Union of General Zionists. In the wake of that step came the affiliation of the United Zionist Association of South Africa, which was then (and had long been) the largest and most influential Zionist organization in South Africa and the most powerful element in the S.A. Zionist Federation. Explaining its reasons for joining, the UZA stated that the party system had outlived its usefulness in the Diaspora and that more and more Zionists outside of Israel now subscribed to this view.

One of the activities in which I was especially honored to participate was the dedication on December 19, 1971, of the Louis Lipsky Chair in Drama at the Hebrew University of Jerusalem, established by our Confederation. Among those present was his son, Elazar Lipsky, a Zionist leader in his own right. At the ceremony, I was afforded the opportunity of paying tribute to one of the greats of our movement and I said in part:

> More than anyone in his generation, Louis Lipsky was the ideologist, teacher, publicist and administrator of American Zionism. Those who knew him most intimately, including his splendid children, felt that the attaching of his name to a Chair in Drama would reflect a phase of his career which was very meaningful to him. May the Louis Lipsky Chair in Drama at the Hebrew University be a recurrent reminder of his stellar role in the great Jewish drama of our time—the establishment of Medinat Yisrael.

In an article I prepared for *Hadassah Magazine* prior to the 29th Zionist Congress in 1978, I took occasion to summarize a few aspects of our Confederation's work that I felt had been of lasting significance in the upbuilding of Israel and in the furtherance of Zionism in the Diaspora. I also mentioned some of the people whose contributions were especially noteworthy:

> Our Confederation has provided top leadership for the Jewish Agency and the World Zionist Organization: Rose Halprin, who served as chairman of the American Section of the Jewish Agency Executive; Charlotte Jacobson, chairman of the American Section of the World Zionist Organization; Ezra Shapiro, who succeeded me as chairman of Keren Hayesod; Kalman Sultanik, a member of the Jewish Agency Executive's American Section and chairman of the Herzl Press; Faye Schenk, former chairman of the American Zionist Federation and now chairman of the Organization Department of the Jewish Agency,* having made her Aliyah in 1978; Melech Topiol, chairman of the Keren Hayesod-United Israel Appeal in France; Sidney Shipton, general secretary of the Zionist Federation of Great Britain; and Dr. Izak Warszawski, who heads our Confederation in Europe. These are a few of the Zionist leaders whom we have given to the World Zionist movement and to Israel.

*To our great sorrow, Mrs. Schenk died suddenly three years later, in August 1981.

The name of Barnett Janner should also have appeared in this roster. From 1931 until 1970, he sat in the House of Commons, first as a Liberal member of Parliament and later as a Labor M.P. For more than half a century, he was a prominent leader of British Jewry, having served as president of the Board of Deputies of British Jews and, until his death in May 1982, as president of the Zionist Federation of Great Britain and Ireland. The knighthood which he received in 1961 explicitly recognized his services to the Jewish community, and the peerage bestowed upon him when he retired from the House of Commons was a mark of his high reputation in British public affairs. Lord Janner displayed constant loyalty to the Jewish people, the Zionist movement generally and to General Zionism in particular. A popular speaker on Jewish platforms in the U.S., he was an honorary vice-president of our World Confederation and a Zionist General Council Virilist. "Barney" Janner helped to found the reorganized Confederation of General Zionists in 1958, on which occasion he said, "Israel party politics are irrelevant to Jews and Zionists in the Diaspora." His passing, one month before his ninetieth birthday, was a loss to World Jewry and Zionism as a whole.

More than any other single constituency, I believe, the World Confederation of United Zionists (WCUZ) holds the promise of a reinvigorated Zionist movement. It is represented in the presidium of the World Zionist Organization by Isaac de Vries, Haim Schachter, and myself, and on the Directorion of the Keren Kayemet by Judge Harold W. Wilkenfeld and Mrs. Sylvia Shapiro. The Confederation's Jerusalem office is ably directed by Haim Schachter, with Pesia Hoffman as his executive secretary and loyal assistant.

At the world conference of our Confederation held in Jerusalem prior to the 29th World Zionist Congress in February 1978, Charlotte Jacobson, Michel Topiol, and Kalman Sultanik were elected co-presidents of the WCUZ, with Sultanik serving as executive co-president. In my opening address before this conference, I availed myself of the opportunity to pay tribute to the memory of Ezra Z. Shapiro and Rose Halprin:

> Ezra was one of the most respected and beloved members of the Jewish Agency Executive and one of the most successful chairmen in the history of the Keren Hayesod, having brought it to the highest levels it has ever attained in income and in prestige. He represented our Confederation, both at home and abroad, with dignity, grace and effectiveness.

> Rose brought to our Confederation not only the luster of Hadassah, which she served with distinction as president on two separate occasions, but her own personal luster, as one of the leading personalities in the Zionist movement. For years she served effectively as chairman of the American Section of the Jewish Agency Executive. In our Confederation, she served as co-chairman at my side, for more than a score of years, with characteristic zest and brilliance.

In the course of my remarks, I noted that, as the Medinah was approaching its thirtieth anniversary, negotiations over a peace treaty with Israel's largest Arab neighbor, Egypt, were now beginning. It was our hope, I said, that this Congress would be remembered as the time when a wider peace began to dawn in the Middle East, "leading to an era when Israel can be tranquil, with no one to make it afraid," and when the Jewish State would be able to play its part in the economic and cultural development of the entire region.

One important step forward is the establishment of Confederation House, our new world center in Jerusalem. Located on a magnificent and historic site opposite Mount Zion, it has been built as an imaginative expansion of "St. George's facing David's Tower," a structure partly dating back to the fifth century. There will be four floors in this new center, providing offices for the Confederation, a library, space for meetings, seminars and film shows, a coffee bar, and social facilities. It is intended to serve as a venue for cultural activities, dialogues, and discussions, and also as a meeting place for tourists and visitors from abroad. Each floor will afford a splendid, uninterrupted view of Jerusalem "Within the Walls" (the Old City) and its environs. Thanks to the initiative and resourcefulness of Kalman Sultanik, who acquired the site in 1980 and has been responsible for all stages of the work, this world center is scheduled to be completed and dedicated by 1984.

I deem it a privilege to have had a hand in shaping and guiding the World Confederation of our movement, from its inception in 1946, into a useful instrument for the strengthening of Zionism in the *Golah* and for the support of constructive enterprises in Eretz Yisrael and Medinat Yisrael.

15

At Home and Abroad: 1971–77

Although the accounts of my involvement in the leadership of both the Keren Hayesod and the World Confederation of General Zionists have brought the story of my life close to the present time, they have done so in a limited and specialized context. I must therefore return to the summer of 1971, in order to restore the proper perspective and give the events and activities of my past twelve years of "retirement" their due place in this narrative.

My wife and I took our customary annual vacation in the United States for visits to our family and our congregation. On August 29, the Jewish Theological Seminary held a convocation at the Park Avenue Synagogue in New York City, where honorary degrees were awarded to graduates who had completed twenty-five years of service in the rabbinate, in Jewish public affairs, or in scholarly fields. Chancellor Louis Finkelstein presided. He had asked me to deliver the principal address and I chose as my subject "Changing Dimensions of the American Rabbinate." After briefly surveying the communal developments since 1946, I presented the view of one living in Israel:

> The problem, as I see it, is not whether American Jewry has a long-range future, but whether it will go on by force of inertia, or by force of momentum; what will be its character and content; whether it will be obliged to rely on anti-Semites to stimulate Jewish consciousness, or whether the stimulation will come from healthy, positive, inspiring sources.

I dwelt on the indispensable and vital motivations of the synagogue, Jewish education, and Medinat Yisrael. However much Israel would continue to need the material and moral support of American Jewry, I said, American Jews needed Israel even more deeply. Those of us who live in Israel were all too aware of the flaws in our own society and were doing our best to correct them. "We do not deny the right of fellow Jews outside Israel to criticize us," I went on, "but the criticism would be more welcome if the critics came to cast in their lot with us." Despite its imperfections, Israel provided a new and vitalizing thrust in a jaded and decadent world. I urged that both the Seminary and the Conservative movement strengthen their physical and spiritual presence in the Jewish State.

244

My High Holy Day sermons at Congregation B'nai Jeshurun in September again touched on the Israeli factor in contemporary Jewish life. "View from One Man's Summit," the sermon marking my seventy-fifth anniversary, which I delivered on *Shabbat Shuvah*, contained a broad hint that U.S. economic and military aid should not be used as a form of pressure on Israel to make concessions that would endanger its security. "As one who lives in Israel, I can testify to the overwhelming desire of its population, which is reflected in the Government as well, to see the day arrive as soon as possible when, under conditions of peace, a climate will be created for reciprocal relations with its neighbors which will fructify the entire Middle East." Israel could never afford to be just another little nation on the map of that region of the world. "It must continue to embody justice, righteousness and peace, and a world vision, which are its heritage from ancient prophetic days."

A few days before Rosh Hashanah, I visited my old friend, David Sarnoff, formerly head of the Radio Corporation of America, whose career was one of America's outstanding success stories. On several occasions, he had demonstrated his staunch friendship and support for Israel. I had also interested him in the Jewish Conciliation Board, where he was able to practice his homely Yiddish, for which there obviously was no outlet in the RCA's daily operations.

Mrs. Sarnoff told me, when I called at their house, that he was seriously ill, and so I knew that my visit must be brief. I sat down at his bedside and did what I could to cheer him. When I conveyed some greetings from Israel, his face lighted up.

David Sarnoff then implored me to pray for him during the forthcoming High Holy Day services. He chanted tearfully a moving passage from the liturgy of the *Yamim Nora'im:* "On Rosh Hashanah it is inscribed and on Yom Kippur the decree is sealed, how many shall pass away and how many shall be born, who shall live and who shall die . . ." He chanted the entire passage by heart, in the traditional prayer mode, as he had been taught in his boyhood years as a synagogue chorister.

A few weeks later, when I had already returned to Israel, David Sarnoff's life came to an end.

My last visit to a man who had come as a child from the Old World to the New, who had risen to international eminence in the field of broadcasting and disseminating classical music to untold millions, and who, on his deathbed, chanted the ancient liturgy of Jewish religious heritage, remains an unforgettable experience.

On October 3, the eve of Sukkot, I delivered an address at the Jewish Agency's observance of David Ben-Gurion's eighty-fifth birthday, held at the Herzl Institute in New York. My address, which incorporated a number of personal vignettes, was a tribute to "the modern David who did more than any other living Jew to convert the *Sukkat David ha-nofelet*, the fallen Tabernacle of David, to *Sukkat David ha-mukemet*, the reestablished Tabernacle of David."

From New York, Bert and I left for the West Coast to see our children. We were in time to participate in the dinner tendered to my brother, Morris, by his congregation, Sherith Israel of San Francisco, after more than forty years of meaningful service as its rabbi. This function also marked his impending retirement.

Our homeward journey, by way of the Pacific, took us to Hawaii, Japan, and

South Korea. In Seoul, we were the guests of Israel's ambassador, Yehudah Horan, and his wife. Mrs. Ruth Horan was familiar to us as a painter whose works had been exhibited at the Jerusalem Artists' House. From Seoul we proceeded to Hong Kong, Taiwan, and the islands of Bali and Java in Indonesia.

My abiding interest in and concern for the small Jewish outposts of the Diaspora, struggling to maintain their religious and cultural identity, had led me to the old synagogue of Dubrovnik when we visited Yugoslavia about three months previously. Dubrovnik had, under its former name, Ragusa, once been a flourishing center of Jewish life on the Adriatic coast and its surviving place of Jewish worship dated back to the sixteenth century. Now, however, fewer than a score of Jews lived in the port and a *minyan* for Shabbat services could only be mustered when there were Jewish tourists thereabouts.

While vacationing in Bali, I decided to spend a day in Sourabaya, the second largest city of Indonesia, where a community of about 600 Jews—mostly refugees from Nazi Germany—had been active in the 1940s, during the period of Dutch rule. I found that a mere eighteen Jewish families remained there, mainly Sephardim of Iraqi origin. The synagogue, built in 1946, was still in use, but only on the High Holy Days and major festivals.

Until his death earlier that year, David Musseri, an ardent Zionist, had been the *parnas* (warden) of the congregation and one of the very few remaining Jews capable of leading the prayers in Hebrew. His widow had been converted to Judaism by an Orthodox rabbi in Singapore. She and the children continued to practice what Jewish observances and customs still survived in Sourabaya.

Visiting the synagogue, which was being painted (a sign that it was in use, albeit infrequently), I learned that, after the death of Mr. Musseri, only one aged man knew how to recite the Hebrew services and he was now barely able to do so. This eighty-year-old recited a *Hazkarah* memorial prayer at the grave of a former community leader, when I was escorted to the local Jewish cemetery. There were about seventy graves there and a *Taharah* house, where the dead were prepared for burial. Some of the tombstones had been vandalized. I was asked if I could find them a prayer book with the Hebrew transliterated into Latin characters, and this I subsequently procured and sent to the community.

A "mass meeting" of the entire *kehillah* that evening brought about thirty men and women to the home of the Musseri family. I began by reciting the *Ma'ariv* service. During the discussion that followed, I warned that there would be no future for them as Jews in this community and urged my audience to explore seriously the prospect of Aliyah for themselves and, more especially, for their children. This was also my theme at a farewell gathering I addressed in the synagogue on the following morning. In reply to questions about the ultimate fate of that house of worship, I advised that the Torah scrolls be shipped to the Ministry of Religious Affairs in Jerusalem and that the building be sold and the proceeds used to construct a new synagogue in Israel.

As I was on the point of concluding my address, I happened to glance at the wall and suddenly noticed a telling symbol of the plight that this remote Jewish community—and so many others like it—now faced. It was a large clock, the hands of which had stopped ten minutes short of twelve. Looking at the pathetic vestiges of Jewish life in that far-off Indonesian city, I said, "You must know that all of you also stand at ten minutes to twelve in your Jewish lives here, so plan your Aliyah without delay!"

After my visit, I communicated with the World Jewish Congress branch in Australia and asked that they maintain contact with this surviving remnant of Jewry in a distant outpost of the *Golah*.

A new stage in my life began after our return to Israel in November 1971. No longer tied down by daily public responsibilities, I was able to enjoy a measure of freedom and to plunge into some long-delayed writing.

At this time, several anniversaries of special significance engaged me. One was the eightieth birthday of Leopold Goldmuntz, who, with his wife, Julia, was the foremost patron of our Jerusalem Youth Village. On the occasion of their golden wedding anniversary in 1972, I took them to the Hebrew University Synagogue for a brief service of thanksgiving, and then to the Youth Village that meant so much to them. We also participated in the golden wedding celebration of our friends, Mr. and Mrs. Max Freilich of Sydney, Australia. A former president of the Zionist Federation of Australia and New Zealand, Max Freilich had also been the "daddy" of the Keren Hayesod–United Israel Appeal, the Jewish National Fund, and numerous other Jewish communal and Zionist causes in his community. A dinner in Tel Aviv was arranged in his honor by the Hebrew University, of which he was a leading activist. Bernard Cherrick, the university's vice-president, chaired the proceedings and tributes were paid by Finance Minister Pinḥas Sapir, Interior Minister Yosef Burg, Jewish Agency Chairman Louis Pincus, and Lou Klein, who represented Australian Jewry. It was my privilege, on behalf of the Keren Hayesod, to share in the felicitations extended.

A melancholy event was the death that year of Edward Gelber, a leading figure in the World Zionist Organization, who had served as president of the Zionist Organization of Canada prior to his Aliyah in 1954. Edward Gelber had assumed his late father's mantle of devoted leadership, especially in the field of Jewish education, in his native Toronto. After settling in Israel, he had distinguished himself as chairman of the executive committee of the Hebrew University and of the board of the Rubin Academy of Music in Jerusalem, as well as in his capacity as vice-chairman of Yad Vashem. It was my sad privilege to deliver the eulogy at his funeral.

About this time, I became involved in the development of Haifa University, initially at the urging of Professor Benjamin Akzin, who was then serving ably as pro-rector of the fledgling academic institution. Professor Akzin, though a staunch Revisionist, had been a friend and colleague of mine from the days when we had both worked on the American Zionist Emergency Council. More recently, he had served with distinction as dean of the Hebrew University's Law School.

Founded as the Haifa University College in 1963, this new institution of higher education was the brainchild of Haifa's dynamic Mayor, Abba Khoushi. It was designed by Oscar Niemeyer, the eminent Brazilian Jewish architect, who planned it as one vast unit housing all the faculty buildings and dominating a picturesque hill overlooking the city of Haifa.

My interest in the university was aroused by a number of factors: it was new and open to new ideas, it lay close to the heartland of Israel's kibbutzim and had taken under its wing the Oranim Training School for kibbutz teachers, and its student body included more Arabs than all the other Israeli universities combined. Additionally meaningful to me was the fact that the chairman of the board was Nathan H. Ancell of New York, who, with his wife and his sister and brother-in-law, Florence and Theodore H. Baumritter, had been friends and congregants at B'nai Jeshurun. They were currently involved in important Jewish philanthropies on the American scene.

Haifa University was fortunate in having the active support of Akiva Lewinsky. He was then a leading official in Bank Ha-Poalim, and his cultural background and financial acumen proved to be important assets. Years later, he served as treasurer of the Jewish Agency. Another important supporter was Dr. Reuben Hecht, who had founded the Dagon grain silo in 1957 and now served as its managing director. Dr. Hecht, once an organizer of the Berihah ("illegal" Jewish immigration from Europe) during the last days of the British Mandate, was one of Haifa's leading citizens and a noted patron of the arts. More recently, as a close friend of Prime Minister Menahem Begin, he has served as one of the Government's chief advisers. A third good friend of the university was Dr. Naphtali Wydra, chairman of Israel's Port Authority, who had been managing director of Zim, Israel's navigation company.

I had the responsibility of serving with Mr. Ancell, Dr. Hecht, Mr. Lewinsky, Dr. Wydra, and Professor Avraham Kaplan, the representative of the faculty, on the committee appointed to select the fledgling university's first president. We chose Eliezer Rafaeli, a trained sociologist, who, as the son-in-law of Israel's late Prime Minister Levi Eshkol, had many influential friends in Government and academic circles. President Rafaeli endowed Haifa University with a wise and liberal administration. Upon his retirement from office in 1979, we chose as his successor Gershon Avner, secretary to the Israel cabinet and former ambassador to Canada. Mr. Rafaeli retained the post of chancellor. He later became the administrator of the Jewish Agency's Urban Renewal Program.

On January 18, 1972, the 28th World Zionist Congress opened in Jerusalem. For the first time in twenty-two years, I attended the Congress not as a member of the Zionist Executive. Considerable attention was devoted by the Congress to Zionist tasks in the *Golah,* and to social problems and the cultural gap in Israel. Yigal Allon, Israel's Deputy Prime Minister, delivered the keynote address and the participation of the nation's political leaders was more impressive than at any time since the establishment of Medinat Yisrael in 1948.

As co-chairman of the World Confederation of General Zionists, I addressed the Congress on January 19. My subject was "Israel and Diaspora Jewry." I stressed the cultural, moral, and spiritual dimensions of their relationship, and observed that, with due respect for the intellectual resources of American Jewry, "there is more

Jewish scholarship and literary excellence in one square mile in Jerusalem than in ten square miles in New York, Philadelphia, Chicago, or Cincinnati." Yet before Israel could become *or la-Goyyim,* "a light to the Gentiles," it must be *or la-Yehudim,* "a light to the Jews." The infiltration into Israel of various un-Jewish forms of decadence was disturbing; it ran counter to Zionist ideals and its effects threatened Israel's moral standing. The fact that 250,000 Israelis were still under-privileged—underfed, underhoused, and undereducated—was another blot on the Zionist badge. It was, alas, an explosive time bomb menacing the country's internal security. All the more welcome, therefore, was the Jewish Agency's decision to tackle some of these grave problems. Responsibility for alleviating them must be shared by Diaspora Jewry: "Their standard of giving," I remarked, "has not affected their standard of living."

Turning to Aliyah, I observed that prospects for increased immigration from North America had somewhat improved, but that the WZO should make greater use of the Association of Americans and Canadians in Israel in the tasks of immigration absorption. I dismissed the argument that American Zionist leaders should not be urged to make Aliyah, lest this weaken their organizations. The six million Jews of the United States, I said, were perfectly capable of producing new and effective leaders, and the example of "Aliyah from the top" was a Zionist imperative.

Three days later, I presided at a special session marking the seventy-fifth anniversary of the First Zionist Congress. I took occasion to note that, since 1897, vast changes had taken place in the structure of the Jewish people as a result of mass emigration from Eastern Europe, the Nazi Holocaust, and the virtually enforced isolation and assimilation of Jews in the Soviet bloc countries. The Jewish State had been established and had enhanced the image of the Jew, but it had not perceptibly reduced anti-Semitism throughout the world. Indeed, Arab hostility to Israel had generated new forms of anti-Jewish activity.

In opening this seventy-fifth anniversary session, I spoke of the response to the "shofar blast" that resounded at Basle in 1897—the building of the Jewish National Home, the establishment of Medinat Yisrael, the Ingathering of the Exiles, and the consolidation of the State. "Consequently, the word and the concept 'Zionism' are now serving as a banner of revival in the land of the Hammer and Sickle, where the hammer has not succeeded in beating down the Zionist longing, and the sickle has not succeeded in extirpating *Hatikvah,* hope, from the Jewish heart."

Immediately after the Congress, on January 28, I retired from the leadership of the World Confederation of General Zionists and made way for my successor, Ezra Z. Shapiro. This marked the completion of twenty-five years of continuous service to the Confederation.

On January 10, a week prior to the Zionist Congress, I delivered my presidential address before the fourth convention of Brit Ivrit Olamit, the World Hebrew Union, in Jerusalem. A full decade had passed since it had last convened, in 1962. A broad representation of delegates—religious and nonreligious, rabbis and secular educators, Zionists and non-Zionists—made this a significant gathering. I referred to imaginative techniques, such as "floating *ulpanim*" on transatlantic liners and

Hebrew columns in many non-Hebrew newspapers and periodicals, as well as to Brit Ivrit Olamit's close cooperation with Kol Zion La-Golah in the planning of Hebrew broadcasts to the Jews of Soviet Russia.

I also pointed out that whereas Hebrew education for the young was specifically the concern of the World Zionist Organization, Hebrew programs for adults primarily involved the Brit Ivrit Olamit, which deserved more than pious resolutions of support bereft of substance. Hitherto, there had been a considerable gap between what was pledged by the Government of Israel and the WZO and what was actually done. I expressed the hope that, with the broadening of the Jewish Agency, a more serious effort would be made to strengthen the hands of the World Hebrew Union.

I continued to head the Brit Ivrit Olamit until President Zalman Shazar retired from office in May 1973, when, according to the terms on which I had accepted his invitation, he returned to the organization's formal leadership.

Time takes its toll of one's friends and makes one increasingly aware of the inevitable limitation on one's future.

On March 12, 1972, at the Jewish Agency in Jerusalem, I spoke at the *Shloshim* memorial meeting for Berl Locker, the veteran Labor Zionist leader, who had died at the age of eighty-five. I paid tribute to him as a leading exponent of his own Po'alei Zion (Socialist Zionist) ideology, and of Zionism in its entirety. He was a forceful debater, gifted with a sense of humor that often served him as a powerful weapon. While in the United States during World War I, he had counteracted the anti-Zionist influence of the Yiddish-speaking Socialist Bund. In England, he served effectively, at the side of Dr. Chaim Weizmann, in the Jewish Agency Executive. He won many supporters for the Zionist cause within the ranks of the British Labor Party. Berl Locker had headed the Jewish Agency's Political Bureau in London from 1938 until after World War II. He had also served as chairman of the Jewish Agency Executive in Jerusalem at the time when I was its treasurer. After his retirement, he found satisfaction in writing his memoirs—"the only paradise from which one cannot be expelled."

Another sad event was the death in late September of Yosef Weitz, a director of the Keren Kayemet and its expert on afforestation. A noted writer as well as a public figure for decades past, Yosef Weitz had devoted most of his life to the reclamation of the soil of Eretz Yisrael. Walking stick in hand, he had covered tens of thousands of *dunams* of land, checking their potential for reclamation. Since 1961, I had been privileged to accompany him on many tours of Israel and its newly developed areas. Speaking at the *Shloshim* memorial meeting, Deputy Prime Minister Yigal Allon aptly remarked, "The staff of Moses brought forth water from the rock; the staff of Joseph [Weitz] brought forth bread from the earth."

Tests of Faith

For Jews in Israel and throughout the world, 1972 will be remembered as the year of escalating terrorist outrages by Palestinian and other murder squads. From 1948 until 1967, within its constricted borders, Israel had suffered from the incursions of *fedayeen* groups based in Egypt, the Gaza Strip, Jordanian-occupied territory west of the Jordan river, Lebanon, and Syria. During the prolonged War of Attrition, which followed the Six-Day War, Arab terrorism and "petrodollars" fostered new and more brutally audacious operations by the so-called Palestine Liberation Organization (PLO) and kindred gangs specializing in the murder of defenseless civilians.

At first, these depredations aroused horror and condemnation, except among the Soviet and "Third World" countries. In the course of time, however, as urban terrorism became an almost daily occurrence in many lands and as an increasing number of Western industrialized states found themselves dependent on Arab oil supplies, Israel received diminishing moral support from the free world.

The terrorist attack on an El Al plane at Munich Airport, on February 2, 1970, was a sign of things to come. On May 9, 1972, four Arabs belonging to the "Black September" group hijacked a Belgian Sabena aircraft, forced it to land at Lod Airport, and threatened to blow it up with all its passengers and crew aboard, unless the Israel Government released more than 100 Arab terrorists under detention for murder or attempted murder. On this occasion, fortunately, an IDF squad managed to storm the hijacked plane and release the hostages, killing two of the Arab terrorists and capturing the others.

Exactly three weeks later, on May 30, three Japanese "Red Army" allies of the PLO, masquerading as tourists, opened fire indiscriminately on other disembarking passengers in the Lod Airport arrival hall, killing twenty-four and wounding seventy-eight. Many of the victims were Christian pilgrims. Among the dead was Professor Aharon Katzir (Katchalski) of the Weizmann Institute of Science, a former president of the Israel Academy of Arts and Sciences and an internationally renowned research chemist and biophysicist. His younger brother, Professor Ephraim Katzir, also a distinguished scientist at the Weizmann Institute, became Israel's fourth President in the following year. Two of the Japanese terrorists were killed by security forces, but the third, Kozo Okamoto, was captured and is now serving a life sentence. Responsibility for this ghastly massacre was claimed by the "Popular Front for the Liberation of Palestine."

Encouraged by the success of their fellow assassins, "Black September" chose the Olympic Games in Munich as the target for their next murderous operation. Eleven members of the Israeli national team, including new Olim from the Soviet Union, were slaughtered at the Olympic Village or at Munich Airport after the Arab "hit squad" had again tried unsuccessfully to use them as hostages for the release of imprisoned terrorists. As television and radio coverage brought us the story of those horrifying events in Munich on September 5, we were all in the grip of a helpless fury—that German security had been so lax, that the Munich police had so mismanaged their rescue attempt at the airport, and, later, that the three surviving "Palestinians" awaiting trial should have been released in order to buy off Arab wrath.

Worst of all was the decision taken by Avery Brundage, president of the International Olympic Committee, that "the games must go on." After such an unspeakable violation of the vaunted Olympic spirit, the only proper course of action would have been for the organizers to hold the memorial assembly and then to have the games abandoned, instead of allowing the Israeli survivors to fly home by themselves. The official decision minimized the gravity of what had occurred and paved the way for a subsequent decision to allow PLO "athletes" representation at the 1980 Olympics in Moscow.

It was that same Avery Brundage who, on December 8, 1935, as president of the American Olympic Committee, helped to defeat a motion that U.S. athletes boycott the forthcoming (1936) Olympic Games in Berlin. Ignoring the recently promulgated Nuremberg Laws, Brundage had welcomed glib Nazi assurances that German Jewish athletes would not be banned from Hitler's propaganda festival.

Israel's reaction was to render it very difficult for terrorists to cross its borders undetected; to keep them "on the run" with periodical search-and-destroy raids into Lebanon and Syria by land, sea, and air; and to develop highly trained anti-terror squads capable of dealing with any situation at a moment's notice. Only when other Western nations learned to their own cost that the PLO and its allies were a menace to humanity in general, and not only to Jews, did they decide to copy some of Israel's security measures.

Reaction from the Christian churches in 1972 was not universally reassuring. In a personal message to President Shazar, Pope Paul VI expressed his horror at the "detestable events perpetrated" at Munich, but the Protestant World Council of Churches issued no such forthright statement. The Israel Interfaith Committee held a memorial meeting for the victims of the Lod Airport massacre, in cooperation with the American Jewish Committee and the Ecumenical Theological Research Fraternity in Israel, which was attended by leading Jewish, Christian, and Muslim personalities. Following the tragedy in Munich, the Interfaith Committee there sponsored a visit to Israel by representatives of the Conference of Christians and Jews in Germany. They came to extend condolences and tokens of friendship to the families of the murdered athletes and trainers. In my capacity as an honorary president of the Israel Interfaith Committee, I chaired the memorial meeting.

In April 1972, under the auspices of the Israel Interfaith Committee, a congress on "Black Africa and the Bible" was held at the Harry S. Truman Research Center of the Hebrew University in Jerusalem. A number of important African organizations, both Catholic and Protestant, sponsored this congress, in which many distinguished religious leaders from Africa and Israel participated. On the international level, the Israel Interfaith Committee continued to organize annual seminars on Judaism, Israel, and Christian-Jewish relations, for visitors from the Afro-Asian countries. On the local level, it sponsored annual awards for outstanding literary and dramatic works aiming to promote Jewish-Arab understanding.

I felt pleased to be associated with my fellow honorary presidents of the Committee—Anglican Archbishop George Appleton, Greek Catholic Archbishop Joseph Raya, and Sheikh Tewfik Mahmud Asleya—and with my Jewish colleagues, headed by Professors Zwi Werblowsky, Shmaryahu Talmon, and André Chouraqui.

On July 11, 1972, in an address before the Interfaith Committee, I said:

This is the motherland of Judaism, Christianity and Islam. Within one square mile in Jerusalem are concentrated the Holy Places sacred to half the human race. In physical contiguity, the adherents and spokesmen of the respective religious traditions are closer than anywhere else in the world. Spiritually, however, they are oceans apart. This constitutes an opportunity and a challenge to cultivate intellectual and spiritual contacts, with a view to a better understanding of one another's traditions, and to exploring areas of common dedication to the religious way of life as opposed to the paganism, hedonism, cynicism and materialism which are a common peril to all of us, separately and together.

On the occasion of Israel's twenty-fifth Independence Day, an interfaith symposium was arranged at Jerusalem's YMCA building on May 16, 1973. Speaking as a Jew, I observed that in Israel, the one place in the world where Jews constituted the majority of the population, Jews had to assume unique responsibilities toward other religious groups. Over and above the guarantees written into Israel's Proclamation of Independence, it was in the person-to-person sphere of voluntary relationships that the nation's character would be fashioned. Instead of the 2,000-year-old confrontation in the Holy Land, we were seeking a way for Jews, Christians, and Muslims to "sit together, talk together and work together" in mutual respect. This was a challenge of no mean relevancy to the future of Israel; and its outcome, if worthwhile, would certainly have repercussions in the wider world.

An event of very special significance for my wife and myself was the opening of the new Conservative synagogue center in Jerusalem, in July 1972. The building in which it is now housed, at the corner of Keren Hayesod and Agron Streets, was purchased from a Christian missionary association by David Zucker and Morris Spiesman, two leaders of the United Synagogue of America. They then donated it to the United Synagogue for the specific purpose of establishing the Center for Conservative Judaism in Israel's capital. Our movement styles itself in Israel *Ha-Yahadut ha-Masortit*—"Traditional Judaism."

The first services were held in this center during the High Holy Days of 5733 (September 1972). Bert and I welcomed the opportunity of resuming the mode of worship which, in large part, accorded with our experience at Congregation B'nai Jeshurun in New York. This congregation in Jerusalem, however, held services without organ accompaniment or women's voices in the choir. With a large constituency of retired American rabbis and frequent visits by others now active in the American rabbinate, our congregation is probably the most rabbinically constituted in the world today. Professor Simon Greenberg, vice-chancellor of the Jewish Theological Seminary of America, dividing his time between New York and Jerusalem, was the spiritual father of the Center for Conservative Judaism. His periodical visits were a source of instruction, stimulation, and inspiration.

Our first regularly officiating rabbi, Joshua Stampfer of Portland, Oregon, was spending his sabbatical year in Israel when the center opened. The first permanent rabbi was Dr. Joseph Green, who made Aliyah with his family in October 1974. He has won our high regard for his devoted ministrations. Professor Abraham S. Halkin enhanced the Torah reading through his expert services as *ba'al-keri'ah* In his absence, Rabbi S. Gershon Levi, a distinguished former president of the Rabbinical Assembly of America, frequently acted in that capacity. Occasionally, this service was also rendered by Professor Gershon Weiner of the Brandeis Institute. Among those who volunteered to preach sermons was Rabbi Dr. Louis Katzoff. Cantor Danny Ziff, who taught at the Rubin Academy of Music in Jerusalem, was appointed *ḥazzan;* Rabbi Pesaḥ Schindler became the center's gifted director and supervisor of its educational program; and Rabbi David Bonder served as our genial synagogue director.

Important convocations of the World Council of Synagogues and the Rabbinical Assembly of America have brought the leaders of our world movement to our congregation in Jerusalem from time to time.

Our most illustrious layman was Judge Louis E. Levinthal, my fellow Philadelphian and colleague, and my predecessor as president of the Zionist Organization of America. The literary pundit among us was Professor Sol Liptzin, noted author and former head of the Department of Comparative Literature in the College of the City of New York. Professor Paul Gould was esteemed as one of our literati. Our most active layman was Meyer Bargteil, who succeeded Rabbi Bernard Segal as chairman of the congregation's administrative board, on which Bert is also a member. Our most learned layman was Judge Harold Wilkenfeld, likewise actively involved in public affairs. Dr. Herbert Shulman, another prominent member, now serves as president of our synagogue's board, and Dr. Harold Blum's wife, Tovah, is president of the sisterhood.

We took pride in the important service rendered to the World Jewish Bible Society by Dr. Louis Katzoff as vice-chairman and editor of *Dor le-Dor*, the society's English-language quarterly.

It was a gladdening day for Bert and for me when Cantor Robert H. Segal, my cherished colleague as *ḥazzan* at B'nai Jeshurun, having retired in 1979, came with his talented wife, Judith, to live in Jerusalem. We were now fellow congregants once again, albeit, at this stage, not on the pulpit but in the pew.

On Sabbaths and festivals, two additional congregational *minyanim* worship on the premises of the center—one, a *Ḥavurah*, in the Bet Midrash, and another group in the adjoining community center, which also houses the Bet Atid youth hostel. On weekdays, there are lectures and study circles, as well as a forum series directed by George E. Levinrew, which make the building truly a center of Jewish religious and cultural activities.

The Center for Conservative Judaism is an important addition to the spiritual and cultural map of Jerusalem. It cannot be said, as yet, that our congregation has developed an indigenous Israeli constituency. That will take time. It does, however, carry the banner of Conservative Judaism in Israel, and it has mothered other Conservative synagogues elsewhere in the country. There is reason to hope that, in the course of time, Conservative Judaism will gain a significant foothold in Israel's religious life.

The Reform movement has also spread, establishing new branches throughout

Israel. Its center is the Hebrew Union College in Jerusalem, originally founded by the late Professor Nelson Glueck and more recently headed by Professor Ezra Spicehandler. Rabbi Richard (Asher) Hirsch, who formerly directed the Union of American Hebrew Congregations in the United States, now heads the World Union for Progressive Judaism, which has its office in that building. Since making Aliyah with his family, Rabbi Hirsch has brought new and spirited impetus to his movement and was instrumental in establishing its first agricultural settlement, Kibbutz Yahel, a novel religious experiment in combining Reform Judaism with *ḥalutziut*.

Mention should also be made of the Reconstructionist movement in Israel. Fathered by Professor Mordecai M. Kaplan in New York, it has become a significant factor in the religious life of American Jewry, with its own rabbinical seminary headed by Rabbi Ira Eisenstein. The Israel base of Reconstructionism is Congregation Mevakshé Derekh in Jerusalem, led by Rabbi Jack Cohen, who is director of the B'nai B'rith Hillel Foundation at the Hebrew University and an important member of the interfaith movement in Israel.

Professor Mordecai Kaplan spent some years in Jerusalem, loved and revered by his disciples and others who have sat at his feet. I count myself one of their number. Bert and I felt greatly privileged to attend his ninety-fifth birthday celebration at a luncheon arranged by his disciples and friends in the Knesset on July 22, 1976.

Though organizationally affiliated with the Conservative movement, I have never felt comfortable with the label of "Conservative," seeing myself as belonging to its "left" periphery. My relations with the Reform group in Israel have been cordial. I have cultivated friendly contacts with all religious trends in Jewish life, and with secular groups as well. In the hope that my terminology will not be misunderstood, I would define myself as a "catholic" Jew, in the special all-embracing sense in which my teacher, Professor Solomon Schechter, used that term.

Should anyone ask me whether the Conservative movement has a future in Medinat Yisrael, I would reply strongly in the affirmative. Obviously, it can never have the importance here it has gained in American Jewry, for the simple reason that Israel's religious establishment, which is Orthodox, looks askance at deviations and refuses to recognize marriages and divorces performed by Conservative, Reform, or Reconstructionist rabbis. It is a tribute to the patriotism of Israel's non-Orthodox rabbinate and laity that they have not used their considerable strength and influence in the United States to try to enforce recognition of their legitimacy in Israel.

I feel that this issue should not be forced, since the Conservative and other non-Orthodox groupings are as yet insufficiently rooted here to offer a serious challenge to a religious establishment backed up by powerful Chief Rabbinates, religious courts, Ashkenazi and Sephardi religious constituencies, and political support including and extending beyond the National Religious Party and Agudat Yisrael. In the meantime, more and more Conservative Jews should come on Aliyah and strengthen their own religious institutions in Israel, taking full advantage of the many opportunities that still exist and beckon.

There are some moderate elements in the Orthodox camp that have, in the past, seemed ready to offer the non-Orthodox a fairer deal. Invariably, however, those on the far right have done their best to extinguish such hopes. One is sometimes tempted to ask whether these Orthodox elements would rather have the nonobservant majority remain secular and irreligious than embrace a non-Orthodox form of Jewish religious self-expression. All of us who are confronted by such problems have good reason to make common cause in the struggle to obtain recognition for alternative religious trends in Judaism.

As President Zalman Shazar's second and final term of office drew to a close in the spring of 1973, Professor Ephraim Katzir of the Weizmann Institute of Science in Reḥovot was elected to succeed him.

Zalman Shazar had been an outstanding President, held in both affection and esteem and admired for his profound Jewish culture in Hebrew and in Yiddish. He was also a Zionist President, an impassioned spokesman for his people, who displayed an all-embracing love for Am Yisrael across its many segments and diversities. The United Jewish Appeal and the Keren Hayesod had special reason to be grateful to him for placing Bet ha-Nasi at their disposal and for giving generously of his time in receiving delegations from all parts of the Jewish world. Such visitors were frequently astonished by Shazar's phenomenal memory of people and events associated with his many Zionist missions overseas.

On May 21, the eve of his retirement, members of his study circle (organized by Professor Moshe Davis, Dr. Eliahu Elath, and other close friends) attended a special farewell evening at Bet ha-Nasi when the newly published "Shazar Library," sponsored by the Hebrew University's Institute of Contemporary Jewry, was presented to the outgoing head of state. Prime Minister Golda Meir attended this gathering and Moshe Davis presided. It was my great privilege to make the presentation and to pay tribute to one who had set an enduring stamp on Israel's Presidency. While extending felicitations to his successor, Professor Katzir, I expressed my conviction that Zalman Shazar would "carry into his private life the *Keter Torah* and the *Keter Shem Tov*, the Crown of Torah and the Crown of a Good Name, which are his in and out of office."

One who played an important part in making such functions meaningful was Mrs. Shulamit Nardi, the President's personal assistant and English secretary, upon whom Shazar leaned heavily for the translation of his Hebrew remarks. Shulamit Nardi was the granddaughter of the Reverend Zvi Hirsch Masliansky, doyen of Yiddish orators and preachers of Zionism in America, who had once taught Chaim Weizmann at the yeshivah in Pinsk. This distinguished Zionist background, combined with her own mastery of Hebrew and English and her familiarity with the world Jewish scene, gave Mrs. Nardi's participation in these Bet ha-Nasi meetings a worthwhile dimension of its own.

Professor Ephraim Katzir, Israel's fourth President, was (like his lamented elder brother, Professor Aharon Katchalsky) a scientist of international repute. Though not as conversant as his predecessors with Jewish and Zionist affairs, he learned

30. Golden Wedding Anniversary celebration in the Israel Goldstein Synagogue, Hebrew University, August 15, 1968. Dr. and Mrs. Goldstein recite a specially composed thanksgiving prayer.

31. At a reception in Jerusalem's City Hall, December 20, 1968. The Goldsteins with their cousins, Yitzhak and Batya Abbady *(left)* and Julius and Roslyn Silver.

32. Professor Benjamin Mazar *(right)* serves as an expert guide to excavations at the Southern Wall of the Temple, Jerusalem, December 1968.

33. At the Conference on Human Needs convened in Jerusalem by Prime Minister Golda Meir and Jewish Agency Chairman Louis A. Pincus, June 1969. Seated around the table *(counterclockwise, left to right)* are Charlotte Jacobson (U.S.A), Michel Topiol (France), Rose Halprin and Kalman Sultanik (U.S.A.), the author, and *(with back to camera)* Donald Silk (Great Britain). Keren Hayesod photo, United Israel Appeal Photo Archives, Jerusalem.

34. Eve of Passover visit to the Falasha community of Ambober, Ethiopia, April 1969. Falasha *Kohanim* pose with the author in front of their synagogue.

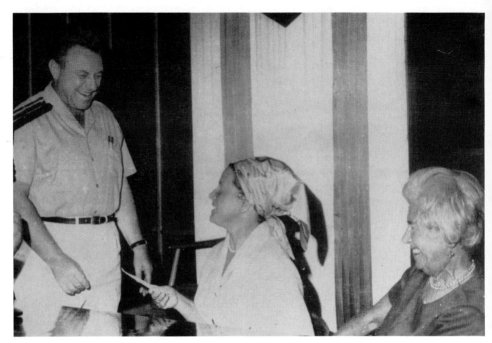

35. Bert Goldstein *(right)* smiles approvingly as Shulamit Catane receives the first Jerusalem Good Citizenship award from Mayor Teddy Kollek, July 1969. Y. Barzilay photo, Jerusalem.

36. Golden Jubilee of the Keren Hayesod, 1970–1971. With Rahel Yannait Ben-Zvi at opening of the Keren Hayesod Jubilee Pavilion in Tel Aviv, May 27, 1970. David Harris photo, Jerusalem.

37. Golden Jubilee of the Keren Hayesod. At conference of the South African Zionist Federation in Johannesburg, March 1970. On dais *(left to right):* Mrs. Itzhak Unna, Lionel Hodes, general secretary of the SAZF, Chief Rabbi Bernard M. Casper, Israel H. Maisels, outgoing chairman of the SAZF, the author, Joseph Daleski, president of the SAZF, Johannesburg's Mayor Alf Widman, Israel Consul Itzhak Unna, Dr. Teddy Schneider, president of the S.A. Board of Jewish Deputies, Bert Goldstein, Chief Progressive Congregations Minister Arthur Saul Super, Mrs. Alf Widman, and former South African Chief Rabbi Louis I. Rabinowitz. Brian Koping photo, Johannesburg, South Africa.

38. Golden Jubilee of the Keren Hayesod. At London conference of the Zionist Federation of Great Britain and Ireland, April 4, 1970. On dais *(left to right):* Lord Janner, ZF president, Hyam Morrison, Donald Silk, ZF chairman, Lavy Bakstansky, ZF general secretary, the author, and Eva, Marchioness of Reading.

39. Presentation of Golden Jubilee medallions to David Ben-Gurion in Tel Aviv, April 7, 1971. Keren Hayesod photo, United Israel Appeal Photo Archives, Jerusalem.

40. Protest rally organized by Soviet Olim at the Western Wall, December 1970, condemning the Leningrad show trials and detention of "Prisoners of Zion." Jewish Agency leaders in foreground, with the hunger strikers, are *(left to right)*: Louis A. Pincus, the author, Zvi Netzer, Ḥaim Finkelstein, Arye L. Dulzin, and *(behind him, in profile, partly obscured)* Moshe Rivlin. Nachum Gutman photo, Tel Aviv.

41. **Jewish Agency Chairman Louis A. Pincus displaying the Scroll of Honor awarded to the author at Binyanei ha-Umah, Jerusalem, June 24, 1971, to mark his 75th birthday and impending retirement from the Keren Hayesod chairmanship. Keren Hayesod photo, United Israel Appeal Photo Archives, Jerusalem.**

ד' ישראל גולדשטיין קיבל את המגילה. על ידו עומדים פרופ' י. כץ, מר אברהם הרנון ופרופ' צבי אדר, דיקן הפקולטה למדעי

42. **At a ceremony held on Mount Scopus, Jerusalem, July 5, 1971, an honorary degree is conferred on the author by the Hebrew University. Pictured *(left to right):* Professor Jacob Katz, rector, Avraham Harman, president, Professor Zvi Adar, and Dr. Goldstein.**

43. Congregation B'nai Jeshurun, New York, marks the author's 75th birthday during the summer of 1971. Presentation of testimonial, with B'nai Jeshurun's Cantor Robert H. Segal *(left)*, President Charles H. Silver *(center)*, and Rabbi William Berkowitz and Board Chairman Leon Singer *(right)*. Archer Associates photo, New York.

44. The author receiving New York City's Medallion for Distinguished Public Service from Mayor John Lindsay, July 10, 1971. Among those pictured are *(left to right)* Leon Singer and David Dubinsky *(2d and 3rd)*, Bert and Israel Goldstein *(5th and 6th)*, Mayor Lindsay and Charles Silver *(7th and 8th)*, Alex Rose and Ruth Richman *(10th and 11th)*, and Dr. David Hyatt *(12th)*. Archer Associates photo, New York.

45. Congregation B'nai Jeshurun. With Charles Silver and Rabbi Berkowitz outside the
Community Center renamed for Dr. Goldstein.

46. Israel Interfaith Committee activities. Memorial assembly in Jerusalem for Professor Ikuro Teshima, founder of the Japanese Makuya movement, January 27, 1974.

47. Israel Interfaith Committee activities. Observance of Israel's 30th Independence year, at the Van Leer Institute, Jerusalem, December 28, 1978. On dais *(left to right)*: Father Marcel Dubois, President Itzhak Navon, the author, Professor Shlomo Avineri, and Yusuf Khamis. Hutmann-J. K. Ben-Josef photo, Jerusalem.

48. Israel Interfaith Committee activities. Dinner guests at the Goldsteins' home in Jerusalem, March 1979. Those pictured include *(left to right, standing)*: Professor Peter Oberlander, Professor Jacob Mann, Motoyuki Fujioka, and *(at end of row)* Mrs. Oberlander, Mrs. Kazuyo Minesaki, and Ya'akov Teshima; *(seated)*: Mrs. Nijiko Jindo, Mrs. Sylvia Mann, Bert Goldstein, Mrs. Chiyoko Teshima (widow of Makuya's founder), and the author.

49. Award of honorary degree at commencement exercises of the author's alma mater, University of Pennsylvania, May 28, 1976. Honorary degree recipients are *(left to right):* Donald T. Sheehan, James A. DePreist, Professor John T. Dunlop of Harvard, Robert G. Dunlop, Board of Trustees Chairman Donald T. Regan, Professor Edward A. Shils of Chicago University, Chief Justice Warren E. Burger, Professor Henry Steele Commager of Amherst College, U.S. Attorney General Edward H. Levi, University President Martin Meyerson, Professor Howard M. Temin of Wisconsin University (1975 Nobel laureate in Medicine), Provost Eliot Stellar, the author, Professor John Bardeen of Illinois University, and former U.S. Senator J. William Fulbright. Frank Ross photo, Ocean City, N.J.

50. Celebration of the author's 80th birthday at Bet ha-Nasi, Jerusalem, June 27, 1976. Pictured *(left to right):* Jewish Agency Chairman Yosef Almogi, Prime Minister Yitzhak Rabin, Bert Goldstein, President Ephraim Katzir, the author, Mrs. Katzir, Keren Hayesod World Chairman Ezra Z. Shapiro, and S. J. Kreutner. Keren Hayesod photo, United Israel Appeal Photo Archives, Jerusalem.

51. Jewish National Fund dedication ceremonies in Israel. Planting of forest honoring Ya'akov and Vera Tsur *(center)*, October 20, 1976. Standing on the right are Reuven Artzi and the author. Dan Schaffner photo, Jerusalem.

52. Jewish National Fund dedication ceremonies. Establishment of the George Eliot Memorial Grove in the International Women's Forest at Turan, Galilee, December 30, 1976, to mark the centenary of *Daniel Deronda*, George Eliot's proto-Zionist novel. The author delivers an address; seated next to him *(right to left)* are Mrs. Mason and British Ambassador John Mason, their daughter and son, Ruth Levitt, and Leah Epstein.

53. With Mrs. Rosalynn Carter at a tree-planting ceremony in her honor, at the Mevasseret Zion Absorption Center for Olim near Jerusalem, during President Jimmy Carter's visit to Israel, March 1979.

54. At the Israel Goldstein Youth Village in Jerusalem. Richard Tucker, U.S. opera star and cantor, enjoys a musical welcome, July 1967. Lonia Liebergall and the author stand to his right and left. Dr. K. Meyerowitz photo, Jerusalem.

55. At the Israel Goldstein Youth Village. "Among my Grandchildren," with Ze'ev Schickler and Lonia Liebergall, at the Village's 25th anniversary celebration, 1975. Werner Braun photo, Jerusalem.

56. At the Israel Goldstein Youth Village. With U.S. patrons Elmer L. and Nan Winter of Milwaukee, November 1981. Israel Sun Ltd., Tel Aviv.

57. Inauguration of the Keren Hayesod 60th Jubilee celebrations at Bet ha-Nasi, Jerusalem, October 25, 1979. Dr. Avraham Avi-ḥai *(left)*, accompanied by the author, hands President Itzḥak Navon a symbolic key "to open the hearts of World Jewry." David Harris photo, Jerusalem.

58. At a gathering in honor of the author's 85th birthday, held jointly by the Hebrew University, Keren Hayesod, and the World Confederation of United Zionists, at Maison de France, Givat Ram campus of the Hebrew University, Jerusalem, June 9, 1981. Greetings are extended by Professor Michael Zand, an eminent Soviet Oleh *(left)*, and Menashe H. Eliachar, Jerusalem Sephardi leader and president of the city's Chamber of Commerce.

59. At gathering in honor of the author's 85th birthday. On dais *(right to left):* Hebrew University Vice-President Bernard Cherrick, Bert Goldstein, Dr. Avraham Avi-ḥai, Keren Hayesod world chairman, the author, and *(far left)* Moshe Rivlin.

60. Association of Americans and Canadians in Israel. The author with *(left to right)* Mayor Teddy Kollek, Abraham Schechter of the AACI, and Bert Goldstein at the site of a new Senior Citizens' housing development in Kiryat Hayovel, Jerusalem, August 1981. Carol Gootter photo, Jerusalem.

61. Installation of Professor Paul Olum, the author's son-in-law, as president of the University of Oregon, October 12, 1981. Pictured *(left to right):* Vivian Olum, Paul Olum, Dora and Avram Goldstein, Bert Goldstein, Kenneth Akiba Olum, the author, and Herbert Scheinberg.

62. Four Generations of the Goldstein Family. The brothers at a family celebration *(right to left):* the author, Rabbi Morris Goldstein, and Isaac Goldstein.

63. Four Generations: The sister of the Goldstein brothers, Mrs. Sarah Lazarus.

64. **Four Generations: The family in Palo Alto, California** *(left to right):* **Michael and his fiancée, Karen Shalowitz, Joshua, Dora and Avram, Dan, Margaret (holding greatgrandson Andrew Eytan) and Brad Wallace.**

65. **Four Generations: Olum family group at granddaughter's wedding, Amherst, August 5, 1980. Pictured** *(left to right):* **Kenneth Akiba, Joyce (the bride) and Philippe Galasky (the bridegroom), Judith Lightfoote (the bride's sister) and Geoffrey Lightfoote (her husband), Vivian and Paul (the bride's parents).**

66. Dr. and Mrs. Israel Goldstein at their home in Jerusalem. R. M. Kneller photo, Jerusalem.

fast. Katzir brought to his high office a natural humility, high-mindedness, and an unaffected, warm character that won many hearts. The outbreak of the Yom Kippur War, less than five months after he assumed office, added to the burdens of his Presidency.

A project that engaged my special interest at this time was Bet ha-Tanakh, the planned World Jewish Bible Center, whose leading advocate was Professor Ḥaim Gevaryahu, chairman of the World Jewish Bible Society. Associated with him in this project was Ben-Zion Luria, treasurer of the Israel Society for Biblical Research and editor of the periodical *Bet Mikra*.

David Ben-Gurion gave this plan the imprimatur of his sponsorship. A magnificent site had been set aside for Bet ha-Tanakh—a hill overlooking the Old City of Jerusalem and the Mount of Olives, mentioned twice in the Book of Joshua (15:8–9 and 18:16). The nine *dunams* of land on which this hill stands had been made available by the Keren Kayemet in 1970, and the project had then received the Israel Government's blessing and wide public approval.

The architects' plans made provision for a complex that would house a complete biblical library, a museum of biblical art and collateral exhibits, and a variety of research and educational facilities. Bet ha-Tanakh was intended to be the international focus of Hebrew Bible study, to attract leading scholars from all over the world, and to cultivate the widest possible popular interest in the Book of Books. In addition to temporary exhibits, permanent displays were planned to demonstrate the Bible's impact on world history and Western civilization. Provision was also made for a garden of biblical flora and fauna to surround the building. Bet ha-Tanakh would serve as headquarters of the World Jewish Bible Society and its affiliated organizations.

Ben-Gurion, a lifelong student of the Bible, had for many years made his home in Jerusalem a meeting place for lovers of the *Tanakh* and this tradition was maintained by President Zalman Shazar, also an enthusiastic supporter of the Bet ha-Tanakh project, who hosted the regular Bible study circle at the Presidential residence.

On October 18, 1970, a ground-breaking ceremony took place on the intended site. Ben-Gurion then affirmed that the Jewish people, which had given the Bible to the world, must now create a center giving concrete expression to the Bible as the fountainhead of Judaism and, additionally, enhancing the prestige of Jerusalem and the honor of the Jewish people. "Such a House of the Bible, built by our own hands, will become a world center for Judaism and for all mankind, here in Jerusalem," he declared.

I deemed it a privilege to respond affirmatively when invited to serve as chairman of the World Council for Bet ha-Tanakh. In that capacity, I accompanied Dr. Gevaryahu and Mr. Luria on a visit to Ben-Gurion at his Tel Aviv home on June 26, 1973, in the hope of securing his permission for the proposed Bible Center to be called by his name. Though not in favor of this initially, he did eventually agree to the compromise formula, "Bet ha-Tanakh, Jerusalem, founded by David Ben-Gurion." He wrote a note to this effect which we later brought to Israel's Finance

Minister, Pinḥas Sapir, trusting that we would secure his help in the realization of the project.

Soon afterwards, Ben-Gurion died. At a *Shloshim* memorial assembly held at Bet ha-Nasi under the patronage of President Ephraim Katzir, on December 29, I made public reference to our visit with Israel's late Prime Minister, in order to place the salient facts concerning Bet ha-Tanakh on record.

On July 20, 1975, after Pinḥas Sapir had become chairman of the World Zionist Organization, Dr. Gevaryahu, Mr. Luria, and I again raised the matter in the course of a meeting at his office. When we showed Sapir a copy of Ben-Gurion's handwritten note, he was obviously impressed. Unfortunately, any favorable steps he may have contemplated were frustrated by his own sudden death in August of the same year.

Owing to the pressure of other responsibilities, I retired temporarily from an active role in this worthy endeavor, but have resumed my interest more recently. Professor Gevaryahu was fortunate enough to enlist additional devotees, notably Ḥaim Finkelstein, a former head of the Jewish Agency's Department for Education and Culture in the Diaspora, who has mobilized considerable support among his friends in the Jewish communities of Latin America and is now chairman of the world executive. S. J. (Shai) Kreutner, following his retirement as director-general of the Keren Hayesod, serves as the executive's vice-chairman. We are hopeful that some day soon this great undertaking will be crowned with the success it deserves.

Numerous projects in Israel now bear the name of Ben-Gurion, yet Bet ha-Tanakh still remains on the architects' drawing board. It will be a day of rejoicing for all of us when "Bet ha-Tanakh, Jerusalem, founded by David Ben-Gurion" will arise on its designated site.

The death of Louis Aryeh Pincus, on July 25, 1973, was a severe blow to the Zionist movement and the Jewish people. He died in his sleep at the King David Hotel in Jerusalem, while in the prime of life and at the height of his powers.

Louis Pincus was a man wholly dedicated to the service of Am Yisrael and Medinat Yisrael. In his native South Africa, where he practiced law, he had been a prominent Labor Zionist and had served as vice-chairman of the S.A. Zionist Federation until he made Aliyah in 1948. A year after his arrival in Israel, he became the first managing director of the newly established national airline, El Al, continuing in that capacity until 1956. After his election to the Jewish Agency Executive in 1961, Pincus served as its treasurer and finally attained the highest office in 1966, following the death of Moshe Sharett, when he became chairman of the Executives of the Jewish Agency and the World Zionist Organization. He also held key positions in the World Jewish Congress, the Claims Conference, and the campaign on behalf of Soviet Jewry, and as chairman of the board of governors of Tel Aviv University.

His ability to translate vision into practical reality was demonstrated throughout his chairmanship of the Jewish Agency and the WZO. The consolidation of Medinat Yisrael, the promotion of Aliyah, and the strengthening of Jewish life in the Diaspora were his three major objectives. Together with Max Fisher, Louis Pincus was primarily responsible for the establishment of the reconstituted Jewish Agency in 1971. It was as a result of his persistence and gifted leadership that Zionists and non-Zionists in all parts of the *Golah* came together and made the Jewish Agency a more powerful and more broadly representative instrument for advancing the welfare of Israel.

He was succeeded in office by Pinḥas Sapir, who had served effectively as Israel's Minister of Finance.

The Yom Kippur War and Its Aftermath

When Bert and I left for New York in August 1973 on our annual visit to our family and our congregation, there was no reason to suppose that grave and fateful events would affect Israel before our return in October. My schedule in the U.S. included, as usual, a number of private and official appointments. I took occasion to meet with Dr. David Hyatt, president of the National Conference of Christians and Jews, and leading members of his staff. The Israel Interfaith Committee figured in our discussion and I urged closer contact and cooperation with that important body.

I paid a courtesy call on Professor Gerson D. Cohen, who had been appointed to succeed Professor Louis Finkelstein as chancellor of the Jewish Theological Seminary. An alumnus of the JTSA, Dr. Cohen was a distinguished academician, having served as professor of Jewish history at Columbia University in succession to Professor Salo W. Baron. Toward the end of our stay in New York, we attended the Seminary convocation on October 21, when Gerson Cohen was formally inducted as the new chancellor. The chairman at this ceremony was Judge Stanley Fuld, presiding judge of the Court of Appeals of the State of New York, who had been one of my friends and congregants in days gone by.

Professor Louis Finkelstein's term as chancellor had been marked by consolidation and expansion. During his period of service, the Seminary had broadened its scope to include the Jewish Museum, for which the late Felix Warburg's family donated their home on upper Fifth Avenue. It also established a West Coast branch, the University of Judaism in Los Angeles. Professor Finkelstein had likewise been responsible for founding the Institute of Religious Studies, the Institute on Ethics, and the Conference on Science, Philosophy and Religion, and for introducing the *Eternal Light* programs on radio and television. At the same time, he maintained the Seminary's high standard as one of the world's foremost centers of Jewish scholarship. It was my own observation that during Chancellor Finkelstein's regime, JTSA had a much more Orthodox complexion than during Solomon Schechter's period, when Louis Finkelstein and I were fellow students.

On October 6, Yom Kippur, I performed my usual tasks at Congregation B'nai Jeshurun, conducting the services with Rabbi William Berkowitz and delivering my sermon, blissfully unaware that the Yom Kippur War had engulfed Israel's population. It was only at the outgoing of the fast that I learned of the concerted Egyptian-Syrian attack that would make this Day of Atonement the most awesome in the history of Medinat Yisrael.

Weeks of mounting tension and hostile declarations had prepared us for the outbreak of the Six-Day War in June 1967. This time, however, we were caught unawares. Egypt's President, Anwar Sadat, had laid his plans with great cunning, realizing what havoc could be wrought on the holiest day in the Jewish calendar before Israel would be in a position to gear itself for full-scale war. In New York, we were heartened by the initially optimistic reports from Israel's Chief of Staff, General David Elazar, suggesting that this would be another brief and successful campaign. Not until we returned to Israel three weeks later, just before the cease-fire, did we fully realize what a costly and precarious victory had been achieved.

The encouraging news bulletins we heard and the fact that my wife was with me made it easier to remain in the U.S. and keep my most pressing appointments in New York and Philadelphia.

On the day after Yom Kippur, we made a hurried visit to Philadelphia to attend a dinner in my honor given by the Hillel Society of the University of Pennsylvania, my alma mater. The address on Israel I was scheduled to deliver at a public meeting following the dinner had to be changed substantially, in view of the unforeseen and grave events back home. Dr. Martin Meyerson, president of the University, extended greetings on both occasions. I spent a few hours with my kin in Philadelphia, visited Gratz College (which had awarded me an honorary degree *in absentia* the previous June), and also called at the Balch Institute, established for the study of America's immigration groups, in order to advise them about Jewish material. The institute was still in temporary quarters, waiting to move to a magnificent new building near Independence Square, which was to be dedicated during the American bicentenary celebrations in 1976.

We returned to Israel on October 24, a day before the cease-fire agreement came into effect. A fuller picture of what had occurred during our absence abroad swiftly unfolded before us. The call-up of army reservists had begun prior to the sudden wailing of the sirens all over Israel at 2:00 P.M. on Yom Kippur afternoon, when the civilian population was brought face to face with the Egyptian and Syrian attack. At the Suez Canal, forward units of the Egyptian army had undermined the "impregnable" Bar-Lev Line with high-pressure water hoses before overwhelming the lightly defended Israeli outposts. On the Golan Heights, both military and civilian installations had to be abandoned as vastly superior Syrian forces pressed forward. With Egyptian troops pouring across the Suez Canal and Syrian tanks coming within sight of Israeli settlements on Lake Kinneret, it must have looked like the Six-Day War all over again, but in reverse.

Israel's reservists—many of them fetched straight from synagogue and still wearing their *tallitot*—helped to turn the tide. For the first time since the establishment of the State, Kol Yisrael began transmitting call-up messages in code and periodical news bulletins on the Day of Atonement. The entire nation was placed on a war footing. Teenagers substituted for teachers away at the front; housewives did duty as drivers or distributed food and drink to soldiers awaiting transport to their units; schoolchildren delivered mail and helped with other vital work. On October 14, the United States began airlifting essential supplies to Israel after Arab losses had been made good by massive Russian supplies. "Friendly" countries in Western Europe proved unwilling, however, to allow the American transport planes landing and refueling facilities at their airports. Only Portugal was ready to assist.

Ferocious tank battles in Sinai and on Ramat ha-Golan finally checked the enemy advance. Ten days after the outbreak of the war, Israeli forces commanded by General Ariel ("Arik") Sharon recrossed the Suez Canal and attacked the Egyptians from the rear. With the Egyptian Third Army completely encircled and Israeli troops only fifty miles from Cairo and half that distance from Damascus, the Russians hastily invited U.S. Secretary of State Henry Kissinger to join them in working out a cease-fire arrangement. A combined U.S.-Soviet resolution calling for direct peace negotiations between the conflicting parties was adopted by the United Nations on October 22, although hostilities on the southern front terminated only three days later.

Considering Israel's state of unpreparedness, the IDF's achievement in turning near-defeat into victory was an astonishing feat. The victory had been won, however, at a tragically high cost: 2,600 dead and thousands more wounded. In terms of casualties, duration, and economic after-effects, the Yom Kippur War proved far more damaging than any other conflict since 1949. Under the impact of these losses, public indignation was directed against the nation's political and defense establishment. A commission of inquiry, headed by Chief Justice Simon Agranat, later arrived at some critical conclusions.

Among the Yom Kippur War casualties were several that distressed us personally, since the bereaved parents were good friends of ours. Rabbi Moses Cyrus Weiler, an esteemed friend and colleague, lost his son, Gideon, the deputy commander of an Armored Corps regiment on the Golan Heights. It was the Weilers' second such bereavement. Gideon's elder brother, Adam, the company commander of a tank regiment, had fallen in battle on the Suez Canal front during the War of Attrition in March 1970. Both sons held the rank of Rav-Seren (major). Professor Haim Gevaryahu, chairman of the World Jewish Bible Society, lost his son, Reuven, a scholarly yeshivah graduate, who was an acting Seren (captain) in the Armored Corps. Another tragedy occurred subsequently in the family of our beloved younger friends, Eliezer and Drora Whartman, whose son, Moshe, lost his life in a retaliatory raid on a terrorist base in Lebanon. It had been my privilege to take part in the Whartmans' marriage ceremony in Israel and to have known Eliezer's parents in Philadelphia, where his father, Isidore, had been one of my *heder* mates.

These three stricken families have borne their grief with exemplary fortitude and have done noble things in memory of their sons.

At the end of October, following our return to Israel, I accompanied Shai Kreutner, director-general of the Keren Hayesod, on a tour of the reconquered Golan Heights in order to visit the Jewish settlements that had been devastated in the course of the fighting. It was a source of regret to me that I had not been in a position to help mobilize funds, as I had done in 1967, but it was good to know that my successor, Ezra Shapiro, and his co-workers had measured up to this new challenge and had set an all-time record for the Keren Hayesod's income.

On November 7, I chaired a War Bond subscription meeting at the home of Jacob

Alkow in Herzlia Pitu'aḥ, where Yitzḥak Rabin, Israel's former Chief of Staff and (until the previous March) ambassador to the U.S., was the main speaker.

Israel's population soon felt the economic effects of the Yom Kippur War. Owing to the mobilization of all available manpower, there was an immediate and drastic fall in productivity. Direct taxation increased sharply and War Bond purchases, both voluntary and compulsory, were introduced. In the longer term, Israel was beset by inflation and by an economic recession.

Side by side with these economic difficulties came the war's traumatic impact on the nation, giving rise to a widespread malaise. It is, I believe, a characteristic of the Jewish people that periods of exhilaration can be followed by periods of deep gloom. Thus, the feeling of elation we had all experienced after June 1967 gave way to introspective melancholy after the traumatic events of October 1973. This swing of the pendulum was unduly prolonged and it resulted in an alarming wave of departures for foreign destinations, where life seemed easier and more attractive. Substantial colonies of Israeli expatriates mushroomed in the United States, Canada, South Africa, and other parts of the world, often with adverse effects on the indigenous Jewish communities. Not a few became permanent Yordim, but others had had their fill of the *Galut* after a few years and decided to return home. Much attention has been devoted to the problem of Yeridah, which can never be eradicated so long as individuals remain free to determine their own futures. Various governmental inducements have succeeded in bringing a proportion of the emigrants back to Israel. It has taken some time for the trauma of the Yom Kippur War to wear off, and one would be loath to predict an early return to the spirit of optimism so prevalent a decade ago.

The death of David Ben-Gurion, on December 1, 1973, was a mournful reminder of the passing of an era, the era of the builders of Medinat Yisrael. Apart from a few exceptions, such as Golda Meir, a new generation of leaders was coming to the fore. Many of them were Sabras, native-born Israelis.

The funeral service for Ben-Gurion took place at Sdeh Boker, his chosen retreat in the Negev. It was my sad privilege to eulogize Ben-Gurion at the *Shloshim* ceremony held at the President's House and, subsequently, at a Haifa University board meeting. I also presided at memorial meetings arranged by the Zionist General Council and by the Association of Americans and Canadians in Israel.* On the first of these two occasions, eulogies were delivered by the Council's chairman, Itzḥak Navon, and by Dr. Nahum Goldmann and Dr. Emanuel Neumann. Brief extracts from Ben-Gurion's own addresses were read.

David Ben-Gurion was a great and complex personality. Not long after his death, I took occasion to ask Professor Ḥaim Gevaryahu, who knew him intimately, if he thought Ben-Gurion had been a religious man. Gevaryahu said that Israel's veteran leader certainly believed in a Higher Force. On one occasion, when they were walking together, "B-G" halted in his tracks as he was about to tread on an insect, which then made good its escape. "Who implanted the instinct in that small crea-

---

*For some personal impressions of Ben-Gurion, see chapter 17.

ture?" Ben-Gurion asked. His inference was clear. I myself recalled that he had once told me, "I may not go to synagogue, but I believe in God." Gevaryahu told me he had formed the impression that Ben-Gurion believed he was, in some mystical way, the reincarnation of Joshua bin Nun, the successor of Moses, who led the Israelites in the conquest of Canaan and settled them on the land.

During this time, I continued to serve on the presidium of the World Zionist Organization's Governing Council. I was also elected to the Directorion of the Keren Kayemet, thereby returning to my first love in presidential Zionist service, the Jewish National Fund, to which I had devoted ten good years of my life (1934–43). In addition, I continued to serve as deputy chairman of the Hebrew University's board of governors and as an honorary president of the Israel Interfaith Committee.

My first engagement in the new secular year, 1974, was a reception in Jerusalem tendered by the Israel Interfaith Committee in honor of a distinguished representative of the World Council of Churches in Geneva, the Reverend Dr. Lucas Fischer, director of the Council's Department of Faith and Order. A visit I much appreciated at this time was that of Professor Jacob Marcus, the director of the American Jewish Archives in Cincinnati. He was interested to hear about my own personal archives, and he made some useful suggestions.

A new and unusual experience awaited me at the end of January, when I was invited to preside at the memorial assembly for Professor Ikuro Teshima, founder of the Makuya ("Tabernacle") sect in Japan. Through his study of the Hebrew Bible, Professor Teshima had come to revere Judaism as the Mother Religion. In May 1948, when Israel was established, he founded Makuya as a tribute to the fulfillment of "Old Testament" prophecy. His followers, the Japanese "New Zionists," are enthusiastically devoted to Medinat Yisrael and regard themselves as "the Gentiles who shall come to thee from the ends of the earth" (Jeremiah 16:19).

On two occasions, Professor Teshima came to Israel with hundreds of his adherents and they marched through the streets of Jerusalem, carrying pro-Israel banners, before offering their tearful prayers at the Western Wall. At the height of the Yom Kippur War, when Professor Teshima was already in impaired health, he led a march of his 50,000 followers through the streets of Tokyo to protest against Japan's unfriendly attitude toward Israel. After his death, a collective leadership took over the direction of the Makuya sect, which has established flourishing centers in the main cities of Japan.

The memorial assembly for Professor Teshima was held under the combined auspices of the Israel Interfaith Committee, the Israel-Japan Friendship League, and the Department of Far East Studies at Tel Aviv University. Twenty-five young men of the Makuya, all wearing blue shirts emblazoned with a large white Magen David, opened the commemorative exercises by chanting the twenty-third Psalm in Hebrew. It was a moving experience and one that led me to form bonds of warm friendship with these devoted friends of Israel.

A JNF forest honoring the memory of Professor Teshima has been planted by the Makuya. Every year, a large Makuya group makes a pilgrimage to Israel. The participants sing Hebrew songs as they march through downtown Jerusalem on their way to the Western Wall. Their obvious devotion to Israel and their colorful attire always attract an enthusiastic response from Jerusalemites and the Israeli media. The annual Makuya pilgrimage concludes with a concert at the Jerusalem Theater, where Hebrew and Japanese songs are rendered with reverence and enthusiasm combined.

Makuya groups visiting Israel have found hospitality at Kibbutz Ḥeftzibah, where they have built one of their "tabernacles." Some learn Hebrew at the kibbutz *ulpan,* while others study the Bible and pursue related courses at the Hebrew University. Makuya publications include a Hebrew-Japanese dictionary. The movement's Israel branch is headed by Dr. Akira Jindo, whose wife is the daughter of the late Professor Teshima. They live in Jerusalem and have a Sabra son. Her brother, Ya'akov, has studied at the Jewish Theological Seminary in New York and has written a doctoral thesis on Ḥasidism.

Despite the vagaries of official policy, there is much grass-roots support for Israel in Japan. "Bet Shalom" centers in Tokyo and Kyoto, sponsored by the Reverend T. Otsuke's Christian Friends of Israel, welcome Jewish visitors and a number of other organizations foster ties with Israel and the Jewish people. Professor Avraham (Setsuzo) Kotsuji, the eminent Japanese Hebraist, who converted to Judaism at the age of sixty, died in October 1973 and his body was flown to Israel for burial in Jerusalem.

For the week of Passover in April 1974, Bert and I went to our favorite kibbutz, Gesher ha-Ziv, not far from Nahariyah. We had been present when it was established in 1949. The ideological leader of Gesher ha-Ziv, Moshe Kerem, directs the Oranim School for training kibbutz teachers, and another leading *ḥaver* is David Coren, a Labor member of the Knesset. Although this is not a religious settlement, the *Seder* conducted there is largely a traditional one and we particularly enjoyed the participation of the kibbutz children in the Passover ritual. A delightful *Bikkurim* (First Fruits) ceremony takes place there on Shavu'ot.

Shortly after Passover, Prime Minister Golda Meir tendered her resignation to President Katzir. Although the Agranat Commission had found no fault with her leadership during the Yom Kippur War, the events of the previous October—and their aftermath—had apparently given her no rest. She was succeeded as Prime Minister by the former Chief of Staff, Yitzḥak Rabin.

As a mother figure and woman of valor, Golda Meir had captured the hearts and minds of her people, in Israel and throughout the Jewish world.

On May 8, I flew with Bert to the United States in order to address a conference of the American JNF, together with Ya'akov Tsur, world chairman of the Jewish National Fund. It was a welcome opportunity to renew a bond dating back forty years to my election as president of the JNF in America, my first major Zionist post. All of us were still in a state of shock following the heinous massacre by Arab terrorist infiltrators of Israeli children and adults at Ma'alot, a sequel to the murderous attack at Kiryat Shemonah a few weeks earlier.

In the course of my conference address at the Waldorf-Astoria Hotel in New York on May 19, I said:

It would only serve the enemy's purpose if we were to permit such tragedies to deflect us from our sacred task of building Israel and of being upbuilded by it. So we go on with the redoubled dedication to defend Israel at every cost, remembering the historic law of our existence, "By thy blood shalt thou live!" One day there will be *Shalom* and an end to the bloodbaths.

Referring to the Yom Kippur War, I observed that the response of World Jewry had been even greater in 1973 than seven years earlier, during the 1967 emergency, because this time the danger had been more menacing. Soon after the fighting was over, it was gratifying to see that the regional office of the JNF, with its telephone connections throughout the Golan Heights, had played an important part as a central communications facility maintaining contact with our forces there. "The roads built by the JNF served well in the first awful hours of the Syrian attack," I went on, "as these roads expedited the mobility of our heavy equipment." Unconditional dedication to Medinat Yisrael must therefore be the watchword of the JNF and all who work for it.

We attended Sabbath services at Congregation B'nai Jeshurun, where Rabbi William Berkowitz and President Charles H. Silver welcomed us at a special *Kiddush* reception. I also attended the sixtieth anniversary reunion of my class of 1914 at the University of Pennsylvania in Philadelphia, and took the opportunity of visiting my brother and sister there, together with their families.

I take considerable pride in my Philadelphia kin. My brother, Isaac, and his wife, Fannie, as well as my sister, Sarah, and her husband, Herman Lazarus, are respected members of the community. Isaac, a realtor, and Fannie, a lawyer, are both artists and art collectors. Sarah, a teacher by profession, has headed the women's committee for Dropsie College; her husband, a prominent lawyer, is involved in community affairs, Israel Bonds, and local philanthropies.

As always, Bert and I most looked forward to visiting our children and grandchildren in the course of our annual vacation in the United States. Our daughter and son-in-law were then resident in Austin, Texas, where he was head of the Department of Natural Sciences at the University of Texas and she taught in the Department of Psychology. We were pleasantly surprised to find not only a chair in Hebrew at the university, but a chair in Yiddish as well. One of the places we visited was the Lyndon B. Johnson Museum, which houses the late President's archives. We were delighted to meet James Michener, the famous author, whose historical novel, *The Source*, has its setting in Eretz Yisrael.

From Austin we proceeded to Stanford, California, where we visited our son, Avram, and his family. Both he and his wife, Dora, are professors of pharmacology at Stanford University. We were interested to make a tour of the Drug Addiction Research Institute, which Avram had established and was directing. It was good to see our grandchildren now grown up and involved in movements to improve the social and political climate of their community. In San Francisco, we visited my brother, Rabbi Morris Goldstein, and his wife, Adeline. Having retired from the active rabbinate, Morris was now serving as a chaplain on the Orient Steamship Line.

On our return to New York in July, we were distressed to hear of the tragedy that had befallen our dear friends in Jerusalem, Israel and Margaret Soifer. Their daughter and son-in-law, Rivkah and Michael Ben-Yitzhak, had been among the victims of an Arab terrorist bomb outrage that devasted part of Zion Square in Jerusalem's central shopping area. Michael, whose original surname had been Isaacs, was a highly cultured young man who had graduated from the University of Oxford before coming to Israel. A fitting memorial to Rivkah and Michael Ben-Yitzhak is a biennial award to the Israeli artist who produces the best illustrations for a children's book published in Israel during the previous two years. The Soifers have given an inspiring example of how grief can be borne with dignity and of how deep personal sorrow can become a source of beneficence.

Fortunately, there was a happier, more cheerful side to life in Jerusalem throughout this period. We were delighted to acquire splendid neighbors in Hyam and Doris Morrison of London, who built their beautiful Jerusalem home next to ours. I had come to know the Morrisons during my term as chairman of the Keren Hayesod, when Hymie served with great devotion as chairman of the Joint Israel Appeal in Great Britain. He led the *magbit* there at the time of the Six-Day War in 1967, when Doris worked energetically at his side. It was a joyous day for me when I was invited to affix the mezuzah on the front doorpost of their new home on Pinsker Street.

Among our other neighbors are the families of Professor Saul Friedlander, Yisrael Zekharyah, and M. Benzion Meiri, Comptroller of the Jewish Agency.

An event of personal significance at about this time was the appearance of *A Lebn fun Shlikhus* ("A Life of Mission"), a Yiddish biography of me written by Aharon Alperin of New York. The author, a leading Yiddish publicist and former editor of the New York *Jewish Morning Journal*, had already published biographies of Baron Edmond de Rothschild, Isaac Naiditsch, and Rabbi Stephen Wise. He had been a friend and colleague of mine during my years of activity on the American scene. That this account of my life and career appeared in Yiddish was especially meaningful to me, since Yiddish was the language in which my beloved parents had raised me. Yiddish was also the language in which I had woven bonds of service to Israel and the Jewish people among numerous *kehillot* during the years of my service in the Jewish National Fund, World Jewish Congress, World Zionist Organization, and Keren Hayesod. Subsequently, in Israel, Aharon Alperin's book was translated into Hebrew and updated by Shmuel Sheharyah, a noted local journalist. As *Ḥayyim shel Shelihut*, this enlarged Hebrew edition of the biography was published in Jerusalem by Rubin Mass in 1977.

An approaching family *simḥah*, to which Bert and I looked forward with keen anticipation, was the Bar Mitzvah of our grandson, Kenneth Akiba Olum. He himself had expressed the desire that it should be celebrated in Jerusalem. On the appointed date, *Shabbat Parashat Balak* (Tammuz 16, 5734/July 6, 1974), the Bar Mitzvah ceremony was held in our new Conservative synagogue in Jerusalem. Rabbi Joshua Stampfer and Cantor Danny Ziff officiated. Just prior to that Shabbat, I went with my grandson to the office of the Jewish National Fund in order to inscribe him in the Keren Kayemet's Bar Mitzvah Book and to plant thirteen trees in his name.

In addition to his parents (our daughter, Vivian, and her husband, Professor Paul Olum) and his older sister, Joyce, we were joined by my sister, Sarah, and her husband, Herman Lazarus, from Philadelphia; Bert's sister, Grace Volpert, and her granddaughter, Adrienne, who was then staying at a kibbutz; our cousin, Enid Silver Winslow, who was on an archaeological dig at Meron; and our Jerusalem cousin, Batya Abbady, who had made Aliyah before us. Many of our friends were present in synagogue, but unfortunately Kenneth's oldest sister, Judith, was not well enough to come.

Our friend and colleague of many years, Professor Simon Greenberg, recited *Shaḥarit* and Cantor Danny Ziff conducted the main portion of the Shabbat services. Dr. Pesaḥ Schindler, director of the Center for Conservative Judaism, also took part and Professor Gerson D. Cohen, the newly elected chancellor of the Jewish Theological Seminary in New York, honored us by delivering a *Devar Torah*. Bert, the proud grandmother, read a Psalm.

The Bar Mitzvah acquitted himself most creditably, and we were all proud of him. It was, needless to say, a moving experience for me to address my own grandson from the pulpit, in both Hebrew and English. "To become Bar Mitzvah in Jerusalem is a special privilege," I told him. "What gives additional meaning to it in your case is that it was your own idea. It so happens that tomorrow, the seventeenth day of Tammuz, is a sad reminder of the destruction of the Temple and of Jerusalem, which brought about our exile. So it is an appropriate time to be made especially mindful of how greatly privileged our generation is to witness Jewry restored and Jerusalem rebuilt, and to feel that it is worth every sacrifice to keep our Jewish Commonwealth alive and flourishing."

The *Kiddush* we gave in the courtyard of the synagogue was followed by a luncheon in our home for the members of our family and a few special friends, including Shirah Nahari, Mr. and Mrs. Ezra Shapiro, Mr. and Mrs. Kalman Sultanik, and Mr. and Mrs. Ze'ev Schickler.

On September 2, I had much pleasure in attending a reception for Professor Alexander Dushkin on the occasion of his eighty-fifth birthday. The reception was held at the International Youth Center in Jerusalem, and Moshe Kol presided. A star pupil of Dr. Samson Benderly, Professor Dushkin had played a central role in the development of Jewish education in the United States, both in Chicago and in New York. He had also been associated with me in the founding of Brandeis University. During the British Mandatory period and immediately after the establishment of the Medinah, he had made an important contribution to the molding of Israel's educational system, particularly at the David Yellin Teachers' Institute in Jerusalem and at the Hebrew University. We were saddened by his death, two years later, in June 1976.

Shortly after the Bar Mitzvah of our grandson, I entered the Hadassah Hospital for minor surgery. It was so close to the High Holy Days that I was unable to leave for New York to be with my congregation. My enforced absence thus broke the hitherto uninterrupted tradition of our High Holy Day visits to B'nai Jeshurun. Since 1974, I have visited the congregation only on special occasions. Rabbi Berkowitz was kind enough to arrange special Sabbath programs to mark significant dates, such as my eightieth birthday and my sixtieth anniversary in the rabbinate, and the congregation's one hundred fiftieth anniversary.

Bert and I have ample compensation, however, in spending the High Holy Day season in Jerusalem. More than once I have had occasion to remark that I would rather be a layman in Jerusalem than a rabbi in New York. In retrospect, I nevertheless found satisfaction in the knowledge that my annual visits not only revitalized the personal bond between the congregation and me but also helped retain within its fold many families which had moved away from the neighborhood. These visits also proved helpful in securing financial support for the congregation's educational program, and they were an important factor in strengthening and refreshing the congregation's bond with Medinat Yisrael.

At about this time, Bert and I decided to bequeath our Jerusalem home and its contents, including the library and art collection, as a "living legacy" to the Hebrew University of Jerusalem. This decision betokened the gratitude we felt for our many blessings, for the privilege of living and working in and for Israel, and for our special ties with the Hebrew University. Most helpful to us in seeing to the legal arrangements were my lawyer, Abraham Angel, and Zvi Schwartz, who served on the university's board of governors.

A mournful event in the last quarter of 1974 was the death of Zalman Shazar, Israel's third President, on October 5. He was accorded a state funeral in Jerusalem. Shazar had the temperament of a Ḥasid, the intellect of a philosopher, and a reformer's passion for social justice. His Presidency added a significant link to the traditions established by Weizmann and Ben-Zvi.

Earlier, on November 2, the centenary of Chaim Weizmann's birth had been observed at the Weizmann Institute in Reḥovot. On the following night, in Jerusalem, a reception was held at the Knesset in honor of Israel's new President, Professor Ephraim Katzir. Golda Meir was one of the principal speakers. In paying tribute to Professor Katzir, she made an interesting and jovial observation. "If we bear in mind that Dr. Weizmann was also a distinguished scientist in the same field, which has given Israel two of its four Presidents, then it would appear that a biochemist has a fifty percent chance of becoming the President of Israel!"

The Youth Village bearing my name in Jerusalem's Katamon neighborhood continued to receive my guidance and help. The twenty-fifth anniversary of its founding was marked by a dinner on February 18, 1975. Addresses were delivered by Yosef Klarman, chairman of the Jewish Agency's Youth Aliyah Department, and by Moshe Kol, Ze'ev Schickler, and myself. Mayor Teddy Kollek was present and U.S. Ambassador Kenneth Keating and his wife came specially from Tel Aviv for the occasion.

On June 16, 1974, a distinguished delegation of friends from Italy, led by Professor Giorgio La Pira, a former Mayor of Florence, attended the dedication of the Einaudi Culture House at the Youth Village. It was named in honor of President Luigi Einaudi, Italy's second head of state after World War II, who had served as honorary president of Youth Aliyah in Italy. When he died, his widow assumed that office. Their son, Dr. Roberto Einaudi, was present at the dedication ceremony, together with Countess Marina Volpi, chairman of the Friends of Youth Aliyah in Italy, Judge Sergio Piperno Beer, chairman of the Union of Italian Jewish Communities, and other notables. Mrs. Esther Ghitis of Milan, whose husband, Jacob, headed the Keren Hayesod *magbit* in Italy, was the moving spirit in the Einaudi House project.

The most beautiful room in the Einaudi House was dedicated, on February 15, 1981, in memory of Raffaele Cantoni, a former president of the Union of Italian Jewish Communities and of the Milan *kehillah*, who was also active in the World Jewish Congress, the Italian Zionist Federation, and the Keren Hayesod. His widow supervised the furnishing of the room and took part in the dedication ceremony.

Another significant date in the first quarter of 1975 was the twenty-fifth *Yahrzeit* of Daniel Frisch, a former president of the Zionist Organization of America. On March 2, a memorial meeting took place at ZOA House in Tel Aviv, and I delivered an address there at the invitation of Daniel's son, Larry Frisch, a U.S. television reporter who lives in Israel. My subject was "American Zionism and Its Place in Israel." An ardent General Zionist and an exponent of private enterprise, Daniel Frisch succeeded in winning the respect of the dominant Labor Zionist element in Israel and the Jewish Agency. Enlarging on his tragically short, but effective presidency of the ZOA, I said:

> Daniel Frisch proceeded to launch a program which his predecessors had not had the imagination or the daring or the know-how to do—a ZOA House in Tel Aviv, to serve as a living link between American Zionists and Israel. He persuaded the Jewish Agency and the World Confederation of General Zionists to provide the basic portion of the funds. I wrote him on November 10, 1949, as President of the World Confederation of General Zionists, pledging our support.
>
> He came here to pick the site and displayed vision in choosing a location which has become the very heart of the city. He worked at top speed, as if he felt intuitively that he did not have much time left. When he died, after a brief nine months in office, he left this House as his enduring legacy to the Zionist Organization of America and to Israel.

In another sense, however, Larry Frisch and his children were the true living memorial to their father and grandfather in Israel. For in one important respect— Aliyah—the leaders of American Zionism had not set a proper Zionist example. As on many previous occasions, I stressed that "holding the fort" in the United States was no substitute for the *mitzvah* of living in Eretz Yisrael.

While vacationing at Kibbutz Gesher ha-Ziv in August, we were visited by Father Elias Chacour, a Christian Arab priest, who took us to the village of Ibillin in western Galilee, where he had his parish. During the Talmudic period, the important Jewish settlement of Avelim had flourished on that spot and the remains of an ancient synagogue can be still seen there. Some two-thirds of the present-day villagers were Christians. In nearby Shefaram, a larger Arab village, where the population included Muslims and Druzes, the Christians were a minority, albeit a substantial one. Father Chacour introduced us to one of the leading Christian Arab families in Shefaram, whose members complained of discriminatory treatment by the Muslims and of not being accorded their fair share of community benefits.

That same month, we attended a reception in Jerusalem for Ḥanokh and Minna Givton, a couple we numbered among our younger friends. They were about to leave for the United States, where he had been appointed Israel's consul in Los Angeles. A brilliant public servant, Ḥanokh Givton had served until recently as director of Israel's Broadcasting Authority. His sudden death on the West Coast in February 1976 came as a great shock to us. Since returning to Jerusalem, Minna Givton, who grew up in England, has taken an active part in cultural and civic affairs.

The nation was particularly affected by the loss of Pinḥas Sapir, chairman of the World Zionist Organization and of the Jewish Agency Executive. He died holding a *Sefer Torah* in his arms while participating in the dedication of a synagogue at Moshav Nevatim, near Beersheba, on August 11. Sapir had rendered immense services to Israel in a dozen spheres and capacities, ranging from civil defense and Negev water supplies to his last governmental post as Minister of Finance. It was hard to believe that this "strong man" of Mapai, tough, vigorous, resourceful, and only in his late sixties, had departed from our midst. Interestingly enough, Sapir could have become Israel's Prime Minister, but declined the offer, preferring to devote his energies to the World Zionist Organization.

Arye L. Dultzin, treasurer of the Jewish Agency, served as acting chairman of the WZO until Yosef Almogi was elected to succeed Sapir early in the following year.

Not long afterwards, in October, I headed a delegation of the Brit Ivrit Olamit that called on President Ephraim Katzir at Bet ha-Nasi to present him with a set of Hebrew publications on Jewish thought in the Diaspora. Professor Aryeh Tartakower, Simḥah Raz, and Ḥaim Zohar accompanied me. Simḥah Raz had gained prominence as the author of *Ish Tzaddik Hayah* ("A Tzaddik in Our Time"), a biography of Rabbi Aryeh Levin, the saintly chaplain to Jewish political prisoners detained by the British during the last years of the Mandate. "Reb Aryeh," a humble, truly pious man who refused all honors, was probably Israel's most beloved figure at the time of his death in 1969.

An invitation I especially appreciated was that extended to me by President Marver H. Bernstein of Brandeis University, and by Ernest Stock, director of the university's Jacob Hiatt Institute, to open their new lecture series in Jerusalem. "Zionist Vision and Israeli Reality" was the subject of my address at the institute on September 17.

I emphasized five major areas where self-criticism was needed in order to build a society worthy of the Zionist vision that Israel's leaders must keep alive. First, much more stress had to be placed on the teaching of civic values and the sense of Jewish peoplehood as the moral basis for our statehood. Second, ethical standards in commerce, industry, and the public sector needed to be improved. Abuses of trust and authority, which besmirched Israel's good name, must be condemned and eradicated. Third, the level of efficiency in both Government and industry had to be raised, and Israel's oversubsidized economy must be seen as a hindrance to progress. East European or Levantine standards were simply not good enough for Israel. While appreciating Ben-Gurion's concern to avoid a *Kulturkampf*, I also expressed my view that the time had come for a modification of the Synagogue-State relationship to allow room for non-Orthodox trends. Finally, I urged that Israel's electoral system, based on party lists, should undergo a reform. Jews immigrating from "Anglo-Saxon" communities of the Diaspora appreciated the value of a constituency system where parliamentary representatives were answerable to their electors and where they accordingly had no choice but to help remedy deficiencies in the public sphere.

I took occasion, however, to stress the unchallenged role of the Jewish State in strengthening the sense of Jewish identity, and hence Jewish survival, throughout the world.

One People—Indivisible

By November 1975, the worldwide chorus of vituperation against Israel, orchestrated by the Arab states and the Soviet bloc, was assuming unprecedented dimensions. It reached a climax that month, when seventy-two member states of the UN voted in favor of a resolution declaring Zionism to be "a form of racism or racial discrimination." In a dramatic gesture of defiance and contempt, Israel's ambassador to the United Nations, Chaim Herzog, concluded his protest speech by tearing up a copy of the resolution before the UN General Assembly. Anti-Semitism, thinly disguised as anti-Zionism, had acquired a spurious respectability—thirty years after the death of Hitler and the boasted defeat of Nazism.

Jews organized mass meetings and protest rallies throughout the world. Even beyond the Iron Curtain they could not be silenced. In Jerusalem, Mayor Teddy Kollek and Ezra Shapiro solemnly removed the "Reḥov ha-Um" ("United Nations") street sign in the city's Kiryat ha-Yovel neighborhood and replaced it with one inscribed "Reḥov ha-Tzionut." The moral authority of the UN had vanished and, for the Jews of Israel, Zionism had become a badge of honor.

I recalled an observation made by Professor Hans Morgenthau, the eminent political scientist and U.S. Government consultant, when the Reuben Hecht Chair in Zionism was dedicated at Haifa University. "Nationalism in our time has proved a failure," said Professor Morgenthau, "but Jewish nationalism is different. It must prove itself through Israel."

A visit to New York in December, at the invitation of the United Jewish Appeal, provided me with firsthand evidence of the infamous UN resolution's effect on Diaspora Jewry. It had galvanized them into new and extraordinary demonstrations of solidarity with Medinat Yisrael. I attended a weekend conference of the UJA and addressed delegates at the fiftieth jubilee session of the United Israel Appeal, during luncheon at the Hilton Hotel, on December 12. Among those present I was glad to see my colleagues and contemporaries, Rose Halprin and Emanuel Neumann, and the treasurer of the Jewish Agency, Arye L. Dultzin. I also attended the Saturday night session of the conference, at which Shim'on Peres was the main speaker.

Vehemently pro-Israel declarations were made by the "non-Zionist" leaders of the United Jewish Appeal. Frank Lautenberg, one of their representatives, who as chairman of the UJA presided at the conference, had no hesitation in proclaiming, "We are all Zionists!" Clearly, much had changed since my days in the leadership of the United Jewish Appeal some two decades earlier. Support for Israel had become a vital credential, the badge of honor worn by Jews everywhere.

There was a heartwarming response to my conference speech, the theme of which was "Medinat Yisrael and Diaspora Jewry—One People Indivisible." Melvin Dubinsky, who presided at this United Israel Appeal jubilee session, introduced me. I had first come to know him as a rising young Zionist *Askan* in St. Louis, a disciple of Professor Gustave Klausner, in the days when I was president of the American JNF. After surveying the role of the Keren Hayesod and of the American Zionist movement in building the Medinah, I declared:

> Israel has not failed you or your children, and it will not fail your grandchildren. To a generation jaded by disillusionments Israel represents something new under the sun, the ever regenerated idealism of the kibbutz, now in its third generation, the redemption of the soil and of the soul, and the unique moral quality and morale of Israel's Defense Forces.

Greater awareness had been shown for Jewish education as a communal responsibility, I said, but the American Jewish leadership should also give more priority to the Hebrew language, to the Israel motif, and to Aliyah as factors in training the young. "One thousand Jewish leaders today can determine the quality of the American Jewish community of five million Jews a generation hence. This is an awesome responsibility." In conclusion, I observed:

> Thus, the Zionist ideal—as ancient as Father Abraham and as futuristic as the Messianism of the Hebrew Prophets, as programmatic as Herzl's *Judenstaat* and as desperate as Jewish homelessness, as local as Eretz Yisrael and as universal as humanity's need for salvation—this Zionist ideal has given birth to the World Zionist Organization and to Zionist organizations everywhere, to the Keren Hayesod, to the United Israel Appeal and its affiliates, and it has come to its climax in Medinat Yisrael.
>
> Our foes may rage, may malign and traduce our vision. The petrocrats may intimidate the councils of the nations, but we Jews everywhere shall wear the badge of Zionism as our proud birthmark, one people indivisible and, as long as indivisible, indestructible, with its battlecry—*Eḥad*, "One!"

Shortly after my return to Israel, the Jewish National-Hebrew University Library held an exhibit of items related to Mordecai Manuel Noah, to mark the one hundred fiftieth anniversary of his "Ararat" project. The exhibit was arranged by Professor Reuven Yaron and I was pleased to make available a large number of Mordecai Noah items in my possession. These I had begun to collect during the early years of my rabbinate at Congregation B'nai Jeshurun, since it was Noah who delivered the oration on the first anniversary of the consecration of B'nai Jeshurun's Elm Street Synagogue, in 1828.

On January 4, 1976, at the opening session of the Zionist General Council, I presided at a symposium closely related to the previous November's anti-Zionist vote at the UN. Professor Moshe Ma'oz spoke on "The Nature of the Arab Attack on Zionism," Dr. Zvi Katz on "The Communist Attack on Zionism," and Professor Nathan Rotenstreich discussed "Zionism Today." Charlotte Jacobson opened the ensuing general debate.

A notable development was the election of Yosef Almogi, the Mayor of Haifa, as the new chairman of the World Zionist Organization and Jewish Agency Executives. He succeeded Pinḥas Sapir, who had died in office several months previously.

It was at this session of the Actions Committee that the World Union for Progressive Judaism, representing Reform congregations in the U.S. and a number of other countries, became affiliated with the World Zionist Organization. This was an event of historic importance both for the Reform movement, once a citadel of anti-Zionism, and for the WZO. Much of the credit for this development was due to Rabbi Richard Hirsch, director of the WUPJ, and to Professor Ezra Spicehandler, director of the Hebrew Union College–Jewish Institute of Religion, both of whom conducted their organizational activities from Jerusalem. The World Council of Synagogues, representing Conservative congregations in many lands, followed suit not long afterwards. To my mind, this sequence was rather ironical, since Conservative Judaism had been firmly committed to Zionism from its inception. The order of affiliation should therefore have been reversed. Nevertheless, the fact that the Conservative and Reform movements would now have a voice in the World Zionist Organization gave me immense satisfaction.

Soon after the beginning of the year, we mourned the loss of Rabbi Solomon David Goldfarb, a leading member of our Conservative synagogue in Jerusalem. A gifted preacher and an excellent Hebraist, he was a devoted colleague and friend. Shortly thereafter, I was especially saddened by the death of Judge Louis Edward Levinthal, another stalwart of our congregation. He and I had been boyhood friends and college classmates in Philadelphia, and in the early 1940s he had been my immediate predecessor in the presidency of the Zionist Organization of America.

On Lag ba-Omer, May 18, 1976, I was asked to deliver the eulogy at his graveside in Sanhedriah, Jerusalem. My thoughts naturally went back to his distinguished father, Rabbi Bernard L. Levinthal, dean of the Orthodox rabbinate in America and a founder of the American Mizraḥi, and to his still vigorous older brother, Rabbi Israel H. Levinthal, who had served as professor of homiletics at the Jewish Theological Seminary and as president of the Rabbinical Assembly.

During his manifold career, as eminent jurist, president of the Jewish Publication Society of America, president of the ZOA, Jewish adviser to the U.S. military government in postwar Germany, and, more recently, as chairman of the board of governors of the Hebrew University, Louis Levinthal had risen to the highest rungs of Jewish and Zionist service. "He was," I said, "influential in converting ignorance into knowledge, lawlessness into law, hopelessness into hope, civic indifference into civic concern, and Jewish homelessness into the Jewish National Home."

Happily, for most of 1976, there were gladdening occasions. In March, while visiting Beersheba, I toured the University of the Negev and met with its president, Yosef Tekoa. Our conversation took me back over a dozen years to 1963, when he had been Israel's ambassador in Moscow at the time of the journey Bert and I made through Eastern Europe. More recently, Yosef Tekoa had served with vigor and effectiveness as Israel's ambassador to the United Nations.

It was, however, the annual convention of the Association of Americans and Canadians in Israel that required my presence in Beersheba on March 23–24, when I presented Henrietta Szold awards to the chosen recipients. A fortnight earlier, I had presided at a special AACI reception in Jerusalem at the President's House to mark the bicentennial of the United States, which happened to coincide with the twenty-fifth anniversary of the AACI. Speaking in the presence of Israel's President, Professor Ephraim Katzir, I said:

> We have before us constantly the challenge that, while Aliyah from some countries is impelled by the push of untoward and even intolerable conditions there, Aliyah from the U.S. and Canada must be impelled primarily by the magnetic pull of Israel. Therefore, it imposes special responsibilities.

With the approach of my eightieth birthday in June, I began to receive gratifying signals from various directions. One day soon after the AACI convention, Rabbi Louis I. Rabinowitz came to see me in his official capacity as Deputy Mayor of Jerusalem. He was accompanied by the secretary of the Jerusalem municipality. A dear and highly esteemed friend, Rabbi Rabinowitz brought me the news that I had been chosen as one of those to be honored with the title of *Yakir Yerushalayim*— Honored Citizen of Jerusalem. In the light of my entire career, and of our sixteen years as active residents in Israel's capital, this honor was particularly meaningful to me. The award ceremony was scheduled to take place on May 26.

Shortly after I received notification of the award, President Martin Meyerson of the University of Pennsylvania, my alma mater, telephoned from Philadelphia and informed me that I had been designated for an honorary degree. He also invited me to deliver the baccalaureate address to the graduating class. It transpired that the degree would be conferred on May 28.

I was able to secure a dispensation from Mayor Teddy Kollek when I mentioned this conflict of dates to him and when I pointed out that the subject of my baccalaureate address would be "A Tale of Two Cities," referring, of course, to Jerusalem and Philadelphia. The bicentennial being observed in the United States would naturally have its focus in Philadelphia. Mayor Kollek agreed that Bert should stand in for me at the Jerusalem exercises, and accept my citation.

Professor Norman Oler graciously hosted me at the University of Pennsylvania baccalaureate in Philadelphia on May 27. President Meyerson introduced Chaplain Stanley Johnson, who presided, and one of the students read a Psalm. Then came my address. "In my childhood," I said, "I lived almost within sight—albeit not within sound—of the Liberty Bell. Now I live in Israel, within sight of a replica of the Liberty Bell which adorns the Liberty Garden in Jerusalem, dedicated to the United States Bicentenary. It is inspiring to behold this memento of the founding of the American nation, in the capital of that old-new land where the biblical injunction of Leviticus (25:10) once resounded: 'Proclaim liberty throughout the land unto all the inhabitants thereof.'"

I traced the spiritual kinship between ancient Israel and the infant United States, between the Torah and the Bill of Rights, the American and the Israeli Declarations of Independence. The Pilgrim Fathers and the New England pioneers had derived inspiration from the biblical Exodus, the concept of Zion, and often also from the Hebrew tongue. This sense of identification with the Old Testament people had motivated Benjamin Franklin, John Adams, and Thomas Jefferson during the American Revolutionary struggle, even as it had guided some of President Harry Truman's decisions in our own time. Thus, William Lecky's oft-quoted remark that "Hebraic mortar cemented the foundations of the [American] Republic" had lost none of its authenticity with the passage of the years.

Faithful to this scriptural tradition, I said, the United States had extended its support to the establishment of the Third Jewish Commonwealth in Palestine and to the moral and material advancement of the State of Israel. "Today, it is an ongoing act of historic justice that America continues to stand by Israel's side when a differently constituted United Nations Organization, majorized, alas, by forces of reaction, seeks by sheer numbers to abjure its firstborn child and to dishonor a decision which gave moral stature to this international body soon after its appearance on the world scene."

Moving on to America's present, especially with reference to matters affecting college youth, I dwelt on the ideal of ethical nationhood underpinning both democracies—the U.S. and Israel—while pointing up some of the defalcations from that ideal during the years of my career in public service. The civilized world's struggle against Nazism, the McCarthyite threat to liberal opinion, the demand of Black Americans for full civic rights, and the folly of the war in Vietnam—these were some of the issues to which I alluded. As the United States entered its third century, I urged, American youth, and most especially collegiate youth, must rededicate itself to the Judeo-Christian ethic and seek an exercise in self-renewal. The challenging vision and idealism of the Prophets still call for a practical response.

In conclusion, I said:

A world which, thanks to the progress of Science, is, in terms of communication and accessibility, incomparably smaller than was the world of 1776, calls for a Declaration of Interdependence among the nations, interdependence in creating and in sharing the material blessings, such as the fructification of the earth, the conquest of disease, advances in the comforts of life, and interdependence in the sharing of the spiritual blessings, the fruit of the human mind and of the human spirit. And it calls for interdependence in the banishment of war, lest our sophisticated instruments of destruction annihilate the entire human race, victor and vanquished alike. "Cooperate or perish!" is the fateful behest to us and to our children.

My address was warmly received and, as I left the assembly hall, a group of Black students came over to express their heartfelt thanks.

The commencement exercises on the following day took place in the university's Convention Center. Chief Justice Warren Burger, one of the recipients of an honorary degree, delivered the commencement address. The fact that 1976 was America's bicentennial year lent a special, added significance to these two hundred twentieth commencement exercises at the University of Pennsylvania.

I was particularly gratified that the citation accompanying my honorary Doctor of Laws degree referred, among other things, to my Zionist career.

Although I was, of course, sorry that Bert could not be with me on such an occasion, it meant much to me that other members of our family were present—my brother and sister-in-law, Isaac and Fannie Goldstein, my sister and brother-in-law, Sarah and Herman Lazarus, my sister-in-law, Grace Volpert, who came in from Lake Placid, and my granddaughter, Joyce Olum, who made the journey from Massachusetts. Our son and daughter-in-law, Avram and Dora, and our daughter and son-in-law, Vivian and Paul Olum, were in touch with me by telephone from the West Coast. Among those whose presence at the degree ceremony delighted me were President Abraham Katsh and Professor Solomon Zeitlin of Dropsie University, Professor Ḥaim Gevaryahu of Jerusalem, and Robert M. Bernstein of Philadelphia, my high-school friend and classmate, now a prominent lawyer and Zionist leader.

I returned to Israel soon afterwards, in time to celebrate the Festival of Shavu'ot.

In thanksgiving for having reached our eightieth birthday, Bert and I presented a *Sefer Torah* to our synagogue and dedicated it in memory of our parents. It meant much to us that several close friends took part in the Torah scroll procession, notably Professor Simon Greenberg, Professor Abraham S. Halkin, Rabbi Theodore Friedman, Professor Abraham Karp, Professor Sol Liptzin, Professor Gershon Weiner, and Ezra Z. Shapiro. Bert led in the responsive reading of Psalm 145.

My presentation address was based on apposite citations from the writings of my revered teacher of blessed memory, Professor Solomon Schechter, and those of my father's teacher, Rabbi Yitzḥak Ya'akov Reines, of blessed memory, founder of the Mizraḥi movement. I also quoted another religious Zionist preacher, Rabbi Yitzḥak Nissenbaum, who perished in the Warsaw Ghetto.

During the next several weeks, my anniversary and my ongoing public involvements were commingled in a succession of meaningful events. On Thursday, June 17, the eve of my eightieth birthday, Ze'ev and Hadassah Schickler, together with Lonia Liebergall and Moshe Kurtz of our Youth Village, came in to extend their congratulations. They invited Bert and me to walk with them to the Rose Garden, only a few steps from our home. There a delightful surprise awaited me—hundreds of children from the Youth Village assembled to greet us with a "Happy Birthday" song. They were accompanied by Yoḥanan Boehm, the noted music critic, conducting his boys' band.

On the following Monday, a three-day symposium on Jewish-Christian relations in Israel, held under the auspices of the Israel Interfaith Committee, began at the Van Leer Institute in Jerusalem. This gathering brought back fond memories, since it marked the thirtieth anniversary of the International Conference of Christians and Jews, established at the conference in Oxford I had attended in 1946. Jewish and Christian leaders from Israel and overseas participated in this symposium. Among them I was glad to see the Reverend William W. Simpson of London, a co-founder of the International Conference and its executive secretary for many years, and Dr. David Hyatt of New York, president of the National Conference of Christians and Jews in the United States. As one of those who had helped to found the International Conference of Christians and Jews at Oxford, I was asked to greet the thirtieth anniversary convention.

Bert and I left for Haifa the next day to attend the dedication of the Julius Silver Institute of Bio-Medical Engineering at the Technion. Five years earlier, we had attended the graduation exercises there at which Julius had been awarded an honorary degree. This was an important event for Israel, making it one of the world's centers for these new techniques in healing and rehabilitation. Julius's wife, Roslyn, and his daughter, Enid, accompanied him. We rejoiced in the significant contribution made to the Technion by our beloved kinsman, colleague, and friend. The main addresses were delivered by Abba Eban and by Dr. Ami Carmon. As in 1971, Julius surprised those in the audience who were not aware that he had graduated from the Teachers' Institute of the Jewish Theological Seminary, by prefacing his remarks with a few sentences in Hebrew. I was given the privilege of affixing the mezuzah.

We entertained the Silver family to dinner in our home on the following Shabbat eve. Our other guests were Ezra and Sylvia Shapiro, Judge Ḥaim Cohn and David Horowitz with their respective wives, and our Jerusalem cousin, Batya Abbady.

To mark my eightieth birthday, the Keren Hayesod arranged a special gathering at Bet ha-Nasi on June 27, hosted by President Ephraim Katzir. It was attended by a galaxy of Israel's leading personalities, including Prime Minister Yitzḥak Rabin, WZO and Jewish Agency Chairman Yosef Almogi, judges of the Supreme Court, and the heads of three academic institutions. A number of our relatives and close friends were also present. President Katzir, Yosef Almogi, and Ezra Shapiro delivered addresses and Shai Kreutner announced the establishment of a prize in my name for the outstanding *Askan* of the year, to be awarded annually by the Keren Hayesod (see also chapter 13).

The next day, I went with Bert to a reception at the Hiatt Institute in honor of Jacob Hiatt, chairman of the board of trustees of Brandeis University. Dr. Marver H. Bernstein, president of Brandeis University, attended and addressed this function.

Birthday greetings were also extended to me on June 30, when President Avraham Harman of the Hebrew University found an appropriate occasion to do so. This was the annual lecture sponsored by the Israel Goldstein Chair in Zionism, which comes within the framework of the Hebrew University's Institute of Contemporary Jewry, headed by Professor Moshe Davis. That year's lecture, delivered by Professor Simon Herman, was entitled, "Zionism and Pro-Israelism—A Destination with a Difference." There was a large and distinguished audience.

A memorable and gratifying aspect of this occasion was the Hebrew Festschrift that Moshe Davis presented to me on behalf of the Institute, published in honor of my eightieth birthday. It was a volume entitled *Studies in the History of Zionism*, incorporating a number of essays by graduate students on a wide range of Zionist topics.

For Bert and me, this birthday marked a new climax in our lives. We naturally missed our kin, especially our children and grandchildren, whose presence would have added to our happiness, but we found compensation soon afterwards in the family reunions that took place during our annual visit to the United States. My wife and I were grateful that we could still continue to serve in the vineyards we had planted and where we had reaped so much over the years.

Over the weekend of July 2–4, we attended a meeting of the board of governors of Haifa University. I was asked to preside at its observance of the U.S. bicentennial program. This took the form of a special evening session, at which I had the honor of introducing U.S. Ambassador Malcolm Toon, Rabbi Arthur Hertzberg, president of the American Jewish Congress, Elmer Winter, president of the American Jewish Committee, and Eliezer Rafaeli, president of Haifa University. We also participated in the dedication of the Strochlitz Chair in Holocaust Studies, named for Solomon Strochlitz, a survivor of the Holocaust, who became a leading supporter of the university. I have known him since he and his wife first came to the United States, when he often attended services at my congregation.

In the course of the following week, America's bicentennial was observed at a special session of the Knesset.

Between the meetings in Haifa, Bert and I returned briefly to Jerusalem in order to attend the Hebrew University dinner in honor of those chosen to receive honorary degrees. Among them were our friends, Zvi Schwartz and Rabbi Philip Bernstein, as well as Rose Halprin, who was awarded the Bublick Prize for outstanding endeavor in the field of Jewish education.

I was also invited to a meeting of the World Jewish Congress Executive, at which Dr. Nahum Goldmann, president of the WJC, extended greetings to me on my eightieth birthday. Similar felicitations were also expressed by Chairman Itzhak Navon, at a meeting of the Zionist General Council, and by Ya'akov Tsur, chairman of the Directorion of the Jewish National Fund, who presented me with a Golden Book certificate.

By a grim quirk of fate, the U.S. bicentennial observance coincided with a week of tense anxiety for Israel that will long be remembered as the Entebbe Affair. At Athens Airport, a gang of terrorists posing as tourists had boarded an Air France plane, on its way from Lod to Rome, and had then hijacked it at gunpoint in midair. Acting on their instructions, the pilot eventually landed at the airport of Entebbe in Uganda. The terrorists, affiliated with the "Popular Front for the Liberation of Palestine," included two Germans, a man and a woman. They threatened to kill all on board the aircraft unless fifty-three other terrorists detained in Israel and other countries were released.

It was soon obvious that the choice of Entebbe for this exercise in extortion was no mere accident, but a deliberate and well-planned scheme. Uganda's notorious, megalomaniacal dictator, "Field Marshal" Idi Amin Dada, assured the 104 hostages that he was negotiating for their release, yet simultaneously berated the "intransigent" Israelis and stationed armed troops around the airport terminal building in which the hijacked passengers and crew were confined. Meanwhile, the terrorists enjoyed freedom of movement and became more menacing. They separated the Israelis and Jews from the non-Jews, who were then released and flown to safety. Throughout the ensuing week, as fruitless negotiations dragged on, we began to fear that this latest Arab terrorist outrage would end in yet another bloodbath.

Behind the scenes, however, Israel's Defense Minister, Shim'on Peres, and Chief of Staff, General Mordecai ("Motta") Gur, were planning their strategy. After nightfall on July 3, a crack Israel army force commanded by Brigadier Dan Shomron, the chief paratroop and infantry officer, flew in three giant Hercules transport planes to Uganda—a distance of nearly 2,500 miles—and landed at Entebbe under cover of darkness. In the ensuing rescue operation, the Israeli troops stormed the terminal building, freed the imprisoned hostages, and killed all seven terrorist hijackers, as well as a score of their Ugandan accomplices. Several Russian-built Mig fighter planes were destroyed on the ground during the battle. Even before Idi Amin could react to this unforeseen development, both rescuers and rescued were on their way home to Israel.

The casualties on the Israeli side included four dead—three civilians and one IDF officer, Lieutenant Colonel Yonatan Netanyahu, who led the attack on the airport terminal building. He was the son of Professor Ben-Zion Netanyahu, a Zionist and Judaica scholar of world renown. It subsequently transpired that "Operation Entebbe" had also cost the life of Mrs. Dora Bloch, whose son, Danny Bloch, a prominent Israeli newsman, I knew well.

On their arrival in Israel, the *Tzahal* rescue force and the freed hostages received a tumultuous welcome. The nationwide jubilation, a mixture of profound relief and joy, took us back to the heady days of June 1967. Prime Minister Yitzḥak Rabin, who headed the welcoming party at Lod Airport, said in a television interview that the operation had restored Israel's self-confidence and demonstrated "the latent power of this nation." Arab reaction was predictably furious. U.S. President Gerald Ford cabled a message of congratulations to the Israel Government. At U.S. Ambassador Malcolm Toon's home in Herzlia, the Fourth of July celebrations became an unprecedented demonstration of Israeli-American solidarity and common rejoicing.

Bert and I first heard the good news on Sunday morning, while we were in Haifa. "Operation Entebbe," which electrified the world, gave new meaning to the popular Hebrew slogan, *Kol ha-kavod le-Tzahal!*—"Well done, *Tzahal!*"

Shortly after this gladdening event, Bert and I had a pleasant and relaxing cruise through the Mediterranean on board a Greek ship, the S.S. *Casteliani*. Our fellow passengers included Judge Yo'el Sussman of the Israel Supreme Court and a Miss Ethel Wallis, who was then engaged in social work among the Circassian villagers in Galilee. Our vessel stopped at various ports en route to Marseilles. One of these was the town of Leghorn (Livorno) in central Italy.

A *kehillah* had been established there by former Marranos and by North African Jews at the beginning of the seventeenth century and it prospered, but a decline set in over a century ago. Leghorn, I discovered, was the birthplace of Sir Moses Montefiore and of Rabbi Sabato Morais, the founder and first president of the Jewish Theological Seminary in New York. The surviving community, reduced in numbers by Nazi deportations during World War II, has been strengthened since 1967 by an influx of Jewish refugees from Libya and other Arab lands.

The original synagogue, a splendid edifice dating from the eighteenth century, had been destroyed by the Nazis and on its site the Italian Government has built an impressive modern edifice. Inside the entrance to the synagogue, we noticed a large *Aliyah le-regel* poster urging people to join the High Holy Day pilgrimage to Israel. We also saw a JNF blue and white box in the secretary's office. While visiting the synagogue, we were told that a *minyan* of worshipers attended services there not only on Sabbaths and festivals but on Mondays and Thursdays as well, and that the local *kehillah* sends an athlete to represent it at the Maccabiah Games in Israel. All of this was in striking contrast to what we had seen on visits to other small Jewish communities, both during this present trip and on previous occasions in various parts of the world. We attributed these signs of active Jewish life to the Leghorn community's living bond with Medinat Yisrael.

In the course of our usual summer visit to the United States, Congregation B'nai Jeshurun held a special Sabbath morning service to mark my eightieth birthday. A warm welcome was extended by Rabbi William Berkowitz, President Charles H. Silver, and a large congregation.

We returned to Israel in good time for Rosh Hashanah. As usual, we worshiped in our Conservative synagogue.

On October 27, it was my sad duty to deliver a eulogy on behalf of the Keren Hayesod at the funeral of Eliyahu Dobkin, a colleague on the Jewish Agency Executive who had been my predecessor as chairman of the Keren Hayesod–United Israel Appeal. Dobkin had played an important role in the organization of Aliyah, both official and "illegal," during and after World War II and had performed much valuable service for the Zionist movement. He was an authority on ancient Jewish glass and there is now an Eliyahu Dobkin pavilion housing his collection at the Israel Museum.

One day during the following week, I went with Bert and Norma Rocker, the widow of our late friend, Louis Rocker, to see the "Good Fence" on Israel's border with Lebanon. Here, Lebanese villagers, mostly Christian Maronites, came to sell the tobacco they grew and to buy gasoline. An Israeli clinic had been set up at this point, which they were at liberty to visit for medical attention. Between the Israeli border and what had come to be known as "Fatahland," an independent Lebanese mini-state stretching from the Mediterranean Sea to Syria was administered by Christian forces under the command of Major Sa'ad Haddad, who increasingly disregarded the ineffectual Government of Lebanon in Beirut. In his ongoing war of survival against the PLO terrorists, Major Haddad had succeeded in enlisting the support of his Muslim Shi'ite neighbors and had proved a useful and effective ally of Israel in a region which UN troops were unable to protect against Palestinian terrorist attacks.

We attended a dinner at our Youth Village on November 4, honoring Shai Kreutner on the occasion of his sixtieth birthday. He and I had been colleagues and friends in and out of the Keren Hayesod for many years, and we were delighted to join in this well-deserved tribute. Apart from myself, the speakers were Dr. Yosef Burg, Minister of the Interior, Moshe Kol, Minister of Tourism, Ezra Shapiro, chairman of the Keren Hayesod, and Zalman Shragai, Jerusalem's former Mayor.

Three days later, I left with Bert for New York to participate in Congregation B'nai Jeshurun's one hundred fiftieth anniversary celebration. The highlight was a dinner at the Waldorf-Astoria Hotel on November 21, 1976, at which President Charles H. Silver was the guest of honor. Rabbi William Berkowitz, my able successor, had planned the event. Among the honored guests were distinguished leaders in the religious, civic, and political life of New York City. The occasion inevitably brought to my mind B'nai Jeshurun's centennial jubilee banquet, held fifty years earlier at the Hotel Astor, on November 26, 1925. In the course of my Shabbat morning address, on the previous day, I spoke of the congregation's origins:

> The twenty-eight men who met in Washington Hall downtown on Pearl Street 150 years ago, to organize the first Ashkenazic Jewish Congregation in New York, seceding from the Sephardic mother congregation, Shearith Israel, when there were enough Ashkenazic Jews to form a congregation of their own—they built better than they knew.
>
> They could not have known that they were starting a process of parturition which 150 years later would become one thousand congregations, large and small, in Greater New York and its suburbs. They could not have known that New York's Jewish population, by 1976, would show a 2,000-fold increase in comparison with 1825, not counting the birth announcements in tomorrow morning's *New York Times!*
>
> Nor could the founders have foreseen that, in 1976, the Rabbi Emeritus of the Congregation would be coming to the Sesquicentennial as a resident of Jerusalem, the capital of a resurrected Jewish State, in the resurrection of which the Congregation they founded has played a not inconsiderable role.
>
> Thus, they built better than they knew.

Mindful of the need to utilize such occasions also for practical purposes, I was glad to be helpful in securing a number of substantial gifts for B'nai Jeshurun. We prolonged our stay until Ḥanukkah, in the latter half of December, when we visited our children and grandchildren on the West Coast before returning to Israel.

Ongoing Commitments

Having renewed my active interest in the Keren Kayemet, I took time for meetings and for periodical visits arranged by the Jewish National Fund in Israel. Earlier in the year, we had toured the new development town of Yammit, southwest of Gaza and beyond the "Green Line" marking Israel's pre-1967 border with Egypt. In nearby Sdeh Nitzan, there were about forty families—including a fair proportion of American Olim—cultivating tomatoes in special hothouse conditions and earning a good livelihood from this agricultural work.

On January 8, 1976, the seventy-fifth anniversary of the KKL-JNF was observed in a festive event at the Jerusalem Theater. President Katzir, Ya'akov Tsur, and Itzḥak Navon, chairman of the Zionist Actions Committee, delivered the addresses.

Some weeks after our return from the United States, Ya'akov Tsur celebrated his seventieth birthday and retired from his post as chairman of the KKL Directorion. Appropriately, the JNF dedicated a forest not far from Jerusalem in honor of Ya'akov Tsur and his wife, Vera. At the dedication ceremony on October 20, I was asked to speak on the Directorion's behalf. Across the years, I had come to appreciate Tsur's Jewish and general culture, his outstanding diplomatic services as Israel's ambassador to France and Argentina, his deep-rooted Zionism, and his years of service to the World Zionist Organization as chairman of the Zionist General Council (Actions Committee), as well as his envisioned leadership over many years as chairman of the Directorion of the World Keren Kayemet Le-Yisrael–Jewish National Fund.

His successor, Moshe Rivlin, was an excellent choice. Scion of an old-established and distinguished Jerusalem family, he combined Jewish cultural assets with experience in Zionist affairs. We had first come to know Moshe Rivlin during the 1950s, when he was Israel's consul in New York. In more recent years, he had served with great ability as director-general of the World Zionist Organization and the Jewish Agency in Jerusalem.

On December 30, I presided at the dedication of the George Eliot Memorial Grove, planted in the Women's International Forest in Galilee to mark the centenary of *Daniel Deronda*, the famous proto-Zionist novel by that British authoress. The 1,000 trees in the grove were contributed by Jewish and non-Jewish donors in Great Britain, South Africa, the United States and Israel. My aid in bringing this excellent scheme to fruition was enlisted by Mrs. Ruth Levitt, who had written a book entitled *George Eliot: The Jewish Connection*. The Women's Division of the Jewish National Fund-Keren Kayemet Le-Yisrael, with Leah Epstein as coordinator, then adopted the project and helped Mrs. Levitt to see it realized. The British ambassador, John

Mason, was present and spoke at the dedication ceremony, which his wife and family also attended.

While spending the week of Passover in Tiberias some months later, in April 1977, we were able to learn more of a minority group that had meant little to us hitherto. Over the years, we had visited the Samaritans on Mount Gerizim, near Nablus, an ancient and once powerful sect that parted company with Judaism and the Jewish people in the days of Ezra and Nehemiah and that had been reduced to a few hundred survivors. We had also visited a Druze village on Mount Carmel, where we were warmly received by these proud and martial folk, whose religion was an offshoot of Islam and who had cast in their lot with Israel since the War of Liberation in 1948. Now, thanks to Miss Ethel Wallis, with whom we had struck up a friendship during our cruise to Marseilles about a year previously, we made the acquaintance of Israel's Circassian community, to which she was dedicating all of her time, energy, and talents.

The Circassians, known in Israel as *Tcherkessim,* are of Caucasian origin and adopted Christianity in remote times, but their ancestors were converted to Islam in the eighteenth century, under pressure from the Crimean Tartars and the Ottomans. Following the czarist invasion of their homeland in the 1860s, the Circassians fled south and found refuge in the Turkish Empire. Their descendants are mainly settled in Israel, Jordan, and Syria. Throughout the period of Arab aggression in 1948–49, the Circassians maintained good relations with their Jewish neighbors and they have since become model citizens, loyal to Medinat Yisrael. Their two principal settlements are the village of Rihaniyya, north of Safed, and Kafr Kama, a more populous townlet southwest of Tiberias in Lower Galilee.

Miss Wallis took us to Kafr Kama, the inhabitants of which earn a livelihood from growing field crops and rearing livestock. They are also great horsemen. Their folk dances and music have influenced Israel's musical culture. What especially interested us, of course, was their current relationship with Israeli society. We discovered that the Circassian boys perform the normal stint of military service in the Israel Defense Forces and that the village schools follow the Jewish—rather than the Arab—syllabus prescribed by the Israel Ministry of Education. Accordingly, since this is the policy favored by the people in Kafr Kama, Hebrew and Circassian are the languages of instruction and a proportion of the teachers are Jews. Senior pupils attend high schools in Afula and other towns and some proceed to university. The desire for integration has led to many profound changes in the inhabitants' way of life, ranging from their local administration to the feeling (among the younger generation especially) that "we are Israelis, not Arabs!"

A different situation prevails in Rihaniyya, where Circassians and Arabs live side by side. No such far-reaching educational changes have taken place and, as a result, the traditional life-style of the Circassians has remained largely intact. One can only hope that the bold experimentation in Kafr Kama will not ultimately weaken those vital and valuable links with an ancestral culture that sympathetic Israeli officials are endeavoring to foster.

At the meeting of the Zionist General Council in June 1977, the Conservative movement—represented by the World Council of Synagogues—was admitted to the World Zionist Organization and allocated a place on the Zionist Executive. Addresses of welcome were delivered by Rabbi Mordecai Kirshblum, on behalf of World Mizrahi, and by Rabbi Richard Hirsch, on behalf of the World Union for Progressive Judaism. As president of the Rabbinical Assembly of America, Rabbi Mordecai Waxman responded in an impressive speech. I had welcomed the movement's decision to affiliate with the WZO in the course of my Rosh Hashanah sermon in Jerusalem several months previously, on September 25, 1976. Professor Solomon Schechter, the founder of the United Synagogue of America, had been a self-affirming Zionist, I said, and that had been true also of his principal colleagues in the Jewish Theological Seminary—Professors Israel Friedlaender, Louis Ginzberg, and Alexander Marx. For more than half a century, therefore, all three major arms of the Conservative movement—the Seminary, the United Synagogue, and the Rabbinical Assembly—had borne the stamp of Zionist identification.

By contrast, I observed, the Hebrew Union College in Cincinnati, the Union of American Hebrew Congregations, and the Central Conference of American Rabbis had long remained predominantly anti-Zionist. Only a handful of Zionist "mavericks," such as Rabbis Max Heller, Stephen Wise, and Abba Hillel Silver, had refused to toe this official Reform line. Not until the Holocaust and the establishment of Medinat Yisrael had made a shambles of anti-Zionism did the character of the Reform movement change, reaching a climax with its formal admission to the WZO in January 1976. "I wish *our* Conservative movement had been the first," I said. "By every historic right, it should have been. If you will pardon my mentioning it, I urged this step, unsuccessfully, fifteen years ago."

Among those who attended the 1977 Actions Committee sessions was Rabbi William Berkowitz, in his capacity as national president of B'nai Zion, a constituent of our World Confederation of United Zionists. Latterly, he had also served as chairman of the Manhattan Committee for Israel Bonds. Bert and I arranged a *Kiddush* reception and luncheon at our home in honor of Rabbi and Mrs. Berkowitz, when our other guests included Mayor Teddy Kollek and the chairman of the Zionist General Council, Itzhak Navon, and his wife, Ophira.

"Reorientation and Rededication" was the theme of my Israel Independence Day address at the Center for Conservative Judaism on April 20, 1977, the eve of Yom Ha-Atzma'ut. I recalled some of the dramatic episodes in which it had been my good fortune to be involved prior to and immediately after the establishment of the Medinah, during the years 1947–49. While paying tribute to the magnificent philanthropic record of World Jewry in recent times, I drew attention to the disappointingly meager response "on the part of Jews who call themselves Zionists" in terms of Aliyah from the free world:

> It is comforting, of course, to hear broad segments of our people proudly announcing their Zionism when Israel is under propaganda attack by its foes, yet, in my view, a Zionist is a Jew for whom Aliyah is part of his life plan. Certainly,

we are desperately in need of a moral and spiritual revival in our national life and in our national institutions. Yet to justify the lack of Aliyah by Israel's shortcomings is to furnish oneself with an alibi. The rejoinder is obvious: Let those who are qualified to do so come and help tone up the quality of our lives, let them join us in the struggle for higher standards, let them come and take "pot luck" with us, for good or for ill. It is not they and we, but all of us together!

Mayor Teddy Kollek was the guest speaker at the Yom Yerushalayim (Jerusalem Day) services held at our synagogue on May 15, to mark the tenth anniversary of the city's reunification. Before delivering his address, he told me that the Municipal Council had just decided by a majority vote, over opposition from the Orthodox bloc (the National Religious Party and Agudat Yisrael), to approve his proposal to grant a plot and a building permit to the newly formed Conservative congregation on Givat Shapira, the northern suburb of Jerusalem also known as "French Hill." Both a synagogue and a school would be constructed on that site. With Mayor Kollek's permission, I conveyed the good news without delay to Rabbi Pesaḥ Schindler, director of the Center for Conservative Judaism, David Zucker, president of the World Council of Synagogues, and Rabbi Richard Hirsch, director of the World Union for Progressive Judaism.

It was an important breakthrough for the non-Orthodox religious constituencies in Israel. Perhaps the most significant impact has been felt in the educational sphere. The new school on French Hill, though part of the officially nonreligious state *(Mamlakhti)* network, caters to parents and children who look for a program that is neither strictly Orthodox nor basically secular in orientation. Thus, prayer services are held at the beginning of the school day, Jewish studies are taught in a religious spirit and with a reverence for traditional values that one does not find in other state schools, and the boys wear *kippot* whenever appropriate. It is gratifying to note the cooperation and encouragement this experiment has received from the Israel Ministry of Education, headed (from 1977) by the National Religious Party's Zevulun Hammer.

Conceivably, there are elements within the NRP and Israel's Orthodox "establishment" which now realize that such a scheme, far from threatening the state religious *(Mamlakhti Dati)* network of schools, provides an opportunity to modify the secular trend and to restore a modicum of Jewish tradition, at least where the demand exists. In this way, Education Minister Hammer and his co-workers may achieve what their predecessors failed to do, in narrowing the gap between the religious and nonreligious sectors of Israel's Jewish population.

One Shabbat in March 1977, not long before Passover, we were invited for afternoon tea to the Jerusalem home of Professor and Mrs. Saul Lieberman. They were about to leave for their annual visit to the United States. Professor Lieberman was kind enough to take note of my eightieth birthday and had apparently read the Hebrew version of my biography, which appeared at about that time. I was touched by this thoughtfulness on his part.

It is interesting to recall that Professor Lieberman and Dr. Chaim Weizmann were *landsleit*, both having been born in the village of Motol, near Pinsk. Whereas Chaim

Weizmann became the leader of the Jewish national revival, Saul Lieberman was destined to become the world's foremost Talmudic scholar and authority on a vast range of Jewish subjects. From 1928, he had lectured at the Hebrew University and at the Mizraḥi Teachers' Seminary in Jerusalem, serving for five years as dean of the Harry Fischel Institute for Talmudic Research before accepting a professorship at the Jewish Theological Seminary in New York, in 1940. He later served as rector of the Seminary's Rabbinical School and was awarded the Israel Prize in 1971.

I had long revered him from a distance as the foremost scholar of Judaica in our time, also sharing the wide appreciation of his qualities as a lovable human being. Blessedly vigorous and stimulating, though close to eighty, he was dividing his time between Jerusalem and New York. Wherever he went, the Crown of Torah went with him.

In the course of our conversation, Professor Lieberman observed that in Europe, before World War II, the rabbinate had been a matrix of Jewish scholarship, whereas in the United States it was essentially a pastoral vocation. I took occasion to reminisce a little about my student days and my teachers at the Seminary, remarking that the atmosphere prevailing there in my time had been more liberal than in later years.

As we were about to leave, Professor Abraham S. Halkin came in with his wife, a sister of Mrs. Lieberman. The father of these two distinguished ladies was the late Rabbi Meir Bar-Ilan, of blessed memory, the onetime leader of World Mizraḥi, whose name is perpetuated in Bar-Ilan University. I had been privileged to know Rabbi Bar-Ilan, enjoying his friendship and cooperation in the Jewish National Fund's Mizraḥi projects and in other Zionist endeavors.

With the tragic death of Ze'ev Schickler soon after Passover, I lost a beloved friend and younger colleague, and the Jerusalem Youth Village bearing my name lost its dedicated and gifted director. A born educator, he loved children and infused into the Youth Village something of his own noble spirit. Ze'ev Schickler died after a prolonged illness, leaving his wife, Hadassah, a son and daughter-in-law, Mikhah and Ettie, and two grandchildren.

The funeral took place at Sanhedriah, Jerusalem, on April 17. Moshe Kol and I delivered the eulogies and a tribute was paid by one of Ze'ev's old comrades in the Haganah, who together with him had been in command of the unit that liberated the Katamon area, where the Youth Village now stands. The older children of the Youth Village came to the funeral services. Among the many who attended were Mayor Teddy Kollek, Yosef Klarman, the head of Youth Aliyah, and his director-general, as well as Shai Kreutner of the Keren Hayesod. Subsequently, at the *Shloshim* memorial exercises held in the Youth Village, the speakers included Gideon Hausner, Moshe Kol, and Yitzḥak Golan.

Lonia Liebergall continues to serve as the village "mother" and Moshe Kurtz as treasurer. Uzzi Kremer, formerly of Rishon Le-Zion, is now the energetic director, and Judith B. Segal is the secretary.

A project was initiated for the building of Ohel Ze'ev, a library in memory of Ze'ev Schickler, adjoining the Lenore and Philip Davidson High School at our

Youth Village. Headed by Shai Kreutner, who had been one of Ze'ev's close friends and colleagues over the years, a special committee took charge of this project. Mrs. Esther Ghitis of Milan, a generous and devoted friend of the *Ḥavvah*, was instrumental in gaining important support for Ohel Ze'ev. Additional assistance came through the good offices of Dr. Avraham Avi-ḥai, world chairman of the Keren Hayesod, and the generosity of a Swiss benefactor, Jean Brunschvig of Geneva.

At the time of its establishment some three decades earlier, the Youth Village was located on Jerusalem's outer periphery, but it is now surrounded by fine apartment buildings in what has become one of the attractive residential areas of an expanded capital city. For the children who live and study in this lovely, verdant spot, it is indeed meaningful to be *be-tokhekhi Yerushalayim*, in the heart of Jerusalem. Nowadays, I might add, scores of local residents attend the High Holy Day services held in the *Ḥavvah*.

An important form of cultural activity maintained on the premises of my Youth Village is the Institute for Zionist Studies conducted by the Zionist Council in Israel, headed by Aryeh Tzimmuki. Youth groups from all parts of Israel attend courses there, and lectures are given by intellectual and political leaders of the Zionist movement. This program enjoys the sponsorship of the Education and Absorption Ministries, as well as of the Israel Information Center and the Jerusalem municipality.

During the summer, boys and girls from North America (together with Israeli youngsters) attend a Camp Ramah program at the Youth Village organized by the Conservative movement's United Synagogue Youth.

Among our foremost patrons I am pleased to mention, in addition to Esther Ghitis, Mr. and Mrs. Leopold Goldmuntz of Antwerp and Monte Carlo, Jean Brunschvig of Geneva, and Mr. and Mrs. Theodore Baumritter of New York. Having built up the Ethan Allen Furniture Company in the United States together with his brother-in-law, Nathan H. Ancell, Theodore Baumritter has taken a special interest in our cabinetmaking shop and has provided it with his expert guidance as well as with up-to-date machinery. The Baumritters, former congregants of mine, are among New York's outstanding philanthropists. An important new patron is Elmer L. Winter of Milwaukee, founder of Manpower, Inc., in the U.S. and formerly president of the American Jewish Committee. The Youth Village receives ongoing support from Youth Aliyah and the Israel Government. It has enjoyed the annual support of the World Confederation of United Zionists and received frequent generous contributions by Hadassah, the Women's Zionist Organization of America.

The Israel Goldstein Youth Center in Kiryat Gat claimed far less of my time, although I visited it occasionally and extended periodic help. Opened in 1958, it provided vocational training for about one hundred boys and girls. Its able director was Yeḥezkel Kimron.

An agricultural settlement I have made a point of visiting at least once a year is Moshav Udim, which I helped to establish during my year as treasurer of the Jewish Agency. In March 1976, I visited the moshav and spoke there at the opening of a new community center. Udim celebrated its thirtieth anniversary in 1978.

One effect of my eightieth birthday was to remind me that there was no time to be lost in organizing my archives and setting to work on some long-delayed literary projects.

I first gave thought to the organization of my archives when I retired from the chairmanship of the Keren Hayesod in 1971. During the six decades of my public service in a variety of areas, Jewish and general, religious and secular, and especially in the Zionist sphere, I had developed the habit of writing memoranda and scribbling notes to compensate for my naturally poor memory. It had been my hope that such an accumulation of documents, records, and memoranda might some day prove of benefit to students of the period covered by such material. This practice of mine has, indeed, proved useful in other ways and has stood me in good stead.

The files and personal papers accumulated over the decades had been stored in the basement of Congregation B'nai Jeshurun's Community Center in New York. Following our Aliyah, these items were transferred from New York to a large room in our Jerusalem Youth Village, where trained archivists proceeded to classify and index the mass of material. I was fortunate to have the expert advice and supervision of Dr. Michael A. Heymann, director of the Central Zionist Archives in Jerusalem, where my archives are about to find their permanent home.

It has been a source of considerable satisfaction to me that these archives, which are still growing, have been visited and consulted by scholars and students in various fields, ranging from Christian-Jewish relations in the U.S. to the American Zionist role in the establishment of Medinat Yisrael. Contact has been established with other Jewish archives in Israel and in the U.S., and there will be facilities for making microfilms available. These archives also contain material relating to my congregation, to the Jewish Conciliation Board of America, the American Jewish Congress, World Jewish Congress, and the wide spectrum of organizations I have been privileged to head.

16

Momentous Changes: 1977–81

On Tuesday, May 17, 1977, Israeli voters lined up at the polling stations. By the early hours of the next morning, it had become clear that Acting Prime Minister Shim'on Peres's Labor-Mapam Alignment, the Ma'arakh, was heading for defeat while the Likud (Ḥerut-Liberal) Opposition, led by Menaḥem Begin, was well on its way to victory. For the first time since the establishment of Medinat Yisrael, a government would be formed without the hitherto dominant Labor Party in control. It was a major political upset, the impact of which we were destined to feel over the next few years.

The final results gave Begin's Ḥerut-Liberal bloc and its allies 45 seats in the Knesset, the Labor-Mapam Alignment 32, Professor Yigael Yadin's Democratic Movement for Change (DMC) 15, and the National Religious Party 12 seats. Although there was some initial talk of a wall-to-wall coalition, the Ma'arakh refused to enter any new government as a junior partner. A coalition of the Likud, DMC, and NRP took over in June, with Menaḥem Begin as the new Prime Minister. Agudat Yisrael lent additional support to this alliance.

A variety of factors was responsible for the change of regime. One could point to the lingering malaise of the Yom Kippur War, popular resentment against a Labor establishment that had been in power for too long and had come to regard itself as the natural ruling party, unedifying squabbles within the Alignment itself, an apparent erosion of U.S. support for Israel and—worst of all—a series of political scandals involving key figures in the outgoing Labor Administration. The Israeli electorate obviously felt that it was time for a change.

This political transition was made easier by the fact that Begin and his supporters had constituted a loyal Opposition throughout the years of Mapai hegemony. The changeover in Government control from the Labor Alignment to the Likud Alliance provided an impressive example of Israel's democracy at work.

Prime Minister Menaḥem Begin's Government represented a novel constellation of forces. As the dominant faction, his Ḥerut-Liberal bloc could have appropriated most of the key ministries for itself, but it preferred to share power and responsibility with Yadin's DMC group and with the NRP, headed by Dr. Yosef Burg. The DMC had, in fact, caused the greatest damage to Labor by winning the support of many disgruntled ex-Alignment voters. Particularly hurtful and dismaying to Labor was Begin's offer of the Foreign Affairs portfolio to Moshe Dayan, who promptly accepted. Begin also displayed political sagacity by making former Air Force chief Ezer Weizman, his election campaign manager, Minister of Defense and General Ariel ("Arik") Sharon, the Yom Kippur War hero, Minister of Agriculture. Shmuel Tamir, Begin's old rival, who had left the Likud to join Yadin's group, became Minister of Justice. One other surprise was the granting of a third portfolio to the National Religious Party, whose Youth Circles leader, Zevulun Hammer, took over the Ministry of Education and Culture.

A new era in Israeli politics had begun and the composition of Menaḥem Begin's Coalition Government would soon find reflection in the leadership of the WZO and Jewish Agency Executives chosen at the ensuing World Zionist Congress in 1978.

A development of peculiar significance to Israel in the spring of 1977 involved a number of hapless "boat people"—refugees then fleeing Communist oppression in Vietnam. Newspaper stories and television reports had focused world attention on the plight of these mainly Christian DPs, thousands of whom were adrift in the South China Sea. As it became evident that most ports were closed to them, ships sailing in the area proved reluctant to take them aboard. The unfortunate Vietnamese on one boat were down to three teaspoonfuls of drinking water per day when they were picked up by an Israeli freighter. Other ships had refused to rescue them. The Israel Government's prompt decision to admit these castaways put the rest of the "civilized" world to shame. Nor was this the last humanitarian act of its kind. I could not help recalling, by contrast, how nearly 1,000 Jewish refugees from Nazi Germany had crossed the Atlantic on board the S.S. *St. Louis* in May-June 1939 and were turned away, even by the United States. Only the 287 refugees finally admitted to Great Britain survived the Holocaust.

I visited one group of the Vietnamese at an absorption center in Ofakim not long after their arrival. Later, Bert and I visited another group of newly arrived refugees from the Far East at the absorption center in Afula. They had come with no possessions whatsoever and some even lacked underwear. After only a few weeks, the children were prattling away in Hebrew; within a few months, the adults had learned enough Hebrew to begin seeking employment. A goodly proportion of them, locating friends or kinfolk in the United States, decided to emigrate and they are free to do so. Enough have remained, however, to make the sight of these Vietnamese newcomers less unusual than it was in 1977. Some have found employment in hotels and restaurants or, with the help of Israeli well-wishers, have opened establishments of their own. In Jerusalem and Tel Aviv, one can now even dine in *kasher* Chinese or Vietnamese restaurants under rabbinical supervision.

This provision of a refuge and home for such non-Jewish victims of war and man's inhumanity to man, when nearly the whole of mankind had turned its back on the Vietnamese "boat people" and left them to perish, is a golden page in Israel's drama-studded history.

The hundredth anniversary of the birth of Louis Lipsky was a welcome opportunity for an observance by our Confederation. On June 30, I headed a delegation comprising Rose Halprin, Charlotte Jacobson, and Kalman Sultanik, that visited

President Ephraim Katzir and presented him with *Memoirs in Profile*, a biography of Lipsky edited by Professor Ben Halprin. Later that same day, a symposium on Lipsky took place at the Hebrew University under the auspices of the Israel Gold-tein Chair in Zionism. I participated, together with President Avraham Harman, Professor Moshe Davis, Professor Aryeh Sachs (incumbent of the Louis Lipsky Chair in Drama), Mrs. Shulamit Nardi, and Dr. Deborah Lipstadt of the University of Washington. Dr. Lipstadt delivered the principal memorial address.

Bert and I made our now customary summer visit to the United States prior to returning to Jerusalem for the High Holy Days. It was an absorbing and a busy time for both of us. On July 14, 1977, I delivered the opening prayer at a session of the House of Representatives in Washington. The necessary arrangements were made by Representative Sidney Yates of Chicago. Sixteen years earlier, at the suggestion of Dr. Abraham G. Duker, he had taken the initiative in having me invited to deliver the prayer marking the hundredth anniversary of the first occasion when a rabbi performed this task before Congress—my illustrious predecessor, Rabbi Mor-ris Raphall of Congregation B'nai Jeshurun.

I took occasion to meet with Chancellor Gerson D. Cohen at the Jewish Theolog-ical Seminary in New York. We discussed the Seminary's past and, more espe-cially, its future. The new chancellor was already displaying his ability there. He welcomed my report of Mayor Kollek's help in making available a building plot to the Conservative congregation on French Hill. He also told me of his own plan to inaugurate a full Seminary course in Jerusalem at Neveh Schechter.

During our visit, Rabbi Judah Cahn, president of the New York Board of Rabbis, interviewed me on television and presented me with a copy of a new book, *The American Rabbi*, edited by Rabbi Gilbert S. Rosenthal, which the New York Board of Rabbis had published to mark the U.S. bicentennial and the Board's ninety-fifth anniversary. Included in this book was an essay I had written on "The Role of American Rabbis in World Jewish Affairs, Zionism and the State of Israel."

As usual, we celebrated our wedding anniversary and Bert's birthday with our children and grandchildren on the West Coast. It has been a source of pride to us that our son, Avram, and his wife, Dora, have won recognition for their work in the fields of drug addiction and alcoholism respectively, and that our son-in-law, Paul Olum, and our daughter, Vivian, have made important contributions in their re-spective fields of education and psychology. Avram, who serves as chairman of the Medical Faculty Senate at Stanford University, was elected to the U.S. National Academy of Sciences in 1980. Paul was provost of the University of Oregon. As usual, too, we visited my brother, Rabbi Morris Goldstein, and his wife, Adeline, in San Francisco. We were interested to discover that our grandsons in Palo Alto, Daniel, Joshua, and Michael, were together involved in a social-service business enterprise—delivering groceries to elderly people unable to do their own shopping. Our other grandson, Kenneth Akiba, was living and studying in Eugene, Oregon.

On our way back to New York, we first stopped off in Denver to see our grand-daughter, Margaret, Avram and Dora's child, and her husband, Bradford Wallace, who live in Boulder, Colorado. She is a dedicated teacher, he, an architect, and they were then building their own home. Our next stop was in Philadelphia, where we visited our kin, my brother and sister-in-law, Isaac and Fannie, and my sister and brother-in-law, Sarah and Herman Lazarus, who took us to see the reconstructed waterfront on the Delaware river. In my childhood days, this had been a slum area of Philadelphia.

Back East again, Bert and I next visited our granddaughter, Judith, and her husband, Geoffrey, in Ithaca and Paul's father, Jacob Olum, a leading citizen of Binghamton, New York. Making our customary round of family visits in New York, we saw Bert's sister, Grace, her daughter and son-in-law, Rose and Bernard Volpert, and our cousins, Julius and Roslyn Silver, and their daughter, Enid.

One of my collateral interests has been the Altschul Foundation, of which I am a trustee. This foundation was established in March 1941 by Louis and Jeannette C. Altschul, who were my friends and congregants. Initially, the other members of the board of trustees were Charles Cohen and Edwin F. Korkus.

The foundation has distributed about $350,000 a year. Its main beneficiaries have been the United Jewish Appeal and the Federation of Jewish Philanthropies of New York, but various philanthropic and educational institutions, both Jewish and civic, in the United States and Israel have received allocations.

Following the death of Mr. Altschul and then Mrs. Altschul, the presidency was held successively by Charles Cohen, Frances Browner, Gershon Reichman, and (presently) Gerald A. Rothstein—all members of the family. Upon the death of Mr. Korkus, Ethel F. Beaver succeeded him as the foundation's attorney and secretary.

When we made Aliyah at the end of 1960, I continued serving as a member of the board of trustees and helped to secure from the Jewish Agency the attachment of the Altschul name to several important properties in Israel, mostly connected with the immigrant-absorption program. Foremost among these are the Louis and Jeannette Altschul *Ulpan* and Merkaz Klitah in Beersheba, the Charles Cohen Hostel for Academicians in Reḥovot, and the Jeannette Altschul State Religious School in Tirat Ha-Carmel, near Haifa. As a trustee, I make periodic visits to these properties and submit annual reports to the foundation in New York.

While in New York, we have always endeavored to visit friends and congregants too numerous to mention individually. From time to time we received gratifying reports about boys and girls, fondly remembered as junior members of my congregation, who were now giving a good account of themselves in business and the professions and in various areas of public service, especially in work for the United Jewish Appeal. Warren A. Silver is a splendid example. As a boy, he was one of the outstanding pupils at B'nai Jeshurun's religious school. He subsequently made his career in the U.S. State Department. It was with keen interest and delight that I received from him in the summer of 1977 a copy of his biographical novel, *The Green Rose*, dealing with Solomon Ibn Gabirol, the philosopher-poet of eleventh-century Spain.

On the first day of Sukkot, following our return to Israel, Meyer W. Weisgal died at his home in Reḥovot. Bert and I went there to attend the funeral service on October 2. Our friendship with Meyer and Shirley Weisgal went back nearly half a century. Meyer and I had been associated with the building of the Palestine Pavilion at the New York World's Fair in 1939 and again, nearly twenty years later, in the American observance of the tenth anniversary of Medinat Yisrael. Subsequently, he was the moving force in the construction of Bet Agron in Jerusalem, honoring the memory of our mutual friend, Gershon Agron.

Meyer's stellar achievement was the building and development of the Weizmann Institute of Science at Reḥovot. Dr. Weizmann had been fortunate indeed to find in Meyer so loyal and enterprising a disciple, while Meyer had proved fortunate in "hitching his wagon to a star." Much of the credit for Meyer Weisgal's success belonged to his wife, Shirley, who never lost faith in him during the early, bleak years.

One delayed eightieth birthday gift that I greatly appreciated was the honorary fellowship awarded to me by the University of Haifa, in the presence of Prime Minister Menaḥem Begin, on October 30, 1977. In my acceptance speech, I said that Bert and I felt privileged to give our active support to this university because it was in the heartland of the kibbutzim, had more Arab students than any other university in Israel, and, being young, constituted a special challenge to educational statesmanship.

On November 30, I was glad to take part in an interesting program at Haifa University. Professor Yosef Nedavah, incumbent of the Reuben Hecht Chair in Zionism, invited me to be one of the panel in a symposium on the chapter of American Zionist activity preceding the establishment of Medinat Yisrael. My fellow panelists were Professor Benjamin Akzin, Dr. Eliahu Elath, Dr. Zvi Ganin, and Hillel Kook.

Though no longer actively involved in the World Jewish Congress, retaining only an honorary vice-presidency in the organization, I was nevertheless interested in the change of leadership that took place about this time, when Dr. Nahum Goldmann retired from the presidency and Philip Klutznick of Chicago succeeded him. No newcomer to Jewish leadership, Klutznick had an excellent record as president of B'nai B'rith and had served the U.S. Government as ambassador to the UN. He was a lifelong Zionist with a firsthand knowledge of Israel. As for Dr. Goldmann, I felt sure that his retirement from the presidency of the WJC did not mean that he would remain detached from—or silent about—the entire range of Jewish affairs.*

Toward the end of the year, on November 3, a ceremony honoring Marc Chagall on the occasion of his eightieth birthday was held at the President's House. Following an address of welcome by President Ephraim Katzir, Mayor Teddy Kollek conferred upon Chagall the title of *Yakir Yerushalayim*. On behalf of the Hebrew University, Rector Gideon Czapski and Dean Shmaryahu Talmon awarded him an honorary doctor's degree.

Chagall's response, in Yiddish, was a memorable one. "As a child in my native Liozno, near Vitebsk," he said, "I would walk home from *ḥeder* in the late winter afternoons, carrying a lantern to light up my homeward path. In my mind's eye, the

*On Nahum Goldmann, see chapter 17.

angels in heaven guided me on my way. Later, when I grew up and became an artist, my pictures were meant to light up the dark corners of Jewish life. Now, Israel is the lamp which brightens the path of the Jewish people."

Visitors from abroad, arriving in the course of 1977, continued to renew some meaningful ties we had forged at one time or another. Thus, in April, we had welcomed Chaplain Stanley Johnson and Professor Norman Oler of the University of Pennsylvania, my alma mater, who were seeking to develop an exchange program with the Hebrew University. I invited them to attend Sabbath services at our Conservative congregation, where Rabbi Green welcomed them, and then to a *Kiddush* in our home, where our other guests included President Avraham Harman and Professor Shmaryahu Talmon of the Hebrew University. A few days later, I took them to visit the Hebrew University Synagogue and our Jerusalem Youth Village.

On another occasion, Dr. William Boyd, president of the University of Oregon, brought regards from our daughter, Vivian, and our son-in-law, Paul Olum, the university's provost. He told me of a plan to establish a Wayne Morse Chair in Law at the University of Oregon, honoring the memory of the eminent Democratic senator from that state who had been a staunch friend of Zionism and Medinat Yisrael. President Boyd sought my advice in regard to the enlistment of Jewish patrons for this project, and I was glad to be helpful.

Just before the end of the year, on December 28, Professor S. Noah Kramer came with his wife from Philadelphia to deliver a series of lectures at the Hebrew University and to receive an honorary fellowship there. As the greatest living authority on the ancient Sumerian civilization, he spoke on "New Light from the Tablets of Sumer." Bert and I attended the lectures and the award ceremony, and we were subsequently glad to welcome Professor and Mrs. Kramer to our home.

This visit provided a charming flashback to our early years together as students at Yeshivat Mishkan Yisrael in South Philadelphia. One day in the late spring of 1973, I had attended a congress in Jerusalem sponsored by the Israel Society for Biblical Research at which Noah Kramer had lectured on Sumerian influences in the Book of Psalms. Having delivered his paper, the lecturer startled me by running across the platform to clasp me in a warm embrace. Until then, I had never even suspected that this professor of Assyriology was the same Noah Kramer who had been a classmate of mine at the "Yeshivah Ketannah" in Philadelphia well over sixty years earlier!

Our paths had diverged, of course, mine toward the rabbinate and Zionist service and his toward academic life and Near Eastern studies. Professor Kramer was never a member of my youthful Zionist circle in the old days, nor was he a Zionist in his maturer years, but latterly, like so many others, he had come to appreciate Israel's meaningfulness and importance for the Jewish people.

A development that brightened the year for us was the arrival of our granddaughter, Joyce Olum, for an extended stay in Israel. A natural gift for languages quickly enabled her to become fluent in Hebrew and to acquire a working knowledge of Arabic. She began teaching a kindergarten class in Jerusalem and another class in a

Bedouin school near Beersheba, devoted part of her time to counseling, and also joined a local *Ḥavurah* group.

The outstanding event of 1977 was the dramatic breakthrough in Israel-Arab relations that culminated in the visit of Egypt's President Muhammed Anwar al-Sadat to Jerusalem. It was the first momentous step along the road to what we hoped would be an eventual overall peace agreement between Israel and the Arab world.

When, in 1971, Sadat had told an interviewer that he was prepared to accept the reality of Israel and to abandon the line of his predecessor, Gamal Abdul Nasser, Prime Minister Golda Meir did not treat the remark seriously. We had heard such statements too often before and learned to regard them as propagandist camouflage. The Yom Kippur War of 1973 appeared to confirm our suspicions. Having "restored Egypt's military honor," however, Sadat again threw out feelers in Israel's direction, particularly when an agreement was reached on the disengagement of forces in January 1974. A number of factors may have motivated Sadat's new strategy: Egypt's disastrous economic situation, its insoluble social ills, disenchantment with the Soviet Union, and the realization that Israel could not be defeated by the military option and that the United States would not abandon its ally. The failure of PLO terrorism to sap Israeli morale and the IDF's brilliant Entebbe operation may have reinforced the Egyptian President's decision to reach an accommodation with the Jewish State.

In fact, however, it was Prime Minister Menaḥem Begin who set things in motion with his "no more wars, no more bloodshed" offer, which prompted Sadat's declaration that he was "prepared to go to the ends of the earth" to terminate the state of hostility between the two countries. On November 15, 1977, Begin sent a formal written invitation to Sadat, suggesting that he come to Israel and almost immediately a positive reply arrived from Cairo. The U.S. embassies in Israel and Egypt facilitated this exchange of communications. The very fact that President Sadat accepted Prime Minister Begin's invitation, considering such a mission "a holy job," astonished the world. No less significant was the fact that Begin had taken Sadat's declaration seriously.

Once arrangements for this historic event had been finalized, Jerusalem became the focus of international interest and attention. The biggest news operation ever mounted in Israel necessitated the conversion of the Jerusalem Theater, just down the road from our home, into a vast communications center for the hundreds of television, radio, and newspaper reporters who arrived to cover Sadat's visit. The tightest security arrangements were also enforced throughout his stay.

On the evening of Saturday, November 19, not long after the termination of Shabbat, the Egyptian aircraft bearing President Sadat and his entourage landed at Ben-Gurion Airport. To the accompaniment of a twenty-one-gun salute and the playing of the Israeli and Egyptian national anthems, the leader of the most powerful Arab state was welcomed by President Ephraim Katzir and Prime Minister Menahem Begin. The two Chief Rabbis, Israel's Cabinet Ministers, the Speaker of the Knesset, Opposition leaders, and members of the diplomatic corps headed the reception party. The tumultuous welcome, particularly by the tens of thousands of schoolchildren waving Egyptian and Israeli flags along the route of Sadat's motorcade over the next two days, heightened the significance of this visit.

That night Bert and I happened to be the guests of our friends, Professor and Mrs. Moshe Goshen-Gottstein, whose home on Jabotinsky Street afforded a grandstand view of the Presidential motorcade. At about 10:00 P.M., we went down to the street outside to see the procession go by on its way to the King David Hotel, where President Sadat and his party would be staying. The motorcade was headed by the car in which Sadat and Begin were traveling and, as the crowds lining the street cheered and clapped, Egypt's head of state waved in response. We were uplifted by a feeling of hope that a new chapter in Israel's history was opening.

Those "Forty-four Hours in Jerusalem"—culminating in President Sadat's address before a packed Knesset—led to Prime Minister Begin's visit to Egypt in late December and to a slow, difficult process of negotiations that would herald a period of lessening tension between Egypt and Israel.

The rest is history. U.S. President Jimmy Carter played a decisive role in bringing President Sadat and Prime Minister Begin together, in securing the Camp David Agreement of September 1978 and in obtaining their signatures to the Israel-Egypt Peace Treaty, finalized in Washington on March 26, 1979. This provided for a phased withdrawal (within three years) by Israeli troops from Sinai, for the return of the Egyptian oil fields, with all the economic consequences this meant to Israel, and for negotiations leading to "full autonomy" for the Arabs in Judea, Samaria, and the Gaza Strip. Following the Begin-Sadat meeting at Aswan in January 1980, diplomatic relations were established, ambassadors were exchanged, and the borders between Israel and Egypt were opened—in the face of furious reactions by the Arab "rejection states."

All of us who had fought for the Yishuv during the years of its political and economic struggle and who had been privileged to serve in the era of fulfillment rejoiced in the prospect of attaining normal, peaceful relations with our most important Arab neighbor. Medinat Yisrael, born and bred amid the fires of war, its existence always fraught with danger, an island of Jewish independence in a sea of Arab nationalism, may now dare to look forward to a day when peace may be established also with other neighboring Arab states. This may still appear to be a distant prospect, but our first occasion for a *Sheheheyanu* blessing makes us hopeful that others may follow. There can be no doubt, however, that we shall continue to need all available resources of mind, spirit, and substance, the backing of World Jewry and of American administrations, to win through successfully.

For Hadassah, American Zionism, the World Zionist Organization, and our Confederation, the year 1978 began on a sad note with the passing of my close friend and colleague, Rose Halprin. Following a religious service in New York, her son, daughter, son-in-law, and granddaughter flew with the body for the interment ceremony in Israel. Charlotte Jacobson, chairman of the American Section of the Jewish Agency Executive, and Kalman Sultanik, a member of that Executive, also came. A funeral service took place at the Jewish Agency on January 12, in the presence of Jewish Agency Chairman Yosef Almogi, members of the Agency Executive and the Zionist General Council, and a large delegation representing the Hadassah Council in Israel and the Hadassah Hospital. Eulogies were delivered by Charlotte Jacobson, Rabbi Mordecai Kirshblum, and myself. I dwelt on Rose Halprin's abiding influence and impact on Zionist affairs (see chapter 17).

A happier occasion was the annual convention of the Association of Americans and Canadians in Israel, which opened in Netanyah on February 5. Charlotte Jacobson was the main speaker, David Breslau chaired the conference sessions, and Esther Zackler was elected the AACI's new president. As honorary president, I was asked to distribute the annual Henrietta Szold awards to Rabbis Theodore Friedman, Richard Hirsch, and Mordecai Kirshblum and to Avraham Schenker, the American members of the Jewish Agency Executive; to Rabbi Emanuel Rackman, president of Bar-Ilan University; and, posthumously, to Ezra Z. Shapiro, the late world chairman of the Keren Hayesod. His widow, Sylvia, accepted the citation. Well over 40,000 Olim have come to Israel from the United States and Canada, and the AACI has played a helpful role in easing the adjustment and integration problems of many Olim over the years.

Two weeks later, on February 20, the 29th Zionist Congress began its deliberations at Binyanei ha-Umah in Jerusalem. Prime Minister Menaḥem Begin addressed the opening session. The political composition of Israel's new Government, dominated by the Likud alliance of the Ḥerut and Liberal parties, was reflected in a changed balance of forces at this Congress. Arye Leon Dultzin, who had served for a number of years as treasurer of the World Zionist and Jewish Agency Executives, replaced Yosef Almogi as chairman of the WZO. A new personality in the Executive was Akiva Lewinsky of Bank Ha-Poalim, who succeeded Dultzin as treasurer.

The elections to the new Zionist Executive produced an interesting constellation of forces. The Likud gained six seats, our Confederation and Labor four each, Mizraḥi-Ha-Po'el Ha-Mizraḥi three, the World Sephardi Federation and the newly affiliated Orthodox, Conservative, and Reform groups two each, and Mapam, WIZO, and Maccabi one each. As a result, our World Confederation of United Zionists—represented by Charlotte Jacobson, Kalman Sultanik, Faye Schenk, and Dr. Avraham Avi-ḥai—emerged as the second largest grouping in the Diaspora. For this success, credit was due mainly to the strength of Hadassah in the U.S. and to Kalman Sultanik's organizational work in other parts of the world.

At the session that took place on February 26, the first part of the evening was devoted to addresses in memory of members of the World Zionist Executive who had passed away since the previous Congress. Moshe Rivlin, chairman of the KKL Directorion, paid tribute to Zalman Shazar, Louis A. Pincus, and Pinḥas Sapir, while it was my sad privilege to memorialize Eliyahu Dobkin, Ezra Shapiro, Avraham Ciegel, and Rose Halprin. The second part of that same evening was given over to a discussion of Israel's social problems. The speakers were Deputy Prime Minister Yigael Yadin and Actions Committee Chairman Itzḥak Navon.

We took Raḥel Yannait Ben-Zvi to another evening session, when a symposium on "The Jewish People and Zionism" took place. The panel comprised Philip Klutznick, president of the World Jewish Congress, Melvin Dubinsky, the "non-Zionist" treasurer of the expanded Jewish Agency, David Blumberg, president of B'nai B'rith, Baron Alain de Rothschild, president of the Conseil Représentatif des Juifs de France (CRIF), Nessim Gaon, president of the World Sephardi Federation, Lord Samuel Fisher of Camden, chairman of the Board of Deputies of British Jews, Rabbi Alexander Schindler, president of the Conference of Presidents of Major Jewish Organizations in the U.S., and Dr. Yosef Burg, Minister of the Interior and spokesman for the Government of Israel. An address by Israel's former Prime Minister, Golda Meir, brought the evening to a climax. Arye L. Dultzin served as the moderator.

An important step in making the World Zionist Organization truly representative of all segments of the Jewish people was the first appearance and participation of the Conservative and Reform movements in Judaism, represented by the World Council of Synagogues (Conservative) and the World Union for Progressive Judaism (Reform). This development had previously encountered resistance from Orthodox elements in the World Zionist Organization, but their opposition had proved of no avail. Rabbi Theodore Friedman, on behalf of the Conservative group, and Rabbi Richard Hirsch, on behalf of the Reform group, were elected to the World Zionist Executive. They represented the Israeli constituencies of their movements, and Rabbi Friedman was later succeeded by another member of our Conservative synagogue in Jerusalem, Rabbi Hertzel Fishman. The (Orthodox) World Conference of Synagogues and Kehillot gained similar representation.

While the Congress was in session, a luncheon was tendered by the Keren Kayemet Le-Yisrael in honor of Rabbi William Berkowitz, the newly elected president of the American Jewish National Fund, on March 3. I was delighted to join Moshe Rivlin, the KKL's new chairman, in greeting my younger friend and colleague. Rabbi Berkowitz held the presidency of the American JNF for a four-year term, until 1981.

On March 29, Bert and I attended a special program at Yad Ben-Zvi to honor Raḥel Yannait Ben-Zvi, widow of Israel's second President, on the seventieth anniversary of her Aliyah. She was then in her early nineties, but still remarkably alert and vigorous. Mordecai Ish-Shalom, the chairman of Yad Ben-Zvi and Jerusalem's onetime Mayor, presided and a lecture describing the Yishuv seventy years earlier was delivered by Professor Yisrael Kollat. At one time, Bert had worked with Raḥel Yannait at her agricultural training farm near Jerusalem. We both admired her greatly as a model pioneering ḥalutzah whose enthusiasm had remained fresh throughout the years. Her death in the spring of 1980 plunged all of Israel into mourning.

In succession to Professor Ephraim Katzir, Itzḥak Navon was elected Israel's fifth President on April 29, 1978. Himself a member of the Labor Alignment, Navon also drew considerable support from other Knesset factions. I had come to know him well in recent years as chairman of the Zionist General Council, and both Bert and I were well acquainted with his beautiful and talented wife, Ophira.

While spending the week of Passover at two kibbutzim in the Galilee region, together with our granddaughter, Joyce Olum, we found ourselves in Presidential company. First, at Kfar Blum, we ran into Professor Ephraim Katzir and his family and then, at Gesher ha-Ziv, we encountered the Navons. It seemed characteristic of Israel that these Presidential families were able to move about quietly among their fellow countrymen.

Ephraim Katzir had served Israel well, even though he had not been as seasoned as his predecessors in Jewish matters. In the Weizmann tradition, he had come to the Presidency from the world of science. In the tradition of Ben-Zvi and Shazar, he had maintained Bet ha-Nasi, the President's House, as a cultural center. Warm-hearted and blessed with an even temperament, he made a serious effort to familiarize himself with the problems affecting all segments of the population in Israel and to achieve a rapport with Jews from the Diaspora. Professor Katzir lent dignity to his high office. When his term was over, he was glad to resume his important scientific work at the Weizmann Institute in Reḥovot.

Itzḥak Navon stemmed from an entirely different background. A large segment of Israel's population took pride in the new President's Sephardic origins. A man of broad Jewish culture and of considerable literary talent, he had begun his career as a teacher and later, having become one of Ben-Gurion's trusted aides, gained experience in diplomatic and political affairs. His service as chairman of the Zionist Actions Committee for some years had familiarized him with Jewish life in the Diaspora. At the time of his election, Itzḥak Navon was also relatively young, in his early fifties. With these qualifications, it seemed likely that he would be at once a popular and vigorous President of Medinat Yisrael. Thus, every one of Israel's Presidents—Weizmann, Ben-Zvi, Shazar, Katzir, and Navon—has brought his own particular gifts to that high office.

Shortly after his inauguration, I visited President Navon at Bet ha-Nasi and recalled some of my contacts and conversations with David Ben-Gurion. When I referred to my presentation of the Keren Hayesod's golden jubilee medallion to "B-G" in 1970, on which occasion we had spoken of the impact made on Louis D. Brandeis by Ben-Gurion's view of the importance of Akaba (Eilat) to a future Jewish State, the President surprised me by pulling a volume of Ben-Gurion's diaries out of his bookshelf and showing me the page where this episode is recorded. I could not help being impressed.

Several events of importance to the Israel Interfaith Committee took place in 1978. The first was a brief visit to Israel soon after Passover by Archbishop George Appleton of London. A liberal-minded churchman, he had served at one time as one of the Interfaith Committee's honorary chairmen and was now pleased to spend an afternoon in our home with some of his former Rainbow Group colleagues. Among those present during our discussion, which ranged over the field of ecumenical relations, were Rabbi Jack Cohen, Shalom Ben-Chorin, Dr. Bernard Resnikoff, the Reverend Dr. Coos Schoneveld, Father Joseph Stiassny, and Mrs. Zwi Werblowsky.

Archbishop Appleton recalled that ours was the first home in Jerusalem he and his wife had visited after their arrival in March 1969. I remembered having gone to meet them at Lod Airport and greeting him with the words: "Theodor Herzl called this *Altneuland*, and we welcome you as an old-new friend of this Old-New Land."

He was hopeful that the Vatican might play a useful role in connection with the Arab-Jewish conflict. This thought came to my mind again at another meeting of the Israel Interfaith Committee that year, when the new secretary of the Vatican Commission on Relations with the Jews made the significant statement that Christian contacts with the Jewish people must necessarily pass through the State of Israel. The relations between Judaism and the Roman Catholic Church were something special, he said, and quite distinct from those of any other faith. The body he represented maintained contacts with the World Jewish Congress, B'nai B'rith, the Synagogue Council of America, and the Chief Rabbis of several important Jewish communities.

Peace and Security

Meanwhile, the new direction being taken by another relationship—that between Israel and Egypt—in no way lessened Arab hostility elsewhere in the Middle East. If anything, Palestinian violence against Israelis and Jews became increasingly desperate and ferocious. In March 1978, a PLO terrorist attack on unarmed civilians returning by bus from Haifa to Tel Aviv left thirty-seven dead and eighty-two wounded. Israeli security forces killed six of the murder gang and captured two others. As a result of this new bloodbath, the Israel Defense Forces were to mount the Litani Operation, in the course of which *Tzahal* destroyed a number of terrorist bases in South Lebanon and temporarily occupied sensitive areas north of the border with Israel.

Other Arab terrorist attacks followed. In May, the victims were El Al passengers at Orly Airport in Paris; in August, two El Al employees were killed and seven wounded in a further outrage in London. Well-informed sources later identified a senior Arab diplomat in the British capital as the man acting as paymaster for PLO agents who had murdered not only Israelis but also two Arab moderates, one of them a former Jordanian Prime Minister.

On May 8, 1978, Yom Ha-Atzma'ut was celebrated in Israel's cities, towns, and villages. Independence Day observances included, as usual, services of thanksgiving in synagogues, official receptions, the International Bible Contest for Jewish Youth, the Israel Song Festival, and the ceremony at which the year's Israel Prizes are awarded for outstanding achievement in the fields of education and culture, public service, medicine, and Jewish scholarship.

This year, however, marked the thirtieth anniversary of Medinat Yisrael. One sign of the times was the participation of Christian villagers from southern Lebanon in the Yom Ha-Atzma'ut festivities held at Metullah. The outstanding event, an open-air concert given by the Israel Philharmonic Orchestra under the baton of Zubin Mehta, took place in the Sultan's Pool area below the Old City walls of Jerusalem. The soloists—Isaac Stern (violin), Mstislav Rostropovich (cello), Jean-Pierre Rampal (flute), and Leontyne Price (contralto)—were, like the conductor, all supreme in their respective musical skills. Those of us whose privilege it was to attend this concert were inspired by such an assemblage of personalities and talents. It is surely no accident that little Israel has proved to be a magnet attracting the world's artistic and creative spirits.

Another special Independence Day event was a symposium held at the Truman Research Center of the Hebrew University on Mount Scopus. Appropriately, this symposium took place in the hall named for Professor Milton Handler, a distinguished New York lawyer and friend of the university, who had played an important role as legal adviser to the American Zionist Emergency Council during the years of our political struggle to win U.S. Government support for the establishment of a Jewish commonwealth in Palestine. The participants in this symposium included Avraham Harman, president of the Hebrew University, Nathaniel E. Goldstein, former Attorney General of the State of New York, Dr. Eliahu Elath, the Jewish Agency's first political representative in New York and Israel's first ambassador to the U.S., "Si" Kenen, executive director of the American Jewish Conference during the pre-State era, U.S. Ambassador Samuel Lewis, Professor Moshe Davis, and Yigal Allon. Owing to a cold, I was unable to appear as scheduled, but my paper on President Harry S. Truman was included in the printed record of this symposium.

Israel's thirtieth anniversary was also celebrated on a grand scale throughout the Diaspora. An estimated one million people attended the festivities in New York, and in London a giant "Twelve Hours for Israel" extravaganza, with Moshe Dayan as the main speaker, attracted vast crowds to the Earls Court Exhibition Hall.

In May, there were several other developments of major Jewish significance. Jews were then emigrating from the Soviet Union at the rate of over 1,000 per month and, of the 150,000 who had left the USSR since June 1967, 125,000 had come to Israel. At the same time, however, a number of Zionist activists had become new *Asiré Tziyyon*, "Prisoners of Zion," in the Soviet Union, having been sentenced to long terms of imprisonment in labor camps for "anti-Soviet activities" and "hooliganism."

A meeting of the Governing Board of the World Jewish Congress took place in Tel Aviv, with Lord Fisher of Camden presiding at the opening session. The WJC reaffirmed World Jewry's feeling of solidarity with Medinat Yisrael. Max Fisher, the non-Zionist co-chairman of the Jewish Agency, proclaimed: "Today, we are all Zionists."

On May 21, as part of a series of lectures on the political struggle that led to the establishment of Medinat Yisrael, I was invited to address IDF officers taking an orientation course at the Military Academy in Jerusalem. Once before, I had been asked to lecture before such a group. This time, the topic assigned to me was the UN partition resolution of November 29, 1947, and the events that preceded and followed it. With Israel now entering its thirty-first year, such background study seemed useful and timely, especially for the country's Sabra generation.

An important project that came to fruition that same month was the long-awaited Museum of the Jewish Diaspora, Bet ha-Tefutzot, on the campus of Tel Aviv

University. To Dr. Nahum Goldmann went the lion's share of credit both for having planned it and for having raised the funds for its construction. Together with President Ephraim Katzir and Philip Klutznick, Goldmann's successor as president of the World Jewish Congress, Nahum Goldmann participated in the dedication ceremony. A touch of meaningful symbolism was provided by the choice of Rumania's Chief Rabbi, Dr. Moshe Rosen, to affix the mezuzah at the museum's main entrance. Bet ha-Tefutzot has been designed to illustrate the entire panorama of Jewish religious, cultural, economic, and social life in the Diaspora, from the destruction of the Second Temple to the foundation of the Third Jewish Commonwealth in Eretz Yisrael. With its historical dioramas, superb models of famous or exotic synagogues, imaginative use of audiovisual aids, and expanding range of films portraying Jewish community life in all parts of the world, this unique museum is, in its techniques, one of the most advanced of its kind. It has fulfilled the hopes of its planners by drawing large numbers of interested visitors from Israel and abroad.

The summer of 1978 had a twofold significance for Bert and me. It marked the sixtieth anniversary of my public service, beginning with my entry into the rabbinate in 1918. It also marked our sixtieth wedding anniversary. We had been the first couple whose marriage in 1918 was solemnized in Congregation B'nai Jeshurun's new house of worship. It was appropriate, therefore, that this double anniversary should be signalized at our congregation in New York on June 10, the Sabbath preceding Shavu'ot. More than a thousand congregants and friends attended the services, and some families were represented by three generations that had "come under my wing." In his address of welcome, Rabbi William Berkowitz reviewed the high points of my career, paid tribute to Bert's role in it, and delivered an ingenious salutation built around the number 60 in Jewish tradition.

In my response, I offered my own assessment of a six-decade involvement in Jewish and general affairs. Our eighteen years in Israel and the recent thirtieth anniversary of the Medinah prompted a measure of stock-taking and self-criticism in regard to social and political problems besetting the nation, I said, but this Yom Ha-Atzma'ut should also be an occasion for a "Declaration of Interdependence" by Israel and World Jewry:

> *Altneuland* should never become for Jews, whether in Israel or elsewhere, an *"Al-tnay"* land, a conditional commitment. Whatever may be the complexion of Israel's Government, whatever may be its blemishes, whoever may be its political leaders, Medinat Yisrael is the inalienable *Ben Yakir*, the precious child of the Jewish people, to be loved and supported, nurtured and encouraged, and never estranged!
>
> For American Jewry, I believe, Israel is more than an inspiration. It is an indispensable, nourishing vitamin.

I concluded with an oft-repeated theme. Assimilation and intermarriage had reached alarming proportions within the American Jewish community. Three forms of medication could be prescribed for this malady. The synagogue and its religious program was one. Another was a communally supported Jewish education system, providing for the needs of every Jewish child, regardless of the parents' ability or willingness to pay for such education. A third was the strengthening and expansion of rabbinical schools and training colleges for Jewish teachers, so as not to be dependent on Israel for teaching staff. A Jewishly educated laity would be the vitamin needed for the survival of American Jewry.

Yet, with all of these, I declared, there were certain other indispensables for the strategy of meaningful Jewish survival in the U.S. and in other Diaspora lands— "the inspiration of Israel, the vitalizing contact with Israel, the steady concern for Israel, and the moral and material support of Israel."

A few days later, the American Section of the World Zionist Organization and Jewish Agency Executive held a reception for both of us at its offices in New York. Isadore (Itzig) Hamlin, executive vice-chairman of the WZO American Section, was helpful, as always, in the arrangements. Charlotte Jacobson, chairman of the American Section, presided with characteristic efficiency and grace. On behalf of their respective organizations, greetings were extended to us by Rabbi Arthur Hertzberg (American Jewish Congress and World Jewish Congress), Rabbi Saul Teplitz (Synagogue Council of America), Herman L. Weisman (Jewish National Fund and Zionist Organization of America), and Kalman Sultanik (World Confederation of United Zionists). Owing to an attack of laryngitis, my voice had deserted me and Bert read my response.

I recalled what former U.S. President Harry S. Truman had said twenty years earlier in Philadelphia, on the occasion of Israel's tenth anniversary. "Our government," he then asserted, "must make it clear that Israel is not *on* the bargaining table but *at* the bargaining table and a full member of the group of nations in the Middle East. . . . The Arab states will be easier to deal with when they learn that they cannot negotiate Israel out of existence or make any backstairs deals with the Soviet Union or the United States." The Carter Administration's wavering policies during the negotiations between Israel and Egypt in 1978 made Truman's cautionary words all the more significant.

My response also dwelt upon the impressive growth in American Jewish unity around Israel. I noted that the American Section of the Jewish Agency had played an important part in this achievement by enlisting the participation of non-Zionist leaders in the United Israel Appeal. I also urged the commitment to Aliyah "as an indispensable part of a Zionist's life plan," the inclusion of the Aliyah motif in educating the Jewish child, and the cultivation of Hebrew as a vital bond with Israel and with *Klal Yisrael*. My final plea was for a communal commitment to the right of every Jewish child to a full program of Jewish education.

For the seventh time in my career, I was honored with an invitation to deliver a prayer before Congress in Washington, this time on the occasion of my sixtieth anniversary in the American rabbinate. Senator Jacob Javits was instrumental in having this invitation extended to me. My prayer before the U.S. Senate was delivered on June 22, 1978.

After spending the rest of our summer vacation with our family and friends, on the East and West Coasts, Bert and I celebrated the new milestone in our lives with a delightful cruise to Alaska.

Ten years earlier, we had marked our fiftieth wedding anniversary by establishing an annual Prize for Good Citizenship in Jerusalem. Now, on the occasion of our sixtieth anniversary, we published a booklet in Hebrew entitled *Anashim U-Ma'asim Bi-Yerushalayim* ("Jerusalem Personalities and Their Deeds"), which contained the biographies of the twenty men and women who had been awarded the prize during the years 1969–78. Its distinguished author, A. H. Elḥanani, whose favorite theme has been Jerusalem, interviewed every one of the prizewinners before writing their life stories. The booklet, which appeared in time for the tenth prize-award ceremony on October 30, 1978, also contained a foreword by Mayor Teddy Kollek and my own remarks on the occasion of each annual presentation. Much of the credit for the arrangement of these award ceremonies was due to Jerusalem's former Deputy Mayor, Yosef Gadish, who had served as chairman of the committee. He was succeeded in this post by Dr. Jack Karpas, former director of the Hadassah Hospital. Every prizewinner, and the families of those who, alas, were no longer in the land of the living, received a copy of this booklet. It was distributed to libraries and also to a number of schools interested in using it for courses in good citizenship.

An important Zionist event that took place in Jerusalem and Tel Aviv that summer was the annual convention of Hadassah, guided by its able and spirited president, Bernice S. Tannenbaum. It was impressive and encouraging to see these thousands of informed and dedicated American women in action. They have brought to Israel the blessings of medical aid and Zionist self-affirmation, and an extensive Youth Aliyah program, in the splendid tradition of their founder, Henrietta Szold. They constitute the greatest single force in the world today for Jewish service and enlightenment.

A distinguished woman Zionist leader whose demise saddened us was Irma Lindheim. I had first met her nearly sixty years earlier in New York. The daughter of wealthy assimilated Jews and wife of a prominent lawyer, she became an ardent Zionist and served as president of Hadassah and as a vice-president of the ZOA before joining the Labor Zionist movement. In 1933, she left America for Eretz Yisrael and spent the rest of her long life at Kibbutz Mishmar ha-Emek, where she mothered and inspired generations of young Zionists. She died in her ninety-second year. Though unable to attend the funeral at her beloved kibbutz on September 24, I sent a message eulogizing this remarkable woman, who had lived to see her people's and her own highest fulfillment in Medinat Yisrael.

Shortly thereafter, an announcement was made by the committee of judges in Scandinavia that it had decided to award the Nobel Peace Prize jointly to President Anwar Sadat of Egypt and to Prime Minister Menaḥem Begin of Israel. The peace treaty between the two countries would not be signed until 1979, but it had already become clear that the process begun in Jerusalem in November 1977 would not be reversed.

A simultaneous award was that of the Nobel Prize for Literature to Isaac Bashevis

Singer, the American-domiciled Yiddish novelist. He was the first writer in Yiddish to receive such international recognition and only the second (after the Hebrew novelist, Shai Agnon) to be honored for Jewish literary achievements. Bashevis Singer has successfully recreated the world of Eastern European Jewry prior to the Nazi Holocaust, imbuing it with elements of mystery, mysticism, and even eroticism.

The revival of interest in both Yiddish language and Yiddish literature undoubtedly owes much to the general upsurge of interest in ethnic roots, as well as to the specifically Jewish impact of the *Sho'ah*. One outcome of this recent development has been a sentimental hankering for the Yiddish language, evidenced by the establishment of chairs in Yiddish literature at a number of American universities.

In Israel, this Yiddish revival is especially noteworthy, in view of the *Kulturkampf* that raged two generations ago, when modern Hebrew was struggling to achieve hegemony in the life of the Yishuv. Today, after the catastrophe that overtook the Jews and their culture in Eastern Europe, there is no ideological resistance to Yiddish. On the contrary, one senses a favoring atmosphere. For my part, I would like to see a concerted effort in Israel's academic circles to foster interest in Yiddish language and literature as a means of enriching our cultural heritage and of weaving a further spiritual-cultural bond with a major component of the Yishuv that has played so vital and pioneering a role in the restoration of Jewish national independence.

On December 8, 1978, Golda Meir died in Jerusalem. The sense of bereavement was universal in Israel and throughout the Jewish world. Next to David Ben-Gurion, Golda had been the nation's most outstanding and forceful personality. She displayed strength, wisdom, and Jewish pride in every post she held—as political secretary of the Jewish Agency before and after the establishment of the State, as Israel's first ambassador to the Soviet Union, Minister of Labor, and Foreign Minister, and finally, at the age of seventy-one, when she succeeded Levi Eshkol as Prime Minister. She was one of the very few women who attained such high office in any country.

Tributes to her memory poured in, not only from the leaders of Israel's political parties but also from heads of state abroad, including U.S. President Jimmy Carter and Egyptian President Anwar Sadat. In deference to Golda Meir's own request, however, there were no eulogies at the funeral, which took place on December 12. After some 100,000 people had filed past her coffin outside the Knesset, a simple burial service was held on Mount Herzl in the presence of President and Mrs. Navon, the Chief Rabbis, and some 300 leading mourners. U.S. Secretary of State Cyrus Vance, his predecessor, Dr. Henry Kissinger, and former British Prime Minister and Labor Party leader Sir Harold Wilson were prominent among the overseas personalities who came to pay their last respects.

During the funeral service, I stood alongside Mrs. Lillian Carter, who represented her son, the President of the United States.

Several of Golda's epigrammatic remarks sprang to my mind. "There should be some place on earth where there is a Jewish majority," she once said. "As a minority, we have quite a history." When some questioned Israel's ability to survive, she revealed "our secret weapon: *En Brerah*, No Alternative."

Prime Minister Menaḥem Begin had recalled Golda Meir's role as "Israel's spokesman before the nations of the world" and Opposition leader Shim'on Peres hailed her as "a proud Jewess, absolutely convinced of the justice of her cause." Deputy Prime Minister Yigael Yadin, in his tribute, had likened her to Deborah, the stern prophetess of Israel in the era of the biblical Judges. Yet there was also a warmth in her character that ignited the first mass expression of Jewish sentiment among Soviet Jews when she appeared in Moscow as Israel's first envoy to the USSR. The Yom Kippur War depressed her in spirit; she never recovered from the ordeal of 1973 and its cost to Israel in human lives. Yet Golda's uncompromising Zionism, her view of Jewish destiny, and the defiance that enabled her to triumph over adversity made her the queen of Jewish womanhood in her time.

A convocation of the Israel Interfaith Committee and several associated organizations took place on December 28, at the Van Leer Institute in Jerusalem, to mark the twentieth anniversary of the Interfaith Committee's founding assembly in 1958. The participants included Professor Benjamin Mazar, a former president of the Hebrew University, and Dr. Simon Agranat, former president of the Israel Supreme Court, both of whom had played an important part in bringing the Committee into existence. It was my privilege to chair this session, at which Israel's President, Itzḥak Navon, extended greetings, and to introduce the main speaker, Professor Shlomo Avineri, the former director-general of Israel's Foreign Ministry, who delivered a stimulating address on "Thirty Years of Interfaith Relations in Israel— Toward a Period of Peaceful Relations in the Area."

My opening remarks were devoted to the purposes for which the Committee had been established and to the hopes aroused, for the first time in thirty years, by the possibility of a new era of peaceful coexistence and development in the Middle East. Negotiations between Sadat and Begin seemed to have reached an impasse at the time, but there was a widespread feeling that they would not be stalled for long. Believing that we should be guided by our hopes rather than by our fears, I said:

> Men of faith may be expected to exercise long-range vision. There was a period in Jewish history some centuries ago when a Golden Age of literature and science resulted from Jewish-Arab cultural relations in Egypt and in Spain. Is it too much to hope that in an era of peace between ourselves and our neighbors—especially our largest and most advanced neighbor, Egypt—cultural contacts and exchanges may once again lead to cultural efflorescence for both?

A good example of ecumenical scholarship and interfaith collaboration was the new French translation of the Hebrew Bible and New Testament by Dr. André Chouraqui, Jerusalem's former Deputy Mayor. It appeared in twenty-six volumes. On its completion, a reception was held in Dr. Chouraqui's honor, at the President's House, on March 2, 1979. Bert and I were happy to attend. With the assistance of eminent Jewish and Christian theologians, Dr. Chouraqui had produced for the modern French reader a Bible that was more faithful to the original than any of its predecessors. He had been awarded the gold medal of the Académie Française, and we rejoiced in his success.

Late into the night of March 21, I sat watching the televised Knesset debate on the terms of the proposed peace treaty with Egypt. Both on the far left and on the far right, voices were raised against the treaty, but Prime Minister Begin secured overwhelming support for his proposals. Some members of his own Ḥerut Party clearly regarded it as a betrayal of hallowed Revisionist principles, and Israeli interests, in return for "a scrap of paper." I subscribed to the view that Begin proved himself to be a courageous patriot and statesman, who dared to modify old political slogans and to call for a great gesture of faith by his countrymen, when historic opportunity beckoned.

On Monday, March 26, 1979, as the Israel-Egypt Peace Treaty was about to be signed in Washington, a festive—though by no means exuberant—atmosphere prevailed throughout the Medinah. Israel had to pay a high price for this break-through: the surrender of irreplaceable oil fields, a phased withdrawal from the vital defense positions in Sinai and the dismantling of flourishing new settlements there, the promise of autonomy for the Arabs in Judea and Samaria (the "West Bank") and Gaza, and a still undefined status for East Jerusalem. In Egypt, the atmosphere was even more restrained. Almost the entire Arab and Muslim world, supported by the USSR, was arrayed against Anwar Sadat, who must have gambled his very life on this bold step.

At 9:00 P.M., Israel time, live television and radio broadcasts relayed the ceremony on the White House lawn where the treaty was initialed. President Jimmy Carter deserved his hour of glory for his share in this achievement. Our thoughts and prayers went out to the two other leaders as well, and to the peoples of the three countries involved.

There were unseen guests at the celebrations that took place in Israel and throughout the Jewish world. We were bound to remember all those young Israelis whose supreme sacrifice in the nation's wars and recurrent battles had made it possible for Medinat Yisrael to endure. Nor could we forget our previous heads of government—Ben-Gurion, Sharett, Eshkol, Golda Meir, and Rabin—who steered the ship of state through troubled waters, and all whose leadership ensured that Israel's democracy would emerge unshaken from every strain and stress.

Israel's mass media took proper note of these many tangibles and intangibles, from the toll of lives in 1948 to the most recent losses and from the role of the founding fathers to the overstrained national economy. Nevertheless, I detected a certain insensitivity to the part played by the World Zionist Organization and by Israel's army of friends and supporters in the Diaspora—"Zionists" and "non-Zionists"—in bringing the Third Jewish Commonwealth into being and in nursing it during the first tender years. Perhaps I was expecting too much of a young, thirty-year-old State preoccupied with its own history and contemplating its own future.

One could not help noticing the contrast between the buoyancy of the Israelis and the audible reticence of the Egyptians. This was, of course, understandable.

Whereas the hitherto beleaguered Israelis could see a door being unlocked before them, the Egyptians were beginning to feel a degree of isolation in the Arab world. One also had to make allowance, perhaps, for a difference in temperament. It was almost pathetic to see the eagerness with which Israeli commentators anticipated rapid developments in the fields of cultural exchange, scientific cooperation, economics, and tourism. All of this shed light on the immense strain that decades of estrangement and hostility had imposed upon a people of world-embracing cultural and spiritual horizons.

One could not help wondering, however, whether the Egyptians altogether welcomed such enthusiastic solicitation. It might be more realistic to gird oneself for a considerable letdown when the implementation of the peace treaty would wrest painful concessions from Israel and when the public would have to face the more controversial and worrying aspects of the new dispensation.

Only one thing was certain. The epoch unfolding before us would call for a combination of steady nerves and imaginative planning. It would inevitably be a time of testing for the Government and the people of Israel.

On April 2, Prime Minister Begin left for further discussions in Cairo. The swiftness with which Israelis had adjusted to the new situation, even before it had assumed definite shape, was amazing. Some of the plans and projects mooted at the time have since become a reality, such as tourism and cultural visits, although most of this traffic has come from the Israeli side. My diary records the thoughts that passed through my mind a week after the signing of the peace treaty:

> What a dazzling series of history-making events we Jews are being subjected to—Sadat's visit to Jerusalem, Camp David, the Knesset's ratification of the Peace Treaty, the final ceremony in Washington, and now the Prime Minister's trip to Egypt! It is almost too much to digest in so short a span of time.
>
> These are revolutionary developments. Could the fathers of Medinat Yisrael ever have imagined that all of this would occur thirty years after Israel was born in fire and blood, and only six years after the Yom Kippur War?
>
> I murmur "Sheheḥeyanu" every morning as I read the paper or listen to the latest news bulletin. It is a zekhut to be alive at such a time and to have witnessed such events.

Perhaps this feeling of exaltation would wear off as the exciting novelty of Israel-Egyptian non-belligerence encountered the frustrating obstacles and irritations that the process of implementation was bound to engender. If such changes of mood should occur (and, by the beginning of 1982, there was already a more tense atmosphere in Israel as the date of the final withdrawal from Sinai approached), I prayed that we might prove capable of the necessary readjustments and that we would remain alive to the significance of the fundamental reorientation that had taken place in Israel's relations with its largest and most prominent Arab neighbor.

These feelings were expressed at a gathering held on May 16, 1979, to mark the tenth anniversary of the Chair in the History of Zionism and the New Yishuv, established in my name at the Hebrew University. I paid tribute to Professor Yisrael

Kolatt, the incumbent of the chair, to Professor Moshe Davis, the former head of the Hebrew University's Institute of Contemporary Jewry, and to his successor, Professor Yehudah Bauer, as well as to the university's vice-president, Bernard Cherrick, who was also present and in whose name a chair in Jewish history had recently been established. After mentioning the significant political events and the change in Zionist climate that had taken place since 1969, when "my" chair was set up, I looked forward to the day "when there will be an Egyptian student in this Institute studying the history of Zionism and the New Yishuv" and facetiously added, "You see, I wish myself a long life!" On a more serious note, I recommended a greater degree of collaboration among the three university faculties—in Jerusalem, Tel Aviv, and Haifa—which fostered the study of Zionism.

On September 21, the eve of Rosh Hashanah, Bert and I made a special point of visiting Professor and Mrs. Mordecai M. Kaplan, to extend our greetings for the New Year 5740. My revered teacher was in his ninety-ninth year, physically bent, but with his spirit unbent and his mind as clear as a bell.* While his wonderful wife, Rivkah, was showing Bert some of her lovely paintings, I began a dialogue with Professor Kaplan, who dwelt on his favorite subject, the Reconstructionist philosophy of Judaism. I kept bringing him back, however, to Israel's ethical, moral, and social problems, which were troubling me. It distressed me to think that general decline in standards of behavior and in Israel's quality of life might obliterate the ḥalutzic image and ideal.

My period of service as treasurer of the Jewish Agency in 1948–49 had made me familiar with some of the contributing factors—unrestricted immigration, primitive absorption facilities in the early years of the Medinah, the uphill fight to integrate Jews from backward societies in a modern environment, overcrowded living conditions, and a shortage of suitable housing for large families in the lower income brackets. Many of Israel's current social ills stemmed from those appalling, albeit wonderful, times.

Latterly, however, other factors had contributed to the erosion of private and public standards in Israeli life. I mentioned the spirit of acquisitiveness and materialism that had infiltrated from abroad and the lack of confidence in Israel's future, which prompted many to seek quick profits in an unstable economy or to live beyond their means. All of these phenomena clashed with the Jewish and general principles and ideals with which the dreamers and builders of Zion had approached the era of Medinat Yisrael.

As I thought aloud, Professor Kaplan listened patiently and then said, "I couldn't agree with you more."

Thus encouraged, I went on to speak of the urgent need for moral leadership in our own day. There were two or three personalities in contemporary Israel who radiated light and attracted a group of disciples, but their influence was limited. In the recent past, both Rav Kook and Martin Buber had lifted a banner, yet they had failed to touch the masses. Ben-Gurion was a practical idealist, but too often

*On Mordecai M. Kaplan, see chapter 17.

acrimony and polemics tarnished the credentials of Israel's statesman-prophet. Israelis and Zionists abroad must work together to make Israel a beacon to World Jewry and "a light to the nations," I concluded, ending my monologue.

By October 1979, I was putting the finishing touches to my book, *Jewish Justice and Conciliation*. Essentially, this told the story of the Jewish Conciliation Board of America during the years of my presidency, from 1930 to 1968, which I regard as having constituted a significant aspect of my Jewish public service in the United States. The history of this tribunal was, in my view, also important for an under-standing of the evolving New York Jewish community. A review of Jewish juridical autonomy through the ages forms an introductory section. The major portion of the volume describes the workings of the Jewish Conciliation Board, the hearings of the cases, and the role of the social-service department. The supplementary appendices contain addresses by Supreme Court Justice William O. Douglas and others, an-niversary greetings by leaders in American public life, and the script of an *Eternal Light* radio program, as well as lists of officers, judges, and patrons. The book was published in New York, by Ktav, in March 1981.

As every author knows, there is a special satisfaction in getting out a book. This is especially so when the author is one whose main occupation and preoccupation has been the spoken word. For better or worse, the written word endures.

Some Varied Events

My life in Jerusalem has not been lacking in an occasional dramatic incident. On the evening of Thursday, January 24, 1980, Bert went to a concert at the Jerusalem Theater, not far from our home, and I remained alone in the house. At about 10:00 P.M., the doorbell rang. When I incautiously opened the door slightly to see who the caller was, two men in stocking masks forced their way in. One of them, holding a revolver to my head, pushed me against the wall and demanded money. I took out my wallet, which contained a few thousand Israeli Pounds (about $50), and handed it over. Much to my relief, the intruders then left after disconnecting the telephone.

As soon as they had gone, I went to the downstairs telephone and called the police. A patrol car arrived almost immediately and I gave the best description I could of my assailants. The police investigators were efficient; by the following morning, they had rounded up the two culprits, who turned out to be youths, age seventeen, as well as a number of others who had been responsible for various burglaries. The two youngsters identified as my assailants were remanded for trial, but my wallet was not recovered.

This incident made quite a story in the Israel press. It was also featured in a New York Jewish weekly, under the headline, "Jerusalem Like All Other Cities." Re-senting the imputation in this headline, I wrote a letter to the editor in which I traced the following course of events.

A few days after the robbery, the mother of one of the arrested boys telephoned to say that she and the other boy's mother would like to come to our home in order to return the money stolen and to apologize for what had occurred. I readily agreed to see them. When they arrived the following day, they not only returned the stolen cash but also brought a huge *sulḥah* (forgiveness) cake, which we later gave away. I made some inquiries about the family background of the two young offenders. What I learned was not favorable.

Next day, the social worker active in their neighborhood called at our home and told me that the youngsters now wished to send me a letter of apology. I said that I would be glad to receive it. When the letter arrived, I wrote in reply that it was not simply a matter of my forgiving them for what they had done. Their offense had also marred the good name of Jerusalem. Since they were young, they could still turn over a new leaf and, if they would make a determined effort and grow up to be good citizens of Jerusalem, forgiveness would be theirs automatically.

The two offenders subsequently received a two-year jail sentence, which was later reduced to six months in view of their good behavior. One of the youths came to see me after his release, accompanied by the social worker, and told me that he was going to join a kibbutz.

"So Jerusalem is *not* like all other cities," I concluded.

Soon after Purim, at the beginning of March, it was my privilege to address the Keren Hayesod's sixtieth jubilee gathering in Antwerp. With the recently celebrated festival in mind, I spoke of the grave danger posed by a modern Haman—the Ayatollah Khomeini—in present-day Persia, Iran. Then, without referring to Chief Rabbi Immanuel Jakobovits of Great Britain by name, I attacked the view "enunciated recently by a religious spokesman in the Diaspora" that if he knew Jews and Arabs "could not come to some accommodation within fifteen years, it would be better for us to liquidate the State of Israel now." Such speculations, I declared, could only be of service to our enemies. "It was a stauncher mettle of Zionism which went ahead with the proclamation of our Medinah at a time when the Yishuv was a beleaguered minority, exposed on all sides to murderous attacks."

That thought came to mind once again a fortnight later, on March 17, when I delivered my annual presidential address before the Association of Americans and Canadians in Israel. This 1980 convention of the AACI, graced by the presence of the U.S. and Canadian ambassadors, took place in Ma'alot, the development town in Upper Galilee where PLO infiltrators had murdered defenseless Israeli schoolchildren in 1974. I could not resist linking our venue with apt texts in Psalms 120–34, which all bear the superscription, *Shir ha-Ma'alot,* "A Song of Ascents" (or "of the Steps"). During the past year, I said, the AACI had taken important steps forward in the interests of Aliyah and Klitah. After paying tribute to Charlotte Jacobson, chairman of the American Section of the Jewish Agency Executive, who had secured substantial assistance from the Agency for carrying out this program, I took occasion to commend Mrs. Esther Zackler, outgoing president of the AACI, for her energetic and progressive administration. I concluded my remarks with a quotation from Psalm 121, which is entitled *Shir la-Ma'alot,* "A Song *to* Ma'alot."

At about this time, I received a telephone call one day from Eliezer Dembitz, informing me that a ceremony would take place on June 3 at the Mount of Olives cemetery in Jerusalem to mark the fortieth *Yahrzeit* of the passing of his father,

Arthur David Dembitz. The invitation he extended to say a few words at the graveside touched a sentimental chord in me and I readily accepted.

Seventy years earlier, Arthur Dembitz had been my teacher in Jewish history at Gratz College, Philadelphia. He taught this subject with infectious enthusiasm. Among those who studied under him were some who later achieved prominence in the rabbinate and in Jewish educational and communal leadership. All of us were united in our affectionate regard for this outstanding teacher and steadfast, lovable Jew. At the memorial ceremony, I also made mention of the Dembitz family's distinguished contribution to American Jewish life. Arthur's father, Lewis Dembitz, had been a prominent lawyer in Louisville, Kentucky, who had used his scholarly talents to promote the cause of traditional Judaism. His cousin, Justice Louis Dembitz Brandeis, was the venerated jurist and world Zionist leader.

Arthur Dembitz and his wife had left the United States in 1933 to settle in Eretz Yisrael, where they raised their son and daughter. It was his son, Eliezer, who asked me to speak at the *Yahrzeit* observance on the Mount of Olives. He held an important post in the Israel Ministry of Justice and adhered to the Orthodox tradition of his late father.

Another event in June was that year's final meeting of the Rainbow Group, which took place in our home. The Reverend Father Francis Furlong presided. Regretfully, we bade farewell to the Reverend Dr. J. (Coos) Schoneveld, who had given years of dedicated service to the Rainbow Group as its secretary, to the Israel Interfaith Committee, and to the Ecumenical Theological Research Fraternity in Israel. He was leaving to become secretary of the World Council of Churches in Heppenheim, Germany, where the onetime home of the late Martin Buber now serves as its office.

To open the meeting, I was asked to read a Psalm and did so in Hebrew, using a Bible in my library that had been printed by the famous Antwerp typographer and publisher, Christophe Plantin, in 1573. This Hebrew Bible once belonged to the Reverend Thomas Shepard, an early patron of Harvard College, and may have been brought to New England by one of the Pilgrim Fathers. Inscribed on the flyleaf are some verses written on July 7, 1853, by the Reverend William Jenks, one of Shepard's descendants, in praise of the holy tongue. I cannot resist quoting these lines:

> Disciple of the Lord, who to His cause
> Would'st give thy life and labor, or dost seek
> In piety to grow, study His Laws
> Not in translations merely; but . . . at the fountain-head;
> Drink the pure waters of eternal love:
> For streams may grow corrupt, as often made
> To bear what flows not from the fount above. . .

After the conclusion of this meeting, I had a nostalgic chat with the Reverend William W. Simpson of London, a former secretary of the British Council of Christians and Jews. We reminisced about the time when we had worked together in establishing the International Conference of Christians and Jews at Oxford in 1946.

The cause of interreligious understanding in Israel suffered a grievous blow in the last week of May with the passing of the Reverend Dr. G. Douglas Young, a Baptist minister and scholar who was the founding president of the Holy Land Bible Institute on Mount Zion. He was also one of the founders of the Rainbow Group and a leading spirit in the Israel Interfaith Committee.

"A Gentile with the heart of a Jew," as Calvin Hanson, his biographer, dubbed him, Douglas Young received his doctoral degree at Dropsie College. Together with his wife, Georgina, he settled in Jerusalem at about the same time as Bert and myself. The institute he founded did not admit Jewish students, lest it be accused of harboring missionary intentions. His love for the Jewish people and his Christian Zionism were rooted in a profound biblical faith. He made frequent visits to the United States, where he addressed Christian and Jewish audiences and countered anti-Israel propaganda. Back home in Jerusalem, he was a volunteer ambulance driver during the Six-Day War of 1967 and relieved Jewish friends of Civil Guard duty on Friday evenings so that they could attend synagogue and enjoy a restful Shabbat with their families. After his retirement from the presidency of the Holy Land Bible Institute, Dr. Young devoted much of his time to "Bridges for Peace," informing Christians of theological errors concerning the Jewish people and adducing biblical evidence for the need to support Medinat Yisrael. The title of *Yakir Yerushalayim* was conferred upon him in 1978. I found in him a kindred spirit with whom any interfaith problem could be discussed with candor and confidence.

It was a joyful day for us when our granddaughter, Joyce, who had been teaching in Jerusalem and Beersheba, became engaged to Philippe Galaski, a Jerusalemite. They came to have a Shabbat eve dinner with us on June 20, when our other guests were Elmer Winter, a former president of the American Jewish Committee, and Dr. Carl Voss, the biographer of Rabbi Stephen S. Wise and the Reverend John Haynes Holmes. Carl Voss and I recalled the days when we were fighting to win over American public opinion for a Jewish State in Palestine and when he helped us greatly in the mustering of Christian support. Elmer Winter told us about his efforts to interest American Jewish businessmen in establishing or joining various business enterprises in Israel. He also urged me to start a course for typists and secretaries at our Jerusalem Youth Village, offering to supply all the proper equipment. Elmer Winter is typical of those "non-Zionists" who give unflagging, devoted support to the Medinah. Later that evening, the Reverend Douglas Huneke, chaplain of the University of Oregon, also came to see us. A student of the Holocaust period, he was in Israel to do some research at Yad Vashem.

On the following night, our World Confederation of United Zionists met at the Hilton Hotel, where a reception for the delegates was hosted by Dr. Avraham Avihai, chairman of the Keren Hayesod. This meeting preceded the opening session of the Zionist General Council on Sunday evening, June 22, at which an address was delivered by President Itzhak Navon. He emphasized the positive aspects of Israel and Israeli life. This, he said, was important because the newspapers gave undue emphasis and coverage to negative manifestations.

An important event at my Jerusalem Youth Village on June 26 was the dedication of Ohel Ze'ev, the library named in memory of the Village's founder-director, Ze'ev

Schickler. Shai Kreutner, chairman of the committee responsible for its establishment, presided at the exercises, which were attended by many guests from Israel and abroad. They included members of the Schickler family, Moshe Kol, Charlotte Jacobson, Faye Schenk, and Kalman Sultanik of the World Zionist Executive, and a large delegation of Hadassah women headed by Bernice Tannenbaum. She, together with Mrs. Esther Ghitis of Milan, Mr. Kol, and myself, were among the speakers at this ceremony.

That same evening, the closing session of the Zionist General Council was addressed by Prime Minister Menaḥem Begin and by Max Fisher, co-chairman of the Jewish Agency. Begin criticized the U.S. and other Western nations for arming states bent on destroying Israel and upheld the right of Jews to settle anywhere within Israel's present borders. He also stressed his view of autonomy for the Arabs living in areas beyond the "Green Line," as meaning administrative autonomy (in accordance with the Camp David Agreement), the security and defense of those areas necessarily remaining in Israel's hands. Begin's vigorous presentation certainly belied rumors about his state of health.

Max Fisher reiterated his new theme, "We are all Zionists." As long as Zionism did not pledge the Zionist to Aliyah, I reflected, Max Fisher was no less entitled to call himself a Zionist than any acknowledged leader of the Zionist movement who had no intention of quitting the *Golah*.

There was active participation by the "non-Zionist" members in the meeting of the board of governors of the enlarged Jewish Agency, which followed the Actions Committee. An important item on the board's agenda was the urban-renewal project, inaugurated two years earlier with the strong endorsement of Prime Minister Begin. Unfortunately, "Project Renewal" had barely gotten off the ground because of the lack of administrative coordination between the Jewish Agency and the Israel Government. Deputy Prime Minister Yigael Yadin, who had taken personal charge of this project, was unable to allay the misgivings of his audience. It accorded a better reception to the address of Eliezer Rafaeli, administrator of "Project Renewal," who spoke on behalf of the intended beneficiaries. Rafaeli, whom I first came to know as Haifa University's president, championed the cause of those living in the urban neighborhoods, praising their dignity and hospitality. "We must not regard them as recipients of charitable handouts," he warned. His resignation as administrator underlined the dangers facing "Project Renewal" and the entire Aliyah absorption program in which the Government and the Jewish Agency are jointly involved. There have been far too many administrative bottlenecks.

A welcome visitor at this time was Rabbi Bruce Cohen, the moving force behind the "Interns for Peace" movement, which in recent years has succeeded in enlisting dozens of idealistic young men and women in the United States. It conducts a two-year bicultural training program for those who enroll, teaching them community and social-work skills in the field. The interns live and work in Arab and Jewish community frameworks in Israel, fostering regional cooperation between Jewish and non-Jewish citizens.

Prominent among our visitors in July was Joseph Linton of London, who for many years had been associated with Dr. Chaim Weizmann in the Jewish Agency Executive. After the establishment of the Medinah, he had served as Israel's envoy in Australia and New Zealand, then in Japan and Thailand, and finally as ambassador to Switzerland.

The summer of 1980 was marked by a number of significant events for me. One was the American Jewish Congress sixteenth Annual Dialogue in Israel. It was held at the Van Leer Institute in Jerusalem in mid-July. Each year, this Dialogue brings leading Jewish intellectuals from the United States for the discussion of important issues with their Israeli counterparts. The overall theme of the 1980 Dialogue was "The Right of American Jewry and Israel to Participate in Each Other's Affairs." It dealt with attempts to influence or change each other's political processes, foreign policies, religious life, and socio-moral character.

Among the speakers on the Israeli side were Interior Minister Yosef Burg and former Foreign Minister Abba Eban. Prominent on the American side were Theodore Mann, who had served most recently as head of the Presidents' Conference in the U.S., and his successor, Howard Squadron, an eminent New York lawyer, who was also president of the American Jewish Congress. Theodore Mann's presentation aroused much controversy and attention, since it expressed outspoken criticism of the Begin Government's policies in regard to settlement in the "Occupied Territories," treatment of the Arabs, and other internal policies.

Though scheduled to participate in the Dialogue, I was on the point of leaving for the United States and could not appear. In my paper, which was entered into the record, I made the point that while—both in the religious and in the political spheres—Israel's Government had formulated and implemented policies which many found objectionable, nevertheless, in my view, only those who had cast in their lot with the Jewish State had the moral right publicly to criticize Israel's Government and to urge a change in its composition. "Israelis alone," I said, "are ready to defend their partisanship with their lives and the lives of their children."

On July 17, Bert and I set out on our annual visit to the United States. We stopped off in France en route to spend a few days in Monte Carlo as guests of Mrs. Julia Goldmuntz, a patroness of our Youth Village, to visit the Chagall Museum in Nice, and then to spend a few days in Paris. A new French Chief Rabbi had just been appointed to succeed Rabbi Jacob Kaplan, who, at the age of eighty-five, was retiring. His successor, Rabbi René Samuel Sirat, was of Algerian Jewish descent. He had done much to introduce and promote Hebrew studies in French universities and was a staunch Zionist. We heard enthusiastic opinions about him. Following the influx of Jews from North Africa in recent years, a vigorous and younger element was coming to the fore in French Jewry, strongly supportive of Israel, outspokenly critical of the French Government's unfriendly policies toward Israel, and impatient with the hitherto unchallenged Jewish establishment in France.

From Paris we flew to New York, where I spent some time with Bernard Scharfstein at the Ktav Publishing House, finalizing arrangements for the publication of my book on the Jewish Conciliation Board. A learned preface had been written by Dr. Simon Agranat, retired president of Israel's Supreme Court. There were approbations by Judges Stanley H. Fuld and Simon H. Rifkind of New York, eminent former members of the judiciary. Favorable prepublication comments were received from Professor Mordecai M. Kaplan and Rabbi Louis I. Rabinowitz in Jerusalem, and from Rabbis Robert Gordis, Leo Jung, and Ronald Sobel in New York. But for the fact that Rabbi Gordis was out of town for the summer, I would have sought him out in order to renew a friendship of many years with common denominators in the Jewish Theological Seminary, where he is professor of Bible, and in the American Jewish Congress, where he serves as editor of *Judaism*.

One afternoon, I went to see Rabbi Leo Jung at his office in the Jewish Center. He is the acknowledged doyen of the modern Orthodox rabbinate in New York. I was amazed and delighted to see how, at the age of eighty-eight, Rabbi Jung continued to be actively involved in the Jewish Center and Jewish community life, and in studying, teaching, and writing. We reminisced about bygone years, when we had collaborated in the Jewish Conciliation Board and in other communal endeavors.

While visiting Rabbi Ronald Sobel of Temple Emanu-El, I was pleased to learn that he was working on a history of his congregation and that he had found it useful to consult my book, *A Century of Judaism in New York*. Glancing around the rabbi's study at Temple Emanu-El, I was intrigued by a picture of his grandfather—a distinguished-looking, bearded Jew from Bialystok, White Russia.

Our grandson, Joshua, Avram's son, came from Stanford, California, to visit us while we were in New York. Like many of his generation, he was eager to discover his Jewish roots and to learn more about his antecedents. We were naturally pleased to see this development of his religious and cultural interests. Since we were staying at an East Side hotel far from B'nai Jeshurun, and he was eager to see Temple Emanu-El, I went with him to Sabbath services there. On a weekday, however, I took Joshua with me to our synagogue. He admired the Oriental style of its architecture. I told him about the beginnings of my own career and about my involvement in Zionism and in liberal, social, and economic movements in New York City. Joshua's forthcoming visit to Israel was a major topic of our conversations.

An important cultural event at the time, a highlight of our stay in the metropolis, was the Picasso exhibition at the Museum of Modern Art. The huge crowds that flocked to it provided gratifying evidence of the successful attempt to educate the public in art appreciation. The exhibit itself was a superb reflection of an amazing creative talent in both conventional and unconventional art forms.

Bert and I were fascinated by the proceedings at the Democratic Party convention, which we watched on television. This method of selecting the party's candidate for the forthcoming Presidential elections was an impressive example of democracy in action. It was a scene that could not be reproduced anywhere else in the world— the almost childish ebullience, the staged and the spontaneous demonstrations of support, and, behind the accolades and showmanship, the overwhelming sense of participation in a momentous event, choosing the man to lead America for the next four years. Although President Jimmy Carter won the Democratic nomination, Senator Edward Kennedy was the real hero of the convention, evidencing qualities that left no doubt as to his credentials when the party's next candidate would be chosen four years hence. That impression was inevitably reinforced when Jimmy Carter subsequently lost to Governor Ronald Reagan of California, the Republican nominee, in the Presidential contest.

Our practice of spending about six weeks in the United States each summer, to which I have referred more than once, has been primarily for the purpose of family visits. In addition, however, it has provided occasions for the renewal of ties with Congregation B'nai Jeshurun, its president, Charles H. Silver, Rabbi William Berkowitz and his family, and a few of its members, as well as with rabbinical, Zionist, United Jewish Appeal, and American Jewish Congress colleagues. The roster of friends whom we have invariably visited in New York, and who have often come to see us in Jerusalem, includes a number of kinfolk and congregants.

Among these, we have retained especially close ties with the Leff families— Philip and Lillian and Carl and Eleanor—who play a leading role in New York's Jewish philanthropies and in the UJA. This bond originated with their parents and now includes their children. Professor Milton Handler and his wife, Miriam, are another of our favorite couples. Milton Handler's primary interest in Israel is the Hebrew University of Jerusalem, whose leading advocate he has been in New York through the years, while Miriam has been prominent in the Hadassah leadership and has headed their Hebrew-speaking circle. Also dear to us are the Sincoff-Kogan-Theodore family alliance, headed by Mrs. Ethel Sincoff, and Mr. and Mrs. Michael Singer, leaders in philanthropic and educational projects in New York and in Israel. Michael Singer, a former board chairman of the Albert Einstein College of Medicine, affiliated with Yeshiva University, was awarded the (Israel) Prime Minister's Medal in 1977.

Throughout the years since our Aliyah, we have maintained warm ongoing contact with Phil Slomowitz, noted publisher and editor of the Detroit *Jewish News*, a leading American Jewish weekly which has distinguished itself as one of Israel's most vigorous protagonists.

We also spent a delightful evening with Theodore and Florence Baumritter, enthusiastic patrons of our Youth Village in Jerusalem. We were delighted to learn about the chairs which they and Mrs. Baumritter's brother, Nathan Ancell, formerly chairman of the board of trustees of Haifa University, had established at Brandeis University, Connecticut College, and Yeshiva University. Their grandson was studying for the rabbinate. This is the third instance within our circle of friends where a young man from a family prominent in the business world has been drawn to a rabbinical career. It may well be a sign of the times in which we live, the reaction of sensitive young Jews to contemporary hedonism and materialistic values, combined with the renewed search for Jewish roots.

In a unique category are Julius and Roslyn Silver, for apart from being cousins— doubly so, because Bert and Ros are cousins also—we have many common interests. Julius is actively involved in the Jewish Theological Seminary, New York University, and the Haifa Technion. He was my principal colleague and adviser in the founding of Brandeis University. The visits we pay to Julius, Roslyn, and their daughter, Enid, and theirs to us, are always very special events in our lives.

The highlight of our stay this time was the wedding of our granddaughter, Joyce Olum, in Amherst, Massachusetts, on August 5, 1980. Her brother, Kenneth Akiba, met us at Springfield and escorted us to the hotel in Amherst where accommodation had been reserved for us. The marriage of our granddaughter, a major family event under any circumstances, was especially meaningful since her *ḥatan*, Philippe Galaski, was an Israeli and a Jerusalemite. Joyce had spent the past two years in Israel working as a teacher and in counseling. Her religious leanings were toward the *Ḥavurah* form of worship. She had originally come under the influence of the Hillel rabbi, Sol Roth, at Amherst and the University of Massachusetts. This accounted for her wish that the wedding ceremony be held in Amherst, where she had studied, taught, and formed her closest friendships.

I was happy to take a significant part in the marriage service, which followed the Reconstructionist pattern, with some traditional features, but which also incorporated modernistic touches denoting the equal role of bride and groom. This family *simḥah* at Amherst was a joyous reunion of relatives and friends, which Paul and Vivian, as well as Bert and I, deeply appreciated.

Following our return to New York, I had a breakfast meeting one day with Kalman Sultanik, who told me that he was about to visit South America with Edgar Bronfman, acting president of the World Jewish Congress. I learned from him that Charlotte Jacobson would be retiring in the near future from her position as chairman of the New York Executive of the World Zionist Organization, and that Bernice Tannenbaum, the president of Hadassah, was to succeed her.

The rest of our time was spent in coast-to-coast visits with our children and grandchildren. Our son's daughter, Margaret, was expecting her first child—our first great-grandchild—and we eagerly awaited the event. I visited Margaret and her husband, Brad, at their home in Boulder, Colorado, but had to return to Jerusalem for the High Holy Days of 5741. Bert remained, however, and was thus able to embrace our first great-grandson, who was born on September 21. By the time he is grown up, mankind will be on the threshold of the twenty-first century.

Back home in Jerusalem, I found our grandson, Joshua, awaiting my arrival. He was visiting Israel in the company of Mark Cartun, his Hillel rabbi at Stanford University, who was influencing him in a positive Jewish way and who had found in Joshua not only an earnest follower but also an able assistant. Our grandson was serving as editor of *Hakol,* the Hillel Society's monthly publication. The few days Joshua and I spent together meant much to me and, hopefully, to him also. He has shown leadership qualities and I trust that these may redound to the benefit of his community.

Israel and the Diaspora

The seventh Plenary Assembly of the World Jewish Congress opened in Jerusalem on Sunday, January 18, 1981, at Binyanei ha-Umah. For the first time since the establishment of the WJC, Dr. Nahum Goldmann was not in attendance. He sent a thoughtful message, stressing what he saw as the weaknesses inside Israel, with particular reference to its spiritual and moral climate.

With the resignation of Philip Klutznick, Dr. Goldmann's successor as head of the WJC, who was taking up an important new post as U.S. Secretary of Commerce, Edgar M. Bronfman became acting president. As the elder son of the late Samuel Bronfman of Montreal, Canada, he had grown up in a tradition of Jewish service and leadership.

I attended the sessions of the Assembly as an honorary vice-president of the World Jewish Congress. It was gratifying not only to meet veteran Congress personalities, but also to see many new faces and hear new voices from communities in various parts of the world. Delegates came, among other places, from Bulgaria, Poland, Rumania, and Yugoslavia.

A WJC study made public by its International Economic and Social Commission, chaired by Baron Guy de Rothschild of Paris, sparked heated debate and controversy. The authors of this report criticized the monopoly exercised by the Orthodox rabbinate in Israel with governmental sanction, Israel's settlement policies in Judea, Samaria and Gaza, the electoral system in Israel, and other matters. They also claimed that Diaspora Jewry had the right to express public criticism of Israel, and rejected the "classical" Zionist position negating Diaspora existence as *Galut* and holding out no long-range hopes for a secure Jewish life outside of the Medinah. Edgar Bronfman, the acting president, assured critics of the report that it did not represent the official outlook or policy of the World Jewish Congress. In fact, the document was not formally presented for adoption.

In my view, a report of this nature, whatever its status might be, was misconceived. It could only do harm to Israel, now under hostile pressure and attack, and to the Zionist cause, which in recent years has been defamed and misrepresented by an assortment of enemies. Legitimate criticism of Israel by Jews, when publicly expressed, is bound to be seized upon by those who deny Israel's right to exist. Whatever needs to be said is better conveyed through channels that will not trumpet it through the public media, with no regard for the consequences.

Among the more important resolutions adopted at the WJC Assembly were those supporting the Israel-Egypt peace process begun at Camp David; calling upon the Soviet leadership to permit the emigration of larger numbers of Jews to Israel, and to grant Jews in the USSR facilities for the practice of their religion and the development of their Jewish cultural heritage; urging a more serious and creative approach to Muslim-Jewish dialogue; and, while expressing shock at the increase in anti-Semitic manifestations throughout the world, particularly in Europe, calling upon all governments, political parties, churches, and communications media to display vigilance and energy in curbing the danger.

Far away from Jerusalem, meanwhile, dramatic events gained the world's attention. Ronald Reagan, having defeated Jimmy Carter in the American elections, was being inaugurated as the new President of the United States. The American hostages in Iran were being released at last, following the negotiation of an agreement with their captors in the closing hours of President Carter's Administration, thanks partly to the Algerian Government's intercession.

I was left wondering about the state of the world and Israel's place in it. Now that the Soviet Union had imposed its military control on Afghanistan, strategically close to the world's chief oil resources, would the United States be able to prevent further erosion of its prestige and mobility in the international arena? Could the danger posed by the capacity of some Arab states to produce nuclear weapons now be contained? How would Israel fare in the middle of this hostile danger zone, and how far would U.S. policymaking take Israel's viability into account? These were only a few of the disturbing questions we would have to face in the period immediately ahead.

An eventful few days awaited us in mid-February. On the morning of the eighteenth, I had a telephone call from the new spiritual leader of French Jewry, Rabbi René Samuel Sirat, whom the Consistoire Central had chosen to succeed Chief Rabbi Jacob Kaplan upon his retirement from office on January 1. I had known Rabbi Kaplan for more than forty years, since the time when he was Chief Rabbi of Paris, and had many opportunities to renew our acquaintanceship in New York and Jerusalem, as well as in the French capital. Throughout his long and distinguished Chief Rabbinate, he displayed the highest degree of Jewish dignity, wisdom, and faithfulness. He made no secret of his Zionism, even in the face of anti-Israel pronouncements by the French Government, yet the non-Jewish public in France held him in high regard.

His successor, Chief Rabbi Sirat, has achieved a position of influence in the French academic world. The initial contact between Rabbi Sirat and myself was made by a mutual friend, Dr. Izak (Warszawski) Varsat, a leader of our World Confederation of United Zionists in Europe and a distinguished professor of law. Rabbi Sirat was visiting Jerusalem and I went to see him at the King David Hotel. His personal qualities, keen interest in American Jewry, and staunch Zionism impressed me, and I offered him my help and cooperation whenever he might need them. French Jewry is today the world's fourth largest *kehillah*, and the Chief Rabbinate of France thus enjoys considerable influence and prestige.

A number of my friends, Zionists and non-Zionists, were circulating in the lobby of the hotel when I arrived. They had been attending a conference of the board of governors of the enlarged Jewish Agency, organized as a three-day "retreat" in Caesarea, with Arye L. Dultzin and Max Fisher presiding. The agenda of the Caesarea Conference dealt with the tasks and objectives of the Jewish Agency in the 1980s, and discussions focused on the new partnership between the World Zionist Organization and the various bodies raising funds for Medinat Yisrael. The Jerusalem Program, adopted by the 23rd Zionist Congress in 1951, was endorsed unanimously. It stated the aims of Zionism to be "the consolidation of the State of Israel, the Ingathering of the Exiles in Eretz Yisrael and the fostering of the unity of the Jewish people."

Certain additions had been made to these stated goals at the 27th Congress, held in June 1968. They read as follows: "The unity of the Jewish people and the centrality of Israel in its life; the Ingathering of the Jewish people in its historic homeland, Eretz Yisrael, through Aliyah from all lands; the strengthening of the State of Israel, founded on the prophetic ideals of justice and peace; the preservation of the identity of the Jewish people through the fostering of Jewish education, the Hebrew language, and Jewish spiritual and cultural values; and the protection of Jewish rights everywhere."

Max Fisher, the non-Zionist chairman of the board, termed the endorsement "historic" and said that it meant "we are all one family . . . we are all Zionists." The Zionist chairman, Arye Dultzin, explained that this endorsement of Zionist goals by leaders of the non-Zionist half of the Agency's board of governors did not mean that the bodies they represented would immediately affiliate with the WZO, but he foresaw that such an affiliation would take place eventually.

Although I regarded this development as encouraging, I still felt that the term *Zionist* was in danger of losing its basic significance. Aliyah received honorable mention in the augmented Jerusalem Program, but it had not been made personally binding. In my view, the reluctance of the World Zionist Organization to face up to this *mitzvah* lay at the root of its present moral weakness. As long as the Program did not commit a Zionist to Aliyah, I believed, our hitherto non-Zionist colleagues of the Jewish Agency Executive were indeed entitled to call themselves Zionists. It was not my definition of Zionism, but it seemed that my position was not the generally accepted one.

At precisely this time, the happy culmination of one momentous Aliyah struggle took place. A Soviet Prisoner of Zion, Yosef Mendelevich, reached Israel on the evening of Wednesday, February 18. Not since Operation Entebbe in July 1976 had Ben-Gurion Airport witnessed such a spontaneous demonstration of enthusiasm. As one of the principal "conspirators" in the Leningrad Trial of 1970, Mendelevich had served more than ten years in various Soviet forced-labor camps for his part in the abortive attempt to hijack a plane and escape from the USSR. He was the last Jewish member of the group to be released from prison.

Devoutly Orthodox, this thirty-four-year-old Jew staunchly refused to make any religious compromises with the harsh regime of a Soviet penal camp. While in jail, he had also managed to conduct an underground Hebrew *ulpan* for his fellow Prisoners of Zion. His readiness to fight and, if necessary, die for his faith made him the hero of Israel's Bnei Akiva youth. Large numbers of them flocked to the airport, where they accorded Yosef Mendelevich a tumultuous welcome.

The scenes, both there, when he was reunited with members of his family, and at the Western Wall, where he pronounced the *Sheheḥeyanu* blessing and recited *Kaddish* for his parents, were unforgettable. So were the Hebrew greetings and the statement Mendelevich made on his arrival: "All my dreams have come true. . . . I now hope to take part in the task of building the holy State of Israel with all of you."

One sensed that he spoke for all of our brethren who demand the free, untrammeled exercise of their Jewish heritage, for all the *Asiré Tziyyon* who continue to fight valorously for their rights and their beliefs. When such a man hugs the stones of the *Kotel*, one becomes newly aware that the Wall is a symbol of our indestructible faith.

The entire dramatic episode was a timely reminder that Israel's *raison d'être* is too often obscured by minor daily irritations which tend to make us lose our sense of perspective. For all its hostility, Soviet Russia, one of the two great world powers, is compelled to recognize Israel as the one and only Jewish homeland.

On March 3, I presented to the Hebrew University a Falasha prayer book that had been in my possession since 1969, when my wife and I visited Ethiopia. It was gratefully accepted by Avraham Harman, president of the university, to be deposited in the Jewish National–Hebrew University Library. Professor Peretz Tishby, chief librarian at the Hebrew University, opined that it was a very rare book, the only one of its kind to enter their collection. The Falasha prayers, inscribed in red and black ink on parchment, are mostly in Ghe'ez, the sacred language of all Ethiopians, but some parts are written in an Agau dialect, Quaranga. This was once current among Falashas of the Quara region, but very few of them still speak or understand it today.

I was glad to know that such a valuable book would now be available to research scholars at the Library.

Toward the end of March, I received a letter from my alma mater, the University of Pennsylvania, informing me that it had established an Israel Goldstein Exchange Fellowship with the Hebrew University. Steven Finestone, the first recipient of this fellowship, would be coming to Jerusalem to pursue his studies in the field of eighteenth-century Haskalah (Hebrew Enlightenment) literature.

An impressive four-day gathering of several thousand Holocaust survivors from all over the world concluded in front of the Western Wall on June 23, with a testament that they would never forget the six million martyrs of the Nazi period and would hand down the memory of Hitler's "Final Solution" to their children. The testament, signed by all the participants, was deposited in Yad Vashem.

An important religious and social factor in our lives has been the Center for Conservative (M'sorati) Judaism here in Jerusalem, where Bert and I attend services regularly and with which many of our friends and colleagues are affiliated. Visitors from New York also keep our bond with Congregation B'nai Jeshurun fresh and strong. More than once, I have derived special satisfaction from the arrival of a grandchild of some former congregant who, fifty or sixty years ago, opposed or grudgingly tolerated my Zionist preachments, when that grandchild came in to tell us that he or she was joining an Israeli kibbutz.

An event of truly historic significance for the Conservative movement took place in Jerusalem over the ten-day period of March 6–15, 1981. It was the Bar Mitzvah International Convention of the World Council of Synagogues, embracing the United Synagogue, the Rabbinical Assembly, the Jewish Theological Seminary of America, the Women's League for Conservative Judaism, the National Federation of Men's Clubs, and the Movement for M'sorati Judaism in Israel.

The numbers and caliber of both rabbis and laymen attending our convention served as an impressive demonstration of the Conservative movement's strength and influence in the United States. Also visible was the movement's growth and impact in Israel, where there are already more than thirty M'sorati congregations in cities and development towns, with active men's, women's, and youth groups.

President Itzhak Navon and Prime Minister Menahem Begin graced the opening session with their presence. Both of them, however, shied away from dealing with the vexed issue of official Government recognition. Leaders of the M'sorati movement justifiably claim the same freedom of religious expression that other Jews in Israel enjoy, in accordance with Israel's Proclamation of Independence. Rabbi Mordecai Waxman, president of the United Synagogue of America, rightly challenged the monopoly enjoyed by Israel's Orthodox establishment in such vital areas as marriage and divorce. It was a call for religious pluralism.

Earlier in the day, Labor Alignment leader Shim'on Peres had come out in favor of recognition for the non-Orthodox streams in Judaism, but he gave no indication as to how far he would go to implement this policy if he headed the next Government. It was clear that, without an absolute majority in the Knesset, no Labor Prime Minister would be able to form a Government coalition without the support of the National Religious Party, and that such an ally would be unalterably opposed. Peres, at any rate, did not have to face such a dilemma. The elections to Israel's tenth Knesset on June 30 returned Begin to power, at the head of a narrow coalition of the Likud, the NRP, Agudat Yisrael, and a new Sephardi group, Tami, also traditionalist in its orientation.

One sometimes hears the argument that "if Conservative Jews from America were to make Aliyah in large numbers, they would change the balance of religious forces in the Medinah." I find this type of reasoning unacceptable, since the question is not one of numbers but of right. Jews, whether Orthodox, Conservative, or Reform, should come to Israel in maximum numbers, for overall Zionist reasons.

A highlight of the convention was the session of the Rabbinical Assembly dedicated to the hundredth birthday of Professor Mordecai M. Kaplan. Much to our regret, he could not be present, having spent the past few months with his family in New York. Addresses on this very meaningful occasion were delivered by Rabbi Jack J. Cohen, head of the Reconstructionist movement in Israel, and by myself. Rabbi Cohen's thoughtful, philosophical paper dealt primarily with Kaplan's theology. I assume that I was invited to speak as Kaplan's oldest living disciple, and I deemed it a great honor and privilege to do so. My paper, based on a rereading of my teacher's major books, dealt with his contribution to Zionist thought, the Zionist program, and the place of Medinat Yisrael in Jewish life. Instead of speaking about Mordecai Kaplan, however, I let Kaplan speak for himself—by citing the views on Zionism and Israel expounded in his books. I concluded with an appropriate Midrash.

Altogether, it was an extraordinary occasion, honoring the extraordinary anniversary of an extraordinary teacher, one who has served as a guide to many of the perplexed in our generation. Even those who could not share Kaplan's Reconstructionist approach to Judaism joined in paying tribute to one of the most remarkable Jewish teachers and thinkers of our time.

Before closing this chapter, I feel bound to say something more about our social life in Jerusalem. Because of its diverse constituency and because it is the Zionist and cultural center of the Jewish world, Jerusalem abounds in kindred spirits.

Our years of service and participation—in the Zionist movement and its fund-raising arms, in the American Jewish Congress and the World Jewish Congress, in the Israel Interfaith movement alongside Jewish and Christian colleagues, in the Hebrew University of Jerusalem and the University of Haifa, for the welfare of Jerusalem itself and our congregational affiliations—have given broad dimensions to our home. Moreover, the kindness and hospitality we have enjoyed from family, friends, and former congregants have brought immeasurable interest and enrichment to our lives.

Irrespective of one's organizational involvements, however, living in Jerusalem is a multifaceted experience and a constant source of inspiration. It would be no exaggeration to say that nowhere else in the world can one find such a range of culture, scholarship, and idealism. Despite its pockets of social and economic problems, this is, on the whole, a peaceful and law-abiding city. Jerusalem possesses a unique charm. Its climate for the greater part of the year is pleasant and salubrious. Scenic delights abound and arresting vistas beckon from every side. History lies at one's doorstep.

Whatever one's cultural, religious, or intellectual bent, Jerusalem, with its Hebrew University campuses and academic life, its multitude of synagogues, yeshivot, and Jewish educational institutions, its churches and Christian theological institutes, its museums and its Western Wall, is a metropolis like no other.

Often, on a Shabbat morning, walking to synagogue when the streets are almost free from the noise and bustle of traffic, I have felt a special kind of Sabbath peace, unlike anything I ever experienced in New York or in quieter Philadelphia. No effort is needed to conjure up visions of King David, who made Jerusalem the nation's capital; of Isaiah, who thundered denunciations and spoke consolations; of Jeremiah, who, with Babylonian troops at the city gates, went to execute a real-estate purchase. And I have often thought to myself, "How goodly has been our lot, to have seen Israel reestablished and to call Jerusalem our home."

Among our cherished friends has also been a relative, my cousin, Batya Abbady (*née* Rothberg). Her mother and mine were sisters. Her first husband, Rabbi Louis Greenberg, ministered to an important congregation in New Haven, Connecticut, and wrote a standard work on Russian Jewry. Batya headed the congregation's religious school. After his premature death, she came to Israel and settled in Jerusalem, where she administered the program of the American Women's League for Israel. Here, she married Yitzhak Abbady, a prominent member of the Sephardi community, who had served as the British Mandatory government's official Hebrew-Arabic translator. Since his demise, she has occupied herself with translating literary works into Hebrew, English, and Yiddish, and with writing and reciting poetry.

Though subsumed under "we," "us," and "our" throughout these memoirs, Bert, my wife, has not only been an inestimable helpmeet over the years but also a communal and Zionist leader in her own right. After graduating from Hunter College and taking higher degrees at Columbia and New York University, she practiced law in New York for some years while serving as my *rebbetzin* at B'nai Jeshurun and as president of the congregation's sisterhood. A wag in our synagogue once quipped,

"The rabbi preaches and the *rebbetzin* practices." Bert went on to become president of the New York chapter of Hadassah and later joined the Labor Zionist movement. She became the first national president of Pioneer Women in the U.S. and the first chairperson of the Women's Division for Israel Bonds in New York. She was a delegate to several Zionist Congresses and served, for a number of years, as a member of the Zionist General Council (Actions Committee). After our Aliyah, Bert took the initiative in organizing and heading the Jerusalem Women's Committee, which aimed to instill civic consciousness and to keep our city clean and beautiful. She has also headed the Jerusalem chapter of University Women in Israel. All things considered, my title of *Yakir Yerushalayim* belongs as much to her as to me.

With the approach of my eighty-fifth birthday and the sixty-third anniversary of our marriage in the early summer of 1981, I counted myself blessed and fortunate to have reached this time of life in health of body and mind, and with my life companion at my side. Throughout our years in Israel, we have numbered among our devoted friends three physicians to whom my wife and I are deeply obligated, namely, Professors Eli Davis, Nathan Saltz, and Marco Caine. Deriving pride and pleasure from our offspring, even to the third generation, Bert and I share one vision of service to Am Yisrael and Eretz Yisrael, and are firmly planted in the capital of Medinat Yisrael. Goodness and kindness have followed us all the days of our lives.

Friends of mine anticipated my birthday by more than a week when, on June 9, the Keren Hayesod and Keren Kayemet, the Hebrew University, and the World Confederation of United Zionists jointly held a reception at Maison de France, on the Givat Ram campus of the Hebrew University in Jerusalem. Some 250 friends, colleagues, and associates attended. A children's choir from my Youth Village provided a bouquet of greetings in song. Addresses were delivered by Bernard Cherrick, vice-president of the Hebrew University, Moshe Rivlin, world chairman of the Keren Kayemet Le-Yisrael, Kalman Sultanik, executive chairman of our Confederation, and by my good friend and collaborator of my Keren Hayesod administration, S. J. (Shai) Kreutner. Dr. Avraham Avi-ḥai, world chairman of the Keren Hayesod, presided. An album of greetings from Israel and abroad was presented to me, including messages from President Itzḥak Navon, Prime Minister Menaḥem Begin, Opposition leader Shim'on Peres, Jewish Agency Chairman Arye L. Dultzin, and many others here and overseas.

It was a touching demonstration of friendship and affection. I declared this to be my wife's celebration as well as my own and, in responding to the host of good wishes, I said:

> The best years of our lives have been the twenty and one half years since our Aliyah. Our preparation for this chapter was the year when it was my privilege to serve as treasurer of the Jewish Agency, immediately after the establishment of the Medinah. It was the most trying, the most difficult and the most rewarding experience of my life. For the deficits created during that year, Mr. Dultzin, who served as treasurer of the Jewish Agency a decade and a half later, must have blessed me. I mean it literally, since the sons and daughters of that Aliyah fought and won Israel's Six-Day War and Yom Kippur War.

Life in Israel is not easy. It will take a generation of persistent, purposeful education of the youth to undo the ills resulting from a generation of inadequate physical and social conditions for large segments of our population.

Israel's merits are great but it is not without faults, and it should be constructively aware of them. Recently, a challenging comment appeared in a popular American weekly, where, after a searching analysis, there was a positive evaluation. "Israel has the ability, if only it can summon up the will, to make the moral horizon, the Jewish people's timeless strength, the ruling priority once again" (*Time Magazine*, May 18, 1981, p. 29).

There is a quaint story in the Talmud (*Megillah* 28a) of how the disciples of Rabbi Nehunya ben ha-Kanah once asked him, "By virtue of what quality have you been privileged to reach length of days?" His answer was, "I never sought honor through the downgrading of colleagues."

While I do not attribute my full measure of years to any special merit, I would like to identify myself as a modern disciple of Rabbi Nehunya. My opponents I respected. My supporters I respected and loved. From both I have benefited, and to both I am obliged.

The generation which has witnessed and worked for the creation of the Jewish State is passing out of the picture. We count ourselves privileged, and our descendants will call us blessed, that we were of that generation. To maintain what has been created is, in some respects, more difficult because it is less dramatic. Yet I have faith in that partnership between World Jewry and the Jews in Eretz Yisrael which brought about the Medinah, that it will ever keep it strong and invincible.

Much to my delight, this birthday observance was topped off a few days later by a dinner at the Israel Goldstein Youth Village in Katamon, presided over by another old friend and colleague, Moshe Kol. A onetime member of the Government as Minister of Tourism, he had led the Independent Liberal Party and served effectively as chairman of Youth Aliyah in the Jewish Agency Executive.

In a sense, this sequence of happy events was symbolic. Faithful to the religious and Zionist tradition in which we were raised, Bert and I are handing on to our grandchildren and their generation the spiritual heritage our parents bequeathed to us. We do so with hope in our hearts and a prayer on our lips—that Israel may dwell securely, that Jews everywhere will preserve and transmit their splendid millenial inheritance, and that mankind, having survived every form of imperilment, may flourish "in a world perfected under the kingdom of God."

Bert and I thus entered upon another year in our lives, filled with thanksgiving for the past and with prayerful hope for the future.

17

Along the Way: Pen Portraits

In the forty-fourth chapter of the Apocryphal book of Ecclesiasticus, Ben Sira, there is a text enumerating the virtues and sterling deeds of those who deserved well of their own generation, which begins: "Let us now praise famous men, and our fathers that begat us."

As one proceeds through life, personalities appear at various junctures to share the journey. Not always do they share the same paths to the common goal. Often, indeed, the broader the kinship of purpose and objective, the keener are the differences in approach.

Like every public servant, my experience in the variety of organizations I have been privileged to serve has been that there were simultaneously colleagues and antagonists, friends and adversaries. Frequently, we were moved by the same purpose, bound in the same direction, and aiming at the same goal; yet we sometimes differed as to methods, nuances, and interpretations. This was human and inevitable.

The subjects dealt with in the following brief pen portraits have been selected not in accordance with any objective criteria, but because they happen to stand out vividly in my personal hall of recollections, having touched my life at one stage or another. A few of the people described have been close to me personally, while others I have admired at a respectful or fond distance. A few have made significant appearances in my life story. All of them, whether living or no longer alive, I salute in retrospect.

Cyrus Adler

Cyrus Adler was in his late forties when, as a youth in Philadelphia, I first came to his notice and under his tutelage. A scholar of no mean attainments, Adler was also a man of practical wisdom. He helped to found the American Jewish Historical Society, of which he was president for more than two decades, and the Jewish Publication Society of America, with which he remained associated until his death in 1940.

With his smooth-shaven face and distinctive pince-nez, Dr. Adler maintained an aristocratic bearing. On his mother's side, he was connected with the prestigious

Sulzberger family of Philadelphia. One often wondered what thoughts and emotions passed through this outwardly dispassionate man. In temperament he was the prototype of the communal *parnas*, a magisterial figure in Jewish life. Cyrus Adler was in fact the *parnas* of Gratz College, Dropsie College and, later, of the Jewish Theological Seminary of America, where he assumed presidential office after the death of Professor Solomon Schechter. He had served with distinction as president of the Seminary's board of trustees while still librarian of the Smithsonian Institute in Washington, D.C. During his years of cooperation with Professor Schechter, he helped to reorganize the Seminary; later he became its acting president and, ultimately, its president.

No one was more aware than I that under Dr. Adler's cold exterior there did beat a warm heart motivating a tremendous sense of responsibility—that of a *parnas* for *Klal Yisrael*—and a deep loyalty to Jewish and Hebrew cultural values. He was a member of the editorial board of the *Jewish Encyclopedia* and played a leading part in having a Hebrew press installed in the headquarters of the Jewish Publication Society.

As will have been apparent earlier in these memoirs, I had reason to remember Cyrus Adler with gratitude. Already a prominent figure in the Philadelphia Jewish community when I was a young student at Gratz College, he took a paternal interest in my future and encouraged me to proceed to the Jewish Theological Seminary in New York. It was as a result of my having been chosen by the faculty to be valedictorian at the graduation exercises in 1918 that I was called to the pulpit of Congregation B'nai Jeshurun, where he was kind enough to install me.

In the years that followed, as my own public career evolved, I often found myself in Jewish and other camps opposed to his. Cyrus Adler was not a Zionist, although he became a non-Zionist member of the Jewish Agency, and in politics he was a conservative. He remained very much the *parnas* in his attitude, not sufficiently sensitive to the importance of democracy in Jewish life. For years he headed the American Jewish Committee, which he had helped to found. When I became actively involved in the American Jewish Congress and the World Jewish Congress, our respective organizations and our views were often at variance, although the personal relations between us remained cordial. As one of my early patrons and mentors, Cyrus Adler will always have a special place in my recollection.

David Ben-Gurion

The man of action par excellence, David Ben-Gurion was also a powerhouse of intellectual and spiritual energy, which he expended in study, contemplation, and exposition. This dichotomy was apt to mislead opponents and critics, because he could swing rapidly from one extreme to another and transpose himself from the sedentary, almost passive scholar at his desk to the decisive commander in the field. If he had any doubts, he never gave any sign of entertaining them and he would take decisions with the speed of a camera shutter.

One always had the feeling in his presence that this man was virtually impenetrable, keeping his own counsel in the midst of the give-and-take of conversation and discussion, that he was essentially a fanatic for his cause—Zionism and Israel— and an uncommonly shrewd strategist in attaining the desired ends.

Ben-Gurion seemed to be utterly lacking in human compassion and he was ruthless in achieving his purpose. He could evoke admiration, confidence, and loyalty, but not affection. His most human moments were those relating no doubt to his children and, in some special way, to his wife, Paula, who alternately sheltered, scolded, and coddled him. He was sometimes prone to exhibitionism, although this took subtle forms, such as his study of Greek and Spanish or his debate with the Burmese leader, U Nu, on Buddhism.

His overriding passions were Bible study, Jewish history, and Aliyah. Hebrew, he insisted, must become the second language of every Jew in the Diaspora. He also believed that Israel's only reliable ally was Diaspora Jewry, and that Jews and Arabs must somehow learn to live and cooperate with each other in the Middle East.

I visited Ben-Gurion at his home in Tel Aviv in 1971 in order to make a presentation of the special medallion struck by the Keren Hayesod to mark its fiftieth anniversary. Ben-Gurion received me cordially and remarked that he had been present at the London Zionist Conference of July 1920 at which the Keren Hayesod was established. He recalled an amusing incident. While he was on the platform addressing the delegates, his wife came in with their baby daughter, Ge'ulah, who shouted "Abba!" when she saw her father standing on the rostrum. Not only did this interruption embarrass Ben-Gurion and halt him in mid-sentence, it also gave rise to a commotion in the packed hall for which "Abba" later chided his wife.

Justice Louis D. Brandeis had attended that conference, Ben-Gurion recalled, an American Zionist leader whom he had held in great esteem. I mentioned my own first meeting with Louis Brandeis in 1931, on which occasion Brandeis disclosed that it was through Ben-Gurion that he had become aware of the strategic importance of Eilat (then called Akaba) for the Jewish National Home.

A charming story was told of Paula's devotion to her husband. Apparently, her dislike of protocol exceeded even his. One morning, she called from her window to the policeman on sentry duty outside the door of their home: "Listen, Tzvi, I'm not dressed. Get me some apples from the grocery store."

"I'm sorry, Ma'am," the policeman replied, "but I can't leave my post. My orders are to guard the Prime Minister."

"You just get the apples," Paula retorted, "and I'll guard the Prime Minister."

Paula never failed him in that respect.

When she was interred at Sdeh Boker, Ben-Gurion's parting words to her were a moving tribute drawn, characteristically, from the Bible:

> I remember for thee the affection of thy youth,
> The love of thine espousals;
> How thou wentest after me in the wilderness,
> In a land that was not sown.
>
> [Jeremiah 2:2]

Eddie Cantor

Born on the Lower East Side of New York, Eddie Cantor became America's leading comedian and a favorite on stage and screen. He raised considerable sums for Jewish and general charities and during the 1930s, when he was at the peak of his career, he did outstanding work in behalf of Jewish refugees from Nazi Germany, particularly for Youth Aliyah. The offices to which he was elected by fellow artists, including his presidency of the Screen Actors' Guild, were a clear indication of the esteem in which he was held by his peers.

At the height of the Zionist struggle in the 1940s, Eddie Cantor joined the ranks of prominent Americans who endorsed the efforts of the American Zionist Emergency Council, and he gave permission for the use of his name on the Council's letterhead. His devotion to the welfare of children anticipated that of Danny Kaye and, on one occasion, he made a special fund-raising trip to England under the auspices of Youth Aliyah, accompanied by his close friend, Emanuel Goldman.

Eddie Cantor divided his time between New York and Hollywood. It so happened that one fine day when he was in the motion-picture capital, he was approached by Peter Bergson (Hillel Kook), who had come from Palestine to organize support for the Irgun's activities. As a result of their meeting, Eddie was persuaded to join the Hebrew Committee for National Liberation, which Bergson headed. When we of the Zionist Emergency Council saw his name on the dissident group's stationery, one of our representatives on the West Coast was sent to express our amazement and to get him to sever his ties with the Bergson group.

Convinced now that he had made a mistake, Eddie Cantor notified the Hebrew Committee for National Liberation of his decision to resign. Someone promptly arrived to persuade him that his resignation was a terrible mistake.

By this time Eddie was completely bewildered. He thereupon telegraphed a plaintive message to us back East: "Please wire me immediately why I resigned."

Eddie Cantor was a great American, a great humanitarian, and a proud Jew with a great Jewish heart. Entertainment may have been his profession, but philanthropy was his way of life. Until his last hours on earth in 1964, the welfare and dignity of the Jewish people remained his unfailing concern.

Levi Eshkol

Israel's Prime Minister, Levi Eshkol, was a man of a markedly different character from that of his predecessor, David Ben-Gurion. I first came to know him as Levi Shkolnik when we were colleagues on the Jewish Agency Executive, where he headed the Agricultural Settlement Department. He later became the treasurer of the Jewish Agency and, in due course, joined the Government of Israel as Minister of Finance in succession to Eliezer Kaplan, later becoming Prime Minister.

Eshkol had a homespun quality of common sense wedded to a talent for getting things done. In later years, especially during the crucial months of 1967 when

Israel was menaced by war, the burden of high office weighed heavily upon him and at times it appeared to have sapped his wonted stamina. During the period of our association on the Agency's Executive, however, he had been a dynamo of action capable of inspiring and motivating great loyalty from those who worked under him. With unruffled calm, he administered huge tasks, such as the development of Israel's water supply, land reclamation, and the settlement program. His quest was for results, not spectacular effects, hence he was frequently underestimated.

Unlike most of his Agency colleagues, Levi Eshkol needed little time to get his points across. His observations were informative, enlightening, and spiced with a Jewish folk wit redolent of the *shtetl*.

It is now common knowledge that the climax of Eshkol's public career, the premiership, was far from the happiest chapter of his life. The barbs directed at him from high places made it especially painful, yet he displayed patience and states-manship in leading Israel through the Six-Day War to a spectacular victory.

Levi Eshkol was a founder and lifelong member of Kibbutz Deganyah Bet, on the shores of Lake Kinneret. At times, when we were together, I sensed that he would rather have been back there, in that beloved alma mater of his pioneering youth, among the fields and groves of Deganyah, than in the halls of state through which destiny had led him.

Nahum Goldmann

An apt description for Dr. Nahum Goldmann might be "Jewish Statesman without a State." Although, next to Weizmann, Ben-Gurion, and Silver, he did more than any other Jew of his time to bring the Jewish State into being, Goldmann apparently could never feel sufficiently at home in Israel to make it his permanent domicile. Perhaps it was not in his character to be provincial, even if the province was Medinat Yisrael. His anchorage seemed, therefore, to be in the Diaspora, where he wielded his baton over the World Jewish Congress and became the roving ambassa-dor of World Jewry. Indeed, he often cast himself in the role of a latterday *Resh Galuta*, "Prince of the Jewish Diaspora."

Of all the eminent Jews with whom I have worked, Goldmann was the most cosmopolitan—not merely by virtue of his command of languages, but in his way of life. He could feel almost equally at home in Geneva, Paris, New York, or Jerusalem.

Nahum Goldmann's passion for Jewish unity was reflected in his decisive role, at the side of Dr. Stephen S. Wise, in the organization of the World Jewish Congress and, later, in fostering the Presidents' Conference on the American scene and the Conference of Jewish Organizations, COJO, in the international arena.

I know of no other contemporary Jewish leader who was so much at home—and so stimulating—in both Jewish and general culture. As a young man, he took the initiative in publishing the German *Encyclopaedia Judaica*, which Hitler's rise to power brought to a halt, and in later years he created the basis for its English-language successor, the new *Encyclopaedia Judaica*. He headed the Memorial Foundation for Jewish Culture, to which the Claims Conference gave birth, and was also the motivating force in establishing Bet ha-Tefutzot, the Museum of the Jewish Diaspora, which stands on the campus of Tel Aviv University and has become one of Israel's major cultural attractions. It deservedly bears his name.

Nahum and I were close colleagues over a period of more than three decades in the Zionist movement, the World Jewish Congress, and a variety of organizations in which these two bodies have figured as constants amid a flux of variables. I was privileged to be at his side in one of the major achievements of his career—the securing, for Medinat Yisrael and the Jewish people, of indemnification and reparation payments from the Federal German Republic. It was an act both of statesmanship and of vision. More than once, however, I found it necessary to diverge from stands which he adopted in inner Zionist politics.

There were issues in which his public pronouncements—regarding the Arab-Israel conflict, the campaign for Soviet Jewry, and relations with the Communist bloc—made Goldmann a center of heated controversy. He was harshly critical of Israel Government policy under Ben-Gurion and Eshkol, and in later years, needless to say, he was likewise vehemently critical of the Begin Administration. Not all of his judgments and forecasts have proved valid, some having been more notable for their boldness than their wisdom, yet most people have tended to underestimate his moral courage. In concluding the Restitution and Reparations Agreement with West Germany, for example, he had to overcome powerful and understandably emotional resistance within Israel itself and among Jewry at large. Nor has sufficient credit been paid to him for his share in winning President Truman's decisive support for the establishment of a Jewish State in Palestine, during the dramatic prelude to the UN partition resolution of November 1947. The contributions he made to Israel's financial viability also deserve to be remembered gratefully.

His *tours d'horizon* at Zionist Congresses and World Jewish Congress Assemblies often proved to be the high point of these gatherings. They were far-reaching reviews of the Jewish and general world scenes, delivered with clarity and urbanity. His easy manner was deceptive: with a few puffs of his cigar he could shatter an opponent's argument. No man of his time had a more extensive knowledge and keener understanding of the world Jewish scene. No one could display more personal charm, intellectual brilliance, and cultural versatility.

Regrettably, however, he did his own past an injustice by choosing to remain a *Galut* Jew.

When Nahum Goldmann died, at the end of August 1982, the Paris daily, *Le Monde*, called him "the last giant among world statesmen." My characterization of him would be "the architect of the Jewish people's unity in our time."

Ḥayim Greenberg

During the more than thirty years in which I knew Ḥayim Greenberg, he was the intellectual leader of American Zionism. Though identified with a particular wing of the movement, Labor Zionism, he preserved an independent spirit transcending party lines. His idealism, learning, and integrity won universal respect.

When an intellectual confrontation was called for, with anti-Zionists of one hue or another, Jewish and non-Jewish antagonists, American radicals or reactionaries, we knew that Ḥayim could be relied upon to enter the lists. He was a chivalrous champion, but a doughty one in any intellectual tournament, commanding several languages and at home in the cultures of both East and West.

It was his view that the Diaspora has played an important part in the epic of Jewish cultural and spiritual creativeness and that its future must not be written off, even though its permanence cannot be guaranteed. He was adept in finding metaphors to adorn his theses. One of those I best recall, from an address he delivered before the World Zionist Congress in 1951, was his characterization of the American *Golah* as "a moonlit night." Israel was the sun.

Ḥayim Greenberg was the apostle of Zionism to the liberal Gentile world— intellectuals, labor leaders, spokesmen for Negro rights, representatives of the Afro-Asian peoples. Unlike most other prominent Zionists, he could not be accused of exclusive involvement in purely Jewish issues. Thus, when he crossed swords with Mahatma Gandhi, insisting that statehood was no less vital to the Jewish people than it had been for India, his liberal credentials were beyond dispute and they enhanced the moral level of his argument.

Despite his affiliation with the "secular" Zionist camp, Ḥayim felt and generated a religious *Stimmung*. His was not a surface religiosity, but a sense of the mystery of life and an awareness of a guiding Force in the universe and in history which defies human comprehension. Rabbis and observant laymen applauded his strictures on those who would dispense with two Jewish fundamentals—God as Reality and Israel as *Am Segulah*, a Chosen People. I believe it is fair to say that Ḥayim Greenberg assigned to the Jewish people a unique place in the human drama and that, to quote Dr. Yeshayahu Aviad (Oscar Wolfsberg), the Mizraḥi leader, "he was not one who submitted to the yoke of traditional observance, but was one who submitted to the yoke of Divine Kingship."

He was the natural choice as head of the Jewish Agency's Education Department in New York, but he revealed unexpected talents in the handling of difficult Zionist assignments. During the 1940s, when the Zionist movement exerted every effort to win friends in all circles so as to attain the *Endziel* of a Jewish State in Palestine, no one was better qualified or more successful than he in influencing the intellectual leadership of the American community. He also played a significant role in the crucial days preceding the November 1947 vote in the United Nations, when the task of winning the support of Latin American countries for the establishment of the Jewish State was placed in his hands.

Later, it was Ḥayim Greenberg who took the lead in warning Israel's leaders against making a cult of the State, against idolizing such externals as the national flag, the army, or the Government apparatus, the glamor and paraphernalia of sovereignty. His demand that the State of Israel justify itself on the moral and spiritual planes was in keeping with his lifelong commitment to the essence, as against the outward form.

Never quarrelsome, he was frequently combative, yet even in combat Ḥayim was always the gentleman. In debate and discussion he was neither superficial nor abstruse. His deep, resonant voice matched the depth and resonance of his ideas, and his lined face seemed to emphasize the labor pains accompanying the birth of his creative ideas. I often think of him, a study in contemplation, with one arm half-folded over the other, two of his long and elegant fingers holding a cigarette to his lips. There were far too many of those cigarettes. They took him prematurely from the scene of intellectual combat, where the Zionist movement could ill spare him.

Rose Halprin

Among the women who entered the front rank of Zionist service during the period of my active involvement, Rose Halprin had a unique place. Throughout her four decades of leadership, no important Zionist gathering took place without our hearing her voice and feeling the impact of her womanly charm, intellectual vigor, and total dedication to the Jewish national cause.

She grew up on New York's Lower East Side in a home imbued with Jewish culture and the ideals of Zionism. Next to Henrietta Szold, her guide and teacher, Rose was perhaps the strongest personality in Hadassah, to the presidency of which she was twice elected—once in the early 1930s and, later, after World War II. The era of her presidency constitutes one of Hadassah's most vital chapters.

Wherever she rose to positions of command, in the American Section of the Jewish Agency Executive and in the World Jewish Congress, and as co-chairman of the World Confederation of United Zionists, Rose Halprin displayed the quality of strong and effective leadership. Several years of her life were spent in Palestine during the 1930s.

It would be out of harmony with the spirit of our time, when so much emphasis is given to "Women's Lib," to offer a woman faint praise by saying that she had a man's mind. More appropriately, one might say that Rose combined personal charm with strength of intellect and strength of character. She was, and remained, strongly partisan in her likes and dislikes. The score of her prejudices for and against people, and of her personal commitments, contained no half-notes; there were only full chords. This faculty of hers made her a fearless advocate and a powerful antagonist. One could not always agree with her views, but one was bound to respect and admire her.

Rose Halprin's *joie de vivre* was reflected in her love of the arts and of people. The resplendence and distinctiveness of her hats was proverbial, but beneath that varied headgear was a *Yiddisher kop*—a brilliant, analytical Jewish mind—together with a warm and sensitive Jewish heart. Her radiant presence and invigorating words were felt in every major center of the Diaspora and in Israel. There were few who could be compared with Rose as devoted servants and indomitable spokesmen of our people.

Mordecai M. Kaplan

When I joined the student body of the Jewish Theological Seminary in 1914, Professor Mordecai M. Kaplan, who held the chair of homiletics there, was probably the youngest member of the faculty, my senior only by about fifteen years. He had a somewhat forbidding exterior, belying his paternal interest in the students and warmth toward colleagues. In his homiletics course at the Seminary, he taught us to look for the meaning behind the scriptural texts and to catch the eternal spirit of Judaism beyond its changing, outward expressions. More than anyone else, he exerted an abiding and formative influence on the thinking and motivations of many of his students, myself included.

Mordecai Kaplan was a trailblazer in American Judaism, and an innovator in modern methods of Jewish education. He headed and fashioned the Teachers' Institute at the Jewish Theological Seminary. He pioneered the American synagogue's new role as a communal center for the entire family. He, together with Judah Magnes, sought to develop the *kehillah* concept in New York Jewry. Above all, he reconstructed the concept and practice of Judaism as an evolving religious civilization.

Some years ago, he and his artistic wife, Rivkah, made their Aliyah. To visit this couple in their Jerusalem home was always an enriching experience. Some of our most rewarding hours were spent in their company.

This phenomenal Jewish teacher and philosopher remained ever alert and incisive, a rebel against "standpattism."

I was flattered when, some twelve years ago, he asked me to take the lead in convoking an assembly of world Jewish leadership to adopt a covenant of Jewish peoplehood centered around Medinat Yisrael. I declined, because I did not feel equal to the task.

Mordecai Kaplan was the Reconstructionist par excellence in Jewish life and thought. The influence of his original ideas will be felt as a guide to the Jewishly perplexed of our modern age who seek to serve God and Israel, and in that service seek to find their highest self-fulfillment.

Louis Lipsky

During the initial phase of my Zionist career in America, I was greatly impressed by Louis Lipsky, whose lucid pen and speech—in the service of Zionism and the American Jewish Congress—had no rival. Through all the years that followed, that impression remained.

Lipsky had the face and demeanor of an artist, heightened by his taste for old-fashioned Bohemian garb, but his manner of dress was simple and unostentatious. His lean figure imparted an air of elegance and quiet distinction to his whole appearance.

A devotee of the theater, Lipsky, in his public career, sometimes gave the impression of being more interested in stage management than in star performance. Yet he himself was a stellar performer when the occasion demanded, and there were many such occasions in the unfolding of the Zionist drama while he was alive.

Among the American Zionist leaders of his time, Louis Lipsky was perhaps unique in his combination of often contrasting gifts. At one and the same time, he was a man of the people and a reserved aesthete; an American born and bred, hailing from upstate New York, and an idol of the immigrant Jewish masses; an exponent of democracy in Jewish life and an aristocrat of the spirit; Machiavellian in his political acumen, yet childlike in the simplicity of his commitment to Jewry and to Zionism.

For a considerable portion of his career, Louis Lipsky was destined to lead and mold the Zionist Organization of America. He, in fact, *was* the American Zionist movement from the dawn of its inception, and he educated two entire generations of Zionists in the United States. A Weizmannist by inclination, he supported the movement's world leader with unswerving devotion.

I served under Lipsky for a time when he was president of the ZOA, later with him in the American Section of the World Zionist Executive and then (with Henry Monsky joining us) as one of the interim co-chairmen of the American Jewish Conference. I was also a colleague of Lipsky's in the American Zionist Emergency Council. We traveled together on the way to and from more than one Zionist Congress overseas.

It was not easy to achieve a close relationship with Louis Lipsky, since he was a many-sided personality and there were moments when one felt that any nearer approach might elicit a rebuff. I admired him greatly, however, not only for his incomparable Zionist record but also for his literary talent.

Sometimes, after theater hours, when he held court with his cronies and admirers at the Tip-Toe Inn at Broadway and 86th Street, a few blocks from my congregation, I would run in there to join them. It was a heartwarming kaffeeklatsch, and I enjoyed the congenial atmosphere in which were were regaled with wit and wisdom.

Lipsky had a consummate knack for political give-and-take and, when in the chair at stormy meetings, he literally was in command of the floor. On one rare occasion, however, I remember his being stumped by Abe'le Goldberg, a keen-witted Zionist propagandist, whose forte was Yiddish but whose humor knew no language barriers. The scene was a meeting of the ZOA Administrative Committee, where the issue under discussion had been especially provocative and Lipsky, the chairman, ruled that each speaker wishing to have the floor should confine himself to three minutes. When Abe'le Goldberg's turn came, he began: "Mr. Chairman, before I confine myself, I would like to say a few words." For once, Lipsky had no retort.

It was an honor for me, at the end of 1971, to dedicate in his memory a chair of drama at the Hebrew University for which the World Confederation of General Zionists had raised the funds. It was a worthy and appropriate tribute to one who had added a new dimension both to the American Zionist movement and to the American theater. Each bears his indelible stamp.

Josef (Yossele) Rosenblatt

The unique place which the *ḥazzan* occupies in Jewish life is one that can be traced back to the Temple singers and musicians of ancient Jerusalem. The cantor's melodious chanting of the synagogue service can still arouse worshipers to a high pitch of religious fervor. In Soviet Russia, after the Bolshevik Revolution, the synagogue fanned dormant sparks of Jewish emotion even in Jewish Communists who slyly entered the derided house of prayer.

Josef Rosenblatt, cantor par excellence, was an embodiment of the highest traditions of *Ḥazzanut*. Among Yiddish-speaking Jews in the "Old Country," a favorite cantor was often referred to by the affectionate diminutive of his first name, and so it was that Cantor Josef Rosenblatt was known to millions in the United States and throughout the world as "Yossele" Rosenblatt.

His sweet tones enhanced the Sabbath services I occasionally attended at the First Hungarian Congregation Ohab Zedek in Harlem, starting from my student days at the Jewish Theological Seminary. I recall the impressive black beard, somewhat out of proportion to the cantor's short stature, which framed a handsome countenance distinguished by large black eyes. He wrote hundreds of compositions, many of which have gained fame through phonograph recordings, yet in the synagogue he excelled as an improviser. From the wellsprings of Jewish piety and emotion he could stir a vast congregation.

Unlike most other leading cantors of the day, Yossele avoided vocal pyrotechnics, although his voice could be tremulous with Jewish sorrow and thunderous with Jewish exultation. It possessed a natural elegance, punctuated occasionally by an audible sigh or sob matching the context of his prayer.

Well versed in Jewish law and lore, Yossele Rosenblatt understood not only the plain meaning of the liturgical text but also the story between the lines—all the grandeur, anguish, joy, and undying hope that fortified his people through its vicissitudes. This tradition he would translate into his people's universal language—Hebrew words tinged with Jewish melody—which found the same response in Pressburg, Hamburg, and New York, in Vilna, Buenos Aires, and Jerusalem.

He was, first and foremost, a noble Jew. This "king of cantors" never played the prima donna, never lost his genial modesty and his responsiveness to the less fortunate. His concerts helped to raise large sums for U.S. War Bonds, Jewish welfare appeals, and Zionist causes. His golden voice was matched by a heart of gold. I knew something of his open house and generous hospitality, of his private benefactions, and of the assistance given by him to musicians and fellow cantors in distress, even when he himself was weighed down by financial burdens.

Kiddush Hashem, the honor of God's Name and of the Jewish people's good name, was so dear to Cantor Rosenblatt that he refused tempting offers to appear on the opera stage and in Hollywood motion pictures. Gentile America learned to respect him as a Jew who set principle above purse. Jews throughout the world took pride in his artistic prestige and loved him for his simple Jewish dignity.

In later years I came to know Yossele as a friend. More than once he told me of his ambition to settle in the Land of Israel. The last weeks of his life that he spent there in 1933, mainly filming *The Dream of My People,* were for him the climax of his career. A thousand times he must have intoned the prayer, "O bring us unto Zion, Thy city, with song." His prayer was granted.

Maurice Samuel

Born in Rumania, Maurice Samuel was raised and educated in Manchester, England. When he came to the United States in 1914, he brought to American Zionism an unusual equipment of broad Yiddish and general culture, sharpened by a keen intellect and expressed in an elegant, albeit incisive English style. A decade of his life was spent in Palestine.

In two of his many popular and provocative books, *You Gentiles* and *The Great Hatred,* Samuel expounded his thesis that anti-Semitism is essentially a problem of the non-Jew, constituting the hostile pagan reaction to a moral law rooted in the Jewish ethic. A popular exponent of Zionism, both through his books and on the lecture platform, he also translated and popularized Hebrew and Yiddish classics. In *The World of Shalom Aleichem* he gave tens of thousands of readers, both Jewish and Gentile, a fascinating insight into the realm of Yiddish culture that otherwise would have remained closed to them. His radio talks on biblical literature also attracted wide audiences.

Maurice Samuel's lecture tours encompassed the entire English-speaking world. On one occasion, in South Africa, a tedious introduction by the local community's rabbi, Moses Romm, caused Samuel to lose patience. Rising to his feet at last, he quipped, "I was burning while Romm [Rome] was fiddling!"

My wife and I enjoyed his friendship and that of his family. I had the pleasure of officiating at his son's Bar Mitzvah in our synagogue.

One sharp encounter with a distinguished anti-Zionist took place in the Community Center of B'nai Jeshurun. I had arranged for a debate on the merits of Zionism between Maurice Samuel and Judge Joseph M. Proskauer, president of the American Jewish Committee. By prior arrangement, my two guests came into my study for a few minutes' preliminary briefing. Their very appearance was a fascinating display of contrasts. Samuel arrived casually dressed, whereas Judge Proskauer appeared in his tuxedo, with a stiff collar and black tie, his hair immaculately parted.

A more striking clash of personalities could scarcely be imagined.

It was agreed that the judge should speak first. I escorted them into the crowded assembly hall and onto the platform, where they took their places on either side of me. After a few introductory remarks, I called on Proskauer to open the debate. He delivered a spirited address, amounting to a diatribe against Zionism, in the course of which he spared neither Samuel nor the cause for which he stood.

Then it was Maurice's turn to speak. As he responded vigorously in kind, I watched his opponent squirming in his chair. Finally, Judge Proskauer rose to his full height and stalked off the platform. As he neared the exit, Maurice Samuel shouted at the top of his high-pitched voice: "Them as can't take it shouldn't dish it out!"

It was no easy task for the chairman to restore order. Whatever the feelings of our two platform debaters may have been, the audience certainly enjoyed this lively set-to.

That contest took place in 1940, several years before Proskauer modified his anti-Zionist position. In fairness to him, as I have mentioned earlier in these memoirs, it should be added that Judge Proskauer redeemed himself in 1946, when he joined Dr. Nahum Goldmann in urging President Truman to support the Zionist program for a Jewish commonwealth in Eretz Yisrael.

Maurice Schwartz

The path to an outstanding stage career was exceptionally hard for Maurice Schwartz, whom drama critics now salute as the last major figure in the Yiddish theater of New York. His experiences as a child emigrant from the Ukraine and as a budding actor were tough and disheartening, but resilience and determination enabled him to overcome obstacles.

After learning his trade in various American companies and on New York's Second Avenue, he set up his own Yiddish Art Theater in 1918 and gained renown as a star performer and then as a producer. Over the next three decades, a golden period in the annals of Yiddish theater, he gained stature as a character actor with a penchant for the humorous touch. A vast array of translated classics and Yiddish plays figured in the repertoire of his company, which toured many parts of the world between the two World Wars. Schwartz was finally obliged to disband the Yiddish Art Theater in 1950. Ten years later, however, at the age of seventy, he attempted a comeback. His bid to create a Yiddish theatrical center in Israel proved unsuccessful. He died in Israel.

When his body was flown back to New York for burial, the Yiddish Actors' Union, knowing of my devotion to the Yiddish theater, asked me to officiate at the funeral service and to deliver the eulogy. I visited the bereaved family on the morning before the funeral in order to express my personal condolences and to obtain some additional information about the deceased for incorporation in my tribute.

I met his widow and their adopted son and daughter, two orphans rescued from the European Holocaust. In the Schwartz home they were reared in the Yiddish tradition and the girl had also begun a career on the Yiddish stage. I looked around the walls of the living room, expecting to see photographs of the actor in various roles. The only picture I saw was one of Maurice Schwartz in the role of Theodor Herzl.

His widow told me the story of how Maurice's father, a traditionally observant Jew, had finally become reconciled to his son's choice of a career. Schwartz senior made no secret of his dislike for the actor's profession. A *balebattisher Yid* such as himself could scarcely approve of the unsettled life, the constant traveling on the road from one city to the next, the love scenes on the stage, and all the other features of such an unconventional existence.

Once, however, he was persuaded to attend a Saturday night performance in which his son, Maurice, figured as the head of a traditional Jewish household. In the course of one scene, the stage paterfamilias chanted *Havdalah*, the prayer recited over a goblet of wine, plaited candle, and spices at the end of Sabbaths and festivals, when reference is made to the *havdalah* (distinction) between "holy and profane, light and darkness, the Seventh Day and the six other days of the week."

Maurice Schwartz recited *Havdalah* with typical aplomb, using the time-honored melody in his basso profundo, obviously aware of the need to impress his father sitting in the front row. Schwartz senior was greatly moved by the performance. When the curtain fell, he ran backstage and embraced his son, bursting into Yiddish: "God bless you, my son! Now I understand what great things you are doing for your people. When *I* make *Havdalah*, it's for myself and my own little household. But you—*you* make *Havdalah* for the whole world!"

Moshe Sharett

A man of unusually keen intellect and broad culture, Moshe Sharett was a Zionist leader whose many exceptional qualities included a pure and delicate soul. He was, however, somewhat inclined to pedantry—in all of the eight or nine languages he mastered. The title, "didactic, sensitive statesman," would have suited him well.

Few of his contemporaries in the Zionist movement, except perhaps for Nahum Goldmann and an eminent predecessor, Nahum Sokolow, could measure up to Sharett's command of languages and familiarity with an array of cultures. Yet because he lacked toughness and a degree of fanaticism in the pursuit of his Zionist aims, he got hurt in the rough and tumble of politics. In that respect, he differed enormously from Ben-Gurion, under whom he had served as head of the Jewish Agency's Political Department and, later, as Minister of Foreign Affairs in the Government of Israel. For a while, he had also been Israel's Prime Minister, a position he found especially difficult under Ben-Gurion's vigilant and critical eye. We felt deeply for him as a result of the treatment he suffered at Ben-Gurion's hands. The "Old Man" could be ruthless to those who differed with him on what he regarded as essential matters.

I sat on the Jewish Agency Executive in Jerusalem when Sharett was its chairman, from 1960 until his death five years later. He towered above us by virtue of his finely honed intellect, linguistic ability, and wide knowledge of many world literatures, but he employed these gifts without ostentation. To be a member of his orchestra when he wielded the baton was an educative experience. At times, however, his didacticism would become somewhat oppressive. He was capable of holding up an Executive meeting for several minutes in order to argue some fine point of Hebrew syntax. He was more than normally sensitive to criticism. These human peccadilloes were, however, outweighed by uncommon intellectual and spiritual qualities and by a comprehensive dedication to the cause of the Jewish people.

The purity of Moshe Sharett's motivations was a constant, glowing inspiration. Many of us felt that for his brilliant services to the Zionist movement before the State and as Israel's first Foreign Minister after Independence, his rewards were not commensurate with his merits.

His last illness was painful and devastating to observe. Though wasting away from an incurable disease, he fought on valiantly from his wheelchair to maintain his duties and responsibilities as chairman of the Zionist Executive. That he found the strength to continue may in large measure be attributed to his wife, Zipporah, who was an unfailing source of comfort, understanding, and support throughout that melancholy but courageous final stage of his life.

Moshe Sharett's death at the age of seventy-one in 1965 was mourned by a host of friends and admirers. It ended the illustrious career of one who had a stellar role in the struggle to establish Medinat Yisrael and in shaping the early, formative years of the State.

Zalman Shazar

It would be both presumptuous and foolhardy to try to summarize in a few paragraphs the amazing and versatile career of the man whom I long knew as Zalman Rubashov, and who later adopted the surname Shazar (acronym for Shneur Zalman Rubashov) by which he is now remembered.

As an author, editor, orator, scholar, statesman, and mystic, he was endowed with a rare combination of gifts, some of which are not ordinarily associated with high political office. In Israel, however, where a different tradition prevails, these gifts did not seem to be out of place. Indeed, during the period of his tenure, they gave Bet ha-Nasi, the President's House, a *Klal Yisrael* character as well as a broad humanistic appeal.

Born in a Ḥabad (Lubavitch Ḥasidic) household in White Russia, Zalman Shazar joined the Labor Zionist movement in his youth and studied first in St. Petersburg and later at German universities. He made Aliyah to Palestine in 1924 and worked on the editorial staff of *Davar*, the Labor daily, of which he eventually became editor in chief. He served as Minister of Education and Culture in the Government of Israel and headed the Department of Education and Culture in the Jewish Agency Executive. In 1963, he was elected President of Israel and, during his two terms in that office, Bet ha-Nasi became a meeting place for scholars, writers, and artists, and a center for Bible study.

A giant of intellect, learning, and broad humanity, Shazar was steeped in Jewish lore and religious mysticism, yet receptive to universal culture and at home therein. Technical responsibilities did not find him at his best, shackling his free spirit. He was much more in his element when studying, writing, and delivering powerful speeches.

Long before he became President, Zalman Shazar was recognized as the Demosthenes of the Zionist movement, the didactic orator par excellence. At Zionist assemblies he dominated the proceedings whenever a cultural topic was under discussion or when a eulogy was called for on the passing of some Zionist leader. His addresses were delivered with fire and passion. The ecstatic gestures, the facial expressions, and the restless pacing to and fro, which accompanied the superb intellectual content and spiritual tone of his speeches, made him a unique phenomenon among the great Zionist orators of his time.

Yet it was not only on the public platform that Shazar excelled. Scholarship and original thought were also the hallmarks of his books and articles, and of the editorials he wrote for *Davar*. He never penned or uttered a banality. One felt that Jewish love, Jewish passion, and the aristocracy of Jewish learning were combined in this man.

As a Socialist, he belonged to the "rationalistic" segment of Jewry, yet no adjective suited him less. Permeated by the mystical approach of the Ba'al Shem Tov and Shneur Zalman of Lyady, he was a Lubavitcher Hasid in chains. The chains fettering him were all the protocol and formalities that accompanied his public responsibilities, especially after his election as third President of Medinat Yisrael.

Time and again, I was among those who were spellbound by Shazar's oratory. It was my privilege to serve under his baton on the Jewish Agency Executive. In personal contact, he was gentle, unassuming, and comradely, although in light conversation one was sometimes left wondering whether his mind had not drifted to more important matters than the subject in hand.

It was, for me, an unforgettable *zekhut* to be among his close friends when we bade him farewell in Bet ha-Nasi, at the conclusion of his second term as President of the State he helped to found, and which he enriched and magnified through his rare gifts of the mind and spirit.

Abba Hillel Silver

Majestic in appearance, imperious in manner, and impressive in erudition, Abba Hillel Silver was one of the giants of American Zionism. He dominated the American Jewish and Zionist scene during the crucial years from 1940 to 1948, when the destiny of the Jewish State hung in the balance.

Whether in the pulpit or on the Zionist platform, Dr. Silver was a matchless orator. His addresses, notable for both their content and their form, were delivered with passion and drama. Having been raised in a Hebrew-speaking environment, he was also one of the foremost Hebraists in the American Reform rabbinate.

Zionism and Hebrew culture were the main causes to which Abba Hillel Silver devoted his energies, yet he also took a leading part in the civic affairs of his community. His political views were usually on the Republican side.

Silver's powerful advocacy of Jewish peoplehood made him a *rara avis* among the Reform rabbis of his time, and the spirit of religious Messianism that inspired so many of his speeches and one of his books was capable, at times, of allying him with Orthodox Zionists of the Mizraḥi. For him, Judaism and Zionism were synonymous.

I worked at the side of Abba Hillel Silver during and immediately after World War II, when he was deeply immersed in the task of building up American public opinion, both Jewish and non-Jewish, in support of the achievement of our Zionist aim—a Jewish State in Palestine. From 1943 onward, with only brief interruptions, his leadership of the American Zionist Emergency Council was responsible in large measure for the passage by the U.S. Congress of meaningful resolutions expressing support for the Zionist cause.

In proceeding toward our common goals our paths sometimes diverged, but my high regard for him remained unalterable.

Silver was more than a brilliant orator; he was a first-class strategist who knew how to maneuver the forces necessary to achieve his purpose. As chairman of the American Section of the Jewish Agency and of the American Zionist Emergency Council, he presented the case for a Jewish State before the General Assembly of the United Nations in May 1947. In that capacity, he orchestrated the Zionist efforts that led to the passage of the historic UN resolution on Palestine of November 29, authorizing the establishment of a sovereign Jewish State in Eretz Yisrael.

As fate would have it, however, that triumphant climax was followed by an anticlimax in Silver's own Zionist career. The infighting and squabbles among his followers, now scrambling for prestige and position, almost left him by the wayside, and the general who had forged alliances and deposed Weizmann and Wise found himself, in the closing years of his life, outside the sphere of significant Zionist influence.

His had been the key role in the Reform movement's transformation from anti-Zionism to pro-Zionism, and he left his mark on the next generation of the American Reform rabbinate.

In his firm support of organized labor, civil liberties, and other social causes, Dr. Silver was more liberal than most people gave him credit for being.

Where personal relationships were concerned, it was not easy to penetrate his outward reserve. He had more admirers than friends.

Abba Hillel Silver will be remembered as a truly outstanding Zionist leader and as one of the prime architects of Medinat Yisrael.

Pierre van Paassen

Born in Holland of generations of Protestant clergy, Pierre van Paassen was himself a pastor by training. As it turned out, the world was his parish and his lectern became journalism and the public platform in many lands. His interviews with Mussolini and with Hitler's aides, to whom he stood up valiantly, aroused worldwide attention. In the battle against prejudice and discrimination he had few equals.

From his home, Pierre van Paassen imbibed a love of the Bible, the Bible land, and the Bible people. Visits to Palestine and Eastern Europe in the 1920s strengthened his warm regard for Am Yisrael. He covered the 1929 Arab riots in Palestine and, in his interview with the Mufti, Haj Amin al-Husseini, accused him to his face of having instigated the anti-Jewish disorders. Like the biblical Pinḥas, whose name Pierre might have borne had he been of Jewish parentage, he was a zealot for the Lord, uncompromising in his loyalties. An ardent Christian Zionist who knew Zionism from the inside, he attended nearly every Zionist Congress during his mature years. With characteristic forthrightness, he criticized Jewish leaders whose attitude toward Great Britain's anti-Zionist policy was one of moderation.

On the American scene, his Zionist endeavors stirred and enlightened Jewish and non-Jewish audiences from coast to coast. A series of books and articles gave expression to the author's staunchly pro-Jewish sympathies. Among his major works, the autobiographical *Days of Our Years* is a classic in its field. The same is true of *The Forgotten Ally*, an indictment of the British White Paper policy that appeared at the height of World War II. "If Palestine is the Jewish National Home," he wrote, "it is my spiritual home." For a short while, in 1942, he headed the American Committee for a Jewish Army of Stateless and Palestinian Jews.

With similar concern for the fate of all his fellowmen, Pierre van Paassen identified himself with the struggle for freedom everywhere. His reportages dealt with momentous and ominous developments—the Fascist takeover in Italy, the revolt in Morocco, the Spanish Civil War, and the Nazi perversion of Germany.

It was often my privilege to introduce Pierre van Paassen before audiences at my congregation and at gatherings of the ZOA and of the American Jewish Congress. He was a temperamental friend and dependable ally in many a contest with the foes we had in common—religious intolerance, narrow Americanism, social injustice, and anti-Zionism.

In a brotherly tribute written when I turned sixty, Pierre said something that is a key to the significance of his own personality: "In the measure that man challenges the conventional, he liberates not only himself but he prepares and contributes to the emancipation of others."* His life and work contributed massively to the emancipation of people in many lands and of many creeds.

Among the world's Righteous Gentiles, Pierre van Paassen has a secure place. In the memory of Jews, Zionists, and fighters for justice everywhere, he deserves a special niche as the unforgotten ally.

Stephen S. Wise

In his time, the first half of the twentieth century, and in his main setting, American public opinion, Stephen Samuel Wise was the peerless champion of the Jewish people.

Stephen Wise cut a striking figure. Tall, graceful, and well built, he had a finely chiseled face topped by a shock of black hair (sprinkled with gray in his later years),

Two Generations in Perspective (New York: Monde Publishers, 1957), pp. 370–71.

parted meticulously in the middle. A prominent nose lent the strength of an eagle to his countenance and, under thick brows, his eyes—ever so lightly crossed—seemed impenetrable to anyone attempting to surmise his thoughts. The use of his large and eloquent hands for gesticulative effect was further dramatized by a deep stentorian voice of wide range that he could manipulate like an organ, from fortissimo to pianissimo.

Dr. Wise was as to the platform born. Hearing him, one often felt that a superb Shakespearian actor was lost when he chose the rabbinate as his vocation and made the espousal of Jewish, American, and general human causes his vocation. For half a century he was the tribune of American Jewry.

Behind the impressive and expressive exterior lay a good mind and a penchant for reform. This embraced Reform Judaism, although Wise started out as rabbi of a Conservative congregation; political reform in New York; and the reform, or reshaping, of Jewish *Galut* psychology into that of Zionist self-emancipation.

A man so abundantly gifted could hardly be less than a prima donna, yet he showed talents as an organizer that were surprisingly effective for one of his volcanic temperament. He knew how to pick men for positions at his side and how to inspire their loyalty. In so doing, he bequeathed to his successors important instruments that he himself fashioned—the American Jewish Congress, the World Jewish Congress, and the Jewish Institute of Religion—as well as his notable contribution to the growth of the American Zionist movement.

My initial contact with Stephen Wise and his family dates back to 1918, when, in my final year as a student at the Jewish Theological Seminary, I taught the senior class of the Free Synagogue's Sunday school. Justine Wise, Stephen's daughter, was my star pupil, then fifteen years of age, bright, intelligent, and impressive. She was in the course of time destined to become a justice in the Domestic Relations Court of New York City and a leader of the American Jewish Congress.

On assuming the pulpit of Congregation B'nai Jeshurun, I learned that one of my predecessors had been Dr. Stephen Wise, whose ministry had extended over a period of seven years until 1900, when he moved to Portland, Oregon. After his return to New York, he more than once observed the *Yahrzeit* date of his late father, Rabbi Aaron Wise, at our synagogue services during Passover week. At B'nai Jeshurun's centenary celebration in 1925, Dr. Wise delivered one of the major addresses.

In common with Louis Brandeis, Stephen Wise taught and personified the thesis that the better the Zionist, the better the American, since idealism is of one piece.

He died in the knowledge that the Jewish State, in the restoration of which he had played a crucial role, was to be at last a fact of history.

Lillian Eigen Sornik

Many noble men and women who have come within the purview of my public career were not leaders but faithful followers, and they served Jewish and human causes with selfless dedication. Without such followers, leaders cannot get far. To these, the unheralded and unsung, I owe a deep debt of acknowledgment.

I have selected one, but their names are legion. I thank and bless them all, living and dead. The joy of their self-dedication has been their reward.

Were she alive today, no one would be more surprised to find her name included in this gallery of pen portraits than Lillian Sornik. She held no prominent communal position and she shied away from honors. Though not even listed in the official roster of my congregation's membership, she was often in synagogue, occupying an inconspicuous seat in the rear.

Because of her girth and a physical ailment, Lillian Sornik found it difficult to get about, but that did not prevent her from coming to Manhattan from her home on Long Island whenever there was a civic, philanthropic, or religious *mitzvah* to be performed. Nor did such disabilities stand in the way of a strenuous visit to Israel that was the spiritual climax of her life.

Although her means were not large, her largesse was great. She gave support to many religious and philanthropic causes, not all of which came to my notice. I had certain knowledge of her devotion to the International Synagogue at Kennedy Airport in New York and to the children of my Youth Village in Jerusalem.

Her artistic taste was exquisite. It is a joy to behold the Bemmelmans picture of a workshop she gave to the Youth Village, the Arthur Szyk portrait of King David she presented to the Hebrew University Synagogue Library, and the beautifully wrought silver mezuzot that found a place in our Jerusalem home.

I cannot tell if Lillian Sornik's code of observance was Orthodox, Conservative, or Reform, but I do know that she was, with every fiber of her being, a dedicated religious Jewess. Among the righteous women of Israel she has a worthy place.

In honoring her memory, I feel that I may, in a sense, be able to honor my debt to the many anonymous "little" people who have crossed and blessed my path through life. The devotion of such men and women—often of humble station but aristocrats of the spirit—has been a source of strength and encouragement to me across the years.

18

A Postscript

Since these memoirs virtually reached their conclusion with my eighty-fifth birthday in June 1981, several events of general significance and a few of importance within my family circle have transpired. These call for brief supplementary mention in this closing chapter.

First, chronologically, was the outcome of what proved to be the bitterest election campaign in the history of Medinat Yisrael, charged with violence, personal abuse, and the exploitation of "ethnic" feelings and grievances. As a result of the ballots cast on June 30, 1981, both major parties increased their representation in the Knesset at the expense of the smaller parties and, by a one-seat margin, the ruling Likud alliance, headed by Menaḥem Begin, succeeded in defeating the Ma'arakh (Labor Alignment), led by Shim'on Peres, and in forming a government. This new coalition included the National Religious Party (Mafdal) and two other groups that attracted religious votes—the ultra-nationalist Hateḥiyah Party and the Tami list, headed by Religious Affairs Minister Aharon Abuḥatzira, which appealed to Jews of North African origin.

The real winner, in the opinion of many, was Agudat Yisrael, the non-Zionist ultra-Orthodox party, which held on to its electorate and thus found itself strategically placed to decide which of the almost evenly balanced major groupings—Likud or Ma'arakh—would receive its four votes and so gain a working majority. Agudat Yisrael's terms for joining Begin's new coalition included substantial funding for its independent yeshivah and school network, and (with respect to the unresolved "Who is a Jew?" question) an amendment to Israel's Law of Return, the existing form of which defined a Jew as "a person born to a Jewish mother, or who has become converted to Judaism, and who is not a member of another religion." Agudah leaders now insisted that this be modified to read: "a person born to a Jewish mother, or who has become converted to Judaism *in accordance with the Halakhah*." Since the Orthodox rabbinical establishment in Israel maintains that it alone can act "in accordance with the Halakhah," such a change in the law would have the effect of disqualifying all conversions performed by non-Orthodox rabbis, even when these are administered according to strict halakhic requirements.

Prime Minister Begin's agreement to this stipulation aroused a storm of protest among leaders of Conservative and Reform Judaism in the United States, where the non-Orthodox constitute a substantial majority in American Jewish life and the most important base of support for Israel.

Chancellor Gerson D. Cohen of the Jewish Theological Seminary, while on a visit to Israel shortly after the election, formulated the position of the Conservative movement in opposing the Agudah's proposed rewording of the Law of Return. This position obtained the support of both the Reform and the Reconstructionist movements, as well as of a large segment of public opinion. Dr. Cohen deplored the fact that the Agudah was "more concerned with who administers and who is empowered to administer the law than with Halakhah." Such restrictions, he said, were an affront to major religious movements encompassing a large proportion of synagogue-affiliated Jews throughout the world, and would both vitiate the fundamental purpose of the Law of Return and diminish the appeal of Aliyah.

Basing himself on the remarks made by Rambam (Maimonides) in his introduction to the *Mishneh Torah*, Dr. Cohen also affirmed that "no group can any longer legitimately regard itself as the authorized spokesman for Jewish law and its administration, nor does any one community have a right to impose its interpretations on any other." It was not for Israel's Knesset to determine the legitimacy of a Jewish religious movement or its posture. "Our commitment to Halakhah is unequivocal," he declared, "but so is our love of the people of Israel and our commitment to religious pluralism."

It would also be apropos to mention the statement published on the eve of Rosh Hashanah 5742 (September 1981) by an organization close to the Jerusalem Chief Rabbinate, claiming that "it is forbidden to participate in prayers held by the M'sorati movement. One cannot fulfill one's obligation to pray by going to a Conservative congregation, either on the High Holy Days or during the year." At present, furthermore, Jewish marriage ceremonies performed in Israel are recognized as valid by the governmental authorities only if they are conducted by rabbis accredited by the Orthodox establishment.

These limitations, which have far-reaching effects on the legitimacy of offspring, inheritance rights, and other matters, need to be changed so as to grant equal rights to non-Orthodox rabbis. Would it not be anomalous if, in the Jewish State, non-Orthodox Jews were to enjoy fewer rights than non-Jews?

Fortunately, Israel's democratic system holds out the possibility of reversing this trend when the nation next goes to the polls. My residual position, however, is that no matter what happens, ours is an unconditional commitment to Israel, whichever party may be in power—as is the case with citizens in all democracies. It is the privilege and duty of every Israeli citizen to fight for the principles and policies he espouses—and against any encroachment on his fundamental rights—but when the die is cast, he must accept the dispensation and "live to fight another day." This is the implication of an "unconditional commitment to Israel." To take Israel on probation, as it were, is an intolerable approach.

In this context, I feel bound to criticize Israel's Jewish supporters abroad who use the public media to ventilate their disagreements with Government policy over here. For although our Jewish friends and supporters abroad have every right to speak out against policies adopted by the Government of Israel, there are channels available outside the media through which such strictures can and should be conveyed.

Israel Bonds, a cause in which both my wife and I had been deeply involved at its inception well over twenty years earlier, brought 400 special guests from abroad to attend its thirtieth anniversary dinner at the King David Hotel in Jerusalem on August 19, 1981. The dinner stirred fond memories of our activity in that sphere ever since the birth of the Israel Bonds campaign. The current program was intended to launch a $100 million campaign for the Mediterranean–Dead Sea Canal project, scheduled to cost $800 million in all. The amount to be raised would be over and above the "normal" target of $450 million that the Bonds organization was hoping to mobilize in 1981. At a ceremony held in Arad, thirty-five "Canal founders," each of whom had purchased $100,000 or more in bonds, signed a scroll that was placed in a capsule to be embedded at the eastern end of the intersea canal.

The moving spirit in this enterprise was the inexhaustible and irresistible Sam Rothberg. Sadly, however, Henry Montor—the man who had been the motive force behind the initiation of the Israel Bonds campaign (and who had previously rendered notable services to the United Jewish Appeal)—could not participate, and has since passed from our midst after a brief residence in Israel.

On August 30, a street in the Jerusalem suburb of East Talpiot was named for Ezra Z. Shapiro, of blessed memory, and a hall and study rooms in his name were dedicated at the Kiryat Moriah complex located on that street, which houses the Jewish Agency's Institutes for Zionist Education and Shliḥim, as well as the Ḥayim Greenberg Institute for Youth Leaders from Abroad. I had the privilege of taking part in the ceremonies and of delivering an address, together with Mayor Teddy Kollek, Dr. Avraham Avi-ḥai, Charlotte Jacobson, Kalman Sultanik, and S. J. Kreutner. Sylvia Shapiro, Ezra's widow, who is a Zionist leader in her own right, also spoke.

The next day, we left for our annual visit to the United States. The highlights of that trip were of an intimate family nature. I was at last able to embrace our first great-grandchild, Andrew Eytan, in Boulder, Colorado, where Bert had attended his birth in the previous year. I naturally found him a beautiful and brilliant addition to the Goldstein clan, and a credit to Brad and Margaret, his father and mother, to Avram and Dora, his grandparents, and to his great-grandparents. In January 1983, I should add, we were equally delighted by the birth in Amherst of a great-granddaughter, Rivkah Ilana. This happy event brought much joy to the baby's father and mother, Philippe and Joyce, as well as to Vivian and Paul, the proud grandparents.

Over the High Holy Days, we attended services on the campus of Stanford University, arranged by the Hillel Foundation rabbi, Mark Cartun. Rabbi Cartun had an important influence on our grandson, Joshua, who became his disciple and assistant. It was gratifying to learn of Joshua's success in the field of computer technology and of his recent visit to China with a group of U.S. computer experts, as well as of the progress made by his brothers, Dan and Michael. At Stanford, we also spent some time with another grandson, Ken, the son of Vivian and Paul Olum, who attended the Hillel services with us. From there we proceeded to Eugene, Oregon, to be with Vivian and Paul for Sukkot, when we worshiped at the local Conservative synagogue. Their daughters, Judith and Joyce, and their husbands, we had already visited in Ithaca and Amherst, respectively.

An important *simḥah* was in store for us in Eugene—the investiture on October 12 of our son-in-law, Professor Paul Olum, as president of the University of Oregon. He had been serving for a number of years hitherto as provost of the university. It was, of course, a great family occasion. All of us, dressed in our academic robes, joined in the procession—our daughter, Vivian, wife of the new president; our son, Avram, and his wife, Dora, who came from Stanford; and I, who had come from Israel to share the joy of this event. Bert, however, preferred to remain in the audience without her academic regalia, to watch us taking part in the exercises. On the previous evening, having been asked to speak in the pre-investiture program, I had brought greetings from President Avraham Harman of the Hebrew University of Jerusalem and took occasion to say:

> Perhaps the message from Mount Scopus, Jerusalem, can remind the intellectual fraternity everywhere of the Old Testament conjuncture, coupled with contrast, between wisdom and knowledge—*Ḥokhmah va-Da'at*—which runs through its pages like a golden thread. Transposed into modern terms, it is the contrast between Wisdom and Science.
>
> In our age of atomic power, where the line between global survival and global extinction is precariously thin, is it not desperately important that higher education should educate the inheritors of our present, not only in the "humanities" but in humanity—namely, a more equitable distribution of nature's bounties multiplied by science, the making of the fruits of knowledge increasingly available to ever growing numbers, and the lifting of the yokes of underprivilege and oppression, wherever these shackle the human spirit?

It was while we were still in the U.S., on October 6, that news of the assassination of Egypt's President Anwar Sadat shocked the world. Israel's Prime Minister Menaḥem Begin was among the foreign notables who attended the state funeral in Cairo. Sadat had proved himself to be a wise and courageous leader of his people— wise, because he understood that Egypt could gain more by peace with Israel than by war; and courageous, because he was willing to take the risk of alienating leaders and public opinion throughout the Arab world in his attempt to come to peaceful terms with the Jewish State.

Hosni Mubarrak, Sadat's Vice-President, replaced the murdered Egyptian head of state and pledged that his policies would be continued. It remains to be seen how firmly, wisely, and successfully this will be done. In the meantime, Israel has already made great sacrifices in its stage-by-stage withdrawal from Sinai, while the autonomy talks between Israel and Egypt on the future of the Palestinian Arabs have been virtually stalled.

The last act in the completion of Israel's withdrawal from Sinai, the obliteration of the lovely coastal town of Yammit, was attended by heartbreaking scenes involving displaced families, conscientious objectors, and threats of suicide *al kiddush Hashem*. The true heroes of the Yammit evacuation drama were the IDF soldiers, boys and girls, who in the face of stubborn, largely passive, resistance accomplished their task sorrowfully and with a minimum use of force.

It was a heavy price to pay for a final settlement with Egypt, but it will be worth all the sacrifices if the peace will hold. Peaceful coexistence with Israel's largest and strongest neighbor will remain an enduring monument to the statesmanship and courage of Anwar Sadat and Menaḥem Begin.

The next hurdle to be overcome on the road to lasting peace in the region, as envisaged by the Camp David Agreement, is the promised autonomy for Arabs living west of the River Jordan. This is an exceptionally difficult and complicated assignment that will tax the patience, resourcefulness, and statesmanship of the leaders of Israel, Egypt, and the United States.

In quite another category, and of special importance to me personally, was an event that can be referred to only briefly in these postscript pages—the Thirtieth World Zionist Congress. It opened with a festive session at Jerusalem's Binyanei ha-Umah on the evening of December 7, 1982 (Kislev 21, 5743). As one of the oldest participants, I was accorded the ceremonial privilege of opening this Zionist Congress with a two-minute address, followed by the traditional three strokes of the gavel.

"The Mountaintop View"

Adjoining the desk in my study, always within sight and reach, lies an object I brought home from Cyprus in 1947. It was given to me by the "Aliyah Bet" internees whom I visited there, survivors of the Nazi Holocaust in Europe, last victims of the heartless Mandatory regime in Palestine, who were soon to emerge from their detention camps and to reach the shores of Eretz Yisrael for which they had long yearned.

This object is a small bas-relief that one of the hapless detainees awaiting the day of release from Cyprus had carved from the local pale brown soapstone. It portrays a scene that must have been indelibly engraved on the mind of its amateur sculptor.

The scene is a Nazi death camp in Poland. Dense clouds of smoke belch forth from the chimney of the crematorium. A German guard stands with his rifle slung over his shoulder and inspects the line of Jews proceeding through the entrance to the death factory, where they are condemned to vanish forever. The faces of the doomed men, women, and children in that procession of victims are indistinguishable, except for the last figure—a man wearing a cap and carrying what may be a bag containing his *tallit* and *tefillin*. He manages to stand erect.

Time and again, this melancholy souvenir has had the effect of bracing me against untoward events, crises, and tragedies in the life of my people. It serves as a reminder of the endless threats and challenges to Jewish survival.

Having reached and passed beyond that stage in life which the Psalmist and our sages termed *gevurot*, "strength" or unusual vitality, I can now appreciate what Cicero wrote in his *De Senectute* about the advantages of the "mountaintop view." My fourscore years and seven have spanned a period in world history when the physical sciences reduced man's conception of our planet to a tiny speck in a vast universe, when politics changed the world's national configurations and balance of power, and when the social sciences made us keenly aware of the perilous gap between the indicative and the optative moods in the relationship of man to his fellowman.

From earliest childhood, while growing up in the ghetto of South Philadelphia and, for a short period, in a Lithuanian *shtetl*, I was sensitive to social injustices. These feelings were strengthened by my American birthright and by the Jewish values instilled in me by parents who had left an inhospitable land of oppression and pogroms for the *Goldene Medine*, a land of freedom and opportunity. Yet even in my native Philadelphia, that "home of liberty" to which I have always remained attached, Jewish immigrant life was marked by stark contrasts, while the wider American scene provided many evidences of the need for social and political reform.

Zionism, a combination of Israel's Messianic hope and Herzl's political program for a Jewish State, was a major formative influence in my boyhood. After the shattering experience of World War I, many young idealists were lured by the brand of Socialism that had triumphed in Russia or soothed by the establishment of the League of Nations, only to have their hopes dashed by the subsequent course of events. The Balfour Declaration and the Jewish National Home in Eretz Yisrael promised Jews a more rewarding prospect, even if far too few heeded Weizmann's call, "Jewish people, where art thou?" On the American scene, Jewish leaders such as Louis D. Brandeis and Stephen S. Wise urged that civic idealism could go hand in hand with work for the Zionist cause.

Judaism was becoming both more inspirational and more programmatic, less a matter for theological controversy and polemics. Challenges posed by the struggle for Jewish survival, by the needs of the individual Jew and of the *kehillah*, by the fight against anti-Semitism, and by Zionist pioneering endeavor in Eretz Yisrael became primary concerns of the religious and lay leadership of World Jewry. This was especially true of America, where a new leadership was coming to the fore, liberal-minded and dedicated to the service of the Jewish people. Some of these younger men were drawn to the rabbinate and assumed positions of responsibility beyond the confines of their immediate congregations.

All of these factors helped to determine my choice of a career in the American rabbinate, where religious leadership and concern for the vitality of Jewish congregational life could be combined with a wider concern—the building of Eretz Yisrael and the achievement of a more just and decent social order.

The American rabbi of my generation who felt the urge to become involved in social reform had to be something of a pioneer. He had to overcome the antagonism of many of his congregants—often the most influential ones—to the very idea of a spiritual leader interesting himself in questions which, they felt, lay outside his parochial sphere of responsibility. In the course of changing such congregational attitudes, he was often in a position to exert a far-ranging influence on people and events. This demanded freedom of expression in the pulpit and a realm of activity into which the rabbinate, by and large, had not previously ventured. Rabbis of my generation were thus often called upon to perform extramural tasks at a time when Jewish lay leaders of caliber and vision were in relatively short supply, even in America. And so, because of those who had hewn out a path before them, rabbis in the following generation who felt impelled to enter the field of social reform encountered less difficulty when they threw themselves into broader spheres of Jewish, civic, and human concern.

As a rabbi, I have always regarded myself not as a cleric ministering only to his flock, but as a servant of the Jewish people carrying the banner of Jewish national revival, enlightened Americanism, and broad social justice. To me, the chief importance of Judaism and the synagogue, in addition to religious motivation, inspiration, and guidance, lies in the fact that they are the "alma mater" of Jewish self-fulfillment and Jewish survival. Jewish self-fulfillment is, in my view, an imperative cognate with Jewish survival and human betterment. These broader involvements have therefore been an essential part of my creed and deed. I believe that the function of the synagogue and the rabbinate must be threefold: to teach Judaism, to preserve Jewish peoplehood, and to strive for a more just and equitable social order.

For the Zionist movement, as I see it, there has been a twofold role: to establish and safeguard the Jewish State, and then to ensure that the Medinah will be the primary, indispensable vehicle for Jewish survival—physically, spiritually, and culturally—with overtones of broad human concern. I would describe myself as a religiously motivated Zionist in the tradition of Solomon Schechter—with Zionism, the lodestar of my life, forming an integral part of my concept of Judaism.

Following the rise of Hitlerism, survival became the central issue for the Jewish people. As once-free nations were submerged in the satanic tide, and as the United States became the arsenal and the embattled leader of the civilized world, American Jewry was catapulted to the position of overarching Jewish responsibility and action. Tasks of an unprecedented magnitude beckoned and commanded—from the rescue and rehabilitation of the Jews who had survived the Holocaust, "brands plucked from the fire," to the consolidation of organized Jewish life in the U.S. and the long struggle to achieve the crowning glory of our people since its exile, an independent Jewish homeland. Out of the ashes of a world destroyed by Hitler's Third Reich, which lasted not for 1,000 years (as he had boastfully predicted) but for little more than a decade, there arose a desperate Jewish effort to end 2,000 years of *Galut* by establishing and building the Third Jewish Commonwealth.

It was American Jewry that took the lead in responding to these great challenges, since World Jewry's center of gravity had shifted to the United States. Regrettably, only a small percentage of Jews in the Western world felt the urge to make Aliyah, despite all the calamities they had witnessed in the *Golah*. Large numbers of Jews have contributed to the development of Medinat Yisrael through donations, investments, and public-relations activities—indeed, through everything short of their own Jewish self-fulfillment in the Jewish homeland. My wife and I are grateful, each day anew, that we made Aliyah and that we have had well over two decades of active involvement, making our lives count for something in the life of Jerusalem and Israel.

I am additionally grateful that here in Israel I have found a congenial framework, the Israel Interfaith Committee, and within it kindred spirits, Jews and Christians, for promoting Jewish-Christian fellowship based on mutual understanding and respect. It is an interfaith fellowship with a great potential of salutary repercussions abroad. Our hope is that it may grow into a threefold fellowship, embracing Muslims as well.

Looking back on my career in the American rabbinate and in Jewish public service, I recognize mistakes I have made, not so much in the formulation of objectives as in the failure to resist well-motivated diversions from basic aims and purposes. Also, I should have devoted more of my time to Torah and to my family. While others may have forgiven my lapses, I am the last to condone them. Yet, if I had to make the choice all over again, I am not sure that, in the hour of decision, I would choose differently.

Not a few of my rabbinical contemporaries have far excelled me as preachers and pastors, and many more as Jewish scholars. There were Zionist leaders of my generation in America whose influence on events exceeded mine. If, however, there is any special merit in my career, it may possibly inhere in the combination of ordinary qualities with an unusual capacity for hard work and the ability to work effectively with others. I think I have always been a better conductor than a soloist.

It is clear to me now that I have always been in a hurry, crowding my days and elbowing aside the years in my haste to get things done. Sheer physical stamina and a relatively even temperament have served me well throughout my life. For these blessings, I am indebted to parents who endowed me with a healthy constitution and a tranquil disposition, and to a beneficent Providence which has kept me alive and robust.

I never cease to be aware that my good fortune has exceeded my merits. All too often, I have seen useful and brilliant lives cut short, inflicting pain and loss not only on the immediate family and community, but on the entire Jewish people. Hence the desperate hurry that has accompanied so many of my involvements and activities. I trust that such haste has not been at the expense of a steady sense of direction. On the whole, I have a grateful feeling that my compass needle has generally guided me toward the right goals—to contribute to the quality of life around me and to serve the best interests of the Jewish community, the American community, and the world community. Through trial and error, it has been brought home to me that the deepest and most abiding satisfactions in life come not from receiving but from giving, and that the most meaningful earthly memorials are the engagements of enduring worth.

I have tried to be a faithful disciple of Theodor Herzl, who taught that "Zionism is a boundless ideal which will continue even after we achieve our land, Eretz Yisrael.

For Zionism is also the aspiration for moral and spiritual perfection." The sentiment expressed in these words, inscribed over the entrance to the Herzl Museum in Jerusalem, close by his grave, has motivated whatever I may have undertaken to improve man's lot on the local, national, and international levels. This broad vision has been part of my Zionism.

My greatest satisfactions have come from the espousal of causes that were not always popular—Zionism, social justice, the cause of labor, civil rights, and racial equality. In the struggle for world peace, I enlisted "for the duration." Inevitably, therefore, I have had little time for those who content themselves with proclaiming generalities and who shun specifics.

My life has been enriched continuously by the opportunities afforded me to travel the world and to become acquainted with people and problems in other lands. At the same time, however, it has also been a source of abiding personal gratification to have served on the local, congregational level and to have been at hand when people looked for their rabbi to share their moments of joy or of sorrow, and to guide them at crossroads in their lives.

What of the Future?

An important question that has been asked of me on many occasions and that now repeats itself at this closing stage of my life is concerned with the future: How do I foresee events affecting Israel and Diaspora Jewry in the coming decades?

We must be prepared for inclement weather. Am Yisrael, the Jewish people, is menaced by intermarriage, assimilation, and an alarmingly low birthrate in most parts of the world outside Israel. To counteract these threats, we must lose no time in implementing the measures many of us have long advocated. We must strengthen our institutes of higher Jewish learning, our rabbinical and synagogue organizations, as well as those secular bodies which promote Jewish life and culture. We must fortify the Zionist movement in all of its ramifications. The most effective safeguard for meaningful Jewish survival is a meaningful program of Jewish education made available to every Jewish child. The improvement, expansion, and consolidation of Jewish education must be regarded as the foremost challenge at present to leaders of World Jewry. As I have often reiterated, one thousand committed Jewish leaders in the United States today can determine the future of American Jewry generations hence. The same holds true, proportionally, of Jewish communities the world over.

If I have a Jewish message for my grandchildren and their generation, it is this. Am Yisrael today is a *she'ar yashuv*, a restored and a restoring remnant. That remnant comprises not only those who survived the *Sho'ah*, but those also who, living in countries untouched by the Nazis, came through the Holocaust years unscathed. The restored remnant must feel a sacred obligation to the *restoring* remnant—helping to build our future everywhere and using every means available to safeguard and enhance the physical, cultural, and spiritual viability of the Jewish people throughout the world.

To maintain and transmit Jewish identity and the Jewish heritage in the midst of all-engulfing alien civilizations is no easy assignment. The forces of assimilation are powerful and ever present. Yet the preservation of Jewish identity is, I feel, not only an obligation of Jewish honor but a desideratum from the broadest human viewpoint, while the specific Jewish contribution to humanity is, in the same way, a categorical imperative. Moreover, the struggle to retain Jewish identity, often in the face of a hostile environment, has generated and can continue to generate special and valuable qualities in the Jewish personality, both collectively and individually.

I also hope and pray that the generation of our grandchildren will develop an appreciation of and personal commitment toward the new factor in Jewish history— Medinat Yisrael—restored after a lacuna of almost nineteen centuries. Israel recently celebrated the hundredth anniversary of Zionist settlement in Eretz Yisrael, which dates from the arrival of the Bilu'im, those idealistic young Jews who came from pogrom-ridden Czarist Russia in 1882 in order to build a new and meaningful Jewish life in the ancient Homeland. Young Jews of today must understand what a national home for the Jewish people has meant, and should continue to mean, for Jews and, indeed, for the rest of mankind. A State of our own is not only a boon for those of our people who do not feel completely at home in the lands of their domicile. It has an even greater significance in terms of creative Jewish values— inspiring and permeating literature and the arts, Jewish scholarship, and the sciences, all of which also represent contributions to humanity in general. And Jews everywhere must find ways of becoming identified with this new phenomenon in Jewish history, Medinat Yisrael, preferably through Aliyah, but at the very least by joining the ranks of Israel's friends, supporters, and champions.

If, therefore, people ask, "When will Israel stop depending on World Jewry?" and "When will World Jewry no longer be dependent on Israel?," I feel bound to give a categorical answer. This interdependence should never cease, because it is essential to the optimum well-being of both.

Medinat Yisrael will continue to have need of World Jewry's material and moral support. In the economy of our modern world, a "land of milk and honey"—even if those commodities were to exist here in abundance—could not hold its own, when forced to compete with lands rich in oil and mineral resources. Israel will, however, also continue to have need of the political support of Jewish communities in the Diaspora, which can influence public opinion, while the Medinah is engaged in its constant struggle for viability and security. Furthermore, Israel will continue to have need of World Jewry's cultural, artistic, and scientific resources, since inter-pollination in these areas—where Jews generally excel and Israel's own credentials are noteworthy—forms part of an essential symbiosis.

As for World Jewry's dependence on Israel, the most obvious need is for a homeland where Jews who are made to feel unwelcome in their existing abodes can find more than a refuge, a permanent home. That, of course, is why many hundreds of thousands of Jews have come to Israel from Arab lands and from the Soviet bloc countries. There are, however, spiritual and Zionist gravitations as well, which beckon to Jews living in the *Golah*. Because of such Zionist considerations, the innermost need to find Jewish self-fulfillment in the Jewish national homeland—Medinat Yisrael and Eretz Yisrael—will always exercise a gravitational influence on Jewish communities abroad.

The relationship between the Medinah and Diaspora Jewry is more than a partnership. These two components of Am Yisrael are, indeed, of one another and will remain inextricably bound together. Thus, the future of the Jewish people will rest on Israel and Diaspora Jewry, according to the extent to which these twin components of Jewish peoplehood interact frankly, fruitfully, and integrally. Such blessed interaction must be based on the will and capacity of each to enter into a covenantal agreement, and to bring to it not only goodwill but familiarity with the Jewish heritage.

The role of Medinat Yisrael in combatting erosive trends abroad is a central one. It provides inspiration, stimulus, and guidance for the World Zionist Organization, the World Jewish Congress, and other bodies concerned with the Jewish present and future. Zionism, which, in its broadest sense, is concern for the Medinah and Diaspora Jewry, has virtually captured the leadership of the Jewish people. It involves not only the mobilization of financial and moral support for Israel among Jews, but the winning for Israel of popular sentiment and the support of governments. The United States, of course, is the major factor. What many people tend to overlook is the fact that American Jewry itself has thereby become revitalized. Israel, Zionism, and a knowledge of Hebrew are desperately needed vitamins for sustaining and vitalizing Jewish existence, and for ensuring Jewish survival in an alluring, predominantly non-Jewish environment.

Aliyah continues to be the most underdeveloped area on the American Jewish landscape. Rank-and-file Zionists will take this imperative more seriously when their own leaders set an example. In an earlier chapter, I referred to a Zionist conference in South Africa where I had the rare privilege of seeing how younger delegates forced through a resolution making it obligatory for those holding the chairmanship of the S.A. Zionist Federation to make Aliyah within a period of two years. This is the kind of approach American Zionists would do well to emulate.

I am not willing to write off the possibility of a more impressive Aliyah from the United States. It would be good for the Olim, for Israel, and for the American Jewish community itself. At the risk of being accused of an "Anglo-Saxon" bias, I am ready to declare that American and other English-speaking immigrants have much to give as well as to receive in Israel. They bring with them habits of efficiency, politeness, civic pride, and good fellowship, qualities nourished in a more relaxed social environment, which can help tone up the quality of life here in Medinat Yisrael.

It may well be that, in an applied sociological sense, *Yerushalayim shel ma'lah*, the "Higher Jerusalem," is an unattainable goal, yet it must remain an indispensable objective. Israel is a miniature world of glaring contrasts—saints and sinners, mystics and materialists, princes and paupers of the spirit. We have our share of adult criminals and reprobates and of juvenile delinquents, the products of our unrehabilitated slums. During the early years of mass immigration immediately following the establishment of the State, the means were simply not available to organize systematically the mass Aliyah that inundated our shores. The Jewish people failed to provide the resources needed to absorb the Olim in an adequate manner. It may take another generation of purposeful social engineering to overcome the problems besetting Israel's society.

Israeli standards, in the labor and business fields especially, may be higher than elsewhere in the Middle East, but they do not as yet approach those of the West. One need only glance at our daily newspapers to be made aware of the decline in the level of our public and private life. We live in a rapidly contracting world where instant communication not only brings us news, but also spreads new fads, fashions, standards, and mores, both good and bad. Israel is thus in danger of becoming less of an *Am Segulah,* a distinctive and distinguished people, and more *ke-khol ha-Goyyim*—like all the other nations.

Is it quixotic to expect otherwise, to believe that this one little Jewish State of ours can remain proof against waves inundating the rest of the world? I am convinced that, by an aroused national will, it can be done. To a degree, it may depend on national leadership. My experience has also taught me to respect the power of inspiration that can emerge from one Rav Kook, one Martin Buber, one Ben-Gurion, like some lighthouse on life's stormy sea. Yet we also need a national strategy in order to make a significant impact on the entire nation.

One might have expected that the Jewish home would be a dominant factor in the battle to improve the quality of our life here in Israel, but—as everywhere else—the home is no longer the influence it was in the past. Many homes are themselves in need of guidance. The major role must therefore be played by our state schools, whether of the general *(Mamlakhti)* or the religious *(Mamlakhti Dati)* trends. Israel's educational system must undertake the primary task of inculcating moral values and civic standards. The teachers will know best how to implement such a program, once the guidelines have been laid down and the objectives have been defined by those in the Government responsible for policy and administration.

Needless to say, my critique of Israeli failings is made out of love and complete self-identification with Medinat Yisrael and its importance for the Jewish people, both now and in the future.

My long-range forecast for Israel is optimistic. I believe that this country's economy will move out of the doldrums, that Jewish intelligence and resourcefulness will stimulate its commerce and industry, and that its remaining backward areas, both social and economic, will be rehabilitated. I believe that Israel will draw ever-increasing numbers of Jews from the Diaspora because of one negative constant—anti-Semitism—and thanks to positive motivations: a sense of Jewish history and destiny, religious sentiments, and the widely shared, though often suppressed, conviction that Israel is the one place on earth where Jews can achieve their true self-fulfillment as Jews.

More than ever before, there is an awakening of Jewish consciousness among that segment of our youth which believes in Jewish survival, manifested in a rejection of alien philosophies and a keen desire to learn what Judaism has to offer. But there is a wide gap between hunger and nourishment, between aspiration and fulfillment. Here is the challenge to our intellectual and spiritual leadership, lay and rabbinic, in Israel and in the Diaspora.

Valedictory

My concluding, residual word is profound thanksgiving.

I am grateful to the Dispenser of the years for a generous allocation; to my parents, of blessed memory, for the Jewish tradition and sense of values they inculcated in me; to my teachers, for the torch of learning and culture; to my life companion, for sharing and stimulating my chosen path; to my children and grand-children, for new outlooks and challenges; and to my congregants, friends, and colleagues, for calls to service in meaningful Jewish, Zionist, civic, social, and humanitarian engagements.

I am thankful that it has been my privilege to live in the most momentous era in nineteen centuries of Jewish history, and to have witnessed and participated in the events leading up to what, I pray, will be the glorious culmination of Israel's national epic.

Why did I and my generation, rather than my father's generation or those before him, merit this *zekhut?* Perhaps it was because my generation, building on the foundations laid by Moses Hess, Leon Pinsker, Theodor Herzl, and other practical visionaries, transformed a mystic faith in *Shivat Tziyyon* into a political program.

For the fact that my life has been cast in the era of struggle and fulfillment, I give thanks to the Author of the universal drama, who has enabled me to have my small share in its unfolding—

Glossary of Hebrew and Yiddish Terms

(Plural forms in parentheses)

ALIYAH: immigration ("going up") to the Land of Israel
ALIYAH (ALIYOT): honor of being "called up" to the Torah
AM YISRAEL: the People of Israel
ASKAN (ASKANIM): Zionist key worker, activist

BAR MITZVAH: Jewish male above age (13) of religious majority
BETH DIN: rabbinical court
BINYAN HA-ARETZ: "upbuilding" of the Land of Israel

DAYYAN: judge in rabbinical court

EL MALÉ RAḤAMIM: opening words of memorial prayer *(Hazkarah)*
EN BRERAH: "No Alternative"
ERETZ YISRAEL: the Land of Israel
ETZEL: Jewish underground movement (Irgun Tzeva'i Leumi)

GABBAI (GABBA'IM): warden of synagogue
GALUT: Diaspora, exile (also *Golah, Golus*)

HAFRADAH: separation of functions
HAFTARAH: prophetical reading in synagogue
HAGANAH: major Jewish underground movement in Palestine
HAGGADAH: traditional "narrative" read at Passover *Seder*
ḤALUTZ *(ḤALUTZIM):* Zionist pioneer; ḤALUTZIUT: pioneering endeavor
ḤANUKKAH: Festival of Dedication and Lights, commemorating Maccabean
restoration of the Temple
ḤASID (ḤASIDIM): member of pietistic Jewish sect
HATIKVAH: "The Hope," Zionist (and Israeli) anthem
HAVDALAH: ceremony marking termination of Sabbath
ḤAVURAH: religious fellowship

ḤAVVAH: farm school

ḤAZZAN (ḤAZZANIM): cantor; ḤAZZANUT: cantorial art

ḤEDER: old type of Jewish religious school

HISTADRUT: trade-union confederation in Palestine and Israel

ḤUMMASH: Pentateuch

ḤURBAN: Destruction of the Temple

KADDISH: form of prayer recited by cantor or mourners

KASHER: ritually fit or religiously valid: KASHRUT: Jewish dietary laws

KEHILLAH (KEHILLOT): Jewish congregation or community

KEREN HAYESOD: Foundation Fund of the Zionist Organization

KEREN KAYEMET LE-YISRAEL (KKL): Jewish National Fund

KIBBUTZ GALUYYOT: Ingathering of the Exiles

KIDDUSH: blessing over wine recited on Sabbaths and festivals

KIPPAH (KIPPOT): skullcap

KLAL YISRAEL: the Jewish people as a whole, World Jewry

KLITAH: absorption of immigrants

KOHEN (KOHANIM): Jew of priestly (Aaronide) descent

KOTEL MA'ARAVI: surviving Western Wall of the Temple

LEḤI: smallest (and most violent) Jewish underground movement ("Stern Gang")

MA'ABARAH (MA'ABAROT): emergency accommodation for immigrants

MA'ARIV: evening service

MAFTIR: last portion of Torah reading in synagogue

MAGBIT: fund-raising campaign

MAGEN DAVID: Shield of David emblem

MAGGID: Jewish preacher

MAMME-LOSHEN: Yiddish "mother tongue" of Eastern European Jews

MATZAH (MATZOT): unleavened bread eaten on Passover

MEDINAH, MEDINAT YISRAEL: State of Israel

MEGILLAH: Scroll of Esther recited on Festival of Purim

MENORAH: seven-branched lampstand or "candelabrum," principal Jewish emblem

MEZUZAH: parchment scroll affixed to doorposts of Jewish home

MIKVEH (MIKVA'OT): ritual bath

MINḤAH: afternoon service

MINYAN: prayer quorum of ten males above Bar Mitzvah age

MITZVAH (MITZVOT): religious precept; popularly, honor allocated in synagogue

OLEH (OLIM): immigrant arriving in the Land of Israel

PALMAḤ: crack troops of Jewish underground in Palestine

PARNAS: community leader or official

PESAḤ: Festival of Passover

PURIM: Festival of Lots, commemorating deliverance from slaughter in Persia

REBBETZIN: rabbi's wife

ROSH HASHANAH: New Year festival

SEDER (SEDARIM): home service on Passover

SEFER TORAH: Torah scroll

SHABBAT: Sabbath day

SHAḤARIT: morning service

SHALI'AḤ (SHLIḤIM): emissary

SHAMMASH: synagogue beadle, sexton

SHAVU'OT: Festival of Weeks, Pentecost

SHE'ERIT HA-PLETAH: the "Surviving Remnant"

SHEHEḤEYANU: blessing said in thanksgiving

SHEḤITAH: Jewish ritual slaughter; *SHOḤET:* slaughterer

SHEMA YISRAEL: "Hear, O Israel!" (confession of faith)

SHI'UR (SHI'URIM): religious study session

SHIVAT TZIYYON: Return to Zion

SHLOSHIM: end of thirty-day mourning period

SHO'AH: Holocaust, Nazi destruction of European Jewry

SHOFAR (SHOFAROT): ceremonial ram's horn

SHTETL (SHTETLAKH): village or township in Eastern Europe

SHTIBL (SHTIBLAKH): Ḥasidic prayer house

SHUL: synagogue

SIDDUR (SIDDURIM): prayer book

SIMḤAH: festive occasion or celebration

SUKKAH: "booth" used as temporary dwelling on Festival of Tabernacles (Sukkot)

TALLIT: prayer shawl

TEFILLIN: phylacteries worn at morning service on weekdays

TISH'AH BE-AV: fast of Ninth of Av

TORAH: "Teaching," Hebrew Bible or (by extension) Jewish religious tradition

TZAHAL: Israel Defense Forces (IDF)

ULPAN (ULPANIM): Hebrew language instruction center

VA'AD LEUMI: National Council of the Jews in Palestine

YAHRZEIT: anniversary of Jew's death

YERIDAH: emigration ("going down") from Israel; YORED: Jew emigrating from Israel

YESHIVAH (YESHIVOT): Talmudical college

YISHUV: Jewish population in the Land of Israel

YOM HA-ATZMA'UT: Israel Independence Day

YOM KIPPUR: Day of Atonement

YOM TOV: Jewish festival

ZEKHUT: privilege

ZEMIROT: Sabbath table hymns

Index

364